Adolescent Development for Educators

Allison M. Ryan
University of Michigan

Timothy C. Urdan
Santa Clara University

Eric M. Anderman
The Ohio State University

Boston   Columbus   Indianapolis   New York   San Francisco
Amsterdam   Cape Town   Dubai   London   Madrid   Milan   Munich   Paris   Montréal   Toronto
Delhi   Mexico City   São Paulo   Sydney   Hong Kong   Seoul   Singapore   Taipei   Tokyo

Vice President and Publisher: *Kevin M. Davis*
Editorial Assistant: *Anne McAlpine*
Executive Field Marketing Manager: *Krista Clark*
Senior Product Marketing Manager: *Christopher Barry*
Developmental Editor: *Gail M. Gottfried*
Program Manager: *Janelle Criner*
Project Manager: *Pamela D. Bennett*
Operations Specialist: *Carol Melville*
Cover Design Director: *Diane Lorenzo*
Cover Art: *Getty Images, Don Mason*
Media Project Manager: *Lauren Carlson*
Full-Service Project Management: *Katrina Ostler, Cenveo® Publisher Services*
Composition: *Cenveo® Publisher Services*
Printer/Binder: *LSC Communications/Kendallville*
Cover Printer: *Phoenix Color/Hagerstown*
Text Font: *10/12 Palatino LT Pro*

Cataloging-in-Publication Data is available on file at the Library of Congress.

1   18

ISBN-10:   0-13-498724-1
ISBN-13: 978-0-13-498724-8

Group Dedication

This book is dedicated to the memory of Carol Midgley and Paul Pintrich. Their wisdom, dedication to students, and generosity created the model of an academic that we strive for in our own work and lives.

Personal Dedications

To Joe, Ella, and Jack. —*A.R.*

To my two favorite adolescents, Ella and Nathaniel. —*T.U.*

To Lynley, Sarah, and Jacob. —*E.A.*

About the Authors

Allison M. Ryan, Ph.D.

Allison M. Ryan is a Professor in the Combined Program in Education and Psychology at the University of Michigan, Ann Arbor. She graduated from Providence College in 1992 and the University of Michigan in 1998, where she earned her Ph.D. in Education and Psychology. Her research interests concern the development of achievement beliefs and behaviors during early adolescence. Her research examines how children's personal characteristics interact with classroom and peer group contexts to influence motivation, engagement, and achievement in school. She has published extensively on these topics in journals such as the *Journal of Educational Psychology* and *Developmental Psychology*. She has been the recipient of numerous honors, including the Psi Chi/Edwin B. Newman Award for Outstanding Graduate Research from the American Psychological Association, the Outstanding Dissertation Award from Division 15 of the American Psychological Association, the Richard E. Snow Award for Early Career Contributions to Research from Division 15 of the American Psychological Association, and Distinguished Scholar and Distinguished Senior Scholar for teaching and scholarship from the University of Illinois at Urbana-Champaign. She has edited *Peer Relationships and Adjustment at School* (with Gary W. Ladd), a special issue of the *Journal of Early Adolescence* on peer relationships and academic adjustment (with Scott D. Gest), and served as an Associate Editor of the *Journal of Educational Psychology* (2009–2012).

Timothy C. Urdan, Ph.D.

Timothy C. Urdan is a Professor of Psychology and Liberal Studies at Santa Clara University. He has conducted research examining academic motivation of adolescent and college-aged students for 25 years, focusing in particular on achievement goal theory, classroom contexts, and student ethnicity. In recent years he has examined how ethnic identity is associated with students' academic identities and has studied both conscious and non-conscious processes that may influence this relationship. He currently serves as the Chair of the Motivation in Education SIG for the American Educational Research Association, is an Associate Editor for the *Merrill-Palmer Quarterly*, serves on the editorial boards of the *American Educational Research Journal*, *Contemporary Educational Psychology*, and *Journal of Educational Psychology*, and is the co-editor (with Stuart Karabenick) of the *Advances in Motivation and Achievement* book series, the *Adolescence and Education* book series (with Frank Pajares), and the *American Psychological Association Handbook of Educational Psychology* (with Karen Harris and Steve Graham). He is the author of *Statistics in Plain English*.

Eric M. Anderman, Ph.D.

Eric M. Anderman is Chair of the Department of Educational Studies and Professor of Educational Psychology at The Ohio State University. He earned his Ph.D. in Educational Psychology at the University of Michigan. His area of research is adolescent motivation; he focuses in particular on (a) academic cheating, (b) the effects of school transitions on student motivation, and (c) HIV/pregnancy prevention in adolescent populations. He has edited the books *Psychology of Academic Cheating* (with Tamera Murdock), the third edition of the *Handbook of Educational Psychology* (with Lyn Corno), and the *International Guide to Student Achievement* (with John Hattie). He also co-authored *Classroom Motivation* (with Lynley Anderman), and recently came on board as a co-author with Jeanne Ormrod and Lynley Anderman on the 9th edition of Ormrod's *Educational Psychology: Developing Learners.* He is currently the editor of the journal *Theory Into Practice,* and is past-president of Division 15 (Educational Psychology) of the American Psychological Association.

Preface

Adolescence is a fascinating time of life characterized by much change. As puberty unfolds, young people undergo dramatic physical transformation. Cognitive development spurs shifts in how they think about themselves and their world. Their relationships become more sophisticated and complex. Adult's expectations of youth evolve, and youth have new rights and responsibilities bestowed upon them. The choices and decisions adolescents make have greater implications and long-term consequences. Thus, it is an exciting but also daunting phase of life.

Teachers play a critical role in the lives of youth at this stage of great change. Through their instruction, middle and high school teachers are in a position to promote critical thinking skills, inspire new ideas and interests, and expand their students' knowledge and understanding of themselves and their world. In their relationships with students, and leadership roles in classrooms and schools, teachers can create safe spaces where students feel comfortable and connect in positive ways with others. At times, teachers provide guidance and support to help adolescents make appropriate choices. Teachers can inspire students to be good citizens not only in the classroom and school, but also within their community. In a myriad of ways teachers can facilitate positive outcomes for their adolescent learners.

However, teaching adolescents can be challenging. Teachers must adapt and respond to adolescents who vary greatly in their abilities and interests. Schoolwork is not always adolescents' top priority. Adolescents can have busy lives outside of school as some take on jobs and others are involved in time-intensive extracurricular activities. Parents can seem uninvolved, or at times over involved, in ways that teachers do not find helpful. Peers and the social scene can dominate the attention of students at school. Technology and media are a powerful distraction in the lives of contemporary youth. As adolescents try out new identities, learn how to relate in more sophisticated ways with others, and improve in self-regulation, their behavior and decisions can, at times, be baffling and frustrating for both teachers and parents.

How can teachers facilitate positive outcomes for their adolescent learners? What strategies can they use? We believe that an understanding of adolescent development will support teachers in their work with their students. We wrote this book to help teachers, future teachers, and others who are interested in the education of adolescents. We have been teaching adolescent development as part of teacher certification or professional development for educators for more than 20 years. In all of our years of teaching we yearned for a book that was geared towards educators. The existing textbooks on adolescent development are predominantly written for undergraduate psychology majors and have little to say about what the theories and research mean for teachers in schools working with adolescent students. The key feature that guided the development of this book and that sets it apart from other textbooks on adolescent development is the focus on application of concepts to educational settings and the practical implications for teachers.

How the Chapters Are Organized

Each chapter in the book includes specific features to help teachers, future teachers, and other readers who are interested in education make the connection between adolescent development and education.

Each chapter begins with an Introduction and an Overview of the Chapter. These serve as advance organizers to help instructors and students gain a quick snapshot of the material that will be covered in the chapter. These are then followed by a series of sections within the chapter that cover the major theories, ideas, and research evidence related to the main topic of that chapter. For example, Chapter 2, *Physical Development*, includes major sections on the physiological changes that occur during adolescence, how the brain develops, the effects of physiological development on social and cognitive processes, body image and eating disorders, physical health and well-being, and school-based services designed to promote health and well-being. These major sections of each chapter represent the key issues in adolescent development.

In addition to the main content, each chapter contains numerous opportunities to help students think more deeply and critically about the content. Each chapter includes brief scenarios that illustrate what some of the issues in the chapter may look like in real-world educational settings. These scenarios were based upon our own experiences as teachers and were developed from discussions that we have had with teachers and students over the years. Each chapter also has several "questions" that are placed in a large font and inserted in the marginal area near related content. These are designed to encourage students to pause and reflect upon what they are reading. They provide an opportunity for students to think about how the material in the chapter applies to real world situations, to themselves as future or current educators, and to the well-being of adolescents. In addition to these, each chapter includes at least two "In-Depth" boxes. The purpose of these boxes is to make explicit connections between concepts from the chapter and examples from contemporary society. For example, in Chapter 10, *Sexuality and Romantic Relationships*, one of the In-Depth boxes examines the issue of how the digital world of the Internet has influenced sex and dating. These In-Depth boxes offer instructors an excellent opportunity to use current topics to generate thoughtful classroom discussions that encourage students to apply what they are learning in class and from the book.

Throughout each chapter there are sections titled "What Educators Can Do." This feature lists recommendations for educators that are closely tied to the material presented in the chapter. Their purpose is to provide another mechanism for linking the content of adolescent development to the real world of schools. These recommendations also provide practical ideas for using what you have learned from the chapter to help adolescents, and their teachers, navigate the challenges of this period of life. Then at the end of each chapter, we summarize the key points about what educators can do in a feature called "Recommendations for Educators."

The organization and structure of each chapter in this book are designed to reflect and advance the goals of the book as a whole. Specifically, the chapters cover the critical theories, concepts, and research that educators should know about adolescent development. In addition, the material is organized in a manner that will promote critical thinking about, and strategies for, how to use knowledge about adolescent development to improve the teaching of adolescents. The recommendations for educators, prompts for critical thinking and reflection, and tests for knowledge will help readers to understand the material deeply and think often about the applications of the material to the real world of teachers, adolescent students, and schools.

Content of the Book

In this textbook we cover topics that are traditionally covered in many adolescent development textbooks, as well as topics that are somewhat less traditional but still highly relevant. Moreover, we focus within each chapter specifically on how these topics are applicable to future and practicing educators. In the first chapter, we introduce some introductory and historical information about adolescence, and we elaborate on how the study of adolescence can greatly benefit educators.

The second chapter focuses on physical development during adolescence. Whereas some educators do not believe that effective instruction is related to their students' physiological development, much recent research indicates that student learning is related to physical development. An understanding of the patterns and types of changes that occur in the human body and brain during adolescence allows educators to better understand their adolescent students' behaviors and challenges and to adapt instruction at times in order to facilitate teaching and learning. We focus in particular in this chapter on the implications of physiological development in terms of adolescents' self-perceptions, social interactions, cognitive development, and overall health and well-being. We offer strategies for how educators can use this information to enhance student learning and motivation.

In the third chapter, we examine various aspects of cognitive development. Specifically, we emphasize that cognitive development is not always a linear, entirely predictable process. Using recent research as well as more classical theoretical perspectives (e.g., Piaget), we examine the ways in which cognitive processes develop, focusing in particular on how instruction can be adapted in order to focus on adolescents' current abilities and strengths, and to facilitate cognitive growth.

The fourth chapter focuses on social and moral development. We examine in detail how adolescents' thinking about social and moral issues changes over time. We also examine how adolescents' ability to understand and appreciate diverse perspectives develops. A section of this chapter is devoted to an examination of service learning (volunteerism); service learning is growing in popularity in schools serving adolescents. Nevertheless, in order for service learning to yield its intended effects, it is essential for educators to understand how it functions within their students' levels of moral and social reasoning. Finally, we discuss academic cheating; we examine its causes, as well as strategies aimed at prevention of cheating.

In the fifth chapter we examine identity and self-perceptions. Adolescents engage in much exploration about "who they are" and "whom they want to be" as adults. This period of exploration is influenced by peers, gender, family, ethnicity, and numerous other variables. In addition to reviewing contemporary research on this topic, we examine the ways in which educators can help adolescents to negotiate their struggles with identity, and to channel that energy into productive learning in school.

In Chapter 6, we discuss families. Rather than thinking of adolescents' families as being removed from students' experiences at school, we examine the current status of family structures and family life, and focus in particular on how they are related to students' school experiences. Educators often complain that parents are not involved enough in schools; we argue that with a more complete understanding of family dynamics and family life, educators can more effectively work with families as partners both inside and outside of the school.

In the seventh chapter, we examine the roles of media and technology. We now live in a world in which adolescents are constantly connected to their friends, their families, and literally the entire world. Rather than seeing technology as an enemy and a burden, we examine its role in the social and academic lives of adolescents. We offer a realistic portrayal of ways in which educators can acknowledge and incorporate new technologies into academia (in a balanced way).

The eighth chapter is about peers and peer relationships. All educators of adolescents acknowledge the tremendous influence of peers on virtually all aspects of adolescent life. We focus first on helping educators to understand the complexities of peer relationships and peer influences. We pay particular attention to social-emotional learning (which is currently very popular among educators), and to bullying and victimization. We again focus on what classroom teachers can do to promote climates in their classrooms and schools that are conducive to the development of positive peer relationships.

We devote the entire ninth chapter to the school experience. In the first half of the chapter, we examine adolescent motivation in detail. We focus on motivation because many of the behavioral problems that occur in schools serving adolescents can be avoided if students are optimally engaged with their work. In addition, many adolescents with the cognitive skills to succeed in school fail to do so because they are not motivated to achieve. There are many urban myths about how to effectively motivate students, so we focus in particular on research-based strategies. In the second half of the chapter, we focus on other aspects of schools and classrooms that affect learning (e.g., school size, school location, transitions into new schools, etc.). When educators understand the research on how these variables affect learning, they can adjust instructional practices and curriculum to meet the needs of their students.

In Chapter 10, we turn to adolescent sexuality and romantic relationships. An understanding of these issues can greatly aid educators in their interactions with students. Sexuality and relationships are extraordinarily important parts of adolescents' lives, and when our students enter into our classrooms, we can't just "turn off" their thoughts, anxieties, and intentions with regard to sexuality. Rather, we need to acknowledge students' feelings and experiences, and help them as best we can to negotiate these feelings and to balance this new part of their lives with their academic learning. Moreover, there are many risks associated with dating and sexual behaviors, and educators can help adolescents understand these risks and develop strategies for avoiding them.

Concerns about the mental health and well-being of adolescents are growing. Whereas some may argue that today's adolescents are more troubled than adolescents of the past, others would argue that our society is perhaps just more aware of these issues, and more willing to acknowledge and discuss them. In Chapter 11, we examine this in some detail. As educators, you will often be on the front lines in terms of observing when your students are experiencing various problems. An understanding of some of the mental health and substance abuse issues that arise during adolescence is essential for educators, so that we can both help them to deal more effectively with their studies, and so that we can refer them for support when necessary.

The final chapter focuses on the transition from high school. We devote part of this chapter to an examination of emerging adolescence (the period from about the ages of 18 through 29). We also discuss the various transitions that adolescents make after graduation. Whereas some do transition into four-year colleges, many of our students choose other options (e.g., entering the workforce, the military, or attending a community college). We examine these various choices, and discuss strategies that educators can use to support their students as they consider options for their futures.

Taken together, the chapters in this book cover the major developments of adolescence and into early adulthood, ranging from physical changes to cognitive growth and from social relationships to mental health challenges. The various contexts of development are considered, including intra-individual, peer, family, school, and the broader society. Perhaps most importantly, this book goes beyond presenting information about adolescent development to consider how educators can understand and use this information to help adolescents navigate the challenges of this period of life and thrive, both in school and beyond school walls. Adolescence is a truly dynamic period of life, and by understanding development during this period, and the challenges and opportunities this development provides, educators can improve their interactions with students and help their students grow.

Digital Features in the Enhanced Etext with MyEducationLab®

Designed to bring readers more directly into the world of adolescents and into the world of the teachers who work with them, integrated media and assessments throughout the etext help readers see the very real impact that developmental psychology concepts have on working with adolescents. These digital learning and assessment resources also

- provide practice using developmental psychology concepts in teaching situations,
- help students see how well they understand the concepts presented in the book and the media resources, and
- help students think about and process more deeply adolescent development.

The online resources in the Enhanced Etext with MyEducationLab include:

Video Examples. Embedded videos throughout the text provide illustrations of adolescent development concepts in action. These video examples show students and teachers working in classrooms, as well individual students or teachers describing their thinking or experiences. See pages 62 and 67 for some examples.

Self-Checks. Throughout the chapters readers will find MyEdLab: Self-Check quizzes. These are meant to help readers assess how well they have mastered the chapter's learning outcomes. These self-checks are made up of self-grading multiple-choice items that not only provide feedback on whether questions are answered correctly or incorrectly, but also provide rationales for both correct and incorrect answers. See pages 57 and 60 for some examples.

Application Exercises. Tied to specific chapter learning outcomes, these scaffolded analysis exercises challenge readers to use chapter content to reflect on teaching and learning in real classrooms. Once readers provide their own answers to the questions, they receive feedback in the form of model answers written my experts. See pages 68 and 71 for some examples.

Ancillary Materials

The following resources are available for instructors to download on www.pearsonhighered.com/educators. Instructors can enter the author or title of this book, select this particular edition of the book, and then click on the "Resources" tab to log in and download textbook supplements.

Instructor's Resource Manual. An Instructor's Resource Manual includes suggestions for learning activities.

PowerPoint® Slides. The PowerPoint slides include key concept summarizations, diagrams, and other graphic aids to enhance learning. They are designed to help students understand, organize, and remember core concepts and theories.

Test Bank. The test bank includes multiple choice and essay questions for each of the chapters.

TestGen. TestGen is a powerful test generator that you install on your computer and use in conjunction with the TestGen testbank file for your text. Assessments, including equations, graphs, and scientific notation, may be created for both print or testing online.

TestGen is available exclusively from Pearson Education publishers. You install TestGen on your personal computer (Windows or Macintosh) and create your own tests for classroom testing and for other specialized delivery options, such as over a local area network or on the web. A test bank, which is also called a Test Item File (TIF), typically contains a large set of test items, organized by chapter and ready for your use in creating a test, based on the associated textbook material. The tests can be downloaded in the following formats:

TestGen Testbank file–MAC
TestGen Testbank file–PC
Angel TestGen Conversion
Test Bank for Blackboard Learning System
Desire to Learn TestGen Conversion
Moodle TestGen Conversion
Sakai TestGen Conversion
Test Bank for Blackboard CE/Vista

Acknowledgments

As always, the production of a book requires the work of many more people than those who get their names on the front cover. We owe a debt of gratitude to our friend and colleague Barbara Hofer who got the ball rolling with this book. We would also like to thank Kevin Davis and Gail Gottfried at Pearson who have worked with us and guided us patiently every step of the way. We have been very fortunate to receive assistance and feedback from several students including Caitlin Courshon, Megan Sanders, Kate Kovach, Colleen Kuusinen, Libby North, Sarah McKellar, Lauren Allport, and Hyo-Eun Bang. This book has been improved by the thoughtful comments of many anonymous reviewers, to whom we are grateful. The production team at Pearson has also been very supportive and helpful, so thank you to Janelle Rogers and Pam Bennett. Finally, we would like to acknowledge and thank our families for putting up with us every time we said, "I can't right now, I've got to work on this book!" We owe you and we know it.

We would like to thank the following reviewers of the manuscript for their valuable input: Teresa L. Branson, University of Southern Indiana; Marsha Joyce Brigman, University of North Carolina, Charlotte; Aerika Brittian, University of Illinois at Chicago; Farah A. Ibrahim, University of Colorado Denver; Rhonda Jamison, University of Maine Farmington; Steve Kucinski, The Ohio State University / Otterbein University; Jodi Burrus Newman, University of Washington; Sharon Paulson, Ball State University; Lynda Randall, California State University, Fullerton; Jacqueline Romano, University of North Texas–Dallas; M. Cecil Smith, West Virginia University; Pamela A. Staples, University of Nevada, Las Vegas; and Mary Waldron, Indiana University.

Brief Contents

Contents

3 Cognitive and Intellectual Development 50

4 Social and Moral Development 82

---

5 Identity and Self-Perceptions   106

---

6 Families   140

7 Technology and Media   170

10 Sexuality and Romantic Relationships   270

11 Mental Health, Coping Strategies, and Problems   296

12   Moving Into Adulthood   324

Adolescent Development
for Educators

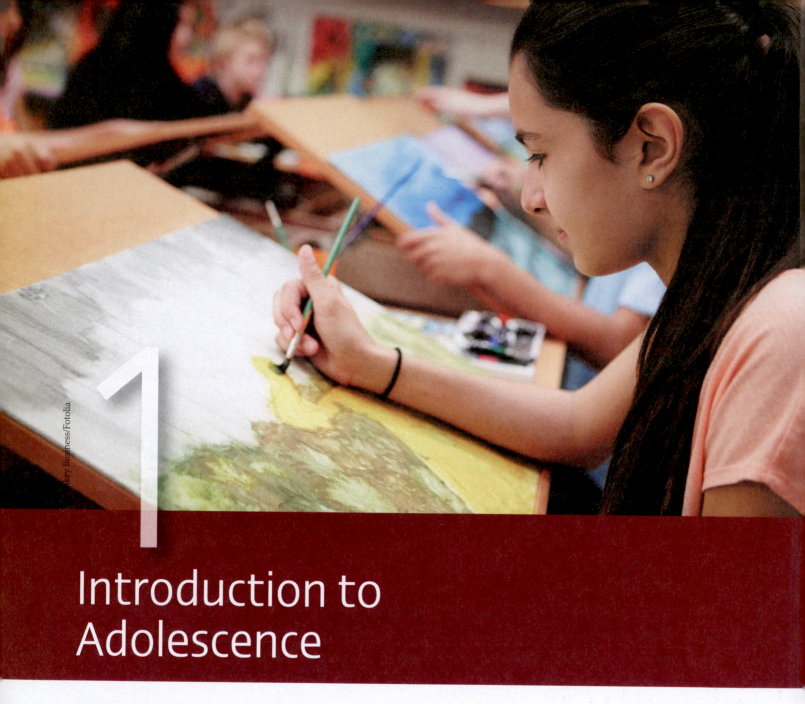

1

Introduction to Adolescence

Learning Outcomes

1.1 You will be able to trace the evolution of the developmental period known as adolescence.

1.2 You will be able to describe the changes inherent in adolescent development and the issues that many adolescents face in contemporary society.

1.3 You will be able to differentiate between bio-psycho-social theories and systems theories of adolescent development.

Introduction

Middle and high school teachers generally instruct students in academic content areas. Indeed, most educators of adolescents study a specialty area and become licensed to teach in a specific academic content domain (e.g., math, language arts, chemistry, physical education, etc.). However, knowledge of your content domain and knowledge about how to teach in that domain are not sufficient. To be an effective teacher, you will also need an understanding of adolescent development to effectively work with your adolescent learners.

Teachers of adolescent students hope that their students will be fully engaged in class lessons, attend to their assignments, prepare for their exams, and take coursework seriously. However, the stage of adolescence presents a plethora of changes to which youth must adapt; developmental changes and transitions often impinge on engagement in academics. Furthermore, most adolescents lead complex and busy lives. Some of our students must balance their academics with extracurricular activities, whereas others must balance their schoolwork with complicated family situations, with work commitments, with medical limitations, and with numerous other issues. Knowledge of the changes inherent in adolescent development and the issues that many adolescents face in contemporary society will help you understand your students and support their engagement in your courses.

Let's consider three different adolescents. As you'll see, although these students are all "adolescents," they are all dealing with different situations in their academic, personal, and social lives.

>>>

RALPH

Ralph was so proud of the B+ average he earned in his first year in high school. He struggled a little with algebra, but excelled in English. Ralph's English teacher recommended that he think about getting involved in the school newspaper the following year. At the end of his freshman year, Ralph was enthusiastic about school and looking forward to his sophomore year. However, his positive attitude dissipated over the summer when his family experienced a series of challenges that put increasing pressure on Ralph to be a caretaker and contribute to family finances. His mom's health declined as her symptoms associated with multiple sclerosis worsened. His dad moved away, supposedly to take advantage of better work opportunities in another city, but the checks he sent home were few and far between. That summer, Ralph assumed increasing responsibility for his 10-year-old brother and for paying the bills. Ralph was able to get a full-time job at the local supermarket, and when fall came around, his manager was able to switch him to the late shift to accommodate his school schedule. Although Ralph continued to get B grades in his courses during the first quarter of the academic year, he started to miss school fairly often because he was so exhausted. His average fell to a low C by the middle of the year, and he was failing several classes by April. Sometimes, Ralph would see his freshman English teacher and think wistfully of writing for the school newspaper. But Ralph knew that writing for the paper was not in the cards for him. Indeed, Ralph could not manage just his classes in combination with his work and family obligations. Ralph didn't return to high school his junior year.

ANIKA

Anika's head hurts from studying. She didn't get home from her away soccer game until 9:00 p.m. and got a late start on her homework. It is almost midnight, and she is exhausted. She is almost done with her biology lab report, but she still has to study for her Spanish test tomorrow. She had hoped to get through the extra-credit problems for geometry tonight, but she decides to save that work until tomorrow's study hall. Her mother comes to her door and tells her she needs to go to sleep. Anika is familiar with her mother's lecture on the importance of sleep, but she won't go to bed until she gets her work done. Despite what her mom says about sleep, she knows her parents want her to keep up her straight A's and get into a prestigious university. After all, it was her parents who encouraged her to take so many honors and Advanced Placement classes. Anika can't wait until the school year is over. It is such a grind. She can't remember the last time she just hung out with friends and had fun.

JOHN

John presses snooze on the alarm clock and goes back to sleep for a few more minutes. Monday mornings are usually tough, but today is especially brutal after such a busy weekend. On Friday night John went to the football game at the school and then to a party that went until 2:00 in the morning. On Saturday John went camping up north with a large group of students. His friend Tim's family has a cabin on the lake. It was a beautiful day, and everyone was out on the water all day. Tim and John built a bonfire, and one of their friends had managed to get a keg, so there was no shortage of beer. In fact, they had enough beer to keep drinking on Sunday afternoon. John didn't get home until after 10:00 on Sunday night. John groans as he thinks about all the schoolwork he did not get to over the weekend. He has a Spanish test second hour and a paper due in American History. Right now the paper is in a pretty rough state. He thinks he should be able to get C's on both of these tasks. That is good enough, he thinks. High school is supposed to be the best years of your life, right?

Now stop and think about the stories of Ralph, Anika, and John. There is much occurring in their lives, and they have to deal with many situations, some highly complex, simultaneously. Many questions come to mind. For example:

- Are they mature enough to make the necessary decisions in these situations?
- Can they weigh the costs and benefits of their decisions now against their future costs and benefits?
- When these students are motivated to excel in multiple domains of their lives, how do they prioritize?
- Are there school, social, or community services that can be of assistance to these students?
- What is the effect of all of this on their psychological and physiological well-being?

In this text, we approach adolescent development from the perspective of educators (i.e., prospective teachers of adolescents). Consequently, let's now think about some questions that might occur to these students' teachers:

- What can I do to support these students?
- Am I, as a teacher, allowed to intervene? Some of these are family issues, so what role do I play?
- As a teacher of a specific content area, how can I help these students to succeed in my course specifically, and in all of their courses in general?
- Are there resources within the school that I can call upon to assist these students?
- What more do I need to know about these students and their development to support them effectively?

Defining Adolescence

The definition and meaning of adolescence is something that varies considerably by cultural context and by historical period. Although we generally think of adolescence as a period of development that roughly covers the teenage years, it is important to note that the concept of an adolescent period of development is a social construction, and a fairly recent one. As such, it is a concept that is riddled with contradictions. Does adolescence begin with the onset of the physical changes associated with puberty? Some children experience these changes before their 10th birthdays, and others not until well into their teenage years. The cognitive development associated with the adolescent period continues well into the early 20s, yet we rarely consider a 22- or 23-year-old an adolescent. In the United States, individuals are considered to be legal adults when they turn 18 years old, even though many physical, cognitive, and social changes associated with adolescence are still occurring at that age. So what is adolescence? And what are the forces that led to the creation of the concept?

Although the odd period of development between childhood and adulthood was discussed as far back as Plato's days in ancient Greece, it was not commonly recognized, or named, as a separate period of development until the industrialization of the Western world occurred. As work moved off the farm and into industrial hubs (i.e., cities), a number of changes transformed the educational and working lives of inhabitants. Some of these changes had the effect of creating a distinct period of development between childhood and adulthood that came to be known as adolescence.

One of the important changes that accompanied the Industrial Revolution at the end of the 19th and beginning of the 20th centuries was the creation of child labor laws (Tyack, 1990). Industrialists' thirst for cheap and manageable labor (i.e., workers who would not go on strike) led to the hiring and exploitation of many children and early adolescents. In the United States, there were no federal laws regulating child labor until 1916 (University of Iowa Labor Center and Center for Human Rights, 2015). Until then, states set their own child labor laws, and some states set few if any restrictions on child labor well into the 20th century. But activists concerned with the debilitating consequences of children working long hours for little pay in unhealthy environments, such as mines and factories, began raising awareness of the issue. Ultimately, this activism led to the passage of child labor laws restricting how many hours children and adolescents could work, the kind of work they could do, and how much they must be paid, at minimum. The first set of federal child labor laws to be passed and not overturned as unconstitutional by the Supreme Court was the Fair Labor Standards Act of 1938 (General Records of the United States Government, 1916). This act set curbs on the number of hours that early adolescents could work, creating a distinct period of adolescent development in the eyes of labor laws.

A second, related development establishing adolescence was the expansion of compulsory education. As the world became more technologically advanced during the Industrial Revolution, more states began passing laws requiring students to stay in school for more years (Tyack, 1990). This extended period of education, along with child labor laws, created a more distinct period of development in which adolescents' daily lives were less likely to be filled with adult-like roles of work or apprenticeship.

As adolescents (and adults) moved to cities for work, and as child labor laws reduced the number of hours adolescents spent at work, there were more opportunities for adolescents to become involved in delinquent behaviors. These delinquent acts were a source of concern for many states, and the desire to curb them was strong. However, there was also a growing recognition that adolescents—who had always been treated like adults in criminal proceedings—were different from adults. As this recognition grew, activists worked to create a juvenile justice system that treated children and adolescents differently from adults. Juvenile courts were established, as was juvenile hall as an alternative to prison for housing more serious juvenile offenders.

Part of the reason for the increasing awareness of adolescence as a period of development that is distinct from childhood and adulthood was the work of scholars conducting research on adolescent populations around the beginning of the 20th century. The most notable of these was G. Stanley Hall, widely considered the father of the study of adolescence. In 1904 Hall published a two-volume book about adolescent development. In this book, he described the physiological, romantic, educational, and criminological development particular to the adolescent period (Hall, 1904). Many of the ideas first presented in this book are still being discussed and studied today, such as the link between adolescent impulsivity and crime, and whether adolescence is a biologically based period of heightened stress and emotionality (i.e., the **storm-and-stress view**). Although Hall had some interesting ideas that have since been discredited (e.g., he seemed to be quite interested in the evils of masturbation), his work and ideas were an important reason that adolescence became recognized as a distinct period of development.

Cultural Variations

In the majority culture in the United States, there are few clear markers of the transition from childhood to adolescence, or from adolescence to adulthood. There are certain transitions built into social structures and laws (e.g., starting middle school, graduating from high school, turning 18, turning 21), but for the most part the entry and exit into and out of adolescence is nebulous. But in many cultures, including some within the United States, there are rituals designed specifically to mark the end of childhood and the beginning of adolescence or adulthood. For example, in many tribal societies there are rituals that involve acts of strength or courage, body piercings or markings, celebrations, and the adolescent moving out of the childhood home. In the United States, different cultures mark the end of childhood and the beginning of adolescence/adulthood with religious rituals (e.g., bar mitzvah or bat mitzvah in the Jewish tradition, confirmation in the Catholic tradition), or with rituals designed to present adolescent girls as ready for the broader roles of early adulthood (e.g., a quinceañera for 15-year-old girls from families of Latin American descent, a debutante ball for wealthy or aristocratic teenage girls, a sweet 16 party for whomever wants one). Most of these traditions date back to the days before adolescence was truly considered a separate period, and marked the age that children were now deemed ready to take on more adult roles, such as getting married (for the girls) or becoming full-fledged members of religious communities. As modern society and globalization have extended the period between the end of childhood and the beginning of adulthood, many of these rituals are considered more as celebratory markers of growing up than as indicators of adolescents' readiness to assume adult roles.

MyEdLab Self-Check 1.1

The Lives of Adolescents

Adolescents balance school with many other personal and social concerns. The issues we saw in Ralph, Anika, and John's stories at the beginning of the chapter are representative of those present in many adolescents' lives. The adolescent of today has to deal with many issues that adolescents of past generations did not face. School, which is a major part of most adolescents' lives, will matter in different ways for different adolescents. For some, academic achievement may be a huge priority, to the extent that we might even worry about some adolescents' perfectionist tendencies; for others, there may be more balance between the importance of academics and of other aspects of one's life. And for still others, school will simply not be a priority.

In Table 1.1, we present recent statistics on some of the challenges encountered by adolescents outside of school. We present this information to give you an idea of some of the variables that come into play in our students' lives. As you will see, many adolescents live in poverty and face severe nutritional and health-related dilemmas. These statistics provide a snapshot of some of the issues that affect adolescents' lives. As a prospective teacher of adolescents, you need to be cognizant of the fact that all of these (and many more) issues exist in our students' lives. Although as educators we can't solve all of our students' problems, it is important to be aware of the larger contexts of our students' lives and the implications of those issues as we work with our students.

MyEdLab
Video Example 1.1

Josh articulately describes some of the challenges that adolescents face, including his early maturation, a friend with an eating disorder, peer pressure, sexual relationships, and his after-school job. We explore these issues, and Josh's views, in more detail in later chapters.

Our goal in this book is to give you, as future teachers, a balanced view of adolescence informed by the latest research and up-to-date evidence. Although Table 1.1 lists some of the challenging situations facing today's youth, adolescents also have many wonderful opportunities and choices available to them. Many schools and communities afford adolescents opportunities to participate in many clubs and activities, to have internships, to learn novel skills through innovative technology, to collaborate and communicate with individuals throughout the world, to learn multiple languages, and to participate in countless other opportunities. As you will see, one of our goals in this book is to provide you with information and strategies that will help you to assist your students in balancing the many wonderful opportunities available to them with the social realities in which our students live.

MyEdLab Self-Check 1.2

TABLE 1.1   **Statistics About Adolescents**

Domain	Statistic	Source
Health	Of adolescents aged 12–17, 6.6% smoked cigarettes in past month.	Centers for Disease Control (2014)
	Of adolescents aged 12–17, 12.9% used alcohol in the past month.	
	Almost 1 out of 4 high school seniors drank some alcohol during the past month.	U.S. Department of Health and Human Services (2015)
	More than 1 out of 5 high school seniors reported binge drinking in the past 2 weeks.	
	By 12th grade, about one-half of adolescents have abused an illegal drug at least once.	
Nutrition	Of individuals with an eating disorder, 95% are between the ages of 12 and 25.8.	National Association of Anorexia Nervosa and Associated Disorders (2015)
	Almost half of adolescent females and one-third of adolescent males use unhealthy weight-control techniques (e.g., skipping meals, fasting, vomiting, taking laxatives).	
	Of adolescents aged 12–19, 18.4% are obese.	Centers for Disease Control (2015)
Poverty	In 2013, 20% of children lived in families with incomes below the poverty line.	Child Trends (2014)
	Adolescents from low-income households are more likely to engage in risky behaviors and to have sex before the age of 16 than are adolescents from middle-income households.	U.S. Department of Health and Human Services (2009)

Frameworks for Conceptualizing Adolescent Development

In the scenarios at the beginning of this chapter, Ralph dropped out of school so that he could earn money after his father left the family, Anika felt compelled to spend all of her time studying so she could earn excellent grades and gain admission to a prestigious university, and John spent a lot of time partying. On the surface, it seems easy to understand the motivation behind the behaviors of Ralph, Anika, and John presented in these scenarios. But if we dig a little beneath the surface and ask a few questions, the complexity of their behaviors, and of adolescent development more broadly, becomes apparent. For example, why does Anika spend so much time studying when other girls at her school, many from similar socioeconomic backgrounds and similar levels of cognitive ability, do not? Why does Ralph decide to drop out of school when other students with full-time jobs find a way to manage both work and school? How are the behaviors and decisions of Ralph and Anika and John influenced by their friends, their families, their own personalities, and the social and economic norms of their cultures and communities?

The gradual unfolding of a human life is so complex, and influenced by so many factors, that it is useful to have an overarching framework in mind to try to make sense of it all. Without such a framework, it can be tempting to ignore the combination of factors that influence behavior and instead settle for simplistic explanations. We will be more effective as teachers when we consider the complexities of adolescent development. Why is Anika so driven to get straight A's? Is it because her parents are demanding? Why does Ralph drop out of school? Is it because his father was a bad role model? Why does John spend so much time partying? Is it because his parents don't pay enough attention to him? From a scientific perspective, these proposed simplistic answers are not satisfying because we understand that human development and behavior are more complex than that. From a less scientific and more person-oriented perspective, these explanations of Anika's, Ralph's and John's behaviors are unsatisfying because they reduce these behaviors to simple cause-and-effect, mechanistic outcomes.

Psychologists have produced numerous theoretical frameworks for interpreting and understanding developmental processes. In this book, we employ two of them: The bio-psycho-social model and systems theories.

The Bio-Psycho-Social Model

The **bio-psycho-social model** of development is based on two principles. First, development is influenced by all three of these factors: *biological* growth and change, *psychological* (the individual's internal thoughts, beliefs, and feelings) growth, and the *social* context within which individuals function. Second, these three areas of development are in constant interaction with and mutually influence one another. The model was developed by Engel (1977) as a new way to think about disease and medical treatment. Since its introduction, it has been adopted by a variety of disciplines, including developmental psychology.

To illustrate how the bio-psycho-social model can help us understand behavior during adolescence, consider the example of Ralph at the beginning of the chapter. Biologically, by the age of 16 Ralph probably has developed physically to resemble a man more than a boy. In addition, changes in his brain—specifically the early development of his prefrontal cortex—allow him to think about more abstract concepts, such as his responsibility to his family and what it means to be a man in today's society. These physical developments that Ralph experiences as an adolescent are associated with psychological changes—how he views himself and his beliefs. Partly as a result of his physical transformation, his identity probably began to shift from that of a boy concerned with childish pastimes to a man with responsibilities. This shift in identity may have increased his desire to be able to land a job. This is an example of the reciprocal nature of the association between these different areas of development, as physical changes influence psychological factors, which in turn influence physical development (see Figure 1.1).

The social part of the bio-psycho-social model is also clearly influencing Ralph's thinking and behavior. He lives in a society that promotes the idea that a man has a responsibility to provide for his family, and this influences his beliefs about identity concerning what it means to be a man, as well as his beliefs about what his obligations are now that his father has left. His own family may also be shaping his beliefs. Influenced by his growing body and more mature cognitive abilities, his mother may believe that he is ready to work full time, and may be encouraging him to do so. In his job he may become friends with older coworkers who encourage him to focus on making money rather than spending time in school. He may pay attention to the many materialistic messages in our culture that emphasize making money now rather than working and planning for the future. The development of his prefrontal cortex is still incomplete, impeding his ability to make long-range plans (such as whether or not to attend college) and to think about the long-term harm he may be

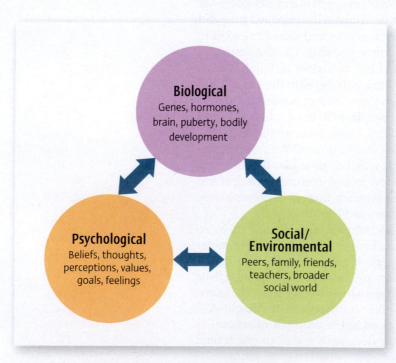

FIGURE 1.1 Bio-Psycho-Social Model

doing to his career and earning potential by dropping out of school at age 16. Indeed, hanging out with coworkers who are older may get Ralph involved in drinking alcohol and experimenting with drugs, and these may actually impair the development of his brain and weaken his capacity for planning and foresight.

Each piece of the bio-psycho-social model has multiple components, and each piece of the model influences, and is influenced by, the other pieces. In the social part of the model, for example, there are friends, family, teachers, messages in the larger society, and cultural influences. This model emphasizes the major areas of development and reminds those who study adolescent development that that major areas of development are in constant interaction with one another and influence one another in direct and reciprocal ways. As teachers, we need to remember that physiological, psychological, and social variables all contribute to our students' complex lives.

Systems Theories

Systems theories are similar to the bio-psycho-social model in that they recognize development and behavior as being influenced by several factors at once, and recognize that those factors influence one another. Systems theories assume that adolescents are part of a complex system, and that each part of the system can influence other parts in the system. In addition, each context in which the adolescent operates is, itself, a system. For example, the family an adolescent lives with is a system. If the parents in the system have an argument and are angry with each other, they may be short-tempered with their children and snap at them. This may cause the children to argue with each other, and their bickering may further enrage their parents. In addition to the reciprocal influences within a subsystem such as the family, the subsystems in the adolescent's life can affect one another. Suppose the adolescent's mother gets a nice raise at work, comes home feeling happy, and takes the rest of the family out to dinner to celebrate, causing everyone's mood to improve and resulting in harmony among the siblings, at least for a night.

MyEdLab
Video Example 1.2

Subsystems are contexts in which an adolescent lives. Family, friends, and community are subsystems in this boy's environment.

Bronfenbrenner proposed an ecological model of a system focused on how individuals develop within a multilayered social and environmental system (Bronfenbrenner and Morris, 2006). He called his model a **bioecological model** (a revision of his earlier **ecological systems theory** model; Bronfenbrenner, 1989), and the levels of the model include the individual; close social systems within which the individual operates, such as family, school, and close friends (the **microsystem**); linkages and processes that take place between two or more microsystems (the **mesosystem**); a larger social system that includes extended family, the neighborhood, and community organizations (the **exosystem**); and the larger society and culture in which one lives (the **macrosystem**). This model is presented in Figure 1.2.

Another systems approach, **dynamic systems theory**, emphasizes the ever-changing nature of the system within which adolescents operate, and the adjustments that individuals make to adapt to the changing system (Fischer & Bidell, 2006; Fogel & Garvey, 2007). Dynamic systems theorists argue that the system is constantly changing and adapting as those within it change. For example, when an adolescent gets his driver's license, he may gain a sense of independence that changes his perception of how much autonomy his parents should grant him. His parents, however, may respond to his new license with apprehension, because a new danger (their son driving) has been introduced. The parents' fear causes them to impose new restrictions on him (e.g., a strict curfew, location monitoring through his cell phone, etc.), causing conflict between the adolescent and his parents. With the family system now out of balance, all the members of the system will have to adapt so that the system can reorganize and function smoothly.

Let's consider how we might apply systems theories to the story of Anika that appeared at the beginning of the chapter. She is working herself to the point of exhaustion in her quest to excel in school and gain entry into a top college. How might we understand this behavior from a systems perspective? First, we might note the salient

FIGURE 1.2
**Bronfenbrenner's
Bioecological Model**

Source: Based on Bronfenbrenner, U., & Morris, P. A. (2006). The bioecological model of human development. In R. M. Lerner (Ed.), Handbook of Child Psychology, Vol. 1: Theoretical Models of Human Development (6th ed., pp. 793–828). Hoboken, NJ: Wiley.

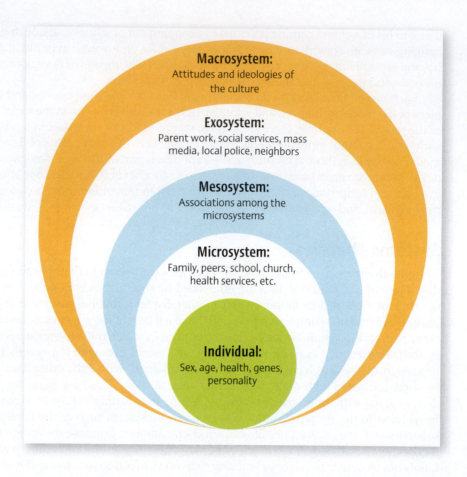

Macrosystem:
Attitudes and ideologies of the culture

Exosystem:
Parent work, social services, mass media, local police, neighbors

Mesosystem:
Associations among the microsystems

Microsystem:
Family, peers, school, church, health services, etc.

Individual:
Sex, age, health, genes, personality

MyEdLab

**Application Exercise 1.1
Theories of Adolescent
Development** Consider how the bio-psycho-social model and systems theories of development can help to explain this adolescent boy's thoughts, feelings, and behaviors.

subsystems within which Anika operates. These include her intrapsychic life (i.e., her goals, her personality, her identity), her family, her peer network, and her school system, among others. In her family system, Anika's role may be that of super-academic-achiever, perhaps because she showed great promise as a child and perhaps because her older siblings had already taken the roles of great athlete and temperamental artist, for example. Striving to make her own mark, and with the encouragement/pressure of her parents, Anika may have developed personal goals and an identity consistent with those of an academic star. At school, Anika has always received good grades and recognition for her academic accomplishments. These accomplishments in her school system have reinforced her identity as academically oriented and her family's perceptions of her as an academic star. When these subsystems are considered within a larger societal system that places tremendous pressure on adolescents to be super-achievers who should accept nothing less than admission to an Ivy League school, Anika feels compelled to push herself to the brink of exhaustion. Teachers who are aware of the multiple systems that are influencing students' daily lives can be more supportive of students like Anika.

Framing of This Book

In this book, we discuss adolescent development in a series of chapters, each with a distinct focus on a particular aspect of adolescent life and development. This focus on particular aspects of the developmental process is necessary to explain these pieces clearly, but it is important to remember that no part of the developmental process occurs in isolation. Rather, the different elements of development occur simultaneously, and often influence one another. One cannot fully understand the physical changes that occur during adolescence without considering the social, cognitive, and environmental factors that affect physical development, or the ways that physical development affects how the adolescent thinks, behaves, and is responded to by others. As teachers, we need to be cognizant of the complexity of the developmental changes that are occurring in our students. Throughout this book, we use the bio-psycho-social model and systems theories to illustrate and understand the development of adolescents.

Why This Book?

We begin this book by introducing information about the complex lives of adolescents because this will serve as a major theme throughout this book. This book is written specifically from the perspective of education and teachers. We contend that teachers of adolescents need to know about all aspects of the lives of adolescents, in order to be effective educators.

A question that you may be pondering right now is whether or not Ralph's complex situation is really the concern of his teachers. Suppose that you are Ralph's math teacher. Your job is to teach math. You might be thinking that, as an educator, as long as you understand the material that you are teaching (e.g., math) and are able to effectively present the material and assess student learning, then you have met your responsibilities. What we hope to convince you of in this book is that you will be an even better teacher if you understand some of the larger issues facing adolescents.

MyEdLab **Self-Check 1.3**

Structure of the Book

This book has been written specifically for individuals who plan to work in educational settings with adolescents. Within each chapter, we discuss current research and issues related to a variety of topics that are relevant for those educating adolescents. In addition, within each chapter, we specifically focus on the implications of the content for educators. Whereas the connections between some of these topics and adolescent education may not initially seem obvious to you, we hope that after you take this journey with us, you will realize that there are many issues that adolescent educators need to know about. We conclude each chapter with implications for educators.

Think again about Ralph, Anika, and John. They are balancing their academic, personal, and social lives in quite different ways. All of them must also contend with other adolescent issues:

- Temptations to engage in various risky behaviors (e.g., smoking, drugs, etc.)
- The use of social media
- Physiological development (i.e., puberty)
- Identity development

Numerous other topics could be added to this list. Below we briefly introduce the topics that we will cover and some of the reasons why these topics are relevant for educators.

Chapter 2: Physical Development

During adolescence, the human body goes through many changes. Nevertheless, physical development is not a linear process—physiological changes do not occur at the same time and even in the same order for all adolescents. In addition, development does not occur in similar ways for males and females. Thus, a teacher of eighth graders may have some students who are over 6 feet tall, and others who are under 4 feet tall; some students may be extremely physically developed, whereas others may have barely entered into puberty. These developmental shifts certainly can and will affect dynamics in your classroom.

Chapter 3: Cognitive and Intellectual Development

You may believe that once childhood has ended, cognitive development is complete. As we will discuss, this is certainly not the case. Many aspects of your students' thinking still develop and change during adolescence. For example, the ability to use advanced cognitive skills and to think about abstract concepts matures during adolescence. Thus, as a teacher, you may find that some of your students are better able to understand complex topics than are others. As an educator, this is extremely important to understand: Some of the differences in your students' abilities may be developmental in nature. If a student doesn't understand a complex topic, it isn't necessarily because the student isn't intelligent enough to learn the topic; it may just be the case that the student isn't ready for that level of complexity at the present.

Chapter 4: Social and Moral Development

Social and moral reasoning also are still developing during the adolescent years. Let's consider students' reasoning about complex issues or problems. A social studies teacher might want to engage her students in a conversation about differences between liberal and conservative political viewpoints. Nevertheless, the teacher may find that whereas some of her students are able to engage in discussions of this nature and appreciate diverse viewpoints, others may not be able to consider multiple perspectives as easily. Thus, the discussions that you have with your students may be complicated by their developing abilities. An understanding of these developmental trends will help you to better manage such discussions.

Chapter 5: Identity and Self-Perceptions

During adolescence, our students begin to seriously consider their futures. Adolescents think about various career options and about their future professional identities—some may see themselves as becoming lawyers, others may be considering careers in music, and others may be completely undecided about the future. In addition, adolescents spend much time ruminating about other aspects of their identities (e.g., some adolescents may want to be seen as being highly athletic, whereas others may want to be perceived as being highly engaged in the arts). Educators who are aware of adolescents' concerns about their developing identities can provide support for adolescents, and also can build identity-exploration issues into lessons and assignments.

Chapter 6: Families

As a teacher, you will work with students from different family backgrounds. We will discuss a wide array of family situations to help you think about your assumptions and approaches in working with diverse families. Furthermore, adolescence is a time of great change for all families. At this stage, students desire autonomy, and how parents and teachers respond to this need has implications for adolescent adjustment in and out of the classroom. The parents of your adolescent learners will differ in their involvement in their children's learning at school. Overall, parental involvement tends to decline during the adolescent years. It is important for educators of adolescent students to learn about a variety of strategies that schools and teachers can use to promote parental involvement.

Chapter 7: Technology and Media

Technology and media have a huge presence in adolescents' lives. Today's adolescents are highly immersed in and interacting with technology and media for many of their waking hours. For many adolescents, easy access to the Internet allows for immediate exposure to a plethora of information. With smaller and more portable devices, watching TV and movies and playing video games are easier than ever. Social media and texting allow for instantaneous communication among peers. Consideration of the role of technology and media for a full understanding of your adolescent students is essential. Teachers are in a position where they can promote responsible and appropriate use of technology. Teachers can also help adolescents develop the skills to navigate and understand the vast array of images and information on the Internet and in the media.

Chapter 8: Peers

During adolescence, the social worlds of youth expand greatly, and they come into contact with a much wider array of peers. For many adolescents, the transition to middle and high school brings changes to their social networks. Adolescents have many different types of relationships with peers—close friends, peer groups, and the larger social scene at middle and high schools. Peer influence is stronger during adolescence than at any other stage of life. Understanding the different facets of adolescents' relationships with peers can help teachers better facilitate positive peer relationships. One of the most important things teachers can do is to work with students to create an emotionally supportive classroom that will enhance achievement and motivation.

Chapter 9: Motivation, Classrooms, and Schools

Adolescents' experiences in classrooms and schools vary widely and have implications for their engagement in academics and extracurricular activities. Teachers are in a position to create a classroom climate that will shape students' motivation in critical ways. Schools differ in their grade configurations, their locations, their sizes, and in numerous other ways. In addition, most adolescents experience transitions as they move from one school (e.g., middle school) to another (e.g., high school). The differences and transitional periods are associated with a host of both positive and negative outcomes for students. Knowledge of these differences, and how they are related to motivation, engagement, and achievement, will help in your work with adolescent students.

Chapter 10: Sex and Romantic Relationships

One of the hallmarks of adolescence is sexual development. Romantic relationships, sexual exploration, and dating become salient aspects of our students' lives. An understanding of the importance of dating and sexuality during adolescence is essential for educators. Teachers need to understand that an interest in dating and relationships is not simply a distraction for our students; it is often a major concern for many adolescents. The emerging romantic and sexual lives of adolescents also bring risks and challenges, including pregnancy, sexually transmitted diseases, dating violence, and managing the emotional ups and downs of romantic relationships. Teachers should be aware of these challenges and what schools can do to address them.

Chapter 11: Mental Health, Coping Strategies, and Problems

Adolescents experience an array of emotions, anxieties, and fears. Many of these represent normal shifts in mood based on the events that occur in our students' lives. But at other times, adolescents experience more significant mental health events, including depression, suicidal ideation, eating disorders, and feelings of aggression. At times, mental health issues become apparent to you as a teacher during the school day. Educators need to be able to recognize potential warning signs of such concerns, so that they can provide appropriate support and consult with and refer potentially serious cases to more qualified experts.

Chapter 12: Moving into Adulthood

When our students complete high school, they do not automatically transition into adult status. Many transitions occur after high school graduation. Some students matriculate to college, some enter the workforce, some join the military, and some choose among numerous other options. Simultaneously, adolescents are still experiencing cognitive, social, and physiological development. Educators can play important roles in providing senior high school students with supports that will help to facilitate such continuing transitions.

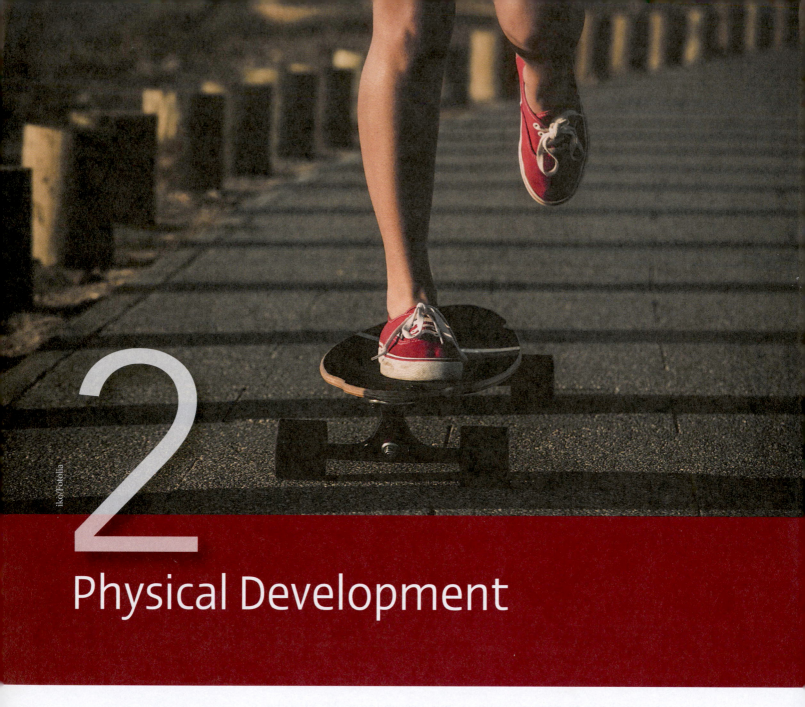
iko/Fotolia

2

Physical Development

Learning Outcomes

2.1 You will be able to describe the physiological changes that occur during adolescence and the systems involved in pubertal development.

2.2 You will be able to identify key changes that occur in the brain during adolescence and describe how these are associated with adolescent reasoning and behavior.

2.3 You will be able to describe how the physical changes that occur during adolescence affect how adolescents think about themselves, how they are perceived and treated by others, and how this differs for boys and girls.

2.4 You will be able to describe how the physical changes that occur during adolescence are associated with the health and well-being of adolescents.

2.5 You will be able to identify ways that educators can help adolescents cope with the challenges associated with physical development and adopt healthy attitudes and behaviors.

Introduction

Adolescence is a period of tremendous physical growth and biological development. It is not uncommon for a middle school teacher to have students who still look very much like children in the same class with students who look more like adults. This disparity in appearance often influences others to treat adolescents quite differently, with mature-looking girls receiving attention from older boys and immature-looking boys being teased, for example. The physical development of adolescents can place teachers in awkward situations. Consider these examples:

>>>

After teaching third graders for 4 years, Ms. Asher is in her first year of teaching at Westbrook Middle School. She is in the middle of a lesson on identifying themes in literature when she notices a scuffle break out between two boys sitting near the back of her seventh-grade classroom. As she moves toward the scuffle to intervene, she realizes that one of the boys is about 6 inches taller and at least 40 pounds heavier than she is. She wants to break up the fight, but hesitates for a moment, fearing for her own safety.

Mr. Wilson is talking with a group of three 10th-grade girls about a homework assignment in his biology class when one of the girls collapses. As he revives her and guides her to a chair, one of her friends says something about an eating disorder and how she has seen the girl purging after meals.

Ms. Hernandez is a new math teacher at the high school. One day after school, she is talking with a veteran teacher about how the first few weeks have gone. "It's going OK, I guess," she says. "But I have to admit that I'm not sure what to make of some of the students. This one girl, Mandy, can be really nice and friendly to me one day, and then all of a sudden she will be sullen or snap at me over nothing. I'm not sure how to handle the mood swings."

As children grow into more adult-like bodies, there are a number of biological developments that can affect their mood, their behavior, how they view themselves, and how they are viewed by others. Sometimes, it can be difficult to remember that the adult-looking person in your class still thinks more like a child than a grown-up. What is important for educators to know about physical development and biological development during adolescence? What kinds of challenges do adolescents face as their bodies develop, and how can educators help adolescents cope with these challenges? These are some of the questions that we consider in this chapter.

OVERVIEW OF THE CHAPTER

Just about all of the really embarrassing parts of adolescence can be traced back to the biological changes that accompany puberty. The pimples, the breast buds, the cracking voices, the wet dreams—all of these are caused by physical changes that mark the transition from childhood to adolescence. The physiological development associated with puberty sets in motion a series of other important changes for adolescents, ranging from how they think about themselves to whom they associate with and to how parents, teachers, peers, and society expect them to behave. The relative innocence of childhood is replaced by pressures to engage in more adult-like behavior, from taking on more responsibilities at home and school to pressure to have sex, drink beer, or defy parental rules. In this chapter, we begin with a description of the biological basis for the shift into adolescence. Next, we consider the cognitive, social, and emotional changes that result from these biological developments. Finally, we consider the role that teachers and schools can and do play in helping adolescent students adapt to their changing bodies.

Physiological Development During Adolescence

Adolescence has been described as a period of raging hormones, happy hormones, and probably a dozen other variations on the hormones theme. So it appears to be common knowledge that there is some connection between hormones and puberty. But what is actually going on? The answer can be found in the endocrine system. Within the **endocrine system** (Figure 2.1), the **pituitary gland** begins producing and releasing hormones into the body at the onset of puberty, sometime between the ages of 7 and 9. The pituitary gland itself is influenced by hormones coming from the **hypothalamus**. Although the pituitary gland and the rest of the endocrine system are in place at birth, the pituitary gland does not really kick into gear until the body is ready to begin the process of pubertal maturation. At this stage, the hypothalamus releases hormones that disinhibit the pituitary gland, essentially telling the pituitary gland it is time to produce and release the hormones associated with puberty (Figure 2.2).

FIGURE 2.1

The Endocrine System

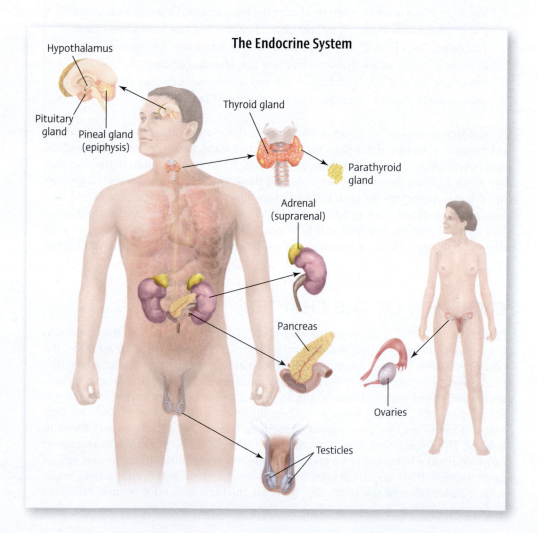

As the pituitary gland gets going, it secretes hormones into the bloodstream that travel to the brain, and this stimulates other glands to begin producing hormones. At first, the endocrine system begins producing small amounts of **hormones** (luteinizing hormone and follicle-stimulating hormone) and distributes them as children sleep. These hormones do not produce any observable changes to the bodies of children but set the stage for later development. Soon, **luteinizing hormone (LH)** stimulates the testes in boys to produce **androgens** such as **testosterone**, and testosterone produces a whole list of more visible bodily changes. These include bodily hair growth, the voice cracking that eventuates in a deeper voice for boys, enlargement of the genitalia, and sperm production. For girls, **follicle-stimulating hormone (FSH)** leads the ovaries to begin producing and releasing hormones, primarily **estrogens**, that lead to the development of breasts, body hair, and menstruation (Susman & Dorn, 2009). Although both males and females produce testosterone, and the amount of testosterone in their bodies is fairly even throughout childhood, in adolescence males produce much more testosterone than do females, creating the marked differences in secondary sex characteristics that emerge in adolescence. Similarly, both males and females produce estrogen and progesterone, but these hormone levels are much higher in girls as compared with boys during adolescence.

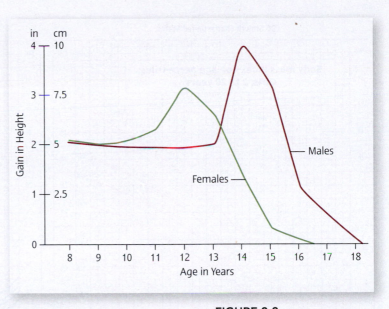

FIGURE 2.2

Average Height Gain at Different Ages During Adolescence (by Gender)

This development of the endocrine system, which brings about changes in **primary sex characteristics** (testes, ovaries, sperm, menstruation), and **secondary sex characteristics** (breasts, pubic and underarm hair), is accompanied by rapid changes in height and weight. After infancy, children grow at a fairly constant rate until they reach puberty. Once the physical changes associated with puberty get into full swing, however, most adolescents experience a growth spurt. Instead of growing the familiar 2 to 2.5 inches per year of childhood, early adolescents grow an average of 3.5 inches (for girls) to 4.1 inches (for boys) during the peak of their growth spurt (Huang, Biro, & Dorn, 2009). This **adolescent growth spurt** typically begins about 2 years earlier for girls than for boys, leading to girls being taller than boys, on average, from about age 11 to age 13 or 14 (DeRose & Brooks-Gunn, 2006). Once boys hit their period of rapid growth (beginning between the ages of 10 to 13), they typically catch up and pass girls in height (Bogin, 2015). Figure 2.2 presents an illustration of growth rates, including peak growth, for males and females during adolescence.

Growth of the physical body during adolescence does not happen proportionally throughout the body. Instead, some parts begin their period of rapid growth before others, with the feet, hands, and head usually leading the way. The last parts of the body to hit the rapid development period are the torso, chest, and shoulders. This uneven sequence of growth produces the awkward, gangly appearance that many adolescents dislike.

The growth of bones is accompanied by a growth in body mass, and the type of body-mass increase differs by gender (Figure 2.3). Whereas boys tend to develop greater muscle mass during the adolescent growth spurt, owing to increases in their levels of testosterone, girls' body-mass increases are largely caused by an increase in fat deposits. So the end result of the adolescent growth spurt for boys tends to be an increase in strength and muscle, whereas for girls the end result is a greater proportion of body fat, although girls also tend to increase their strength during adolescence as well. Boys develop shoulders that are broader than their

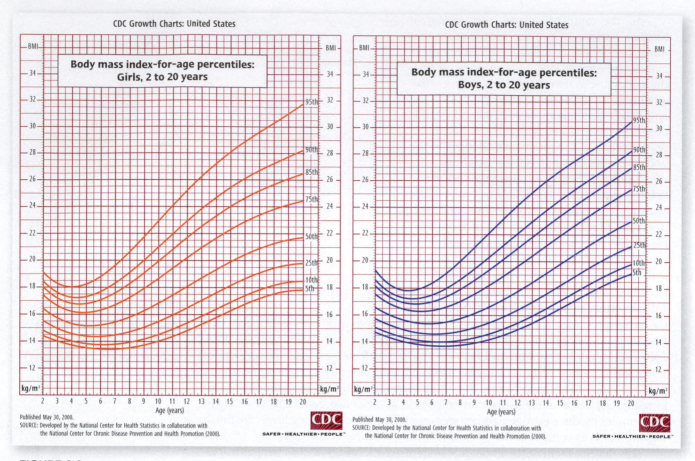

FIGURE 2.3

Body-Mass Index, by Age and Gender

Source: Centers for Disease Control and Prevention, U.S. Department of Health and Human Services.

hips, whereas girls develop hips that are typically wider than their shoulders. The muscle-to-fat ratio is about 3:1 for boys by the end of adolescence, compared with the 5:4 ratio typical for girls (Archibald, Graber, & Brooks-Gunn, 2003). Whereas boys and girls enter adolescence with roughly equal physical strength and athletic abilities, boys exit the adolescent growth spurt with superior strength and athletic ability, on average (Ramos, Frontera, Llopart, & Feliciano, 1998). Table 2.1 summarizes the physical changes associated with puberty for boys and girls.

Researchers and pediatricians use a system known as the **Tanner Scale** (or Tanner Stages) to gauge sexual development. This system, originally developed by Dr. James Tanner in the United Kingdom in 1969 and based on a longitudinal study

TABLE 2.1   **Summary of Physical Changes Associated with Puberty for Boys and Girls**

Girls	Boys
• Increase in hormones, most notably estrogen • Lengthening of limbs, body • Increase in muscle mass and body fat • Development of primary sex characteristics (ovaries, menstruation) • Development of secondary sex characteristics (breasts, body hair, and some facial hair)	• Increase in hormones, most notably androgens such as testosterone • Lengthening of limbs, body • Increase muscle mass • Development of primary sex characteristics (penis length, testes) • Development of secondary sex characteristics (body and facial hair) • Sperm production • Voice cracking

of girls, charts the developmental stages of secondary sex characteristics in girls (e.g., breast development, pubic hair growth) and boys (e.g., penis growth, testicular development, pubic hair growth). Photographs of children and adolescents at different stages of development allow researchers and physicians to determine where children and adolescents are in their pubertal development and whether they are within normal age ranges. (See Figure 2.4 for illustrations of the different Tanner stages.)

Research using the Tanner Scale and other measures of puberty (e.g., rapid growth, menarche, semenarche) has revealed that, in many countries, children are beginning adolescence and progressing through the Tanner Stages earlier now than did adolescents in previous decades (Herman-Giddens et al., 1997, 2012). This pattern of earlier onset of puberty is known as the **secular trend**. In the United States, boys are showing the first signs of puberty 6 months to 2 years earlier than did boys of a few decades ago. Today, Caucasian and Hispanic boys are showing the first signs of puberty at 10.4 years of age, and African American boys are showing signs of pubertal maturation at an average age of just 9.14 years (Herman-Giddens et al., 2012). Among girls, research has documented a decline in the age of the onset of puberty, both in terms of Tanner Stage development and the experience of the first menstrual period (Greenspan & Deerdorff, 2014). Whereas less than 5% of girls had begun puberty (i.e., breast and pubic hair development) by age 8 a generation ago, today 27% of 8-year-old girls have the beginnings of breast development, and 19% have pubic hair development. As with African American boys, African American girls begin pubertal development sooner than do Hispanic and Caucasian girls. In a recent study, 25% of African American girls showed signs of breast development at age 7, as compared with 15% for Hispanic girls and 10% for White girls (Greenspan & Deerdorff, 2014).

The causes of early pubertal onset are not yet known. Researchers have identified a number of possible causes, including chemicals in the environment that mimic hormones such as estrogen and testosterone (Greenspan & Deerdorff, 2014), two of the hormones associated with puberty; increasing numbers of children who are overweight or obese (Burt Solorzano & McCartney, 2010); and evolutionary processes associated with better nutrition (Gluckman & Hanson, 2006). Whatever the cause, the increasing gap between the age at which secondary sex characteristics develop and the age at which adolescents develop the cognitive ability to recognize and avoid risky situations and behaviors is troubling. Adolescents with more adult-looking bodies are often encouraged to engage in risky behaviors such as drinking, drug use, and sex. As we discuss later in the chapter, there are a number of costs, particularly for girls, of early physical development.

MyEdLab
Video Example 2.1
The secular trend and its potential causes are defined and described.

Menarche and Semenarche: Developmental Milestones

In many cultures there are rituals to clearly demarcate the end of childhood and the beginning of adulthood. The Jewish tradition has the bar mitzvah for boys and the bat mitzvah for girls, both of which occur at the age of 13 regardless of where the child is in the process of biological development. Catholics have the tradition of Confirmation in which the adolescent, usually at age 13, confirms his or her faith as an adult, of one's own volition. In many Latin American countries, families celebrate the quinceañera for girls who are 15 years old. In many tribal societies, the transition from childhood is marked by elaborate ceremonies that sometimes involve physical alterations, such as circumcision or scarring of the face, and changes in living arrangements, such as moving out of the parental dwelling and into one shared with peers (Arnett, 2012).

Compared to many cultures and societies throughout the world, the United States has relatively few ceremonial markers of the transition to adolescence, especially for those who are not active members of religious organizations.

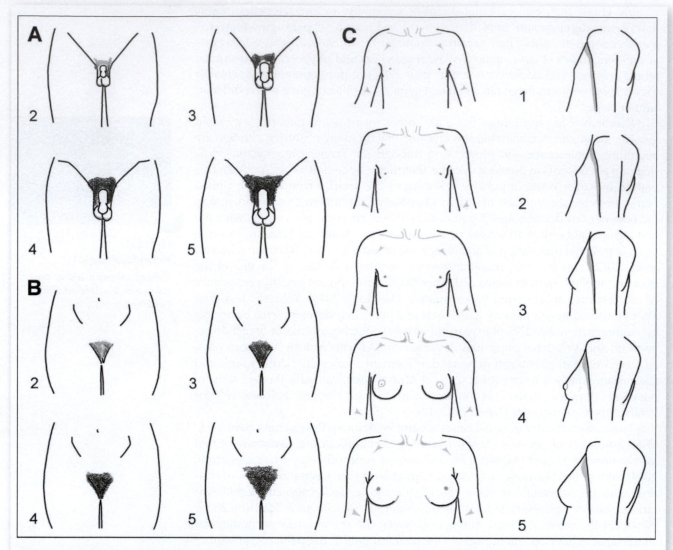

A. The normal progression of male puberty. Sexual Maturity Rating (SMR) 1 (not shown) is prepubertal, with testicular volumes less than 4 mL, a thick and rugated scrotum, and an immature penis. By SMR 2, coarse, sex steroid-dependent hair has appeared on the pubis, but it is sparse and does not typically meet in the midline. The penis remains immature, but scrotal thinning and testicular enlargement have begun. SMR 3 is characterized by pubic hair meeting at the midline and the start of penis growth, predominantly in length. At SMR 4, the pubic hair growth is dense and continuous, but has not reached a full adult pattern. The penis has enlarged in both length and circumference. SMR 5 is that of full adult development. **B.** Normal pubic hair development of the female. The descriptions are similar to those for male pubic hair growth. **C.** Normal progression of breast development. Stage 1 is the normal prepubertal state. Tender "buds" are felt and seen at stage 2, and stage 3 is characterized by further development of breast tissue well beyond the areolar diameter and incomplete nipple development. Stage 4 is easily recognized by secondary elevation of the areola above the contour of the breast, and by stage 5, this areoloar elevation recedes to the plane of the surrounding breast.

FIGURE 2.4

Stages of Normal Puberty Described by Marshall and Tanner.

Source: Figure 1, Muir, A. Precocious Puberty. Reproduced with permission from Pediatrics in Review, 27:373. Copyright © 2006 by the AAP.

For these boys and girls, perhaps the most distinct developmental milestone is menarche for girls and semenarche for boys. **Menarche** refers to the beginning of the process of ovulation, resulting in having one's first menstrual "period." **Semenarche** refers to the beginning of the production of sperm by the testicles, often resulting in boys' first ejaculation. Menarche and semenarche indicate the beginning of sexual maturity for boys and girls, and both are met with a wide variety of responses by the adolescents themselves as well as those in their social circles.

Of the two experiences, semenarche is certainly the less remarkable. Boys often experience their first ejaculation in their sleep (the notorious "wet dream") and awake confused, disgusted, and maybe a little proud. There is nothing really to be done about it, and many boys do not share the news with anyone (Stein & Reiser, 1994). Families rarely take their sons out for ice cream to celebrate their first ejaculation. It is one of those things that just sort of happens, with little fanfare. Some research indicates that boys who knew what to expect experienced semenarche with less confusion and anxiety than did those who were surprised by the development (Stein & Reiser, 1994).

> What is the role of ceremonial transitions to adulthood, and how does their absence in many American adolescents' lives affect the transition from childhood to adulthood?

Menarche is a whole different story. For centuries, the onset of menstruation in girls has been a pivotal point in their development (Ruble & Brooks-Gunn, 1982). Although people often associate menarche with sexual maturity or with the beginning of puberty, it is neither. The first menstrual period occurs well after the processes of pubertal maturation have begun, and other markers of this process usually appear before menstruation, such as the development of breast buds and pubic hair. And the first menstrual period usually occurs about 2 years before the adolescent develops a regular menstrual cycle or is able to become pregnant. Nevertheless, menarche has historically been viewed as an indicator of sexual maturity and has often influenced when adolescent girls are offered up for marriage by their families.

In modern U.S. society, where arranged marriages are rare and girls are generally not expected to assume the role of adult until well after menarche, this developmental milestone is greeted with reactions ranging from excitement and celebration to horror, repulsion, and depression. Many adolescent girls count their first period as among the most embarrassing or shameful events of their lives, something that they hid from parents and peers for as long as they could. But the onset of menstrual periods requires action to be taken, in the form of purchasing and learning how to use products like tampons and pads, so adolescent girls usually share the news of menarche with someone and seek advice on what to do about it. Some families make a big deal out of the occasion, celebrating with dinner and proclamations that the adolescent girl is officially becoming a woman. Others treat it as a shameful or burdensome development to be shrouded in secrecy. Unlike semenarche, menarche has generated a number of nicknames, ranging from the "monthly visit from a friend" to "the curse." These nicknames illustrate the range of reactions different people in contemporary society have to menarche. Research indicates that girls, as with boys' experience of semenarche, tend to have more negative reactions to menarche when they are not prepared for it or when it occurs early (Beausang & Razor, 2000; Ruble & Brooks-Gunn, 1982). Whether adolescent girls view menarche as a positive, negative, or neutral event, most remember their first menstrual period as a noteworthy developmental milestone. There are even websites dedicated to the sharing of menarche stories. For example, a website called We Heart This offers detailed stories from adults who remember their menarche story (http://weheartthis.com/2010/02/16/my-mortifying-first-period-story-2/). Whether it was experienced as scary, embarrassing, funny, or an important developmental milestone, menarche is often recalled as a meaningful and memorable event for adolescent girls.

Research examining reactions to menarche reveals both similarities and differences among adolescent girls from different cultures. In most cultures, for example, girls are more likely to discuss their first periods with their mothers than with anyone else. Similarly, most adolescent girls across cultures get their information about menstruation from their mothers (Uskal, 2004). Across cultures, many women remember their first period as being accompanied by somewhat negative emotions, and many remember feeling unprepared. However, research has also found interesting difference across cultures. For example, some research indicates that adolescent girls' concerns regarding menarche differ by culture. In one study, American girls expressed concern that their periods may interfere with their daily activities, such as athletic participation, whereas eastern European girls expressed more philosophical issues, such as the meaning of the transition from girlhood to womanhood (Chrisler & Zittel, 1998; Uskal, 2004). There are also some interesting differences between more traditional cultures and more westernized or industrialized cultures. Although women across cultures tend to remember menarche as a private event, sometimes even shrouded in some level of secrecy, the taboos in traditional societies against discussing menarche with men have created some practical problems for certain women. For example, in one study, going to the store to buy products such as tampons or menstrual pads was perceived by women in more traditional cultures to be more difficult than it was by women in more modern cultures (Uskal, 2004).

The "Storm-and-Stress" View of Adolescence

Adolescence is a period of rapid changes in hormone levels for both boys and girls. Because most people associate hormones with mood, any mood fluctuation displayed by a teenager often is immediately attributed to their raging hormones. G. Stanley Hall, widely considered the father of the study of adolescent development, was the primary proponent of this model (Arnett, 2006; Hall, 1904). He argued that adolescents are essentially ruled by their hormones, and that these caused a period of "storm and stress" that adults should try to control. Hall's hypothesis, referred to as the **storm-and-stress view**, seems to be shared by many teachers and parents who often complain about the erratic mood swings of adolescents.

Does the research evidence support this common perception of adolescents as more moody than children or adults? And if the evidence does show that adolescents are prone to more frequent and extreme moods than are people at other periods of development, how do we know whether this moodiness is caused by hormones rather than some other cause? The answer to the first question seems to be a qualified yes. Using a research technique called the **Experience Sampling Method (ESM)**, Larson and his colleagues (Csikszentmihalyi & Larson, 1984; Larson & Lampman-Petraitis, 1989) did find evidence for increased mood fluctuation among adolescents (Figure 2.5). By "beeping" participants at random points throughout the day for several days and asking them to report their activity and their mood each time they were beeped, Larson and his colleagues found that adolescents reported more frequent and more extreme positive and negative moods than did adults. A study of adolescent

FIGURE 2.5

Graph Showing ESM Data for Emotionality, by Grade Level

Source: Larson and Lampman-Petraitis, 1989.

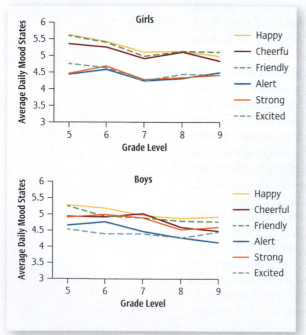

emotionality in India produced similar findings, suggesting a biological under-pinning of the increased emotionality (Verma & Larson, 1999). In addition, there is an increase in mood disorders such as depression during adolescence, espe-cially among girls (see Chapter 11). As the data presented in Figure 2.5 reveals, there are differences between the moods of adolescents as they progress from 5th grade through 9th grade, but on average these changes are not particularly dramatic.

The answer to the second question, about whether these changes in emo-tionality are caused by hormonal changes associated with puberty, is more com-plicated. There is evidence that puberty brings changes to hormone levels and to the brain that are associated with increased emotional intensity (Dahl, 2004). We discuss this in more detail in the following section on brain development. How-ever, research also suggests there are other factors that may contribute to the emotional displays of teenagers. For example, adolescents' daily lives are simply more complex than those of most children, and this complexity often carries emotionality with it. Whereas 9-year-olds do not often hear about their girl-friends kissing someone else, adolescents sometimes do. The intimate nature of adolescents' social relationships often adds an emotional edge to them. Similarly, the cooperative and relatively noncompetitive elementary school experience of most children is replaced by high-stakes, competitive, evaluative classrooms in middle and high school, and these evaluations cause fluctuations in affect throughout the day and over weeks (Eccles & Midgley, 1989). Adolescence is also a period of rapid cognitive development, and the increased cognitive sophisti-cation of adolescents can lead to intense moods. For example, adolescents are better able than are children to understand the consequences of big issues, such as war, environmental degradation, and the rising costs of college tuition, and this understanding can cause fluctuations in mood. Finally, some of the appar-ent emotionality of adolescents may be due to changes in the way that others, such as peers, parents, and teachers, view the growing teenager. This factor is discussed in greater detail later in the chapter. Although adolescents may be a bit moodier than children, changes in hormone levels associated with puberty are only one of several factors that contribute to increased fluctuations in mood (Buchanan, Eccles, & Becker, 1992).

It is also important to note that the image we have of the moody American teenager who argues with parents constantly and challenges the authority of teachers is not a universal phenomenon. In many cultures, the adolescent years are not marked by increased levels of conflict with parents, teachers, and other adults. Indeed, adolescents in many cultures are expected to respect adults as much in adolescence as they did in childhood, and they usually comply (Arnett, 2012). Because the biological processes

> How does the apparent emotional volatility of adolescent students affect the way that teachers view and interact with their students?

of puberty are the same across cultures, the fact that these processes do not lead to the same kinds of emotional volatility and conflict with adults sug-gests that many of the behaviors we think of as biologically determined may, in fact, be largely influenced by cultural factors. For example, in the United States, the dominant messages to teens emphasize rebelliousness and indi-viduality (Frontline, 2002). White, middle-class values emphasize independent thinking and separation from adult control during adolescence, leading many American teenagers to question the authority of parents and teachers. In other cultures, however, unity and obedience are emphasized, even in adolescence (Arnett, 1995, 1999; Triandis, 1995). There is some evidence that within the United States, most of adolescence is marked by *decreases* in conflict with par-ents from ages 13 through 17, but then increases from ages 17 through 19 for some groups, such as boys and African Americans (Guttman & Eccles, 2007).

What Educators Can Do

When a teacher is confronted with a moody or temperamental teenager, it can be tempting to simply chalk it up to raging hormones. However, this attribution can be disempowering for both the teacher and the adolescent. Once moodiness is blamed on the internal biological mechanisms of the adolescent, there is nothing that the teacher or the adolescent can do to resolve the situation. In addition, in many cases the moodiness of adolescent students is caused by factors other than the hormonal changes associated with puberty. A more profitable approach may be for the teacher to remain open to other possible explanations for the adolescent's behavior, such as frustration with performance in a class or a difficult social interaction. These are issues that can potentially be addressed by educators and resolved through discussion with the adolescent. Attributing adolescent moodiness to causes such as a dynamic social life or increased cognitive sophistication has the added benefit of allowing teachers to view their adolescent students as rational rather than merely as slaves to their raging hormones. Although interacting with emotionally charged adolescents can be frustrating, the sense of hopelessness that many teachers (and parents) express when discussing their interactions with teenagers can be reduced if the actual causes of the emotional fluctuations of adolescents are identified and taken seriously. Here are a few tips for handling the moodiness of adolescent students:

- Don't jump to conclusions. Attributing moodiness to hormones does not allow you to help your student cope with whatever is causing the mood swing.
- Don't take it personally. Although adolescent students may snap at you, be disrespectful, or test your boundaries, both you and the student will respond better if you try to remain calm. Remembering that some of this kind of behavior is normal for the age can help you remain calm.
- Offer to listen. Although adolescents may appear to be reacting dramatically to trivial problems, remember that you can be a stabilizing presence by listening and reacting calmly.
- Don't trivialize. Adults often try to calm adolescents down by assuring them that they are overreacting and that the problem is much smaller than the adolescent is making it. This simply adds to the adolescent's perception that adults do not understand adolescents and creates distance. Try to show the student that you are taking the issue seriously and want to help him or her resolve it if possible.

MyEdLab **Self-Check 2.1**

Development of the Brain During Adolescence

In addition to the visible parts of the body, a tremendous amount of growth also occurs in the brain during adolescence. The development of the brain during adolescence can be divided into two different types (Spano, 2003). The first type involves the development of neural pathways that connect neurons to one another and connect different parts of the brain to one another. Through experience and repetition, neural pathways are created and reinforced. For example, when a teenager learns to drive, she develops a series of new thoughts and behaviors that involve several different areas of the brain. Pulling a car out of a parking spot involves checking mirrors and looking over the shoulder for oncoming traffic (visual), and remembering instructions from a driving instructor (e.g., "Use your blinker, check your mirrors, look over your shoulder."). She must remember to put the car in gear, step on the gas, turn the steering wheel, and follow the rules of driving, such as staying in the correct lane and going the proper speed. All of these are new behaviors for the developing driver, and at first each of the steps in the process requires conscious awareness. Any distractions—the car radio, a talking passenger, a bicyclist traveling in the opposite direction—can interfere with the new driver's concentration.

As the driver gains experience, many of these behaviors become automatic. The process of using the turn signal, checking the mirrors, and looking over the shoulder becomes one smooth and integrated process. The process of putting the car into gear and stepping on the accelerator happens unconsciously and can be done while the driver is changing the radio station or talking on the phone. (Although you should not use your phone while you drive!) What happens in the brain that allows this complicated, new process to become a smooth, easy, and largely automatic (i.e., unconscious) process? First, new neural pathways are created that connect the various parts of the brain that are involved in the driving process. Second, the **axons** in these new neural pathways become covered in a fatty sheath of **myelin** in a process known as **myelination**. Myelination allows the electrical signals that cause the **neurons** to "fire" (i.e., release neurotransmitters across the synaptic gap and connect to other neurons) to travel more quickly down the axon, and the myelination process appears to reach its peak during adolescence (Giedd et al., 1999). With more practice, the firing process becomes quicker, and the behaviors that are tied to these neural pathways become easier and more automatic. Whether it is driving a car, remembering your daily schedule in school, or learning the recipe for a cake, the process in the brain is essentially the same: Create the neural network and then reinforce and speed up this network with practice and repetition.

It is also important to realize that old neural pathways fade away (in a process known as **pruning**) as they are no longer used. A sixth grader who spent hours learning the capitals of each U.S. state or how to play his favorite song on the guitar will become the 10th grader who struggles to remember the names of those capitals or the chords to the song if he has not practiced them in the intervening years. Just as the process of developing neural pathways is important for mastering new skills and learning new information, the process of pruning unused pathways is also important. Pruning increases our efficiency of thinking and behavior, as energy is not being wasted on pathways that we no longer use.

The Prefrontal Cortex

The second type of brain growth during adolescence is the actual physical growth of certain regions of the brain. For example, the **parietal lobe**, which is responsible for visual-spatial acuity and the subsequent motor response (e.g., hand–eye coordination, awareness of one's position relative to others and to, for example, the ball on a soccer field) grows during adolescence (Leany, 2013). Similarly, the **temporal lobe**, the center of language production and processing, grows during adolescence. As a result, adolescence is a period of burgeoning verbal skills that is unparalleled in any period of development besides early childhood.

Perhaps the most interesting area of brain growth during adolescence and early adulthood is the development of the **prefrontal cortex**. As the brain develops from the center (i.e., the brainstem) outward, the last area of the brain to develop is the prefrontal cortex (see Figure 2.6). It is such an interesting area of the brain because this is where our abilities to regulate our impulses, to develop plans, and to engage in abstract thought are all centered. This is the region of the brain

MyEdLab
Video Example 2.2

Sarah, a runaway teen, finds herself in court after her impulsive plans turned into a nightmare. As you watch the video, consider how developments in the brain affect adolescents' abilities to make sound decisions. Also think about how decisions are influenced by older peers.

FIGURE 2.6

Graphic of the
Developing Brain

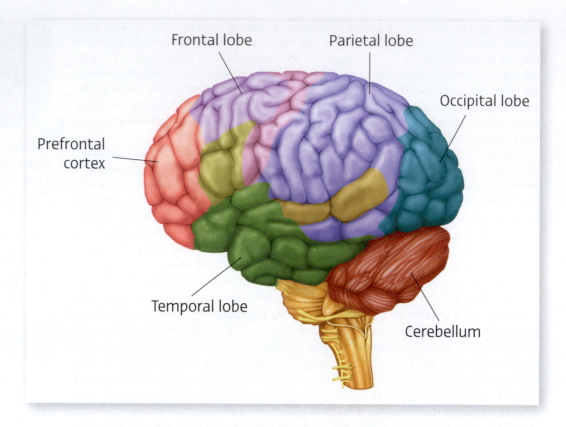

that is associated with so much of the thinking and behavior that distinguishes adolescents from children. Because it is still growing and developing in adolescence and early adulthood, and not fully formed, it is also the area of the brain that is associated with many of the impulsive and risky behaviors that distinguish adolescence from adulthood.

In a landmark longitudinal study, Jay Giedd and colleagues (Giedd et al., 1999) used neuroimaging to track cortical development from childhood through adolescence. They found that the **gray matter** in the frontal part of the brain—the part that is associated with planning, making sound judgments, and strategizing—grows tremendously throughout late childhood and peaks at early adolescence, around 11 or 12 years old. More specifically, they found that there was a thickening of the gray matter, indicating the formation of more and more connections among the neurons. After the peak of gray-matter thickening in early adolescence, it begins to thin as connections between neurons are pruned. Giedd et al. have argued that that tremendous buildup of gray matter during late childhood and into preadolescence provides the brain with tremendous capacity to become skilled in a wide variety of areas, but pruning occurs as adolescents put more of their time and energy into certain activities and not others. The pruning follows a "use-it-or-lose-it" principle. Those neural pathways that are used survive for a long time, and those that are not used disappear. Because this process of developing long-term neural pathways is so critical, some of the risky behavior that adolescents experiment with—especially drug and alcohol use—can be particularly damaging, as they can interfere with this neurodevelopmental process.

Brain Development and Adolescent Risk Taking

There is an interesting paradox that occurs during the teenage years. At the same time that the brain is developing new capacities in the prefrontal cortex for impulse control, abstract and hypothetical reasoning (e.g., "If I smoke pot before I drive, I might crash"), and self-regulatory skills, as well as better integration of visual stimuli with motor responses (i.e., coordination and reaction time), there is a tendency for adolescents to engage in risky behaviors that can lead to injury, illness, and death (Leany, 2013; Spano, 2003). Why would this be? The answer to this riddle is most likely a combination of factors that includes social influences as well as physiological changes associated with puberty.

On the social side, it is important to remember that as teenagers mature, they look older and are able to think in more sophisticated ways. This causes the people around them, from friends to family to government institutions, to treat them differently. For example, teenagers are allowed to drive for the first time, and driving carries with it many risks. Adolescents are given a lot more freedom and time that is unsupervised by adults, and this unsupervised time can promote risk-taking behaviors (e.g., substance use, sex, launching oneself down a flight of stairs on a skateboard). As we discuss later in this chapter, adolescents who appear to be more mature based on their physical development are often encouraged by their peers to engage in behaviors, such as sexual activity and substance use, that are quite risky. In short, teenagers are afforded with more opportunity and encouragement to engage in risky behavior than are children.

But why don't the developing brains of adolescents, specifically their impulse-inhibition and self-regulatory powers, simply cause them to say "no" to these risky opportunities? There are at least two explanations. First, we need to remember that although these new capabilities for reason and self-regulation are developing in adolescence, they are not a finished product until well into adulthood. These inhibition and regulatory abilities are *emerging* in adolescence, but there are still many times when they will fail (Schwartz, 2008). Second, research evidence indicates that hormonal changes associated with puberty are linked to changes in mood and increases in appetitive, drive-oriented motivation (Bessant, 2008). For example, adolescents often experience increases in sensation seeking, pleasure seeking, novelty seeking, the intensity of their emotions, and romantic desires (Dahl, 2004). Some of these changes are associated with certain chemical **neurotransmitters** in the brain (e.g., dopamine) that fluctuate during adolescence (Ernst & Spear, 2008). Steinberg (2010) found evidence for a **dual-systems model** of risk taking during adolescence. Whereas impulsivity decreased in a linear fashion beginning at about age 10, as the executive control areas of the brain begin to develop, reward-seeking (which is associated with risky behavior) increased from preadolescence to mid-adolescence, then began to decline. This suggests that reward seeking may be more strongly associated with the hormonal changes of puberty and impulsivity with physical development in the brain.

These puberty-linked changes in the sensation seeking, reward seeking, and emotional volatility of adolescents are occurring earlier as the age of pubertal onset continues to drop, especially in the industrialized world (Greenspan & Deardorff, 2014; Herman-Giddens et al., 1997, 2012). But other changes in the adolescent brain, such as the increases in impulse control, logical reasoning capabilities, and self-regulation that are associated with the development of the prefrontal cortex, are more closely tied to age than to the stage of puberty one has reached. As a result, the gap between the appetitive desires that develop in adolescence and the adolescent's ability to control these desires is widening. Coupled with the fact that earlier pubertal onset leads to more social pressure at earlier ages to engage in risky behaviors, this combination of internal and external forces leads many adolescents to take risks. And some of these risks (e.g., drinking, taking drugs) increase adolescents' susceptibility to taking additional risks (e.g., driving recklessly, engaging in unprotected sex).

What Educators Can Do

The neurological developments that occur during adolescence are remarkable, and can have profound implications for education. Some of these developments, such as the increased ability to think abstractly and burgeoning verbal skills, allow teachers to assign tasks and engage in discussions that are much deeper than was possible before adolescence. (See Chapter 3, Cognitive Development, for more information about the implications for teachers of the increased cognitive sophistication of adolescent students.) In addition to these curricular and pedagogical recommendations for teachers, we also have some recommendations regarding how teachers might approach brain-based changes in sensation seeking, mood intensity, pleasure seeking, and the developing impulse and self-regulatory controls of adolescents:

- Keep in mind that looks can be deceiving. Although many of your students may look like young adults, the development of their prefrontal cortexes, and the abilities of reason and self-control that are regulated therein, is still a work in progress. Your 11th-grade students should be more mature and less impulsive than middle school students, but they are still prone to serious lapses in judgment and impulsive behavior. Set a high standard for behavior and thoughtfulness, but expect lapses.
- Help your adolescent students develop awareness of risky situations and behaviors, and help them develop strategies for avoiding them. As adolescents face increasing pressures and opportunities to engage in risky behaviors, and may simultaneously develop increased appetites for sensation and pleasure, it is important for teachers to help them recognize these risky situations and know how to avoid them. Although teens often underestimate the likelihood of their own injury or illness due to feelings of invincibility (see Chapter 3), there is evidence that programs designed to teach teens about risks and avoidance strategies can increase their awareness about the dangers of certain behaviors (Kisker & Brown, 1996).
- Exercise patience and support. The increasing emotional volatility, romantic interests, and argumentativeness of adolescents can be trying for the parents, teachers, and other adults with whom they interact. Keep in mind that some of these characteristics are the result of changes in the brain that are beyond the control of adolescents to regulate. By remaining patient and supportive, you can serve as a resource for adolescents as they develop the necessary skills for better regulating their emotions and behavior.

MyEdLab **Self-Check 2.2**

How Physical Development Affects Social and Cognitive Change

Changes in Perceptions of Self and Others

In addition to the physiological changes, the changing bodies of adolescents often create cognitive changes, both within the minds of developing adolescents as well as with the perceptions of others in the adolescents' social sphere. Within the adolescent, the realization that one is becoming bigger and stronger may lead to several new thoughts. For example, a boy who has grown from a 70-pound, 4-foot-10-inch preteen into a 130-pound, 5-foot-8-inch teenager tends to think of himself as stronger and more capable than he used to be. This often leads to a desire to engage in new activities, from physically demanding sports to sex. It can also lead the adolescent boy (or girl) into a new and challenging relationship with parents. Whereas children often acquiesce to parental demands because of differences in physical stature (and, at times, physical force used by parents), as the size of the adolescent begins to approximate the size of parents, adolescents are less likely to be persuaded by physical means alone. As the adolescent looks in the mirror, he or she may think, "I look like a grown-up, so it is time I start receiving the rights and privileges of adulthood."

The changing appearance of adolescents often elicits new responses from people with whom adolescents interact. For example, parents and teachers expect adolescents to behave more responsibly than children, and teens are often given more responsibilities, such as household chores. Research indicates that the changing physical appearance of adolescents is associated with greater emotional distance between adolescents and their parents, in part because parents and adolescents both expect the more mature-looking adolescent to be more independent (Steinberg, 1988). Behaviors more typically associated with children, such as playing with dolls or having temper tantrums, are not as easily accepted once the early adolescent develops physical attributes of adulthood, such as secondary sex characteristics. In addition, as adolescents develop physically, they often gain the attention of older adolescents and early adults. When girls develop some of the curves associated with adolescence, older boys and men take notice and begin inviting girls to participate in behaviors that they may not be ready for, such as sex and substance use. Similarly, as boys develop physically, they often enter a new social realm that can include new expectations for athletic prowess or new opportunities to interact with older adolescents in social and antisocial activity. These new expectations from those in the adolescents' social sphere can be a useful and important part of the social and psychological development of adolescents. After all, it would be difficult to mature if one were treated like a child for his or her entire life. But the attention and expectations of older adolescents and adults are also fraught with potential risks, especially for early adolescents whose bodies develop early. These risks are considered in more detail in the next section as we discuss the timing of pubertal development.

MyEdLab
Video Example 2.3
Camila, 16, describes her desire to make independent decisions and how that leads to frequent conflict with her parents. Notice how this desire for independence is related to Camila's changing self-perceptions as she has become physically mature.

Timing of Physical Development

The timing of the physical developments associated with puberty varies widely among adolescents. This variability in the timing of puberty is a classic example of the way that genetics interact with contextual factors to shape how genotype (the genes one is born with) are expressed as phenotype. Boys and girls are born with a genetically determined "program" to change, physically, from a child into an adult during adolescence. But when in the child's life this process gets triggered into action, and how quickly it unfolds, are affected by environmental factors. We do not yet know all of the factors that can influence the timing of puberty, or how they affect it, but we do know some of them. For example, nutrition and weight influence the timing of puberty. Girls who are severely underweight often experience a delay in the onset of puberty. It appears that a certain amount of body fat is needed to trigger pubertal onset for girls (Anderson & Must, 2005).

One particularly interesting, and potentially troubling, example of the interplay between genes and context involves the decreasing age at which girls experience menarche (i.e., get their period for the first time). For decades, researchers have

Think about your own reactions to adolescent students who differ in their physical development. How might you react differently to two students who are similar in age, but one looks more like an adult and the other more like a child? What effect would your different reactions to these two students have on their attitudes and behavior?

observed that the age of menarche has fallen. A study of French women (Clavel-Chapelon, 2002; Clavel-Chapelon et al., 1997) found that the average age of menarche fell from 13.2 years old among women born in 1929 to 12.7 among women born in 1950. Research in the United States has found similar declines, and that the age of menarche continues to decline (Anderson & Must, 2005). At the same time that age of menarche has declined, the age at which girls develop regular cycles of menstruation has increased (Clavel-Chapelon, 2002). This is potentially troubling because the gap between menarche and first pregnancy may be a risk factor for developing breast cancer. There is also evidence that earlier onset of menarche is associated with an increased risk for developing psychopathology (Ge & Natsuaki, 2009).

As noted earlier, researchers have developed a number of hypotheses to explain the decreasing age of menarche (Ellis, 2004). Perhaps the most popular explanation is that changes in dietary habits, including easier access for more people to cheap food, has increased the body fat of girls at younger ages, thereby triggering menarche (Clavel-Chapelon, 2002; INSERM, 2007). There is also speculation that increasing levels of physical activity among girls has triggered menarche at earlier ages (Clavel-Chapelon, 2002). Some have even speculated that growth hormones given to animals, such as those given to cows to spur the production of milk, are passed to humans through consumption of animal products, accumulate in girls, and trigger menarche at earlier ages. All of these explanations, however, have counterarguments and evidence. For example, Demerath and his colleagues (2004) examined longitudinal data and found there was no association between average age at menarche (which declined) and average body-mass index during childhood and adolescence (which did not change) over a 50-year period. Although the evidence shows that the age of menarche has steadily declined over the last 80 years, and there is good reason to suspect that environmental factors are at least a partial cause of this decline, a widely accepted explanation has remained elusive.

The effects of pubertal timing also have dramatic consequences for the behavior and emotional well-being of youth. Because puberty ushers in a period of marked physical development, including changes in height, weight, and secondary sex characteristics such as body hair, depth of voice, and breasts, people in the adolescent's social sphere notice these changes and begin treating the adolescent differently as a result. As but one example, girls are much more likely to be approached by boys with sexual/romantic interests after they develop secondary sex characteristics than before. In addition, because of the cognitive changes associated with puberty (see Chapter 3), adolescents become hypersensitive about how they compare to others, and physical development is one easily visible criterion upon which social comparisons can be made. Being the first one or the last one among a group of friends to "hit puberty" can be extremely awkward for adolescents. Interestingly, recent research in Australia has shown that some of the problems associated with early pubertal onset, such as difficulties with psychosocial adjustment and, for boys, behavioral problems, may actually appear well *before* puberty (Mensah et al., 2013). This research suggests that the effects of starting puberty early are not solely due to how others treat early-developing adolescents.

Timing of Puberty for Girls. For girls, the effects of early physical maturation can be quite difficult. Early-maturing girls tend to have lower levels of satisfaction with their bodies and are more likely to be depressed, develop eating disorders, and become involved in delinquent activities such as fighting, substance use, and truancy than are later-maturing girls (Mendle, Turkheimer, & Emery, 2007). There are many possible explanations for these differences, but two of the most common are cultural definitions of beauty and the attention of older boys. In the United States, the mass media often depict beautiful women as those who are thin

(Cusumano & Thompson, 1997). Because puberty causes an increase in body fat for most girls, those who mature first are also the first to develop bodies that do not conform to the thin-body ideal. Interestingly, early-maturing girls from cultural backgrounds that are not associated with this thin-body ideal (e.g., African American and Latina) do not report the same levels of body dissatisfaction as their White peers. In addition to changes in body image, early-maturing girls are also more likely than other girls to attract the attention of older boys. Older boys are more likely than younger boys to be engaged in sexual activity, delinquent behaviors, and drug, alcohol, and tobacco use, so girls who associate with them are also more likely to become involved in these kinds of activities. This is particularly a problem for early-maturing girls because their cognitive development may not have kept pace with their physical development, making them less likely to make wise decisions and more likely to be influenced by the older boys with whom they often associate (Phinney, Jensen, Olsen, & Cundick, 1990). All of these factors contribute to higher rates of conflict with parents. In addition, because romantic and sexual relationships carry with them quite powerful emotions, early-maturing girls often report more emotional distress than do later-maturing girls, who are less likely to be involved in romantic relationships.

Late-maturing girls tend to avoid the problems of early-maturing girls, but there are some negative consequences of their later development. Whereas their peers are developing breasts and hips and other markers of sexual maturity, late-maturing girls maintain a childlike appearance and, as a result, are perceived as younger. This can have social costs, as late-maturing girls are less likely to be included in mixed-gender social events such as parties and dating. Late-maturing girls can begin to worry about whether their bodies will ever develop and attract the attention of boys, and they can sometimes envy their earlier-maturing peers. On the positive side, in addition to avoiding many of the pitfalls of early development (e.g., early sexual activity, drug use, etc.), later-maturing girls also tend to avoid some of the parental conflict that early-maturing girls experience. It seems that peers and adults in the adolescents' social network treat adolescents differently depending on their level of physical development.

There has been little research into the long-term consequences of early or late maturation among girls. Some research suggests that early-maturing girls, perhaps because of the more grown-up experiences they have at a relatively early age, are more psychologically advanced in early adulthood (Peskin, 1973). But other research indicates that early-maturing girls are more likely to discontinue their education at an earlier point than are later-maturing girls (Magnusson, Stattin, & Allen, 1986) and are more likely to experience psychological distress during adolescence or early adulthood (Graber, Seeley, Brooks-Gunn, & Lewinsohn, 2004).

Timing of Puberty for Boys. The first boys to develop in any given school tend to enjoy several advantages. Because early-maturing boys are bigger, stronger, and generally more coordinated than their peers, they are often better at sports and, partly as a result, enjoy higher social status than their later-developing peers. Early-developing boys are admired by their peers and are more likely to be selected for leadership roles, get invited to parties, and become popular with girls. Early-maturing boys tend to feel better about themselves than do later-maturing boys and are more likely to report feeling good and being in love (Richards & Larson, 1993). Given the value that society places on masculinity for boys, it makes sense that those boys who reach puberty earliest are likely to enjoy some social advantages from their more adult-like appearance, and this increased attention and admiration from others helps early-maturing boys feel better about themselves.

But maturing earlier than one's peers is not all positive for boys (Mendle & Ferrero, 2012). As is true for girls, there are some costs associated with early maturation among boys, although these costs tend to be less severe for boys. Early-maturing boys are more likely to associate with older friends, and older adolescents have a penchant for engaging in antisocial activities. Early-maturing boys are more likely than their later-maturing peers to get into trouble at school, become involved in delinquent acts and truancy, use drugs and alcohol, and be sexually active. There is also evidence that early-maturing boys express more hostility and feel more internalized psychological distress than do their later-maturing peers (Ge, Gonger, & Elder, 2003; Mendle & Ferrero, 2012).

Late-maturing boys (i.e., those who do not develop secondary sex characteristics until most of their peers have) experience a number of negative consequences, but the news for them is not all bad. These boys do not enjoy the same admiration from as their early-maturing peers, are not as successful in either the athletic or romantic arenas, and often report feeling distressed about their lack of physical development (Spencer, Dupree, Swanson, & Cunningham, 1998). In short, being smaller and less developed than most of their peers makes many later-developing adolescent boys feel weak, and they tend to be treated in a more childlike way than are their earlier-maturing peers, especially by girls and athletic coaches.

Despite the difficulties experienced by late-maturing boys, their extended preadolescence seems to have advantages as well. As already noted, the physical maturation associated with puberty causes others to put pressure on adolescents to behave in more adult-like ways. A boy who hits puberty at age 13 may suddenly be pressured by older peers to cut school, drink alcohol, smoke pot, or steal a video game from a store. Similarly, the early-maturing boy may be expected to take more leadership roles in the classroom, in the home, or on the athletic field. But a more mature body does not mean the early-maturing boy is any more cognitively sophisticated, and these pressures from peers and adults to behave in a more adult-like manner are difficult for the early-maturing boy to resist, and to handle. In contrast, a boy who does not hit puberty until 15 or 16 years old has more time to develop the cognitive resources to cope with the sudden changes associated with puberty, and to resist peer pressure to engage in antisocial acts. As a result, later-maturing boys tend to engage in less antisocial behavior and report fewer mood swings and temper tantrums at the onset of puberty than do early-maturing boys (Ge, Conger, & Elder Jr., 2001).

Interestingly, research indicates that the difference in the timing of pubertal onset among boys is associated with different types of personality and behavior well into adulthood. Early-maturing boys, who were often pushed into leadership roles and more adult-like behaviors during adolescence, were more likely to grow into men who are responsible and cooperative but are also more conforming and conventional. Late-maturing boys, who had a longer period of preadolescence to engage in more childlike behavior without the pressures of leadership and responsibility, were more likely to grow up to be more creative, insightful, and inventive (Livson & Peskin, 1980). It appears that being asked to behave more like an adult at an earlier age may have turned the early-maturing boys into somewhat more stodgy, more risk-avoidant adults, whereas the later-maturing boys were able to maintain some of their extended childhood tendencies well into adulthood.

Differences Between Boys and Girls in the Effects of Pubertal Timing.

Although early-maturing boys have some difficulties (more difficulty managing their emotions in early adolescence, more drug and alcohol use, etc.), the research clearly indicates that early-maturing girls have a tougher time than do early-maturing boys. There are several possible explanations for this. First, because girls tend to hit puberty earlier than boys, early-maturing girls are usually the first in their grade level to mature. It can be very awkward to begin looking like an adult when all of your classmates, boys and girls, still look like children. Second, keep in mind that one source of problems for early-developing adolescents is the mismatch between their physical maturity and their cognitive maturity. Early-maturing

TABLE 2.2   **Summary of Outcomes Associated with Early and Late Physical Maturation, by Gender**

	Girls	Boys
Early maturation	• Lower body satisfaction • Depression • Eating disorders • Delinquency • Substance abuse • Sexual behavior • More conflict with parents • Emotional distress	• Higher self-esteem • More admiration from peers • More likely to be selected for leadership roles • Physical coordination, strength • More popular • Delinquency • Truancy • Drug and alcohol use • Sexual behavior • Hostility and psychological distress
Late maturation	• Some social costs due to perception as younger • Less conflict with parents • Less emotional distress • Less delinquent behavior • Less substance use • Lower rates of sexual activity, dating	• Distress about lack of physical development • Less admiration from peers, popularity • Not as successful athletically or romantically • More resistant to peer pressure • Lower levels of risky, antisocial behavior • Less moody • More creative, insightful, inventive as adults

adolescents, because of their appearance, often receive pressure from older adolescents to engage in risky or antisocial behavior. If they lack the cognitive sophistication to resist this pressure, they can quickly get into trouble. Because early-maturing girls hit puberty at even younger ages than do early-maturing boys (about 2 years earlier, on average), they tend to be even more immature cognitively and less able to resist pressure from peers or to weigh the risks of certain behaviors. Finally, the high value placed on thinness for girls in mainstream U.S. culture may place early-developing girls at particular risk for developing problems with body image and self-esteem. Puberty tends to add a layer of fat to girls' bodies, moving them away from the thin body type prized by society. Early-developing boys, in contrast, develop a more muscular physique that is in line with societal values. Table 2.2 summarizes the effects of pubertal timing for girls and boys.

What Educators Can Do

Although educators are powerless to influence the timing of puberty among their students, they can and should be able to monitor and control their own reactions to it. In addition, educators may be able to help their adolescent students cope with the challenges they face as their bodies change.

Perhaps the most important step educators can take is to learn about the various difficulties adolescents face when puberty begins, or doesn't. All adolescents must learn to cope with their changing bodies, including awkward appearance, menstrual periods, fluctuating hormone levels, and the changing pressures and expectations of others. These challenges are often exacerbated among those who are either early or late maturers, and educators who make themselves aware of the specific difficulties early and late maturers face can develop strategies for helping adolescents cope with these challenges.

Teachers are important adults in the lives of their adolescent students, so their opinions and behaviors toward their students carry significant weight. It is a natural reaction to view more physically mature adolescents as more emotionally capable as well. Educators often respond to mature-looking adolescents by assigning them more leadership responsibilities and expecting them to behave more responsibly. But early-developing adolescents are often not able to fulfill these expectations,

MyEdLab
Video Example 2.4

Josh describes his experience as an early-maturing teenage boy. Notice how his social experiences are tied to his physical development.

MyEdLab

**Application Exercise 2.1.
Effects of Early Development**
In this exercise you can identify how one adolescent boy's experience with early maturation affects his self-perceptions, others' perceptions of him, and contrast it with the experience of early-developing girls.

leading to disappointment and conflict with teachers. Moreover, early-developing adolescents are often struggling under the weight of new expectations and pressures from older adolescents and from parents to act more grown up. Teachers who make themselves aware of these struggles can work to manage their own expectations of their more physically mature students and can serve as a resource to help these students handle the new pressures created by their physical development.

It is also helpful for educators to keep in mind that the behaviors adults often think of as an unavoidable part of puberty—moodiness, low self-esteem and body-image issues, conflict with adults—are highly dependent on context. When an adolescent seems hostile or depressed, it is not enough for the teacher to simply think it is part of adolescence and there is nothing to be done about it. Instead, educators should think of these behaviors as something that may be partly the result of the contexts that adolescents are in. Research comparing early-developing girls who attend coeducational schools with those attending single-sex schools find fewer problems among those in the single-sex context (Caspi, Lynam, Moffitt, & Silva, 1993). Educators who make themselves aware of the challenges puberty presents, especially for early-developing girls, can take steps to alleviate these challenges. Some of these steps might include the following:

- Questioning their own assumptions about the cognitive maturity of early-developing adolescents and their ability to take on more responsibilities
- Listening to the concerns of adolescents who are angry or depressed, rather than writing them off as inevitable behaviors during adolescence
- Understanding the kinds of pressures that early maturers are under to engage in risky or delinquent behaviors and remaining alert for the signs that adolescents may be engaging in such behaviors
- Creating opportunities, on the school grounds, for adolescents who are experiencing adjustment problems to seek counseling
- Developing a curriculum to help adolescents understand the physical changes associated with puberty, how those changes might affect their social and cognitive development, and how to cope with the challenges these changes present
- Recognizing that the problems associated with early maturation are especially pronounced among adolescents with other life stressors, such as poverty or ineffective parenting, and aim counseling and health resources at these groups in particular

The onset of puberty can be awkward for any adolescent, especially those who develop earlier or later than their peers. But these challenges do not necessarily lead to serious problems. Educators can take steps to help students navigate this sometimes bumpy road and experience a smooth transition into adolescence.

MyEdLab **Self-Check 2.3**

Body Image and Eating Disorders During Adolescence

Try to remember how you felt about your body as it began to change once you hit puberty. If you are male, chances are you were happy about the changes, even if you went through periods where you felt somewhat gangly and awkward. If you are female, however, it is most likely that you viewed your body more negatively as you gained the weight and curves associated with adolescence. Over 25% of adolescent girls report being highly dissatisfied with their bodies (Kelly, Wall, Eisenberg, Story, & Neumark-Sztainer, 2005). Over 60% of American high school girls report that they are actively trying to lose weight (Centers for Disease Control and Prevention (CDC, 2013). Yuan (2010) found that changes in one's body were particularly worrisome for early adolescent White girls, but were not related to psychological well-being for boys. Although some adolescent boys do struggle with body-image issues and some even develop eating disorders (Furnham & Calnan, 1998), these issues tend to be more common among adolescent girls. Why are so many adolescent girls, especially White girls, so unhappy with their bodies?

One likely source of this dissatisfaction is the media. There was a time, not too long ago, when the ideal woman's body type presented in Hollywood and magazines was women with curves. In the 1950s and 1960s, many of the female movie stars who were so-called "sex symbols" were full-bodied and curvy. Since then, the women presented as beautiful in movies, television, and magazines have become thinner and thinner (Wiseman, Gray, Mosimann, & Athens, 1992). The typical fashion model today is approximately 6 inches taller than the average American woman and weighs 45 pounds less. These are physical measurements that are unachievable for the vast majority of American women and adolescent girls. Unfortunately, many girls, even before they hit adolescence, internalize this beauty standard and become increasingly dissatisfied with their bodies the further they grow away from it. Research has found that magazines aimed at adolescent girls, such as *Seventeen* and *Teen Vogue*, have a disproportionate number of articles about appearance and dieting. In addition, girls who read fashion magazines, particularly those aimed at adolescents, are more likely to be dissatisfied with their bodies and to develop eating disorders (Jones, Vigfusdottir, & Lee, 2004). In one study of adolescent girls, 69% reported that pictures in magazines influenced their perceptions of the ideal body type, and 47% reported that the pictures in magazines made them want to lose weight (Field et al., 1999). There is also evidence that exposure to thin women in other forms of media, such as television and movies, is linked to body dissatisfaction and eating disorders among adolescent girls (Botta, 1999; Harrison & Cantor, 1997). It should be noted, however, that the effects of media on body image may not be the same across all ethnic groups. Although African American girls tend to watch more television than do White girls, African American adolescents respond somewhat differently to the images of thinness that they see, internalizing the thinness ideal less than their White peers, particularly if they watch a lot of television dramas with thin actresses in them (Botta, 2000).

Although the media is an easy (and deserving) target for criticism regarding the promotion of unrealistically thin body types for girls, there are other contributors to body dissatisfaction. One important predictor of **body dissatisfaction** among adolescent girls is how their friends think about beauty and diet. Girls who spend their time with friends who have a **thin-body ideal** and are actively trying to achieve it through dieting or **disordered eating** behaviors are more likely to report body dissatisfaction and symptoms of disordered eating themselves (Crandall, 1988). There is also evidence that parents, particularly mothers, influence the body images of adolescent girls. Parents who are less educated have adolescent daughters who are more aware of, and more likely to internalize, societal ideals of beauty than are children of more highly educated parents (Abrams & Stormer, 2002). (For a more detailed discussion of eating disorders, see Chapter 11.)

MyEdLab
Video Example 2.5

In this video, 12-year-old Kianna, her best friend, and her mother describe some of the influences on adolescent behavior. As you watch, notice the perspectives about body image expressed by Kianna and her friend. Also notice their view of the negative influence of the media.

Given the negative effects that exposure to media portrayals of beauty can have on adolescent students, what could you do, as a teacher, to minimize these effects?

Ethnic Differences in Body Image and Eating Disorders

In popular music and movies, there are often references to ethnic differences in ideal body types for women. For example, some music and movies include African American musicians or characters deriding the thin-beauty ideal of White women and declaring a preference for more curvaceous, fuller-figured bodies. Are these observations and personal preferences referred to in popular culture supported by the research on ethnic differences in body image? Only partially, research suggests. A number of studies

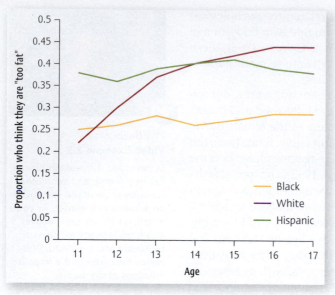

FIGURE 2.7

Percentage of Girls with Body-Image Issues, by Race

Source: Mikolajczyk et al., 2012.

Note: These numbers are estimates based on graph 2 in the publication.

in the 1980s and 1990s revealed that African American adolescents and women enjoyed a more positive body image than did their White peers (Abrams & Stormer, 2002). Some evidence supports the assertion that adolescent White girls are more likely than either African American or Latina adolescent girls to have high levels of dissatisfaction with their bodies and to develop eating disorders (Abrams & Stormer, 2002; Barry & Grilo, 2002; Story, French, Resnick, & Blum, 1995). Although African American women are more likely than White women to be overweight, roughly twice as many White women report being dissatisfied with the shapes of their bodies (Abrams, Allen, & Gray, 1993). For example, Abrams and Stormer (2002) found that African American adolescent girls who had friends from various ethnic groups were more likely to be aware of and internalize societal beauty ideals than were African American girls with mostly or only African American friends. Similarly, in a qualitative study, evidence emerged that African American girls were more flexible in their perceptions of what counts as beautiful than were White girls (Parker et al., 1995). African American girls in this study suggested that beauty was a matter of working with whatever body type one has, whereas White girls were more likely to believe one must have a certain body type to be beautiful.

In a study of U.S. adolescent high school girls, Mikolajczyk, Iannotti, Farhat, and Thomas (2012) found that between the ages of 11 and 17, the proportion of White girls who believed that they were "too fat" increased, but the proportion of African American and Hispanic girls who thought they were "too fat" did not change. The proportion of White girls who thought they were too fat increased steadily from age 11 to 15, then leveled off. Hispanic girls were more likely than African American girls to believe there were "too fat" at every age from 11 through 17, and African American girls were less likely than White girls to believe that they were "too fat" beginning at around 13 years of age (see Figure 2.7).

For many years, eating disorders and unhealthy eating habits were thought to be a problem primarily constrained to middle- and upper-middle-class White girls (Yuan, 2010). But the evidence suggests that disordered eating may affect girls across ethnic groups. In a study comparing different ethnic groups, Shaw, Ramirez, Trost, Randall, and Stice (2004) found that there were no differences across ethnic groups in their reported eating disorder symptoms or the relationship between various risk factors and the development of eating disorders. In their words, "Ethnic minority groups have reached parity with Whites in this domain" (p. 12). Similarly, research from the CDC (2013) found that Hispanic adolescents were more likely than White adolescents to use diuretics, laxatives, and vomiting to control their weight.

Summary

The physical changes that adolescents experience affect how they think about themselves and how they are viewed and treated by others in their social circles. As adolescents gradually become more adult-like in their appearance, parents, peers, and educators expect them to behave in more mature ways, for better and for worse. These expectations and pressures to engage in more grown-up behavior, ranging from taking on more responsibilities at home to engaging in risky or antisocial behavior, can be difficult for adolescents, especially early-maturing adolescents, to handle. These difficulties may be especially pronounced for early-maturing girls, who are often pressured to engage in behaviors they are not ready for. There is considerable evidence that adolescent girls, much more than boys, are dissatisfied with their bodies, wish they were thinner, and sometimes take drastic measures to attain thinness. By making themselves aware of these challenges many adolescents face as they try to come to terms with their developing bodies, educators can help ease this transition by monitoring their own expectations of, and reactions to, their students who have s more grown-up appearance.

Physical Health and Well-Being During Adolescence

The physiological changes that adolescents experience, combined with the greater autonomy adolescents are afforded, place a premium on the factors that influence their health. These include sleep patterns, what and how much they eat, and exercise habits. Teachers and school programs can influence each of these contributors to healthy physical development and overall well-being. In this section of the chapter, each of these factors is discussed in turn.

Circadian Rhythm

As parents of teenagers know well, adolescents tend to keep very different hours than children. Whereas children often follow a set bedtime and wake-up schedule for most of their childhood, and tend to sleep the same amount every night, adolescents like to stay up late into the evening, wake up early on school days, and sleep until noon on the weekends. What are the causes of this change in sleep patterns during adolescence, which is known as **delayed phase preference** (Caskadon, Vieira, & Acebo, 1993), and what are some of the consequences?

The shift toward later bedtimes that often accompanies adolescence probably has both biological and social causes. Biologically, it appears that the internal clock that is within each person and controls sleep and wake cycles (i.e., **circadian rhythm**) shifts during adolescence. Whereas children and adults generally begin to feel tired in the early evening and eventually go to sleep somewhere between 8:00 and 11:00 p.m., adolescents are wide-eyed and active in the evening and often do not feel sleepy until after midnight (Carskadon & Acebo, 2002; Millman, Working Group on Sleepiness in Adolescents/Young Adults, & AAP Committee on Adolescence, 2005). Research indicates that this shift toward greater wakefulness at night and later onset of sleep occurs across cultures, and even across species, during adolescence (Hagenauer, Perryman, Lee, & Caskadon, 2009), providing further evidence that it is based, at least in part, on biological factors.

The likely culprit in this circadian shift during adolescence is changes in the production of **melatonin**, a hormone that helps the body determine the time of day and, therefore, when to go to sleep. With the onset of adolescence, there is a delay in when melatonin is secreted, causing a delay in the onset of sleep at night. Recent evidence suggests that exposure to bright screens, such as those found on mobile phones, tablets, and computers, further delays melatonin release and sleep (Wood, Rea, Plitnick, & Figueiro, 2013). Because adolescents and emerging adults often spend a lot of time looking at bright screens in the evening—on their phones, working on computers—there is a concern that the social world may be having harmful effects on the circadian rhythms of adolescents, resulting in sleep deprivation. Even without the potentially harmful effects of glowing screens at night, adolescents also experience a number of new social demands that keep them awake late into the night. Completing hours of homework, instant messaging with friends, talking on the phone, and participation in activities that occur at night (such as athletic events, movies, and dates) all conspire to keep adolescents awake late at night.

Unfortunately, there is a cost to the late-night schedules of adolescents. Teenagers still need a lot of sleep, and the early start times of school, coupled with the late bedtimes of adolescents, create a lot of sleepy high school students. Whereas adults generally need 7.5 to 8.25 hours of sleep per night to be fully rested, adolescents need roughly 9.5 hours of sleep. During the week, many adolescents accumulate a large **sleep debt** as they go to bed at 1:00 a.m. and wake up at 7:00 a.m. for school. Although they make up some of this debt on the weekends, sleeping an average of 90 minutes longer than they do on weekdays (Randler, 2008), it is not enough to make up for all of the sleep that they have lost during the week. As a result, adolescents are often tired, especially during morning classes, and this sleep deprivation can lead to irritability, problems paying attention in class, and decreases in attendance rates (Giannotti et al., 2002).

Because of the problems associated with adolescents' lack of sleep, several people have suggested that high schools should begin the day later. Minnesota public schools pushed the start time of seven high schools back from 7:15 a.m. to 8:40, and teachers reported that students were more alert in the morning classes as a result (Wahlstrom, 2002). The apparent success of this program has led other school districts to consider later start times for their high schools and prompted Zoe Lofgren, a congresswoman from California, to introduce legislation that would offer school districts a financial incentive for starting the school day later. The timing of the school day is influenced by many factors, such as parental work schedules and the availability of school buses, so changing the start times of high schools is a complicated proposition. But it appears clear from the research that the circadian rhythms of adolescents shift toward greater alertness later in the day and at night rather than in the morning, so a shift to a later start time would likely benefit the attention and achievement of adolescent students.

Nutrition

As adolescents begin spending more time outside of the home and away from adult supervision, their eating habits often change. Adolescents, especially boys, snack more than children do, and the snacks they choose tend to be high in salt, fat, and sugar. Adolescents also drink a lot more soda than children do, in part because of the relentless marketing campaigns of soda companies aimed at adolescent consumers. Until recently, vending machines selling soda were ubiquitous in American high schools. An initiative spearheaded by former president Bill Clinton has led many soda producers to remove vending machines from high schools. Still, 78% of high school students reported drinking at least one soda during the previous 7 days (CDC, 2013).

In addition to eating more unhealthy snacks, adolescents are also prone to skipping breakfast (Shaw, 1998). In one study, 62% of high school students said they did not eat breakfast every day during the week (CDC, 2013). Socioeconomic status (SES) is closely linked with what adolescents eat as well. Families with lower incomes tend to eat more processed foods that are high in energy (e.g., processed sugar) but low in fiber and **complex carbohydrates** (Darmon & Drewnowski, 2008). Adolescents from higher-SES backgrounds tend to eat more fresh fruits and vegetables, lean meats and fish, and lower-fat dairy products than do their lower-SES peers. One reason for this may be that highly processed foods that tend to be lower in nutritional value are cheaper than are fresh foods and lean meats (Darmon & Drewnowski, 2008). Some research also suggests that lower-SES mothers are less likely than are more affluent mothers to consider the health properties of the foods they buy and are more likely to consider the cost (Hupkens, Knibbe, & Drop, 2000). In modern society, it is simply cheaper to eat food that is less healthy, so those adolescents from lower-income families are more likely to eat unhealthy foods and to suffer the negative health consequences associated with eating such foods. See Table 2.3 for a summary of the eating habits of high school students.

School Lunches

For decades, advocates of healthy eating have battled with school districts and government agencies about what should be served in school lunches. In 1981,

TABLE 2.3	Eating Habits of U.S. High School Students, by Ethnicity			
	Asian	Black	Hispanic	White
Did not eat fruit*	2.9	6.9	4.1	4.9
Did not eat vegetables*	2.3	11.3	9.3	4.5
Drank a sugary soda*	65.5	79.6	78.6	77.9
Drank at least one sugary soda per day*	12.2	30.2	22.6	29.0
Did not eat breakfast at all during previous 7 days	12.8	16.0	17.4	11.5
Did not eat breakfast on at least one of previous 7 days	56.3	69.9	64.2	59.0

Source: Data from Centers for Disease Control and Prevention, 2013.

*During previous 7 days.

President Ronald Reagan and members of his administration were widely criticized for proposing that ketchup be classified as a vegetable in school lunches. To this day, nutritional experts frequently criticize school lunches as offering too many processed and fried foods that are high in fat and sugar content and not enough fresh foods, such as vegetables and fruits. A study published in the *Journal of the American Dietetic Association* (Crepinsek, Gordon, McKinney, Condon, & Wilkinson, 2009) found that only 6 to 7% of school lunches served in the subsidized school lunch program met all of the nutritional standards developed by the United States Department of Agriculture (USDA). Nearly half of the schools in the study offered no fresh fruits or raw vegetables in their school lunches. Pizza, French fries, hamburgers, and other high-fat foods were common on school lunch menus. In addition to the unhealthy foods offered in school lunches, schools often have vending machines that are filled with candy, potato chips, and sugary drinks, such as soda.

Some experts worry that the high fat and sugar content of school lunches may be contributing to the rising numbers of **overweight** and **obese** children and adolescents. Although unhealthy lunches in the subsidized school lunch programs may be a contributing factor, evidence suggests that it is probably not the main factor. The subsidized lunch program serves low-income youth across the United States. Research indicates that low-income families tend to eat more high-fat, high-sugar, and processed foods than do wealthier families. In addition, in one study the school-provided lunches were more nutritious than were the lunches that students brought from home or bought on their own, outside of school (Food Research and Action Center, 2010). Nonetheless, the history of unhealthy school lunches, combined with rising concerns about the health of children and adolescents, has created a growing movement to improve the quality of school lunches.

Perhaps the leading voice in the healthy-lunch movement is renowned chef and restaurant owner Alice Waters. She has owned and operated a celebrated restaurant, *Chez Panisse*, in Berkeley, California, for over four decades. In recent years, she has become a food activist, regularly encouraging people to frequent their local farmer's markets, to shop locally, and to eat fresh food. She has also become an activist for healthier foods in schools. She founded the **Edible Schoolyard** program, beginning with one middle school in Berkeley. The goal of the program was to help students better understand where food comes from, what is in it, how to prepare it for eating, and how food affects health. Students at a participating school grow fruits and vegetables in a garden on the school grounds, harvest the food, help to prepare and cook the food, and then eat the food they have grown in school lunches. The program also involves integrating information about cooking and gardening throughout the school curriculum, improving the overall nutritional quality of school lunches, and creating a more pleasant dining atmosphere in school cafeterias. A longitudinal study found evidence that students who participated in well-implemented Edible Schoolyard programs developed increased nutritional knowledge, ate more fruits and vegetables (especially in the earlier grade levels), and had more positive attitudes about the taste and health benefits of healthier school lunches (Henry, 2010). Although the sample is small and the evidence is modest, this research provides hope that adolescents can be encouraged to eat healthier food, especially if they participate in producing it.

Less comprehensive programs have sprung up in school districts across the country, resulting in more fresh fruit and vegetable offerings and the introduction of whole grains to replace breads, pastas, and pizza crusts made white flour. To date, little research has been conducted to determine the effects of these healthier school lunches on kids' eating habits and health outcomes. But the evidence so far indicates that some benefits are beginning to emerge. For example, Wojciki and Heyman (2006) examined the effects of the San Francisco school district's nutrition policy, specifically the district's offering of healthier food in school lunches. They found that offering students healthier menu options led to an increase in the number of students participating in the federal school lunch program. Much more research is needed to determine how changes in the nutritional values of school lunches affect the health and eating habits of adolescent students.

Athletic Participation

As discussed earlier in this chapter, the physical changes associated with puberty are quite different for boys and girls. Whereas girls tend to add more fat than muscle when they hit puberty, the opposite is true for boys. The conventional wisdom has often pointed to this difference as the likely explanation for why boys are so much more likely than girls to participate in sports in high school. But recent trends in athletic participation among boys and girls suggest that the conventional wisdom is wrong. Instead of differences in physique, it is most likely differences in societal expectations of girls and boys that create the different levels of participation in sports between adolescent boys and girls. As those societal expectations and norms of behavior have changed over time, so have the athletic participation rates of male and female adolescents.

According to a survey of high school athletic programs conducted by the National Federation of State High School Associations (2014), the 2013–2014 academic year saw the highest percentage of students participating in organized athletic programs ever: 55.5%. Of the nearly 8 million high school students who participated in some sort of organized sporting activity in school, 42% were girls. Although this percentage is still well below the percentage of boys who participated in sports that year, the historical trends show a rapid increase in the number of girls participating in athletics in high school. Girls' participation in high school athletics has increased every year for 25 years. Over the last 20 years, the number of boys who participate in high school sports has increased 31%, but the number of girls participating in sports has increased 63%. Going back even further, the changes in participation rates for girls and boys are even more striking. Forty years ago, during the 1971–1972 school year, more than 3.5 million boys participated in high school sports, as compared with only 294,015 girls. In other words, 40 years ago boys were more than 10 times as likely as girls to participate in high school sports. By the 2010–2011 school year, nearly 3.2 million girls participated in high school athletics, an increase since 1971–1972 of roughly 1000%! Over this same period, the increase in the percentage of boys participating in high school sports was about 20% (Figure 2.8).

Because the changes that accompany puberty in the bodies of girls and boys have been consistent for centuries, the recent upward trend in girls' participation in high school sports is not attributable to changes in body type. Instead, the increase is likely due to changes in societal attitudes about what constitutes appropriate behavior for adolescent girls. Whereas it used to be considered unfeminine for a young woman to engage in sports after puberty, that attitude has clearly changed in the United States over the last 40 years. The women's liberation movement of the 1960s and 1970s paved the way for important legislation, such as **Title IX**, which mandated equal funding for girls and boys sports programs in public schools. With increased opportunities and decreased social stigma, high school girls have been participating in athletic programs in ever-increasing numbers.

There are many benefits of participation in athletic programs during high school. One clear benefit is physical health. Students who participate in school-sponsored sports tend to exercise more (Greenleaf, Boyer, & Petree, 2009). But research indicates that participation in sports during adolescence has a number of additional benefits beyond more frequent exercise. For example, in one study, high school students who participated in sports tended to have more positive perceptions of their bodies (i.e., positive body image), regardless of their gender or which sport they played, than did nonathletes (Hausenblas & Down, 2001). In addition, there seem to be academic benefits from participation in interscholastic sports during high school. Athletes tend to get better grades, are more likely to graduate from high school, are more likely to enter college, and are more likely to graduate from college (Troutman & Dufur, 2007) than are nonathletes. Moreover, research shows that athletes tend to have higher self-esteem (Delaney & Lee, 1995; Greenleaf et al., 2009; Shaffer & Wittes, 2006), are less likely to develop eating disorders (Wilkins, Boland, & Albinson, 1991), and develop broader social networks than do nonathletes (Broh, 2002).

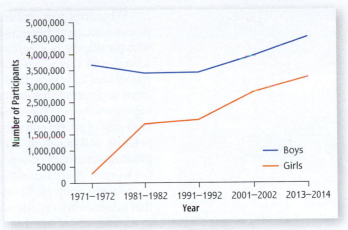

FIGURE 2.8

Athletic Participation in High School, 1971 to 2014, by Gender

Source: National Federation of State High School Associations, 2014.

In-Depth 2.1

Should Schools Limit Who Participates in Sports?

Most high schools put limits on who can participate on interscholastic athletic teams. For example, students are often required to maintain a minimum grade point average (GPA) to remain eligible for participation on sports teams. In addition, by high school, most teams are competitive and only have space for a certain number of participants. Those students who wish to play but are not deemed competent (i.e., get "cut" after trying out for the team) must search for opportunities outside of school. Given the many benefits of participating in high school sports, are these exclusionary practices wise? This is a difficult question to answer. Some might argue that the higher achievement levels of athletes are a result of the minimum GPA requirement. Students who might excel at sports but not care about their athletic achievement are motivated to at least pass their classes so they can remain eligible for the team. Others argue that eliminating eligibility for lower-achieving students removes their only remaining connection to school and makes dropping out of school a more attractive option. Similarly, there are two sides to the competitive nature of selection for high school teams. On the one hand, students who might benefit from being on a team miss out on these benefits if they are not competent enough to make the team. On the other hand, some of the advantages of participating in high school sports appear to stem from feeling competent and being on a team that wins, at least occasionally. Is it better for a less skilled player to make the basketball team but never play or to never make the team at all? The research needed to answer that question has not yet been conducted. What do you think?

Why does participation in athletic activities, especially interscholastic sports, produce so many benefits for adolescents? One explanation may be that students who participate in sports tend to develop connections with peers and adults in the school, and this social bonding creates a greater sense of identification with the school and its values (Broh, 2002). Because these values include academic achievement and continuing education, athletes tend to try harder in school and aspire to higher levels of achievement and education. It also appears that participating in high school sports enhances participants' body image, perceptions of athletic competence, and beliefs about the benefits of physical activity. These, in turn, promote physical activity in college and greater overall well-being (Greenleaf et al., 2009). For women, these benefits of sports participation were especially pronounced when the women enjoyed the sports experience. Taken together, the evidence indicates that adolescents experience numerous benefits from participating in sports while in middle school and high school, and these benefits extend beyond the physical realm to include social, self-esteem, and academic benefits. And the benefits last.

Obesity

Much has been reported in the media about the rising rates of obesity in the U.S. population. Numerous potential contributing factors have been proposed to explain this phenomenon, including increased consumption of processed and high-fat, high-sugar foods; increased time sitting in front of computers or video games; and reductions in athletic programs in schools. One well-orchestrated attempt to address the problem of obesity is the **Let's Move** campaign begun by First Lady Michelle Obama (http://www.letsmove.gov/). This campaign approaches the problem of childhood obesity from several angles, including healthier eating, more exercise, and increased awareness of the problem. But what does the research show about the number of obese and overweight adolescents and the factors that may contribute to being overweight? Are American adolescents really getting fatter, as the frequent media reports suggest?

According to the CDC, using data from the 2013 National Youth Risk Behavior Survey, the percentage of high school students who are obese (i.e., a body-mass index <BMI> at the 95th percentile or higher) is 13.7%. This was up slightly from 2009 (12%), but roughly equal to the percentages reported in 2005 and 2007. In 2013, boys were substantially more likely than girls to be obese. In addition, obesity was more common among African American high school students (14.8% for boys, 16.7% for girls) and Hispanic high school students (19% for boys, 11.2% for girls) than among White students (16.5% for boys, 9.2% for girls). (Asian- Americans tend to be much less likely than Whites to be overweight or obese, except for native Hawaiians, CDC, 2013). In addition to these obesity rates, nearly 17% of U.S. high school students were classified as overweight (BMI between 85th and 95th percentile). These percentages were almost identical for males and females. Again, Whites were less likely than African American and Hispanics to be classified as overweight. Although the percentages of high school students classified as overweight in 2013 was up slightly compared to 1999 data and about a percentage point compared to 2009 data, it is interesting to note that since 2009, the percentage of overweight high school students has actually decreased slightly for African American and Hispanic students, but risen for White students (Figure 2.9).

As the percentages reported in Table 2.4 reveal, there are some very interesting differences between perceptions and reality regarding weight. For example, although over 33% of male high school students are either obese or overweight, only 25.9% of males consider themselves to be even slightly overweight. In contrast, 27.5% of female high school students are either obese or overweight, but 36.3% perceive themselves to be overweight. There are also some interesting differences between ethnic groups in perceptions of being overweight, relative to the actual percentages within each ethnic group that is overweight. Only 26% of African American high school students consider themselves to be overweight, despite the

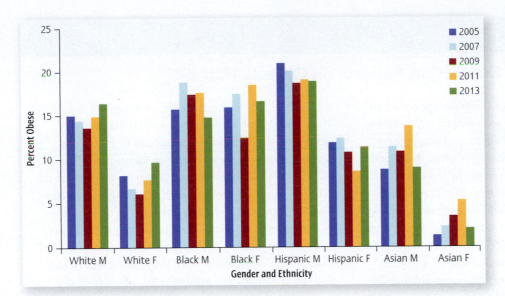

FIGURE 2.9

Obesity Rates of U.S. High School Students, by Gender and Ethnicity, 2005–2013

Source: Data from Centers for Disease Control and Prevention, 2013.

fact that 34.8% of this ethnic group is either obese or overweight. In contrast, White and Hispanic adolescents tend to perceive themselves as overweight in roughly the same percentages as their actual obesity and overweight statistics. These ethnic and gender differences in perceived and actual rates of being overweight and obese point to interesting cultural differences in conceptions of physical attractiveness. African Americans, in general, are less likely to adopt the view that the ideal body type for women is very skinny. Media depictions, particularly in magazines, of extremely thin models generally include images of White women, and it appears that White adolescent girls are more likely than African American adolescent girls to have a gap between their perceived and actual body weight. As discussed earlier in the section on body image, African American adolescent girls are more likely than White or Hispanic adolescent girls to report being satisfied with their bodies.

It is also worth noting that there are some mismatches between perceptions of weight and reported behaviors regarding weight. As the numbers in Table 2.4 reveal, only 31.1% of U.S. high school students perceive themselves to be overweight, yet almost half (47.7%) indicate that they may be trying to lose weight, including over 60% of females. In other words, nearly twice as many girls report trying to lose weight as report perceiving themselves to actually be overweight. Thankfully, most students do not report turning to unhealthy methods of weight management, such as fasting for at least 24 hours (13%), taking diet pills or powders (5%), or vomiting or taking laxatives (4.4%).

Eating Disorders

As noted in the previous section, many adolescents, particularly girls, experience a mismatch between their actual weight or body type and their ideal weight or body

TABLE 2.4 **Percentage of High School Students Who Are Obese and Overweight, by Ethnicity**

	Females	Males	White	Black	Hispanic	Total
Obese	10.9	16.6	13.1	15.7	15.2	13.7
Overweight	16.6	16.5	15.6	19.1	18.3	16.6
Describe selves as slightly or very overweight	36.3	25.9	31.8	26.0	33.8	31.1
NOT trying to lose weight	37.4	67	52.9	59.1	45.5	52.3

Source: Data from Centers for Disease Control and Prevention, 2013.

In-Depth 2.2

Making Sense of Conflicting Reports on Obesity Rates

In recent years, numerous stories have appeared on television, on the Internet, and in print, all declaring that Americans, including children and adolescents, are getting fatter. Indeed, obesity is often described as the most serious health concern facing U.S. children and adolescents today (Steinberg, 2010). According to the Institute of Medicine (2006), obesity rates among American adolescents have tripled since 1970, including an increase of roughly 50% from 1994 to 2002. But data from the Center for Disease Control and Prevention (CDC) indicate that obesity rates among U.S. high school students increased only slightly from 1999 to 2013. In addition, research examining changes in body-mass index (BMI) among children and adolescents from the 1960s to the 1990s found only modest increases at most age levels (i.e., increases of 0.2 to 1.2 points in median BMI within each age group; Flegal & Troiano, 2000). A study published in the *Journal of the American Medical Association* reported that there was no change in the obesity rates for children, adolescents, or young adults between 2002 and 2012 (Ogden, Carroll, Kit, & Flegal, 2014). And in February 2015, researchers from the CDC reported that obesity rates actually declined among young children, but this was quickly followed by another report in April 2015 arguing that obesity rates were, in fact, increasing, especially the number of severely obese children (CBS News, 2015).

Why is there so much confusion regarding whether the numbers of obese and overweight U.S. children and adolescents is rising, falling, or remaining stable? There are a number of reasons. One is that different reports use different time periods to determine whether these rates are changing. Some look at the last 10 years, whereas others at longer periods, such as 20 or 30 years. Different studies also use different samples. For example, there is evidence that obesity rates are increasing most among Hispanic girls and African American boys. Studies that have larger percentages of children and adolescents from these populations may find larger increases in obesity rates, whereas studies with smaller samples from these populations may report no changes in obesity rates. When you read, see, or hear stories about obesity among adolescents, check the source of the information carefully.

Here are a few examples of different kinds of reporting about obesity:

Charts of BMI in childhood and adolescence over time: http://www.halls.md/bmi/nhanes.htm

Story from ABC News on adolescent obesity: http://abcnews.go.com/Health/Wellness/obese-us-kids-teens-fatter/story?id=11446419

Story from CBS News on adolescent obesity: http://www.cbsnews.com/stories/2003/05/12/health/main553370.shtml

Report in the *Journal of the American Medical Association* on childhood and adult obesity: http://jama.jamanetwork.com/article.aspx?articleid=1832542

type, and more than 6 in 10 American high school girls report that they are actively trying to lose weight. This mismatch between one's ideal and actual body type leads some adolescents, mostly girls, to develop eating disorders. (Note that we will only mention eating disorders briefly here. A more detailed description of eating disorders, their causes, and their treatment is offered in Chapter 11.)

The two most common eating disorders are **bulimia nervosa** and **anorexia nervosa**. Bulimia is defined as **binge eating** (usually in secret) followed by inappropriate methods of weight control, such as inducing vomiting or taking laxatives. In a study of college students in 1986, Zuckerman and his colleagues found that 4% of women were classified as having bulimia, and 0.4% of men had the disorder. But bulimic symptoms, such as fasting or vomiting, were much more frequent (Zuckerman, Colby, Ware, & Lazerson, 1986). More recent data show that about 6.6% of high school girls have symptoms of bulimia, including binge eating and **purging** (CDC, 2013). It is still more prevalent among women than men. Anorexia nervosa is a severe eating disorder that is defined by aversion to food, distorted views about the body (i.e., perceiving even thin bodies as fat), and marked weight loss. Females are about 10 times more likely than males to develop anorexia, and it affects approximately 1% of female adolescents (National Association of Anorexia Nervosa and Associated Disorders).

In addition to differences in the frequency with which anorexia and bulimia occur, the rates of recovery from these two disorders are also quite different. Horzog and his colleagues (1999) followed a group of women with eating disorders for several years after they received treatment for their disorders. Seven and a half years after receiving treatment, nearly three-quarters of women treated for bulimia were categorized as fully recovered, compared to only one-third of women treated for anorexia. About 33% of bulimics and anorexics relapsed after having achieved full recovery. The authors also found that there were high rates of partial recovery from both disorders, but anorexia was the more difficult disorder to recover from, either partially or fully. Although both of these eating disorders are serious illnesses, anorexia nervosa has a higher fatality rate and is more difficult to overcome. Sullivan (1995) found that 5.9% of adolescents and young adults with anorexia nervosa between the ages of 15 and 24 died during that age period, a rate 12 times higher than the rate for females in that same age group who did not have anorexia.

MyEdLab **Self-Check 2.4**

Adolescent Health and School Health Services

Most adolescents are very healthy. Indeed, adolescents tend to be the healthiest of any age group and very rarely die of natural causes. Among infants, the second leading cause of death is birth defects. But if a child is healthy enough to reach adolescence, he or she is very unlikely to die from causes that were present at birth. In adulthood, the leading causes of death tend to be disease caused by a combination of genetic and environmental factors. But among adolescents and young adults (ages 15 to 24), the top-three causes of death are accidents, homicide, and suicide (National Institutes of Health, 2015). In other words, the leading causes of death in adolescence and early adulthood are largely preventable. Yet adolescents die much more frequently than do children and early adolescents (between the ages of 1 and 13). Why is that? And what are some of the health concerns that adolescents do have?

The primary contributor to major health concerns among adolescents may be cognitive rather than physical. As discussed in Chapter 11, adolescents tend to develop a sense of **invincibility** and a belief that bad things will not happen to them. This, along with the increase in **sensation seeking** and **novelty seeking** in adolescence discussed earlier in this chapter, leads to more frequent involvement in risky behavior, and such behavior often has health consequences. For example, adolescents are notoriously risky drivers, often driving too fast, with too many distractions (such as texting), and while under the influence of drugs or alcohol. This leads to an inordinate number of automobile accidents among adolescents and early adults. Similarly, adolescents often engage in risky sexual behavior, such as having sex without using a condom. Sexually transmitted diseases and pregnancy are two consequences of such behavior, both of which require medical attention. A third example of how the lack of cognitive development, especially in the planning and foresight regions of the brain, affects adolescent health involves what adolescents put into their bodies. Adolescence is the time when most people begin drinking, smoking, and using drugs. Although it would be difficult to find an adolescent who is not aware of the health risks of such consumption, the false sense of invincibility common among adolescents leads many into taking risks with what they consume. Similarly, as discussed earlier, adolescents tend to enjoy junk food that is high in fat, salt, and sugar. Frequent consumption of these kinds of foods contributes to the population of overweight and obese teenagers in the United States.

It is important to note that adolescent health is closely linked with the contexts in which adolescents live. Poor and minority youth in the United States (and throughout the world) tend to experience more health problems than do their wealthier peers. In the United States, this can be attributed to several factors. First, poor youth are less likely to have medical insurance, and are therefore less likely to receive preventative care. Second, wealthier families tend to have easier access to fresh fruits and vegetables and to be more knowledgeable about nutrition, leading to differences in diet that can compromise the health of poorer adolescents. Minority youth in the United States suffer from more food-related illnesses, such as obesity, high blood pressure, and high cholesterol levels (National Heart, Lung, and Blood Institute, 1992). Third, poor and minority youth are more likely to live in higher-crime neighborhoods. As a result, African American and Latino youth are more likely to be murdered than are White adolescents (Ozer, 2005). Because poor and minority youth have more health problems and less access to medical care, schools that serve these (and all) students may need to provide these services for their students.

Health-Care Services in Schools

Schools generally approach the topic of student health in three ways: (1) information/education; (2) physical exercise; and (3) direct provision of health-care services, such as mental health counseling and school-based physicians and nurses. Perhaps the approach that is most common, and has been most studied, is the health education curriculum. In a comprehensive review of the effects of health education programs, the effects of school-based health education programs depended on both the characteristics of the program and the health behavior that was targeted (Inman, Bakergem, LaRosa, & Garr, 2011). For example, sexual health (i.e., the prevention of **sexually transmitted diseases [STDs]** and unwanted pregnancies) was best promoted when the health goals were very clear (e.g., preventing HIV infection) and the specific behaviors necessary to achieve these goals were explicitly discussed (e.g., abstaining from sex, using condoms when having sex, etc.). For promoting social-emotional health, school programs that focused on helping students develop strategies for building their social competence, monitoring and awareness of bullying behavior, teaching conflict resolution skills, and managing emotions were most effective. For healthy behaviors regarding substance use and abuse, such as alcohol and drugs, Inman and her colleagues found that there is good evidence that information can reduce the use of these products, but few schools have programs in place to provide adolescents with this information. The evidence suggests that teaching students about the dangers of drugs and alcohol before they begin using them is the most effective at reducing their use. They also found that although there are a number of effective curricula for promoting healthy behavior, schools often have difficulty successfully implementing these programs. In fact, Inman et al. (2011) refer to implementation as the "missing link" in school-based health programs.

Does providing adolescents with information about health actually improve their health-related behavior? The evidence is mixed. Although adolescents who receive information about such things as the risks of smoking and drugs, how to avoid STDs and pregnancy, and how to eat healthier foods are often able to display increased knowledge in these areas, changes in their actual behavior are more difficult to produce (Kisker & Brown, 1996). This mismatch between knowledge and behavior is found among adults as well as adolescents. After all, everyone knows that smoking is bad for health, but many smoke anyway. To actually produce changes in behavior, more than knowledge may be needed. So called "sin taxes" associated with cigarettes, thereby making them more expensive, have reduced smoking (Gruber & Zinman, 2001), as has the ever-growing list of places where smoking is prohibited. It appears that although providing information to adolescents about the advantages of healthy behavior has benefits, to truly change behavior this information should be paired with policies that make engaging in unhealthy behavior more difficult.

In addition to information, schools can, and often do, provide direct health-care services to students. In some schools, these services can be simple, such as a school nurse putting bandages on scraped knees or distributing aspirin for headaches. But in some schools, the health-care services are quite a bit more involved. In recognition of the fact that many low-income youth are at greater risk for injury and illness as compared with their wealthier peers, and are also less likely to have health insurance, many schools in lower-income districts have created health-care clinics that are inside of or next to schools. These health-care centers provide both information and direct care to students. For example, California has 231 **School Health Centers**. These health centers come in various forms, including health centers based in schools, community health centers that are linked to specific schools, and mobile health vans that travel to schools. They also provide a variety of services, including comprehensive health screening, prescription drug services, mental health services, immunizations, and lab tests. Responsibility for the administration of these School Health Centers falls to several agencies, including school districts, hospitals, federal and county health agencies, and community health centers. Research suggests that School Health Centers have several benefits for students and result in fewer student absences, lower dropout rates, and reduced disciplinary problems (see http://www.schoolhealthcenters.org for more information on these centers).

Integrated Health-Care Services. The overall health of adolescents involves integrating and coordinating health information and services across the different contexts in which adolescents live. For example, promoting healthy nutrition at school is more effective when it is paired with the availability of healthy foods at home, and for that to happen parents often need to be educated about nutrition and how to prepare healthy meals. Similarly, it is important for health-care services offered in schools to work in partnership with health-care providers in the community. If a student is diagnosed with a medical condition by his doctor in the community, it may be important for the nurse at his school to understand the diagnosis and treatment so that continuity of care can be managed throughout the adolescent's day. In addition, because various aspects of health influence each other (e.g., mental health, nutrition, exercise, knowledge about risk behaviors), the best health-promotion programs are those that are able to integrate information and services across these multiple areas of health.

As this book is being written, school budgets are being tightened in districts across the United States. As a result of budget cuts, many of the school-based programs and services designed to improve the mental and physical health of adolescent students are being reduced or eliminated. This is unfortunate. Because many of the illnesses adolescents experience are preventable, providing children and adolescents with information they might use to avoid developing these problematic behaviors is important. In addition, because many poor students lack access to health care, especially preventative health care, and are at more risk for disease, school-based health-care services may be the only access many of these students have. As funding for school-based health care dwindles, the opportunities for many adolescents to remain healthy dwindle as well.

Recommendations for Educators

Because physical development and biological maturation are natural processes that occur at their own rate and time, it may seem that there is little teachers and schools can do to address these changes. But the fact that physical maturation brings changes in adolescents' self-perceptions, social interactions, and health behaviors creates a window of opportunity for educators to help make the process of physical development as smooth and healthy for adolescents as possible. Our recommendations for educators can be divided into three general areas: awareness, providing information, and creating healthy opportunities.

Awareness

It is important for teachers to make themselves aware of the physical and biological changes associated with puberty and the concomitant changes in self-perceptions, social interactions, and behaviors among adolescents. For example, teachers should be aware of the following:

- Changes in hormone levels can create heightened moodiness, but changes in adolescents' moods often have other causes.
- Changes in physical appearance do not always mean adolescents' cognitive maturity has increased.
- Physical development is often associated with both decreases in body satisfaction and increases in social pressures, especially for girls.
- Increased autonomy afforded to adolescents' due to their more mature appearance can be associated with unhealthy choices about food, exercise, and other behaviors.
- Lethargy among adolescent students may be due more to changes in their circadian rhythms and sleep patterns than to laziness or disrespect.

By making themselves aware of the changes associated with puberty and adolescence, teachers can place themselves in a better position to understand the behavior of their adolescent students, the social pressures they may be encountering, and the opportunities to provide help and support as adolescents try to manage these new pressures.

Information

One of the ways that teachers can support adolescents as they cope with their changing bodies is to provide relevant information to their students. For example, many teenagers become voracious consumers of media images that portray body ideals that are impossible to achieve. These body ideals (i.e., thin for women, muscular for men) can lead to body dissatisfaction for adolescents, and subsequently to unhealthy behaviors (e.g., dieting, smoking, bulimia, use of muscle-building supplements). We recommend that teachers use their awareness of the various challenges adolescents face as a result of their physical maturation to provide relevant information to help them cope with these changes and make smart choices about their behaviors. Specific recommendations include the following:

- Provide adolescents with information about what normal, healthy adult bodies look like to counter the thin-body ideal presented in media images.
- Provide information about how to resist the social pressure many early-developing girls receive to engage in risky behavior.
- Provide information about the health risks of dieting, disordered eating, and supplements such as diet pills or muscle-building supplements.
- Provide information about healthy eating, how to cook, and how to recognize unhealthy ingredients in food.
- Provide information about the amount and kinds of exercise adolescents need to maintain health.
- Provide information about how to get enough sleep.

Although providing relevant information to adolescents is no guarantee that they will use the information to maintain healthy attitudes and behaviors, it is clear that adolescents' misperceptions about what healthy bodies look like and the risks associated with certain behaviors designed to achieve body ideals can lead to unhealthy behaviors among adolescents.

Healthy Opportunities

In addition to providing information, it is important for teachers and schools to provide opportunities for adolescents to engage in healthy behaviors. As described earlier in the chapter, these can range from opportunities for all students to engage in exercise regularly (e.g., physical education classes, athletic teams) to the Edible Schoolyard programs that provide adolescents with knowledge about nutrition and cooking.

Some schools have gone a step further to provide students with integrated health services. The CDC has developed a **Coordinated School Health Plan** that describes the need for, and parameters of, a coordinated health-care system. The main idea is that the various components of health (e.g., nutrition, exercise, mental health, etc.) need to be coordinated, and that in-school health promotion services need to be coordinated with family and community efforts to keep adolescents healthy. There are eight components to the CDC's Coordinated School Health Plan:

- Health education: Giving students knowledge about health through a health curriculum and teaching
- Physical education
- Provision of health-care services, either at school or through referral to health providers in the community
- Nutrition services, including access to healthy meals at school and information about healthy eating
- Mental health services
- A healthy and safe school environment, including schools free from contaminants and a nurturing psychosocial environment free from bullying
- Health promotion of school staff
- Coordination between school, family, and community health efforts

The goals of the Coordinated School Health Plan are lofty and will require a concerted effort for schools to achieve them. The CDC offers several suggestions for how schools can implement this program. These include securing the support of the administrators of the school, including the superintendent; identifying a school health team with a single school health coordinator; prioritizing the health needs of the students in the school; developing a plan and implementing it incrementally; and providing training for school staff.

MyEdLab Self-Check 2.5

Conclusion

The onset of puberty sets in motion a series of physiological and physical changes that dramatically alter the appearance of adolescents. These changes in appearance usher in a set of changes in the ways that adolescents are perceived and treated by others, and these changes can influence dramatically the way that adolescents think and behave. Although educators cannot do much to alter the process of physical development, they can become informed about the effects of these changes and use this information to develop behaviors and programs that will help adolescents adjust to this transition in a healthy way.

Cognitive and Intellectual Development

Learning Outcomes

3.1 You will be able to describe the four stages of Piaget's theory of cognitive development, particularly focusing on the stages that are applicable to adolescents.

3.2 You will be able to describe Vygotsky's theory of cognitive development, and how it can be applied to instruction.

3.3 You will be able to compare and contrast the Piagetian and Vygotskian theories of cognitive development.

3.4 You will be able to identify and describe 21st-century skills.

3.5 You will be able to describe human memory from an information-processing perspective, and how teachers can use this information to improve student learning.

3.6 You will be able to compare and contrast current theories of intelligence.

3.7 You will be able to describe metacognition, and explain how teachers can facilitate metacognition in adolescent students.

Introduction

Many educators assume that students' abilities to "think" are completely developed when students reach adolescence. This assumption yields very important implications for the education of adolescents. Consider the following example:

>>>

Mr. Ryan is a ninth-grade social studies teacher. He is working with his students on a unit examining American involvement in the Middle East. He engages his students in a discussion about involvement in Iraq specifically. He asks his students to do some research on the history of U.S. involvement in Iraq, and then he asks them to form an opinion about current U.S. policy. One of his students (Amanda) provides a detailed history and critical analysis of U.S. involvement in Iraq throughout both the 20th and 21st centuries; Amanda provides a thorough analysis of historical and current issues, and concludes that involvement is not justified. In contrast, another student (Seth) provides a somewhat less critical analysis (he just reports factual information), and concludes that involvement is justified.

As illustrated in this example, an assignment given to a group of adolescents can lead to different types of responses from the students. Amanda's response involves critical analysis, whereas Seth's is more or less just a reporting of facts. Based on their research, these two students expressed different opinions about U.S. involvement in Iraq. Is one of them "right" and the other "wrong"?

Although it is possible that Amanda and Seth did not spend equal amounts of time on this assignment and that one may have exerted more effort than the other, there is another possibility as well. What if Amanda and Seth, who are the same age chronologically, are not able to cognitively engage with this task as equals? What if Amanda is able to think about these issues in a qualitatively different manner than Seth? Does this have implications for how Mr. Ryan evaluates the assignment? Does it have implications for instruction? Does it have implications for students' self-concepts?

Clearly, the answer to all of these questions is "yes." This example serves as a preview to many of the concepts that we will explore in this chapter. Specifically, this chapter focuses on cognitive and intellectual development during adolescence. A theme that will recur throughout this chapter is that chronological age and cognitive development are not perfectly correlated. Although most students may get to certain levels of cognitive development by the time they reach adulthood, the rates at which students achieve cognitive milestones during adolescence vary, sometimes quite widely. Thus, two students may both be in the ninth grade, but one may be more able to critically examine complex issues than another. In addition, the ability to engage in complex thinking may vary across subject areas for some students, and thus the ability to engage in complex thinking in math may develop more quickly in some students than the ability to engage in complex thinking in language arts, for example.

OVERVIEW OF THE CHAPTER

We review several important aspects of cognitive and intellectual development in this chapter, keeping a close eye on implications for educators. First, we examine two theoretical frameworks that are often considered in discussions of cognitive development: the theories of Jean Piaget and Lev Vygotsky. Although these theories often are viewed as competing models, we examine important implications of each theory, and how effective educators of adolescents acknowledge and consider aspects of both theories. We also examine 21st-century skills, which in recent years have emerged as outgrowths of the work of Piaget and Vygotsky (and others).

Second, we examine information processing during adolescence. The term *information processing* basically refers to memory. There are many important implications of research on this topic for educators. In particular, a strong knowledge of the capacities and limitations of human memory during adolescence has ramifications for how instruction is developed and presented, and how knowledge is assessed.

Third, we examine intelligence. There are many conceptions of intelligence, and there are many popular educational interventions that have been developed based on notions of intelligence. Whereas some of these interventions are important and rooted in research, others are not; it is important for educators of adolescents to understand the state of current research on this topic, in order to be able to make informed decisions about instructional methods and interventions.

Fourth, we discuss metacognition. Metacognition refers to how students think about their own thinking. Some students carefully consider their own thought processes, whereas others do not. Educators can incorporate research-based strategies to help adolescents develop effective metacognitive strategies that can be applied across different subject domains.

One final note: For all of the aforementioned topics, it is important to realize that adolescent cognitive development does not occur in a vacuum. Rather, adolescent cognition is part of a longitudinal process that begins before birth and continues throughout one's lifetime. Recall our discussion in the last chapter about changes that occur in the brain during adolescence; these changes are preceded by vast brain development that occurs throughout infancy, childhood, and adolescence. We introduce some of the important topics related to both earlier and later stages of cognitive development throughout this chapter so that you can appreciate the larger context of adolescent cognition; however, the focus will remain on the adolescent years.

Piaget's Theory of Cognitive Development

Jean Piaget, who lived from 1896 through 1980, was one of the most influential scholars in the field of cognitive development. His theoretical framework has influenced educators around the world. Although more recent research has identified concerns about some of Piaget's original ideas, his work yielded important contributions and set the pathways for many subsequent researchers (Scholnick, Nelson, Gelman, & Miller, 1999).

In this chapter, we review some of the basic components of Piaget's theory that for the most part have stood the test of time (Piaget, 1929, 1952, 1954, 1972; Piaget & Inhelder, 1973). In particular, we focus on some of these that are particularly relevant to adolescent development, because they are important themes that will recur throughout this this chapter and others in the book.

It is important to understand the concept of a **schema** before discussing Piaget's theory in depth. The term *schema* refers to the ways that individuals represent concepts in their memories. Schemata (the plural of schema) include a great deal of information that helps learners to organize their knowledge about a topic (Schraw, 2006). Schraw suggests thinking about a schema as a file cabinet, where we store different types of information about a topic. When we think about that topic, we open that filing cabinet and retrieve the information related to that topic. For example, an adolescent's schema for *restaurant* might include tables, food, serving staff, busing staff, maître d, dishes, good smells, music, and a variety of other pieces of information.

An understanding of schemata allows us to delve into Piaget's theory, and how it relates to adolescent learning and development. Piaget's notions of *assimilation* and *accommodation* are relevant concepts that describe how students' thinking changes and develops as they encounter new information. **Assimilation** occurs when individuals acquire new information and fit that information in with their current thinking; in contrast, **accommodation** occurs when individuals change their current ways of thinking as a result of acquiring new information. Assimilation and accommodation, which occur simultaneously, exemplify how learners construct knowledge based upon their experiences with novel phenomena. Imagine an early adolescent who gets an iPhone at the age of 11. The adolescent, who may already have used an iPod, will probably assume that the iPhone is similar to the iPod, and will easily *assimilate* new information about the iPhone into his or her existing knowledge about such devices. However, after using the iPhone, the adolescent may realize that there are some important differences between the iPhone and iPod, and that they are not nearly as identical as she had thought. Thus the adolescent needs to change her current way of thinking to *accommodate* the new information about how the iPhone functions.

When new information has been accommodated, the learner reaches a state of **equilibrium**. Flavell (1985) noted that Piaget's discussions of *equilibration* have made important contributions to our understanding of how learning occurs; indeed, Piaget's was one of the first attempts by any scholar to explain the processes underlying cognitive development. The notion of *equilibration* refers to the fact that when individuals encounter situations that are novel and do not make sense, they try to make sense of those situations. This is similar to what social psychologists refer to as *cognitive dissonance*; **cognitive dissonance** occurs when learners encounter new information that contradicts what they already know; that new information causes a sense of discomfort, which leads learners to try to resolve those conflicting feelings (Festinger, 1962). For example, a seventh grader who understands the mathematical process of *subtraction* knows that the process involves taking one quantity away from another quantity; this represents a state of equilibrium. However, at some point the student will learn that when one subtracts a negative number from a positive number (e.g., 3 – <–2> = 5>, the two quantities actually need to be added. This new information conflicts with the student's understanding of *subtraction*, and induces a state of **disequilibrium** (or *cognitive dissonance*) As the student comes to understand that both processes represent subtraction, a new state of equilibrium has been reached.

Finally, one of the most important contributions that Piaget made was that he clearly articulated the fact that children and adolescents of different ages think "differently." As we will review in the next section, young children think differently than do children in middle childhood, and adolescents think differently than do younger children. As we noted in the example at the beginning of this chapter, this has extremely important implications for instruction.

Early Development

Piaget posited that children and adolescents pass through four stages of cognitive development, although the final two stages are most relevant for discussions of adolescence. As teachers of adolescents, it is helpful to understand how your students developed into the young adults with whom you interact daily. Thus we will very briefly mention the first two stages of Piaget's theory before discussing the aspects that are most relevant to adolescent students.

The **sensorimotor stage** occurs from birth through approximately the age of 2. During this stage, young children develop rudimentary forms of logical thinking, and the ability to recall the existence of objects after they are no longer visible or audible. The **preoperational stage** occurs from the age of 2 through about the age of 7. During this stage, children truly start to think about their actions and interactions with others and with various objects. Probably the most important aspect of this period is the development of language.

Piaget's Explanations of Cognitive Development During Early, Middle, and Late Adolescence

The stage of cognitive development that Piaget called **concrete operations** occurs between the ages of 7 through about 11. During this stage, children begin to move into early adolescence; thus, the changes that occur during the concrete operations stage are particularly relevant to teachers of early adolescents (e.g., students in grades 5 through 8).

During this stage, students become better able to use more complex mental operations. For example, during this stage, children and early adolescents become able to reliably reverse their thinking. Thus, a 12-year-old who hurts her friend's feelings who is able to "reverse" her thinking would understand what she could do to undo the bad feelings that she caused with her friend; in contrast, a younger child who cannot engage in reversible thinking might not understand how to apologize to or make up with the friend.

In addition, at this stage children and young adolescents generally master the principles of **conservation**. Before conservation is developed, children do not fully understand that various forms of matter remain constant in quantity, even when the form of matter is changed. Imagine taking a large page from your daily newspaper, laying it out on a table, and showing it to a student; then imagine crumpling the page up into a tiny ball. If you ask a student who has not developed the ability to conserve which paper is "bigger," the child will say that the full page that is laid out on the table is bigger; however, a student who has developed principles of conservation will understand that both pages are actually the same size, and that the overall mass of the paper has not changed. Younger children focus on only one aspect of the paper at a time (e.g., the length of the paper), and are unable to focus on more than one feature simultaneously. According to Piaget, the younger children (pre-adolescents) center their attention on this one aspect (e.g., length), whereas the children who have developed principles of conservation can focus on several aspects simultaneously. This phenomenon in which young children tend to focus on one specific aspect of an object is referred to as **centration**.

One of the most interesting aspects in the development of conservation is a phenomenon known as *horizontal decalage*. **Horizontal decalage** is the phenomenon wherein an aspect of cognitive development emerges in some domains prior to others. Piaget noted that conservation does not emerge as a cognitive ability simultaneously across domains. Youth are first able to conserve numbers, then matter, then weight, and finally volume (Piaget, 1952). Implications for educators of children are plentiful. For example, particularly within the domain of science, it is important for educators to realize that sixth graders may be able to understand that if you have twelve pennies lined up in one row and you move the pennies so you have three rows with four pennies in each, there are still twelve (of the same) pennies present. However, the same sixth graders may all not understand that if one pours a pint of milk from a tall glass into a flat bowl, there is still a pint of milk. Horizontal decalage is indicative of the fact that some aspects of conservation develop during the preoperational stage, whereas other aspects develop during the concrete operational stage. This is very important, because, as we will see later in this chapter, these differences are related in important ways to the development of memory in children and adolescents. Although older children and early adolescents can perform many more mental functions than they could during the preoperational stage, they are still unable to think abstractly until they reach Piaget's fourth stage.

Formal operations (from approximately the age of 12 onward) represents the final stage in Piaget's model of cognitive development, and the one that is most applicable to discussions of the education of adolescents. During this stage, adolescents are finally able to engage in complex, hypothetical thinking. As we will discuss later, this is the result of both experience and biological maturation. Adolescents have greater memory capacity than do younger children, and they also have more fully developed schemata than do younger children; the combined greater memory capacity and more developed schemata allow for the occurrence of more complex reasoning in adolescents.

As it is with the other stages, the emergence of formal operations is gradual; thus the cognitive developments that we describe in this section will emerge gradually and differentially across your students. Although there is some evidence that these abilities may emerge earlier in students who have been identified as gifted (Thornburg, Adey, & Finnis, 1986), there aren't many clear indicators of when specific abilities will emerge for any given adolescent. It is extremely important to keep this in mind—not all of your students will be able to engage in formal operations equally! Several hallmarks of formal operations, all of which have important implications for the education of adolescents, are as follows:

1. *Hypothetical-deductive reasoning.* During this period of development, adolescents become able to postulate and test hypotheses. Whereas younger children might try to solve problems through trial and error, an adolescent is able to formulate an idea and then systematically reason through the idea to arrive at a conclusion. Adolescents have the ability to reason about both concrete situations with which they are confronted (e.g., a scenario presented to them in a science classroom) and about more abstract situations (e.g., engaging in reasoning about what the characters in a novel might do in the future). Piaget demonstrated the development of this type of reasoning by presenting both children and young adolescents with a pendulum and asking them to figure out what determines the speed at which a pendulum swings. Piaget argued that younger children who are still in the concrete operational stage approach this problem through trial and error, whereas those who have entered the stage of formal operations are better able to experiment with the task and develop logical explanations (Inhelder & Piaget, 1977). Adolescents can move beyond simple trial-and-error approaches to problem-solving strategies because they have a more fully developed memory system (which we discuss later in this chapter), and because they have had more experiences and thus have more fully developed schemata that they can rely upon.

2. *Complex concepts.* During this period, adolescents become able to explore complex concepts, and educators are better able to engage adolescents in discussions of complex and controversial topics. For example, a science teacher who wanted to engage her students in a discussion about varying opinions on evolution could potentially attempt such a conversation at this stage. Whereas a 10-year-old who is in the stage of concrete operations might not be able to consider the many opinions and issues surrounding evolution, an older adolescent could explore multiple perspectives (e.g., those who adopt a strictly biblical interpretation of evolution and those who accept a purely scientific explanation).

3. *Metacognition.* During this period, adolescents develop the ability to think about their own thinking (Piaget, 1964/1968). Thus, if a teacher is engaging students in a conversation about evolution, a presupposition is that the students can truly reflect on their own statements and thoughts. An adolescent who is metacognitively aware should be able to reflect on his thinking and arrive at the conclusion that "what I just said doesn't make any sense." This is related in important ways to hypothetical-deductive reasoning, wherein an adolescent needs to be able to think about her own thought processes in order to arrive at reasonable conclusions (we discuss metacognition in greater depth later in this chapter).

The cognitive abilities that develop during formal operations clearly have important educational implications for adolescents. Curricula that focus on

TABLE 3.1	Piaget's Four Stages of Cognitive Development	
Stage	Ages	Description
Sensorimotor	Birth until about 2	Very simplistic thought characteristic of infants and toddlers; they are only able to focus on what they can attend to ("out of sight, out of mind").
Preoperational	2 until about 6 or 7	Children are able to use symbols (and thus language) to represent both what they attend to in the moment as well as ideas or objects that are not present (e.g., things that they remember).
Concrete Operations	6 or 7 until about 11 or 12	Older children develop conservation (i.e., the ability to understand that entities do not change in mass or volume, even if shapes or containers are changed), and the ability to use simple logic to solve problems.
Formal Operations	11 or 12	Early adolescents begin to develop the abilities to think logically and to reason about abstract, hypothetical, and theoretical concepts.

higher-order thinking and complex problem-solving skills, which often begin to be introduced during middle school, often require that students have developed the ability to reason about complex issues. In addition, the skills that are associated with formal operations are associated positively with academic achievement (Hudak & Anderson, 1990; Mwamwenda, 1993).

To summarize, Piaget's theory of cognitive development introduced many important concepts that led the way to future research on the development of cognition in children and adolescents. Piaget demonstrated that children think "differently" at across the four stages of cognitive development (as summarized in Table 3.1), and he showed that children's and adolescents' interactions with various stimuli lead to these developmental shifts. Piaget's work offers implications for the education of adolescents. In particular, Piaget's work sensitizes educators to the fact that two adolescents of the same chronological age may in fact think about a topic or a problem in qualitatively different manners.

What Educators Can Do

Piaget's theory offers some practical suggestions for teachers of adolescents. Think about how you might be able to implement some of these ideas in your own teaching:

1. *Be aware that some adolescents may be more able to think about complex, abstract topics than others.* Because formal operations emerge gradually, it is important to always remember that your students may not be able to engage equally with complex topics. For example, if you are reading a novel and discussing a complex theme in a language arts class, some students may be better able to engage in the discussion than others. Interestingly, Piaget's theory suggests that teachers may need to wait for students to develop abilities that they have not yet attained; as we will see

later in this chapter, there are other points of view (e.g., those related to the student's lack of prior knowledge and the limits of working memory) that are more facilitative to helping students to become ready to learn about complex topics.

2. *Consider asking your students to develop and test hypotheses when possible.* One of the hallmarks of formal operations is the ability to engage in hypothetical-deductive reasoning. Provide your students with opportunities to form and test hypotheses, but be sure to provide support and assistance so that they don't become frustrated.

3. *Introduce discussions of controversial topics when appropriate.* Teachers of younger students may refrain from engaging their students in controversial or politicized topics. Obviously, all educators must be sensitive and cautious when engaging their students in such discussions; however, adolescents may be able to engage in these discussions in a productive manner. For example, you might engage your students in a friendly debate about the differences between Republicans and Democrats.

MyEdLab **Self-Check 3.1**

Vygotsky's Theory of Cognitive Development

Lev Vygotsky was a Russian psychologist who lived in the early 20th century (1896–1934). Vygotsky proposed a theory of cognitive development that, as we shall see, both contrasts and aligns with Piaget's theory. Vygotsky's theory emphasizes the interactions between individuals, and focuses on the socialization of cognition through interactions with more experienced others. Although Vygotsky's theory spans aspects of childhood through adulthood, he did argue that adolescence represented a period in which particularly complex concepts are acquired (Van der Veer, 1994). Vygotsky's theory has many implications for the education of adolescents. Indeed, Vygotskian ideas have been applied to adolescent populations in a variety of subject domains, including foreign language education (Faltis, 1990), mathematics (Cesar, 1998), literature (Taliaferro, 2009), and reading (Palincsar & Brown, 1984).

One particularly important term that is used to describe many of the facets of Vygotsky's theory is *scaffolding*. **Scaffolding** occurs when supports are provided to a learner, in order to help the learner develop a particular skill or ability. Teachers often scaffold student learning by providing students with hints, clues, or strategies when students are working on solving various problems. However, scaffolding can be provided by many other individuals besides teachers, including parents, peers, and even technological aids (e.g., computer programs or tablet applications).

A few core concepts are associated with Vygotsky's theory. These include the existence of both elementary and higher mental functions, the use of cultural signs and tools (e.g., language) to help individuals to acquire more complex psychological functions, and the importance of social interactions in the developmental process (Gauvain, 2009). Each of these, and their importance in adolescent cognitive development, is discussed in the following sections.

Elementary and Higher Mental Functions

The concept of the **zone of proximal development (ZPD)** is paramount to Vygotsky's perspective on cognitive development. The ZPD represents the difference between an individual's ability to solve various problems independently versus when working in collaboration with more experienced peers or adults (Vygotsky, 1978). For example, an adolescent learning Spanish may find it difficult to combine a noun, a verb, and an adjective into a meaningful sentence when working on the task alone. However, the same adolescent may be better able to construct a meaningful sentence when working with a more experienced Spanish speaker or with a teacher. The difference between the student's ability to construct the sentence when working alone and when working with a more experienced peer or teacher is the "zone" in the ZPD.

Elementary mental functions occur first, and through social interactions, higher mental functions are formed. Learners acquire higher-order mental functions through interactions with adults and more experienced peers. As students use language, it serves as a tool that can help students to direct their attention toward specific phenomena or problems. Although language is the primary tool that is most often considered in discussions of Vygotsky's theory, numerous other social tools also exist, including number systems, objects, and other socially constructed markers.

As a teacher of adolescents, what are some examples of academic tasks in which you can pair your adolescent students with elementary school students from a neighboring school? How will such pairings benefit the elementary students and the adolescents?

Cultural Signs and Tools

One of the central ideas in Vygotsky's theory is that cultural signs and tools are necessary for the emergence of higher-order cognitive functions. Signs are symbols created by humans to help us to organize and master various behaviors (Gredler, 2009). The most basic of these is *language*. Language is a "tool" because it helps

In-Depth 3.1

Adolescents Working with Younger Children

Adolescents can have beneficial experiences interacting with younger children in school settings. This can be beneficial to both the adolescents and to the younger children. Through having to learn how to explain information to novice learners, adolescents may gain important insights into their own abilities, and may enhance their own understanding of various topics. In one interesting study, Gray and Feldman (2004) examined the naturally occurring social interactions among young children (ages 4–11) and adolescents (ages 12–19) who attended a multigrade school. Many instances of adolescents interacting with younger children were recorded, and many of these evidenced adolescents contributing to the intellectual development of the younger children (i.e., helping them to move into the ZPD). In many cases, younger children were observed to engage in more complex and advanced behaviors when they were with adolescents as compared with when they were with their same-aged peers.

In one example, they describe an 18-year-old boy named Alan who helped a 5-year-old girl named Bridget to find her lost shoes; Alan asked Bridget where she might have left the shoes, and asked her to think about where she already had looked. Bridget may not have been able to find her shoes by herself, but through Alan's scaffolding, she is more likely to find the shoes (Gray & Feldman, 2004). Although Bridget appears to have benefited more from this interaction than Alan did, it is important to note that Alan may have experienced benefits as well. For example, Alan may now feel more efficacious at interacting with younger children, and this could be particularly important given the multigrade nature of the school. In addition, Alan may have improved his self-regulatory skills because he needed to carefully think about how to structure his interactions with Bridget so that she would be better able to find her shoes by herself. In what other ways might Alan have benefited from this interaction?

learners to make sense of and reason about the stimuli that we encounter. Other tools are less abstract in nature; for example, smartphones that allow users to make phone calls, send text messages, check e-mail, and surf the Internet (sometimes simultaneously) also are tools.

In Vygotsky's view, concepts are obtained through a combination of interacting with the environment and through the use of tools such as language. For example, an adolescent in a mathematics class might learn about the concept of using a compass by both physical manipulation of the compass and also through the language that math teachers and other peers use. Another adolescent might want to learn how to play the saxophone; she could learn techniques for playing the saxophone through experimenting with her new instrument (i.e., blowing into it and pressing the various keys), and through lessons with her band teacher. Thus, from a Vygotskian perspective, she is learning how to play the saxophone both through her interactions with the environment (i.e., playing the saxophone and watching others play similar instruments) and through language (e.g., conversations with her teacher, reading in her music book).

What Educators Can Do

Vygotsky's theory also has important implications for educators of adolescents:

1. *The idea of the zone of proximal development can be implemented across all academic content areas.* The notion of the ZPD can be incorporated into many lessons and academic tasks. Many students are asked daily to complete worksheets independently. Adherents to Vygotsky's theory might argue that when the students are presented with complex problems on such worksheets, they will learn more efficiently if they can work in pairs. Thus, one adolescent who has slightly more expertise than the other adolescent can help the other student to understand the complex issues involved.

2. *Use technology to lure students into the ZPD.* Given the abundance of technology in today's classrooms, educators can think of many technological tools as "partners" for their students. When selecting software, look closely for programs that provide scaffolding and assistance to students, and thus act as a partner, helping students to reach higher levels of understanding.

3. *As the teacher, you are always engaged in partnerships with your students, and you are always helping to move them into the ZPD.* Both when you interact individually with students and with the entire class, you are providing scaffolds for your students, and helping them to move forward in their thinking. It may take quite a bit of effort on your part, but you can think about almost all of your interactions with students using a Vygotskian lens!

MyEdLab **Self-Check 3.2**

Integrating Piaget's and Vygotsky's Theories

The perspectives put forth by Piaget and Vygotsky often are contrasted. However, many researchers and educators agree that the similarities between the two theories are more important than are the differences (Dockett & Perry, 1996).

One of the similarities between the two theories is that both emphasize the importance of *social interaction*, although in different ways. Vygotsky emphasized the idea that social interaction is in fact the starting point for cognitive development; it is through the shared solving of problems (with more experienced learners guiding the learning of novice learners) that cognitive development occurs. In contrast, Piaget emphasized cooperation between individuals, so that individuals could develop understandings of others' viewpoints and opinions, which ultimately would help children and adolescents to achieve equilibrium and develop more advanced cognitive abilities (Rogoff, 1990).

Both theories also have been criticized. A common criticism of Piaget's theory is the notion of there being four discrete stages of cognitive development. As many parents and teachers would attest, development in children and adolescents isn't straightforward. Rather than occurring in discrete stages, development more likely occurs differentially across various mental domains (Gelman, 2000). In addition, research indicates that individuals are capable of mastering some cognitive skills earlier than Piaget had originally posited (Kuzmak & Gelman, 1986); thus, Piaget may have underestimated some abilities.

Finally, there has been much criticism of Piaget's ideas about *formal operations* (e.g., Smith, 1987; Strauss & Kroy, 1977). This is particularly important when one considers the implications of the theory for the teaching of adolescents. Specifically, later researchers have argued that there is much individual variation around the emergence of formal operations. Keating (1975) compared formal operations in fifth- and seventh-grade boys who scored between the 45th and 55th percentiles and boys who scored at the 98th or 99th percentiles on a standardized mathematics exam. Results indicated that formal operations emerged earlier in both grades for the students from the higher percentile groups. These results suggest that formal operations do not emerge uniformly during early adolescence.

Vygotsky's theory also has been criticized, although perhaps less than Piaget's. For example, whereas Vygotsky drew a distinction between lower psychological processes and higher psychological processes, this distinction may have been more dramatic than necessary (Van der Veer & van Ijzendoorn, 1999). In addition, some criticisms have been raised about the fact that Vygotsky may not have fully considered how well some of the children whom he studied understood the activities that were being studied (Matusov & Hayes, 2000).

MyEdLab **Self-Check 3.3**

Adolescent Cognitive Development in the 21st Century

The empirical and theoretical work of Vygotsky and Piaget paved the way for much of the current research on adolescent cognition. Developmental researchers have continued to study adolescent cognitive development, and although the groundbreaking work of Piaget and Vygotsky still provides us with very important information about how adolescent thinking changes over time, some newer ideas also have emerged in recent years.

One of the more recent conceptions of adolescent cognition is the notion of the adolescent learning to think like a scientist. Rather than having different abilities that change over time (as posited by Piaget), adolescents, with their greater memory abilities (as discussed in the next section), are better able to construct and test theories about how the world works (Bartsch, 1993).

Specifically, adolescents (and adults) construct theories and test hypotheses about novel phenomena that they encounter; they then revise those theories as they come across new information. Although younger children also construct and test hypotheses (Gopnik, 2012), adolescents, who have acquired a great deal of knowledge and have more developed memory abilities than do young children, are able to construct and test more advanced hypotheses than can younger children. Thus, more advanced thinking can be attributed to the fact that adolescents and adults have generated more advanced theories as they have matured, rather than to the fact that they are in different stages of development, as put forth by Piaget (Bartsch, 1993).

Research has demonstrated that merely making small suggestions to students may lead to important changes in adolescents' theoretical thinking. For example, Kuhn and Dean (2005) demonstrated that early adolescents could learn the principle of scientific control (i.e., holding most facets of an experiment constant while only manipulating one facet at a time) from merely providing a suggestion to students about controlling such variables; they argue that this may be more effective in producing cognitive growth than direct instruction in how to control variables in science.

21st-Century Skills

During the past decade, there has been particular emphasis on developing **21st-century skills** in adolescents. Given that the requirements to enter into and be successful in the workforce are changing all the time, it is imperative for adolescents to be cognitively prepared to be competitive in the workforce.

Much of the emphasis on 21st-century skills has come from those concerned with science, technology, engineering, and mathematics (STEM) education (e.g., Duran, Yaussy, & Yaussy, 2011; Suh & Seshaiyer, 2013). The National Research Council (NRC) Board on Science Education introduced five specific 21st-century skills that are important for the education of adolescents (NRC, 2010). In this section we describe each of these skills, and how they can be nurtured during adolescence. It is important for educators of adolescents to be aware of these skills, because much of the focus of instruction in schools in the ensuing years will be directed toward helping adolescents to develop these cognitive skills. Moreover, these skills can be taught across all academic domains, not just in science (i.e., they also can be taught in social studies, language arts, music, etc.).

Adaptability. Knowledge in today's world is changing at a dramatic pace; consequently, it is extremely important for adolescents to learn to be adaptable in their thinking (Burbules, 2010). **Adaptive thinking** involves the ability to use **background knowledge** to alter one's thinking in order to effectively solve problems. *Background knowledge* refers to the prior information that is prerequisite for the learning and understanding of more complex information. For example, learners need to have mastered background knowledge in the areas of multiplication and division of integers before they can learn how to multiply and divide complex fractions. Thus, before teachers can work with students on practicing adaptive thinking skills, teachers must ensure that students have the appropriate background knowledge on a particular topic.

Adolescents also must be willing to put forth the effort to adapt their thinking across various situations. Thus adolescents must see the value in considering alternative perspectives and points of view. They also must be willing to accept that some of their novel ideas may not be correct, and may even be challenged by others (Anderman, Sinatra, & Gray, 2012). For adaptive thinking to be valued and viewed as important by adolescents, teachers need to create a classroom climate in which **intellectual risk taking** is valued and not derided by fellow students. For example, an adolescent might be presented with the task of analyzing whether or not U.S. involvement in a civil war in an African nation is advisable. The student might be tempted to say that participation is advisable, and the student might also be able to justify that response; however, the student may only offer this suggestion if the student feels that she will not be teased or derided for providing that answer—in other words, it might be *risky* to give that response, although it might be what the student truly believes.

Complex Communication Skills. Much work in STEM disciplines (and in other disciplines) in the 21st century occurs in collaborative group settings. The idea that the "sum is greater than the parts" is particularly important in the ability to solve problems and make discoveries in STEM disciplines. Indeed, professionals from various related fields often will work together in teams on projects and problems. For example, in order to develop an artificial limb, a team might consist of medical doctors, engineers, biologists, kinesiologists, and sports psychologists all working together. Given the prevalence of groups working together, the need to be able to effectively communicate becomes particularly important. Thus, teachers of adolescents will be expected to develop the cognitive skills needed to enhance adolescents' communication skills. This not only will be expected of teachers in content areas typically associated with communication skills (e.g., language arts and foreign language), but expected of teachers in all disciplines.

Such communication is complex. Indeed, effective communication involves the ability to communicate in both writing and speaking. The act of writing, in particular, is complex and involves multiple skills (e.g., being able to spell, form paragraphs, present a logical argument, provide evidence to support arguments, etc.). Effective writers need to plan, revise, understand how writers within a specific field communicate, and know how to target their writing toward a particular audience (Graham, 2006).

Nonroutine Problem-Solving Skills. Many of the problems that individuals encounter do not conform to standard algorithmic solutions. Thus, one of the important cognitive skills that individuals need in the 21st century is the ability to solve nonroutine problems. An example of a nonroutine problem might be the following:

>>>

> You are given a cardboard box, some duct tape, and a large black plastic bag, and must create a raft or boat that will be able to hold at least a 100-pound person; the boat needs to be able to be paddled across a 400-foot distance in a swimming pool, without sinking, while the person sits on top of the raft, without falling off.

This is a nonroutine problem for many reasons. First, there is no simple algorithm that can be easily applied to the scenario. Second, solving this problem involves knowledge from a variety of domains, including physics, engineering, and mathematics. Third, this is, for most students, probably a truly novel/unique situation that has never been previously encountered. In order to be effective at such problems, adolescents need to develop positive feelings toward nonroutine problems. Thus, educators can work with adolescents to reduce anxiety and increase efficacy in such situations.

To solve nonroutine problems, adolescents need to be able to monitor their own thinking about problems; later in this chapter, we discuss metacognition, which is an important ability that teachers can nurture and develop in their students. Mayer (1998) has noted that individuals are more likely to persist with challenging problems when they are interested in the problems. Thus, when teachers can adjust problems so that they tap into students' interests, the motivation to persist with nonroutine problems may be enhanced (see Chapter 9).

Self-Management/Self-Development. Self-regulation is an important 21st-century skill. A **self-regulated learner** is able to monitor and control the use of various learning strategies (Boekaerts, Pintrich, & Zeidner, 2000; Zimmerman, 1990, 2002; Zimmerman & Moylan, 2009). In order to engage effectively in STEM and other disciplines, adolescents need to be able to think about and adjust the ways in which they approach and solve various problems. Research indicates that

MyEdLab
Video Example 3.1

In this video, the teacher asks his students to figure out how pendulums work. This is an example of nonroutine problem solving since the teacher does not provide the students with an algorithm or a specific way to solve the problem.

adolescents can become self-regulated learners (Wolters & Rosenthal, 2000). Numerous programs have been developed that can assist educators in the development of self-regulatory skills in adolescents (Ramdass & Zimmerman, 2011a, 2011b; Tuckman, 2003).

One particularly useful way to help adolescents develop these skills is through homework (Ramdass & Zimmerman, 2011a). When students are engaged in homework, they must use a number of important strategies. In particular, they need to be able to (a) avoid distractions, (b) set goals, (c) stay on task, (d) manage their time, and (e) think about their progress on assignments. Teachers and parents can work with adolescents on developing these skills. In particular, as a teacher of adolescents, you may want to incorporate statements in homework assignments that remind students about these important considerations.

Systems Thinking. Problem solving in the 21st century requires adolescents and adults to be able to think about how multiple systems interact. Anderman et al. (2012) discussed the examples of tornado forecasting, predicting the effects of a pandemic, and examining the causes of the decline in the bee population as examples of scientific problems that require systemic thinking. For example, in order to predict the potential effects of a pandemic, scientists need to consider population demographics, geographical features, statistical probability, genetic mutation of viruses, and the nature of the immune system. The potential effects of the pandemic may be determined only after a careful consideration of the interactions between and among these multiple systems. Thus, teachers of adolescents will need to work with their students on developing the abilities to recognize the need to think systemically, and to develop the skills and efficacy beliefs necessary to accomplish such tasks. **Efficacy beliefs** refer to students' beliefs about their confidence in their abilities to accomplish a task (see Chapter 9 for a more detailed explanation). Research indicates that the presentation of abstract representations of phenomena may be helpful in developing systemic thinking in adolescents. For example, Moreno and her colleagues demonstrated that students were best able to learn about electrical circuits when they were exposed to abstract representations of those circuits, and then presented with opportunities to relate those abstract representations of circuits to more concrete representations (Moreno, Ozogul, & Reisslein, 2011).

Teaching All of the Skills. We acknowledge that it is difficult to nurture the development of all of these skills in any given lesson. Sometimes as educators we may choose to focus on one of the skills at a time, whereas in other lessons, we may be able to integrate the skills. Given the five domains identified by the NRC (adaptability, complex communication skills, nonroutine problem-solving skills, self-management/self-development, and systems thinking), think about how you could structure lessons around the topics in the following list, in order to enhance the development of these skills. Consider specific instructional techniques that you could you use to promote 21st-century skills in each of these areas:

- Finding a cure for lung cancer
- Understanding why there is social and political unrest in the Middle East
- Preventing the extinction of the giant armadillo
- Developing the technology to keep vaccinations potent when they are transported to remote regions
- Preventing the spread of white-nose syndrome in the American bat population

---

How might you develop a homework assignment that would include reminders to students about self-regulation?

MyEdLab
Video Example 3.2
This student discusses some of his feelings and thoughts about learning in high school. Note that he does not demonstrate effective self-management strategies. Can you think of some suggestions that you could make to him to help him to better manage his time and study more effectively?

How will you, as a teacher of adolescents, encourage the development of 21st-century cognitive skills in your students?

MyEdLab **Self-Check 3.4**

TABLE 3.2	Examples of Memory in Educational Settings
Subject Domain	**Memory**
Mathematics	Memorization of formulas
Science	Memorization of human anatomy
English	Memorization of details from literature
Foreign language	Memorization of vocabulary and pronunciation
Social studies	Memorization of historical facts
Physical education	Memorization of rules for various sports
Art	Memorization of techniques
Music	Memorization of notes, chords, and scales

Memory

The concept of **memory** is something that educators of adolescents must consider daily. During adolescence, memory comes into play in all subject domains, in a variety of different ways. Recall our discussion of schemata from earlier in the chapter, particularly in relation to the theories of Piaget and Vygotsky. The formation of schemata is memory development in action! As students develop a deeper understanding of a concept and fill their "file cabinet" with information related to that concept, they are developing and categorizing memories. Consider the examples presented in Table 3.2.

As we discuss in this section, some of the topics that adolescents need to commit to memory are simply factual in nature, whereas others are more procedural. Thus adolescents need to learn and remember much information, but they also are expected to be able to manipulate and use that information in novel ways. Some of these skills may be challenging for adolescents, and as an educator, there are many strategies that you can employ to assist adolescents in improving various memory skills.

Memory Development

Memory in humans changes and develops over time. The memory capacities of an infant are different than those of a young child, and the memory capacities of children differ from those of adolescents and adults (Kail, 1990). Recall our earlier discussion of Piaget; the different stages that were posed by Piaget all are related to the development of memory. Thus, the emergence of formal operations during adolescence is tied directly to the enhanced capacity of human memory that is associated with adolescence. As an educator, it is important to realize that adolescents are developing new memory capacities that they may not have utilized strategically or effectively during elementary school.

There is much research indicating that different facets of memory develop at different rates during childhood and adolescence. The research on memory development is extensive, but the important message for teachers is that memory development is not complete at birth; rather, memory skills develop over time. For example, research indicates that adolescents are better able than younger children to use categories (e.g., "food") to remember lists of words (e.g., "spaghetti, apples, potato chips"; Kobasigawa, 1974). In addition, as children mature, they are better able to direct their attention toward specific tasks and not become distracted by other stimuli; this ability improves in particular between the ages of 6 through 12

(Lin, Hsiao, & Chen, 1999). Adolescents also are better able to use strategies such as alphabetizing lists of words to aid memory than are younger children (Kenniston & Flavell, 1979). In addition, memory is related to our prior knowledge—we are more likely to store information for the long term if we can relate newly learned information to prior knowledge. Because adolescents have more overall knowledge than do younger children (i.e., more prior knowledge), they may be able to more effectively relate newly learned information to that greater storehouse of prior knowledge.

Information Processing

The system that helps us to remember information is referred to as **information processing**. This system consists of three major components: the sensory register, short-term memory, and long-term memory. This system has been posited in a variety of related forms (Broadbent, 1958, 1963; Phillips, Shiffrin, & Atkinson, 1967; Shiffrin & Atkinson, 1969). The basic ideas behind information processing-models of memory are straightforward.

Sensory Register. When you encounter any type of stimulation through your senses, that information enters the **sensory register**. This includes visual information that you see, auditory information that you hear, tactile information (i.e., impressions of things that you touch), and even information about what you smell. In order to demonstrate this, try doing the following right now (don't stop to think about this—just do it!):

1. Freeze.
2. Consider each of your senses, and write down *everything* that you can perceive with each sense right now—what you see, what you hear, what you smell, what you feel, and so forth.

Now look at what you have written down. You probably have created a list with several items in each sensory category. Now ask yourself the following question: *Would I have remembered all of these observations if I had not made a special effort to do so?* Probably not!

This is a nice demonstration of how sensory memory works. Your senses are exposed to many stimuli, all the time. However, only the information that you pay attention to is actually transferred to other levels in the information-processing system. The sensory register is believed to hold an exact sensory image of information, albeit for a very short time span (probably less than .025 second; Mayer, 2012).

The implications for educators of adolescents are quite profound. The major message that research on sensory memory offers for educators is that *paying attention is extremely important* (Norman, 1969)! Therefore, as an educator, you need to consider actions that you can take to focus students' attention and to minimize distractions. Much information enters the senses, but only a small amount of that information is remembered.

It is important, however, to be careful about what your students are paying attention to. Often teachers may try to use some hook or dramatic action to grab students' attention; however, as teachers, we want our students to remember the content of what we are teaching, and not just the dramatic "hook." So it is particularly important to focus your students' attention on the information that you want them to remember.

Let's consider an example. A high school science teacher wanted to demonstrate how water molecules cling to each other. He took a bucket of cold water, stood up on his desk, and threw the water all over the room. Students were surprised, and many got quite wet. This got the students' attention! However, he then focused the students on all of the puddles that had formed on the classroom floor. He specifically pointed out the puddles, and used these as a way of helping his students to remember the principle about molecules sticking together. Thus, although most students probably remembered getting wet, the teacher used this as an opportunity to grab their attention, and then to focus it on a scientific principle that he was trying to teach; consequently, they probably also remembered the principle.

What strategies can you use in the classroom to focus your students' attention appropriately?

Working Memory. **Working memory** (also referred to as **short-term memory**) is the component of memory in which we temporarily store information that we are paying attention to. Whereas much information enters the sensory register, only the components that you readily concentrate on and pay attention to are moved into working memory. As we discuss in this section, working memory is related to academic achievement in important ways (Swanson & Packiam-Alloway, 2012).

Whereas virtually unlimited information can enter the sensory register, working memory is quite limited. Although the basic structures of working memory are in place by about the age of 6 (Gathercole, Pickering, Ambridge, & Wearing, 2004), research indicates that the *capacity* of working memory increases during childhood and adolescence (Cowan & Alloway, 2009; Cowan, AuBuchon, Gilchrist, Ricker, & Saults, 2011). Recall our discussion of Piaget from earlier in this chapter; we discussed the fact that adolescents are able to think abstractly, whereas younger children are not able to engage in abstract, complex thinking. This can be explained by the fact that adolescents have more well-developed working memories; they can hold multiple pieces of information in working memory, whereas younger children are unable to do this. Indeed, whereas younger children may have a more limited capacity to briefly store small amounts of information, that capacity improves during adolescence. Working memory generally can hold information for about 15 to 20 seconds; learners can hold between five and nine bits of information at a time. (A good example that is often used to describe this is being able to briefly recall a seven-digit phone number.)

Working memory probably consists of several subsystems. In addition, different types of sensory memories may be stored in working memory in different ways (e.g., sounds may be stored differently than images of visual stimuli). Thus, humans are often described as having dual channels that are used in the processing of information—one for auditory input and one for visual input (Mayer, 2012). Although some researchers have posited that there is only one working memory system (Atkinson & Shiffrin, 1968), the more likely scenario is that working memory consists of several subsystems (Baddeley, 2001).

Baddeley (2001) describes three components of working memory. One of these is the **phonological loop**. This is the component of the system that allows us to temporarily store small bits of information. Next is the **visuospatial sketchpad**; this is the component that allows us to temporarily hold and manipulate images. For example, picture a trampoline in your mind; now try to invert the trampoline, and picture what it would look like it if were upside down. The "place" in working memory where you perform this manipulation is the visuospatial sketchpad. Finally, the **central executive** component of working memory is the component that oversees all of the processes involved in working memory. This is the part of memory that oversees how you pay attention, how you temporarily store and manipulate information in working memory, and how you ultimately transfer newly acquired information into long-term memory.

Although the aspects of working memory may seem complex, it is important to note that we engage in many tasks without exerting much mental effort. Whereas some aspects of working memory are called upon to engage in daily routines, we often are not aware of these processes. Indeed, many of the things that we do on a daily basis occur automatically. **Automaticity** refers to the ability to engage in highly familiar tasks without exerting much mental effort. For example, if you traverse the same 10-minute walk every day from your apartment to the bus stop, you often may find yourself at the bus stop without really knowing how you got there. This is because the walk has become so routine that you do not have to exert much mental effort to perform this task. The walk has become automatic to you; although aspects of working memory certainly are called upon during your walk, on most days you are probably completely unaware of these mental processes!

Long-Term Memory.   When you think about something and recall a thought or an image, that thought or image is coming from **long-term memory** (LTM). LTM is where we store vast amounts of information throughout our lives, and is virtually unlimited in its capacity. LTM consists of three distinct types of memories or knowledge. These are important distinctions for educators, because, as we will see, they have implications for how curricula are developed for and presented to adolescents. These three types of knowledge generally increase modestly across all school-related subject areas between the fourth grade and college entry (Wigfield, Byrnes, & Eccles, 2006). The first type of knowledge is **declarative knowledge**. Declarative knowledge is quite simply the knowledge of facts. Declarative knowledge would include vocabulary words, symbols on the periodic table of elements, the capitals of European nations, the names of the planets in the solar system, and the rules for classroom behavior.

The second type of knowledge is known as **procedural knowledge**. This is the knowledge of how to do things. Procedural knowledge would include knowing how to ride a bicycle, how to conjugate a verb in Spanish, how to find the area of a triangle, how to bake a cake, how to operate a laptop computer, and how to watch a Netflix video on a smartphone. Interestingly, procedural knowledge is reliant upon declarative knowledge, in that an individual can only carry out procedures using factual information that has already been learned. For example, the procedural knowledge necessary for baking a cake requires the declarative knowledge of being able to identify the ingredients used in the recipe (e.g., flour, eggs, butter, etc.).

The third type of knowledge is **conditional knowledge** (Paris, Lipson, & Wixson, 1983). This is the knowledge of when and how to use other types of knowledge (i.e., procedural and declarative knowledge), or, as Paris and his colleagues state, "knowing when and why to apply various actions" (Paris et al., 1983, p. 303). A student would be applying conditional knowledge in a mathematics classroom when she understands that it is appropriate to use the Pythagorean theorem in that setting (as opposed to trying to play volleyball during math class!).

A key factor influencing how and whether students store information in LTM is how they attach meaning to the new information. As your students acquire new information, you will be able to help them to more effectively store that information in LTM if you can help them to relate the new information to prior knowledge that they

MyEdLab
Video Example 3.3

In this video, notice how the teacher focuses on the need for her choir students to remember specific procedures that will enhance the quality of their music. The students need to remember these procedural strategies and not just facts in order to be successful in this class.

The development of memory is related to both one's prior knowledge and biological maturation. Thus, an 11-year-old may remember a great deal of information about baseball, but not as much about math. This may be partially explained by the fact that the 11-year-old likes baseball and spends much time watching baseball, playing baseball, and reading about baseball players; in contrast, the same 11-year-old may spend very little time engaged in mathematics. Thus, the repeated exposure to information about baseball facilitates memory development in this area.

TABLE 3.3	Examples of Mnemonics Commonly Used with Adolescents
Mnemonic	**Explanation**
SOHCAHTOA	Used in trigonometry: Sine = Opposite/Hypotenuse Cosine = Adjacent/Hypotenuse Tangent = Opposite/Adjacent
HOMES	To remember the Great Lakes (Huron, Ontario, Michigan, Erie, Superior)
All Students Take Chemistry	Used in mathematics; the first letter of each word indicates the function that is positive in a quadrant on a grid (All, Sine, Tangent, Cosine)
TLH	Used in Spanish to remember the uses of the verb *estar* (temporary, location, health)

already possess. As the teacher, when you remind students about information that they already have learned (prior knowledge), the students will temporarily bring that previously learned information into working memory. By helping them to link the new information to their prior knowledge, you will be helping your students to be able to remember that new information.

Consider the following example. Suppose you are a high school math teacher, and you are teaching your students how to calculate means (averages) using a new software package that your school has just purchased. Let's also assume that your students already know how to calculate means using calculators and using Microsoft Excel. If you want your students to learn and remember the procedures for calculating means using the new software, you will assist them by reminding them that they already know how to do this using other forms of technology (i.e., calculators and Excel); by relating the new information (calculating means with the new software) to their prior knowledge (calculating means using calculators and Excel), you will help to move the new information into LTM.

MyEdLab Self-Check 3.5

MyEdLab
**Application Exercise 3.1
Procedural and Declarative
Knowledge** In this exercise, you will be able to examine procedural and declarative knowledge applied in a classroom setting with adolescents.

What Educators Can Do

It is possible to improve one's memory (Willingham, 2008–2009). It has been suggested that one of the reasons that students often report that they don't like school is because they don't find lessons very memorable (Willingham, 2010). Researchers have identified specific strategies that both teachers and students can employ to improve both working and long-term memory:

1. *Encourage the use of mnemonics.* **Mnemonic devices** are ways of summarizing information, often with the use of acronyms, to assist with the memorization of larger amounts of information. Examples of several mnemonics that are commonly used with adolescents are presented in Table 3.3. Research indicates that mnemonic strategies may be particularly effective for students with mild disabilities (Scruggs, Mastropieri, Berkeley, & Marshak, 2010).

2. *Encourage students to summarize and review information that they have learned.* When students encounter new information, it is beneficial to have them summarize and review that information. When summarizing information, students need to actively think about what they have learned, which may solidify this information in long-term memory. Interestingly, although many educators have argued that "overlearning" (i.e., learning information repetitively well beyond the point of mastery) improves memory, some

recent research calls this belief into question (Rohrer & Taylor, 2006; Rohrer, Taylor, Pashler, Wixted, & Cepeda, 2005).

3. *Limit distractions in the classroom.* As we reviewed, when individuals pay attention to sensory input, they are best able to move that input from sensory memory into working memory, and to ultimately remember the information. For adolescents, this is particularly important, because there are many possible distractions that can divert attention. In the classroom, these distractions may include daydreaming, whispering or writing notes to friends, or using various forms of communicative media (e.g., texting, e-mail, etc.). Whereas teachers can successfully limit distractions in class, adolescents obviously are faced with myriad distractions at home, which can affect their ability to study and do homework. Therefore, it would serve educators well to inform parents (through conferences, communications, and meetings) about the importance of helping students to avoid distractions at home. In addition, teachers also need to be mindful about the distractions that they may introduce into lessons. Engaging students in activities that distract the students from the relevant meaning of the lesson may undermine opportunities for your students to commit information to long-term memory.

4. *Promote physical activity.* This may seem unusual, but recent evidence from the field of neuroscience suggests that memory is enhanced when adolescents are active. For example, research indicates that different brain regions are active during memory tasks when comparing adolescents who are physically fit with adolescents who are less fit (Herting & Nagel, 2013). Other research also indicates that physical fitness may be related to enhanced cognitive functioning. For example, results of one recent study indicated that being aerobically fit is related to learning from an experimental computerized task for male adolescents (Herting & Nagel, 2012). Educators can infuse movement into academic tasks in a number of ways. For example, a science teacher could have students hike around school grounds to find materials that will be studied in class; language arts teachers can have students physically act out scenes from stories and books; social studies teachers can have students re-enact various historical events. Requirements for movement that facilitates aerobic fitness can be included in such activities.

5. *Encourage adolescents to study before they go to sleep.* During adolescence, many students develop problematic study patterns. Some sleep for a while, and then awaken in the middle of the night to study; others pull "all-nighters," and study large amounts of information for many hours before an exam (instead of sleeping). Still others awaken early in the morning and study after sleeping. Research generally indicates that memories are consolidated during sleep, and that studying should occur before going to sleep (assuming that one will then have a good night's sleep!) (Dewald, Meijer, Oort, Kerkhof, & Bögels, 2010; Diekelmann & Born, 2010; Potkin & Bunney, 2012). Research on the relations between sleep and memory represents a relatively new area of scholarship; nevertheless, such research is yielding information that may yield important recommendations for the teaching and learning of adolescents. For example, there is current evidence for the effective consolidation of procedural memories that are learned in the evening, although some research also suggests that declarative information may be better learned in the afternoon (Holz et al., 2012). Nevertheless, educators should emphasize to adolescents that memory will be enhanced (and learning will be more effective) if studying occurs before going to bed in the evening. Although it is difficult for many adolescents and college students to believe, it is often better to study for 4 hours and

then sleep for 8 hours, rather than studying for 8 hours (and probably getting tired as the night goes on) and then sleeping for only 4 hours.

6. *As an educator, constantly remind yourself that working memory is limited!* Once information enters into the sensory register and is transferred to working memory, students will be able to retain only small amounts of information, for short periods of time. Therefore, it is extremely important to think about how you present information to students. If you present too much information in too short of a time period, students are likely to be unable to effectively move that information into long-term memory. Go slowly, and give students the chance to construct meaning out of what you have taught them!

7. *Acknowledge that some adolescents may have memory-related disabilities.* Some adolescents may have special needs, and may need extra tutoring, coaching, or support from teachers, parents, counselors, and school psychologists. There are many reasons why memory deficits may occur during adolescence. For example, recent research indicates that infants who are born preterm are more likely to experience memory problems during adolescence than are infants who are born at full term (Luu, Ment, Allan, Schneider, & Vohr, 2011). If you suspect that a student is experiencing difficulties with aspects of memory, it is important for you to consult with other professionals (e.g., school psychologists) so that appropriate diagnoses can be made and effective services can be provided.

8. *Encourage the use of strategies to enhance memory.* Research indicates that there are several types of strategies that individuals can use, either naturally or with coaching, to enhance memory. As a teacher, you can demonstrate and encourage students to use these strategies, which include the following:
   a. **Rehearsal:** This is a strategy that can be used to keep information active within working memory. If an individual continuously repeats newly perceived information, the information will remain active in working memory. For example, suppose that a mathematics teacher is instructing adolescents about the concept of pi, and teaches the students that pi is approximately equal to 3.14. The teacher can ask the students to repeat "3.14" silently to themselves in order to keep the number series active in each student's working memory.
   b. **Elaboration:** This is a strategy that students can use to improve long-term memory. Elaboration involves relating newly learned information to knowledge that one already has stored in memory. For example, suppose that a social studies teacher is conducting a lesson on U.S. military involvement in Iraq. If a student relates the newly learned information to previous knowledge about U.S. involvement in other nations (e.g., Korea), the student is more likely to remember and later recall the newly learned information. Teachers can encourage elaboration by asking students to think about, discuss, and write about how newly learned information relates to prior knowledge. One particularly useful way of doing this with adolescents is through online discussion rooms or blogs. Blogs have been used successfully to encourage adolescents to discuss the relations between literature that has been read in language arts classes and aspects of their personal lives (Witte, 2007).
   c. **Organization:** The media often portrays adolescents as being notoriously disorganized. In reality, some adolescents clearly have better organizational skills than do others. Nevertheless, the organization of information can greatly enhance memory. When information is well organized, students tend to study that information and ultimately remember it more effectively. As a teacher, it is important to encourage your students to keep their work well organized. This often requires modeling. One of the authors of this book recalls a high school foreign language teacher who taught students to organize their notebooks into seven sections: (a) vocabulary, (b) grammar, (c) verbs, (d) culture,

(e) homework, (f) quizzes, and (g) tests. Notebooks were graded quarterly, simply to ensure that they were organized in this manner. Although we note that it is important to provide adolescents with opportunities to make choices and experience autonomy (see Chapter 9), it is also important to acknowledge that they may need scaffolding and assistance in some areas. Reminding students about organizational skills and modeling such skills for them will benefit students greatly.

   d. **Chunking:** Chunking is a technique that can be used to enhance working memory. Suppose that your students need to memorize a string of letters: A, C, D, E, G, U, R. This string of letters doesn't convey much meaning, and may be difficult to memorize. You could help your students to memorize this string by breaking it into two smaller "chunks." One possibility would be to group "ACE" together and then to group "DRUG" together. The students now only have to remember two words ("ACE" and "DRUG") as opposed to memorizing seven unrelated letters.

9. *Provide context for new material.* When you introduce new material to your students, always make sure to provide a broader context for that information. Remember that information is best stored in long-term memory when students can relate new information to their prior knowledge. Therefore, when you introduce new lessons to your students, always spend a few minutes explaining how the new lessons are related to the broader issues that you are teaching in your course.

MyEdLab
Application Exercise 3.2
Memory and School Work
Consider how this student uses a variety of memory strategies to help her remember what she is learning in her classes.

Intelligence

The concept of intelligence is significant in the study of adolescent development for many reasons. First and foremost, intelligence is something that teachers, parents, administrators, and students hear about and discuss often. From very young ages, some children are referred to as being more or less intelligent than others. Although this may have limited effects when children are young, various indicators of intelligence are used by many schools to sort students within their schools. Thus students who are deemed "more intelligent" may be able to take advanced or honors courses, whereas students who are deemed "less intelligent" may not be afforded those opportunities.

Being labeled as intelligent (or not intelligent) during adolescence has significant ramifications. Perhaps most important is the fact such labels can confirm beliefs about one's ability and one's potential, and can affect decisions and major life choices. Consider the following two examples:

>>>

Beth is in the ninth grade. She is a hardworking student who gets good grades in school. She is told by a school counselor that tests have identified her as being very intelligent because of her scores on some standardized tests. Beth feels great about being identified in this way, and when she gets into 10th grade, she chooses to enroll in advanced chemistry, mathematics, and English classes. The fact that she was told that she is highly intelligent influenced her decision to enroll in these classes.

George is in the ninth grade. He also is a hardworking student, and he also generally gets good grades in school. He is told by the same school counselor that he did not earn impressive scores on the latest standardized tests that were administered at school. When George hears this piece of news, he is somewhat distraught. He decides to enroll in regular (as opposed to advanced) courses in the 10th grade, because he begins to doubt his academic abilities.

George and Beth react differently to the information that they hear about their levels of intelligence, and these reactions affect their subsequent decisions. George and Beth might in fact both be earning identical grades in school, but the information that they have been told about their intelligence may affect their long-term plans differently. Think about your own experiences as an adolescent. How did your beliefs about your own intelligence affect decisions that you made?

Measured Intelligence and Beliefs About Intelligence

It is important to distinguish between *measures of intelligence* and *beliefs about intelligence*. Many assessment instruments have been developed to measure children's and adolescents' intelligence. These purportedly represent external, unbiased measures of ability. However, we all also have our own beliefs about our own intelligence. Some of these beliefs are based on data that have been reported to us through assessments, whereas other beliefs have formed based on our experiences and on feedback provided to us about our abilities and performance (we will also discuss beliefs about intelligence in greater depth in Chapter 9).

It is essential to keep this distinction in mind as you read the following sections. The results from a measured intelligence test can be used by teachers to place students into various courses, and can be used by parents and other professionals to make other important decisions. However, one's beliefs about one's intelligence can affect the choices that the individual makes—for example, how hard he works, what courses he will take, and so forth.

Is There One Intelligence, or Are There Multiple Types of Intelligence?

One of the oldest/most persistent debates in psychology is that related to the overall nature of intelligence. Is intelligence really just one general concept (i.e., an indicator of the overall ability of one's brain), or are there multiple aspects to intelligence? This is an important question for scientists because it has implications for research on the human brain, but it also has equally important implications for educators because it can affect how we structure schooling for children and adolescents.

In the early 20th century, Charles Spearman introduced the notion of g, or general intelligence (Spearman, 1904, 1927). Spearman posited that intelligence can be broken down into an overall general measure of intelligence, as well as more specific factors that are related to specific areas of intellect. The notion of generalized intelligence has been criticized on the grounds that the specific tests use to measure g often are limited and artificial (Sternberg, 2013).

Subsequent intelligence researchers broke the concept of g down into more specific aspects of generalized intelligence. One of the most commonly used distinctions is between **crystallized** and **fluid intelligence** (Cattell & Horn, 1978; Horn & Cattell, 1966, 1967). Fluid intelligence refers to cognitive processes that are directly related to the physiological functions of the brain, whereas crystallized intelligence refers to what has been learned through interactions with others and with the environment in which one lives. Fluid intelligence generally increases throughout childhood and adolescence, whereas crystallized intelligence can increase beyond the adolescent years, as it is directly related to the types of experiences that individuals encounter. Thus, a 50-year-old adult who learns calculus may display an increase in crystallized intelligence, but not in fluid intelligence.

Gardner: Multiple Intelligences. Howard Gardner developed the notion of **multiple intelligences**. Rather than conceiving of either one general form of intelligence or the dichotomous notions of fluid and crystallized intelligence, Gardner posited that there are several distinct domains of intelligence. Individuals may display high levels of intelligence in some domains, whereas they may exhibit lesser intelligence in other domains. Gardner originally proposed seven domains. These are described as follows (Gardner, 1993, 1999, 2006; Gardner, 2013):

1. *Linguistic intelligence.* This refers to the ability to use language to communicate. It involves written and oral language. Individuals who excel in this area include writers, poets, and journalists.
2. *Logical/mathematical intelligence.* This refers to the ability to think mathematically and logically. Individuals who excel in this area can think about complex logic problems and causal systems, and can use mathematics with skill and efficacy. Individuals who excel in this area include engineers, mathematicians, and accountants.
3. *Musical intelligence.* This refers to the ability to think cogently about music. Individuals who excel in this area can manipulate musical pieces, apply rhythmic patterns, and create new music. Musical intelligence is evident in musicians and conductors, but also in many individuals who simply enjoy music.
4. *Kinesthetic intelligence.* Individuals who excel in this domain are able to use their bodies in highly controlled manners. Such individuals tend to excel at various forms of athletics. Some may be talented across a variety of sports, whereas others may have highly specific skills in certain areas (e.g., gymnastics, boxing, long-distance running, etc.).
5. *Spatial intelligence.* This is the ability to manipulate objects in your mind. An individual high in spatial intelligence can look at an object, form a mental image of the object, and manipulate it mentally (e.g., imagine it upside down, inside out, turned on its side, etc.). Individuals who use spatial intelligence in their work include architects, engineers, and artists.
6. *Interpersonal intelligence.* This is the ability to communicate and interact well with others. Individuals high in interpersonal intelligence work well in groups and in social and cooperative settings. Individuals who use this ability might include counselors, teachers, and lawyers.
7. *Intrapersonal intelligence.* Individuals high in this domain of intelligence truly understand themselves. They understand their strengths and their weaknesses. They understand their goals and have a good sense of how to achieve those goals.

    Subsequently, Gardner added two additional domains. Whereas naturalist intelligence is often acknowledged as one of the domains, the addition of existential intelligence is a relatively novel, exploratory area at this point.
8. *Naturalist intelligence.* This is the ability to understand nature and the natural world. Individuals high in naturalist intelligence understand and appreciate

the world around them. Individuals who enjoy camping, mountain climbing, and hiking may excel in this domain.

9. *Existential intelligence.* Individuals high in this domain think about the philosophical nature of the world. They ponder big questions, and wonder about the meaning of life and death, the nature of the universe, and the nature of time.

Gardner's theory has much appeal for educators. It allows for the unique talents of students to emerge and be celebrated. There are a plethora of books, articles, and curricula espousing the use of multiple intelligences to enhance the educational experiences of children and adolescents.

Nevertheless, it is important to note that the research evidence supporting the existence or utility of multiple intelligences is limited. There have been no empirical tests of the theory; much of the evidence that has been provided has been descriptive and anecdotal. Although this theoretical framework provides an important reminder to educators (i.e., that students have talents in different areas and that multiple domains of knowledge should be valued), the empirical evidence for the theory is quite limited (Waterhouse, 2006). In fact, Gardner himself has been critical of some of the ways in which the theory has been applied to education. He and his colleagues have argued that the idea of multiple intelligences is a useful way to think about the multiple talents that students have, but is not necessarily a panacea for all of the problems in today's schools (Moran, Kornhaber, & Gardner, 2006).

Sternberg: Successful Intelligence.

Robert Sternberg has proposed that intelligence should be considered in terms of the skills that individuals need to have, referred to as **successful intelligence** (Sternberg, 2009, 2011, 2013). Although specific skills will vary for individuals across regions and cultures, there are a few components of intelligence that are important for all humans.

Metacomponents of intelligence refer to the abilities to recognize problems, identify the type of problem that one has encountered, select an appropriate strategy to solve the problem, and evaluate one's solution to the problem. **Performance components** refer to the ways that individuals carry out the metacomponents (i.e., making comparisons between two problems). **Knowledge-acquisition components** refer to how individuals learn to solve problems and to acquire information (Sternberg, 2013).

Sternberg argues that in order to solve problems (in school, at home, and in any aspect of life), individuals need to use three different types of abilities: creative abilities, practical abilities, and analytical abilities. We use analytical abilities to identify problems, decide upon strategies to solve problems, and evaluate responses to problems; we use creative abilities to assist ourselves in coming up with novel solutions to problems; and we use practical abilities when we use our cognitive abilities in the real world (Sternberg, 2003, 2013).

Sternberg's work on successful intelligence has been applied in the education of adolescents. In one example, the theory was used to successfully develop new versions of Advanced Placement examinations in the areas of statistics and psychology (Stemler, Grigorenko, Jarvin, & Sternberg, 2006). Items were developed to assess memory, as well as analytical, practical, and creative intelligence. One of the most significant findings in this research was that achievement gaps between ethnic minority and White students were lower in some domains (e.g., for creative abilities) than was evidenced when using more traditional exams. Sternberg and his colleagues also have developed lessons that can be used to engage students in

MyEdLab
Video Example 3.4

In this video, a seventh-grade science teacher uses Gardner's multiple intelligences as a means of providing different types of assessments in his class.

TABLE 3.4	Teaching for Successful Intelligence
Domain	**Lesson Ideas**
Analytical thinking	Present individual lessons on the six skills involved in effectively solving problems: *Identify the problem; allocate resources; represent and organize information; formulate strategy; monitor problem-solving strategies; evaluate solutions.*
	Examples for allocation of resources could include (a) having foreign language teachers ask students to decide upon how much time it would take to effectively memorize a list of words, (b) having math teachers ask students to divide their time in completing different parts of a math exam in order to effectively complete the exam during one class period, and (c) having science teachers ask students to determine how much time it will take to complete an experiment.
Creative thinking	Provide lessons that allow students to learn to tolerate ambiguity. Creative solutions to problems may not be straightforward; they may be ambiguous—and that is okay!
	Examples could include (a) having mathematics teachers continue to encourage students to try to solve a seemingly unsolvable problem; (b) having physical education teachers ask students to play a game that they are familiar with, but applying a new set of rules; and (c) having social studies teachers get students to discuss the reasons why the United States entered into the Vietnam War.
Practical thinking	Provide lessons that allow students to learn to avoid stumbling blocks to practical thinking.
	An example would be helping students to learn not to procrastinate. Thus, (a) a language arts teacher could encourage students to set daily goals for completing a long novel; (b) an art teacher could ask students who are working on portraits to create a grid and try to complete a set number of squares each day; and (c) a foreign language teacher could encourage the learning of new vocabulary by asking students to practice using several words each day, in preparation for a quiz on all of the words at the end of the week.

Adapted from Sternberg, R. J., & Grigorenko, E. L. (2000). Teaching for succesful intelligence. Arlington Heights: Skylight Professional Development..

analytical, creative, and practical thinking (Sternberg & Grigorenko, 2000). Several examples are presented in Table 3.4.

MyEdLab Self-Check 3.6

Metacognition

One of the most important skills that academically successful adolescents have is the ability to think about their own thinking. The term **metacognition** refers to our abilities to think about our own thoughts (Armbruster, Echols, & Brown, 1982; Brown, 1987; Campione, Brown, & Connell, 1988; Flavell, 1979, 1985). Metacognition has a long history, and even Piaget and Vygotsky discussed aspects of metacognition in their theories (Fox & Riconscente, 2008). Metacognition encompasses a number of educational strategies and abilities that are particularly important for academic success during adolescence. These include (a) the ability to think about one's memory (sometimes referred to as **metamemory**), (b) the ability to make decisions about how to divide one's time among tasks, (c) the ability to focus on a particular task and not become distracted by other tasks, and (d) the ability to allocate mental resources effectively and to regulate strategy use (Pressley & McCormick, 1995). Consider the following two students:

>>>

Sarah and James are both eighth graders, and they are both taking Algebra I. They are in the same class, and have the same teacher. Both find the class challenging, and know that they will have to work diligently in order to do well in the class and to really understand the material. Sarah and James both get home at 3:30 p.m. every afternoon. Sarah gets herself a snack, rests for 10 minutes, and then devotes 40 minutes to doing her algebra homework. While she is working on her assignment, she thinks about each problem, considers the types of strategies that she will need to use to solve the problems, and adjusts her strategies accordingly. When Sarah encounters a difficult problem, she considers how to adjust her strategies and approaches so that she can better try to solve the problem. James also gets home at 3:30. However, when James works on his assignments, he does not think about how he will approach the various problems that have been assigned. When he encounters novel problems, he does not consider adjusting the types of strategies that he will have to use to solve those problems. When James encounters a difficult math problem, he tries to think about why the problem is difficult, and then he usually just writes down the first thing that comes to mind, because he knows that the teacher will go over the problem in class the next day.

What is the difference between Sarah's approach and James's approach? The main difference is that Sarah is highly metacognitive in this situation, whereas James is not. Sarah thinks about her own thinking—she searches her memory for additional strategies that might be helpful to her in solving novel problems.

In contrast, James is not metacognitive in this situation. He does not think about his approaches to the problems, and about ways to adjust his strategies. Instead, he just steamrolls ahead without considering other options, and decides to wait until the next day, when the teacher will show the students how to solve the problems.

Metacognition develops throughout childhood and adolescence (Larson & Armstrong, 2014; Schneider, 2010; Weil et al., 2013). Younger children are not as readily able to monitor their thinking, planning, and comprehension, whereas older children and adolescents are better able to manage these skills and strategies. Think about how children and adolescents monitor their own progression on tasks. A 3-year-old who is working on making a sculpture may quickly become frustrated and squish the sculpture; a 6-year-old may be a bit more systematic in making the sculpture; a 12-year-old begins with planning, and might first draw a picture of what she is trying to sculpt, and then carefully create one part of the sculpture at a time. Thus, as children get older and move toward adolescence, they become more able to monitor their actions and to engage in planning (i.e., they are becoming more metacognitive!).

Luckily, metacognitive and self-regulatory skills can be taught. These strategies can be particularly effective with adolescents. For example, Palincsar and Brown (1984), in a now classic study, taught students a technique called *reciprocal teaching*, in which adolescents learned from one another how to approach reading with metacognitive strategies. Specifically, they demonstrated that students can be taught to *summarize* ideas, *generate questions*, *clarify* confusing parts of text, and *predict* what will happen next in a text. This technique is based in the work of Vygotsky, wherein the teacher demonstrates these strategies, and then the students adopt the strategies and integrate them into their own reading habits. Research indicates that students' reading comprehension skills greatly improve with they learn and adopt these strategies (Palincsar & Brown, 1984, 1989; Rosenshine & Meister, 1994).

In-Depth 3.2

Do Video Games Affect Adolescent Cognition?

There is much debate about the effects of playing video games on a variety of outcomes during adolescence. For example, there has been much talk in the media about the potential effects of watching and playing violent video games on engagement in violent and risky behaviors. Nevertheless, some research suggests that playing video games may actually enhance some cognitive abilities during adolescence. Whereas some research suggests that playing video games may enhance cognitive abilities such as spatial cognition (Feng, Spence, & Pratt, 2007), other studies indicate that there is no relation between video game playing and enhanced cognitive skills (Ferguson, Garza, Jerabeck, Ramos, & Galindo, 2013), and still others suggest that playing video games may lead to inattention, which can be negatively related to academic performance (Chan & Rabinowitz, 2006).

Clearly, there is still much research to be completed on this topic. Nevertheless, given the popularity of video games with today's adolescents, it is important for educators to consider the potential effects of video games on cognitive abilities. As a teacher, it is particularly important to think about how much time some of your students might spend at home playing such games. Whereas the effects on cognition are still debatable, one thing is certain: If students spend hours at home playing video games instead of studying or doing their homework, academic performance will suffer.

Limitations of Adolescents' Cognitive Abilities

Although adolescence represents a time when many important cognitive skills develop, it is important to acknowledge that there are some limitations to adolescents' cognitive abilities. As a teacher, you will want to put much trust and faith in your students' emerging cognitive capabilities. However, it is important to note some important limits.

First, as we already discussed, adolescents vary in terms of their prior knowledge. Because prior knowledge is extremely important (recall that learners need to relate newly learned information to prior knowledge in order to more effectively store the new information in long-term memory), it is important to recognize that adolescents will vary in the amounts of prior knowledge that they have about topics that you introduce to them. Thus, students in a first-year French class who already spent 2 years studying Spanish as a foreign language will have some prior knowledge about how to successfully study a second language; in contrast, students who have never studied a foreign language do not have this prior knowledge, and may take longer to learn new information (e.g., how to pronounce words, how to memorize vocabulary, etc.).

Another particularly important area in which adolescents may experience variation in abilities relates to **decision making**. Consider the following example:

>>>
Josie and Frank are both 11th graders. One of their friends offers them some marijuana. Frank quickly agrees to try the marijuana, whereas Josie stops and really thinks about the potential consequences of marijuana use. Josie wonders if she might get caught and get into trouble; she also wonders if this might lead to her using more illegal substances. She thinks deeply about whether or not to partake, and after a few minutes, despite encouragement from Frank and her other friend, she decides not to.

In-Depth 3.3

Strategies for Working with Impulsive Students
Alyssa Emery, The Ohio State University

Students who struggle with impulse control can prove challenging for any teacher's classroom management; however, there are some ways to help students meet behavioral expectations. For instance:

1. Movement may help some students stay focused. Build movement into your lessons, give stretch breaks, or consider accommodations such as permitting students to work while standing at a podium or sitting on an exercise ball.

2. Teach students appropriate ways to get attention or help—impulsive or disruptive behaviors are often the result of boredom or frustration.

3. Be clear with your directions, and make sure that you have students' attention before giving instructions. Announcing to the class, "please behave" can be vague and less effective than concisely detailing your expectations. Try making eye contact and saying, for example, "Taylor, please quietly find your textbook and turn to page 23."

4. Visual cues can help some students stay focused. These can be as simple as a note taped to a student's desk with "RYH"—a reminder to *raise your hand*, but one that won't draw attention from others.

5. Offer choices, and model thinking through decisions. Especially for unstructured time, remind students of the purpose of the activity—for example, "Jordan, we're going to the library to work on our essays. Using time wisely means finding about five sources while we're there. Would you like to start with books, or the Internet?"

For more strategies, see the website of the American Psychological Association (http://www.apa.org/education/k12/classroom.aspx).

What is the difference between Josie and Frank in this situation? Josie thinks deeply about the potential costs of smoking marijuana, whereas Frank just goes for it. We can describe Frank as someone who made an impulsive decision—he did not draw on his many available cognitive resources to make a rational decision; rather, he sought immediate gratification, and chose to use the marijuana without considering the consequences.

Impulsivity is a personality trait that is related to impulsive decision making. Decision making during adolescence may be seen as running along a continuum, wherein some adolescents make very rational decisions, and others are quite impulsive. An impulsive decision maker reacts quickly to novel situations, and does not always consider the potential outcomes (particularly the negative ones) associated with a decision (recall our discussion of the biological aspects of impulse control in Chapter 2). Adolescents who tend to make impulsive decisions are more likely to engage in a variety of problematic behaviors; such individuals are more likely to engage in risky sexual behaviors (Donohew et al., 2000), to engage in academic cheating (Anderman, Cupp, & Lane, 2010), to be overweight (Fields, Sabet, Reynolds, 2013), and to attempt suicide (Ghanem et al., 2013).

Students may also make impulsive decisions in the classroom as well. As educators, it is important for us to be aware of this limitation in some adolescents, and to help them to make more effective decisions. For example, as a teacher, you might give your students an assignment and ask them to work in self-selected groups. Some of the more rational decision makers might think about working with partners who have similar interests, and who will probably help the group members achieve their goals. In contrast, some of the more impulsive decision makers may just quickly gravitate toward working with their friends. As a teacher, you can help your students to make more rational decisions by providing appropriate guidance. For example, before they rush to form groups, you could ask each student to follow a rubric that would encourage the student to carefully consider the selection of partners. Some questions in the rubric might include the following:

- Whom can you work with who has expertise in the topic?
- Whom can you work with who will not distract you from your work?
- Can you think about forming a group where each member can make unique contributions?

By encouraging all of your students to use a rubric of this nature and to think about their decisions before rushing into a novel situation, you may help them to more effectively use their cognitive resources and make more rational decisions.

Recommendations for Educators

In this chapter, we have explored many of the thought processes of adolescents. We have examined how thinking develops and changes over time and how memory operates, both in the moment and over the long-term. We have examined different theories of intelligence, and we have examined students' abilities to actively think about, monitor, and control their thought processes. All of these clearly have implications for the education of adolescents. In the following sections, we discuss some of these implications.

Remind Yourself Constantly That Cognitive Development Varies Greatly

We discussed several different perspectives on cognitive development. Whether, as an educator, you subscribe to Piaget's views, Vygotsky's views, a synthesis of the two, or some of the newer theories of cognitive development, the main message is clear: *Cognitive development does not occur at the same time and in the same manner for all children and adolescents!*

As a teacher, you must acknowledge that your students will be at different levels of cognitive development. This should not be seen as a deficit on the part of some students; in contrast, this is just one of many ways that students may differ from one another at any given time period. If you are a high school social studies teacher and you want to have a discussion about the Tea Party and its role in American politics, some of your students will be able to engage in a sophisticated discussion wherein they truly understand some of the complex issues and nuances regarding what it means to be politically conservative or liberal. In contrast, others may see this as a very concrete, black-and-white issue, and may not be able to engage in the same level of discussion. Nevertheless, you could use the discussion as an opportunity to expose the students to a wide array of ideas about this topic. From a Vygotskian perspective, conversations between the students with the deeper understanding and others may lure students into their zones of proximal development, which ultimately may lead to cognitive growth. From a Piagetian perspective, the discussion may lead to disequilibrium for some students, and as they assimilate and accommodate information from the discussion, their thinking about the Tea Party may move to a new level of understanding.

Consider Techniques to Improve Students' Memory Skills

In the section on memory, we presented eight recommendations for improving memory skills and abilities in adolescent populations. As a teacher, you can incorporate many of these suggestions into your daily or weekly routines. By doing so, you may greatly improve your students' abilities to learn and remember information.

For example, you can demonstrate elaboration techniques to your students to help them to draw connections between newly learned information and prior knowledge. A Spanish teacher might help students to learn vocabulary words by relating Spanish words to similar words in English. For example, the word *carta* means "letter" (i.e., the kind of letter that you send in the mail to a friend). The teacher might ask the students to think of a card that one might send to a friend in the mail for a birthday. The meaning is not exactly the same (*card* versus *letter*), but there is enough similarity between the two concepts to allow for the improved likelihood of remembering what the word *carta* means.

Having students write about a topic can also help them to elaborate and better remember information (Bangert-Drowns, Hurley, & Wilkinson, 2004; Hamilton, 1989). When students are asked to write about a topic, they need to come up with language to describe their thought processes. Thus, if a student is required to write a paragraph about the Tea Party, the student will have to at some level elaborate upon the topic, potentially by drawing connections to some form of prior knowledge. By forming these connections (through writing), the process of elaboration may enhance the student's ability to embed the new information in long-term memory, and to recall the information at a later time.

Teach and Model Metacognitive Skills

As a high school or middle school educator, your specialty is your subject domain (e.g., math, science, language arts, etc.), and you clearly have effectively learned your content. You inevitably developed skills and strategies that enabled you to become a successful learner. Just as it is your job to teach the content, you also have a responsibility to teach students *how to learn the content*.

Thus, you can teach your students to be metacognitive. You can demonstrate to your students how you approach various academic tasks, and you can literally think aloud and show them how you make decisions within your subject area. For example, reading or language arts teachers can teach students metacognitive strategies (e.g., the ones mentioned earlier in the discussion of reciprocal teaching) to help them to become strategic readers. In particular, teachers can first assess students' current metacognitive strategies for reading (e.g., by asking them about what they do and observing them during reading tasks), and then teachers can demonstrate and practice various strategies with their students (Paris & Flukes, 2005).

Conclusion

In this chapter, we have examined the cognitive abilities of adolescents. We have learned in particular that cognitive development occurs over a long period of time—it begins in infancy, continues throughout childhood and adolescence, and some aspects even continue into adulthood. Thus, new cognitive abilities emerge during adolescence, and educators need to work with adolescents to develop and practice these newly emerging skills.

We also need to recognize that development occurs at different times and at different rates for adolescents, and that development may be advanced in one area, but less advanced in another area for any given student. It is particularly important for us to be careful about academic decisions that we make during adolescence. Preventing a student from signing up for an advanced biology course may be beneficial if the student does not have the complex thinking skills necessary to succeed, but it also may be highly problematic, because it may lead the student to believe that he or she is not "good" at science, and thus lead the student to not consider science as a viable career option. In this situation, perhaps a compromise would be to allow the student to take the advanced biology course during either the 10th or 11th grade—if students can have some autonomy and make choices, they may elect to take courses when they are ready to, and experience success in those courses.

Finally, we discussed the fact that teachers can assist students with various cognitive skills. As an educator of adolescents, you can provide instruction that may improve students' memory skills, metacognitive strategies, and ability to understand seemingly complex topics. You will have many opportunities to help adolescents to become effective and efficient learners, but you must always keep this responsibility in mind as you plan your daily lessons in order to truly make a difference in this area.

Devan Georgiev/Fotolia

4

Social and Moral Development

Learning Outcomes

4.1 You will be able to describe Kohlberg's and Gilligan's theoretical frameworks for moral development, and how they can be applied to the education of adolescents.

4.2 You will be able to explain the development of the ability to appreciate diverse perspectives during adolescence, and how this ability affects learning and instruction.

4.3 You will be able to explain the role that religion and religious beliefs play in the lives of adolescents.

4.4 You will be able to explain how educators can involve adolescents in volunteering and service-learning activities.

4.5 You will be able to describe the prevalence of academic cheating during adolescence, and how educators can deter cheating.

Introduction

n this chapter, we continue to examine some of the ways in which adolescent thinking develops. In particular, we reflect on several nonacademic facets of adolescents' lives. Consider the following description of an adolescent male:

>>> ─────────────────────────────────

> Joel is an 11th grader living in a suburban community. Joel earns good grades in school, but there are many other issues in his life that he must balance with his academic work. Joel spends time every Saturday volunteering at a local nursing home. He visits with residents, reads to them, plays cards with them, and helps them with some of their daily tasks and activities. This is an important part of Joel's life, and he tries to never miss a Saturday at the nursing home, despite his other academic, family, and social needs and responsibilities.

Why does Joel volunteer at the nursing home? Why does he choose to spend his Saturdays involved in this voluntary activity, when there are many other ways in which he could be spending his time? Why has Joel made a commitment to this work, when he could be spending Saturday with his friends or his family or working at a part-time job?

As we will see in this chapter, Joel's decision is reflected in several different facets of his life. Some of the variables that might influence Joel's decision include his beliefs about morality, his ability to empathize with others and consider diverse perspectives, his religious background, and his parents' attitudes toward volunteering. These aspects of development affect both adolescents' nonacademic and academic lives.

Although one's beliefs about moral issues and religion certainly affect choices about how one spends time, these beliefs also affect the ways in which adolescents interpret, understand, and analyze issues that arise in school. Consider a case in which an adolescent who has mild intellectual disability bullies other students at his school. This is not atypical, as there is evidence that students with disabilities may be involved in bullying (both as victims and as perpetrators of bullying) to a greater extent than are students without disabilities (Rose, Forber-Pratt, Espelage, & Aragon, 2013; Rose, Monda-Amaya, & Espelage, 2011). How would other students react to such bullying? Would students be angry at the perpetrator? Would they feel sorry for the perpetrator because of his disability? Would they fear that the perpetrator might not be "smart enough" to know what he is doing, and might pose a danger to others? Would they feel like the victim of the bullying might have instigated the situation, because a mentally impaired student would probably not provoke such a situation?

These are all legitimate questions, and the ways that students react in such situations may be related to their moral development, their abilities to assume other perspectives, their religious backgrounds, the influences of their families and friends, and numerous other factors. The message for educators is that situations of this nature are highly complex, and the ways in which adolescents think about and react to such occurrences may vary widely.

OVERVIEW OF THE CHAPTER

In this chapter, we examine how a sense of "morality" develops during adolescence, and the implications for educators. We also discuss a related body of research examining how adolescents develop the ability to appreciate diverse perspectives on a variety of issues. We explore the ways in which students' religious beliefs and behaviors interact with their developing abilities to engage in moral reasoning and perspective taking. We also discuss two contemporary examples of how these issues play out in today's schools. First, we discuss student volunteering, which is sometimes referred to as service learning. Finally, we examine academic cheating, which is a problem that any prospective teacher of adolescents should understand in depth.

Moral Development During Adolescence

As an educator of adolescents, you will notice that your students will encounter many seemingly "**moral**" issues. Some of these will be encountered within the curriculum, whereas others will be encountered in their everyday lives. One of the most ingtriguing aspects of adolescence is that adolescents differ greatly in the ways that they think about moral issues. Although you may be tempted to think that two students' different thoughts or beliefs about a moral issue may represent a "right" and a "wrong" way of thinking, in actuality it is a bit more complicated than being an issue of simple "right" or "wrong."

Let's examine the list of moral issues presented in Table 4.1. Table 4.1 is divided into issues that might occur during school, as part of the curriculum or daily school life, and issues that occur in the "real world." Although we have made this distinction, discussions of any of these issues could easily arise in your classroom.

Let's look at one of these issues in greater depth: *There is discussion of the military starting a draft.* Although mandatory military service is required in many nations, it has not been mandated in the United States since the early 1970s. Understandably, if the government were to mandate military service and require adolescents to register for service at the age of 18, there would be much controversy and discussion. Imagine that three of your students get into a debate about this issue. Here are their comments:

>>>

Student 1: I think the draft is sensible. We are at war, and it is every person's duty to serve his or her country. If the government says that we have to serve, who are we to question that? It's our duty, and that's that.

Student 2: The draft is ridiculous. If I serve in the military, I might be forced to kill innocent civilians. I will have no part of that. Innocent civilians did not ask for war, and they should not suffer the consequences. I could never raise a weapon against an innocent person, and because a draft might force me to be in that situation, I think that the idea of a draft is ridiculous. That's what I believe, and I don't care what anybody else thinks.

Student 3: No way! I'm not going to get hurt or killed. Wars are dangerous, and I just won't do that. Period. End of discussion!

MyEdLab
Video Example 4.1
Moral reasoning can occur in any classroom; note how this middle school science teacher integrates one of the moral dimensions of science into this lesson.

TABLE 4.1	Moral Issues That Adolescents Might Encounter
From the curriculum:	In a language arts class, students are viewing the classic movie *Sophie's Choice*. They have a discussion about whether Sophie's actions were appropriate.
	In a social studies class, during a presidential election year, students have a heated debate about the conservative versus liberal views on same-sex marriage.
	In a biology class, some students feel that it is sinful to discuss "evolution," whereas others feel that it is entirely appropriate.
	In an economics class, students discuss the issues of taxation based on income.
	The student council debates punishments for truancy.
From the "real world":	An adolescent in your town who was found guilty of a serious assault on another individual is tried as an adult and found guilty.
	A local political election is fraught with allegations of racial discrimination.
	A trial that receives national publicity divides the nation on the dialog about the right to own a gun and carry a concealed weapon.
	There is discussion of the military starting a draft.

Clearly these three students have very different ideas about the draft. Is one of them right and the others wrong? In order to answer that question, you, as the classroom teacher, have to think about where you stand on this issue—how do you feel about the draft? Do you think that one student is "right" and the others are "wrong"? If you do, can you separate your own beliefs from those of your students so that you can mediate the discussion effectively?

We will now discuss some theories and research about adolescent **moral development**. These theories offer perspectives that will help you to understand how adolescents think about issues involving morality. We will return to the draft example as we discuss various aspects of moral development.

> How will you, as a teacher, negotiate the differences between your own personal feelings about various social issues and your students' opinions?

Kohlberg's Theory of Moral Development

Lawrence Kohlberg was a developmental psychologist who derived a theory of how moral reasoning develops. He proposed that children and adolescents (and later adults) pass through a series of different stages of moral development; thus, the ways in which individuals think about moral situations change as one matures. As we will see, much of the development in moral reasoning mirrors cognitive development (see Chapter 3).

Kohlberg used a very famous scenario called the **Heinz dilemma** to assess moral development. He asked people to think about the following scenario:

>>>

In Europe, a woman was near death from a special kind of cancer. There was one drug that the doctors thought might save her. It was a form of radium that a druggist in the same town had recently discovered. The drug was expensive to make, but the druggist was charging ten times what the drug cost him to make. He paid $200 for the radium and charged $2,000 for a small dose of the drug. The sick woman's husband, Heinz, went to everyone he knew to borrow the money, but he could only get together $1000, which is half of what it cost. He told the druggist that his wife was dying and asked him to sell it cheaper or let him pay later. But the druggist said, "No, I discovered the drug, and I am going to make money from it." So Heinz got desperate and broke into the man's store to steal the drug for his wife. (Kohlberg, 1969, as cited in Durm & Pitts, 1993, p. 1400)

Kohlberg analyzed individuals' responses to the Heinz dilemma as a means of understanding moral development. Based on responses to the dilemma, Kohlberg developed his stage theory of moral development. Specifically, he suggested that progression through the stages occurs in a sequence, and that as individuals are able to reason at higher levels, they are still able to understand how thinking at one of the lower stages could occur (although their preference will be to use the higher level of moral reasoning). Kohlberg's theory contains three levels, each of which contains two substages (Kohlberg, 1975). These are presented in Table 4.2.

Students in the **preconventional stage** are at the most basic level of moral development. Students in stage 1 (**punishment/obedience orientation**) are focused on themselves, and consequences that they might face. Stage 2 is similar to stage 1, although a student at stage 2 might obey a rule if such adherence to rules would benefit the student or someone else. In our example about the draft, student 3 would be at the preconventional stage; that student is simply focused on not getting injured or killed; there is no consideration of a higher moral code, or the effects that wars might have on others.

TABLE 4.2   **Kohlberg's Levels and Stages of Moral Reasoning**

Level	Stage	Description	Example
Level I: Preconventional	Stage 1: Punishment/obedience orientation	Decisions are made based on obedience to authority and avoidance of punishment. There is no consideration of a higher moral code.	Susan will not steal a piece of candy from the candy bowl because she knows she will get punished by her parents if she does.
	Stage 2: Instrument/relativist orientation	An individual subscribes to rules if the rules will lead to a benefit for the individual. Another person's needs also may be met if it will benefit the individual (as Kohlberg puts it, "you scratch my back, and I'll scratch yours").	Susan obeys the rule (not to take candy from the bowl) because she knows that she will get to have a donut on Friday if the candy bowl remains untouched all week.
Level II: Conventional	Stage 3: Good-boy/nice-girl orientation	Individuals behave appropriately in order to receive the approval of others.	Susan helps her brother with his math homework because she wants her parents to think that she is a kind sister.
	Stage 4: Law-and-order orientation	Individuals behave appropriately because they are respectful of authorities, rules, and the social order.	Susan will not steal a candy from the bowl because she knows that stealing is illegal.
Level III: Postconventional	Stage 5: Social contract/ legalistic orientation	Laws are respected, but individuals' own values and opinions also matter. Moral reasoning is based on ideas that have been rationally derived by members of a society. Laws are seen as changeable if necessary.	Susan doesn't agree with her school's strict policy about not being late for class. Susan truly believes that sometimes there are legitimate reasons to be a bit late for a class, but she adheres to the rules because she knows that it is important to maintain agreed-upon standards of behavior in order for the school community to function effectively.
	Stage 6: Universal ethical principles	Individuals who reach this level think about moral issues in terms of what their own conscience knows to be correct. "Right" and "wrong" are determined individually, based on justice and human rights, and the notion that all people should be treated ethically.	Susan leaves school in the middle of the day without permission when she gets a text message from her older brother indicating that he had been in a car accident and has been taken to the emergency room. Susan thinks that she might need to provide a blood donation, and her concern for her brother's well-being takes precedence over school policy.

Source: Adapted from Kohlberg, L. (1975).

The **conventional stage** consists of the **good-boy/nice-girl orientation** (stage 3), and the **law-and-order orientation** (stage 4). Students who are at stage 3 obey rules in order to receive approval from others. Many students in elementary school could be characterized as being at this stage—they obey the rules in school because they want their teachers and their parents to think well of them. Think of a middle school student who desperately wants to earn her teacher's approval; that student might obey class rules (e.g., stay seated, have work completed on time, don't chew gum in class) simply in order to receive positive affirmations from her teacher. Stage 4 is similar to stage 3, but in stage 4, there is an acknowledgement of the roles of authority figures, and of the need for a larger social order. Thus, students who conform to school rules because they respect their teachers and school administrators are at stage 4. Student 1 in the example about the draft is probably at stage 4. That student believes that service in the military is a responsibility of citizens, because it is the law of the land; if the government says that service is mandatory, and if individuals respect the government, then they should not question service.

Finally, the **postconventional stage** consists of the **social contract/legalistic orientation** (stage 5) and the **universal/ethical principles orientation** (stage 6). At stage 5, laws are still respected, but the individual also understands that his or her own opinions also matter; thus, a law could be changed if there is reason to do so. At stage 6, the individual makes truly independent decisions about what is "right" and what is "wrong." These decisions are a matter of individual choice, and emanate from the belief that all humans have rights, and should be treated well. In the draft example, student 2 is probably at stage 6; that student feels very strongly about the values of others' lives, and has arrived at this position on his or her own.

In summary, Kohlberg posited that there are qualitatively different ways in which individuals think about moral issues. Some people move through these stages and reach high levels of moral development, whereas others remain at lower stages. Kohlberg's theory has received much attention and has been very influential for many years. However, there has been some critique of his theory. In particular, much of this critique has been focused on Kohlberg's use of males to develop his framework. There has been considerable debate about whether Kohlberg's theory applies to all individuals universally. In particular, there has been much discussion about the applicability of this theory to females.

Gilligan's Theory of Moral Development

Carol Gilligan proposed an alternative perspective on moral development. She argued that much of Kohlberg's work might not apply to females. In particular, she argued that Kohlberg's theory focuses on **justice**, and that focus might not be entirely applicable for women. Rather, she proposed that women approach moral reasoning from the perspective of **care**, rather than justice (Gilligan, 1982; Gilligan & Attanucci, 1994). An orientation toward morality that comes from a care perspective involves a focus by the individual on the importance of relationships between individuals. Consider the following example:

>>>
> Jordan and Amanda, who are 14 years old, are in the grocery store with each other. They are in the candy aisle, and they notice that there are open bins of individually pre-wrapped candies right in front of them. Jordan encourages Amanda to reach into one of the bins and quickly grab a handful of candy and stick it in her pocket. Amanda at first appears nervous, but then decides to grab some candy.

How would you assess Amanda's decision? From Gilligan's perspective, one might argue that Amanda took the candy because she cares about Jordan and her relationship with Jordan. In contrast, from Kohlberg's perspective, one would probably explain Amanda's decision based on one's own current level of moral reasoning; the overall focus, however, would probably be on justice (i.e., was it "wrong" for her to take the candy?). Gilligan has argued that females are more likely to think about situations such as the one just described from a *care* perspective; in contrast, males may be more likely to think about this scenario in terms of *justice*. How did you assess the situation? Do you think that there are gender differences in how individuals might think about such scenarios?

Gilligan's critiques of Kohlberg are important. In addition to arguing that Kohlberg's theory does not work well for females, she and her colleagues also have argued that the higher stages in Kohlberg's theory also may be problematic, particularly for older adolescents and young adults (Murphy & Gilligan, 1994), chiefly because of Kohlberg's strong emphasis on justice.

Critiques of Gilligan's Theory. Although Gilligan's ideas are intuitive and appealing, there is debate about the empirical support for her conclusions about justice and care orientations. Results of a **meta-analysis** (i.e., a study examining the cumulative results of many other empirical studies) examining 113 separate studies of

MyEdLab

Application Exercise 4.1 Kohlberg's Theory of Moral Development Let's take a closer look at some of Kohlberg's stages of moral development; consider in particular that adolescent students in your classroom will not all be at the same levels of development.

moral reasoning, conducted by researchers at the University of Wisconsin, indicated that there actually are only small gender differences in justice and care orientations (Jaffee & Hyde, 2000). Other research (e.g., Garrod, Beal, & Shin, 1990; Walker, 1984) also indicates that gender differences in moral reasoning are not large.

In summary, moral development during adolescence is complex, but extremely relevant for educators. The ways that adolescents react to lessons about history, science, literature, current events, and numerous other topics are reflections of their own current levels of moral reasoning. The message for educators is to understand that your students will be at different places in their moral reasoning, and that these differences are normal. Thus, a teacher should not suggest that a student is "wrong" because she thinks about an issue differently than does another student; rather, the teacher should use such events as opportunities to point out the different opinions about such issues, and to encourage students to think about the different perspectives that their peers have. Indeed, most of our students think about moral issues across a variety of social domains (e.g., Turiel, 1989, 2008); therefore, students may think about issues differently across different classes, inside and outside of school, and when present with family members. In the next section of this chapter, we more closely examine how and why adolescents assume varying perspectives.

> Are Kohlberg's and Gilligan's theories compatible? Are there useful points that you can garner from each theory?

Referring back to Table 4.1, you hopefully can now see that students in your classes might react very differently to some of those issues. For example, a discussion of taxation based on income in an economics or social studies class could become very complicated if some students think about this strictly as an issue of equity (i.e., the rich should pay more), whereas others discuss the nuances of the system, including the fact that wealthier individuals who make charitable contributions can deduct those from tax payments. Students who just see this issue as one of right or wrong may say that charitable donations are unfair, but students who also consider the benefits to society from such donations may think about and respond to this discussion differently. As the teacher, your job is to serve as the mediator of the discussion; although you may side with the student who thinks about the issue of charitable deductions being acceptable, you need to acknowledge the thoughts of the other students, and to make sure that the other students don't feel that they are being reprimanded or looked down upon for having different opinions. Rather, as we discuss in the next section, this may be a wonderful opportunity to ask both students to try to assume the other's perspective on the issue, to gain a greater appreciation for other points of view.

What Educators Can Do

Whether you espouse Kohlberg's or Gilligan's theory or a mixed view of adolescent moral development, it is essential as a teacher to acknowledge that there is much diversity in how your students will think about issues related to morality. An awareness of these differences can help teachers to develop positive relationships with their students. Educators who are aware of differences in how adolescents think about moral issues can better manage class discussions, and can more easily understand why some students may express positive emotions (e.g., happiness) while others express negative emotions (e.g., sadness, anger) over an identical situation. Moreover, as teachers, we also need to acknowledge that our students come from different cultural heritages, and that their cultural histories also may impact how they think about moral issues (e.g., López-Pérez, Gummerum, Keller, Filippova, & Gordillo, 2015; Zhang et al., 2013). The moral dilemmas presented in Figure 4.1 provide you with an opportunity to discuss some of these issues with adolescents, and to analyze the types of responses that different students provide.

FIGURE 4.1
Moral Dilemmas

In order to more fully appreciate that there may be age and gender differences in how adolescents think about moral issues, choose one of these scenarios, and present it to at least four different adolescents. Try to vary the adolescents to whom you present the scenarios (e.g., choose some younger and some older adolescents; choose some female and some male adolescents; etc.). Ask identical questions to your respondents, and compare their answers. Then discuss what you have learned with the other students in your class. Did everyone answer the questions in the same way? What similarities and differences in responses were evident? Can either Gilligan's or Kohlberg's theory help you to explain some of what you observed?

Scenario 1: The Heinz Dilemma
Try using the actual Heinz dilemma.

Scenario 2: Cheating
You notice that a close friend of yours is using a cheat-sheet during an exam in one of your classes at school. Is your friend's behavior acceptable? Would you report your friend's actions to the teacher?

Scenario 3: Helping a Struggling Student
Imagine that you are a teacher, and one of your colleagues tells you that she has a student who was struggling on a specific math problem on the state-mandated standardized test. The student was extremely anxious and started to cry. The teacher felt terrible for the student, who has a documented learning disability. Your colleague informs you that she whispered a "clue" to the student to help the student solve the problem, and then the student calmed down. The teacher felt that this was in the student's best interest, given the high levels of anxiety being experienced. Is this acceptable?

Perspective Taking During Adolescence

One of the hallmarks of adolescence is the ability to take different perspectives on issues. Although this may be easy for some students to do, it may be cognitively difficult for other students to accomplish. Let's look at an example:

>>>

Imagine that you are a ninth-grade high school social studies teacher, and you are teaching your students a unit about the Middle East. On one particular day, you are working on a lesson on the conflicts between Israelis and Palestinians. After discussing some of the general issues and some of the historical facts surrounding this part of the world, you divide your students into two groups (Group A and Group B). You ask the members of Group A to imagine that they are Israelis, and you ask those in Group B to imagine that they are Palestinians. You then ask students in each group to write a paragraph about how they feel about the Israeli–Palestinian conflict from the perspective of the assigned group. Later, you switch the groups, so that Group A represents the Palestinians, and Group B represents the Israelis; you again ask the members of each group to explain the conflict, but from the newly assigned perspective (i.e., so that all students get to think about this issue from both perspectives).

Ninth graders typically are about 14 or 15 years old. Would most ninth graders be able to take on one of these perspectives, and then switch to the other perspective? Clearly, for some students this would be an easy, fun task, whereas for others this might be a stressful, anxiety-invoking task. In addition, certain background variables might affect the students' abilities to take on these varying perspectives. Some of these might include:

- The students' religious backgrounds (i.e., if a student were Jewish or Muslim, would that affect the activity?)

- Prior knowledge about the conflict
- Personal acquaintance with an Israeli or a Palestinian
- Relationship with someone who is highly opinionated about the conflict
- Having recently seen a story on the news about the conflict
- Knowing that one's parents were strongly opinionated about this topic

Robert Selman proposed a theory to explain the development of perspective taking during childhood and adolescence. Some of his work focused on the general development of **perspective taking** (Selman, 1976, 1980; Selman & Byrne, 1974), whereas some focused specifically on how perspective taking develops within the context of friendships (Selman, 1981). He posited that prior to adolescence, children are not readily able to assume others' perspectives (i.e., they look at the world only through their own eyes). As children develop, they come to realize that other individuals do hold different perspectives from theirs, and they come to see that their own personal perspectives may differ from those of others. Eventually, near the onset of adolescence, children become able to perceive how others might perceive situations. At early adolescence, youth are able to understand both that others hold different perspectives and that other people acknowledge that perspectives differ among individuals. Thus, whereas an 8-year-old child might assume that everyone has the same opinion about an issue, a 12-year-old is more likely to realize that perspectives do, in fact, vary.

Throughout adolescence, youth also become able to see how social interactions with others might be viewed by third parties; in addition, ultimately they are able to see that the perspectives held by others are influenced by social forces (e.g., societal norms, classroom rules, etc.). Thus if Jerry (who is 16) wants to ask Diana (who is 13) to go out with him, he will probably think about how other students at school, and how his parents, will think about this. Jerry might wonder if some of his friends would think it was "weird" to ask out a much younger student; he also might wonder if his parents would perhaps prefer him to date a younger student than an older one. The point is that Jerry would be able to realize that various individuals in his life would think about his social interactions with Diana in different ways; Jerry's realization of the different perspectives that other individuals would have about his dating behaviors might affect his ultimate decision about whether or not he would ask Diane to go out with him.

Benefits of Being Able to Take Perspectives

As children develop into adolescents and become better able to understand diverse perspectives, they accrue numerous benefits. Being able to understand other viewpoints during adolescence can have a positive impact on one's physical and psychological well-being, one's social interactions with peers, and one's relationships with parents. As we discuss later in the chapter, when teachers understand how these abilities develop, they are better able to guide discussions with adolescents about a variety of academic and nonacademic issues.

Adolescents are able to make decisions more carefully when they are able to entertain other perspectives. The ability to consider a range of perspectives can be particularly beneficial to adolescents as they encounter opportunities to engage in various risky behaviors. In fact, research indicates that adolescents' abilities to take on other perspectives may be related to their abilities to make decisions

MyEdLab
Video Example 4.2

This high school literature teacher asks her students to assume the identities of characters that they are reading about in order to help her students to appreciate diverse perspectives.

In-Depth 4.1

Should We Teach Morals and Values in Schools?

There is much debate about whether or not we should teach morals and values in school. There is much variation in the beliefs of teachers, parents, policymakers, religious leaders, and others about this topic. As a prospective teacher, you may think that this will never come up as an issue for you. Nevertheless, morality and values come up both during regular curricular content as well as part of specialized programs designed to enhance moral behavior in students.

Consider the following curricular examples:

- In a social studies lesson, a discussion emerges about whether or not the United States should maintain military involvement in the Middle East.
- In a science class, in a lesson about ecology, students debate how much responsibility individuals have for maintaining the environment.
- In a language arts class, students question the actions of a character in a novel.

These and other exemplars will certainly arise in your classes. But as a teacher, how much should you encourage and facilitate these conversations? Should you encourage students to debate these issues? In addition, if you have a specific opinion about one of these issues, should you share your perspective? Should you suggest that one perspective might be "better" in some ways than another?

There are many ways to teach about morals and values, if you are going to do so. For example, in Hong Kong, moral education is often presented in the form of didactic lectures; however, such lectures demonstrate only weak links to valued outcomes (Cheung & Lee, 2010). There also are many "character education" curricula available. Some of these curricula focus on teaching students how to be responsible citizens, to be honest, and to strive for social justice. But there is debate about whether or not these programs actually affect moral behavior (Weissbourd, 2015), and research on many of these programs is scant.

When issues involving morality arise, there are several factors that you'll need to consider:

- From a moral development perspective (i.e., Gilligan, Kohlberg, etc.), are all of your students equally able to engage in discussions of the issues?
- Can your students fully understand the varying perspectives that others might have about these issues?
- Can you present the material to your students without letting your own personal feelings shine through? Or, if you have strong feelings about a particular topic, should you share those feelings with your students?

about important safety- and health-related topics. If adolescents can think about a risky situation both from their own viewpoints as well as from the viewpoints of other individuals, they may be less likely to choose to engage in risky behaviors that might adversely affect their health and well-being. Research indicates that younger adolescents and adolescents who are **high-sensation-seekers** (i.e., those who like exciting, stimulating activities) are more likely to choose to engage in risky behaviors than are older adolescents or low-sensation-seekers; however, when younger adolescents and high-sensation-seeking adolescents are asked to think about situations from another person's perspective, they are better able to see that others might perhaps not choose to engage in such behaviors (Crone, Bullens, van der Plas, Kijkuit, & Zelazo, 2008). Thus, as a teacher, your students will benefit when you ask them to think about various issues from multiple perspectives.

What Educators Can Do

There are many ways in which teachers of adolescents can encourage students to examine various perspectives on issues. As teachers, we must realize that activities that encourage adolescents to consider a variety of perspectives are complex—as the teacher, you need to be able to manage what could become a heated discussion. However, such discussions can lead to wonderful learning opportunities for adolescents. And adolescents can be encouraged to consider multiple perspectives in any of their classes. Examples of perspective taking across a range of subject areas are presented in Table 4.3.

Consider the following example. A high school teacher from Michigan used the example of a pregnancy prevention campaign that had been implemented in New York City as a topic for discussion with her students. She asked her students to read a neutral description of the campaign. Next, students examined campaign posters, and some conversations about the messages being conveyed in the campaign were initiated. Finally, students were provided with editorials that had been written both in favor of and against the campaign. Students were then encouraged to form their own opinions and take a position on the campaign; they then had to write a response to an opposing opinion (Doyne, 2013).

This type of activity provided many benefits to students. First, it encouraged them to understand diverse perspectives on an issue that most adolescents could relate to. Second, in order to defend their positions, they had to actually learn content—the information from the campaign had to be mastered in order for students to understand the editorials, and to write effectively about their own viewpoints.

Next, consider the decision to get into a car with a driver who might be intoxicated. Clearly, there are adolescents who would be willing to get into the car; recent data indicate that in 2011, 24% of adolescent drivers who were killed in car crashes had been drinking (U.S. Department of Transportation, 2013). Nevertheless, students might benefit from conversations in their schools about making such decisions; in particular, by asking students to role-play various perspectives about the decision to get into the car, students might be able to make safer decisions if eventually confronted with such a situation. Several additional examples of topics that can be explored with adolescents are provided in Table 4.4.

TABLE 4.3 Perspective Taking Across Academic Domains

Subject Domain	Example
Language arts	Students read one of the books from *The Hunger Games* series, and are asked to consider the perspectives of citizens from two different regions about the importance of the games.
Social studies	While studying the American Civil War, students are asked to consider the views of a 25-year-old female from the South and a 25-year-old female from the North about the reasons for the war.
Music	Students listen to a musical piece played first by an orchestra and then by a band, and are asked to provide perspectives on which presentation is preferable.
Physical education	Students are learning about running, and they are asked to discuss their perspectives on distance running versus sprinting.
Science	Students are asked to consider a variety of perspectives on the origins of the universe.
Math	Students are asked to consider two different methods of solving the same problem.

TABLE 4.4 Perspective Taking

As a teacher of middle or high school students, you will quite likely engage in many conversations with your students about complex and sometimes controversial topics. For this activity, develop a short lesson in which you could ask students to take on two different perspectives. In other words, the students should have to explain their answers in their own voices, and then from another person's perspective (e.g., from a parent's perspective, from a peer's perspective, etc.). After you design this activity, try it out with a partner; each of you should take on a different perspective, and then compare your responses. Some possible topics include:

1. The overcrowding of animal shelters necessitates the euthanization of some animals.
2. Evolution should be studied in schools.
3. Drinking soda (pop) is bad for one's health.
4. Exercise is important.
5. Alcohol should not be used until one reaches the age of 25.

It is also plausible that students may be more likely to assume other perspectives when they feel connected to school (i.e., they feel as though they fit or belong in their schools). Batanova and Loukas (2012) found that feeling connected to school was related to a greater self-reported ability to take on other perspectives among adolescent males; although the same result did not emerge for females, results did indicate that the negative relation of parent–child conflict to perspective taking was lessened for females who felt connected to their schools. Thus, adolescents who feel connected to their schools may adopt some of the values and belief systems that are prevalent in their schools, which may be related to a greater likelihood of taking on other perspectives.

One of the areas in which adolescents may have different perspectives is in their conceptions of religion. Students' religious beliefs and practices may vary greatly, and the ability to understand and appreciate a variety of perspectives may be particularly beneficial to adolescents. We turn to this topic next.

MyEdLab **Self-Check 4.2**

Religiosity During Adolescence

Religion plays a significant role in the lives of some adolescents (King, Ramos, & Clardy, 2013; King & Roeser, 2009). When we consider religion, we need to remember that there are many different aspects to how adolescents can be involved with religion. For some, participation consists of involvement in social activities (e.g., a youth group); for others, participation involves attendance at religious services and religious educational activities; for others, participation may not involve participation in any type of organized activities, but rather may reflect a deep spiritual connection. And for others, religion may simply not be an important part of their lives.

Adolescents affiliate with numerous religions. Data from the National Study of Youth and Religion, conducted by the Carolina Population Center at the University of North Carolina at Chapel Hill, summarized in Table 4.5, are indicative of the diversity of adolescent religious affiliations.

Although there is some variation, studies suggest that about half of U.S. adolescents (i.e., about 50%) consider themselves to be quite religious. More recent data on young adults (aged 18 to 29) indicate that 68% report affiliations with Christianity (e.g., Protestant, Catholic, Mormon, Jehovah's Witness, Orthodox, and Orthodox Christian), 6% with other religions (e.g., Jewish, Muslim, Buddhist, Hindu), and 25% report no affiliation (Pew Research Center, 2010). There also is some evidence that religiosity declines during adolescence (Rostosky, Danner, & Riggle, 2008). Thus, the centrality of religion in adolescents' lives may decline over

TABLE 4.5	Adolescent Religious Affiliations in the United States, 2002 and 2005	
Religion	2002 (Ages 13–17), %	2005 (Ages 16–21), %
Protestant	56.43	48.27
Catholic	19.27	20.27
Latter-Day Saints/Mormon	2.36	2.19
Jewish	1.46	1.29
Jehovah's Witness	0.45	0.52
Muslim	0.36	0.39
Buddhist	0.34	0.19
Hindu	0.13	0.18
Pagan or Wiccan	0.14	0.13
Native American	0.09	0.04
Eastern Orthodox	0.02	0.04
Christian Science	0.00	0.04
Unitarian Universalist	0.07	0.00
Miscellaneous other affiliations	1.80	1.90
No affiliation	15.18	23.51
Don't know or refused	1.39	0.87
Two affiliations reported	0.23	0.19

Source: Adapted from Denton et al., 2008. Used by permission from University of Notre Dame.

time. Recent data indicate that there is some stability in the percentage of adolescents reporting that religion is a very important part of their lives; specifically, 31.4% of 8th graders, 25.9%% of 10th graders, and 28.1%% of 12th graders indicate that religion is very important to them (Child Trends, 2013a). The majority of adolescents report believing in God, and believing that many religions may be true, as opposed to there being only one true religion or religions having little truth at all (Denton, Pearce, & Smith, 2008). Nevertheless, as noted in Table 4.5, almost one in four adolescents reports no formal affiliation with any religious group; similar results have been found from other surveys of adolescent religious affiliation (e.g., Pew Research Center, 2010).

There is much diversity in attendance at religious services: Whereas 42% of young adolescents reported attending religious services at least once per week, 18% reported never attending, and 13% reported attending only a few times per year (Denton et al., 2008). Adolescents also appear to attend religious services less often as they progress through their schooling; data indicate that whereas 41.3% of 8th graders attend religious services weekly, only 33.5% of 10th graders and 30.6% of 12th graders attend weekly (Child Trends, 2013b). In addition, 39% reported being involved in youth groups, although that decreased to 25% later in adolescence (Denton et al., 2008).

There are some patterns evident in adolescent religiosity. For example, research indicates that African American adolescents are more likely to attend church than are Caucasian adolescents (Molock & Barksdale, 2013). There also are some gender differences in religiosity. Research indicates that, overall, female adolescents are more involved with participation in religious activities than are males (Molock & Barksdale, 2013). Adolescents who live in the southern part of the United States tend to report being more religious than do other adolescents in the United States (Wallace, Forman, & Caldwell, 2003).

Religiosity during adolescence also has been linked to lesser engagement in some types of risky behaviors. For example, research suggests that drug use is lower among adolescents who are somewhat religious (Amey, Albrecht, & Miller, 1996; Neymotin & Downing-Matibag, 2013). However, some research suggests that the beneficial relations between religiosity and engagement in some risky behaviors (e.g., alcohol abuse) may not be as powerful among sexual minorities (i.e., adolescents who later identify as gay, lesbian, or bisexual; Rostosky et al., 2008) as they are in the general adolescent population. Interestingly, the relations between sexual activity and religiosity are quite weak (Neymotin & Downing-Matibag, 2013). Research also indicates that adolescents who truly feel that religion is an important part of their lives and who are genuinely interested in religion are less likely to use abuse illicit drugs (Fletcher & Kumar, 2014), and also are less likely to experience depression as a result of victimization by peers (Helms et al., 2015).

What Educators Can Do

As a teacher, you will bring your own religious beliefs to the classroom. Effective teachers need to consider how their own beliefs and belief systems relate to their students' beliefs and practices. Consider the following scenarios:

- You have some Jewish and Muslim students in your class who will be absent in order to celebrate holidays that the majority of your students do not recognize.
- You have a very outspoken student in your classroom who proselytizes, and believes that everyone should believe in Jesus Christ as the savior; that student is very outspoken about these beliefs, and shares those beliefs with everyone else daily.
- You have a student who claims to be a devil worshipper in your classroom.
- You have a Muslim student in your classroom, and your class gets into a heated discussion about Middle Eastern politics.
- You have a student who is very spiritual and adopts a "New Age" approach to religion and spirituality; this students likes to discuss topics such as near-death experiences, altered states of consciousness, and feelings of oneness with the universe.
- You have a student who is an atheist and often talks about the fact that she does not believe in God.

How would you deal with these situations? Is it your job as a teacher to worry about these and related issues?

There are several matters to consider. First, if you are teaching a core academic subject (e.g., mathematics), you may just choose to focus on the topic at hand; consequently, if and when issues of religious diversity come up, you could just direct your students back to the topic that you are teaching that day. However, you shouldn't fool yourself into thinking that these topics just won't ever come up in your classrooms; issues of religion can emerge in class (as well as in other settings outside of the classroom but in the school setting) in many ways; for example, a sentence or photograph in a textbook might lead to a comment or observation that may allude to religion.

Second, you may decide to acknowledge that some of your students are dealing with issues of identity development, and that religion is simply one of many aspects of adolescent development (we discuss this in greater detail in Chapter 5). Thus, you may decide to allow for some brief discussions of these varying belief systems, with the overall goal of helping students to understand and accept diversity in ideas about religion.

Another issue to consider is how your own religious beliefs affect the ways that you interact with your students. Consider the following situation:

>>>
You personally hold very strong spiritual beliefs attached to a particular religion, yet there are several students in your classes who hold very different beliefs.

Would your beliefs affect your interactions with your students? Perhaps, but what is most important is to acknowledge these differences, and to carefully consider them as well as how you might react if a student brought up the topic.

Consider the following true story:

>>>
Mr. Hunter is a high school biology teacher. He has been teaching biology for many years, and the state curriculum requires him to teach a unit on human evolution. Mr. Hunter attends church weekly, and believes in the Bible and in the word of God. However, he also is a biology teacher, and he believes in science and accepts that there is strong evidence for human evolution. Mr. Hunter struggled for many years to reconcile his personal beliefs with his scientific knowledge; in addition, he struggled even more so with how (or if) to communicate this personal conflict to his students. After several years of thinking about this, he came to personal terms with these two sets of beliefs. Interestingly, he shared his personal journey with his students, so that they could learn about how an individual can reconcile two contrasting belief systems. Specifically, he told his students that although he did believe in the story of Creation across 7 days, he also believed that evolution had occurred. He personally came to believe that the "days" that are described in the Bible represent long eras in the Earth's history, and that he was able to personally reconcile the biblical story as being a symbolic way of telling the story of evolution. He believed that the story of Creation actually mapped onto the theory of evolution quite well, and he was able to reconcile these two belief systems by acknowledging to himself that he could accept that both the biblical story and the science of evolution could coexist.

This story represents a teacher's struggle to deal with his own identity as a teacher, his personal beliefs about religion, and the sensitivity of the topic for his students (and perhaps their families). Indeed, teacher identity is a growing area of research; such research examines the ways in which teachers come to understand their beliefs and conceptions about themselves as teachers (Woolfolk Hoy, Davis, & Pape, 2006). As educators, we need to seriously consider our personal beliefs (i.e., beliefs about religion), and if and how those beliefs might affect our interactions with our students. Although we may want to share some personal information (as Mr. Hunter did), we may also choose not to share our beliefs; nevertheless, as professionals, we must at least consider how those beliefs might affect our interactions with students.

MyEdLab Self-Check 4.3

Volunteering and Service Learning

There is much discussion in schools about the importance of **volunteering**. One of the terms that is often used to describe one type of volunteering is *service learning*. **Service learning** is an educational experience in which students participate actively in activities that meet community needs, while being simultaneously integrated into the academic curriculum and allowing students to apply skills and to develop a sense of caring for others (Commission on National and Community Service, 1993, as cited in Kraft, 1996). Service learning has been defined as "a teaching and learning strategy that integrates meaningful community service with instruction and reflection to enrich the learning experience, teach civic responsibility, and strengthen communities" (National Service-Learning Clearinghouse, 2013). It is important to note that, technically, there is a distinction between service learning and volunteering, in that service learning often (but not always) may be required of students, whereas volunteering may or may not be required. Although educators and researchers often do not distinguish required from truly voluntary activities, it is important to realize that this distinction does exist. It also is important to note that there is debate about what constitutes volunteering during adolescence. Crocetti and colleagues note that volunteering is just one of numerous forms of civic engagement. The larger notion of civic engagement includes a number of activities, including both community-oriented and political pursuits (Crocetti, Jahromi, & Meeus, 2012).

> If a school requires students to engage in some type of service-learning activity, will that increase or impede students' desires to volunteer later in life?

Volunteering is related to moral development and perspective taking in many ways. As adolescents develop the abilities to engage in complex moral reasoning, and to appreciate diverse perspectives on social issues, they become better able to make rational decisions about whether or not to engage in volunteer work. For example, younger children and adolescents may only engage in volunteer work when it is required, or when they feel that they will "get something" in return for volunteering (e.g., recognition, a prize, etc.); however, older adolescents may engage in volunteer work because they have a broader understanding of how such activities benefit other individuals and the larger society.

Many adolescents endorse various forms of **civic engagement**, and acknowledge that these endeavors are important (Metzger & Ferris, 2013). About one-third of adolescents seem to participate regularly in volunteering activities. Data indicate that about 27.1% of 8th graders, 34.4% of 10th graders, and 38.8% of 12th graders report volunteering once per month (Child Trends, 2015). Of those who volunteer, 33% volunteer in education or youth organizations, 28% in religious organizations, and 39% through other types of organizations (Child Trends, 2015). Most of the service-type activities in which adolescents engage are voluntary in nature, although some adolescents participate because their schools may require such participation (Child Trends, 2015; Schmidt, Shumow, & Kackar, 2007).

Volunteering for political organizations tends to increase between the ages of 18 through 21 (Rosenthal, Feiring, & Lewis, 1998), most likely corresponding to college attendance and the ability to participate as a voter in elections. Some research suggests that female adolescents participate in volunteer activities more than do males (Cemalcilar, 2009; Crocetti et al., 2012). Research also indicates that adolescents who were characterized during childhood as effectively being able to regulate their emotions and who were more highly socially skilled are more likely to volunteer during adolescence (Atkins, Hart, & Donnelly, 2005). In addition, when adolescents' families believe in volunteering and support such activities, adolescents' intentions to volunteer, and subsequent volunteering behaviors, tend to be higher than those of adolescents from less supportive families (Law & Shek, 2009).

Participation in activities such as volunteering is related to other valued behaviors and attitudes (Schmidt et al., 2007). Adolescents who report feelings of social responsibility are more likely to volunteer (Cemalcilar, 2009; Crocetti et al., 2012; McGinley, Lipperman-Kreda, Byrnes, & Carlo, 2010). Thus, adolescents who, for example, care about their communities, about the environment, about the elderly, and about the homeless may be more likely to volunteer. There also is evidence that adolescents who engage in volunteering activities *become* more socially responsible (Hamilton & Fenzel, 1988) over time. In general, civic engagement during adolescence is correlated positively with academic achievement (Davila & Mora, 2007), although it isn't clear whether civic engagement causes students to achieve at higher levels or whether higher-achieving students are simply more likely to engage in volunteering activities. Some recent research indicates that there may be other socially beneficial outcomes of volunteering; for example, results of one recent study indicate that adolescents who volunteer are less likely to bully others (Gebbia, Martine, & Camenzuli, 2012).

MyEdLab
Video Example 4.3

Dr. Hudson involves her high school English students in a project that integrates what they are learning in the classroom with direct involvement in the community.

What Educators Can Do

There are several ways that educators can encourage and facilitate volunteering during adolescence. First, research suggests that engaging students in sessions in which students discuss and debate the merits of volunteering can lead to enhanced intentions to engage in volunteering activities among adolescents (Wilson, Allen, Strahan, & Ethier, 2008). Although some volunteering is required of adolescents via service-learning initiatives, an outcome that would benefit society at large would be the nurturing of positive feelings and intentions toward volunteering in the future. Teachers in all subject areas can engage their students in such discussions. For example, a biology teacher could discuss the merits of volunteering at a local zoo or aquarium, a social studies teacher could discuss ways that students can volunteer to assist during local elections, and an English teacher could mentions ways that adolescents could volunteer to tutor children in reading in the local elementary school.

Second, it may benefit adolescents to become involved in volunteering activities in which a responsible and knowledgeable adult serves in a supervisory role. Research indicates that adolescents appear to be particularly satisfied with volunteering experiences when they are supervised by professionals (Kulik, 2008). Thus, simply putting an adolescent into a volunteering position (e.g., working 1 day per week in a nursing home) without any supervision might lead the adolescent to become bored or frustrated; however, if the adolescent worked with an adult who supervised the experience and was available for brief consultations and discussions, the experience might be much more positive, and that adolescent might be more likely to remain in the placement. Consider two adolescents who are volunteering to tutor third graders in reading. Now imagine that one of those students is assigned to tutor but primarily works independently with her tutee, whereas the other student receives feedback after each session from a teacher who offers suggestions and comments about what went well and what could have gone better during the tutoring session. The adolescent who is supervised by and receives feedback from the classroom teacher may be more likely to persist with the tutoring, and more likely to want to engage in more tutoring opportunities in the future. Particularly if this is the first time that the adolescent is involved with tutoring younger children, the feedback from the teacher will build a sense of efficacy (confidence) in the adolescent; as she begins to feel more competent as a tutor, she will be more engaged with the task of tutoring, and she will be more likely to want to continue tutoring.

Third, educators can facilitate volunteering by presenting students with specific opportunities to volunteer. Merely telling students that it is "good" to volunteer probably won't be enough to motivate some students to engage in such activities; however, if, for example students were presented with an opportunity to volunteer at a local hospital, and if a representative from the hospital came to the school to talk about the opportunities and how to sign up for them, then an introduction of this nature might ultimately facilitate participation.

There is one important caveat to our discussion of volunteering. Interestingly, recent evidence suggests that *requiring* students to engage in service-learning-type volunteering activities may lead to decreases in volunteering behaviors later in life (Helms, 2013; Sparks, 2013). This is a concern, because

many states are beginning to require participation in such activities for graduation. For example, the state of Maryland and the District of Columbia currently
require participation in service-learning activities in order to graduate from high
school. However, several other states (i.e., Colorado, Iowa, Minnesota, Missouri,
Rhode Island, Tennessee, and Wisconsin) allow individual school districts to
adopt service-learning requirements for graduation (Sparks, 2013).

MyEdLab **Self-Check 4.4**

Academic Cheating

Did you ever see anyone cheat on a test or an assignment when you were in high
school? Did a friend of yours ever tell you that he was going to cheat on some
academic work? Or perhaps at some time during your many years of schooling,
you engaged in some type of cheating activity. As a teacher, you will probably be
surprised by how often you will encounter various forms of academic dishonesty.
   Let's consider a few situations. Would you characterize all of these as "cheating"?

- You notice a student copying another student's homework assignment just
  before your class starts.
- You catch a student using a cheat-sheet during a test.
- During an in-class exam, you notice that one of your students tends to gaze
  to the left rather often.
- A student uses material found on a website without giving proper credit to
  the source.

MyEdLab
Video Example 4.4
As children move into adolescence and moral reasoning
develops, changes emerge in
how students think about academic cheating.

   Some of these examples are flagrant examples of cheating (e.g., catching a student using a cheat-sheet). But in some of the examples, there may be some debate
regarding the severity of the situation. For example, if you see a student gazing to
the left, that may be indicative of copying from another student's test, but it may
also just be because the student is not concentrating on the test (i.e., the student
is not using efficient self-regulatory strategies). Moreover, the student who does
not give appropriate credit to a website may be plagiarizing, but the student also
may not realize that websites need to be appropriately referenced; indeed, adolescents today are living in a world in which one can Google just about anything,
and therefore students may not understand the need for documentation of sources
when using the Internet. Thus, as you can see, "cheating" during adolescence is not
straightforward—the issues are complex, and as educators, we need to understand
why cheating happens, how it happens, and how it can be prevented.
   Academic cheating is related in important ways to moral development and to
the ability to appreciate diverse perspectives. As adolescents develop, their beliefs
about cheating, and the likelihood of engaging in academic cheating, may change
dramatically. Indeed, much attention has been paid in recent years to high reported
rates of academic cheating in schools and colleges. Adolescents in particular are
more likely to engage in academic cheating than are younger children (Anderman
& Midgley, 2004; Franklyn-Stokes & Newstead, 1995; Jensen, Arnett, Feldman, &
Cauffman, 2002; Sheard, Markham, & Dick, 2003), although some data suggest that
rates of cheating may decline somewhat in college (Jensen et al., 2002). Data vary
depending on the study, but in general, available data suggest that many adolescents cheat at some point during their academic lives, with reports ranging from
about half of all students engaging in some form of cheating (Kelley, Young, Denny,
& Lewis, 2005) to somewhere between 75 and 98% of all students engaging in academically dishonest behaviors at some point in time (Educational Testing Service,
1999). One estimation is that for any given exam, approximately 3 to 5% of the
students taking the exam engage in some type of academic cheating (Cizek, 2001).

It is important to note that these statistics do not indicate that all students cheat all of the time; rather, some of the students in these studies may be repetitive cheaters, whereas others may have only cheated once or twice. In addition, whereas some students may engage in flagrant cheating (e.g., standing in for someone and taking an ACT or SAT test for someone else), most instances of cheating are less severe in nature, and involve incidents such as copying another student's homework assignment. Thus, there is much variation in the rates and types of cheating.

The increase in cheating as children become adolescents and progress through school has been attributed to many variables, but most notably to the increased focus on grades and test scores that is emphasized as students progress through school (Anderman & Midgley, 2004). Research indicates that when educators are perceived as emphasizing grades and test scores during adolescence, students are more likely to report engaging in cheating behaviors (Anderman, 2007; Anderman, Griessinger, & Westerfield, 1998; Anderman & Midgley, 2004). Research also indicates that when students report that their teachers emphasize mastery (as opposed to grades), students are less likely to report that they cheat (Anderman, 2007; Anderman & Danner, 2008; Anderman et al., 1998; Anderman & Midgley, 2004).

In addition to older adolescents cheating more than younger adolescents, research indicates that males tend to cheat more than do females (Calabrese & Cochran, 1990; Davis, Grover, Becker, & McGregor, 1992; Miller, Murdock, Anderman, & Poindexter, 2007). However, these differences often are quite small, and there are other studies in which no gender differences in cheating have been found (Anderman & Turner, 2004; Genereux & McCleod, 1995). Because, as already mentioned, cheating is highly prevalent during adolescence, we know that both males and females do engage in academic cheating. One possibility is that statistics may suggest that males cheat more than do females either because males may be more likely to admit having cheated, or because males may be caught more often than are females.

High-Stakes Testing and Cheating

The increase in the use of high-stakes testing in academia has resulted in many reports of academic cheating. High-stakes testing occurs across the United States, as well as in many other nations. In Table 4.6, we provide some examples of state-level high-stakes examinations.

MyEdLab
Video Example 4.5

This student used technology to cheat; he and a college administrator discuss the consequences of this decision.

TABLE 4.6	Examples of High-Stakes Assessments in the United States	
State	**Test Name**	**Description**
California	Standardized Testing and Reporting (STAR)	Administered each spring to students in grades 2–11
Ohio	Ohio Achievement Assessments (OAA)	Administered each spring to students in grades 3–8
Florida	Florida Comprehensive Assessment Test (FCAT 2.0)	Administered to students for reading in grades 3–10, math in grades 3–8, and science in grades 5 and 8
Illinois	Illinois Standards Achievement Test (ISAT)	Administered to students in grades 3–8 every March
Wyoming	Proficiency Assessments for Wyoming Students (PAWS)	Administered to students in grades 3–8 and 11 for reading, writing, and mathematics, and in grades 4, 8, and 11 for science

High-stakes exams are first administered to children during the early elementary grades, and continue throughout adolescence. These exams are considered to be "high stakes" because scores almost always are reported to the public (i.e., printed in the newspaper), aggregated for all students in a school, and these aggregated scores are then used to evaluate the effectiveness of schools. These test scores can affect teachers' and principals' jobs, and can even affect real estate prices, wherein homes that are zoned in neighborhoods in which residents will attend consistently high-achieving schools may be worth more money (Chiodo, Hernandez-Murillo, & Owyang, 2010).

Although the results of these exams have very important implications for schools and for staff in schools, they often don't mean much to students. However, results of other types of high-stakes exams, including college admissions exams such as the ACT and SAT, do have very significant implications for students. A high score on the ACT or SAT can lead to admission at more selective colleges and universities. Thus, the temptation to cheat on those exams may be high for some students, and the decision of whether to cheat or not is dependent on the adolescent's ability to engage in moral reasoning and perspective taking.

Assessments that are given by teachers in schools also may be considered as high-stakes tests to some students. For example, final exams in middle school or high school classes may count for large percentages of final grades in a course, and thus the temptation to cheat on such exams may be high. As mentioned earlier, if students are learning in classrooms in which grades and test scores are emphasized, or if the students are extrinsically motivated (i.e., students know that a good test score will lead to certain privileges), students will be more likely to cheat and to justify cheating as acceptable (Anderman et al., 1998). In addition, assessments given in class by teachers may be high-stakes assessments for adolescents because the students perceive pressure from their parents to do well on these exams. A parent might tell a 16-year-old adolescent that if the student earns A grades on all of her final exams, the parents will buy her a car. When the results of a test are related to highly valued extrinsic incentives (e.g., getting a new car), the temptation to cheat will be much higher (Murdock & Anderman, 2006).

> **What might you do in your classroom to prevent cheating from occurring?**

It is important to note that in recent years, numerous high-profile cases of academic cheating have been highlighted by the media. Although many occurrences of academic cheating involve students, some of these also have involved teachers or school administrators who have been implicating in cheating scandals. In those situations, educators have been accused of changing students' answers or scores after tests had been administered. Some recent examples are described in Table 4.7.

TABLE 4.7 Examples of Cheating on High-Stakes Assessments

1. *Cheating on the SAT*. In Long Island, New York, students from five high schools were arrested for cheating on the SAT. Some students served as imposters and took SAT exams for other students in exchange for payments. Both the students who served as imposters and the ones who paid the imposters were arrested. The imposters were paid between $500 to $3600 per exam (Anderson & Applebome, 2011). The imposters generally went to test sites that were located a large distance from their neighborhoods (Caulfield, 2011).

2. *Cheating in Atlanta, Georgia*. Teachers in Atlanta had the opportunity to earn up to $2000 in bonuses for improving their students' test scores (Vogel & Perry, 2009); 178 educators were accused of having been involved in changing students' scores after exams had been completed.

3. *Cheating in Columbus, Ohio*. School personnel in Columbus City Schools were accused of changing scores by tampering with students' enrollment records. Specifically, students were artificially withdrawn from schools and then re-enrolled in the same schools; this allowed those students' test scores to be discounted from annual calculations of school improvement, because state regulations required students to be continuously enrolled in order for their scores to be counted (Smith Richards, 2012).

What Educators Can Do

There are many actions that teachers can take to lessen the likelihood of cheating. First, it is important to acknowledge how much cheating occurs during adolescence. Although rates do vary, data suggest that many students engage in cheating during their adolescent years. Teachers need to let students know that cheating is unacceptable. In addition, when a teacher catches a student cheating, it is important to do something about it—do not ignore the cheating! As a teacher, you will need to establish a balance; you don't want to humiliate a student in front of everyone else if you know that cheating is occurring during an exam in your class, but at the same time you don't want other students to perceive that you tolerate cheating. Consider the following example:

>>>

> You are a 10th-grade math teacher. You are giving a unit examination, and during the test, you notice that one of your students keeps looking at the right side of his desk. You walk over and discover that there are formulas written on the desk.

How would you respond? There are several different actions that you could take:

- You could yell at the student, take his exam away, and say, "I don't tolerate cheating."
- You could walk over to the student, pick up his exam, and say, "See me after class."
- You could walk over to the student, stare at him to let him know that you are aware of the cheating, shake your head in disapproval, and then allow the exam to continue.
- You could call the student over to speak with you after class.

From these four options, which would you choose? Different teachers may make different choices, but probably the wisest choice would be the second one (pick up the exam and say, "See me after class."). This would (a) stop the cheating, (b) send a message to other students that you do not tolerate cheating, and (c) not humiliate the student. If you yelled at the student in front of everyone else, that would certainly cause additional embarrassment; if you either shook your head in disapproval or just spoke to the student after class, that would send a message to other students suggesting that students might be able to get away with cheating in your class. Thus, you need to establish a balance between demonstrating your intolerance of cheating with sensitivity to the humiliation that could be caused for the perpetrator. This can and should be a learning opportunity for everyone!

Second, be aware that students are more likely to cheat when there is a strong emphasis on grades and test scores. If you constantly make statements like "There will be a quiz on Friday"; "If you don't do well on the test, your grade for this semester will be ruined"; "Getting a good grade in this class is essential if you want to get into a good college"; or "At least half the class always fails the test," then you will be doing a lot to encourage cheating to occur in your classroom.

As mentioned earlier, students are less likely to cheat when teachers emphasize *mastery* rather than test scores (Anderman, 2015). This does not mean that you will need to eliminate tests; rather, you need to think about how much you talk about tests, and what you emphasize as being the most important outcomes of learning in your class. One way that teachers can emphasize mastery and lessen cheating is by allowing students to re-take exams or rewrite assignments. If students know that the ultimate goal is learning, and that they will be given multiple opportunities to learn (i.e., to re-take an exam if they don't pass), over time they will see that cheating does not help them to truly learn the material.

If your assessments truly require students to demonstrate learning, and if they realize that they can redo assignments in which they have not demonstrated mastery, cheating is unlikely to be a serious problem.

Third, carefully consider how you will respond when you catch a student cheating. Will you treat all cases of academic dishonesty in the same manner? Would you handle the case of a student who copied one answer on a nightly homework assignment in the same way that you would treat a student who had been caught plagiarizing a major term paper? These are important considerations, and there are diverse ways that educators can respond when students are caught cheating.

Some teachers will adopt the attitude that this is a learning opportunity, and they will attempt to use the fact that the student was caught cheating toward deterring cheating in the future and fostering learning. For example, if a student is caught with a cheat-sheet during an exam, as the teacher you could just give the student a grade of zero; however, another alternative would be for you to give the student a zero (so that there is still a consequence for cheating), but then also allow the student to re-take the exam, and have the student's final grade be an average of the zero and the new grade that was earned fairly—that way you might convey the message that although cheating is unacceptable, learning the material is still the most important outcome.

MyEdLab **Self-Check 4.5**

MyEdLab
**Application Exercise 4.2
Cheating in School** What should teachers do when they catch a student cheating? In this exercise, we will explore how teachers can handle these situations effectively.

In-Depth 4.2

Zero Tolerance

The term **zero tolerance** refers to policies in which predetermined punishments are consistently applied when certain behavioral infractions occur. These consequences are enforced regardless of any extenuating circumstances. Thus, if a teacher has a zero-tolerance policy for cheating, and the consequence for cheating is a grade of zero on that assignment, then any student caught cheating, *for any reason*, would receive the zero grade—no exceptions. Similarly, if a school has a zero-tolerance policy toward bullying, and if the mandatory punishment for bullying is a 3-day suspension from school, then any student involved in any case of bullying would be removed from school for 3 days—no exceptions.

Due to the popularity of zero-tolerance policies in the United States, the American Psychological Association (APA) appointed a task force to examine the research on the effectiveness of these policies (APA Zero-Tolerance Task Force, 2008; Skiba et al., 2008). The task force discovered that there is actually very little scientific research supporting the effectiveness of zero-tolerance policies in schools. Further, the task force found that although there is a widespread belief that removing "bad" students from school will improve the school climate for other students, this is simply not supported by the data; in fact, in schools where suspension and expulsion are used frequently, schoolwide academic achievement often is low, even when controlling for socioeconomic status. In addition, although there often is an assumption that zero-tolerance policies will have a deterring effect on other students (i.e., if students know that the school has a strict policy about a certain type of misbehavior, students will be less likely to engage in that behavior), research results do not indicate that these policies serve as effective deterrents.

The task force provided many recommendations for the use of these policies, and also offered some useful alternatives. Some of the recommendations that are most applicable to schools serving adolescents include the following (APA Zero-Tolerance Task Force, 2008; Skiba et al., 2008).:

- Be more flexible in the use of zero-tolerance policies (i.e., acknowledge that sometimes there truly will be good reasons to make an exception to the policy).
- Allow teachers and/or other professionals who have regular contact with students to be the first ones to communicate with parents when disciplinary infractions occur.

- Train educators to respond to infractions appropriately, based on the severity of the infraction.
- Evaluate all school policies to ensure that all are focused on positive outcomes for students.
- Only implement zero-tolerance suspensions or expulsions for the most severe infractions.
- Require police officers who work in schools to be trained in adolescent development.

- Try to prevent violence from occurring by improving school climate and creating a sense of belonging for all students.
- Create a strong network of communication between schools, parents, mental health professionals, and law enforcement agencies so that these entities can work collaboratively with adolescents who commit serious behavioral infractions.

Recommendations for Educators

In this chapter, we have examined several different aspects of adolescent development and behavior. In particular, we discussed various aspects of moral development, how adolescents learn to appreciate different perspectives, and how religious participation and the importance of religion change during adolescence. We then looked at the specific example of adolescent volunteering within the larger context of service learning. We also discussed academic cheating, which is an issue that all educators must confront.

The implications for educators are vast. Although many educators may feel that these represent nonacademic areas of students' lives in which teachers should not be involved, others will recognize that student moral and social development and students' beliefs in these areas are related to how they think, act, and behave in and out of school. In addition, students' reactions to and interpretations of classroom discussions will most certainly reflect some of these underlying developmental issues. Several recommendations are as follows:

1. *Acknowledge and embrace that your students will be at different places developmentally in these noncognitive domains.* As we reviewed in this chapter, development in the moral and social domains is not necessarily linear; some students ultimately reach higher levels, whereas others don't. It is not "wrong" for a student to think about a moral issue in a less complex manner than do other students. It is important for you, as the teacher, to acknowledge these differences, and to help your students to understand the different perspectives that are expressed by classmates.
2. *When varying perspectives are evident in your students, use those variations in viewpoints as learning opportunities.* Rather than pointing out that there are differences and emphasizing dissimilarities, use differences in opinion as a means of examining alternative points of view. For example, in a heated discussion about the Middle East, attempt to get your students to understand the myriad and diverse opinions about sensitive political issues; in particular, you might want to focus your discussion on historical facts that led different groups to have different current opinions about political issues.
3. *Acknowledge the importance that religion may play in some of your students' lives.* We all know about the separation of church and state, and few administrators would encourage you to discuss personal issues of religion in the classroom. Nevertheless, as a teacher of adolescents, you need to fully understand the larger worlds in which your students live. For some adolescents, participation and attendance in church or other religious activities may be very important. Such knowledge may help you in being able to hold meaningful

conversations with students, in helping them to find interesting assignments, and in understanding some of their extracurricular commitments.

4. *Remember that all volunteering opportunities are not created equally.* Some opportunities to volunteer may in fact be mandated service-learning requirements. Your students may approach such experiences differently than self-initiated volunteering activities. When adolescents participate in voluntary activities, it will be helpful to discuss their responsibilities, time commitments to those activities, and reasons for participating.

5. *Be aware of the fact that students cheat.* Students will have many different reasons for engaging in academic cheating, but the primary reason why students cheat is because they are motivated to get a high grade on an exam or in a class. Keep in mind that when a teacher focuses on mastery (i.e., the focus is on learning the material and truly understanding it—not on just getting a good test score), students will be less likely to cheat.

Conclusion

In this chapter, we have examined various aspects of social and moral development during adolescence. We noted that moral reasoning changes over time, and that our students think differently about moral issues as they grow older. Moreover, we also noted that there are different ways of framing adolescent moral development. For example, whereas Kohlberg posed a stage theory, Gilligan frames cognitive development in terms of how people think about moral issues in terms of "justice" and "care."

We also examined perspective-taking. Adolescents develop better abilities to understand and assume diverse perspectives as they mature. Whereas an early adolescent may not be able to appreciate diverse perspective on an issue (e.g., rationale for a war), older adolescents will be better able to understand that diverse perspectives do exist, and they may be better able to understand why some individuals may interpret situations differently than they do.

As educators, we need to understand that our students' involvement with various activities also changes during adolescence. For example, involvement with religious activities, as well as the reasons that adolescents have for participating in religious activities, change at this time. Similarly, adolescents often are afforded opportunities to engage in volunteer and service-learning activities for the first time; whereas some of these may be required for school, others may be strictly voluntary. Finally, we examined academic cheating. We noted that academic cheating occurs quite often, and that students engage in cheating for a variety of reasons. Cheating at times is related to a perceived emphasis on grades and high-stakes assessments.

danr13/Fotolia

5

Identity and Self-Perceptions

Learning Outcomes

5.1 You will be able to describe the multifaceted nature of identity and the different specific parts of identity that make up the whole.

5.2 You will be able to describe how identity development is influenced by multiple factors, including intrapersonal, social, and societal factors.

5.3 You will be able to describe how gender affects identity and behavior.

5.4 You will be able to describe how culture and ethnicity affect identity and behavior.

5.5 You will be able to describe what educators can do to help adolescents through the identity-development process and alter aspects of identity that may interfere with optimal development and functioning.

Introduction

Adolescence is a time of rapid development and change in all aspects of life. The onset of puberty heralds physical changes that transform childlike bodies into those that more closely resemble adults. These changes in physical appearance, as well as societal expectations about how teenagers should act, affect the ways that others, including friends, same-age peers who are not friends, and adults, interact with adolescents. Unlike young children, when 15-year-olds interact with adults they may be peppered with questions such as these: "How are you doing in school?"; "What are your plans for the future?"; "Are you dating anyone?"; "Why did you dye your hair pink and pierce your eyebrow?"; and "Isn't it about time you got a job, at least for the summer?" Similarly, the expectations and requests from friends and peers change as children morph into adolescents. Whereas the 8-year-old may be faced with relatively inconsequential choices, such as choosing between playing Legos or having a water fight, the 16-year-old is likely to confront requests from friends that carry the weight of long-term consequences: "How about we skip the study session and go to that party?"; "Do you want to make out?"; "Do you want a hit of this joint?"; "Are you going to sign up for this AP class?"

Along with physical changes and different social expectations, adolescence is also marked by tremendous changes in cognitive abilities. The ability to think abstractly allows adolescents to ponder different futures for themselves, and the different costs and benefits of those alternate futures—for example, "I could become a doctor, but do I want to be in school for that long? Or I could become a musician, but what are the chances I could really make money doing that?" This ability to think about hypothetical futures is made possible by a related cognitive development: the ability to reason about complex issues due to increased cognitive capacity (see Chapter 3). Whereas a younger child may think, "I want to be a firefighter so I can ride in a shiny red truck," the more cognitively developed adolescent may think, "Being a firefighter involves helping others, which is great, but it also involves serious physical danger, lower pay than many other jobs, and perhaps disappointing my parents, who want me to become a lawyer. Still, the red trucks are cool." This ability to think about options for the self in complex ways, and the demands of friends and family to begin thinking seriously about one's future, encourage adolescents to spend a lot of time thinking about who they are, and who they will become. In short, one of the important tasks of adolescence is to develop an identity.

The identity-formation task of adolescence has direct implications for educators. Consider the following hypothetical exchange, one that will sound familiar to just about every high school teacher and is probably similar to thoughts you've had at some point in your educational career:

>>>

In Mr. Riggins's 10th-grade geometry class, the students had been working on the process of developing proofs. One day, in the middle of the period, Jeremy dropped his pencil and sighed. "Man, this is a waste of my time," he said. "I'm going to be a writer. Why do I need to learn how to do proofs in geometry? I'll never do this stuff again in my life after this class."

Mr. Riggins dusted off the same explanation he'd used for years whenever this complaint was raised. "Jeremy, you are only in 10th grade. You don't yet know what kind of career you will have. Our job, as teachers, is to prepare you for lots of different career options. Next year you may discover that you are fascinated by robots and decide you want to become an engineer. You need to learn this kind of math now so you will be prepared to pursue that interest in case it arises in the future."

"Whatever," Jeremy responded, unconvinced. "Any job that wants me to do geometric proofs is not the job for me."

In many ways, the ongoing efforts of adolescents to develop their identities affect every aspect of their behaviors and attitudes in school. As adolescents figure out who they are, who they want to become, and what they value, they will regularly ask questions about the relevance of schoolwork, the importance of academic achievement, and their place in the social structure of school and society. Educators need to understand this identity-development process so they can respond to the questions raised by students like Jeremy and so they can think about ways to help adolescents develop identities that open, rather than close, doors of opportunity.

OVERVIEW OF THE CHAPTER

There is quite a long history of research examining adolescent identity formation. This chapter begins with a review of the different ways that identity has been defined and conceptualized and the various theories of identity development. This section includes a discussion of the different aspects of identity (e.g., the physical self, the social self, the academic self) as well as concepts that are related to identity (e.g., self-esteem, self-concept, possible selves). Next, we consider two particularly salient features of identity that come into sharper focus during adolescence and influence many aspects of adolescents' lives: gender identity and ethnic/cultural identity. The chapter concludes with suggestions for ways that educators can help adolescents explore their own identities and develop healthy attitudes and behaviors that are consistent with their self-definitions. Throughout the chapter we pay particular attention to the ways that different dimensions of identity, and the identity-development process, influence adolescents' attitudes toward, and behavior in, school.

Theories, Conceptualizations, and Definitions of Identity

Identity Versus Role Confusion

Erik Erikson (1963, 1968, 1980) thought of human psychosocial development as occurring over eight distinct stages (Table 5.1). Each stage was marked by a particular conflict, and the successful resolution of that conflict (or the lack of a resolution) would have a lasting impact on the individual. Erikson argued that the primary conflict in the adolescent period of development is the struggle to develop an organized and coherent sense of self—an identity. This is the fifth stage in his model, and he labeled the conflict of this stage as identity versus role confusion. A healthy and successful resolution to this conflict, which Erikson thought occurred in most people in their late teens or early to mid-20s (i.e., young adulthood), would leave the individual with a secure sense of what she values, who she is, and what she wants to do with her life. The successful resolution of this stage of development would lay the groundwork for establishing a fruitful career and for developing long-lasting intimate relationships. It allows the individual the ability to *commit* to a pathway, be it in the area of romantic relationships, religious beliefs, or career. In contrast, the unsuccessful resolution of this stage would leave the individual feeling confused about her role in society and unsure about career goals and personal values, which Erikson called **role confusion**. This enduring lack of a cohesive sense of self and one's values would leave the individual ill-prepared for making lasting commitments to career, religious path, or intimate relationships.

TABLE 5.1	Erikson's Stages of Psychosocial Development	
Age	**Crisis**	**Resolution**
Infancy	Trust versus mistrust	**Hope:** A positive resolution produces a sense of safety and trust that one's needs will be met. A negative outcome produces mistrust and lack of faith.
Early childhood	Autonomy versus doubt	**Will:** A positive resolution produces a sense of self-determination, pride, and self-control. A negative outcome produces withdrawal and self-doubt.
Preschool age	Initiative versus guilt/shame	**Purpose:** A positive outcome produces a belief in one's ability to initiate action, and self-reliance. A negative outcome produces embarrassment and feelings of inadequacy.
Elementary school age	Industry versus inferiority	**Competence:** A positive outcome produces a sense that one is competent, able to learn and master new skills and knowledge. A negative outcome produces feelings of inferiority and the inability to learn and understand.
Adolescence	Identity versus role confusion	**Fidelity:** Positive outcome produces clear, organized sense of self and one's values. Negative outcome produces confusion about one's beliefs, pathway, and clear identity.
Early adulthood	Intimacy versus isolation	**Love:** A positive outcome produces the ability to commit to and love others. A negative outcome produces fear of commitment and difficulty forming and remaining in loving relationships.
Adulthood	Generativity versus stagnation	**Care:** A positive outcome results in caring for the welfare of others and society, and a desire to nurture and protect. A negative outcome produces self-centeredness and concern with one's own prosperity.
Old age	Integrity versus despair	**Wisdom:** A positive outcome produces sense of fulfillment and satisfaction with one's accomplishments, and a lack of regrets. A negative outcome produces bitterness, fear of death, and regrets.

Erikson believed that the key to developing a strong and coherent identity was through exploration. It is quite common for teens to "try on" different identities by experimenting with their looks, trying out different peer groups, and becoming involved in different activities. Although Erikson thought this kind of exploration was a healthy part of identity development, he also recognized that society often puts constraints on the acceptable identities for adolescents, and experimenting with identities can have costs. For example, despite the advances toward gender equality in contemporary American society, adolescent girls still receive frequent messages about how they are supposed to look and dress (Durham, 1998). Adolescent girls who experiment with a different style (e.g., punk, tomboy) may be ridiculed by some of their peers or disparaged by teachers or parents (Eder, 1995). Similarly, the role of brainy nerd is generally reserved for White or Asian American students, so students from other ethnic groups who take on this role may suffer the insults of their peers (Ogbu, 1992). Although these difficult experiences are part of the process of developing an identity, these social costs may cause adolescents to abandon self-definitions that would have made them happy as adults. In addition, the frequent experimentation with different roles causes many adolescents to recognize that they act differently in different situations, or with different groups of people, and they can begin to wonder who their "true" self is (Harter, 1990). We address this in more detail later in the chapter.

Refining and Expanding Erikson's Ideas

Building on Erikson's idea of exploration leading to a stable identity, James Marcia (1966) examined the various pathways that individuals take to develop a sense of self. Erikson's theory posits that the stage of identity versus role confusion is successfully resolved when adolescents explore different identity options and ultimately reach a commitment regarding who they are, what they value, and what they want to do with their lives. Marcia recognized that adolescents and young adults often differ from one another in how much exploration they do and in how committed they are to a path at the end of the process. To examine these differences, Marcia (1966) developed the **identity interview**. In this interview, Marcia and his colleagues asked adolescents and young adults questions about a specific domain (e.g., career aspirations, political beliefs, religious beliefs). Specifically, they asked about the level of commitment to the aspiration or belief as well as the amount of exploration adolescents had undertaken within the domain.

For example, consider the following hypothetical interview between a researcher and a college senior, using the Marcia interview technique:

Researcher:	Do you know what you'd like to do for a career after college?
Student:	I want to become a lawyer.
Researcher:	How sure are you that this is what you'd like to do?
Student:	I'm pretty sure that's what I want to do. I've begun applying to law schools.
Researcher:	How long have you known that you wanted to become a lawyer?
Student:	Since high school, I guess. My parents are both lawyers, and they've encouraged me pretty strongly to become a lawyer and carry on the family business.
Researcher:	Did you ever seriously consider a different career?
Student:	Not really. When I was little I wanted to be a singer but that was more of a childhood dream than a career plan.

In this abbreviated example of a Marcia interview, you can see that the researcher asks about commitment ("How sure are you that this is what you'd like to do?") and exploration ("Did you ever seriously consider a different career?"). Marcia used the responses to these interviews to identify four types of identity status: identity achievement, identity foreclosure, identity moratorium, and identity diffusion. These four identity statuses are categorized along the two dimensions of commitment and exploration (see Table 5.2). **Identity achievement** represents a high level of commitment after a period of high exploration. For example, a young adult might decide to pursue a law degree after carefully considering other possible career options. **Identity foreclosure** indicates a high level of commitment to a path but without much exploration. The hypothetical college student in the hypothetical interview represents identity foreclosure because she has committed to the career path of lawyer without ever really considering other options. **Identity moratorium** involves high levels of exploration without any lasting commitment to a particular path. And **identity diffusion** reflects an absence of exploration and commitment. Identity achievement most closely matches what Erikson had in mind

TABLE 5.2 **Marcia's Stages**

		Exploration	
		Yes	**No**
Commitment	Yes	**Identity achievement:** Confronted with doubts, explored various options, committed to a path	**Foreclosure:** Decided on a path early, possibly based on parental beliefs and values, never had doubts or seriously explored other options
	No	**Moratorium:** Considering different options and paths, but not ready to commit to one yet	**Identity Diffusion:** Not actively exploring options and not committed to a path

when he described the successful resolution to the conflict of identity versus role confusion, and identity diffusion is analogous to Erikson's idea of role confusion.

Since Marcia's creation of the identity interview and his identification of the four identity types, hundreds of studies have been conducted using this model (Marcia, 1993; Sneed, Schwartz, & Cross Jr., 2006). The theory and interview method have been applied to other domains, such as social relationships and romantic commitments (Grotevant, Thorbecke, & Meyer, 1982). The theory has been critiqued in terms of its cross-cultural relevance (Sneed et al., 2006), and compared to other perspectives on identity (Côté & Schwartz, 2002). For over 50 years it has offered a useful and interesting way to think about the process of identity formation among adolescents, young adults, and older adults as well.

Think about your own identity formation. How did you decide that you wanted to become a teacher? How sure are you now that teaching is the career for you? What other options did you consider?

The Multidimensional Self

Although individuals begin developing their identities in infancy, the combination of physical, social, and cognitive changes that occurs during adolescence makes this a particularly interesting and important period of identity development. The cognitive ability to recognize how one is treated differently by different groups of people and how one acts differently depending on the context is an ability that really takes hold in adolescence. In addition, adolescents spend more time than children in thinking about and weighing their different values, in part because there are more demands for them to make commitments to certain paths. Friends will demand that they try to fit in with the style and beliefs of a particular social group. Adults will demand that they begin to think seriously about future plans, such as college and career.

The consequence of these increasing social demands and greater cognitive capacities is that adolescent identities become more multidimensional and differentiated, leading to the **multidimensional self** (Harter, 1999). Whereas the younger child tends to think of himself in somewhat global terms ("I'm pretty cool, I guess. I'm good at sports."), the adolescent begins to realize that his "self" is actually a collection of different "selves." The adolescent's answer to the question "Who are you?" is likely to be several answers, not one—for example, "I'm pretty good-looking, but a little skinny. I'm really funny, but only with my close friends. I tend to be pretty quiet around my parents and other adults. I'm a decent student, but I really see myself as more of a writer than a math or science guy." In short, adolescents are more likely than children to consider the context, their own values, and who they are with when thinking about their own identity, and are therefore more likely to think about themselves as having several parts rather than just one or two global attributes (Harter & Monsour, 1992).

Another consequence of increased cognitive sophistication is a better ability among adolescents, as compared with children, to consider the perspectives of other people. This allows adolescents to realize that who they are really depends on perspective, and how one views herself may differ from how others view her. For example, an adolescent may view herself as somewhat moody and emotional, but realizes that others tend to view her as upbeat and happy. Similarly, a teenager may be well known for her athletic accomplishments, but tends to think of herself more as an academic person.

The multidimensionality of identity creates a difficult developmental task for adolescents: organizing these different pieces into an integrated, coherent identity. When you consider that adolescents often have different self-conceptions about their physical appearance, their athletic abilities, their social selves, their academic selves, their gender, and their ethnic identity and then combine that with their awareness that they act quite differently in different contexts, and that others view them in ways that differ from how they view themselves, you begin to get an idea of how daunting the task is of forming an integrated, unitary identity.

Research has revealed that there is an interesting pattern of identity development during adolescence. Although adolescents of all ages recognize that their identities vary across social contexts and times, their feelings about this variety change as they get older. Harter and her colleagues (Harter, Bresnick, Bouchey, & Whitesell, 1997) found that early adolescents did not really care about their apparently contradictory personality traits, and viewed it as normal or inevitable that they were friendly and outgoing in some situations but moody and withdrawn in others. Harter et al. (1997) argued that early adolescents may lack the cognitive capacity to simultaneously compare different abstractions about their personalities, and are therefore not bothered by them. As adolescents develop the cognitive sophistication to engage in such comparisons around mid-adolescence, however, the contradictions do begin to upset them (Harter & Monsour, 1992). Now they are able to recognize that they feel and behave quite differently in different contexts, but they are not yet able to create a unifying theory for why this might be. The result, often, is feelings of confusion about who they "really" are, what their "**true self**" is, and whether they are just phonies.

Thankfully, around late adolescence and into early adulthood, most individuals are able to develop an integrated sense of self through the employment of more abstract identities. Whereas the 15-year-old may be confused by his tendency to feel happy at some times and angry at others, the 18-year-old may resolve this conflict by defining himself as being a moody or emotional person. Similarly, whereas the 15-year-old may question her genuineness when she notices she is outgoing and loud with friends but shy and reserved in her romantic relationships, the 18-year-old may resolve this conflict by noting that different roles call for different behavior, or that she has known her friends much longer than she has known her romantic partner. Older adolescents have the cognitive ability to both recognize the apparent contradictions in their personality and to resolve them by integrating them into a coherent whole (Harter et al., 1997).

The Dynamic Self: Past, Present and Future Selves

One additional feature of identity that complicates the task of creating an integrated and coherent sense of self is the fact that identity is dynamic, not static. In other words, when thinking about the self, individuals consider who they want to be in the future (or fear becoming), in addition to who they are now (Markus & Nurius, 1986). These **possible selves** can take many forms. For example, they can be **hoped-for selves** ("I would like to be a doctor in the future") or **feared selves** ("I am afraid of being unemployed after college"). Possible selves can also be perceived as being more, or less, likely to occur. Possible selves tend to be more grandiose and general among adolescents and young adults (e.g., "I want to be rich and famous") than they are among the middle-aged (e.g., "I hope to get that promotion at work") or the elderly (e.g., "I hope I can avoid hip surgery"; Markus & Nurius, 1986). Possible selves, both hoped-for and feared, can serve a motivational function for adolescents by providing them with a goal, an image of where they want to be in 5 or 10 years. They provide a method for bridging the gap between how one views herself now (the **actual self** or the **real self**) and what one wants to become (the **ideal self**). Of course, achieving this ideal self requires being able to both imagine it (i.e., to formulate a positive future self) and the ability to identify and overcome the obstacles to attaining that future self. This can prove difficult for adolescents who do not have a history of achievement in socially valued domains (e.g., school) and who lack role models of success in these domains (Oyserman, Terry, & Bybee, 2002). Even when adolescents are able to formulate clear hoped-for future selves, these may not always influence current behavior. For example, a 15-year-old who wants to become a doctor in the future may still fail to study for an upcoming biology exam because that future doctor self is either not salient (i.e., the 15-year-old is instant messaging with friends and not thinking about her future self) or is too far in the future to be deemed relevant in the moment (Oyserman, 2014). We will return to this idea later in the chapter when discussing what educators can do to promote healthy identity development.

Self-Esteem, Self-Concept, and Self-Worth

Self-esteem refers to global feelings about oneself (Rosenberg, Schooler, Schoenbach, & Rosenberg, 1995). Generally speaking, it involves the answers to questions such as these: Am I happy with myself? Do I feel like I am a good person? Or do I generally feel unsatisfied with myself and who I am? Self-esteem among adolescents has been a key area of research for many years. As we discuss later in this chapter, some of this research has examined gender differences in self-esteem, and some research has explored the association between self-esteem and academic performance. In this section of the chapter, we focus on different kinds of self-esteem, some of the factors that influence self-esteem during adolescence, and how self-esteem differs from other, closely related concepts such as self-worth and self-concept.

For several decades, researchers have wondered and debated about whether self-esteem is a stable trait or something that fluctuates across time and situations. Rosenberg (1986) argued that there are actually two different kinds of self-esteem: **baseline self-esteem**, which tends to be stable over time and situations, and **barometric self-esteem**, which involves short-term fluctuations over time and situations. As adolescents experience many physical and social changes, struggle to define their identities in different contexts, and are in a general period of flux and change, it is reasonable to expect that their self-esteem may fluctuate as well. There is some evidence that supports such expectations. For example, research indicates a general decline in overall self-esteem during early adolescence, possibly related to the transition to middle school and a greater tendency to compare oneself to others (Crain, 1996; Eccles & Midgley, 1989). This general decline is followed by an average increase in self-esteem during the high school years, as adolescents gain more autonomy (Harter, 1999).

The view that fluctuations in barometric self-esteem are an inevitable feature of adolescent life has been challenged by some researchers. For example, Harter and Whitesell (2003) argued that for some adolescents, self-esteem is quite stable over time and across situations, but other adolescents experience frequent shifts in their feelings about themselves. In research with both older (college-aged) and younger (middle school) adolescents, Harter and Whitesell found that self-esteem was stable for some adolescents and variable for others. This research revealed that when adolescents felt like they were succeeding in domains (e.g., social, academic, physical, etc.) that they valued, and that they were being judged favorably (i.e., approval) by others, they were able to maintain steady and high levels of self-esteem. Those adolescents who experienced changes in self-esteem were those who reported changes in their success in valued domains and changes in their approval from significant others. When adolescents experienced increases in success and approval, their self-esteem went up. But when they experienced failure or lack of approval, their self-esteem decreased.

Two concepts that are closely related to, but slightly different from, self-esteem are self-concept and self-worth. **Self-worth** (sometimes referred to as *global self-worth*) is quite similar to self-esteem in that it refers to global, overall judgments

Think about yourself 5 or 10 years into the future. What do you want to be doing with your life and career? Think about the obstacles you will have to overcome to get there and what you can do to overcome those obstacles. How clear is your plan? And how confident are you that you can achieve these hoped-for possible selves?

about the self. However, it is focused on a slightly more narrow set of questions than is global self-esteem (Covington, 1992). Self-worth refers to feelings about one's general value: Do I have value? Am I an important member of this group (e.g., family, classroom, society, peer group)? Or am I feeling worthless? **Self-concept** tends to be more specific than self-esteem or self-worth (Marsh, Byrne, & Shavelson, 1988). Unlike those two more global self-assessments, self-concept is tied to a specific domain, such as academics or athletics. Academic self-concept, for example, refers to feelings of competence within the domain of academics: Am I a good student? Do I tend to do well in school? How well do I do compared to other students?

It is quite interesting and informative to consider how these three types of self-perceptions are associated with academic engagement and achievement during adolescence. For several years, researchers and educators believed that one reason students may not do well in school was because they had low self-esteem. If true, this is particularly problematic for early adolescents, as many young people (11 to 15 years of age) experience a decline in self-esteem as they engage in more **social comparison** and struggle to figure out their identity (Harter, 2006). The goal of helping students develop and maintain high self-esteem was deemed so important that schools famously began incorporating self-esteem-building activities into the curricula. In 1986, the legislature in the state of California established a self-esteem task force. The legislation was promoted by the belief that increasing students' self-esteem would promote academic achievement, reduce antisocial behavior, and even increase economic productivity (Billingsley, 2010). The document produced by the task force, *Toward a State of Self-Esteem* (California State Department of Education, 1986), identified six problematic areas of behavior that could be improved by boosting the self-esteem of children and adolescents and contained recommendations for how to do so, including making self-esteem protection and enhancement a focus of K–12 education.

In-Depth 5.1

Self-Esteem in California Schools

In 1986 the state legislature of California created the California Task Force to Promote Self-Esteem and Personal Social Responsibility. This 25-member task force operated from 1987 to 1990 with the goal of identifying the key components to building stronger self-esteem with the hope that improved self-esteem would solve a variety of social ills, from crime to low academic achievement (Rodota, 2014). The driving force behind this effort was a state assemblyman named John Vasconcellos. Although the work of the task force (indeed, its very existence) was lampooned mercilessly in Garry Trudeau's *Doonesbury* comic strip, the members of the task force took the work seriously and were genuinely optimistic about the potential social benefits of boosting the self-esteem of Californians.

The final report of the task force was released in 1990 and sold 60,000 copies, the best-selling state document of all time. Despite the hopes and promises of Vasconcellos and many members of the task force, there has never been strong evidence that improving self-esteem can solve social ills or improve academic achievement. There is also no solid evidence that superficial programs designed to promote self-esteem, such as instructing students to tell themselves that they are good and likeable people, ever did anything to raise self-esteem. Critics of the self-esteem movement argued that the work of the task force led California to adopt practices in schools, such as avoiding criticizing student work and promoting students to the next grade even if they have not mastered the material, that have ended up hurting students and the state (Billingsley, 2010). Although the task force was formed and worked with good intentions, enhancing self-esteem is a difficult process, and the benefits of enhanced self-esteem are not clear.

Although self-esteem is positively associated with academic achievement and with overall well-being, it is not clear that high self-esteem *causes* higher academic achievement (Baumeister, Campbell, Krueger, & Vohs, 2003). Nor is there a consensus about how to help students develop healthy self-esteem if they do not already have it (Baumeister et al., 2003). In addition, there is evidence that many adolescents who engage in unhealthy or negative behaviors (e.g., bullying, vandalism, truancy, and dropping out of school) often have quite high global self-esteem (Baumeister et al., 2003). Moreover, feelings of self-esteem tend to increase in later adolescence and into adulthood, even without improvements in academic performance (Harter, 2006; Shapka & Keating, 2005). All of this suggests that global self-esteem may not directly influence things like academic engagement and achievement. Thirty years after the creation of the California self-esteem task force, the efforts of this task force are widely viewed as having produced few benefits for students or schools (Billingsley, 2010).

One reason for the unclear and fairly weak association between self-esteem and academic outcomes is that self-esteem depends on a variety of factors, and people are pretty good at manipulating those factors so that they can avoid feeling badly about themselves. For example, we tend to base our self-esteem on our values, and if we are not good at something, we often devalue it. A student who chronically fails in school may be able to maintain a generally positive view of himself by putting less value on academic achievement and more value on activities and traits in which he feels successful, such as his appearance or athletic accomplishments. Because academic accomplishment is highly valued in most industrialized cultures, it is difficult for students to completely devalue it, and low achievement is associated with slightly lower self-esteem. But the association is quite modest, and it is likely that academic performance influences self-esteem as much as self-esteem affects academic performance.

A much stronger predictor of academic motivation and achievement is how one feels about one's academic abilities (**academic self-concept**) and one's confidence in his or her ability to succeed (**self-efficacy**). Because these judgments about the self are tied more specifically to academic outcomes than is general self-esteem, they tend to exert a stronger influence on actual academic behavior (Bandura, 1986; Marsh et al., 1988; Pajares, 1997). Not only are academic self-concept and self-efficacy stronger influences on academic engagement and achievement than self-esteem, they are easier for teachers to adjust as well. Instead of encouraging students to look in the mirror and tell themselves how great they are (this was an actual assignment in many schools in California during the self-esteem movement), teachers can boost students' academic self-concept by providing frequent opportunities to succeed, reminding students of how much they have already learned, teaching them effective strategies for overcoming challenges in their learning, and encouraging them to focus on their own growth and development rather than how they compare with other students (Anderman & Maehr, 1994). These are particularly important strategies for teachers of adolescents because adolescence is the time when social comparison reaches its peak, and comparing one's academic performance to peers' can reduce academic self-concept and self-efficacy for students who are not among the highest achievers in the class. (See Table 5.3 for a comparison of self-esteem, self-efficacy, and academic self-concept.)

Independent Versus Collectivist Selves

It is important to note that how one defines the self depends on the social context in which one lives. Recognizing this, some researchers have examined how the definition of identity differs in different cultural contexts. Triandis (1989, 1995) noted that in the United States and many western European countries, the self is defined mostly in terms of independence from others. Personal goals and accomplishments

TABLE 5.3	Differences Among Self-Concept, Self-Esteem, and Self-Efficacy		
	Self-Concept	**Self-Esteem**	**Self-Efficacy**
Definition	How one feels about one's self in various domains (e.g., academic, physical appearance, athletic ability, social skills)	How one feels about one's self overall; global self-concept (e.g., "I am a good person. I like myself.")	Confidence in one's abilities to achieve specific outcomes (e.g., get an A on a test, run a mile in less than 7 minutes, get a date for the prom)
Association with academic variables	Moderately correlated with achievement and motivation; in general, more motivated and higher achievement for those with higher academic self-concept	Very weakly associated with motivation or achievement because not specific to academic domain; can do poorly in school and still like one's self as a person	Strongly associated with motivation and achievement for the specific task or outcome; one who is confident he will get an A on a test is often motivated to study for it and often will get a good grade on that test

are emphasized, and a major goal of becoming an adult is becoming self-sufficient, moving out of the parental home, and establishing a place for oneself in the world. Triandis called this cultural definition of the self **individualism.** In many other countries, most notably East Asian countries (e.g., Japan, China) and in many other cultures (e.g., Latin American, Native American), the self is defined more in terms of one's connections to others and roles within a larger group. Instead of striving to set oneself apart and establish a path of independent accomplishment, individuals in these cultures are primarily concerned with doing their part to further the interests and well-being of their group (e.g., family, tribe), even if this means sacrificing personal goals. Triandis referred to this kind of self-definition as **collectivism**. Other researchers who have examined cultural differences in identity have used different terms, such as an **independent self** versus an **interdependent self** (Markus & Kitayama, 1991). It is important to note that when families move from one kind of culture to another (e.g., from a collectivist culture to a more individualistic culture), their self-definition does not change overnight. In the United States, for example, there are many families that continue to emphasize a more collectivist view of the self, even as the larger society promotes a more individualistic view.

Research examining these cultural differences in self-definition has revealed that they influence a wide range of beliefs and behaviors. In the area of education, teachers may notice that schools tend to promote values that are congruent with individualistic values. Students are often encouraged to view school as a vehicle for pursuing their goals, gaining recognition for their good work, and distinguishing themselves from others as they strive to get into prestigious colleges. But adolescents from more collectivist cultures may not be motivated by such individualistic goals. Rather, such students may strive to do well for the sake of bringing honor to the family or to become better prepared to further the interests of their cultural group. Some research has found that students from collectivist cultures confounded their teachers and school counselors because they often did not follow the traditional path to college (Valadez, 2008). Rather than applying to the most prestigious colleges they could get into, some high-achieving Mexican immigrant adolescents selected less prestigious colleges that would allow them to stay closer to home, fulfill family obligations, and allow them to attend college without sacrificing cultural values such as collectivism. Teachers should be aware that such differences in

MyEdLab
Video Example 5.1

Gary, a Vietnamese-American young adult, describes his experience growing up in a family with collectivist values and pursuing his individualistic goals.

self-definition can have profound effects on adolescent students' aspirations and motivation in school.

What Educators Can Do

The development of a coherent identity that integrates the many parts and values of the individual and creates a clear, committed path for future careers, relationships, and values is a fundamental task of adolescence. The physical, social, and cognitive changes associated with this period of life allow and force adolescents to question who they are, try on new roles, and carve out their own sense of self. In particular, the ability to think about various possible roles, both now and in the future, and to compare one's self to others creates a window of exploration and experimentation unlike any other during the developmental life course. But this exploration involves risk—for example, of being ridiculed for a silly style choice or for behaving in ways that are not socially acceptable by one's gender or cultural group, of prematurely committing to a path that one may later regret, and of feeling like an imposter or a phony when the adolescent recognizes how differently he acts and feels in different situations.

Teachers can help their adolescent students as they struggle to figure out who they are, particularly as students, in a variety of ways. Here are some ideas for how to do that:

- *Encourage exploration by providing opportunities for students to think about different possible selves and by encouraging students to consider how school subjects are personally relevant.* Flum and Kaplan (2006) and Kaplan, Sinai, and Flum (2014) argue that schools are settings that can and should be used to help adolescent students explore their identities. Specifically, they make the point that, in ways both subtle and explicit, school experiences are constantly affecting how students think about themselves and their relationship to what they are learning. For example, the student who sits bored in his history class day after day is doing more than occasionally dozing off; he is also developing a current and future identity that does not include the roles of historian or seeker of knowledge about history. A number of researchers, including Flum and Kaplan, have argued that schools should encourage students explicitly to engage in identity exploration, and they have provided several models for how this can be done.

- *Create opportunities for students to think about the personal meaning and relevance of the work.* This can take many forms. Hulleman and Harackiewicz (2009) asked high school students to think about the relevance of their science work as a means of encouraging them to find meaning and personal relevance in their schoolwork. Sinia, Kaplan, and Flum (2012) created an in-class activity to encourage adolescent students to explore their own identities by reflecting on a poem in their literature class. Lakin and Mahoney (2006) engaged early adolescent students in service-learning projects as a means of helping them explore and develop identities as active agents for change.

- *Create a safe space for exploration, and scaffold it appropriately.* Identity exploration is often an implicit process that adolescents are not consciously engaging in. Asking students to explicitly think about their own identities and how that may be related to what they do in the classroom requires creating an environment in which students feel safe to think about and discuss their identity exploration (Flum & Kaplan, 2012). Methods for doing this can include allowing students to reflect on their identity formation privately (e.g., in journals) and taking time to create a safe environment for sharing ideas publicly. Teachers can model how to talk about their own identity exploration and can provide frameworks for a safe discussion, such as developing procedures and guidelines for appropriate responses when people share their thoughts.

- *Provide opportunities to explore multiple and unlikely paths.* As Erikson (1968) and Marcia (1966, 1993) argued, identity foreclosure is not an ideal outcome of identity formation. To prevent students from settling on a single path before exploring alternatives, teachers should provide opportunities for students to explore multiple identities. For example, before a student decides that he doesn't care about English literature because he has no plans to become a writer, help him consider other uses of English literature to help him fulfill his goals. Alternatively, encourage adolescent students to spend some time learning about people and careers that are quite different from how students currently perceive themselves to be. For example, a student who has not developed a future self as scientist may have little knowledge about what professional scientists actually do. Encouraging students to explore several alternative pathways can help them develop more informed and well-articulated identities, thereby increasing their commitment to those identities.

- *Help students identify potential obstacles to achieving hoped-for selves and developing strategies for overcoming those obstacles.* Adolescents are often better at thinking about who they want to become than about how to actually achieve those goals. Helping students to identity potential barriers, and to develop strategies for overcoming those barriers, makes the goal feel more achievable and provides a pathway for students to follow.

- *Focus on developing students' academic self-concept and self-efficacy rather than their global self-esteem.* Adolescents' self-esteem is multifaceted and often depends on factors beyond the realm of the classroom (e.g., feelings about appearance, social relationships with peers, athletic accomplishments, etc.). Academic motivation and achievement are much more closely tied to academic self-concept and self-efficacy than to global self-esteem. Teachers can help build academic self-concept and self-efficacy by helping students succeed in the classroom; breaking challenging tasks into smaller, more manageable pieces; and helping students recognize and reflect upon their academic growth and learning over time.

- *Recognize that students will actively protect their feelings of self-worth by reducing effort in and valuing of school if the costs of failure (e.g., public humiliation) are perceived to be too high.* Teachers are often tempted to highlight the achievements of students in a public manner. Although this may be gratifying for some students, it can also be embarrassing for the high achiever and demoralizing for the lower achievers. In general, it is more powerful and effective when teachers provide feedback to students privately rather than in a public manner (Brophy, 1981).

- *Reduce the emphasis on social comparison.* Many adolescents feel self-conscious and vulnerable. While they are trying to develop an identity that is unique and personally meaningful, they can become inhibited if they are frequently asked to compare themselves to their classmates. Teachers can reduce this inhibition by encouraging students to focus more on their own interests and ability development rather than on how they compare to others.

Teachers cannot eliminate all of the growing pains associated with identity exploration and development during adolescence, but there is much they can do to reduce the risks adolescents feel as they try on different identities and provide adolescents with opportunities to explore their possibilities.

MyEdLab **Self-Check 5.1**

MyEdLab **Self-Check 5.2**

Gender Identity

In 1982, Carol Gilligan published *In a Different Voice*. In this book, she argued that theories of moral, identity, and cognitive development presented by such luminaries of psychology as Kohlberg, Erikson, and Piaget all gave higher status to boys' thinking and socialization processes than to girls'. According to Gilligan, girls are socialized to develop and maintain harmonious and caring relationships with others. Boys, in contrast, are socialized to develop identities that are separate from others, independent, and self-reliant. Moreover, Gilligan argued that as girls age into early adolescents, they become increasingly aware that their values and worldviews are given lower status than those of boys. The result is that the confident, boisterous young girl becomes the quiet, passive, and self-conscious adolescent. Gilligan referred to this change as girls "losing their voice."

Although several scholars and commentators have questioned Gilligan's assumptions and her research (e.g., Harter, Waters, Whitesell, & Kastelic, 1998; Sommers, 2000), Gilligan's ideas struck a chord with many people and provided one framework for understanding the process of gender identity development. Specifically, she emphasized the differences in expectations that American society has for boys and girls. In addition, she raised an important question regarding which traits and characteristics—those associated with masculinity or those associated with femininity—are more valued in society. These questions have been examined extensively through research on correlates of different gender-role beliefs, gender differences in self-perceptions, and the effects of stereotypes on mental health and academic outcomes.

Gender Roles and Gender Identity

It is important to note the difference between *gender roles* and *gender identity*. **Gender roles** refer to societal expectations and messages about gender-appropriate attitudes, beliefs, and behaviors. Gender roles represent the information that adolescents receive from various socializing agents (parents, teachers, media, friends, the larger society) about how males and females should act and how they should think. **Gender identity** refers to how individuals think about themselves in terms of their gender. For example, Mary may have been told from an early age that a woman's role is to look beautiful, be nice, and devote her life to caring for her husband and children. These are gender-role messages that Mary has heard from various sources for most of her life. However, Mary may develop a gender identity that involves challenging the dominant role of men in high-tech industries, breaking through glass ceilings, and serving as a role model for girls and women who would like to follow in her footsteps. In this example, the gender roles that were most commonly presented to Mary and the gender identity she has created for herself are quite different from each other.

MyEdLab
Video Example 5.2

In this video, two stories are presented of children who were born with male anatomy but identified as female. Think about what these stories suggest about where gender identity comes from and the difference between one's gender and one's sex. Also think about how others in the child's environment respond to transgender children.

Some of Gilligan's claims about society placing more value on masculine than on feminine traits are supported by research examining adolescents' sex roles. As adolescents become more concerned with figuring out who they are and how they should behave, they may become increasingly sensitive to social cues about appropriate style, behavior, and attitudes for their gender. The idea that adolescents become increasingly concerned with gender-appropriate behavior is known as the **gender-intensification hypothesis** (Hill & Lynch, 1983). According to this idea, the impetus for behaving in gender-stereotypical ways comes from a variety of social sources, ranging from friends to romantic partners to magazines aimed at teenage girls (Maccoby, 2002). Teachers also seem to hold and promote beliefs that boys and girls have different interests and skills (Basow, 2004). In more traditional cultures, both within the United States and in other countries, as children move into adolescence, they are expected to assume the more gender-specific roles of their culture. In the dominant cultures in the United States, where gender roles are considerably less rigid, the pressure to behave in gender-stereotyped ways during adolescence may be less intense, but it is still present. Indeed, views about gender-appropriate behavior become more flexible from childhood into early adolescence but then grown increasingly rigid throughout high school (Alfieri, Ruble, & Higgins, 1996).

Despite the relatively liberal attitudes of mainstream American society regarding gender roles, there are still some traits and behaviors that are considered to be more feminine and some more masculine. Bem (1974) developed an inventory of characteristics that are classified into **masculine** and **feminine** categories. Those who score higher on the feminine traits (e.g., expressiveness, empathy, nurturing tendencies) are thought to be more feminine, whereas those who score higher on the masculine traits (e.g., assertive, aggressive, ambitious) are thought to be more masculine. Those who have high levels of both masculine and feminine traits are called **androgynous**.

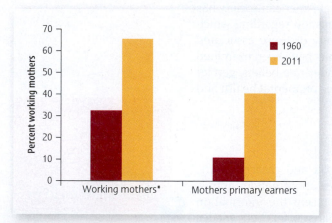

FIGURE 5.1

Trends in Mothers Working and Being Primary Breadwinners

* Mothers in a couple.

Source: Data from Wang, W., et al., 2014.

One of the interesting questions regarding gender roles is how socialization processes influence the gender roles adolescents adopt. Specifically, adolescent boys and girls may receive mixed messages about how sex-stereotypically they should behave. On one hand, American society has steadily moved away from the strongly sex-stereotyped expectations of men and women that prevailed prior to the 1970s (Davis, 2011; National Opinion Research Center, 2011). Today, most women are in the workforce (47% of the U.S. workforce, according to 2010 U.S. Census data [U.S. Department of Labor, 2014]), women are the primary money earners in 40% of U.S. families (Wang, Parker, & Taylor, 2014; see Figure 5.1), and there are many prominent female role models in traditionally male-dominated fields such as sports, business, and law. On the other hand, according to the gender-intensification hypothesis described earlier in this chapter, adolescents may become increasingly concerned about behaving in gender-appropriate ways, and may be pressured by their peers to be more feminine (girls) or masculine (boys). One way that this apparent conflict has been resolved is that the definitions of gender-appropriate behavior have changed. For example, whereas girls were once explicitly dissuaded from playing sports because it was viewed as being not feminine, now girls are often encouraged to play sports, and are doing so in record numbers (Stevenson, 2007). Similarly, it is no longer considered unusual for men to be actively engaged in caring for their children.

Despite these changes in stereotypes about appropriate behavior for males and females, adolescents still differ in their masculine and feminine traits, and these differences appear to have consequences. For example, research indicates that girls who are relatively high in both male and female traits (i.e., androgynous) are more highly satisfied with themselves than are either very feminine or very masculine girls. For boys, however, self-acceptance is highest when they are very masculine (Frome & Eccles, 1996; Markstrom-Adams, 1989; Orr & Ben-Eliahu, 1993). Similarly, although peer acceptance is highest for adolescent boys and girls when they behave in **gender-stereotypical** ways, the *costs* of behaving in ways that do not conform to gender stereotypes are higher for boys than for girls. Boys who display a relatively large amount of female-stereotypical traits and behaviors are more likely to be ostracized by their peers and more likely to have negative self-perceptions than are girls who display a relatively high number of male-stereotypical traits and behaviors (Egan & Perry, 2001; Frome & Eccles, 1996). As Carol Gilligan (1982) noted, there appear to be fewer costs for adolescents who behave in more stereotypically masculine ways than for those who behave in more stereotypically feminine ways.

Stereotype Threat

Many have noted and lamented the shortage of women in certain science, technology, engineering, and math (STEM) fields, most notably math, physics, and engineering (Beede et al., 2011; Eccles, 2007; see Table 5.4). Although the majority of U.S. college students are female, and female high school students receive better grades in their math and science classes than do their male counterparts (Voyer & Voyer, 2014), males still greatly outnumber females in math, physics, and engineering programs in college and in these professions. A number of possible explanations for this phenomenon have been offered, including the idea that female students are less likely than male students to be encouraged by their teachers to pursue these areas of study; the belief that these fields are too demanding to allow women to also pursue their goals of raising children; the belief that men are intimidated by women who excel in these areas; and the idea that females value professions that will allow them to help others, and they do not view these fields as providing such opportunities (Eccles, 2007).

What are some of the messages in society about what is gender-appropriate behavior for adolescents today? Where are these messages coming from, and what are they doing to either reinforce or break down gender stereotypes?

Another possible contributor to the shortage of females in these STEM fields is the debilitating effects of **stereotype threat** (Walton & Spencer, 2009). According to stereotype threat theory, performance can be inhibited when one is a member of a group about which there is a negative stereotype for the task being performed (Steele, 1997; Steele & Aronson, 1995). For girls and women,

TABLE 5.4 Percentage of Workers in STEM Fields by Gender

	Male		Female	
	2000	2009	2000	2009
All workers	53	52	47	48
College educated	54	51	46	49
STEM workers	76	76	24	24
College educated	76	76	24	24

Source: Data from U.S. Department of Commerce, Economics and Statistics Administration, 2011.

there is a negative stereotype about their abilities in math and some sciences. When they are confronted with an achievement task in these domains, they may experience feelings of threat—that they will fulfill the negative stereotype about their group. This stereotype threat can dampen performance in these areas (Steele & Ambady, 2006; Walton & Spencer, 2009). For stereotype threat to have its harmful effects, it must somehow be activated. For example, girls who are asked to indicate their gender before completing a math test performed 33% worse than girls who were not asked to indicate their gender (Danaher & Crandall, 2008). Because stereotypes come from the environment, there is some evidence that the stereotypical beliefs regarding girls' lack of ability in math and some scientific fields is transmitted to them, in part, from parents and teachers (Shapiro & Williams, 2011).

What can be done to reduce the negative effects of stereotypes on girls' achievement and desire to pursue STEM careers? Because stereotype threat occurs in specific situations, researchers have focused on introducing elements into the achievement situation to counteract it. For example, some research has found that when women are asked to simply think about something that they value before taking a test in math or physics (what's known as **values affirmation**), they perform better on the

In-Depth 5.2

Stereotype Threat, Women, and Science

In recent years, there has been a lot of concern regarding the relative scarcity of women in certain math, science, and technology fields, such as physics, engineering, and mathematics. As described in this chapter, there is very interesting research that has demonstrated the negative effects that stereotype threat can have on high school and college women's scores on mathematics and physics exams. Now, some fascinating research is being conducted to examine how stereotype threat may be driving some female scientists out of the profession (National Public Radio, 2012). Using an audio recording device to track the speech of male and female scientists as they went about their work during the day, researchers found that when male scientists discussed their work with their colleagues, they became energized and excited. In contrast, when women discussed their work with their colleagues, particularly their male colleagues, they became less energetic and enthusiastic. In fact, the more female scientists discussed their work with their male colleagues, the more disengaged they reported being in their work. And disengagement with work is a strong predictor of leaving the profession. In addition, the recordings revealed that female scientists sound less competent when discussing their work with male colleagues than when discussing their work with female colleagues.

Why would female scientists become less engaged with their work, and sound less competent, as a result of talking with male colleagues about it? One possible explanation is stereotype threat. When female scientists discuss science with male colleagues, the stereotype that men are better than women at science becomes activated, and the female scientist becomes concerned, perhaps subconsciously, about fulfilling this stereotype. This concern draws mental resources away from the task (e.g., performing well on a test, sounding competent in a conversation), thereby causing female scientists to sound less competent when discussing science with men than with women. Concerns with stereotype threat are also draining, thereby reducing female scientists' enthusiasm and engagement when talking with male colleagues about science. The stereotype threat explanation is bolstered by two additional findings from this research: The female scientists were fully engaged and enthusiastic when talking with male colleagues about non-science topics, and when talking with their female colleagues about science. In both of these situations, stereotype threat was not activated, and its debilitating effects were not present. (To listen to a National Public Radio story about this research, go to this link: http://www.npr.org/player/v2/mediaPlayer.html?action=1&t=1&islist=false&id=156664337&m=156689258)

test (Martens, Johns, Greenberg, & Schimel, 2006; Miyake et al., 2010). These beneficial effects of values affirmation were only found for women who were experiencing stereotype threat. A second approach to reducing stereotype threat has been to make use of role models. For example, college women performed better when they believed that their math test was created by a female math professor (Marx & Roman, 2002) or when they read biographies of successful women before taking the test (McIntyre et al., 2003). Teaching female students about stereotype threat can also reduce its negative effects (Johns, Schmader, & Martens, 2005).

Gender Differences in Self-Perceptions

Perhaps the area of identity-related gender differences that has received the most attention by researchers is self-esteem. Scores of studies have been conducted, and they have produced a mixed bag of results. Although several studies have found that adolescent boys' self-esteem is higher, on average, than girls', others have found no significant gender differences in self-esteem. In a meta-analysis that combined the results of many studies of adolescent self-esteem, a small but statistically significant gender difference emerged, indicating that males had slightly higher self-esteem than did girls and that this difference peaked in late adolescence (Kling, Hyde, Showers, & Buswell, 1999). Robins and Trzesniewski (2005) reported similar results, with a gender gap in self-esteem emerging at about age 12 and remaining roughly constant throughout adolescence (see Figure 5.2). However, a more recent study of a large, nationally representative sample of Americans found that there were no gender differences in self-esteem during adolescence. In addition, this study revealed that self-esteem increased at the same rate for males and females throughout adolescence and into early adulthood (Erol & Orth, 2011).

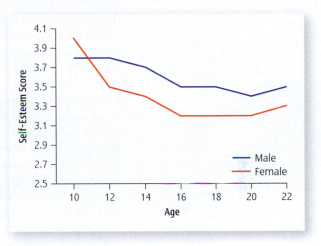

FIGURE 5.2

Trends in Self-Esteem by Gender

Source: Data from Robins and Trzesniewski, 2005.

When we move away from global self-esteem and consider gender differences in specific domains, we do find fairly consistent gender differences. For example, boys generally feel better about their physical attributes (i.e., appearance, athletic ability) than adolescent girls do (Harter, 2006; Ruble, Martin, & Berenbaum, 2006). Adolescent girls, in contrast, tend to feel better than boys about their social skills (Harter, 2006). A **meta-analysis** of self-esteem studies found that males scored higher than females on physical appearance, athletic, and self-satisfaction self-esteem, but females scored higher than males on behavioral conduct and moral-ethical self-esteem (Gentile et al., 2009).

There is also a considerable amount of research that has focused on gender differences in the academic domain. The identity-related research has examined gender differences in self-efficacy beliefs and academic self-concept. Regarding self-efficacy, most of the evidence indicates that adolescent boys are more confident in their mathematical abilities than are adolescent girls, despite not performing better in their mathematics classes (Huang, 2013; Pajares, 2005). In contrast, research has either revealed no gender differences in adolescents' self-efficacy for language arts (Pajares & Valiente, 1999) or slight differences favoring girls (Huang, 2013), despite the fact that girls generally outperform boys in their language arts classes.

Research on gender differences in academic self-concept has often found stereotypical gender differences, with girls having higher self-beliefs in language arts and boys feeling better about their abilities in math (e.g., Fredricks & Eccles, 2002; Marsh & Yeung, 1998). Eccles (1987) reported that these gender differences first emerged in early adolescence and that the differences between boys and girls grew throughout the high school years. More recently, however, research has indicated that differences between the self-concepts of boys and girls in math, language arts, and sports appear well before adolescence, and that the gender differences do not grow wider during adolescence (Jacobs et al., 2002). In fact, gender differences in math self-concept largely disappeared in high school.

Vulnerabilities of Adolescent Boys

Much of our discussion so far has focused on the challenges of adolescent girls (e.g., stereotype threat, lower levels of global self-esteem). But adolescent boys also experience a number of identity-related challenges, many of them centered around the idea of what it means to be masculine. As mentioned earlier, many people, especially the peers of adolescents, react particularly negatively to adolescent boys who behave in stereotypically female ways. There are many examples of adolescent boys and early adults being punished for behaving in stereotypically feminine ways or from being encouraged to "man up" and behave in more masculine ways. For example, a **transgender** teen, Gwen Araujo, was murdered in California when some men she was with discovered she was anatomically male. A similar tale was told in the movie *Boys Don't Cry* that dramatized the real-life story, and murder, of Brandon Teena. In one high-profile story involving professional football players, Jonathan Martin was allegedly bullied by his teammate, Richie Incognito, for not being tough enough. In another story that received a lot of media attention, freshmen on a high school football team were assaulted by older players on the team as part of a violent hazing ritual (Schweber, Barker, & Grant, 2014).

All of these incidents, and countless others that have not seen the light of media attention, indicate that adolescent boys are often pressured to equate masculinity with being tough, disregarding their own feelings and those of others, and sometimes being violent, either as a method of making others see them as more masculine or as a reaction to having one's own masculinity compromised. What are the consequences of defining masculinity in these terms? According to several recent books, when society equates manhood with being tough and ignoring the emotions of the self and others, there is a cost to both adolescent boys and the communities in which they live. For example, in the book *Lost Boys*, Garbarino (1999) argues that parents and teachers who ignore signs of trouble among adolescent boys, such as a callous attitude toward others, may pave the way for later violent behavior. Similarly, in the book *Raising Cain: Protecting the Emotional Life of Boys*, Thompson and Kindlon (2009) argue that socializing boys to be stoic and neglect their emotions puts many boys at risk for developing depression, anger, and potentially destructive behavior toward themselves and others. Although we have long known, both from research and our own observations, that adolescent boys and young men often pay a price for behaving in stereotypically feminine ways, it is now becoming clear that there is also a price to be paid for defining manhood and masculinity in a manner that suppresses the feeling and expression of emotions, empathy, and caring.

Gender Identity by Ethnic Group

It is important to note that gender roles and gender identity differ for various cultural and ethnic groups. Several researchers have noted that there is a difference in the gender-specific expectations of more traditional cultures as compared with more Western, affluent cultures. For example, in more traditional cultures, adolescent males and females are expected to spend their time in quite different ways. Whereas females are expected to take on more of the home and childcare responsibilities as they move into adolescence and early adulthood, adolescent and young-adult males often experience a broadening of their social and experiential worlds. This can include going off to work or school and spending more time with male peers than with their families (Schlegal & Hewlett, 2011). Relatedly, as adolescent girls in traditional cultures develop physically and become sexually attractive to males, their roles often become more tightly restricted. In contrast, as adolescent boys become sexually mature, they are often afforded more freedoms and exposed to a broader world (Larson, Wilson, & Rickman, 2009; Regan, Durvasula, Howell, Ureno, & Rea, 2004).

Within the United States, there are also differences between ethnic and cultural groups in the gender roles and gender-role identities of adolescents. For example, some research has found that African American female adolescents and young adults are more likely than their White peers to have more androgynous gender-role identities that combine self-reliant traits with strong characteristics of nurturance and expressiveness (Basow & Rubin, 1999). Although White adolescent and young-adult females are likely to have more liberal views about their gender roles in the home, the history of repression and economic difficulties may explain why it is common for African American adolescent girls and women to develop complex identities that include independent agency combined with their role as anchors of family life (hooks, 1981; Ward, 1996).

Social and economic history in the United States has also influenced the gender-role identities of African American and Hispanic adolescent males. Belittling racism and economic injustice have made it difficult for many African American and Hispanic men to fulfill traditional male roles as providers for their families and as respected members of society. The frequent slights and humiliations of racism and economic struggle, combined with traditional views of masculinity, may lead to the adoption of extremely masculine gender identities that include an emphasis on being tough and aggressive, and suppression of vulnerable emotions (Hall, 2009; Stevenson, 2004). Examples of these extreme masculine gender roles can be found from popular culture (e.g., rap lyrics that frequently reference toughness and violence) to high rates of gang affiliation in low-income African American and Hispanic neighborhoods. The influence of cultural and ethnic experiences and values on gender roles and gender identity in adolescence is clear.

What Educators Can Do

Over the last half century, there have been tremendous changes in U.S. gender stereotypes and gender roles. Whereas in the past adolescent girls were generally socialized to become nurturing caregivers and men were socialized to be competitive and ambitious providers, today most women are in the workforce, and men are often actively involved in childrearing. Despite these changes, children and adolescents are still socialized by their parents, peers, teachers, and society to think of themselves within gender-specific roles, and there are social costs for behaving in non-gender-conforming ways. One implication of these gender stereotypes is that adolescent students, particularly girls, may steer away from certain areas of study and work (i.e., STEM fields), despite having talent in those areas. Another implication is that adolescent boys may be socialized to avoid feeling and expressing caring and empathetic emotions, or to ostracize and humiliate those boys who do express such emotions. Teachers should be aware of, and actively confront, these stereotypes so that students are able to develop beliefs and aspirations that are aligned with their abilities rather than with stereotypes about the abilities of their gender. Teachers who work to minimize and counteract, rather than perpetuate and transmit, stereotypical gender beliefs will help their adolescent students develop gender identities that are compatible with positive academic self-concept in any domain and reduce the anxiety, ostracization, and potential physical harm associated with behaving in ways that do not conform to rigid gender stereotypes. Here are a few specific strategies:

- *Help students see how their values can be realized in careers they may not have considered (e.g., engineering for girls).* Despite performing as well as boys in high school math and science classes, and recognizing the value of these fields, girls are much less likely than boys to pursue college majors and careers in math, physics, computer science, and engineering (Eccles, 2007). One important reason for this decision is that many girls and young women do not believe these fields will allow them to pursue their values, such as working in careers that will allow them to help others (e.g., medicine, counseling, teaching; Eccles, 2007). Such beliefs are usually based on an incomplete understanding of the nature of these fields. For example, a fundamental goal of most engineering programs is teaching students how to design products that solve important human problems. Helping students understand how their own values can be realized in fields they may not have considered can help adolescents solve the difficult problem of integrating their social identities (e.g., gender, ethnicity) with their academic identities.

- *Encourage students to pursue courses and careers that they may not pursue on their own.* Sometimes, adolescents simply need caring adults to encourage them to persist in an academic subject or develop future academic identities. There are several anecdotes from successful scholars who were strongly encouraged by a teacher to think of themselves as college material and to develop high academic goals (e.g., Jordan-Irvine, 2008; Walker, 2008). Some have argued that there are so few women in math and physics majors and careers simply because they have not been encouraged by teachers and professors to persist in these male-dominated fields (Pollack, 2013). In recent years there has been an explosion of charter schools that have the mission of encouraging and supporting low-income students to graduate from high school and gain admission to college, perhaps best exemplified by the **Knowledge Is Power Program (KIPP)** schools (Mathews, 2009).

  Effective encouragement must go beyond the occasional pat on the back. It must be mindful of the challenges some students face. For example, girls in math and physical sciences may benefit from opportunities to engage in these activities away from boys, perhaps through camps or discussion groups. In addition, encouragement needs to be accompanied by support as students struggle to develop positive academic identities. For example, encouraging low-income students to think of themselves as future college graduates would be ineffective if it were not accompanied by long hours of instructional support and college counseling.

- *Reduce and counteract the effects of negative stereotypes and stereotype threat.* Researchers and educators have tried a few strategies to reduce the negative effects of stereotype threat. One strategy is to make frequent use of role models who defy the stereotypes (e.g., women who are mathematicians or scientists, professionals from modest backgrounds who excelled in college, etc.). Providing students from stereotyped groups with frequent opportunities to meet, learn about, and be mentored by adults who defy the stereotypes but are from similar backgrounds as the students can help reduce the effects of stereotype threat (Marx & Roman, 2002; McIntryre et al., 2003).

- Keep in mind that role models are most effective when students can relate to them. If possible, use role models that are similar to students in ethnicity, gender, and background.

- Another approach to breaking the cycle of anxiety and self-doubt caused by stereotype threat is to reduce the threat. One way to do this is to have members of the stereotyped group remind themselves of what they value (i.e., values affirmation) before taking tests (Miyake et al., 2010). Similarly, presenting students with evidence that counteracts the stereotype, such as stories about high-achieving members of stereotyped groups, can reduce the effects of stereotype threat. In addition, helping students develop the mindset that academic ability is something that can grow (i.e., is not a fixed trait) can reduce the negative effects of stereotype threat (Aronson, Fried, & Good, 2002).

Gender socialization is strong in adolescence and can influence how male and female students perceive the value of different academic subjects and the career pathways that are available to them. By making yourself aware of gender-identity processes, how they influence the values and perceptions of your students, and what you can do to counteract harmful gender stereotypes, you can help your students develop gender identities that are broad and encompass a wider variety of academic and career pathways.

MyEdLab **Self-Check 5.3**

Ethnic and Cultural Identity

Many teachers and school communities feel that issues of race and ethnicity are the third rail of education. These are hot-button issues for many students and teachers, rife with political overtones and a history of discrimination in the United States. But for many students, particularly members of ethnic minority groups, ethnic identity is an integral part of overall self-concept that influences many aspects of life, including education. Consider the following example:

>>>

At the beginning of a unit on immigration to the United States around 1900, Ms. Wilson asks her students to write a brief essay about their own family history and where their relatives emigrated from when they came to the United States. As part of this assignment, she asks students to reflect upon their connection to their families' native cultures and to think about how their relatives handled the cultural transition to life in the United States. Erika, a Caucasian student, was stumped by the assignment. "What do you mean?" she asked Ms. Wilson. "My family is American. We've never really talked about where we came from before. I have no idea what to write about."

For many Caucasian adolescents in the United States, as for adolescents in the ethnic majority in other countries, their ethnic identity is not a particularly salient feature of their overall identity (Cross, 1995). In other words, most adolescents in the ethnic majority spend little time thinking about their ethnicity. But for students from ethnic and cultural[1] minority groups, ethnic identity is often a

---

[1] Ethnicity and culture are different. Ethnicity refers to racial heritage, and culture refers to shared customs, beliefs, and behaviors among groups of people. There is often considerable overlap between these two constructs, and in this chapter we refer to both somewhat interchangeably.

very important aspect of overall self-concept. In this chapter, we focus primarily on the ethnic identity of adolescents in the United States and other countries who are not members of the ethnic or cultural majority in the countries in which they reside.

Definition and Developmental Models of Cultural and Ethnic Identity

Ethnic identity refers to how individuals think about and define themselves in terms of their connection to their ethnic heritage. Although there are subtle differences between ethnic, racial, and **cultural identity**, for the purposes of this chapter we use the term *ethnic identity* and assume that it incorporates elements of race, ethnicity, and culture. In this manner, adolescents from the same racial group (e.g., Hispanic) may differ in their ethnic identity due to differences in the families' countries of origin (e.g., Guatemala versus Mexico) and to other factors, such as how many generations of the family have lived in the United States (Hudley & Irving, 2012).

Most current conceptions of ethnic identity recognize that it is a multidimensional construct. The Multidimensional Model of Racial Identity (MMRI) includes four dimensions that represent the content of identity at a given point in time (Rivas-Drake, Hughes, & Way, 2008; Sellers et al., 1998). Two of these dimensions focus on the importance of race/ethnicity in the overall definition of the self. Specifically, **salience** refers to how conscious a person is of her ethnicity in a given situation. For example, a Latina woman who may be the only Latina in her college classroom is likely to be acutely aware of her ethnicity in that situation but may not think about her ethnicity at all when at home. **Centrality** refers to the place of one's ethnic identity in his or her overall identity. For example, many Caucasian adolescents would place their ethnicity at the end of a long list of personally important attributes, after more central characteristics such as gender, roles (student, friend, athlete), and personality characteristics. In contrast, an African American adolescent may feel that his ethnicity is a more central feature of his self-definition. Whereas salience is a perception that fluctuates with the situation, centrality is a more stable aspect of ethnic identity.

The other two dimensions of ethnic identity are **regard** and **ideology**. These dimensions involve the subjective value judgments of one's ethnic identity. Regard refers both to how one feels about her ethnic group (e.g., "I am proud of the accomplishments of my ethnic group") and to her perceptions of how others view her ethnic group (e.g., "Other people hold negative stereotypes about the academic abilities of my ethnic group"). The fourth dimension of ethnic identity, ideology, refers to beliefs one has about how members of his ethnic group should think and behave. For example, the belief that members of one's ethnic group should not date or marry members of other ethnic groups represents the ideology dimension of ethnic identity. Similarly, the idea expressed by some African American adolescents that performing well in school was akin to **acting White** and therefore subject to ridicule and ostracism (Fordham & Ogbu, 1986) is another example of the ideology dimension of ethnic identity. Table 5.5 summarizes these dimensions of ethnic identity.

There are a number of theories regarding how individuals develop their ethnic identities. Several of these have adopted stage models, much like the general identity model of Erikson (1968) discussed earlier in this chapter or the cognitive development stage model of Piaget (Piaget & Inhelder, 1969; discussed in Chapter 3 of this book). For example, Quintana (1998) argued that ethnic identity unfolds across four stages that are closely tied to cognitive development. Young children are aware of their ethnicity based on physical cues

TABLE 5.5	**Dimensions of Ethnic Identity**			
	DIMENSIONS			
	Salience	Centrality	Regard	Ideology
Definition	How conscious one is of his or her ethnicity in a given situation	How important one's ethnicity is to one's overall self-definition and identity	How one feels (positively or negatively) about one's ethnic group; one's beliefs about how others judge one's ethnic group	One's beliefs about how members of his or her ethnic group should think and behave

(e.g., skin color, hair type), but are unaware of the social construction of race and ethnicity. As they move into middle childhood, however, children begin to recognize race and ethnicity as social labels that are associated with certain behaviors (e.g., ways of speaking) and customs in addition to physical features. Early adolescents begin to understand the consequences of belonging to various ethnic groups as they become aware of stereotypes, differential status between ethnic groups, and discrimination. Finally, in mid-adolescence, as teenagers are beginning to integrate the various aspects of their identities, they develop an awareness of what their own ethnic group's values are and the importance of their ethnicity in their overall identity.

Phinney (1996) presented a model of ethnic-identity development that was more closely aligned with the identity theory of Marcia (1980). In her view, the development of ethnic identity involves two dimensions: *exploration* and *commitment*. **Exploration** involves seeking out information about the beliefs, behaviors, values, and mannerisms of one's ethnic group. **Commitment** refers to the importance of one's ethnicity to one's sense of self. According to Phinney, ethnic identity unfolds during adolescence in a three-stage process. First, adolescents are in an unexamined ethnic-identity stage in which they have not really considered what their ethnic identity means. Next, they enter a stage of searching for information about the values, beliefs, behaviors, and status of their ethnic group, and consider how salient their ethnic identity is to their sense of self. Finally, after the search phase, adolescents and early adults move into the achieved stage of ethnic-identity development. In this stage individuals have a clear sense of what their ethnic group is and how important their ethnicity is to them (Hudley & Irving, 2012).

The development of a clear ethnic identity may depend on encountering certain **triggers** (Cross, 1971; Cross & Vandiver, 2001; Helms & Cook, 1999). One may not really think about her ethnic identity until she encounters a racist comment or finds herself to be the only member of her ethnic group in a room full of people. For Caucasian adolescents, most of whom have infrequent experiences of prejudice and attend schools that are majority Caucasian, such encounters may be rare, and there will be little need to deeply explore their ethnic identity. For adolescents who are members of ethnic minorities, however, these triggers are quite common. Experiences of racial discrimination, either directly or indirectly through media portrayals, occur frequently for ethnic-minority adolescents. As a result, minority adolescents are forced to engage in the search stage of ethnic-identity development. Ethnic identity is often a much more salient part of the overall identity of adolescents from ethnic-minority groups than it is for Caucasian adolescents (Fuligni, Witkow & Garcia, 2005).

How salient is your ethnic identity to you? How do you think the centrality and feelings about your own ethnic identity will help or hinder your ability to understand the role that ethnic identity might play in your students' engagement and achievement in school?

Integrating Multi-Ethnic Identities

>>>

"Growing up, I always went to private schools that were almost all White, and all of my friends were White. I knew that my family was Indian, and that I was Indian, but I never really thought about it. I pretty much thought of myself as White. Then one day at the end of high school, some of my friends started making fun of me, talking about how dark I am and using these exaggerated Indian accents. It was the first time that I realized that they saw me as different from them. I felt like I was not connected to them in the way that I thought I was. But I also felt like it was too late to really feel connected to my Indian culture. I didn't really feel like I fully belonged in either culture; that I would not be accepted by either one. I still don't feel like I belong to either one. I am not White enough and I am not Indian enough."

—"Sam," age 21

Adolescents who are members of ethnic-minority groups are confronted with a complex identity problem: how to coordinate aspects of their families' ethnic culture with aspects of the dominant culture in the society in which they live (Phinney & Devich-Navarro, 1997). For example, an African American adolescent must figure out what it means to him to be African American and how that part of his identity fits within the cultural norms of the larger society in which he lives (Ogbu, 1992). Of course, these judgments will be influenced by a number of social factors, including information from his family about what it means to belong to his ethnic group, messages from his peers, and how he is treated and portrayed by various people (e.g., teachers, police, store clerks, etc.) and media (e.g., television, magazines, music) in society (Gitlin, Buendia, Crosland, & Doumbia, 2003).

Several scholars have examined how adolescents and early adults have tried to combine different cultural and ethnic identities (Berry, 1990, 2006; Berry, Phinney, Sam, & Vedder, 2006; LaFromboise, Coleman, & Gerton, 1993; Phelan, Davidson, & Cao, 1991; Phinney, 1992; Phinney & Devich-Navarro, 1997). Most models have identified several patterns of ethnic identity formation that include some combination of the following:

- **Full assimilation**, in which the ethnic-minority individual identifies fully with the dominant culture in society;
- **Full separation**, in which the ethnic-minority individual identifies fully with his or her ethnic group and not at all with the dominant culture in society;
- **Bicultural identity**, in which the ethnic-minority individual either views him- or herself as having an identity that blends his or her ethnic culture with the dominant societal culture or he or she "switches" between the two cultures in different situations; and
- **Marginalized**, in which the ethnic-minority individual does not feel like he or she identifies with either the ethnic culture or the dominant culture in society.

These different patterns of ethnic identity are presented in Figure 5.3.

The type of ethnic identity that adolescents from minority groups develop has implications for a range of outcomes, including mental health, physical health, peer-group affiliation, career aspirations, and academic achievement.

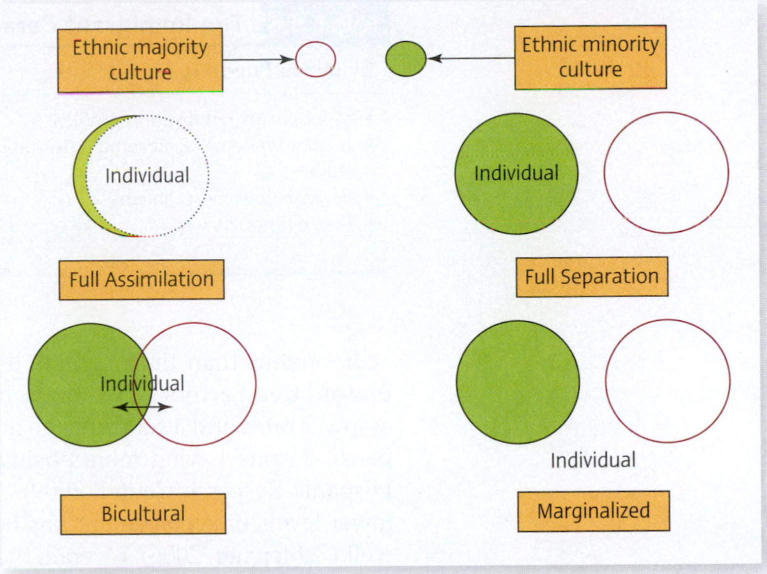

For example, it can be quite distressing for adolescents and early adults, as in the example of "Sam" presented earlier, when they feel like they are not fully accepted by, or do not belong to, either their own ethnic group or the dominant cultural group in society (i.e., marginalized). On the other hand, there can be benefits for those who are able to maintain a strong connection to their native culture while also taking advantage of the affordances made possible by adapting to the cultural norms and values in societal institutions such as schools (e.g., bicultural identity; Gibson, 1988; Ogbu, 1992; Suarez-Orozco & Suarez-Orozco, 1995). The balancing act of trying to fit into contexts that emphasize different cultural values can be quite challenging, for a couple of the reasons discussed earlier in this chapter. First, as adolescents switch their behaviors to adapt to the cultural norms of different contexts, they can experience the confusing feelings associated with the **false self** and be confronted with the challenge of trying to decide which self is real. Second, the self is not static; it changes with time and experience. As ethnic-minority adolescents become more adapted to dominant cultural values and norms, they may grow more distant from their native ethnic values and behaviors (Gonzalez, Fabrett, & Knight, 2009; Padilla, 2006).

This process of becoming more familiar with the beliefs and behaviors of the dominant culture is known as **acculturation**, and it has both benefits and costs. For example, the children of immigrant parents in the United States are often fluent speakers of English from an early age, and this provides them with a better opportunity to succeed in school. But language provides a critical connection to one's culture, and many immigrant parents in the United States. lament that their children speak English more than they use their native language, becoming less connected to the family's native culture as a result. There is also evidence that with each successive generation in the United States, adolescents become more likely to identify themselves using some form of American label (e.g., Mexican American) than a non-American label (e.g., Mexican) (Fuligni et al., 2005). Some research has found that immigrant children, compared to their native-born peers of the same ethnic background, are less likely to be diagnosed with significant behavioral problems (Jutte, Burgos, Mendoza, Ford, & Huffman, 2003) or to engage in antisocial or delinquent behavior (Rumbaut, 1997). The pattern of positive outcomes among immigrants relative to their native-born peers, despite their relative disadvantage (lower income, less fluency in English), has led some researchers to use the term **immigrant paradox** (Coll et al., 2009).

In the area of education, evidence for the immigrant paradox is somewhat mixed. Some have found that immigrant Latino students have more positive motivational profiles than do their native-born peers (Fuligni, 1997; Fuligni & Tseng, 1999; Urdan & Garvey, 2004) and perhaps better achievement in school as well (Coll et al., 2009; Suarez-Orozco & Suarez-Orozco, 1995). Yet there is other research indicating that native-born Hispanic children have higher levels of academic

FIGURE 5.3

Varieties of Assimilation and Accommodation

TABLE 5.6	The Immigrant Paradox: Does the Evidence Support it?
Evidence Favoring Immigrants	**Evidence Favoring Non-immigrants**
• More positive motivation profiles • Higher academic achievement (in some studies) • Fewer behavioral problems • Less delinquency	• Higher graduation rates • More likely to attend college • Higher academic achievement than their parents • Higher academic achievement than immigrants (in some studies)

achievement than their parents did (Waldinger & Feliciano, 2004), indicating an upward trend across generations. In addition, immigrant children tend to graduate at lower rates and attend college at lower rates as compared with their native-born peers, despite having more positive attitudes about school (McMillan, 1997; Pew Hispanic Research Center, 2009). A similar pattern of more positive attitudes but lower levels of achievement has been found for immigrants in other countries as well (Schleicher, 2006). Overall, the evidence for the "immigrant paradox" is mixed (see Table 5.6).

It is also important to note that many adolescents are not a single race or ethnicity (e.g., Black, White, Hispanic). Data from the 2010 U.S. Census reveal that the number of **multiracial** children in the United States increased 50% compared to 10 years earlier, making this the fastest-growing ethnic group in the country (Saulney, 2011). According to projections from the U.S. Census Bureau, the percentage of Americans who identify themselves as **mixed race** will grow from 2.4% in 2012 to 6.4% in 2060 (U.S. Census, 2012). Similarly to single-race adolescents, multiracial adolescents are theorized to develop their ethnic identity in a stage-like progression from low awareness to a searching phase and finally to a stage of ethnic identification. Unlike single-race adolescents, however, multiracial adolescents are also faced with the opportunity to choose which ethnicity to identify with most strongly (Root, 1998). Whereas some multiracial adolescents may choose to identify most strongly with a single ethnicity (e.g., African American or Caucasian), others may strongly identify themselves as **biracial**, and still others may not identify with race at all (Rockquemore & Brunsma, 2002). There is also evidence that compared to mono-racial college students, multiracial students are more aware that race is socially constructed (rather than biologically determined), and their academic performance is less susceptible to stereotype activation (Shih, Bonam, Sanchez, & Peck, 2007).

Ethnic Identity and Education

What is the connection between ethnic identity and academic achievement and engagement for adolescent students? The answer to this question involves a complex comingling of several factors. How strongly does the adolescent identify with her ethnic group? What are the societal stereotypes about the academic abilities of her ethnic group? Are most of the other students in her school of the same or different ethnicity than her? What does her school do, if anything, to reduce potential barriers between her ethnic identity and her academic self-concept? And how do her peers and family support her academic efforts and ambitions?

One useful framework for thinking about the association between ethnic identity and academic outcomes such as achievement and effort was offered by Phelan and her colleagues (Phelan, Davidson & Cao, 1991; Phelan et al., 1994).

MyEdLab
Video Example 5.3
This teen recognizes that "there are certain things that people expect" from Asian children. Try to identify where she is in the process of her ethnic identity development and how stereotypes about her ethnic group may affect her self-perceptions and behavior.

They argued that the different contexts in which adolescents operate daily—school, family, peer groups—represent different worlds (see Figure 5.4). For some students, the borders between these worlds are small and porous, so it is easy to move between them. For example, many middle-class Caucasian students have highly educated parents who encourage and support their children's academic aspirations and achievement. They also attend schools where most of the teachers and other students are Caucasian and where behaviors and values that are common among middle-class Caucasians in the United States are promoted, such as certain ways of speaking and faith that getting a good educa-

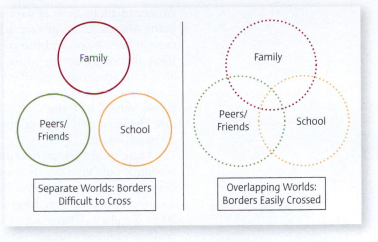

FIGURE 5.4

Model of Multiple Worlds and Boundaries

tion will result in a good career and high life satisfaction. These students tend to associate with peers and friends who share these values and behaviors. The similarity of cultural values and behaviors across these worlds allows middle-class Caucasian adolescents to move between them easily, with little friction or need for cultural adjustment.

For comparison, consider the case of low-income Latino adolescents attending a majority-Latino high school. Many of the students attending this school may have parents who immigrated to the U.S. from Mexico or a Central American country. They may speak mostly Spanish at home and live in neighborhoods with relatively few college graduates. Most of the teachers in the school are Caucasian, and students are not allowed to speak Spanish in their classes. The values promoted by the school of independent accomplishment and attending a prestigious university on the path to prestigious careers are not necessarily shared by many of the adolescents' peers in the school. And some of the more traditional beliefs that their parents have about how adolescents should behave are undermined by the more liberal attitudes toward dress, dating, and respect for adults promoted in popular U.S. culture. For many of the adolescents in this school, the borders between family, school, and peer worlds are difficult to cross because the values and norms differ in each world, so adolescents are forced to either reject one or more of these worlds or become adept at quickly adapting to the norms and values of each context as they move through them daily.

In the 1980s and 1990s, researchers generally focused on the difficulties some cultural and ethnic groups experienced in school. In their articulation of **segmented assimilation theory**, Portes and Zhou (1993; see also Portes & Rumbaut, 1996, 2001) argued that many immigrant families in the United States live in low-income neighborhoods with few models of high academic achievement or career success. Rather than assimilating with the dominant American culture and adopting the dominant cultural values (i.e., the American Dream), many immigrant families become acculturated to the beliefs, values, and behaviors of an underclass that is resistant to the majority values of high academic achievement and college aspirations. Instead of striving for success as typically defined by mainstream Americans, adolescents who engage in **downward assimilation** disdain hard work in school. Ogbu (1992; Fordham & Ogbu, 1986) made a similar argument regarding African American adolescents. According to his theory, a history of discrimination has led many African American youth to develop a stance toward academic achievement that is in direct opposition to the values of middle-class Caucasians. Trying to do well in school, according to Ogbu and his colleagues, is often perceived by African

American adolescents as a form of selling out and trying to "act White." As a result, many African Americans are actively discouraged by their peers from trying to succeed academically, and the costs of academic striving are too high. According to these theories, a strong ethnic identity would be predicted to be *negatively* associated with academic aspirations and achievement. After all, if doing well in school is perceived to be turning one's back on one's ethnic values in favor of mainstream White values, a strong connection to one's ethnicity would lead African American, Hispanic, and other oppressed ethnic groups away from embracing academic accomplishment.

More recent research examining the association between ethnic identity and academic outcomes paints a somewhat different picture. For example, there is evidence that adolescents who have positive feelings about their ethnic group and a strong ethnic identity have more positive attitudes about school (Fuligni et al., 2005). Similarly, Chavous and her colleagues (2003) found that ethnic identity was positively related to academic motivation and persistence among African American adolescents. A number of scholars have examined whether certain ethnic groups really do have oppositional positions against academic achievement, as Ogbu, Portes, and their colleagues suggested. More often than not, this research has found little evidence to support these claims. Specifically, research evidence indicates that, on average, there are no differences between students of various ethnic groups in their valuing of academic achievement or feelings about school (Ainsworth-Darnell & Downey, 1998; Cook & Ludwig, 1998).

It appears that the association between ethnic identity and school-related variables is too difficult to capture with blanket statements about whole ethnic groups. Rather, it may depend on the confluence of several different variables. For example, Portes and Fernandez-Kelly (2008) found that second-generation youth (i.e., children born in the United States to parents who were immigrants) were both more successful in school and able to maintain a strong ethnic identity when their parents were highly educated and when they lived in multi-ethnic neighborhoods. Similarly, research with low-income Latino adolescents revealed that students who developed an ethnic identification with both the larger society and their home culture had relatively high academic achievement (Altschul, Oyserman, & Bybee, 2008). In general, research indicates that maintaining some connection with one's native culture and having positive regard for one's ethnic group are associated with positive educational outcomes for a variety of ethnic groups, but these associations depend on other factors such as the socioeconomic status of the family, the socialization practices of the parents, and the home obligations of the adolescent students (Fuligni & Tseng, 1999).

Although much of the emphasis in research and the media regarding adolescents who adopt a negative stance toward academic achievement has focused on minority youth, it is important to note that White students often regard school as a waste of time. In a landmark ethnographic study of adolescent life in a housing project, Jay MacLeod (2009) described two groups of adolescent boys who lived in the project. The Hallway Hangers was a group of mostly White boys who spent their days drinking and hanging out in the project. As a group, the members of the Hallway Hangers had largely given up on education and believed that, even with a high school diploma, they were destined for the kinds of menial labor that required little education anyway. Many members of this group had dropped out of school, and they largely rejected the ideal of the American Dream as a hoax. In contrast, a predominately African American group of adolescent boys, the Brothers, held fast to the belief that education was the key to improving employment opportunities and their station in life. They had disdain for the attitudes and behaviors of the Hallway Hangers and tried to stay away from them as much as they could. These two groups of adolescent boys, who shared a housing project but little else, serve as a reminder that sweeping generalizations about the achievement beliefs and behaviors of certain racial and economic groups can distract us from the wide variability within these groups.

Ethnic Identity and Stereotype Threat

There is also research indicating that the association between ethnic identity and academic outcomes may depend on stereotype threat activation (see Figure 5.5). As discussed earlier in the section on gender identity, stereotype threat involves the performance inhibition that can result in situations where individuals may confirm a negative stereotype about their group (Steele, 1997; Steele & Aronson, 1995). For certain ethnic minority groups (e.g., Hispanics and African Americans in the United States, Koreans in Japan, Turkish students in the Netherlands), there are negative stereotypes in the society about the academic abilities of students from those groups. When students who are members of these ethnic groups have a strong sense of ethnic identity and are in situations in which the stereotypes about their ethnic group are activated, such as being in a college classroom with mostly White and Asian American students, achievement can suffer (Armenta, 2010; Guyll, Madon, Prieto, & Scherr, 2010). There is also some evidence that students in those situations (e.g., high-achieving Latino students in a mostly White university) may subconsciously separate their ethnic identities from their academic self-concepts (Urdan & Morris, 2010). It is important for teachers to find ways to minimize stereotype threat. The methods for doing this that were described earlier regarding gender stereotypes can also work to reduce the negative effects of stereotype threat for different ethnic groups.

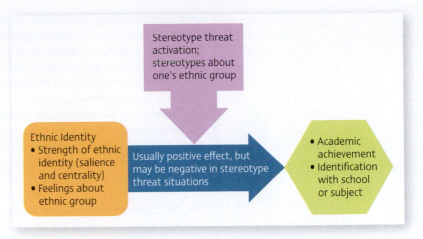

FIGURE 5.5

Associations Among Ethnic Identity, Stereotype Threat, and Academic Outcomes

What Educators Can Do

Ethnic identity is a multidimensional construct that includes how salient one's ethnicity is in a given situation, how central a part of one's overall identity his or her ethnic identity is, how positively one feels about one's ethnic group, and beliefs about how members of one's ethnic group should think and behave. For adolescents in the cultural or ethnic majority, ethnicity is not usually a salient feature of the situation and not a central feature of one's overall self-concept. But for members of ethnic-minority groups, ethnic identity is often a very salient and central part of overall identity. As adolescents from ethnic-minority groups try to coordinate the values of their ethnic group with those of the dominant cultural group in society, they are often confronted with choices about how to behave and what they should value that can have profound consequences for their social relationships with family and peers and can influence academic engagement, achievement, and aspirations. Educators should be mindful of the challenges many students face when navigating the boundaries between their cultural worlds of family, peers, and school and create strategies for helping students develop healthy academic self-concepts while maintaining a strong ethnic identity. In addition, educators should be aware of the ways that stereotypes about different ethnic groups can undermine academic engagement and performance, and take steps to reduce the activation of these stereotypes. Such steps can include providing students with information about how well members

MyEdLab
Video Example 5.4

As this teacher learned from a student, respecting a student's culture is very different than expecting a student to have particular interests, skills, or behaviors simply because he or she has a particular cultural background.

of their ethnic group perform on academic tasks, telling students about the effects of stereotype threat on performance, and minimizing references to differences in academic performance related to ethnicity or ethnic group. (Strategies for reducing the effects of stereotype threat are essentially the same as those for stereotypes about race or gender, and several were presented earlier when discussing gender identity.)

In addition to reducing the negative effects of stereotype threat, teachers can engage strategies to help students of various ethnicities deepen their feelings of belonging in school, promote positive feelings of ethnic and cultural identity for all students, and increase their chances of success. Here are some of those strategies:

- *Help adolescent students develop positive academic self-perceptions.* For teachers, perhaps the most important aspect of identity development during adolescence is how students come to think of themselves in the academic domain, both currently and in the future. For a variety of reasons that we have discussed earlier in the chapter, many adolescents do not think of themselves as good students, are only weakly identified with the academic domain (i.e., their academic self is not an important part of their overall self-concept), have difficulty developing a positive or successful academic future self, or have ruled out certain areas of study that they might enjoy and be good at. Some of these reasons include a history of low achievement in school, leading to low self-efficacy and poor academic self-concept; negative stereotypes about their group and the associated effects of stereotype threat that these produce; a lack of academically successful role models to whom the student can relate; and the devaluing of certain subjects, domains, and careers because of a perceived lack of fit with one's current values or future goals. As teachers try to help all of their students develop positive academic identities, it is important to be aware of the many barriers students face in developing such identities.
- *History of low achievement:* Adolescents with a history of academic difficulties often develop low self-efficacy for school and poor academic self-concept. Over time, these negative self-perceptions can reduce the centrality of students' academic identities to their overall self-concept. To improve self-efficacy and academic self-concept, students should be provided with genuine opportunities to succeed (Pintrich & Schunk, 2002). Here are three strategies for doing this:
    - Break larger tasks down into smaller, more manageable pieces. Struggling students often find assignments too challenging and give up in frustration. Breaking assignments down into smaller pieces can be less daunting and can provide students with several little victories, thereby improving self-efficacy (Pajares, 1997; Schunk & Swartz, 1993).
    - Provide more **scaffolding**. Students who lack confidence often want and need more support. Using a combination of online resources and face-to-face tutoring, struggling students can get the support they need to begin succeeding and gaining confidence.
    - Implement a peer-tutoring program. Research suggests that students can benefit from being tutored by peers, and this is a good way to support struggling students without overwhelming teachers (Kunsch, Jitendra, & Sood, 2007). There is also very interesting evidence that low-achieving middle school students gain skill, confidence, and an increase in identification with school when they are involved in tutoring elementary school children (e.g., Coca Cola Valued Youth Program).

- *Encourage development of a positive future academic self.* For many students, the absence of academically successful role models at home and in their neighborhoods makes it difficult to develop a vision of themselves as academically successful high school or college students. This may be particularly true for adolescents whose peers openly devalue academic effort and achievement. To help such students develop positive future academic selves, Oyserman et al. (2002) developed a 9-week after-school program to help at-risk African American middle school students develop positive academic future selves. Key features of the program included helping students think about what kinds of future academic selves they would like to attain, helping students view their social identity as congruent with a positive academic identity, identifying potential obstacles on the path to attaining positive academic future selves, and developing strategies for overcoming these obstacles. By the end of the program, students felt more connected to school and had developed strategies for attaining positive academic future selves. They also had better school attendance and fewer behavioral problems in school. A similar project conducted with Hispanic and African American eighth graders produced additional benefits, including improved test scores and grades and lower levels of depression, effects that persisted for at least 2 years (Oyserman, Bybee, & Terry, 2006).

- *Provide opportunities for students to integrate academic and ethnic identities.* Some students perceive that the barriers between the various worlds in which they operate (e.g., home, peer, school) are high and difficult to overcome (Arunkumar & Midgley, 1999; Phelan et al., 1991). Teachers can reduce these barriers by incorporating material from a variety of ethnic groups (e.g., books from authors of several ethnic groups, highlighting the achievements of people from different ethnic groups in math, science, literature, etc.). Teachers can also learn about and incorporate culturally responsive teaching practices (Delpit, 2012; Gay, 2010) that value the ethnic identities of all students and do not favor those of the ethnic or cultural majority.

It is important to note that several of the recommendations in this section are not tied to any particular ethnic or cultural group. Indeed, developing positive academic self-perceptions and feelings of being valued in the classroom is important for all students. But for many students of color, particularly lower-income students, a history of low achievement and feelings of marginalization in school are acute problems that influence how ethnic identity and academic identity influence each other. It is particularly important for teachers who work with minority students to be aware of these issues and to develop and implement strategies that reduce barriers for students in developing positive academic identities and are consistent with positive ethnic identities.

MyEdLab **Self-Check 5.4**

MyEdLab
Application Exercise 5.1
Identity: Where Does It Come From? In this exercise you will have the opportunity to consider where identity comes from and how much socially constructed labels contribute to how adolescents think about and define themselves.

Recommendations for Educators

The development of a coherent sense of self is one of the critical and inevitable tasks of adolescence and early adulthood. It can be a difficult and confusing process for many adolescents. Teachers can help their adolescent students to better understand who they are, who they want to become, and how to integrate the various aspects of their identity with a positive academic self-concept. Throughout this chapter, we have offered suggestions for how teachers can use what we know about the identity-development process, gender identity, and ethnic identity to help their students develop integrated and healthy identities that include positive academic identities. In this section, we offer a brief summary of some of the broad ideas about identity that educators should keep in mind.

The most important step educators should take in helping their adolescent students develop positive and integrated self-systems is to learn about the process of identity development. As we have discussed throughout this chapter, there are certain features of the identity-development process that are important to keep in mind when trying to understand, teach, and inspire adolescent students. Through understanding this process, teachers can develop proactive plans for helping adolescents navigate this sometimes confusing and difficult period of development. In addition, teachers can use their understanding of the identity-formation process to interpret and cope with some challenging behavior. For example, it is useful to know that some students in your class may be disengaged and uninterested because they have decided the subject that you teach does not fit into their future self-perceptions. Similarly, students who are trying on identities such as "class clown" or "authority defiant" may be handled with more patience when teachers realize these are more likely to be temporary personas rather than enduring identities.

Some of the key aspects of identity development during adolescence and early adulthood include the following:

- Many adolescents experiment with different identities and personas.
  - Some of these may include things that are troubling for teachers, such as "too cool for school" or "class clown" or "defiant."
  - These are often temporary and quickly outgrown.
- Some adolescents, particularly those who are not middle-class Caucasian students, may be experiencing difficulties navigating boundaries between family, school, and peer worlds.
- Identity includes current self-perceptions *and* future self-perceptions.
  - How students think about and value what you are teaching in your classroom depends both on how they view themselves now (e.g., "I am not really a math person") and their perceptions of their future identities (e.g., "I don't see myself going to college, so algebra is not really important to me").
- Because identity formation is so active during adolescence, it is an excellent time for teachers to expose students to a variety of possible identity options.
  - Encouraging students to explore various identity options is useful and important.
- Students often differ in their perceived identity options depending on their ethnicity, gender, socioeconomic status, peer socialization processes, and family socialization processes.
- Adolescents often form beliefs about possible future directions for themselves based on limited information or misperceptions.

By understanding the process of identity formation and the complex, multifaceted nature of identity, teachers can better cope with some of the challenging aspects of adolescent identity formation and also help students develop coherent, integrated, and positive identities, both in the present and for the future.

MyEdLab Self-Check 5.5

MyEdLab
Application Exercise 5.2 What Teachers Can Do To Help Immigrant Students In this exercise you will think about what educators can do to help immigrant students succeed in school.

Conclusion

The task of developing an integrated and stable identity that incorporates the self across multiple roles and contexts takes center stage during adolescence. This can present challenges for teenagers and young adults as they try on different identities, struggle with feelings of being phony or unsure of who they really are, and try to meet the demands of different social groups and institutions, many of which have different expectations and demands. It can also be a challenging process for teachers of adolescent and young adult students, as many students develop identities that are at odds with high academic effort and achievement, at least in some academic domains. Fortunately, the search for a clear identity also provides educators with a number of opportunities to help adolescents explore their identity options, develop more positive current and future academic identities, and support students as they overcome challenges to developing academic identities that can produce long-term academic and life benefits. Although the challenges are daunting, the rewards are many.

Jaren Wicklund/Fotolia

6

Families

Learning Outcomes

6.1 You will be able to describe the current circumstances of adolescents and their families in society and why this matters for educators.

6.2 You will be able to describe how adolescence brings about changes in families from a family systems perspective.

6.3 You will be able to compare and contrast the nature and effects of different parenting styles on adolescent development (including cultural and ethnic differences) and the implications for educators.

6.4 You will be able to describe how early attachment affects adolescent development.

6.5 You will be able to describe how emotional, behavioral, and cognitive autonomy develop during adolescence and the implications for educators.

6.6 You will be able to describe the importance of parental involvement in adolescents' learning and what educators can do to increase it, with attention to optimal parental involvement.

Introduction

There is tremendous variability in families, including how they support adolescents' learning and interact with teachers and the school. Compare the following examples of a middle school teacher's experiences with her students and their parents:

>>>

Ms. Drake opens her e-mail to find yet another inquiry from the mother of Maria, one of her eighth-grade students. Maria is a good student, but she is somewhat inconsistent in her performance. She does well on most assignments, but she sometimes doesn't follow directions or turn in all her homework. Ever since Maria's first-quarter report card went home with a B in Algebra, her mother has been relentless in her communication. Maria's mother insists that her daughter is an "A" student. To help her daughter she wants daily updates that go beyond the information on the school-based website where parents can check attendance, homework completion, and exam grades.

Ms. Drake is having a quite different experience with the parents of Robert, another student in the same class. Robert started off the school year doing well in Algebra. However, his attitude and effort have changed recently. He often seems tired in class. He has not been turning in his homework. When Ms. Drake asks him about his homework, he says he doesn't have time. His mom got a new job and he has to take care of his younger siblings after school. On his last exam, Robert got a D. Ms. Drake has left e-mail and phone messages for his parents, but they have not responded.

As Ms. Drake is contemplating how to best reach Robert's parents, she gets an e-mail from the mother of Shaquel, a student in her Pre-Algebra class. Shaquel's mom thanked her for the opportunity to visit the classroom yesterday. Ms. Drake had invited parents via e-mail and print letters to attend class when students would be presenting their group projects. Ms. Drake happened to run into Shaquel and her mom in the office as Shaquel was getting dropped off at school. She took the opportunity to tell Shaquel's mom how much she enjoyed having Shaquel as a student. Shaquel's mom seemed to appreciate the information, and so Ms. Drake reminded her about the opportunity to visit the classroom. Shaquel's mom mentioned in her e-mail that she would not have visited if she had not run into Ms. Drake that day, but she was so glad that she did.

In these examples, we can see that see that the parents of adolescent students can vary a great deal. For teachers, some parents may seem overinvolved and even demanding, whereas others seem absent and hard to reach. Others parents are receptive to suggestions to learn about and support their adolescents' efforts in school. Overall, parents are less involved in middle and high school as compared with elementary school (Hill & Tyson, 2009). However, the vast majority of parents still value communication with teachers and want to support their children's success (Epstein, 1995). Much research indicates that parental involvement increases the chances that an adolescent will be successful at school (Hill & Tyson, 2009; Jeynes, 2007). Given the benefits, it is important for teachers and schools to promote positive parental involvement when it is possible.

The overall goal of this chapter is to enhance your understanding of families as a context of adolescent development. As a teacher, understanding the nature of families and the role they play in adolescent development can provide insights into your students' adjustment at school. Further, research and theory on parent–adolescent relationships has implications for nonparental adults who work with students during this stage of life. Finally, an appreciation of adolescent development in relation to parents can inform teachers in the way they interact with parents and help promote parental involvement during the middle and high school years.

OVERVIEW OF THE CHAPTER

In this chapter we review important aspects of adolescent development in the family context. First, we consider the wide array of family circumstances for adolescents in contemporary society. We review how families and society have changed in recent decades in the United States. As a teacher, it is important to appreciate the variety of parents and caregivers with whom you will work.

Second, we examine the family system and common changes that occur when families have adolescent children. When you teach adolescent students, you will be working with students and their families during a time of much change. An appreciation of these developmental issues will give you insights and facilitate your work with students and their families.

Third, we present parenting styles, which refers to the different approaches parents have to raising their adolescent children. Knowledge about parenting styles and their effects can help teachers to better understand adolescent behavior in the classroom. We discuss how effective parenting styles are similar to effective teaching styles.

Fourth, we examine attachment and autonomy, which are critical components of the parent–child relationship during adolescence. We consider the development of attachment to parents and caregivers early in life and the implications for adolescent adjustment. We discuss what it means to achieve a sense of autonomy during adolescence. We also examine the role of adolescent–parent conflict in this process. We discuss how school is an important setting where adolescents are establishing autonomy, and what teachers can do to support the development of autonomy.

Fifth, we examine parents' involvement in adolescents' learning. We consider the nature of parental involvement in student learning, variations in involvement depending on parents' financial and educational background, and changes in parental involvement in student learning during the adolescent years. We review what constitutes optimal parental involvement. We discuss recommendations for schools and teachers to promote parental involvement.

Changing Circumstances of Adolescents and Families in Society

As a teacher, you will be working with adolescents and parents from many different types of families. The diversity that characterizes families today is greater now than it has ever been in our nation's history. The variety seen in today's families is due to many changes that have taken place over the last half century in the United States. In the 1950s, most children were born to and grew up with their biological parents in a home tended to by a stay-at-home mother. Since that time there have been increases in children born out of wedlock, divorce, cohabitation, and maternal employment, and declines in marriage and remarriage, making the family experiences of American children and adolescents more complex (see Figure 6.1). Although the majority of children and adolescents will live with both of their biological parents for some period of time, more than half will spend some time in another family arrangement or multiple arrangements as their youth unfolds (Kennedy & Bumpass, 2008). The flow of immigration to the United States and racial and ethnic differences in fertility and marriage have also transformed characteristics of families and contributed to the diversity we see today (Crosnoe & Cavanagh, 2010). In recent years legal changes in same-sex marriage are making families led by gay and lesbian parents more visible. In this section, we consider the changing circumstances of families in American society and the implications for adolescent development. We examine divorce, single parenthood, remarriage,

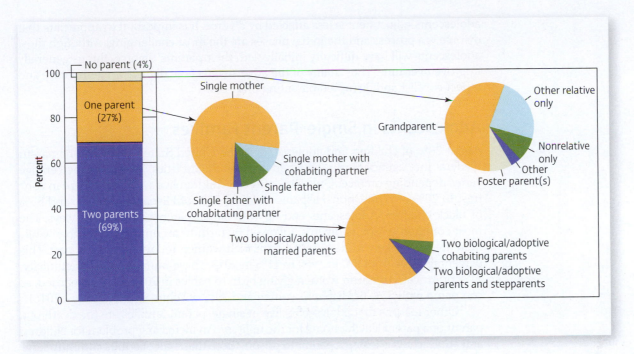

FIGURE 6.1

Percentage of Youth Ages 0 to 17 Living in Various Family Arrangements, 2014

Source: U.S. Census Bureau, Current Population Survey, Annual Social and Economic Supplements.

maternal employment, gay and lesbian parents, poverty, and immigration, and then discuss the implications for educators.

Adolescents and Divorce

Today, about 43% of first marriages end in divorce within 15 years, and about 60% of those divorces involve children under the age of 18, which means that approximately 1 million children and adolescents each year experience the divorce of their parents (Amato, 2010). The divorce rate was less than 30% in the 1950s and early 1960s and increased significantly from 1960 through 1980. It hovered around 50% in the 1980s and into the 1990s. From 1996 on there has been a decline, and the most recent data indicate that just above 40% of first-time marriages end in divorce (Vespa, Lewis, & Kreider, 2013). Divorce rates differ by education level. For adults with a college degree, fewer than 1 in 3 marriages end in divorce.

Divorce is usually a challenging experience for a family, and much research has shown that it is associated with diminished well-being for adolescents. Adolescents from divorced families have lower academic performance, more behavioral and emotional problems, and less positive family relations than do adolescents from nondivorced families (Amato, 2010). However, the magnitude of the effects of divorce is small, and there is much variation in adjustment for adolescents who experience the divorce of their parents. The extent of problems due to divorce depends, in large part, on the level of marital conflict, diminished parenting practices, and financial strain (Potter, 2010). As you might guess, when there is more conflict and hostility between parents, adolescents are more likely to have problems (Amato & Cheadle, 2008). When parents are divorcing they are often distracted and emotionally drained, and the quality of their parenting practices can suffer, which also increases the chances of negative outcomes for adolescents (Schoppe-Sullivan, Schermerhorn, & Cummings, 2007). Dividing up a household costs money and can introduce financial stress for parents and their children. However, there is variability in how divorce unfolds in families, and when these issues are less salient, adolescents' adjustment is less affected by divorce. It is important to appreciate that divorce is a process and the initial phases are the most challenging. Although most adolescents will have difficulty initially with their parents' divorce, things generally improve over time. Thus, many of the adverse effects of divorce are temporary and reflect conflict and disrupted parenting practices.

Adolescents in Single-Parent Families

About 28% of children and adolescents in the United States live with one parent (Federal Interagency Forum on Child and Family Statistics, 2015). This percentage varies depending on race: Only 11% of Asian children live with one parent in contrast to 20% of White, non-Hispanic children, 31% of Hispanic children, and 55% of Black children. Adolescents end up with single parents in different ways. The most common reason is divorce, followed by birth to an unmarried mother. Children are more likely to be born to unmarried women today than in the past. This percentage rose from 5% in 1960 to 41% in 2013. These numbers vary by ethnicity: 71% of African American women giving birth to babies in 2013 were unmarried, as compared with 53% of Hispanic women and 29% of White women (Coles, 2016).

Other reasons that adolescents live in single-parent families are the death of a parent or a parent leaving home for the military. An increasing problem for children and adolescents is losing a parent to prison. More than half of adults currently serving time in prison are parents of children and adolescents under 18, which equates to 2.7 million children and adolescents, or 1 out of every 28. This is a dramatic increase from the 1 in 125 children in 1990, and is likely due to harsher drug laws and mandatory minimum sentences (Pew Charitable Trust, 2010).

When adolescents are raised in single-parent homes it is usually by their mothers (of the 28% of single-parent homes with youth, 24% are mother-only, as compared with 4% that are father-only). Adolescents with single mothers are more likely to experience economic strain and stress in the household. As you can imagine, it is harder when all of the caregiving and financial resources fall on the shoulders of one parent rather than being shared between two parents. Adolescents from single-parent homes are often expected to assume more responsibility around the house and have more input into family decision making (Hetherington, 1999).

Adolescents and Remarriage

Most adults who get divorced will remarry (about 65% of women and 75% of men) so many adolescents who experience divorce will also experience living as part of a stepfamily at some time. Divorce is more likely to happen in remarriages and happens sooner than in first marriages, meaning that many youth will experience a second divorce (Amato, 2010). Some children and adolescents will experience remarriage in which both parents bring children from previous marriages, called a **blended family**.

Remarriage has the potential to bring benefits to the family. With the addition of another parent there is likely to be increased economic resources, more help with parenting, and the addition of a role model. However, research has found that, in general, adolescents' adjustment suffers when their mothers remarry and their new partners move into the house. Remarriage is associated with declines in academic performance and increased behavioral and emotional problems for adolescents. The highest levels of problems are in blended families (Hetherington & Stanley-Hagan, 2000, 2002; Jeynes, 1999). Why does remarriage lead to problems for adolescents? Despite the potential benefits, it seems that remarriage is challenging because it is another disruption to a family that has already been strained by the experience of divorce. With a blended family there is even more change to accommodate. Adolescents are generally more reluctant than are their parents to accept another adult into the home (Silverberg

Koerner, Kenyon, & Rankin, 2006). Similar to divorce, there is variability in how adolescents handle the remarriage. Research has found two factors that are associated with more positive outcomes for adolescents in the context of remarriage (Buchanan, Maccoby, & Dornbusch, 1996; Hetherington, 1999). First, authoritative parenting can help, especially when stepparents are consistent and supportive in their parenting. Second, when adolescents have positive relationships with their noncustodial biological parent and the parenting style is similar among all of their parents, it helps adolescents adjust.

Multiple Transitions. Research has examined how youth experience multiple family structures and transitions—parental marriage, divorce, single parenthood, cohabitation, remarriage—over time (Crosnoe & Cavanaugh, 2010). Children and adolescents who experience one type of family transition are more likely to experience subsequent transitions. Children and adolescents who go through numerous transitions experience more stress and threats to their well-being than those who do not experience any transitions or experience just one. For all adolescents, but especially boys, family transitions are associated with increased behavioral problems across all stages of childhood (Cavanagh & Huston, 2008; Fomby & Cherlin, 2007) and with early sexual behavior in adolescence (Cavanagh, Crissey, & Raley, 2008).

Maternal Employment

The number of women who work outside the home has increased steadily over the last several decades. Today, about two-thirds of U.S. children (63%) live in a two-parent household with both parents working outside the home (compared to 48% of children with this scenario in 1970). When both parents work, about three-fourths of mothers work full-time (Pew Research Center, 2015). Research on maternal employment has examined differences between youth from homes with dual earners as compared with homes with stay-at-home mothers. The focus on stay-at home mothers is due to the fact that in most families when one spouse stays at home to care for the family it is the mother, although about 5% of the time it is the father (Vespa et al., 2013). Overall, research has found few differences in the quality of parent–child relationships or in adolescent adjustment in dual-earner versus stay-at-home-mother homes (Galambos, Berenbaum, & McHale, 2009). One positive finding has been that adolescent girls who are in dual-earner families have higher career aspirations as compared with girls whose mothers do not work.

Another area of research on maternal employment has focused on the effects in low-income families, which are often headed by single mothers. Welfare reform in the mid-1990s increased the number of poor mothers moving from welfare into the workforce. The rationale behind the legislation was that working mothers would not only increase family income but provide children and adolescents with positive role models and increase structure in their family routines. One large-scale study that took place in three cities found that mothers' entry into the workforce had few effects for children and some positive effects on adolescent adjustment (Chase-Lansdale et al., 2003). However, this pattern varied depending on the nature of the work. Women who left welfare and moved into paid work were more likely to have nonstandard work schedules that did not conform to standard schedule of 5 days and 40 hours per week. Nonstandard schedules were more likely to undermine the quality of parent–child relationships, disrupt organization in the home, and lead to poor outcomes for children and adolescents (Dunifon, Kalil, & Bajracharya 2005). Further, maternal employment was more likely to negatively affect adolescents' grades and attendance in school when they had younger siblings, likely due to increased childcare burdens that fall to the adolescents in such family situations (Gennetian et al., 2004).

Adolescents of Gay and Lesbian Parents

The estimates of how many children and adolescents have gay and lesbian parents vary widely. Although the total is not known for sure, some have estimated that between 2.7% to 5% of current children and adolescents have a LGBT parent while a smaller number (less than 3%, about 200,000) are being raised by two same sex parents in the same household (Angier, 2013; Gates, 2015). Many adolescents of homosexual parents are in families that originated with two heterosexual parents before one parent identified as gay or lesbian. With society becoming more accepting of homosexuality, there are increasing numbers of single and partnered gay and lesbian adults choosing to become parents with the help of donors, surrogates, and adoption. In 2000, only 10% of same-sex couples reported raising children, a number that almost doubled to 19% in 2009 (Gates, 2013).

Research has examined whether the outcomes for children and adolescents raised in same-sex couples vary as compared with those for children and adolescents raised in other types of families. There has been opposition to same-sex parents on the grounds that such families would create a disadvantageous situation for children. However, research has found that these fears are not warranted (Gates, 2015). Children and adolescents from same-sex parents are similar to youth from heterosexual parents in terms of emotional well-being and academic progress in school (Gates, 2015; Rosenfeld, 2010; Tasker, 2005).

Adolescents and Poverty

For adolescents aged 12 to 17, about 19% grow up in poverty. An additional 22% grow up in low-income families (Jiang, Ekono, & Skinner, 2015). Ethnicity affects an adolescent's chances of growing up in poverty or in a low-income household. Sixty-one percent of African American adolescents live in low-income households, as compared with 60% of Hispanics, 58% of American Indians, 33% of Asian Americans, and 28% of White adolescents. The percentage of children and adolescents living in poverty and low-income families has been on the rise—increasing from 35% in 2007 to nearly 41% in 2013 (Jiang et al., 2015).

Poverty is perhaps the greatest threat to adolescent well-being because it puts adolescents at risk for social, emotional, and behavioral problems. Poverty contributes to health problems and limits adolescents' ability to learn and do well at school (Jiang et al., 2015). Much research on poverty and adolescent development has used a **family process model** that conceptualizes that a family's economic circumstances affect child and adolescent well-being by influencing interpersonal dynamics within the family (see Figure 6.2). Economic status (defined in terms of poverty or family income) affects parents' emotional well-being, creates behavioral problems (for example, conflict between family members or withdrawal from the family), and alters relationships, and in turn these changes affect parenting practices (for example, harsh, inconsistent, or uninvolved parenting), which in turn affect children's emotional well-being, social behavior, and academic achievement (Conger et al., 2002; Linver, Brooks-Gunn, & Kohen, 2002). For the most part, research has found that the family process model applies to different ethnic groups (Raver, Gershoff, & Aber, 2007).

Immigration

Immigration trends into the United States have changed the social landscape of cities, neighborhoods, and families. For the last decade, immigration and the corresponding foreign-born population have continued to rise and have reached

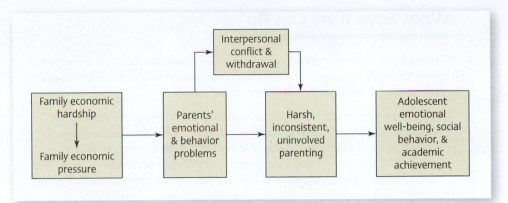

FIGURE 6.2

Family Process Model

Source: Adapted from Conger, Conger, and Martin, 2010.

near-record levels in the United States (Kandel, 2011; Zong & Batalova, 2015). Immigration to the United States has undergone dramatic changes in terms of numbers of immigrants and their countries of origin. In 1960, the foreign-born population was about 9.7 million, or 5.4% of the population, and was mostly from countries in Europe. In 2013, the foreign-born population was about 41.3 million and made up about 13 % of the population. There is tremendous diversity in today's immigrant population, with the majority being Hispanic (46%) and Asian (26%), and among Hispanics, Mexicans are the largest nationality group (Zong & Batalova, 2015).

Adolescent immigrants can face unique issues related to language proficiency, cultural adaptation, and poverty. The pressure to learn English quickly is quite high for many new adolescent immigrants in American schools. English-proficiency issues vary by country of origin, with Mexican and Hispanic immigrant adolescents being more likely to have limited English skills than are Asian immigrant adolescents. For adolescents of limited English proficiency, the dropout rate is higher than for those who have mastered English skills. For immigrant adolescents who have mastered English, a challenging issue can be parents who rely on them to translate or interpret so they can communicate. Despite counting on their adolescents for communication, immigrant parents are often resistant to their adolescents' becoming too American and independent (Dorner, Orellana, & Jiminez, 2008; Qin, 2006). Adolescent immigrants are more likely to be in poor families and have parents who work nonstandard hours or multiple jobs; thus, the family process model of disadvantage described in the previous section is relevant to understanding adolescent immigrant outcomes.

Despite these challenges, immigrant families are likely to have many strengths, including two-parent families with at least one working parent, an extended family network, and connection to a community of immigrant families from the same country of origin (Smith-Davis, 2004). This may be why adolescent immigrants do just as well as do adolescents born in the United States in terms of avoiding high-risk behaviors such as alcohol and drug use or sexual behavior. Further, in terms of academic achievement, scholars have described an **immigrant paradox**, which refers to evidence that adolescents from immigrant families outperform their peers in school despite higher-than-average rates of social and economic disadvantage in the population as a whole (Crosnoe & Lopez-Turley, 2011). The immigrant paradox is more apt to apply to Asian and African immigrants groups, and it is stronger for boys than for girls. For adolescent immigrants from Asia, the paradox is in part due to the fact that those who come to the United States from Asia tend to be from higher educational and socioeconomic backgrounds than those who stay.

What Educators Can Do

As an educator in contemporary society, it is likely your students will come from a variety of family situations. The following suggestions will facilitate your work with parents and caregivers from diverse backgrounds:

1. *Avoid making assumptions about students' family lives.* Given the increasingly diverse nature of our society, you will teach students from many types of family structures and backgrounds. Get to know your students and the community you teach in so that you understand some of the strengths and challenges of the families and students enrolled in the school. Ask questions and show a genuine interest in your students' family cultures.

2. *Listen.* At times, some of your students will experience challenges in their family lives that will spill over into school and affect their performance. Although you cannot solve your students' problems, you can listen to their thoughts and support them at school.

3. *Work to create a culturally inclusive classroom.* As a starting point, reflect on your own cultural beliefs and behaviors and educate yourself about other cultures that are represented by the students you teach. Look for commonalities (people are more alike than different!), but appreciate the differences that exist among students and families from different cultural backgrounds. Try to incorporate the perspectives of many cultures into your curriculum. Talk about important historical figures from different cultures and try to discuss legitimate contributions, rather than trivializing other cultures or treating them as a curiosity.

4. *Recognize that being sensitive to diversity is an ongoing process that teachers need to engage in continuously to understand families and try to meet student needs.*

MyEdLab
Video Example 6.1

As they enter adolescence, Kianna and her best friend, at age 12, find that they are influencing family dynamics as much as their parents are.

Can you recall a major change to your family when you were a child or adolescent? What was the catalyst for the change? How did it affect different members of your family? Did it affect you or your siblings' adjustment at school?

The Family System During Adolescence

Development is often thought of as what happens to an individual person as he or she progresses from infancy to childhood and then adolescence. The family unit also moves through predictable developmental changes of its own. A family with young children will have particular tasks to address, such as how to incorporate children into the marital relationship and connect with extended family. Families with adolescents are helping individuals prepare for leaving the family and developing independence, when they will enter the stage of "launching" as children move out on their own.

One view of families is that they are a system in which all members are interconnected (Gavassi, 2011). The members of a family have different roles but operate together as a complete system. Change to any member has an impact on the whole system. Any kind of change can require the whole family to readjust. For example, even something simple, such as one family member getting sick, causes changes; consequently, the other family members might have to readjust to that person staying at home and not performing normal daily activities. More substantial changes, for example, the birth of a new child or a parent getting a new job, may require long-term adjustments by the family system.

Adolescent Changes and the Family System

Adolescence can be thought of as introducing changes to the family system that require accommodation for balance to be restored to the system (Martin, Bascoe, & Davies, 2011). Think of the different developmental issues you have read about and how they might require families to change. Cognitive, pubertal, and social changes instigate new needs, interests, and activities in adolescents that affect those around them. With cognitive changes, adolescents desire more explanations about family decisions and may desire changes in family rules and expectations that they did not question just a year or so earlier. Their more sophisticated reasoning abilities allow them to engage in questioning and debating with their families in a new manner. With pubertal changes, adolescents desire more privacy. Whereas it might have been fine for Mom or Dad to walk into their child's bedroom or bathroom at any time, adolescents' want their personal space, often behind locked doors.

Adolescents' behaviors at home and with their peers also affect family dynamics. Puberty ushers in romantic interests, and many adolescents will desire to spend time with the opposite sex either on dates or in social gatherings with peers. As adolescents' time spent with peers increases, their time spent with family decreases (Larson, Richards, Moneta, Holmbeck, & Duckett, 1996). Further, there is generally less parental supervision or involvement in peer relationships during adolescence. Adolescents stay out later with peers, and even when they are home, adolescents start staying up later in the house. Thus, the extent and nature of "family time" change during adolescence (see Figure 6.3), and parents and siblings have to adjust.

All of these changes necessitate new roles, routines, and communication for family members during adolescence. The overarching task during this stage for a family is to shift the balance of power to allow for increased independence and more egalitarian relationships to emerge as adolescent children move toward adulthood. However, it is not just children who are entering a different developmental phase. For a full appreciation of families during adolescence, we also need to consider the developmental issues for parents at midlife that also contribute to changes in the family system.

Parents at Midlife and the Family System

With rising ages of marriage and childbirth, most parents of adolescents are in the midlife period of development, generally regarding as beginning around age 40. Parents are likely to be addressing their own developmental issues during this period. In spite of the popularity of the phrase **midlife crisis**, the number of individuals who report an actual age-specific crisis (as opposed to divorce or job changes that might occur at any time during adulthood) is relatively small. In fact, several positive changes are reported by adults during this period, including increased wisdom and improved ability to regulate one's emotions (Lachman, 2004).

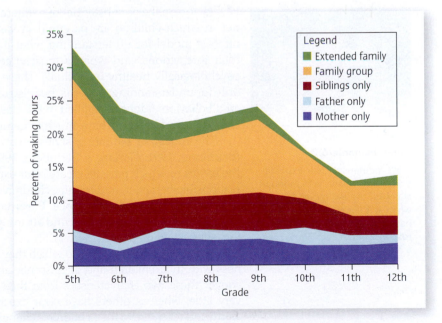

FIGURE 6.3

Changes in Time with Family During Adolescence

Source: Larson et al., 1996.

What seems most common to the experience of midlife in the United States is more a period of re-evaluation than of crisis. This is a time when individuals may assess their own achievements against their early plans and dreams and may reconsider where they are headed in their jobs and careers. Witnessing the potential of the adolescent who still has all of the choices ahead can be a reminder of the limitations in one's own life, the impact of earlier choices, and the limited number of years left for actualizing aspirations. The mother who put a career aside or took a step down to have more time at home with family may bristle when her child describes ambitions that exceed her own accomplishments. On the other hand, she may also feel uneasy about seeing the period of time when having children at home comes to an end, necessitating a redirection of attention and purpose. Conversely, she may be looking forward to the opportunities this represents for her, yet feel uneasy about how to navigate the transition. Fathers and mothers both may become aware of their own physical limitations as they watch growing children begin to eclipse them in sports they nurtured. This is also a period when illness, disease, and physical problems begin to surface as signals of aging (Lachman, 2004) and, ultimately, as reminders of mortality.

Parents at midlife are busy people, likely to be juggling multiple roles with extended family, work responsibilities, and community and civic roles. At this time in life they become more aware of the aging of their own parents, and may be involved not only in taking care of their children but may be beginning to worry about the health and well-being of their parents. Such midlife parents are often dubbed the "**sandwich generation**," caught in the middle of responsibilities for both older and younger generations and feeling stretched to meet the expectations of others. As a teacher, if you can offer opportunities for parental involvement that are flexible and require a minimal time commitment, you may have more success in getting greater numbers of parents involved.

MyEdLab Self-Check 6.2

Parenting Styles

Few factors make as substantial of a difference in individual outcomes as the manner in which children are parented. A vast body of research on parenting styles offers a model for understanding what it is that parents do and the patterns of their interactions, and what is most effective in raising competent, responsible, psychologically healthy individuals. These parenting styles have implications not only for understanding students, but also can illuminate how aspects of the associated behaviors might be applied in the classroom. Effective parenting and effective teaching of adolescents have much in common.

The model of parenting styles involves two basic dimensions of parenting (Baumrind, 1991; Darling & Steinberg, 1993). **Parental demandingness** refers to the extent to which parents create clear expectations and rules, expect mature and responsible behavior, and require children and adolescents to comply, with a willingness to confront disobedience. **Parental responsiveness** involves recognizing the adolescent as an individual and attuning to the adolescent's needs in an accepting, supportive manner.

Parents vary in the degree to which they employ demandingness and responsiveness with their children and adolescents, and the extent to which their interactions convey these two characteristics form their parenting style. Some parents demand very little, whereas others have clear expectations for behavior. Some parents are warm and receptive to their children's changing needs, negotiating when appropriate, while others believe that only parents know what is best and set down strict rules that must be obeyed without exception.

Research on parenting styles conducted by Diana Baumrind and others who have based their research on her work (Baumrind, 1991; Darling & Steinberg, 1993) suggests that the combinations of demandingness and responsiveness create four

MyEdLab
Video Example 6.2

Tim's mother set clear expectations for behavior, and although she was "the evil mom" for a while, it is likely that the combination of demandingness and responsiveness led Tim to make a major change.

distinct parenting styles that are common among families in the United States (see Figure 6.4).

Types of Parenting Styles

Parents who are high in both demandingness and responsiveness are classified as **authoritative parents**. They set clear rules and expectations for mature, responsible behavior, with consequences for violations. They also provide reasons for the rules that they set, and are open to discussion of those rules. In addition, rules and expectations are likely to evolve with the child's growth and development, rather than remaining rigid. Compromise and negotiation are possible, and communication is bi-directional, characterized by verbal give-and-take. Parents who are authoritative are confident in sticking to rules that may not appeal to their adolescents, however, when they know that the rules are in their best interest. Authoritative parents convey support. Support can be conveyed in different ways—acceptance, nurturance, warmth, and positive regard.

Authoritarian parents, by contrast, are those who are high in demandingness and low in responsiveness. As a result, they make rules that they own and enforce, based on their ultimate authority as parents, with little explanation or discussion. Rules—and parents—are to be obeyed unquestioningly, with no room for negotiation. Although "because I said so" may slip out of many a parent's mouth, this is the bottom line for authoritarian parents, and infractions are likely to be handled with punishment. Authoritarian parents differ from authoritative parents in how they employ demandingness. Although both exhibit behavioral control, only authoritarian parents engage in restrictive, psychological control (Darling & Steinberg, 1993). In the extreme, authoritarian parents may be harsh, punitive, and controlling.

Permissive parents are the opposite of authoritarian parents, as they are low in demandingness but high in responsiveness, and are generally perceived as indulgent. There is little or no effort to control their adolescents' behavior. Rules may be viewed as impinging upon adolescents' freedom, discipline is relatively lax, and punishment is rare. These parents strive to attune themselves to adolescents' needs, and allow them to blossom without too much interference. They display warmth and support, but offer little guidance.

Indifferent parents, low in both demandingness and responsiveness, are generally disengaged from their adolescents and their role as parents. With this type of parenting style, too, there is little or no effort to control their adolescents' behavior. They provide few rules and expectations, know little about what is going on in their adolescents' lives, and may be more focused on their own needs. Taken to an extreme, indifference may become neglect.

An important point to appreciate is that parenting styles are not totally determined by the parents. Each parent responds to his or her adolescent's personality and temperament (Albrecht, Galambos, & Jansson, 2007; Beaver & Wright, 2007). If an adolescent is difficult or aggressive, or tends to break the rules, a parent may be more likely to respond in an authoritarian manner. If an adolescent is responsible and tends to follow the rules, a parent may be more likely to respond in an authoritative manner. Parent–child relationships are interactive and reciprocal, rather than unidirectional, and neither the parent nor the child is totally responsible for parent–adolescent interactions (Lansford et al., 2011).

The Effects of Parenting Styles on Adolescent Development

There has been much research on how the different styles of parenting affect child and adolescent development. The results of the research are quite consistent

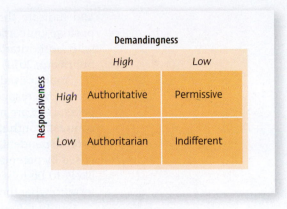

FIGURE 6.4

Parenting Styles

and indicate that youth from homes with authoritative parents have the most positive outcomes and the least problems as compared with youth from homes with authoritarian, indulgent, or indifferent parents (Laursen & Collins, 2009; Steinberg, 2014).

Youth raised by parents with an authoritative parenting style tend to be more confident, responsible, and self-reliant. They have better social skills with their peers. They are more successful in school and overall more curious and creative. In contrast, youth raised by parents with an authoritarian style tend to be more insecure, dependent, and passive. They are less socially adept with their peers. Youth raised by parents with a permissive style tend to be less responsible. They are more likely to be followers than leaders among their peers and are more likely to conform to what their friends want to do.

Youth raised by parents with an indifferent style tend to be more impulsive in their decision-making and are more likely to get involved in delinquency. They are more likely to be involved with alcohol and drug use and sexual behavior at earlier ages (see Chapter 12 for additional discussion of this point).

With a few exceptions, the evidence that authoritative parenting fosters healthy and adaptive adolescent development is strong. Research has been conducted over many decades and includes samples of families and adolescents from many different ethnicities, social class backgrounds, and countries around the world. Authoritative parenting is thought to be associated with positive outcomes for several reasons. First, authoritative parents have a nice balance between allowing autonomy and setting restrictions. Having some autonomy allows adolescents to develop self-reliance and the confidence that they can care for themselves. Having some restrictions provides limits at a stage when adolescents are still learning and need some guidance. Second, authoritative parents tend to discuss the reasons behind the rules, which can help adolescents develop reasoning skills and the ability to take another person's perspective. Discussions rather than commands make adolescents feel like their opinions matter, which fosters confidence. Third, authoritative parents tend to be warm and loving, which increases the chances that adolescents will identify with and admire their parents, making them more open to their parents' opinions. When adolescents are close to their parents, they are more likely to want to be like them and to adopt their values.

Cultural and Ethnic Differences in Parenting Styles

Parenting styles have been found to vary between different ethnic groups. One way researchers have investigated this issue is to examine the extent to which the frequency of parenting styles differs for different groups. Such work found that African American, Asian American, and Hispanic American parents are less likely to use an authoritative parenting style and more likely to use an authoritarian parenting style, as compared with parents of European American students. Another approach has been to examine variations in the effects of parenting styles for different groups, with attention to the meanings of and motivations for parenting within specific groups (Hill, Bush, & Roosa, 2003). The authoritarian parenting style has received the most attention, likely due to the fact that the negative effects of an authoritarian parenting style are worse for European American youth as compared with African American, Asian American, and Hispanic American youth. One reason is that ethnic-minority youth are more likely to live in impoverished areas, and in such areas authoritarian parenting might be necessary to help protect adolescents from harm. In situations that are dangerous, parents might prioritize safety rather than autonomy as the priority to ensure well-being.

Another explanation is that the distinction between authoritative and authoritarian is harder to make in African American, Asian, or Hispanic cultures. Scholars have shown that positive parenting practices in different ethnic groups can be misinterpreted as overly controlling or disengaged because they are different from the practices of European American culture. For example, the control and restrictiveness that are seen as characteristic of Chinese families reflect a different set of underlying beliefs than for European American parents. For many Chinese parents, strictness is rooted in a notion of training (*chiao shun* and *guan*) that reflects Confucianism. The goal is to assure harmonious family relationships rather than to dominate or control the child (Chao & Otsuki-Clutter, 2011). In Puerto Rican and Mexican families, there is high value placed on characteristics associated with *respeto* and *educacion*, which refer to maintaining self-dignity, responsibility, and proper demeanor toward others as the means to maximize potential in the world (Arcia, Reyes-Blanes, & Vazquez-Montilla, 2000). Thus, parenting styles need to be understood in terms of their sociocultural context. In some cultures, high levels of warmth may be combined with high levels of strictness or insistence on obedience, but it is not hostile.

Whereas the meaning and effects of an authoritarian parenting style vary across groups, an authoritative parenting style is consistently found to have positive effects for all adolescents, regardless of ethnic background. In light of these findings, Collins and Steinberg (2006) note that the most important conclusion from research on cultural and ethnic differences in parenting styles is not that authoritarian parenting is less negative for some, but rather that authoritative parenting is good for all. Although it will not look identical across cultures and families, the combination of high levels of demandingness and responsiveness promotes positive outcomes for adolescents.

Related to that point is research showing that parents' expression of responsiveness toward their children may vary depending on cultural values. For example, overt affection and praise seem to be less prevalent in the way parents show support in African American and Asian American families (Chao & Otsuki-Clutter, 2011; Hill et al., 2003). In Mexican families, parents are more likely to describe parental support as "being there" for their children rather than displays of warmth (Gil-Rivas, Greenberger, Chen, & López-Lena, 2003). What does seem to be common across cultures is the notion that parental support involves parents' acceptance of their children and being responsive to their needs (Chao & Otsuki-Clutter, 2011).

Implications of Parenting Styles for Effective Teaching Styles

Effective teaching styles have much in common with effective parenting styles (McCaslin & Good, 1991; Wentzel, 2002). Teachers vary in how demanding and responsive they are in the classroom. An authoritative teaching style, high in both demandingness and responsiveness, is thought to be the most effective style for adolescent students. Similar to authoritative parents, authoritative teachers are "firm but flexible." They set high expectations, discuss their standards, teach adolescents how to meet them, and value when adolescents can learn to regulate their own behavior. Authoritative teachers value communication with their students; they solicit, inquire, and respond to student perspectives (McCaslin & Murdock, 1991). Authoritative teachers help students understand the rationale that underlies classroom assignments and rules, which promotes a feeling of mutual respect and community in the classroom.

Research has found that an authoritative teaching style promotes adolescents' motivation and academic achievement as well as positive social behavior in the classroom (Wentzel, 2002). Similar to parenting styles, it seems that when teachers are responsive to students' needs, their students are more likely to adopt and pursue the goals and values promoted by their teachers, as compared with when teachers are harsh or critical of their students. Further, when teachers hold high expectations and actively teach and provide constructive feedback to students, their students are more likely to learn academic content as well as appropriate social behavior. Overall, an authoritative teaching style is thought to be effective because it enables adolescents to become independent and responsible in managing their own behavior.

What Educators Can Do

Adolescent students will benefit from teachers who relate to them in an authoritative manner, whether they have an authoritative parent at home or not. To achieve an authoritative teaching style, educators need to do the following:

1. *Offer a reasonable amount of structure so that students know what is expected of them.* Be clear about the rules and consequences for not following the rules. Be consistent in applying consequences when students do not do their work or follow the rules. As a teacher, you should strive for reasonable standards for behavior and performance and clear, fair, and transparent means of evaluation.

2. *Value student input in your decision making in the classroom.* Be sensitive to your students' needs and respond to them in a supportive manner. In the beginning of the year, consider creating some classroom rules through negotiation and discussion by the class. Provide a rationale for rules that aren't negotiable, such as those that are schoolwide policy. Find a means of checking in with your students on a regular basis so that you understand how students are experiencing your classroom.

3. *Strive for a balance between demandingness and responsiveness.* Achieving an authoritative style means finding that delicate balance between exerting your control and authority as a teacher and responding to student perspectives and incorporating their ideas in the classroom. This is not an easy task, as it is sometimes appropriate to be heavy-handed and take control. However, if the focus becomes too much on compliance, it is likely to alienate students and hinder the development of self-reliance. Achieving the right balance involves experimentation and reflection. As a teacher, you can ask yourself, "Am I being clear about my expectations for my students?"; "Am I listening to my students?"; and "Is there a way to allow student input that would achieve my learning objectives?"

4. *Remember that an authoritative style applies to instruction as well as classroom management.* Strive for a balance between demandingness and responsiveness for students' academic performance in the classroom. Set high expectations so that students feel challenged, but provide support to help them meet the challenge.

5. *Be aware that the families of your adolescent students from different ethnic and cultural groups may have different expectations than your own in regard to student behavior.* For example, as mentioned earlier, some ethnic and cultural groups place a greater emphasis on obedience to adult figures, and that might differ from the approaches of some teachers in middle or high schools. Or you might be from an ethnic or minority group that differs from those of your students. Remember that most parents want what is best for their children. Make an effort to communicate, listen, and keep an open mind to find ideas that work for everyone.

MyEdLab **Self-Check 6.3**

MyEdLab
Application Exercise 6.1
Family Systems Reflect on the family system that includes 14-year-old Ryan, his parents, and his younger sister.

In-Depth 6.1

Parenting, Achievement, and Well-Being: Can We Learn Something by Comparing Chinese and Americans?

My kids were maybe seven and four and my husband had forgotten my birthday so at the last minute we went to this mediocre Italian restaurant and he said "O.K. girls you both have a little surprise for mommy." And my daughter Lulu (younger one) pulls out a card, but the card was just a piece of paper folded crookedly in half with a big smiley face on it and it said Happy Birthday Mom. And I looked at it and I gave it back and I said "This isn't good enough. I want something that you put a little bit more time into."

This is a quote from Amy Chua's (2011) best-selling book titled *Battle Hymn of the Tiger Mother*. In her book, Chua raises some provocative points about differences between American and Chinese parenting. In general, she views American parents as too concerned about protecting their children's self-esteem. In contrast, she views Chinese parents as most concerned with promoting high achievement. In Chua's view, the path to high achievement does not begin with positive feelings, and most things are not fun until you are good at them. To get good at something you have to work extremely hard, and children, on their own, will not want to work that hard at something. Chua's book is based on her own parenting experiences and the success of her two daughters, particularly in music. Chua's book generated much controversy about the nature of American and Chinese parenting and what is best for children and adolescents.

What does the research show? A recent review of the research concludes that there are differences in practices between Chinese and American parents (Pomerantz, Ng, Cheung, & Qu, 2014). Although

there is variability within each country, there are differences between the two countries. First, Chinese parents are more involved in their children's learning than are American parents, starting at early ages and lasting through adolescence. Second, Chinese parents are more controlling in their interactions with their children. Third, Chinese parents focus on the correctness of the work, do not hesitate to point out errors or mistakes, and discuss ways children and adolescents can improve. In contrast, American parents tend to give their children more choice and autonomy in learning situations. Overall, American parents minimize attention to failures and focus more on what children do well. Thus, although Amy Chua's descriptions of Chinese parenting in her book may be extreme, they do align with some differences documented by research.

What are the consequences for children and adolescents? Research has found that there are costs and benefits associated with both styles of parenting (Pomerantz et al., 2014). The Chinese style may benefit youth academically but has emotional costs. For example, a study that followed youth in China for several years found that parents' heightened control around schoolwork led to decreased happiness in adolescence (Pomerantz & Wang, 2009). The American style may benefit children emotionally without the academic benefits. Considered more broadly, these differences reflect cultural values about the priority of achievement and feelings of self-worth.

Pomerantz and her colleagues (2014) suggest that both Chinese and American parenting practices have strengths and weaknesses, and that rather than debate which is better, it might be most fruitful to think about how to integrate the best of each style. From their research conducted in both countries, the ideal combination is parents who are highly involved but in an autonomy-supportive, rather than controlling, manner. Emphasizing success and strengths builds confidence. Attending to mistakes and weaknesses identifies areas that need attention and improvement. Thus, an integrated style could give children the resources for academic achievement while facilitating autonomy and self-worth, thus supporting emotional well-being as well.

What do you think? Is it possible to raise happy children who achieve at high levels? What role does culture play? What was your experience in high school? As a teacher, how will you strike a balance in encouraging high achievement but supporting students' feelings of self-worth? How will you promote this balance in the parents of your adolescent students?

Attachment and Autonomy

A popular parenting manual entitled *Get Out of My Life, but First Would You Drive Me and Cheryl to the Mall?* (Wolf, 2002) captures the push-and-pull nature of the changing relationships with parents during adolescence. This is a period when the tension between attachment and autonomy is often paramount, and parents may struggle to both celebrate the growing independence they witness and maintain a close connection. Earlier views of this process suggested that adolescents needed to break away from parents in order to become autonomous, but more recent research shows the value of maintaining a healthy attachment while becoming independently competent and emotionally autonomous (McElhaney, Allen, Stephenson, & Hare, 2009). Parents and teachers can support this developmental process in a host of ways.

In this section, we first consider what attachment is, how it develops early in life, and the implications for adolescent adjustment, particularly for achieving a sense of autonomy. Second, we consider the nature of autonomy and what exactly it means to develop autonomy during adolescence. Third, we discuss recommendations for educators.

Attachment

Attachment concerns the emotional bond with one's parents or primary caregivers (Roisman & Groh, 2011, 2009). Attachment theory was initially an explanatory means of understanding how infants responded to their caregivers, and early research focused primarily on very young children and their mothers (Ainsworth, Blehar, Waters, & Wall, 1978; Bowlby, 1969). Many attachment theorists consider the attachments formed early in life to be critical to understanding social, emotional, and romantic relationships in adolescence. There are three types of attachment: *secure, anxious-avoidant*, and *anxious-resistant*. The classic assessment of attachment in young children is a laboratory procedure known as the Strange Situation Protocol devised by Mary Ainsworth (Ainsworth et al., 1978). In this procedure the child and the child's caregiver are placed in an unfamiliar playroom and the child experiences separation and then reunion with the caregiver. Researchers examine how the child explores and interacts with the caregiver in the strange room and reacts to the stress of being separated from the caregiver and left with a stranger.

Infants and children with a **secure** attachment seem comfortable exploring the room. They use their caregiver as a secure base for exploration and check back periodically. When the caregiver leaves, the child protests the departure. When the caregiver returns, the child seeks physical proximity and consolation. After being comforted, the child will return to exploring the room. Infants and children with an **anxious-avoidant** attachment exhibit low levels of emotion and sharing behavior when playing in the room with their caregiver. When their caregivers leave, they show no distress. When their caregivers return, they seem indifferent, ignoring and making no effort to make contact with their caregivers. Infants and children with an **anxious-resistant** attachment are not comfortable exploring the room away from their caregivers. They cling to their caregivers and are unable to use the caregivers as a secure base for exploration. When their caregivers leave, they are distressed. When their caregivers return, they are ambivalent or show anger. They hesitate to return to play with their caregivers in the room.

The different types of attachment are related to parent behavior. Overall, a secure attachment is characterized by trust and is built from a caregiver who responds consistently and appropriately to a child's needs. An anxious-avoidant attachment is characterized by a lack of an emotional bond with a caregiver and is the result of a caregiver who is neglectful even when a child is distressed. An anxious-resistant attachment is characterized by anxiety in the child and is due to an inconsistent pattern alternating between appropriate and neglectful caregiving behavior.

Psychologists who first studied attachment, such as John Bowlby (1969), thought that the emotional bond with one's caregiver in the early years of life was the foundation for relationships throughout the life span (Bowlby, 1969). Bowlby theorized that the interactions between children and caregivers contribute to the development of an **internal working model** that is a mental representation for understanding the self with others. Memories and expectations based on interactions with the primary caregiver form the working model that guides future social interactions and emotional bonds with others. Other scholars suggested that an insecure attachment during early childhood leads to a heightened sensitivity and fear of rejection in romantic encounters in adolescence, a trait known as **rejection sensitivity** (Butler, Doherty, & Potter, 2007).

Is early attachment important to adjustment in adolescence? Researchers who have asked adolescents to recall their childhood relationships with their parents has indicated that individuals who recall secure attachments in the past do report closer friendships and more stable romantic relationships as compared with those who recall insecure attachments. It seems that when there is a secure attachment in infancy, it sets the stage for better social relationships in early childhood, leading to increased confidence in later childhood and more intimacy in adolescent friendships and romantic relationships. Some longitudinal studies that followed samples from infancy to adolescence have found that attachment classifications early in life do predict peer relationships in adolescence, but results are not entirely consistent and are stronger in early as compared with late adolescence (Roisman & Fraley, 2012).

The current view by psychologists is that the attachment formed as an infant and young child is important to later development, but so are the experiences and relationships that individuals have when they are actually adolescents and adults. For many adolescents there is similarity in the parenting they receive that continues to contribute to their attachment and adjustment in a similar manner. However, for some adolescents there may be changes in their caregiving situation (for example, divorce, death, or remarriage of a parent), and their current situation will contribute to their adjustment in a different manner. In addition, in recent years scholars have pointed out that the quality of attachment between parents and adolescents is not solely determined by parent characteristics, as adolescent characteristics and behavior contribute (Roisman & Groh, 2011). It is not just the parent that determines the parent–child relationship; both parent and adolescent characteristics matter.

Consistent with this focus, recent work has assessed the attachments of individuals during adolescence. Adolescents with secure attachments to their parents are more socially skilled and form positive relationships with other people in their lives (Collins & Steinberg, 2006). Adolescents with secure attachments and positive internal working models of their relationships with their parents are more likely to have secure attachments and positive working models of relationships with close friends and romantic partners (Roisman & Groh, 2011).

Another benefit of a secure attachment with parents during adolescence is that it supports the development of autonomy. Just as in childhood, a secure attachment to parents provides a safe base for adolescents. Explorations in infancy may involve crawling across the room and back to seek parental reassurance. In adolescence, the explorations involve considerably greater distance and risks, and are more multifaceted, involving the exploration of new friends, ideas, and places. Although adolescents have less need for a caregiver's immediate presence, they continue to need the safe base that parents provide, with acceptance, boundaries, and support. Over the course of adolescence, individuals rely increasingly less on their parents for comfort and support and more on peers, but the need for parental support does not disappear. Secure attachment offers the opportunity for autonomy, a process that occurs gradually across adolescence (Laursen & Collins, 2009). Ultimately, healthy individuals learn to conduct themselves independently but know when and how to rely on others (Steinberg, 2014). As we have noted several times in this chapter, there is a reciprocal relation between adolescents' behaviors and parenting behaviors that unfolds over time: Adolescents feel secure to explore, but are also given the freedom to explore by their parents, partly because they have demonstrated rational decision making and social competence before and during adolescence.

Autonomy

Establishing autonomy encompasses the transformation from a child who is dependent on his or her parents to an adult who is independent and self-sufficient. Although establishing autonomy is a central concern in adolescence, the process begins in childhood and continues into adulthood. Autonomy is multifaceted and complex (Zimmer-Gembeck, Ducat, & Collins, 2011). There are three basic types of autonomy to be considered: emotional autonomy, behavioral autonomy, and cognitive or value autonomy. These types of autonomy are related but have their own unique features.

Emotional autonomy involves feeling independent, especially within close relationships. Emotional autonomy is characterized by self-sufficiency and feeling comfortable and confident when making decisions without excessive guidance from parents. Over time, adolescents have decreased dependence on their parents for their emotional regulation and support. Emotional autonomy also includes the feeling of being one's own person. The process of gradually achieving a sense of self separate from parents is known as **individuation** and is intertwined with identity development. Part of de-individuation is the **de-idealization of parents**, which refers to adolescents' realizing that their parents are not perfect and, like other adults, they have their unique strengths and challenges.

An example of emotional autonomy is an adolescent girl who has an incident with a teacher at school and is upset that the teacher misunderstood her actions and gave her a lower grade for being off task during class time. Although she is quite distraught over what she thinks is unfair treatment, she is able to calm herself

MyEdLab
Video Example 6.3

Eighteen-year-old Tim and his mother are still negotiating the boundaries of his autonomy, in what his mother calls the "modern world."

down and think about how to improve the situation. Instead of rushing to her parents for support, she talks to the teacher after school and explains her side of the story. At dinner that night, she tells her parents what happened.

Behavioral autonomy involves acting independently. Behavioral autonomy is characterized by more mature decision making and taking responsibility for one's own behavior. Mature decision making involves having an awareness of risks; having an awareness of future consequences; consulting with others who may have experience or knowledge that is relevant to the decision, including parents, peers, and teachers; revising attitudes in response to new information; and considering that other people have their own motives or limitations when they provide advice. An issue for many adolescents' decision making is not being overly susceptible to peer influence. Conformity to peers has been found to peak around age 14 and is thought to be part of the process of establishing independence from parents (Steinberg & Monahan, 2007). Part of establishing behavioral autonomy involves an adolescent making his own decisions and being his own person among friends.

An example of behavioral autonomy is an adolescent boy who arrives at his locker one morning to find his friends talking about skipping school. It is the first nice spring day, and they all want to go do something fun outside. As the idea gains traction in the group, the excitement grows. He is so tempted to join because it sounds fun, but he knows he should stay in school because he has a quiz first period and he studied really hard for it. He also just got in trouble for getting home late last weekend and knows that if he gets caught it will cause big problems with his parents. His friend Eddie is adamant that they won't get caught, but he recalls that Eddie said something similar last weekend before he got in trouble. He decides to stay in school and heads to class early to avoid further temptation.

Cognitive or value autonomy involves thinking independently. Cognitive or value autonomy is characterized by the development of one's own opinions guided by a personal set of principles and values. At school and other places outside the home, individuals are exposed to new perspectives about people, places, and things. During adolescence, individuals become aware that their parents' view of the world is not the only view. Cognitive or value autonomy involves adolescents forming their own opinions on moral, religious, or political issues. It is supported by cognitive development, especially advances in the abilities to think abstractly, take others' perspectives, and think in multiple dimensions. Cognitive autonomy tends to occur later than emotional or behavioral autonomy.

An example of cognitive autonomy is an adolescent girl who has grown up in a politically conservative family but is starting to form her own opinions about government and what laws and policies are best for the United States. This year in her American Government class, her teacher has invited in a wide variety of speakers encompassing liberals, conservatives, independents, socialists, and libertarians to share their views on a range of contemporary issues, such as immigration, taxes, welfare, and charter schools. On some social issues she has decided she has a more liberal viewpoint than her parents, and this has led to several lively discussions in the home.

Although it is sometimes depicted as breaking away from one's parents or an act of rebellion, research indicates that autonomy development is a far more gradual process that unfolds across the adolescent and young-adult years. Over time, adolescents regulate themselves more, and parents need to reduce their monitoring. Although the process does not always go smoothly, and adolescents may test the boundaries of their autonomy, research indicates that it is not inherently or consistently stressful for most adolescents and their parents.

How does students' autonomy relate to the 21st-century thinking skills discussed in Chapter 3?

What Educators Can Do

Schools and classrooms are settings where students have an opportunity to gain autonomy and learn to manage themselves away from their parents. As nonparental adults, teachers can play an important role in helping adolescents adjust to being more independent and autonomous. The information on attachment and autonomy covered in this section has important implications for how teachers can help adolescents' develop autonomy, including the following:

1. *Provide your students with opportunities for choice in the classroom.* There are many ways teachers can provide students with choices in the classroom. For example, students might be allowed to select from a list of possible paper topics or chose alternative approaches to completing a task. When appropriate, you might allow students choices about where to sit or whom to work with on an assignment.

2. *Encourage students to develop their own opinions and values.* Assignments, activities, and discussions that expose students to different perspectives can help them reflect on their own values. As a teacher, you can have students explain their position to help them form their own opinions.

3. *Encourage students to become more independent learners.* Helping students develop autonomy means helping students become self-sufficient. The expectation for adolescent students is that they can set goals, organize their time, monitor their progress, and make adjustments when necessary. However, most students need support and guidance to operate independently, especially in early adolescence. Teachers can help students develop effective strategies and work habits (e.g., keeping a planner, making charts or lists, breaking down larger projects into smaller tasks). Part of being an independent learner involves seeking help when it is needed. Encourage students to ask questions when they are not clear about the directions or do not understand the content. Importantly, focus students on asking for the kind of assistance that helps them learn—not just get done with their work—because this will support them being independent in the future.

4. *Develop positive relationships with your students.* As we have discussed, close personal relationships can support the development of autonomy. During adolescence, individuals are branching out and forming important attachments beyond their parents. Personal and supportive relationships with teachers can also contribute to the development of autonomy. Similar to in parent–adolescent relationships, trust between teachers and adolescents is facilitated by care and consistency.

5. *Recognize that not all children have been raised in a responsive and consistent environment.* Students who have not experienced a secure attachment with parents, either in childhood or in adolescence, may be wary of adult authority. Some students' internal working models of relationships with others will not lead them to readily trust others, including teachers and peers. Some students may have heightened rejection sensitivity and readily notice cues that others do not accept them. For such students, it is especially critical to have a safe and predictable classroom environment. It is only when students feel secure that they might overcome fears of rejection or low expectations that others care about them as a person. It is important for educators to remember that adolescents' present experiences can triumph over previous experiences that may have been lacking in support. A positive, predictable, and safe experience in your classroom can make a difference.

Conflict with Parents

Parent–adolescent conflict was once viewed by psychologists as not only common and nearly inevitable, but the absence of such conflict was seen as a problem for normal development. Adolescents were expected to separate from their parents, and interpersonal struggle and conflict were expected to erupt in the process of what was viewed as detaching from parents. This psychoanalytic view from Anna Freud (1958) and others is no longer in favor, as psychologists now see that adolescents can remain attached to parents while they become autonomous individuals. Research from multiple studies, beginning in the late 1960s and 1970s, suggests that the majority of teenagers, roughly 75%, have positive relationships with their parents (Douvan & Adelson, 1966; Steinberg, 2001). They may argue, disagree, and have their differences, but overall the interaction is pleasant. There is not a serious breach in the parent–child relationship during adolescence. Relationships that were close and affectionate in childhood do not change dramatically. For the 25% of families who experience more serious conflicts, it is likely that they had difficulties in their families prior to adolescence.

Take a look at any of the books on how to "survive" adolescence as a parent, however, and it is hard to know that four decades of research have overturned the expectation that adolescence can be anything but difficult and conflictual. This may be in part because conflict does exist, and it rises sharply during early adolescence (Arnett, 1999), so the experience of parents is a comparative one, with the once-compliant child now finding much more to argue about with parents. In general, conflict with parents remains high into middle adolescence and then declines in late adolescence (Dworkin & Larson, 2001; Larson & Richards, 1994). The intensity of conflict is highest during mid-adolescence (Arnett, 1999). This is likely due to parents and adolescents negotiating the amount of freedom and choice that is appropriate when adolescents enter high school, gain drivers' licenses, and experience expansions in their social lives and ties. Conflict with mothers is more frequent and intense than conflict with fathers (Laursen & Collins, 2009). However, adolescents report feeling closer to their mothers than fathers, so it does not seem that the conflict hurts the overall relationship. Further, conflict seems to be more pronounced for firstborn children, suggesting that parents might learn from experiences with an older child, which helps them negotiate the adolescent stage more smoothly with their younger children (Laursen & Collins, 2009).

What are most conflicts between parents and adolescents about? The most common sources of conflict for adolescents and their parents are household chores, keeping one's room clean, personal appearance, clothing, leisure activity and choice of friends, curfew, and time spent on homework (Smetana, Daddis, & Chuang, 2003). Adolescents and their parents do not tend to disagree on core values and important matters such as the importance of education, career aspirations, religion, and what it means to be a good and moral person. To some extent, conflict in families with adolescents can be characterized as bickering over mundane issues. However, it is important not to minimize the toll that this kind of bickering can have on families. Research has shown that it is not just major events that affect well-being, but that persistent daily hassles can cause stress (Kanner, Coyne, Schaefer, & Lazarus, 1981). Conflict is less frequent in ethnic-minority families, but research has found that the issues causing disagreement are quite similar across ethnic groups (Smetana et al., 2003).

Jeffrey Arnett, a scholar of adolescence, points out that some of these issues are really not as trivial as they might seem (Arnett, 1999). Issues such as choice of

Think back on your time at home as an adolescent. What did you argue about with your parents? How frequently did you disagree? Would you describe the relationship as a positive one?

MyEdLab
Video Example 6.4

Conflict between adolescents and parents most often occur over minor issues that come up in the course of daily life, although sometimes they are more serious.

friends, where to go and what to do with friends, curfew, and clothing and personal appearance represent more serious issues such as sex, drugs and substance use, and driving safety. Given that many parents do not talk openly with their children about certain issues, such as sexuality, conflict may represent parents struggling to exert control and protection over their children in these areas. However, research in Latino and Asian immigrant families has found that conflict does often emerge directly around the sensitive topics of sex and drugs, and often leads to domineering behavior and use of threats by parents (especially with daughters) as they struggle to exert their more conservative values in what is generally seen as a more permissive American society (Lau et al., 2005).

Judith Smetana's research has found that adolescents and their parents tend to differentially define the issues that cause conflict (Smetana, 2011). Issues of conflict are often viewed by parents as matters of social convention, in that there is a right versus wrong way to act. In contrast, adolescents tend to view these issues as a matter of personal choice. Adolescents think matters such as how clean their rooms are and who their friends are should be left up to them. Smetana suggests that conflict peaks in early adolescence because that is when adolescents first press for autonomy, and parents are figuring out how much independence should be granted.

Overall, conflict plays an important role in how the family system adjusts to changes in adolescent development. For most families it does increase, but this does not displace closeness and affection between adolescents and their parents. Conflict is a part of all relationships at one time or another. Conflict can bring about change. During the transitional time of adolescence, conflict is part of the process of adolescents becoming more autonomous and the overall family system developing a new equilibrium (Laursen & Collins, 2009).

MyEdLab Self-Check 6.4

MyEdLab Self-Check 6.5

MyEdLab
Application Exercise 6.2
Apply your knowledge about parent-adolescent conflict to describe and evaluate one teen's perceptions of her relationships with her parents.

Parental Involvement in Adolescent Learning

Parents vary in their involvement in adolescents' learning. Parental involvement can happen both at school and at home. At school, parents may attend parent–teacher conferences as well as volunteer or take part in school events such as science fairs and open houses. At home, parents may assist with homework and course selection, react to performance on tests or assignments, discuss how school is going, inquire about what topics are being studied, and emphasize the value of doing well in school. Parental involvement in intellectual activities, such as recommending books or visiting museums, can also support learning and motivation even if it doesn't directly concern schoolwork.

Much research has shown that parental involvement enhances students' performance in school (Hill & Tyson, 2009; Lee & Bowen, 2006). This is true for parents and students from all socioeconomic backgrounds (Jeynes, 2007). Eva Pomerantz, a scholar who has done much research on families, explains that parental involvement enhances student achievement because it provides children and adolescents with assets that allow them to perform at their full potential (Pomerantz, Kim, & Cheung, 2011). Parental involvement nurtures four different types of assets: cognitive skills, adaptive motivation, appropriate behavior, and positive emotions.

Cognitive Skills. Parents can nurture the development of cognitive skills through practice and instruction. For example, a parent may quiz an adolescent on her Spanish vocabulary words or show her how to do an algebra problem. Cheung and Pomerantz (2012) found that higher parental involvement of early adolescent students predicted positive learning strategies (such as planning their work) 2 years later.

In-Depth 6.2

Siblings

Family life for most adolescents includes the presence of siblings, with 77% of U.S. families having more than one child (U.S. Census Bureau, 2010). Sibling relationships are important to adolescent development (Kramer, 2010). Sibling relationships vary in their characteristics. Sometimes an older sibling acts as a caretaker and provides parent-like functions for a younger sibling. Some siblings treat each other as friends and enjoy spending time together. Other siblings view the other as a rival and tend to compete and to compare themselves to each other. Some siblings spend little time together and don't have a strong emotional connection. Other sibling relationships are contentious and have high levels of arguments and teasing.

Conflict between siblings is common. Adolescents report more conflict with their siblings than with their parents, extended family, friends, or teachers. Conflicts between siblings often concern name-calling or teasing, privacy and possessions (e.g., going into siblings' room or borrowing their things without permission), household chores, and perceived unequal treatment or attention from parents (Noller, 2005). The amount and intensity of conflict with siblings tend to decrease from childhood to adolescence as youth spend more time out of the house and away from the family.

If you have a sibling, you may have wondered how the two of you could have grown up in the same home yet have the number of differences that you do, or perhaps you have wondered this about friends and their siblings. Researchers have also been curious about this phenomenon, and they have examined both environmental and genetic influences. Those who study behavioral genetics examine how genes may influence sibling behavior, as well as how genes and the environment interact. Scientists no longer assume that behavioral outcomes are a result of simply "nature or nurture," but now know that the environment can affect those with different genes in different ways, and that genetic makeup can also evoke differing responses. For example, an adolescent who has a difficult temperament and displays hostile behavior is more likely to elicit negative responses from her parents.

Researchers who study genetic and environmental influence often compare identical versus fraternal twins, as well as examine individuals who have been adopted or raised in stepfamilies. Such research indicates that characteristics that are strongly influenced by genes are aggressive behavior and depression (Spotts, Neiderhiser, Hetherington, & Reese, 2001; Jacobsen & Rowe, 1999). Genetic influence is strong for intelligence but not for actual school performance (Teachmann, 1997). Remember that among siblings who are not identical twins, only a portion of genes are shared.

It is not uncommon for teachers to teach children from the same families over time. It is important for teachers to avoid making comparisons between siblings. Making assumptions about students based on their siblings can foster rivalry and competition. Some adolescents may find it hard to follow an older sibling into a classroom, knowing that the teacher may remember the older sibling's behavior and accomplishments, whether they were problematic or praise-worthy. When educators treat each child as an individual, it lets adolescents focus on their own progress without concerns about expectations to live up to or live down the reputation of a sibling.

Did you have an older sibling? Did you ever feel like you had to contend with a sibling's reputation at school? What do you think is important for teachers to appreciate about sibling relationships?

Adaptive Motivation. When parents are involved it demonstrates to their adolescents that they value school, and it can foster student motivation. Over time, adolescents are likely to internalize the values of their parents regarding school. Parents serve as models for their children, and parental involvement shows an active approach to learning and conveys the idea that with effort, one can bring about positive outcomes. With positive feedback from parents, adolescents are more likely to view themselves as competent and capable to do their schoolwork.

Appropriate Behavior. When parents are involved, they often communicate appropriate expectations about behavior. Teachers and principals inform parents when rules are broken or a student is disruptive. Parental involvement can reinforce expectations at home. Positive behavior supports achievement. One study found that parental involvement in seventh grade led to fewer disruptive problems in eighth grade, which in turn led to improved achievement in ninth grade (Hill et al., 2003).

Positive Emotions. Parental involvement validates a child's sense of worth and increases positive emotions. Parental involvement can diminish anxiety and depression (Pomerantz, Moorman, & Litwack, 2007). Parents can help adolescents learn to regulate their emotions around schoolwork. When parents help with homework, they can model how to deal with challenge and frustration.

Parents' Income Level, Educational Background, and Parental Involvement

Poor, less educated parents are less likely to go to school events and attend parent–teacher conferences as compared with more affluent, educated parents. This is due to the fact that such activities are more difficult for parents with less financial resources because they already stretched thin—perhaps working multiple jobs or figuring out how to pay bills and buy food without enough money (Grolnick, Benjet, & Kurowski, & Apostoleris, 1997). These issues can be especially challenging for single parents (Benner, Graham, & Mistry, 2008). Parents with less educational background feel less confident that they can help their children succeed at school. This lack of confidence diminishes their involvement in their children's learning (Hoover-Dempsey, Bassler, & Brissie, 1992). Further, poor and less educated parents are more likely to think it is not their role and view their child's achievement as up to teachers and school personnel, which can also contribute to a lack of involvement (Lareau, 1987).

Changes in Parental Involvement During Adolescence

Parental involvement declines as children move through elementary school and into middle and high school (Hill & Tyson, 2009). The decline during adolescence may come in part from adolescents who desire more autonomy as well as parents who think adolescents should be more independent and responsible for their own learning. Notes, newsletters, and telephone calls from school to home decline as children progress through the school system. Information about what students are learning as well as how to help with homework declines as children age. The structure of middle and high school may contribute to decreased parental involvement, as these are much bigger settings and students have many more teachers.

What Educators Can Do

Given the importance of parental involvement for student achievement and success, schools and teachers need to try to increase involvement. Families are often busy and have many circumstances that can make it difficult for them to invest time in their students' schooling. This can be especially true for poor or less educated parents. Nonetheless, most parents want their children to succeed. During adolescence, an additional challenge is that parents feel less informed about how to get involved in their children's middle or high school. As we noted, information from schools tends to decline during the adolescent years. However, it does not have to be this way. There is much that schools can do to increase parent and family involvement in schools. In 2010, the Virginia Department of Education surveyed 450 parents, teachers, and school administrators about what schools can do to partner with families and promote student success; here is an overview of some of the key strategies schools can use to promote parental involvement (Virginia Department of Education, 2010):

1. *Host events and activities to bring parents and families into the school.* Schools can sponsor fun and/or educational events to build community and promote academic success. Examples of events include open houses, musical concerts by the students, ice cream socials, and Halloween parties. What events work best will depend on the community that the school is serving. Parent–Teacher Association groups can be helpful to gain parental input. Adolescents can contribute ideas and assist in the planning. The beginning of the school year is the time when families have the most questions as well as enthusiasm.

2. *Communicate with parents frequently, using a variety of methods.* Newsletters, web pages, blogs, and calendars of events can keep parents informed and solicit involvement. Mailing, phone calls, e-mails, information sent home with students, and face-to-face meetings are the variety of methods schools and teachers can use.

3. *Create a warm, respectful, and welcoming environment.* When parents e-mail, call, or enter the school, how they are treated is a big determinant of whether they will continue to respond or initiate contact with school personnel. It is also important to respond promptly to parents' inquiries, which shows that parents' questions and concerns are a priority for school personnel. This is especially important when working with parents from diverse backgrounds or limited economic means because they may not feel as comfortable or knowledgeable about how to engage with the school and teachers.

4. *Be flexible in accommodating parents and families.* Schools can provide transportation for parents who need it and even hold events or activities at other locations when possible. An example is offering parent–teacher conferences at a community center in the neighborhood in addition to the school. Offering childcare can help families with younger siblings. Translators are needed for families whose language is different from that of school personnel.

5. *Provide a variety of resources for parents.* Well-advertised information sessions can be helpful. Materials in easy-to-access places can inform parents about frequently asked questions and concerns. A well-organized and frequently updated website will be helpful to many parents. Others may need information delivered in a different manner.

These strategies show that there are things schools can do to promote involvement, but it is not a simple or easy process. Families will vary greatly from school to school and within any school. Multiple strategies and trial-and-error approaches are usually needed. There is not one sure way to promote involvement. However, not trying different strategies will surely dampen involvement.

What were ways your middle or high school promoted family or parental involvement? What ideas do you have for promoting parental involvement in school?

Optimal Parental Involvement in Adolescents' Learning

So far we have described the possible benefits of parental involvement in adolescents' learning. However, the quality of parental involvement plays a role in the

Structure	Parents provide clear and consistent guidelines, expectations, and rules regarding schoolwork for adolescents.
Autonomy-Supportive	Parents allow adolescents to take an active role in their own learning.
Process-Focused	Parents focus on effort rather than innate ability.
Positive Affect	Parents display positive affect by showing interest, providing encouragement, and being supportive when adolescents experience challenges or setbacks.

FIGURE 6.5

Characteristics of Optimal Parental Involvement

extent to which it is beneficial for adolescent development. This is especially true when it comes to parental involvement in students' learning in coursework. There are four characteristics that make parental involvement optimal: structure, autonomy-supportive practices, process-focused practices, and positive affect (Pomerantz et al., 2007). This is important for teachers to appreciate so that they encourage the kind of parental involvement that is most beneficial for their students. You'll likely notice that the characteristics of optimal parental involvement, shown in Figure 6.5, are consistent with authoritative parenting.

Structure. Structure refers to the extent to which parents provide clear and consistent guidelines, expectations, and rules regarding schoolwork for adolescents. Parents who provide structure provide routines about when and where homework is completed and have consequences if it is not completed. An adaptive amount of structure would be characterized by guidelines, expectations, and explanations that take into account adolescents' capabilities and are appropriate for their level of competence and skills. Structure predicts the development of cognitive skills, motivation, and appropriate behavior (Skinner, Johnson, & Snyder, 2005).

Autonomy-Supportive Practices. Autonomy-supportive practices allow adolescents to take an active role in their own learning. Autonomy-supportive practices involve parents encouraging adolescents to take initiative and generate their own solutions to problems. Parents who support autonomy also make an effort to take their child's perspective. In contrast, giving commands and threatening love withdrawal is highly controlling and undermines adolescents' sense of autonomy. Support for autonomy predicts the development of cognitive skills, motivation, appropriate behavior, positive emotions, and emotional regulation (Skinner et al., 2005).

Process-Focused Practices. Process-focused practices involve a focus on effort toward learning rather than innate ability. Process-focused practices emphasize adolescents' personal mastery of the material in contrast to their performance relative to other students. Parents with a focus on process emphasize the important role of effort and draw attention to progress toward goals. When parents are focused on process, attention is on developing skills rather than on attributes the child already has. A focus on process predicts the development of cognitive skills, motivation, and positive emotions and emotional regulation (Pomerantz, Ng, & Wang, 2006). The more process-focused practices parents use when their children are in elementary school, the less their children's motivation declines in adolescence (Gottfried, Marconlides, Gottfried, & Oliver, 2009).

Positive Affect. Positive affect is important for parental involvement to be beneficial. Parents may display positive affect by showing interest, offering encouragement, and being supportive in the face of challenge. However, this is not always easy for parents to achieve with adolescents. Parents are busy, and homework is often being done while parents are trying to get household chores or their own work done. Often parents get involved when things are not going well and adolescents are frustrated, confused, or upset about the work or their grade. Or parents might get involved because an adolescent is procrastinating or apathetic. It is challenging for parents to maintain positive affect in these interactions.

What Educators Can Do

Previously in this chapter we discussed some general strategies that schools and teachers can use to promote parental involvement. Here we focus more specifically on what teachers can do to promote parental involvement in their courses. There are many ways that teachers can help parents get involved in their adolescents' learning. First, and foremost, teachers need to know the communities that they are teaching in, as the norms and values of families can vary a great deal. In this section, we describe several different ways that teachers can communicate with families and encourage parental involvement throughout the school year. All strategies need to be tailored to the needs of specific communities.

As we have noted, certain types of parental involvement are more beneficial than others. As a teacher, when you communicate with parents you want to try to encourage optimal parental involvement. In the following list we describe five concrete ways that teachers can communicate with parents and affect parental involvement in adolescents' learning in coursework. As you read about the different ways teachers communicate with parents, think about how, as a teacher, you could promote parental involvement that is structured, autonomy-supportive, process-focused, and positive, such as by using the following strategies:

- **Structure**: As a teacher, provide clear information about the expectations for homework in your class so parents can know what to expect and provide a routine that would support adolescents' effort.
- **Autonomy supportive**: As a teacher, encourage parents to help adolescents figure out what strategies or routines works best for them to foster independence.
- **Process-focused**: As a teacher, provide information about resources for students who are struggling or doing poorly so parents know what to do if the need arises.
- **Positive affect**: As a teacher, convey enthusiasm about your course to help parents have a positive attitude.

1. *Introduction Letter to Families.* At the beginning of the year, teachers have the opportunity of introducing themselves to the parents of their students. An introduction letter sent home during the first week of school opens the line of communication for future interactions and provides information about you, your classroom, and goals for the year. When parents perceive a teacher as warm and inviting, they are more likely to get involved. Take advantage of this opportunity to give parents a positive impression of you as an educator.

2. *Open House Presentation.* Most schools hold an open house for parents to meet teachers and see the school and classroom. This kind of event may take place in the spring of the year before students enroll in the school to prepare them for the following year. It may be an event to help families decide about attending the school. Open houses are also held early in the school year for parents to meet the teachers that their children will have for the year. For example, in some middle and high schools, this is held in the evening and parents follow a condensed version of their children's schedules (e.g., rotate on a 10-minute schedule). Open houses are an important opportunity for you

to introduce yourself in person to parents. Open houses are also a time when you can learn more about the parents of your students and concerns and hopes they have for their children in your classroom.

3. *A System for Routine Communication.* Teachers need to think about how they will communicate with parents on a regular basis throughout the year. Many middle and high schools now have online systems that record students' homework completion, attendance, tardiness, and grades. If your school does not have such a system, how will you communicate these issues to parents? Some teachers provide information about major units of study and due dates for assignments on a website or via group e-mails. Hard copies of this information may be appropriate if you do not think all parents have access to the Internet. At the middle school level, it is helpful to give parents information about key dates, major assignments, and goals for student learning so that parents can help students adjust to managing multiple teachers with different expectations.

4. *Feedback on Student Work.* Teachers comment of the quality of students' work and, if needed, what they need to do to improve their performance. Your primary audience may be the student, but bear in mind that parents often read the feedback. Teachers need to think about how their feedback will be read, interpreted, and used to inform both students and parents. All too often parents only hear from teachers when there are problems. This often contributes to negative affect dominating parental involvement in their adolescents' learning. Contemplate reaching out to parents once during the first semester of the year to share a positive observation. This can be especially important if you have had a prior communication about negative behavior or poor performance. Has there been any improvement? Such communications do not need to be long. A quick e-mail about positive behavior can boost parents' (and adolescents') morale.

5. *Request Parental Involvement.* Schools and teachers can increase involvement with invitations to volunteer and participate in school events. When teachers request assistance, parents are more likely to get involved. Provide multiple opportunities and different ways that parents can get involved. Many parents work or at times will be too busy to devote time to volunteer, but if invitations go out at different times during the year and ask for small amounts of time, it increases the chances that a parent will help out. Requests can involve volunteering on a regular basis (weekly or bi-weekly) or be more limited, such as helping with a special project or event in the classroom (e.g., a mock trial, debate, performance, or experiment) or chaperoning a field trip.

Recommendations for Educators

In this chapter, we have examined the role of the family in adolescent development. We discussed the wide array of family structures in contemporary society. We examined the common changes that occur for families of adolescent children. We learned about family dynamics such as parenting styles and their importance for adolescent development. We considered the nature of parental involvement in adolescents' learning. Next, we review the important implications that these topics have for teachers of adolescents.

Families Differ: Don't Make Assumptions, and Use a Variety of Approaches to Communicate with Parents and Caregivers

We examined the diversity of family structures that adolescents experience, and how family structure has changed in recent decades. As a teacher, you will work with a variety of parents and caregivers. Some students will have two parents at home, some will navigate between parents in two households, some will only have one parent to rely on, and others will have an extended family that is part of their daily home life. For some adolescents, it may not be a biological parent who is the caregiver. You are likely to have students from different socioeconomic and cultural backgrounds. As a teacher, do not make assumptions about your students' family environments. Get to know the community and your students. You will need to have a variety of ways of approaching and communicating with parents and caregivers that you tailor appropriately for different situations.

Adolescence Is a Time of Great Change for Families: An Appreciation of Parenting Styles, Autonomy, and Attachment Will Help Your Work with Students and Their Families

When you teach adolescents, you will be working with students and their families at a time of great change. As we learned in this chapter, adolescence is a stage when students desire autonomy, and how parents and teachers respond to this need has important implications for adolescents' well-being. We discussed theory and research showing that an authoritative parenting style with high levels of demandingness and responsiveness is most effective in raising competent, responsible, and happy adolescents. Teachers are in a position to promote student well-being with authoritative teaching in the classroom (Wentzel, 2002). At school and in the classroom, teachers can provide structure and set high expectations but also allow room for student input and choice. We discussed how close personal relationships facilitate the development of autonomy for adolescents. As a teacher, investing time in getting to know your students is likely to make them more amenable to your goals and make you more aware of their reasoning, allowing for their input and choices when appropriate.

Build Partnerships with Parents to Support Optimal Parental Involvement That Promotes Adolescents' Learning and Achievement

As a teacher, you will have students whose parents vary dramatically in their involvement in their adolescents' learning. We learned in this chapter that research has shown that parental involvement boosts students' engagement and achievement in school. Thus, it is important for schools and teachers to build partnerships with parents to increase involvement. This can be challenging during the adolescent years because students are more independent from their parents, and the larger nature of most middle and high schools can act as an impediment to teachers and parents getting to know one another. However, as we discussed, there are strategies for schools and teachers to promote parental involvement. It is often the case that schools and teachers provide less information to families at the middle and high school levels as compared with elementary school, and this contributes to the problem. As an educator of adolescents, you have many opportunities to promote optimal parental involvement.

MyEdLab **Self-Check 6.6**

Conclusion

In this chapter, we discussed the importance of families as a context for development. Teachers can benefit from an awareness of family dynamics, adolescent development, and diversity among families during adolescence, as it can inform their work with students and their parents. Ultimately, as a teacher, you will want to draw on this information to find effective ways to work with your students and promote parental involvement in school.

Ikoimages/Fotolia

7

Technology and Media

Learning Outcomes

7.1 You will be able to describe current technology ownership, Internet access, and technology use by adolescents.

7.2 You will be able to explain how changes in technology have brought about both new opportunities and causes for concern for adolescents.

7.3 You will be able to describe digital citizenship and what educators can do to promote it in their adolescent students.

7.4 You will be able to describe the contemporary media landscape for adolescents.

7.5 You will be able to compare and contrast the different theories and models (cultivation theory, social cognitive theory, schematic information-processing theory, media practice model) of how the media affects adolescent development.

7.6 You will be able to describe what research has found for media effects on different aspects of adolescent development.

7.7 You will be able to describe media literacy and what educators can do to promote it in their adolescent students.

Introduction

Adolescents today are developing in a digital world where technology and media dominate much of their attention. The last 25 years have seen great advances in technology and a proliferation of media devices. The nature and pace of change in recent years have been startling. Media devices are now smaller, more portable, and integrated such that adolescents with smartphones have continuous access to friends and family as well as the Internet, music, and video. On their devices, adolescents have more choices than ever before. With the exceptions of school and sleeping, adolescents today spend more time with media than any in other activity. Inside school, adolescents increasingly use technology to support their learning. The technology-intensive and media-saturated world of students is often evident to teachers in the classroom. Consider the following examples:

>>>

Mr. Purcell is about to start his first-period biology class when he notices Anthony texting on his iPhone. Despite the school policy that phones should not be seen or heard in the classroom, he often has to ask students to put away their phones. When he asks Anthony to put away his phone, Anthony replies that he really needs to communicate with his mom about something. Mr. Purcell wonders how strict he and the other teachers should be about students' phones. More and more, it seems students are lost without their phones.

Mr. Burke is a first-year teacher at a large suburban high school. He is an outgoing and energetic teacher who is excited to try new techniques to engage students in his history classes. He established an interactive website for the purpose of communicating about course material and assignments. He is pleased with how engaged his students have been with the site and impressed with the quality of most students' comments and questions. However, a few students' posts have been more personal than professional. He realizes he needs more specific guidelines to help all students use the site appropriately.

Mrs. Howard sits amused, but also somewhat concerned, by the antics of a group of girls in her seventh-grade advisory period. She has rewarded their good behavior with some free time, and the girls are using it to sing and dance. Their dance moves are entertaining but somewhat suggestive, inspired by the latest Miley Cyrus video. When the girls start "twerking" and the boys start to make comments about different girls' physical attributes and "twerking" talent, Mrs. Howard calls an end to free time and has everyone return to their seats. She can't help worrying about her students and their exposure to and interest in entertainment and media that in her opinion is far more sexualized and violent as compared with when she was an adolescent. She contemplates engaging her class in an activity to promote their critical thinking around the values they see in the media.

In these examples, we see the presence of technology and media in students' lives and how it can present itself to teachers. As a teacher, you are likely to engage in a range of behaviors (e.g., limiting, managing, embracing, discussing) around a host of possible scenarios with technology and media and the role they can play in your classroom and instruction. The overall goal of this chapter is to enhance your understanding of the role of technology and media in adolescent development and appreciate the implications for your teaching. We would like to note at the outset that it is beyond the scope of this chapter to provide in-depth coverage of issues surrounding teachers' use of technology in planning, instructing, and assessing students. Our focus here is adolescent development and implications for teachers of adolescent students.

OVERVIEW OF THE CHAPTER

This chapter is divided into two main sections. First, we examine current trends in technology and media use by adolescents. We consider how it has changed in recent years and how such changes represent both new opportunities and cause for concern. We discuss the role that teachers and schools can play in promoting students' responsible and appropriate use of technology to facilitate learning and well-being (referred to as *digital citizenship*).

Second, we consider how the media affects adolescent development. We examine the nature of the contemporary media landscape that youth experience. We describe different theories about how the media influences youth and review evidence to date about media effects on adolescent development. We consider how adolescents select, interact with, and interpret the media. We discuss the role that teachers and schools can play in helping adolescents develop the ability to understand, analyze, and evaluate the images, words, and sounds that make up our contemporary mass-media culture (referred to as *media literacy*).

The concepts of digital citizenship and media literacy are garnering increased attention due to the growing role of technology and media in the lives of youth (Boyd, 2014; Chakroff & Nathanson, 2008; James et al., 2009; Ribble, 2011; Strasburger, 2014). Given that issues related to technology and media affect youth in schools (either due to the use of technology in schools and classrooms or due to issues that arise in schools and classrooms stemming from use outside of school), educators are increasingly being called upon to foster such knowledge and skills in students. In some school districts, these topics may be addressed within technology and health courses. The amount of attention these topics get varies dramatically. Whether or not digital citizenship and media literacy are a specific focus in health or technology classes in the middle or high school where you work, you will need to address these issues within your own courses. As a teacher of adolescents in contemporary times, you need to decide how to best support students' responsible and appropriate use of technology for learning as well as foster their critical thinking skills in an online world. How you do so will vary depending on the subject you teach, the nature of assignments, and your interests and goals as a teacher. The objective of this chapter is to provide foundational knowledge for you as an educator around these issues. Being aware of current trends and relevant research and theory about how technology and media affect adolescent development will help you to make more informed decisions about how you can support digital citizenship and media literacy in your adolescent students.

Technology and Media Use

It is helpful for teachers to be aware of how their students are using technology and media. Most adolescents and young adults today are **digital natives**, meaning they were born and grew up immersed in digital technology and therefore have high levels of familiarity with computers and the Internet. Youth often lead the way and embrace new technology in greater numbers than do older generations. Educators and parents can feel at a disadvantage when they are unfamiliar with adolescents' technology habits and media use. In this section we review current trends to inform you, as a teacher, about the role technology and media play in contemporary adolescence. We take advantage of several large-scale studies that describe adolescents' digital world. It is important to note at the outset of this section that due to the rapid changes in technology and media, it is challenging for researchers to capture the patterns of media use among youth. By the time the results of a survey have been collected and reported, some changes in what is available and how it is being used have already happened. As a teacher, you will always have to observe and talk to your students about their technology use and media habits to stay abreast of their behavior and the current norms and latest trends in your community. However, the information in this section provides an important foundation and overview regarding technology and media use by adolescents in contemporary America.

Technology Ownership and Access to the Internet

The Pew Research Center's Internet and American Life Project is an ongoing effort to understand the evolution of the Internet, how Americans use the Internet, and how such use affects their lives. The Pew project's website is a good resource for staying informed about technology and media issues (see http://www.pewInternet .org). In 2015 the Pew project released a report on teens and technology based on surveys conducted in late 2014 through early 2015 with a nationally representative sample of over a 1000 teens aged 13 to 17 years old and their parents living in the United States. The survey asked teens if they have or have access to five types of technology devices: desktop or laptop computer, smartphone, basic phone, tablet, and game console.

In-Depth 7.1

Cell Phones in Schools and Classrooms

Cell phone use at school is a controversial topic. Michael Bloomberg faced much pressure during his time as mayor of New York (2002–2013) for actively enforcing a ban on all cell phones at school. In 2007, New York City schools started using metal detectors to search for and confiscate not only weapons, but phones as well, resulting in much outrage among parents and students. Many parents criticized the policy, saying it violated their rights to monitor, contact, and communicate with their children. Many students resisted the ban and smuggled their phones into school. Students went to great lengths to keep their phones by smuggling them in their socks, underwear, and even buried in their sandwiches. Bloomberg and his administration refused to drop the ban, insisting that previous generations of students and parents managed just fine without phones. They viewed cell phones as a distraction in the classroom and too often used to cheat, take inappropriate photos in bathrooms, and organize gang activity. In addition, when fights break out, cell phones can summon a large crowd in minutes. Allowing cell phones in schools is also problematic because they are a top target for theft.

In 2015 New York City Mayor Bill de Blasio announced he would lift the ban and allow schools to decide their own policies. Schools around the country vary greatly in their policies: Some ban phones completely from school, others allow phones at school but not in the classroom, and others leave it up to the teacher whether to allow students to use phones in the classroom. With the increasing presence of cell phones in adolescents' and adults' lives, it becomes more challenging to ban phones from schools. Further, computers, iPads, digital gaming, and other types of technology are increasingly being integrated into students' learning experience in the classroom. Some educators advocate for use of phones in the classroom. Cell phones can be a useful resource to do calculations, take pictures, and search online. Banning phones may be a missed opportunity to teach students to be responsible with their phones. There are also many apps available that can be used as learning tools. For example, Poll everywhere (http://polleverywhere.com) allows teachers to poll students' opinions on multiple-choice quizzes.

The opposing view is that adolescents today need less screen time, not more, and the classroom is now one of few places where students can be quiet and focused and not distracted by their phones. Advocates of this view think we should preserve the classroom for contemplation and face-to-face social interaction. It can also be challenging for teachers to manage 25 students using phones and making sure they stay on task and do not use the phones inappropriately during class. Further, although many students today have phones, not all students have phones or have smartphones that allow Internet access, which could put some students at a disadvantage if phones are used in the classroom.

What do you think schools and teachers should do about phones in school? Ban them outright? Require them to be turned off in the classroom? Require them to be left in lockers? Allow them to be used at the teacher's discretion in the classroom? If given the choice, what would you do in your classroom?

FIGURE 7.1

Most Adolescents Ages 13–17 Have Access to Technology

Source: Lenhart, A., 2015.

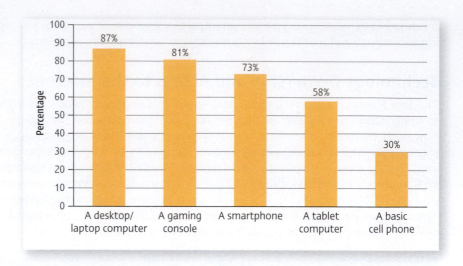

The results indicate that teens today are avid users of technology, highly immersed in the digital world, and taking advantage of the mobile nature of technology (see Figure 7.1). The majority of American teens have access to computers, cell phones, smartphones, game consoles, and tablets (Lenhart, 2015). Overall, 70% of teens reported having access to three or four of these tech devices, 4% reported having access to only one, and only 1% reported having access to no devices.

Most teens have some kind of cell phone (88%), and 73% have smartphones. There are some differences in smartphone access based on age and race. Older teens are more likely to have smartphones (76% of 15- to 17-year-olds) than are younger teens (68% of 13- to 14-year-olds). African American teens are more likely than any other racial group to have smartphones (81% compared to 71% of White and 71% of Hispanic youth).

Most teens have access to a desktop or laptop computer (87%) or tablet (58%). White teens are more likely to have a computer (91%) as compared with Hispanic (82%) and African American youth (79%). Most teens also have access to a game console such as Xbox, Wii, or PlayStation (81%). Boys (91%) are more likely to have a game console than are girls (70%). White and African American teens (85%) are more likely to have game consoles as compared with Hispanic youth (71%).

The vast majority of teens, some 95%, are online (Madden, Lenhart, Duggan, Cortesi, & Gasser, 2013). The high percentage of teens online has been consistent since 2006. What has changed dramatically is the nature of teens' Internet use. Internet use has gone from stationary connections through desktops to always-on, mobile access that travels with them throughout the day. In 2014, 91% of teens reported that they go online from a mobile device, at least occasionally. All African American youth (100%) reported going online at least occasionally compared to rates of about 90% for White and Hispanic youth (Lenhart, 2015).

The term **digital divide** is used to describe the gap between groups of people who have access to and knowledge of technology and the Internet and those who do not. The digital divide has lessened between groups in the United States over time but still exists, primarily in relation to groups that differ in family income level. Adolescents from lower-income families are less likely to have computers (80% of families with incomes less than $50,000, compared with 91% of teens from families earning more than that). Similarly, teens from lower-income families are less likely to have smartphones (64%) as compared with teens from families with higher income (77%).

Schools are increasingly spending money on technology, but that does not address the problem that many low-income students lack computers with Internet access at home. Low-income students are often forced to rely on public resources such as libraries or after-school programs that are often unreliable and inadequate due to high demand and time limits. Imagine a student Stacey, who, because she does not have Internet access at home, goes to the library on Saturday to do research and write a paper for her social studies class. Upon arrival she learns there is an hour wait. When she finally gets her turn, she has a 30-minute time limit. She finds several relevant resources but has just begun writing when she runs out of time. She must stop her work and sign up again, with another hour-long wait. When we think of Stacey in contrast to her peers who can do their work at home, we see the disadvantage that faces many low-income students. Given these issues, many have expressed concern that as schools embrace technology it will become harder and harder for low-income youth to succeed in school (Monahan, 2013). As a teacher, it is important to be aware of your students' computer resources and Internet access at home and take this into account for homework assignments, as well as how you communicate with parents and students.

Technology and Media Use

Mobile devices have facilitated teens' use of the Internet. Going online is a daily event for 92% of teens, and for 24% of teens it is something they report doing "almost constantly" (Lenhart, 2015). More than half of teens (57%) go online several times a day, and 12% report that they go online once a day. Only 6% of teens report going online weekly, and 2% report going online less than weekly. African American and Hispanic youth report more Internet use than White teens. About a third of African American and Hispanic teens report going online "almost constantly," compared with 19% of White teens (see Figure 7.2).

Social Media.   Social media use is pervasive among American youth. Most teens (90%) have used social media (Common Sense Media, 2012) and most have their own site (76%; Lenhart, 2015). Since the emergence of Facebook in 2004, social media has been evolving. Adolescents and young adults are often the predominant demographic to initially lead the way in use of social media sites. For example, Facebook originated and took hold among college students but expanded to wide use among adults of all ages. In recent years, adolescents' use of Facebook is changing. Adolescents are more enthusiastic about Instagram and Twitter as compared with Facebook (Madden et al., 2013). Adolescents' waning enthusiasm for Facebook seems due to the large adult presence, too many negative social interactions, and feeling overwhelmed by friends who share too much on the site (Madden, 2013).

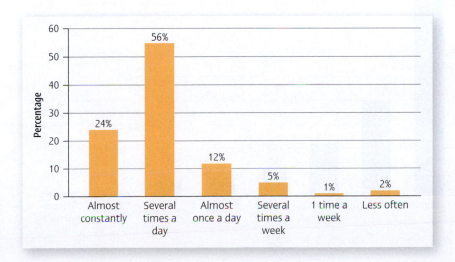

FIGURE 7.2

Adolescents Ages 13–17 Are Frequent Users of the Internet

Source: Lenhart, A., 2015.

FIGURE 7.3

Facebook, Instagram, and Snapchat Are Top Social Media Platforms for Adolescents Ages 13–17 (Lenhart, 2015)

Source: Data from Pew Research Center's Teens Relationship Survey conducted Sept. 2014–March 2015.

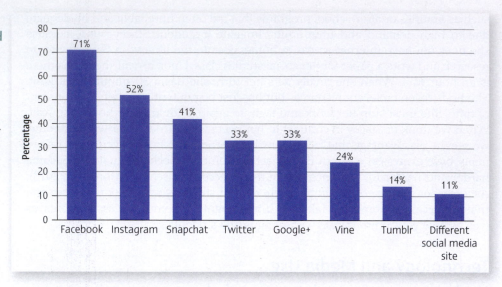

However, adolescents still use Facebook more than any other social media site, with 71% reporting they use Facebook as compared with 52% for Instagram, 41% for Snapchat, and 33% for Twitter (Lenhart, 2015; see Figure 7.3). Most teens (71%) report using more than one platform. When asked what social media site they use most often, Facebook still emerges at the top (see Figure 7.4). There are some interesting differences by age, gender, and family income in what social media site is used most:

■ Older teens (ages 15 to 17) are more likely than younger teens (13 to 14) to say Facebook is their most-used site (44% versus 35%), whereas younger teens are more likely than older teens to say Instagram is their most-used site (25% versus 17%).
■ Boys are more likely to say they use Facebook the most (45% of boys versus 36% of girls), whereas girls are more likely to say they use Instagram the most (23% girls versus 17% boys).

FIGURE 7.4

Facebook, Instagram, and Snapchat Are Used Most Often by Adolescents Ages 13–17 (Lenhart, 2015)

Source: Data from Pew Research Center's Teens Relationship Survey conducted Sept. 2014–March 2015.

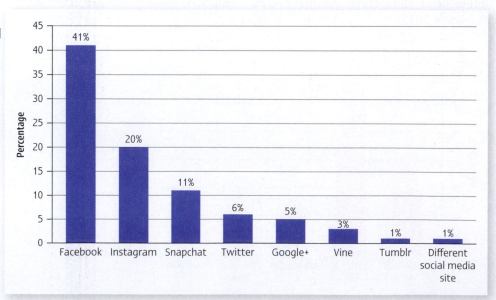

- Adolescents from lower-income families (49% of those earning less than $50,000 a year) are more likely to use Facebook the most, compared to 37% of adolescents from families who earn more than that.

Communication. Texting is a key form of communication for adolescents today. Overall, 91% of teens who have cell phones report using text messaging (Lenhart, 2015). For teens who text, the median number of texts sent in a typical day is 30. Girls tend to text more than boys. Older adolescent girls (ages 15 to 17) are the most active texters, with a median of 50 texts a day.

Text messaging apps have grown in popularity in recent years, and about a third of teens report using apps like Kik or Whatsapp on their phones (Lenhart, 2015). White teens (24%) are less likely than their African American (47%) or Hispanic (46%) peers to use such apps.

Another interesting trend is the use of anonymous sharing apps or sites where teens can ask questions or post texts or images not identified by their names. Such apps have received media attention and stirred up concern in recent years, but few teens report using such sites. Of teens with cell phones, 11% report using anonymous sites such as Whisper, Yik Yak, and Ask. FM (Lenhart, 2015).

Most adolescents (49%) still prefer face-to-face communication with their friends as compared with any form of electronic communication (Common Sense Media, 2012). When asked why, teens were most likely to say that they prefer face-to-face communication because it is more fun or because it is easier to understand what people mean. Some adolescents report that hectic schedules due to extracurricular activities can make it hard to see friends in person, but social media and texting allow them to stay connected to their friends (Boyd, 2014). Adolescents do recognize some drawbacks to electronic communication (and cell phones in general), and 43% agree or strongly agree with the statement that they wish they could sometimes unplug. As shown in Figure 7.5, almost half (45%) strongly or somewhat agree that they get frustrated with friends for texting or social networking when hanging out together. Interestingly, adolescents' frustration extends to their parents as well. Of adolescents whose parents have cell phones, 28% consider their parents addicted to their phones, and 21% wish their parents spent less time with their cell phones.

Inevitably, by the time you read this chapter there will be changes in technology and the popularity of different sites and apps. What new trends have you noticed in the last year or two among adolescents? What new benefits and challenges do you see?

Television. Over the last decade, there has been an increase in the amount of TV and video that teens watch due to the increased flexibility of when, where, and how shows and movies can be watched. The average time spent viewing TV shows and movies on television (or any electronic device) is about 3 to 4 hours a day (Bleakely, Vaala, Jordan, & Romer, 2014; Flint, 2012; Rideout, Foehr, & Roberts, 2010). Contemporary teens (similar to adults) are less likely to view shows at their original broadcast time on a television set and more likely to do their viewing on laptops or cell phones (Bleakely et al., 2014; Rideout et al., 2010).

There are important differences in heavy TV viewing depending on adolescents' parents' education level. In a nationally representative sample, one study found that

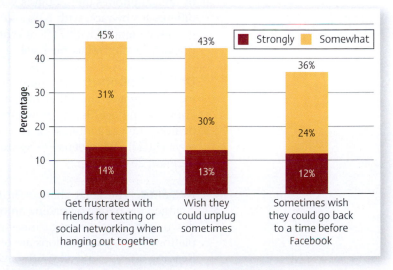

FIGURE 7.5

Adolescents Ages 13–17 Have the Desire to Unplug

Source: Common Sense Media, 2012.

FIGURE 7.6

Whether Adolescents View Television More Than 4 Hours or More on Weekdays Varies by Parental Education Level

Source: Child Trends, 2013.

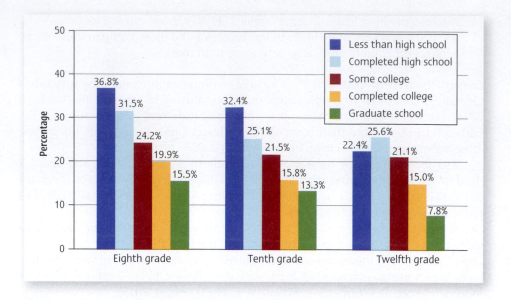

the more education adolescents' parents had, the less likely they were to watch 4 or more hours a day of TV on weekdays (Child Trends, 2013; see Figure 7.6). This was true for 8th-, 10th-, and 12th-grade students. Four or more hours of TV is considered excessive and known to be associated with decreased school performance (Child Trends, 2013).

Video Games. Playing video games is widespread among American adolescents. In a nationally representative sample, parents of teens estimated their youth spent an average of an hour and a half day playing video games (Bleakely et al., 2014). For most, playing video games is a social experience, with friends either in the same room or online (and half of those who play online say they already know their online friends from their offline lives). Only 25% report that they only play video games alone (Lenhart et al., 2008). There are marked gender differences in owning a game console (70% of girls versus 91% of boys) and playing video games online or on cell phones (59% of girls versus 84% of boys; Lenhart, 2015). There are also differences by race, with 83% of African American teens reporting that they play games, compared with 71% of White teens and 69% of Hispanic teens. Patterns do not vary by family income level.

Online Pinboards. The number of sites where users can upload, save, sort, and manage images and other media content (known as "pins") through collections known as pinboards has grown in recent years. About 1 in 5 teens (22%) use pinboards (such as Pinterest or Polyvore). Girls (33%) are more likely to do so than boys (11%). Older teens (25%) are more likely to do so than younger teens (16%; Lenhart, 2015).

Reading. The great changes in technology and media in recent decades have changed the nature of reading among youth. Whereas reading used to mean sitting down with a book or magazine, it now often takes place on a screen on a variety of platforms where distractions are only a click away (Common Sense Media, 2014b). Reading rates among all youth have declined greatly in the last 30 years. According to a large study conducted by the government, rates dropped for youth of all ages (see Figure 7.7). From 1984 to 2013, the proportions of youth who read at least once a week for pleasure dropped from 81 to 76% for 9-year-olds, from 70 to 53% for 13-year-olds, and from 64 to 40% for 17-year-olds. In contrast, the proportion who report that they never or hardly ever read increased from 8 to 22% for 9-year-olds

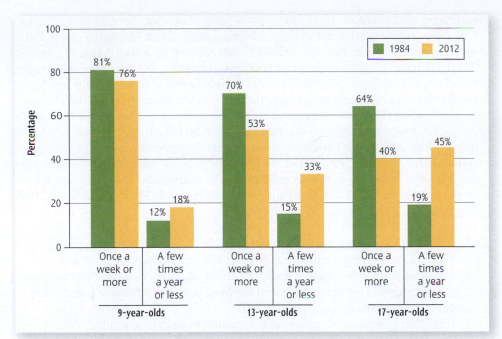

FIGURE 7.7

The Frequency of Reading Declined Between 1984 and 2012, Especially for Older Adolescents

Source: Data from U.S. Department of Education, National Center for Education Statistics, 2013.

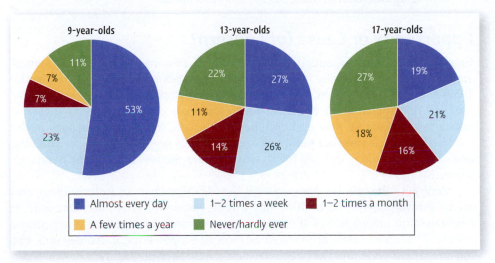

FIGURE 7.8

Frequency of Reading for Fun Declines During Adolescence

Source: Data from U.S. Department of Education, National Center for Education Statistics, 2013.

and from 9 to 27% for 17-year-olds. Across all ages, girls spend more time reading than boys (Common Sense Media, 2014b; Rideout et al., 2010). Among teenagers, 18% of boys are daily readers, compared with 30% of girls (Scholastic, 2013). The amount of time spent on daily reading drops greatly from childhood to adolescence (Scholastic, 2013). As shown in Figure 7.8, more than half of 9-year-olds read for fun each day, compared with 19% of 17-year-olds. E-reading has the potential to alter the nature of reading for youth. Most children and adolescents have some experience with e-reading (Common Sense Media, 2014b; Wartella, Rideout, Lauricella, & Connell, 2013; Scholastic, 2013). E-reading is growing in popularity (Zickuhr, 2013). However, it is not yet clear what the impact of that growing popularity will be (Common Sense Media, 2014b).

Advertising. During their time with various media, adolescents today are exposed to an unprecedented level of advertising. TV ads continue to be a prime way companies reach adolescents. Given that time watching TV is increasing, it is not surprising that exposure to TV ads is increasing (Common Sense Media, 2014a). One study estimated that the average adolescent saw about 16 ads per day in 2011, up from about 13 ads per day in 2004 (Rudd Center for Food Policy & Obesity, 2012). With the great changes in technology and media, the nature of advertising has changed too. Often advertising is inextricably linked with entertainment. Many companies are now integrating their products into the programming that audiences are viewing (TV, movies) or playing (games). Instead of featuring a company's product or brand in a separate ad, companies pay to have their products and logos appear during the program itself. Online advertising encompasses not only more sophisticated and enticing ads but also features such as "advergames," online videos, branded websites, virtual worlds, and social marketing. Today's online advertising is different from TV or print ads for several reasons (Moore & Rideout, 2007; Montgomery, Grier, Chester, & Dorfman, 2013):

1. It is often interactive, meaning youth actively engage with the brand (for example, by playing a game that involves the brand's logo or product).
2. It is often immersive, meaning that youth are in a fully branded "environment" for an extended period of time, and the lines between advertising and other content are blurred.
3. It is often personalized, meaning it is created from data about the child or adolescent that allows it to be targeted to that youth based on his or her demographic characteristics, interests, and locations.

Opportunity or Cause for Concern?

Changes in technology and the introduction of new media have often generated controversy, especially in regard to child and adolescent well-being. In the 1950s some thought rock 'n' roll would change the world, whereas others thought it would ruin the children. Similarly, today some see changes in technology and media as representing new opportunities and a force for positive changes in the world (dubbed the **utopian perspective**), and others see the changes as troubling and cause for concern (dubbed the **dystopian perspective**; Jackson, 2008; Livingstone, 2014).

Central to the utopian perspective is the idea that changes in technology and media provide new opportunities for learning, communication, and creativity. It celebrates the emergence of the information age and the rise of the networked society. Electronic media are viewed as tools of empowerment. Adolescents can interact with a wide array of people beyond where they physically live, which can enhance perspective-taking ability and facilitate relationships that would otherwise not be possible (Tynes, 2007). There is endless information online that they can access to pursue their interests and worldviews. For example, changes in technology provide new opportunities for youth to select and interact with media that can foster identity development. In past decades adolescents' "identity experiments" with media consisted of pictures on their bedroom walls or lockers (Brown & Bobkowski, 2011). Social media sites provide youth today with broader access to more numerous resources and increased flexibility in constructing and changing their online identities. Changes in technology also allow the collection of personal information that can be used to provide insight and motivate change. For example, activity trackers like the "fit bit" are wireless wearable devices that measure how many steps a person takes throughout the day as well as the amount and quality of the person's sleep.

An example of the utopian perspective would be a website like Change.org, which allows individuals to post petitions aimed at bringing about social change. The website is available in different languages and multiple countries. Among the many successful petitions launched on Change.org was one by teenager Sarah

MyEdLab Self-Check 7.1

MyEdLab
Application Exercise 7.1
Use of Technology in Adolescence Reflect on the ways in which contemporary adolescents use technology to interact with friends.

MyEdLab
Video Example 7.1

Tara Gander, the technology facilitator at East Mooresville Intermediate School, describes how teachers can address new opportunities and causes for concern within a single lesson.

Kavanagh from Mississippi, who launched a campaign asking for removal of the ingredient brominated vegetable oil (BVO) from Gatorade and PowerAde. BVO contains bromine, an element found in flame retardant that is not approved for use in food products in Europe or Japan. Kavanagh, who was only 12 when she started the petition, got over 250,000 signatures for her petition and ultimately was successful in getting both companies to agree to drop the ingredient (Strom, 2014).

In contrast, the dystopian perspective highlights the potential negative effects on youth. First, there is concern that the time that youth spend with technology and media is time away from family and friends and time spent outdoors. This is known as the **displacement effect:** Technological devices and media have negative effects because they often replace more positive activities. Time with cell phones would be better spent doing schoolwork, exploring nature, being active, or interacting with others in person in more meaningful pursuits such as sports, band, or theater. In regard to adolescents' peer relationships, there is concern that electronic communication with friends is replacing talking and spending time together in person.

Second, there is concern with multitasking and the extent to which youth (and adults!) constantly divide their attention on computers or cell phones and how it may diminish the quality of work, social interactions, and overall well-being. Many teachers and parents are concerned that children and adolescents' use of technology and media while doing homework has an adverse effect on their learning. The effects of media multitasking are not fully understood, and are likely to depend on the extent of multitasking and what kind of tasks and outcomes are being considered. Concerning academic work, there is growing evidence that multitasking during such work is associated with reduced attention and ability to filter distractions, which diminishes memory and learning (Baumgartner, Weeda, van der Heijden, & Huizinga, 2014; Ophir, Nass, & Wagner, 2009; Sana, Westen, & Cepeda, 2013).

Third, there is concern with the content of the media and that it exposes children and adolescents to inappropriate and harmful images and information, such as violence or explicit sexual material (a topic we consider in depth in the second part of this chapter). Information in the media can be biased or inaccurate, but youth do not bring a critical eye to much of what they encounter in the media. In their more immediate social world, easy and instant access to peers can bring costs in terms of shared information that one would rather keep private (i.e., the inevitable mistakes one makes growing up are amplified in public spaces). All of this contributes to the viewpoint that it is harder growing up today, and the main reason is the media.

Of course it would be overly simplistic to think one perspective is correct and the other wrong. There is truth to both the utopian and dystopian perspectives on changes in technology and the media, in general and specific to adolescent development. Danah Boyd, a scholar who spent years interviewing American adolescents and observing how they use technology, notes that the reality of technology and adolescent development is nuanced and complicated, with both pros and cons (Boyd, 2014). It is not all magical and wonderful, nor is it all terrible and ruining youth today. Further, it is important to remember that many aspects of American teen culture remain unchanged in the digital age. In many ways the school experience is similar to what it was decades ago. Just as in the past, adolescence is an often awkward time when individuals are searching for identity while feeling self-conscious and striving to develop meaningful friendships. Boyd reminds us that although technology has changed much about the adolescent experience, there is much that remains the same.

"Today's students are really no different than those of previous generations—they just have different tools through which to express themselves." Do you agree with this statement? Why or why not?

Teachers' Views of Adolescents and Technology. A study on teachers' views of how changes in technology have affected adolescents' research skills highlights some of the opportunities and causes for concern that have accompanied the advances in technology in the academic domain (Purcell et al., 2012). Overall, the majority of teachers view the Internet and digital search tools as having a "mostly positive" impact on their students' research skills. However, the teachers' responses to more specific issues about the Internet and adolescents' research skills show that their views are quite mixed. On the positive side, almost all teachers agreed that the Internet has allowed students to access a wider range of resources than would otherwise be available (99%), and most agreed that the Internet makes students more self-sufficient researchers (65%). However, in tandem to these benefits, teachers reported some concerns. The majority (87%) agreed that the Internet has created an "easily distracted generation with short attention spans" and that the amount of information available online to students is overwhelming (83%). Specific concerns that teachers worry about include students' overdependence on search engines; the difficulty many students have in judging the quality of online information; increasing distractions pulling at students and poor time management skills; students' potentially diminished critical thinking capacity; and the ease with which today's students can borrow from the work of others. Teachers report that for today's students, "research" means "Googling."

The teachers in the sample for Purcell et al.'s (2012) study included over 2,400 teachers from different regions of the United States as well as urban and rural schools. They were predominantly high school Advanced Placement teachers as well as some middle and high school teachers who were part of the National Writing Project (see http://www.nwp.org). Thus, the results are not generalizable to all teachers and students. The fact that these teachers' views were so mixed when they teach some of the brightest and most hard-working students is notable.

To address the concerns they have with their students' research skills, the teachers in Purcell et al.'s (2012) study reported that they spent class time instructing students in the following areas:

- How search engines work
- How to assess the reliability of the information they find online
- How to improve their search skills

In addition, the teachers reported constructing assignments that point students toward the best online resources and encourage the use of sources other than search engines.

What Educators Can Do

MyEdLab
Video Example 7.2
Mr. Dunleavy uses a WebQuest in his lesson on Edgar Allan Poe. Note the ways in which he encourages students to become good digital citizens who can navigate and evaluate Internet resources.

Promoting Digital Citizenship in Adolescent Students

Given the strong presence of the digital world in adolescents' lives, there is increasing advocacy for the idea that educators should promote digital citizenship in their students (James et al., 2009; Ribble, 2009, 2011). In general, citizenship refers to the status of being a citizen in a particular place and the qualities that a person is expected to have as a responsible member of a community. In today's world, billions of people interact online in a digital world each day, and their collective interactions in this space can be thought of as a digital society. **Digital citizenship** refers to the norms of appropriate and responsible technology use and the information and skills that one needs to be active, informed, and responsible in the digital world. It is a proactive approach to educate the next generation, not just react when there are problems. Digital citizenship is multifaceted. We describe five key elements of digital citizenship: (1) communication,

(2) privacy and safety, (3) technical skills, (4) information navigation, and (5) operating in a culture of relentless multitasking. We also discuss what educators can do in regard to each of these elements. In some middle or high schools students may be exposed to issues of digital citizenship in technology or health classes, or in advisory periods in middle school. However, digital citizenship is an issue that all teachers have to attend to in various ways, as students will have new social and learning experiences in each class and school in general. A helpful (and free) resource for teachers at all levels is the Digital Literacy and Citizenship Classroom Curriculum, which is available on the website of Common Sense Media.

The five key elements of digital citizenship are as follows:

1. *Communication.* Digital citizenship includes making appropriate decisions about how to communicate with others in the digital world. The nature of communication in today's digital world is that adolescents are able to keep in constant contact with almost anyone else. Educators can help adolescents by teaching them about etiquette and respect when communicating online. This can include discussion about rules and norms for e-mail communication with you as their teacher, as well as how to pose questions and make comments when working in groups or in forums where their classmates are also participating. More broadly, educators can help adolescents think about all of their communications online, including texting and social media with peers. Adolescents' cognitive and social skills that help them appreciate others' perspectives are still developing, and so teachers can help their students by reminding them about how their use of language, pictures, and humor can affect their peers. See Figure 7.9 for a sample poster that promotes reflection in adolescents regarding their online communication.

2. *Privacy and Safety.* Digital citizenship includes making appropriate decisions in regard to one's privacy and safety, including posts, privacy settings, and the sharing of personal information, such as one's address, online. Adolescents need help to appreciate the wide scope of an online audience. Information and images shared online can be spread quickly, and it may become beyond their control to remove or alter the things that they post. Colleges and employers may judge prospective students and employees based on their online profiles. Some adolescents are unaware that adults can access the information that they post to social media sites. Educators can help students by teaching them about their **digital footprint**, or the traces one leaves in the electronic environment, and setting the appropriate privacy settings and making good decisions about what to share online. Further, students need to think about the possibility of information being hacked and the importance of saving their information in a secure way but also limiting the extent to which they share personal information, even in private communications.

3. *Technical Skills.* Digital citizenship involves technical skills. Technology is constantly evolving in today's world, and adolescents need to be comfortable with learning new skills. In many contemporary workplaces adults are expected to use an ever-expanding array of technology and programs. When it is possible and fits in the curriculum, educators can help adolescents by using new technologies, programs, and applications.

4. *Information Navigation.* Digital citizenship involves learning strategies for information navigation. The amount of information available online is vast. Although this represents many opportunities for adolescents to learn about new topics, it can also be overwhelming. Educators can help adolescent students with strategies for searching online, evaluating different online sources, and organizing and processing the results of their online searches. This is in line with the Common Core State Standards, 2010, which state

Before you...

THINK!

T - Is it true?
H - Is it hurtful?
I - Is it illegal?
N - Is it necessary?
K - Is it kind?

FIGURE 7.9
Digital Citizenship Poster
Source: Retrieved from http://ictevangelist.com/digital-citizenship/

MyEdLab Self-Check 7.2

MyEdLab Self-Check 7.3

MyEdLab
**Application Exercise 7.2
Digital Citizenship in Adolescence** Consider the ways in which a lesson linking classrooms in Hawaii and New Hampshire fosters digital citizenship.

that students need to be skilled in using technology to produce and publish writing and interact and collaborate with others.

5. *Operating in a Culture of Relentless Multitasking.* Digital citizenship involves learning to operate in a digital culture where everything is easily and simultaneously accessible. For adolescents, it is hard to resist checking one's favorite sites and communicating with others while doing homework, hanging out with peers, or just about anything. However, multitasking can drain our focus and hinder performance. Constantly checking one's phone or moving from window to window on the computer undermines learning. Educators can help adolescents by teaching them to be mindful and engage in strategies to do their best on homework. It is unrealistic to expect adolescents to resist multitasking all together. However, adolescents need to realize that they must engage in some strategies to regulate their attention and focus to succeed in school—for example, putting one's phone in another room for a half hour while completing an assignment.

Media and Adolescent Development

In this section of the chapter we turn our attention to how the media affects adolescent development. The content of the media may have special significance for development during adolescence. The media is a vast source of information at a time when individuals are trying to better understand themselves and the world around them. Given the pubertal, cognitive, and social changes that unfold during this stage of life, adolescents experience uncertainty and questions that spur them to self-reflect and seek information. Identity development is a central feature of adolescence, and at this time individuals may be more likely to incorporate ideas they encounter into their own personal views. Even when not actively seeking information, adolescents may be more receptive to ideas in the media if they concern issues that are salient to them. Topics like sex, drugs, and pop culture are rampant in the media and of high interest to most adolescents. Such topics are not frequently addressed by parents. Further, adolescents are more likely to engage in media away from their parents and when they are alone or with friends.

Media, in its variety of forms—movies, TV shows, video games, music, books, websites—simultaneously entertains and distracts with its delivery of nonstop messages about life, love, beauty, family, friends, food, clothes, gender, sex, violence, what's cool and what's not, and just about every other topic imaginable. It is a powerful force in the lives of youth, and there has been much attention to how it affects development. In this section of the chapter we consider what the media landscape is like for adolescents, how it influences their development, what aspects of development are affected, and how adolescents' selection of different media plays an important role. We also consider issues related to social media, which has some features that differ from those of traditional media. We conclude this section of the chapter with a discussion of how schools and teachers can support media literacy skills in their adolescent students.

MyEdLab
Video Example 7.3

Eighteen-year-old Tim is a digital native. He describes the typical media landscape for adolescents in the mid 2000s.

The Media Landscape

Before we can examine whether the media affects adolescent development, we need to appreciate the type of content that adolescents are exposed to in the media. We consider several topics that have received much attention: violence, sex, substance use, gender roles, body image, and ethnicity. We also consider the content of food advertising aimed at youth.

Violence. Violent imagery in television, movies, music videos, and video games is prevalent (Roberts, Henricksen, & Foehr, 2009; Prot, Anderson, Gentile, Brown, & Swing, 2014). A study of prime-time TV shows airing between 1993 and 2001 found that 61.2% of shows contained violence and that violent acts happened an average of 4.5 times per program (Signorielli, 2003). Violence on television is seldom punished, frequently justified, and often carried out by attractive characters (Strasburger, Wilson, & Jordan, 2009). A study on advertising for video games found that 56% of advertisements in popular gaming magazines contained violent imagery or language (Scharrer, 2004). There is much concern over video games because of their interactive nature, in which virtual violent actions are often rewarded. For example, one of the most popular video games to date, *Grand Theft Auto* has drawn criticism for its violent content, including torture scenes and degrading depictions of women. In a nationally representative sample of 1102 youth aged 12 through 17, the two reported most widely played games in 2008 were racing and puzzle games that contained little violent content (e.g., *NASCAR, Tetris*). However, almost two-thirds of the teens in this study reported playing action or adventure games that did contain violent content (e.g., *Grand Theft Auto, Tomb Raider*). Most parents reported that they always or sometimes know what games their children play (90%; Lenhart et al., 2008).

Sex. Scripts of romantic and sexual relationships are plentiful in the media (Milbrath, Ohlson, & Eyre, 2009). Research on prime-time TV shows and movies has found that sexual content is frequent and that typically sex is portrayed as risk free and recreational, with little attention to negative outcomes (Kunkel et al., 2007; Wright, 2011). Physical attractiveness is portrayed as important to sexual behavior, especially for females (Ward, 2005). Portrayals of homosexual relationships are increasing, but still are rare as compared with portrayals of heterosexual relationships (Fisher, Hill, Grube, & Gruber, 2007). Sexual content is also common in music videos, with recurring themes that men are dominant and women are sex objects and subservient to men (Roberts et al., 2009; Ward, 2003). The Internet has provided greater access to sexual content. Two-thirds of male U.S. adolescents aged 12 to 14 and one-third of females report having seen at least one form of sexually explicit media (pornography site or X-rated video or magazine; Brown & L'Engle, 2009). About 28% of U.S. youth report having experienced unwanted pornography (e.g., popups with explicit content) in the last year (Wolak, Mitchell, & Finkelhor, 2007).

Substance Use. The media often portrays tobacco, alcohol, and drug use as normal behavior, which works against many policies and programs that focus on minimizing youth substance use (Brown & Bobkowski, 2011; Strasburger, 2014). Alcohol is the substance featured most often in TV programs. It is hard to find a televised sporting event that doesn't break for an entertaining beer commercial. Substance use is often featured in movies as well. In a study focused on the main characters in teenage movies released between 1999 and 2001, 40% of the teenage characters drank alcohol, 17% smoked cigarettes, and 15% used drugs (Stern, 2005). An analysis of movies rated PG-13 or R released between 1996 and 2004 found that half contained alcohol use (Tickle, Beach, & Dalton, 2009). The amount of smoking by main characters increased from the 1980s into the 2000s and was equal to that of movies in the 1950s but has declined in recent years (Strasburger, 2014). Alcohol and tobacco companies also have an increasing presence on the Internet (Strasburger, Jordan, & Donnerstein, 2010). The tobacco and alcohol industries spend billions on marketing and promotion (National Cancer Institute, 2008; Strasburger, 2010). Of recent concern is the high prevalence of drug and alcohol references and imagery on social media sites and YouTube (Strasburger, 2014).

Gender Roles. Conventional gender roles are prevalent in the media, with women appearing less frequently than men and having fewer speaking roles than men (Hust & Brown, 2008). The majority of men are depicted as employed professionals, whereas women are more often depicted as staying at home (Glascock, 2001). When they do work, female characters are just as likely to have roles in professional and white-collar occupations but are less likely to be shown as leaders (Signorelli & Kahlenberg, 2001; Lauzen & Dozier, 2004). Some have argued that even when women are depicted in professional roles, their status is diluted by a focus on romance and looks (Hust & Brown, 2008). Female characters are more likely to be affectionate and show concern, whereas male characters are more likely to be physically aggressive (Glascock, 2001). Women are more likely to be depicted as sex objects, especially in advertising (Reichert & Carpenter, 2004).

Body Image. Our cultural ideals of the slim female and muscular male are rampant in the media. As we discussed in Chapter 2, the content in many forms of media typically represents thin as normative and attractive and fat as aberrant and repulsive. There has been much concern about magazines aimed at adolescent girls, in which the majority of articles focus on dating in heterosexual relationships and emphasize the importance of physical attractiveness for young females. The message to girls is that being beautiful leads to happiness (Saraceni & Russell-Mayhew, 2007). The thin ideal dominates television too, especially in commercials that tout the benefits of weight loss and beauty products (Borzekowski, 2014). Regarding the Internet, there is concern about websites that describe and support eating disorders (known as "pro-ana" and "pro-mia" sites (Peebles et al., 2012).

Ethnicity. The U.S. Census Bureau reported that in 2013 our population was 62% White, 17% Hispanic or Latino, 13% African American, and 5% Asian. The media does not reflect the diversity of our nation. Casts of prime-time shows are more likely to be White, and this is especially true when it comes to lead roles (Greenberg & Mastro, 2008). African Americans are most likely to be characters in sitcoms and crime dramas. When sitcoms feature African Americans, the entire cast is often African American. Characters in television ads are 83 to 86% White, 11 to 12% African American, 1% Hispanic, and 2% Asian (Coltrane & Messineo, 2000; Mastro & Stern, 2003). In an analysis of the 101 top-grossing children movies released between 1990 and 2004, 72% of the speaking roles were male, and of those 86% were White, 5% were African American, 3% were Asian, 2% were Latino, and 1% were Native American (Greenberg & Mastro, 2008). Minority characters were more likely to be physically aggressive and violent (62%) as compared with White characters (38%).

Advertising of Food Products. It is ironic that the same media venues that promote the thin ideal for women and the muscular ideal for men also promote fast food and junk food. Using Nielsen data to quantify the number of ads seen in specific product categories, the Rudd Center for Food Policy & Obesity (2012) found that in 2011, fast-food restaurant, candy, and sugary cereal ads accounted for just under half of all food and beverage ads seen by children and adolescents. Foods and beverages of low nutritional value are increasingly being advertised though new online technology and use promotional techniques such as attention getting, repetition, and branded characters (Borzekowski, 2014).

Theories of Media Influence

There is little doubt that the media landscape contains questionable and possibly harmful content for adolescents. Of course we should point out that scholars have tended to focus on topics of concern for adolescent health. We do not want to forget that in addition to problematic content, much of the media landscape is mundane or innocuous as well as positive and inspiring. How does all of this content in the media affect developing adolescents? According to Roberts et al. (2009), there are three main theories that are most frequently applied to understanding how adolescents (or people of all ages) are affected by the media: cultivation theory, social cognitive theory, and schematic information-processing approaches.

Cultivation Theory.

Cultivation theory concerns the way that the mass media shape, influence, and reinforce a viewer's perceptions of social reality (Gerbner, Gross, Morgan, Signorelli, & Shanahan, 2002). The main idea is that certain ideas and images are salient in the mainstream media, and the more time people spend with media, the more they believe such ideas and images reflect the real world. It was initially developed by George Gerbner in the 1960s to understand the effects of television viewing on people's worldviews. In his classic studies, Gerbner compared people who watched more than 4 hours of TV a day ("heavy" viewers") to those who watched less than 2 hours a day "light viewers") and found that heavy viewers had a higher fear of crime than did light viewers. Content analyses of TV consistently find that the world as depicted on TV is far more violent than the everyday world, so these findings supported Gerbner's idea that TV viewers come to believe the television version of reality the more they watch it.

Video Example 7.4

Twelve-year-old Kianna, her best friend, and her mother describe some of the ways in which media influence adolescent behavior. Notice that, in accordance with cultivation theory, some of the messages that the teens receive about beauty from the magazines do NOT resonate with the girls.

Such findings have been called the **mean world syndrome** because media exposure can cultivate the belief that world is a meaner place than it really is. This effect has been replicated many times with adults, children, and adolescents (Gerbner et al., 2002). Research has found evidence for cultivation theory in other topics as well. For example, heavy soap opera viewers are more likely than light viewers to overestimate the rates of extramarital affairs, divorces, and abortions (Gerbner et al., 2002). Such findings have been referred to as the **sexy world syndrome** because media exposure can cultivate the belief that people have more sex and sex-related issues than is typical in real life. Research has also found evidence of cultivation theory in relation to gender and racial stereotypes. In all of these areas, cultivation theory assumes the process is subtle, with small, gradual, and indirect effects that slowly accumulate over time to have an impact on people's views.

An idea within cultivation theory is that certain ideas and themes will have different relevance for different individuals. When a theme resonates with a person, it reinforces his or her experience, giving the individual a double dose of the message, and the cultivation of the theme or idea is even stronger. For example, the message that the world is a dangerous place might resonate with people from poor neighborhoods who have experienced this issue, and thus the mean world syndrome can be even stronger for them. Alternately, an idea in the media can have relevance for an individual because it provides information that is not available in the individual's daily life. In this regard, youth may be more impressionable to messages in the media because they have less experience in the real world to compare with media depictions, and thus are more likely to believe the ideas they see or read. For example, young teens who have never had sex may be more likely to believe that a portrayal of a sexual encounter is realistic because they have nothing to compare it with.

Social Cognitive Theory.

Social cognitive theory concerns social influences on cognitions and behavior (Bandura, 2002). The main idea is that people acquire knowledge, skills, strategies, and even emotions from observing others. The media provides symbolic models (e.g., TV characters) or print models (e.g., instructions) from which adolescents can learn new ideas and behaviors. Albert Bandura is a prominent psychologist who developed much of social cognitive theory. To show that youth learn from watching others, he conducted a series of experiments in which he exposed children to different videos (Bandura & Walters, 1963). He found that children who had watched videos in which a person had been aggressive with a doll were more likely to display such behavior following the video as compared with children who had not observed such behavior. Furthermore, children who saw a model rewarded for aggressive behavior were more likely to behave aggressively as compared with children who saw a model who was not rewarded or for whom there were no consequences.

These processes related to observation are known as **vicarious learning**, or learning that takes place without firsthand experience. With vicarious learning, behavioral consequences do not have to be personally experienced to motivate behavior. When adolescents observe models engaged in behavior that has a successful outcome, they are more likely to engage in that behavior. When adolescents observe models engaged in behavior that incurs negative results, they are less likely to engage in that behavior. Social cognitive theory distinguishes learning from performance; adolescents may not demonstrate new beliefs and behaviors at the time of learning, but store the information away and use it a later time when it is appropriate or they are motivated to do so. Bandura emphasized that observational learning affects people's outcome expectancies associated with different behaviors and their personal self-efficacy, or the belief that they can execute a behavior successfully.

Observational learning does not happen automatically. Adolescents must pay attention and be motivated to learn from examples they see in the media. An important factor is similarity, or the extent to which a viewer identifies with a model. Similarity increases the probability that a viewer can expect similar results to those achieved by a model. For example, if an adolescent views a character of a similar age building a skateboard ramp, the adolescent is more likely to think that building a ramp is something that he or she could also do as compared with viewing an adult character doing the same thing. This is why public ad campaigns geared toward adolescents often have teen celebrities promote an idea.

Schematic Information-Processing Approaches.

Schematic information-processing (SIT) approaches concern the schemas that people store in memory and how they affect interpretation and judgment (Shrum, 2002). The main idea is that the media plays a major role in the development of the schemas that adolescents have for how the world works. A schema is a mental representation of experience that includes a particular organized way of perceiving cognitively and responding to a situation (Fiske & Taylor, 1991). A schema could be a script about how people typically interact in certain situations, such as dating, sexual intimacy, coping with stress, or conflict resolution. For example, if an adolescent repeatedly sees stories in which the guy initiates sexual contact, the adolescent starts to form a similar script for such situations. Or a schema could be a more simple cognitive association between stimuli. For example, if an adolescent repeatedly sees alcohol paired with a pleasurable mood, the adolescent starts to form that association. Although similar to cultivation theory, schematic processing approaches focus on more specific cognitive and memory processes.

The relationship between the media and schemas is reciprocal. Media experiences shape schemas, and in turn schemas shape media experiences. Schemas guide how adolescents process media content, including what they select, what they attend to, how they organize information, and how they create meaning out of what they read, hear, and see. Activating schemas can strengthen them, and continued exposure to similar schemas reinforces them. Schemas are more readily shaped by the media when adolescents lack direct experience with or knowledge of the content depicted in the media or, alternately, when content resonates closely with an adolescent's life experience. Schematic information-processing approaches have been applied to understanding the role of the media in regard to aggression (Huesmann, 1986), gender roles (Calvert, 1999), and sexuality (Gagnon & Simon, 1974). Although beliefs and behaviors in all of these realms have roots in biology and personal experience, they also differ widely between culture and time. Schematic information-processing approaches assume the media is a major agent of socialization that conveys what is normative and acceptable.

MyEdLab Self-Check 7.4

MyEdLab Self-Check 7.5

Media Effects

What does the research show for media effects on adolescent development? There has been much research in this area, but before we discuss it, we must point out how challenging it is to do research on the media. The media is ubiquitous from early on, especially for members of younger generations, who are often digital natives. It is hard to isolate and quantify the effects of a vast, complex, and omnipresent media world. Much of the research showing "media effects" is correlational in nature, revealing an association between certain types of media experiences and different aspects of adolescent development. Correlation is not causation. For example, if a study shows that watching porn online is associated with the view that women are sex objects, it could be that the activity of watching porn online led to this view, or it could be that individuals with this view are more likely to seek out porn online. Longitudinal research studies showing that certain media experiences predict changes in certain outcomes over time provide better evidence for media effects, but are less common.

Other research on media effects is experimental and involves randomly assigning subjects to conditions with different media experiences. With random assignment, experiments can rule out preexisting individual differences and provide better evidence of cause and effect. However, it is not clear that the short-term effects of specific aspects of media experience capture the far more complex processes of real-world media exposure. Given these challenges, it probably will not surprise you that there is some controversy among scholars about media effects on adolescent development. However, challenges and controversy notwithstanding, there has been some consensus among experts in this area on some issues regarding media effects and adolescent development. It is worth noting at the outset, however, that all behaviors are caused by numerous factors. Even when a link is established between media and behavior, there are numerous other causes (e.g., genetic, personality, situational) that always need to be considered.

Violence and Aggression. Probably the most controversial and researched topic on the media is whether violent content influences aggressive behavior. There have been hundreds of studies, including longitudinal and experimental research with a wide variety of measures, showing a link between the viewing of violent media content and subsequent aggressive behavior (Paik & Comstock, 1994). In 2000, six professional medical associations (e.g., the American Medical Association, the American Academy of Pediatrics) issued a statement that "Viewing entertainment violence can lead to increases in aggressive attitudes, values and behavior, particularly in children" (American Academy of Pediatrics, 2000; the full statement is available at http://www.aap.org/advocacy/releases/jstmtevc.htm).

The topic of whether playing violent video games leads to aggression is still debated. In a U.S. Supreme Court case in 2010 (*Brown vs. Entertainment Merchants*) the Court did not find sufficient evidence that video games make adolescents more aggressive and ruled that a California law banning the sale of violent games to minors was unconstitutional. Soon after that, a meta-analysis (i.e., an examination of the results of all prior studies) of over 136 studies concluded that violent game play is associated with increased aggressive cognitions, emotions, and behavior (Anderson & Bushman, 2001). The link to cognitions and emotions is more agreed upon than the link to aggressive behavior, which continues to be debated (Ferguson, Garza, Jerabeck, & Galindo, 2013; Gunter & Daly, 2012).

Visual–Spatial Skills and Attention. Although it has not received the extensive attention devoted to aggression, there has been research on the effects of video games on other types of outcomes. In a review of the research to date, Prot et al. (2014) concluded that playing video games has been associated with improvement in and superior performance on many visual and spatial tasks. Gamers show better skills in these areas as compared with nongamers. Experiments show that even 10 hours of video game play can improve spatial attention and mental rotation skills (Feng, Spence, & Pratt, 2007). On the other hand, video game play is related to attention problems, such as impulsiveness, and less cognitive control; experiments have found diminished performance on cognitive tasks that involve cognitive control (Bailey, West, & Anderson, 2010).

Prosocial Behavior. Prosocial video games focus on helping other characters, in contrast to hero-centered violent video games, in which the player kills enemies. In a review of the research to date, Prot et al. (2014) concluded that prosocial video games have been shown to increase prosocial thoughts, empathy, and cooperation while also decreasing aggressive thoughts, emotions, and behavior. Short-term results have been found in the laboratory, and long-term results have been documented outside of the laboratory indicating that these effects are not transitory. Beyond video games, it also seems that prosocial content in other media can have a positive effect. For example, prosocial lyrics in songs can increase prosocial thoughts, prosocial behavior, and positive affect (Greitemeyer, 2009).

Sex. Research has found that media content is related to adolescents' sexual attitudes and behavior (Brown & Bobkowski, 2011). For example, frequent exposure to sexual content on TV is positively associated with adolescents' views that sex is recreational, that men have a higher sex drive, and that women are sexual objects (Ward & Friedman, 2006). More research has established links between the media and beliefs as compared with links between media and behaviors. However, increasing numbers of longitudinal studies show links to behavior as well (Brown, El-Toukhy, & Ortiz, 2014). In one longitudinal study of adolescents aged 12 to 17, it was found that more frequent viewing of TV shows with sexual content increased the likelihood of the initiation of sexual activity (Chandra et al., 2008). In another longitudinal study of adolescents aged 12 to 14, it was found that adolescents with greater exposure to sexual content across TV, magazines, music, and movies were more than twice as likely as those with less exposure to sexual content to have had sex by the age of 16 (Brown et al., 2006). Exposure to sexually explicit media in early adolescence has also been found to be related to sexual behavior in later adolescence, as well as less progressive gender roles (Brown & L'Engle, 2009).

Substance Use. Much research has examined exposure to tobacco and alcohol marketing and adolescents' reported attitudes and behaviors regarding smoking and drinking. Increasing numbers of longitudinal studies are showing that exposure to smoking ads is related to youth smoking (Roberts et al., 2009). For example, young adolescents who had never smoked but could name a favorite smoking brand were more than twice as likely as peers to be a smoker 4 years later (Biener &

Siegel, 2000). In a review of the studies to date, Strasburger (2014) concluded that there is now sufficient evidence to conclude that alcohol advertising affects adolescent alcohol use and brand preference. There has been scant research on whether exposure to illicit drug use on TV or in movies affects adolescent behavior, although this is a growing concern (Roberts et al., 2009).

Gender Roles. A meta-analysis of 30 studies found that the more individuals watch television, the more they endorse stereotypical, conventional gender roles (Herrett-Skjellum, & Allen, 1996). One study found that children who frequently watch TV were more likely to identify household chores with gender stereotypes (e.g., men do yardwork and women do laundry) as compared with children who infrequently watch TV (Signorielli & Lears, 1991). More recent work has found that the effects are even stronger for talk shows, soap operas, and music videos (Ward, Hansborough, & Walker, 2005).

Body Image and Eating Disorders. Over a hundred studies have found that exposure to ideal-body media imagery diminishes females' body satisfaction (Brown & Bobkowski, 2011). Frequent exposure to such thin-positive and heavy-negative characters in TV and magazines leads to decreased body image for girls and disordered eating for boys and girls, although more so for girls (Levine & Harrison, 2009). For male adolescents, exposure to muscular men in the media increases body dissatisfaction (Agliata & Tantleff, 2004). Some studies found that African American girls might be less susceptible to these effects; however, recent work finds similar patterns across ethnicity. This may be because depictions of African American females in the media have become thinner in recent years (Baker, 2005). Recent research finds that a thin-body ideal can lead to body-image disturbances, but also that girls with body-image and eating problems seek out thin-ideal media (Thomsen, McCoy, Gustafson, & Williams, 2002).

Obesity. The obesity rate among adolescents has more than tripled (from 4.6 to 17.6%) in the past 40 years (Ogden, Carroll, & Flegal, 2008). Many factors contribute to this trend, including increased reliance on cars and fast food that is inexpensive and high in calories. There is concern that increases in screen time have contributed to decreases in the activity levels of youth. Beyond the "couch-potato" hypothesis, there has been attention to the link of increased marketing to youth and the rising obesity rates. The World Health Organization and the Food and Agriculture Organization concluded there was enough evidence to report that such advertising was a "probable" causal factor in obesity among youth (Borzekowski, 2014). The U.S. Institute for Medicine has called for limiting food marketing aimed at children (Vandewater & Cummings, 2008). Companies persist in such marketing to build brand loyalty early in life and because children's preferences affect their parents' purchasing behavior. Starting in early adolescence, youth have more discretionary money, and much of it is spent on food and beverages. With changes in media, marketing is expanding to new mediums all the time, but it is not known how newer strategies are affecting adolescents.

> In the United States, our government exerts little regulation in terms of content or advertising aimed at youth. What is your opinion—should there be more regulations on marketing to children and adolescents?

Ethnicity. Greenberg and Mastro (2008) note that little research has examined how the media affects children and adolescents' beliefs about race and ethnicity, especially for minority children. However, experimental research with adults indicates that media portrayals of minorities affect race-related beliefs for Whites and minorities. In one study, watching undesirable media portrayals of minorities led Whites to make more stereotypical evaluations of minorities

(Mastro & Kopacz, 2006). In contrast, research shows that watching well-liked African American celebrities (e.g., Oprah) leads to more favorable views of minorities and greater recognition of the fact that discrimination is an important social problem (Bodenhausen, Schwartz, Bless, & Wanke, 1995). For minorities, the effects may be more complex. Viewing unfavorable images of one's ethnic group can lower expectations that certain groups can accomplish what they want (Greenberg & Mastro, 2008). Viewing stereotypical images can initiate race-based comparisons that favor the group that viewers belong to (e.g., Latinos; Mastro, 2003). One study with children examined the effects of a *Sesame Street* episode in which a White child has a play date at an African American child's home. After watching just the one episode, 70% of children (African American and White) reported that they wanted to play with an African American Barbie doll (Fisch, Truglio, & Cole, 1999).

MyEdLab **Self-Check 7.6**

Use of Media to Promote Adolescents' Health

People invested in the well-being of adolescents have tried to capitalize on the power of the media to promote healthy behaviors among youth. Every year millions of dollars are spent on ad campaigns aimed at reducing negative behaviors such as smoking and drug use. In an attempt to understand the extent to which such ad campaigns can really affect adolescents' behaviors, a group of researchers conducted a meta-analysis. They found that, on average, 4 to 8% of individuals exposed to ad campaigns will change their health-related behavior (Snyder & Hamilton, 2002). Although this is a small proportion, it can translate to a large number of individuals if the ad campaign reaches a large audience.

Research has identified several characteristics of health-related ad campaigns that can increase the ads' effectiveness with adolescents. Ads with messages that emphasize the social risks of smoking are most effective with adolescents. Examples of social risks are that smoking harms others and people look down on smokers (Pechmann, Zhao, Goldberg, & Riebling, 2003). Ads that evoke strong emotions are the most likely to be remembered by adolescents (Biener, Ji, Gilpin, & Albers, 2004). In this vein, a successful anti-smoking ad campaign that ran in 2012 and 2014 showed in graphic detail the serious health problems that can result from smoking (see http://www.cdc.gov/tobacco/quit_smoking/). Anti-drug ads that use intense images, loud and fast music, and rapid scene changes are also more likely to be remembered by adolescents (Niederdeppe, Davis, Farrelly, & Yaresevich, 2007).

There have been attempts to use the mass media to address health issues other than substance use. For example, the Dove Campaign for Real Beauty is a marketing campaign that celebrates the natural physical variation of women. This campaign aims to combat the rampant media message that only skinny is beautiful. The ads have focused on a range of issues: what the widespread use of photo-shopping has done to our beauty ideals, notions of beauty in girls, raising daughters in our media culture, and women's anxiety about and dissatisfaction with their looks. The 2013 ad "Real Beauty Sketches," which shows women describing themselves to a forensic sketch artist, has been viewed more than 64 million times on YouTube. Of course, this campaign has not been without its critics (Dove is a company that sells health and beauty products, after all!), but there is no doubt that it has garnered much attention. You can read about evolution of the campaign at http://www.dove.us/Social-Mission/campaign-for-real-beauty.aspx.

Researchers have also identified how ad campaigns can bring about unintended negative effects. The National Youth Anti-Drug Media Campaign was one of the largest media campaigns ever run in the United States. In the third phase of the program (1999–2004) TV, radio, print, and online ads were run extensively. A nationally representative survey indicated that most adolescents recalled seeing the ads. However, the campaign was so widespread that seeing the ads was associated with adolescents' perceptions that many youth used marijuana, and actually increased adolescents' intentions to try marijuana! Although the campaign's direct message was about *not* using marijuana, it indirectly communicated the idea that marijuana use was widespread (Orwin et al., 2004).

Social Media

There have been much interest and speculation about how contemporary adolescents' wide use of social media sites affects their social relationships. Social media has made communication among teens more public and shared. An entire school community might see photos or videos and have the opportunity to comment. There is also an element of permanency, as such interactions often cannot be erased. Research has found that Facebook has the potential for increasing people's feelings of connection with others and positive emotions, but also has the potential for increasing negative feelings such as envy, loneliness, and depression, especially if individuals spend a lot of time alone passively reading others' posts and not sharing their own content (Feinstein, Herschenberg, Bhatia, Meuwly, & Davilia, 2013; Valenzuela, Park, & Kee, 2009). There is also concern about **cyberbullying**, or harassing, threatening, or embarrassing peers on social media sites. As discussed in Chapter 6, cyberbullying is associated with school problems, depression, and suicide ideation (Juvonen & Graham, 2014; Tokunaga, 2010).

One recent survey from a nationally representative sample of 13- to 17-year-olds provides insights to adolescents' view of social media (Common Sense Media, 2012). Youth generally have a positive perception of social media, reporting that it helps them keep in touch with friends they can't regularly see, allows them to get to know other students at their school better, and facilitates connecting with people who share a common interest. The majority of adolescents do not think social media has any effect on their well-being (80%), and very few (4%) reported that using social media made them feel depressed. Of course it is possible that adolescents are not aware of how social media sites make them feel and/or cannot distinguish the effects of social media from those of other activities that they often engage in at the same time as social media. There is increasingly a fusion of different media into social media; many users post and read links to websites, and social media sites like Facebook now contain advertising. In addition to multitasking, adolescents may use social media sites in very different ways (e.g., time spent, active versus passive use, number of posts, types of posts, motives for posting).

The implications of adolescents' different motives and use of social media were examined in a recent study of seventh- and eighth-grade students (Nesi & Prinstein, 2015). Adolescents who reported that they use technology-based communication (Facebook, Instagram, and texting) for the purposes of social comparison and seeking feedback were more likely to be depressed 1 year later. Thus, when a primary goal of adolescents is to find out what others think about them or compare their lives with other people's lives, it can make them feel worse about themselves over time. This association was found to be far greater than the link with overall frequency of technology use and the link with prior levels of depression. This association was particularly strong for females and adolescents who were low in popularity.

Social media, in all its forms, seems to be here to stay. What benefits and problems do you think social media use poses to the social relationships of middle and high school youth? How might these benefits and problems affect teachers of middle and high school students?

In-Depth 7.2

Teachers and Social Media

Some teachers are gaining inspiration from social media to get ideas about how to make their classes and assignments more engaging for students. Others are actually using social media sites as a tool to support their teaching. Consider the following examples:

- Mr. Burke has his ninth-grade students write "tweets" on sticky notes as exit tickets from his science classroom.
- Ms. Gonzalez has her eighth-grade students create short videos to augment their creative essays in English class.
- Mrs. McCreadie has her 12th-grade students use Pinterest to organize their resources for their history project.
- Mr. Limon is using a site called the Global Classroom Project (see http://theglobalclassroomproject.wordpress.com) to have his sixth-grade students connect with students in a classroom in Australia about their social studies projects.

- Ms. Schwartz uses Pinterest to pin current events to a board for students in her 11th-grade American government course to read each day.
- Mr. Jackson uses Twitter to deliver short bursts of information to his 10th-grade students in his chemistry class.
- At the end of each year, Mrs. Smith suggests that her seventh-grade math students use the Khan Academy site (see https://www.khanacademy.org/) to support and extend their math skills over the summer months. She coordinates with the eighth-grade math teachers to provide incentives for students who do so.
- Mr. Cramer asks his 12th-grade history students to follow elected officials on Twitter and report back on what the officials tweet.

What other examples can you think of? What do you see as the benefits and challenges of teachers using such practices? As a teacher, how might you learn from and use social media in your teaching?

Adolescents' Selection of Different Media

To understand how the media may or may not affect an adolescent, it is also important to consider how individuals select different types of media. This is especially important in today's media world because the media is increasingly specialized and offers more choices to consumers. A change in the last few decades has been the increase in content specifically created for adolescent audiences. There are a myriad of choices in entertainment for today's teen, and there is variability in what teens choose.

Jane Brown, a prominent researcher who specializes in adolescent media habits, describes the contemporary media scene as a "smorgasbord" of media from which teens choose their own "media diet" (Brown, 2000). Some things are elements of common culture—content that most youth will attend to (e.g., hit TV shows, top-10 songs, blockbuster movies, best-selling books). In the past, common culture made up a larger part of the teen diet because there were not as many choices. In the 1950s there were three TV channels, compared with the hundreds available on cable today, in addition to the ever-increasing video options available through iTunes, Hulu, Netflix, and other providers. Further, the media is now produced for different ethnic audiences.

Media Practice Model. Brown and her colleagues (Brown, 2000; Shafer, Bobkowski, & Brown, 2013) developed the Media Practice Model to describe how adolescents choose, interpret, and interact with the mass media in today's society. As shown in Figure 7.10, an adolescent's identity leads to differing motives and selection of media, which affects how much the adolescent pays attention to and

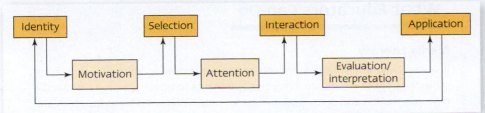

FIGURE 7.10
Media Practice Model

interacts with media. As adolescents interact with the media, they evaluate, interpret, and may or may not apply what they are learning. Application could involve an adolescent incorporating new information into his or her identity or resisting the information as not part of his or her identity. There are three important features of this model to note. First, most media use is active: Adolescents select certain media and interact with it and make sense of it in their own ways; they may embrace or reject some media and its content. Second, the nature of media use and effects is reciprocal: Adolescents choose media, which affects their beliefs and behaviors, which affects their subsequent choices; media effects cannot be oversimplified and thought of as a linear process whereby the media affects a passive user. Third, an adolescent's current and emerging identity is central to understanding his or her selection of and interaction with different media in everyday life; adolescents choose media and interact with media based on who they are or who they want to be.

In the Media Practice Model (Brown, 2000; Shafer et al., 2013), ethnicity and gender are factors of identity that contribute to adolescents' identity beliefs and media choices. The types of media used by boys and girls are quite different, so much so that some have claimed that by adolescence, boys and girls are living in different media worlds (Rideout, Foehr, & Roberts, 2005). For example, in regard to TV shows, girls prefer shows with family-oriented, romantic, or comedic content, whereas boys prefer sports programs and shows with action (Hust & Brown, 2008). Ethnicity affects media selection too. African American adolescents are more likely than White adolescents to watch television shows with African American cast members (Brown & Pardun, 2004). African American, Hispanic, and White adolescents tend to listen to different types of music, especially in late adolescence (Roberts et al., 2005).

The Media Practice Model also notes that identity affects how individuals interact with the media. This is called **selective perception**: Adolescents see and interpret media messages in different ways. For example, one study showed links between ethnic identity, age, and perceptions of rap music. Older adolescents and those who had a stronger sense of ethnic identity were more likely to view rap music as empowering, or to report that it inspired them to consider the experiences of others, think critically about the world around them, and want to make a difference in their communities (Travis & Bowman, 2012)

The Media Practice Model (Brown, 2000; Shafer et al., 2013) highlights that media effects may not be uniform for all adolescents. Depending on how they interpret media messages, media may or may not affect their beliefs and values. Adolescents may critique or resist certain messages even if they dominate the media landscape. How adolescents interpret and respond to the media varies depending on their personal characteristics as well as other contexts that they experience. Adolescents' media experience does not occur in a vacuum but alongside experiences with family, peers, and school. These experiences affect the critical thinking skills that adolescents bring to the media and are important to the role that the media plays in development. Critical thinking skills relevant to the media are often called *media literacy,* the topic we turn to next.

What Educators Can Do

Media Literacy

It seems clear that engagement with media is at unprecedented levels in contemporary youth. There are many positive things to gain from time with media—new information and many possibilities for entertainment. However, youth are also exposed to much questionable content. Heavy marketing to adolescents is unlikely to abate. With this landscape in mind, there has been growing interest in developing media literacy skills in adolescents (Chakroff & Nathanson, 2008; Ribble, 2011; Strasburger, 2014). Many national organizations in the United States call for media literacy education as a way to prepare youth for life in the 21st century. These organizations include the American Academy of Pediatrics, the National Middle School Association, the National Council for the Social Studies, and the National Council of Teachers of English. In this section, we define and examine the core elements of media literacy and consider how schools and teachers might foster media literacy in adolescent students.

What is media literacy? **Media literacy** refers to the ability to access, analyze, evaluate, create, and participate in the images, words, and sounds that make up our contemporary mass-media culture (Thorman & Jolis, 2005). Advocates for media literacy see it as helping youth develop the critical thinking skills necessary for active engagement in the 21st-century media culture. According to Thorman and Jolis (2005), a media-literate adolescent is an individual who can:

- Use the media wisely and effectively
- Engage in critical thinking when evaluating media messages
- Evaluate the credibility of information in the media
- Understand the power of visual images
- Appreciate multiple perspectives on media content
- Express him- or herself using different forms of media
- Recognize media influence on beliefs, attitudes, values, behaviors, and the democratic process

What do you think—is media literacy a critical 21st-century skill? In what ways can you imagine it being integrated into middle and high school classes? What advantages and challenges do you see?

Several key principles are often emphasized to support media literacy. First, the media presents representations that are constructed by people. The media does not reflect reality, but rather represents someone's version of reality. The extent to which the media is realistic, selective, biased, or stereotypical reflects choices made by producers. For example, certain actions may not be typical but are often the focus because directors, writers, and producers think they have high entertainment value. The images we see in the media are often distorted and do not accurately depict regular people, appearances, or behaviors, but are used because they are memorable or appealing. Second, media content is created for an audience and with a purpose. Media content is often circulated or distributed with an intended audience in mind. The purpose is often commercial, with the aim to promote and sell a product. Third is the idea that audiences negotiate meaning. The effects of the media on individuals depend on how they use it and think about it. Media literacy exploits this principle—if adolescents are critical consumers, they are more likely to recognize that media content is often created for entertainment or commercial purposes and does not reflect reality or truth.

Thorman and Jolis (2005) recommend that educators frame media literacy around five guiding questions to support adolescents' understanding of these principles. Teachers can have adolescent students examine a wide variety of media forms and consider these five guiding questions:

1. Who created this message?
2. What techniques are used to attract my attention?
3. What lifestyles, values, and points of view are represented in, or omitted from, this message?
4. Why was this message sent?
5. How might different people understand this message differently from me?

For the most part, scholars who advocate for media literacy do not see it as its own subject, but rather as relevant to many subjects and something that can be integrated with existing curriculums. Broadly, it enhances students' critical thinking skills, which are a concern in all subjects. Media literacy has many natural connections to language arts and social studies. For example, an important skill in language arts is understanding the point of view of an author. Practice with this skill by adolescents could incorporate media literacy in many ways, such as through evaluating websites and advertisements. Media literacy is also relevant to many topics covered in health classes (e.g., substance use, nutrition, sexuality, body image, aggression, bullying). A helpful resource for teachers is the website of the Center for Media Literacy (see http://www.medialit.org/), which, in addition to professional development materials, offers sample lesson plans for teachers in a range of subjects and at all grade levels.

Critics of media literacy think it puts too much responsibility on children and adolescents to be critical consumers, when it should fall on advertisers and the entertainment industry to minimize the extent to which they contribute to a harmful media landscape for youth (see Klass, 2013). They worry that too much focus on media literacy will diminish media activism, or advocacy for positive change. What do you think?

Recommendations for Educators

In this chapter, we have examined the role of technology and media in adolescent development. In the first half of the chapter, we reviewed current trends in technology and media use by adolescents. We considered how changes in recent years have introduced both benefits and challenges to adolescents and the educators who teach them. We discussed the role schools and teachers can play in promoting digital citizenship in adolescent students. In the second part of the chapter, we analyzed the contemporary media landscape for adolescents, how and what effects the content of the media has on development, and how schools might foster media literacy in adolescents. There are important implications for educators.

Strive to Learn New Things and Stay Familiar with the Latest Trends in Technology and Media Among Your Adolescent Students

Technology and media are constantly evolving, and you cannot possibly know it all, but with even a little effort you can stay informed. If you are not a tech-savvy person, don't give up or get overwhelmed. Start with small goals. Talk to colleagues who are knowledgeable about technology. And remember that your students are a great resource and often love to share their interests, opinions, and knowledge.

Appreciate the Importance of Technology and Media in Your Students' Lives and Use It as a Way to Engage and Connect with Students

Just as parents and peers are important to understanding adolescent development, so are technology and media. Recognizing this fact will help you better understand your students. As a teacher, you can use this as a source of motivation or a way to make a personal connection to students' life outside the classroom. For example, you might draw on popular shows or games (as appropriate) in examples or activities in class. For instance, a math teacher might draw on the March Madness basketball tournament for examples related to probability or statistics. Or a language arts teacher might have students compare a character from a book read in class to a character from a television show. To make a personal connection with students, you might ask them about their favorite movie or television show.

Strive for a Balanced Perspective of Technology, Media, and Adolescent Students

There are opportunities and concerns associated with advances in technology and the emergence of new media. A positive attitude and willingness to try new things is likely to lead to fruitful learning opportunities for you and your students. However, as we discussed, there are real challenges for adolescents in a fast-paced changing digital world that cannot be ignored. Some awareness of the challenges can inspire educators to think ahead about how to approach potential problems with technology and media, especially the Internet, and adolescent students.

Remember That Adolescent Students Need Guidance to Be Responsible Digital Citizens in a Rapidly Changing, Vast, and Complex Digital World

To harness the possible benefits of technology and new media in your teaching and students' learning, you will need to provide scaffolding to your students. As we discussed in the section on digital citizenship, teachers can help adolescents to be active, informed, and responsible in their technology use by supporting their emerging knowledge and skills regarding communication, privacy and safety, technical issues, information navigation, and operating in a culture of multitasking.

When Possible, Empower Adolescents with Media Literacy Skills

Adolescents continually make choices about how they engage with the media. If they can bring critical thinking skills to their involvement with the media, they can be savvier consumers, learners, and citizens. As we have discussed throughout the chapter, adolescents are deeply steeped in the online world and may have more knowledge of gadgets, apps, or websites than the adults around them. However, being a "digital native" is not the same as critical thinking (Boyd, 2014). By asking questions, having discussions, and creating opportunities for adolescents to reflect on and analyze the media, teachers can help them to develop their media literacy skills.

MyEdLab **Self-Check 7.7**

Conclusion

n this chapter, we discussed the nature and importance of technology and media as a context for adolescent development. Because technology and media change at a rapid pace, adolescents' media world can feel foreign to parents and educators alike. However, given the salient and important role it plays in adolescents' lives, it cannot be ignored. Our discussion of digital citizenship and media literacy illustrated that there is much you can do to help your adolescent students navigate and thrive in the digital world.

pressmaster/Fotolia

8

Peers

Learning Outcomes

8.1 You will be able to describe each of the different types of peer experiences students may have at school (friends, peer groups, crowds, and popularity) and why they are important to adolescent development.

8.2 You will be able to describe what teachers can do to support the development of positive friendships, peer groups, and popularity dynamics in their classrooms.

8.3 You will be able to explain the nature and consequences of bullying and victimization at school

and describe what teachers and schools can do to minimize bullying and victimization.

8.4 You will be able to explain the nature and potential impact of social-emotional learning programs in schools.

8.5 You will be able to describe the importance of an emotionally supportive classroom environment and what teachers can do to establish such a climate with their adolescent learners.

Introduction

Adolescents spend almost the entire day at school among peers. From conversations in the hallways, to well-established seating patterns in the cafeteria, to classroom interactions, to help with homework on the bus, to camaraderie in drama club or teamwork on the playing field, the social relationships of adolescents are an important part of their school experience. Peers can inspire positive behavior or antisocial behavior, make a student feel safe and valued or threatened and victimized, and serve to bolster motivation and engagement or distract and lead to off-task behavior (Ryan, Kuusinen, & Bedoya-Skoog, 2015). Situations often arise in regard to adolescents' peer relationships at school and require a teacher's intervention to restore or achieve harmony. Consider the following examples.

>>>

Mrs. Messman teaches social studies to sixth graders at a large middle school. Naomi, a student in her third-period class, has become increasingly withdrawn over the past few weeks, and her grades are suffering. Naomi was a little anxious in the beginning of the school year, which Mrs. Messman attributed to the fact that she was new to the school. When Mrs. Messman walks by the cafeteria and notices Naomi sitting at the end of a lunch table, not engaged with any other students, she realizes Naomi is having trouble making friends. Mrs. Messman thinks about the other girls in her third-period class and recalls that when Naomi was in a group with Chandra and Erin, they got along well. She considers how she might facilitate some friendships for Naomi.

Ms. McKellar teaches language arts at a large urban high school. Her fourth-period class is proving to be a challenge this year. There is a group of boys who have recently been off task and boisterous during class. Ms. McKellar often uses group work and lets students choose their groups. However, despite repeated warnings, Kyle, Chris, Michael, and Omar do not get their work done. Even worse, their attitude and behavior seem to be spreading to others in the class. Yesterday, Evan, who is usually a model student, was drawing cartoon pictures instead of doing his work. This drew much laughter from the whole class and encouragement from Omar, the group's leader. Ms. McKellar believes changing Omar's behavior would be a major boost in improving the behavior of the group and ponders her next steps.

Mr. Staples teaches seventh grade at a small private school for students in kindergarten through eighth grade. Mr. Staples has his class for most of the day. He enjoys teaching and considers himself both a serious and fun teacher. He is serious about students' learning and doing their work but also likes to have fun with his class, and when appropriate he jokes around and allows students some socializing time. He prides himself on knowing his students well. Yesterday he was quite surprised when a heated argument broke out among several girls during math and concluded with Mia shouting "I hate all of you" and running out of the room. After school, when he talked to Mia's mom, he learned that there has been some exclusion and gossiping among the girls in his room. Mia's feelings have been getting hurt a lot lately, her mother tells him, and this morning she didn't even want to go to school. Mr. Staples thought Mia, Shoshanna, Colleen, Amaya, and Ellen got along fine and were good friends. Mr. Staples wonders how he missed this situation.

In these examples, we can see the complexity of peer relationships and how they affect students' adjustment at school as well as teachers' ability to manage their classrooms, instruct, and motivate their students. The power of peers during adolescence can be intimidating for teachers and parents alike. Indeed, educators and parents are often concerned that the peer culture in middle and high schools contributes to low value for academics as well as mean and aggressive behavior among youth. However, the power of peers also holds great promise for teachers of adolescent students. Decades of research have shown that peers can be a positive force in adolescents' development. Teachers are in a unique position to create a social climate and structure learning tasks in ways that facilitate peer relations, achievement, and adjustment at school. To understand how teachers might do this, in this chapter we consider the nature and development of peer relationships during adolescence.

There are many important changes in social development during this stage for teachers to appreciate. As children develop into adolescents, their social worlds expand greatly and they come into contact with a wider array of peers. For many adolescents, the transition to middle and then high school represents a dramatic shift in the social scene they are part of each day. Adolescents have many different types of relationships and experiences with peers in and out of school. Adolescents often spend time with a close friend, many hang out in groups, and all must navigate classes and the larger social scene at school that is comprised of a wide array of students. All of these social experiences with peers matter for adolescents' adjustment at school.

OVERVIEW OF THE CHAPTER

In this chapter, we examine the different facets of adolescents' experiences with peers and the important role that teachers play in facilitating positive peer relations in classrooms and schools. First, we consider the importance of friendship, how it changes during this stage of life, and the provisions that friends offer to one another, including cross-ethnic and same-ethnic friendships. We discuss the significance of friendships for adolescents' engagement in the classroom and what teachers can do to support the development of positive friendships.

Second, we explore peer groups (also known as cliques) and how they change during adolescence. We discuss the nature of peer influence and how teachers' attunement to peer groups can lead to better management of peer groups and their influence on achievement beliefs and behaviors in classrooms and schools. We also discuss the notion of a crowd, or the labels that adolescents assign to large groups of students at school (for example, "the jocks" or "the nerds") and the role that such labels play in adolescent identity development.

Third, we examine the nature of popularity during adolescence. We distinguish two forms of popularity: peer acceptance and a popular reputation. We discuss how the characteristics associated with popularity change during adolescence. We consider how, as a teacher, you can manage the social dynamics surrounding popularity and steer them toward supporting, rather than impeding, effort and achievement in your classroom.

Fourth, we examine what is currently known about bullying and victimization. The problem of bullying and its potentially severe consequences on students' mental health and academic achievement has received a great deal of attention in recent years. We discuss recommendations for schools and teachers to minimize bullying among adolescent students.

Fifth, we discuss how educators can support students' peer relationships at school. We consider the nature and impact of social-emotional learning programs that are being adopted more widely by schools and school districts. Then, we discuss the importance of an emotionally supportive classroom environment and what teachers can do to establish such a climate with their adolescent learners.

Friends

"We'll be there, Harry," said Ron
    "What?" said Harry.
    "At your Aunt and Uncle's house," said Ron, "And then we'll go with you wherever you're going."

"No-" said Harry quickly; he hadn't counted on this, he had meant them to understand that he was undertaking the most dangerous journey alone.

"You said it once before," said Hermione quickly, "that there was time to turn back if we wanted to. We've had time, haven't we? We're with you whatever happens."

—J. K. Rowling, *Harry Potter and the Half-Blood Prince*

As much as it is about wizardry and the battle between good and evil, the Harry Potter series is about the importance of friendship. Whatever the circumstances—learning new spells, standing up to the bully Malfoy, or battling the epitome of evil itself—Harry, Hermione, and Ron stand by one another. They offer each other companionship, mutual affection, loyalty, understanding, and trust. They sometimes get annoyed with each other and even fight upon occasion. But ultimately, they have one of the most important interpersonal bonds humans can have: the bond of friendship. Although the circumstances may not be quite as dire as they were at Hogwarts, friends are an important part of most adolescents' school experience. When students walk into a classroom, one of the first things they do is look around for their friends. When students are new to a school they are not likely to feel comfortable until they make some friends. When asked what they like best about school, most adolescents will reply seeing their friends. When there is a problem with friends, school can be miserable. Friends matter for adolescents' adjustment at school. In this section, we describe the nature of friendship, its importance, and changes during adolescence. We consider how the provisions of friendship affect adolescents' adjustment at school and what educators can do to facilitate positive friendships in their classrooms and at school.

Friendship refers to a mutual, close, and voluntary relationship (see Figure 8.1). When asked to list their close friends at school, most adolescents list between 4 and 8 friends, although 3% do not list anyone and about 7% list more than 10 friends (Molloy, Gest, & Ruilson, 2011; Ryan, 2001). However, not all friendship choices are reciprocated, meaning both individuals listed each other. With that criterion, about 10 to 15% of adolescents do not have a mutually agreed-upon friend at school. The number of students without a reciprocated friend tends to be a little higher in the beginning of the school year and a little lower by the end of the school year. Friends tend to be similar in age, race, socioeconomic background, and gender. However, during the course of adolescence, having friends of the opposite sex becomes more common.

Friendships provide adolescents a context in which they can feel closeness, enjoyment, acceptance, validation, security, and satisfaction. Much research has documented the importance of friendship for adolescent development. Having friends is associated with higher levels of self-esteem, greater school satisfaction, increased academic engagement, and protection from peer victimization. Adolescents who are chronically without friends are at risk for anxiety, loneliness, depression, and withdrawal from school (Rubin, Bukowski, & Bowker, 2014). Being friendless in adolescence may even have long-term consequences. One study found that the nature of friendships in early adolescence had lasting effects on an

Friendship	A mutual, close, and voluntary relationship
Peer group (or clique)	Groups of students who tend to hang out and talk to one another and often do activities together
Crowd	Larger, reputation-based groups of similarly stereotyped individuals who may or may not spend much time together (e.g., jocks, brains, druggies)
Peer acceptance	One form of popularity among peers at school, referring to the extent to which a student is generally liked or disliked by peers at school
Popular reputation	Another form of popularity among peers, referring to which students are seen as popular at their school

FIGURE 8.1 Definitions of Different Peer Relationship Terms

individual's sense of self-worth more than 10 years later, when individuals were young adults (Bagwell, Newcomb, & Bukowski, 1998).

Changes in Friendship During Adolescence

Friends are important at all stages of development but are thought to have special significance during adolescence. During adolescence, the nature of friendships becomes more intense and complex, changes that are intricately related to puberty, autonomy, and cognitive development, and that set the stage for the emergence of intimacy and mutual responsiveness.

Intensity. The time and emotional investment that adolescents put into their friendships make them more intense at this stage of life. In general, as individuals move from childhood to adolescence, time spent with their friends increases and time spent with their family members decreases. As individuals move from childhood to adolescence, ownership of cell phones increases (Madden, Lenhart, Duggan, Cortesi, & Gasser, 2013), which gives youth near-continuous access to friends via texting and social media (topics we discuss in Chapter 7). Adolescents describe themselves as happiest when they are with their friends (Larson, 1983). Friends are an increasing resource for improving their mood when something goes wrong in their lives (Levitt, Guacci-Franci, & Levitt, 1993). However, friendships are also the source of adolescents' most negative emotions. Because they rely on their friends so much, when something goes wrong in a friendship it can be a catalyst for intense feelings of anxiety, anger, or sadness (Larson & Richards, 1994).

Why are friendships more intense during adolescence? Puberty and increased autonomy are likely reasons. The physical changes that come with puberty usher in new romantic and sexual feelings. It makes sense that adolescents would turn to their friends, who are experiencing similar changes, to share these novel thoughts and feelings. Further, adolescents are more self-sufficient and independent as compared with children. There is less supervision when they are with their friends, both in and outside of school, which allows for more personal and intimate conversations. Additionally, adolescents' friendships are more egalitarian as compared with their relationships with parents or teachers, so asking for advice or opinions from peers may not be as threatening to their emerging autonomy as seeking advice from parents, although it is worth noting that most adolescents continue to seek support from parents during adolescence. Support seeking from parents remains stable, whereas support seeking from peers increases greatly from childhood to adolescence (Levitt et al., 1993).

Who was your closest friend when you were a child? How about when you were an adolescent? How were those relationships similar and different? How and why were those friendships important to you? What types of activities did you do with those friends?

Complexity. The nature of friendship becomes more complex during adolescence. In childhood, friendship is activity oriented and rooted in similar expectations about how to play and interest in the same types of games. Adolescent friendships are marked by increased understanding and knowledge of each other as well as more sophisticated expectations. Researchers have studied how conceptions and expectations of friendship develop from childhood to adolescence by asking youth "What is a best friend?" or "What do you expect from a best friend?" Comments about spending time together and prosocial behavior are seen at all ages, but comments about loyalty, trust, and intimacy are absent in young children's answers and increase dramatically as children approach early adolescence (Berndt, 1982). Why do conceptions of friendship become more complex? Cognitive development allows early adolescents to understand friendship in this more sophisticated manner.

Adolescents' increasingly complex view of friendship reflects that they are better able to think about abstract concepts and consider multiple perspectives at the same time.

The intensity and complexity of adolescent friendships can be seen in two key attributes of friendships that emerge during this stage of life: intimacy and mutual responsiveness.

Intimacy. In a broad sense, **intimacy** refers to the closeness of a relationship. Intimacy encompasses any features of a relationship that make it close. Shared experiences, support, or help or nurturing between two people contributes to an emotional bond that represents a mutual concern for each other's well-being. Scholars have highlighted two specific dimensions that comprise truly intimate friendships: **self-disclosure**, or the sharing of personal or private thoughts and feelings with friends, and knowledge of personal or private information about the other friend. Sharing and listening from both parties leads to deeper understanding between friends. However, these two dimensions are distinct, as knowledge of a friend is not limited to conversations, and information can be learned about friends from observation or during activities.

Robert Selman is a prominent psychologist whose work has informed our understanding of the development of intimacy. As you learned in Chapter 3, Selman studied the development of social cognition, particularly social perspective taking. According to Selman, preadolescents know that others may have different ideas and feelings than their own. It is not until early adolescence that mutual perspective taking begins to develop, which allows the understanding that others, too, understand that their ideas and feelings are different from their own. In Selman's view, intimacy is not possible until adolescence because it requires mutual perspective taking, which is not typically present prior to adolescence (Selman, 1980).

Harry Stack Sullivan (1892–1949) was an American psychiatrist whose theory of interpersonal relationships has had a profound influence on our understanding of the development of intimacy. In Sullivan's view, each stage of life has distinct interpersonal needs (Sullivan, 1953). As children grow into adolescents and then adults, satisfying the different interpersonal needs is a critical developmental task that can result in feelings of security (when needs are met) or feelings of anxiety (when needs are not met). Sullivan differentiated the following interpersonal needs around the adolescent stage:

- Middle childhood (approximately ages 6 to 9) is characterized by the need for playmates and acceptance into peer groups.
- Preadolescence and **early adolescence** (sometime between 8 and 14 years of age) is characterized by the emergence of the need for intimacy in same-sex friendships.
- Adolescence (sometime between 12 and 18 years of age) is characterized by the need for intimacy with a romantic partner and sexual contact.

Sullivan viewed the preadolescent/early adolescent stage as pivotal. During this stage children form a special friendship with a **"chum,"** in Sullivan's words (Sullivan, 1953). Children become interested in truly supporting their chums and develop sensitivity to the needs of their chums. Sullivan thought it was often seen in 8 1/2- to 10-year-olds, but for many youth it doesn't appear until later. In Sullivan's view, these intimate same-sex chumships are crucial to the subsequent development of intimacy in sexual relationships. Intimacy within same-sex friendships provides a secure base to then explore sexual needs without excessive anxiety. Sullivan thought chumship was so powerful in social development that even one chumship could overcome and repair relationship problems with parents or peers that existed in childhood. Conversely, not forming a chumship at this stage can

In-Depth 8.1

Gender Differences in Intimacy

In numerous ways the friendships of girls are more intimate than are those of boys. In a review of the research on peer relations, Rose and Rudolph (2006) concluded there was much evidence that girls and boys have different goals, behavioral styles, and relationship experiences with friends. Girls are more likely than are boys to endorse intimacy goals, desire closeness and dependency, and worry about hurting or losing a friendship. Girls report more self-disclosure and emotional expression in friendships than do boys. Girls are more sensitive to distress in their relationships and are more likely to seek support from friends when problems arise. Overall, girls are more likely to report that their friendships are close and nurturing. These gender differences reflect the different socialization experiences, discussed in Chapter 5, that encourage greater emotional expression in girls compared to boys.

The greater intimacy in adolescent girls' friendships has trade-offs for their adjustment. With their friends, adolescent girls are more likely than are boys to engage in **co-rumination**, which refers to the extensive discussion of problems. When girls experience stress, they are more likely to frequently discuss problems, encourage friends to discuss problems, revisit their problem repeatedly, speculate about the causes and consequences of a problem, and focus on negative feelings. This higher level of co-rumination seen in girls' friendships leads to greater feelings of closeness between friends but also leads to higher levels of depression and anxiety. It seems that having friends to talk with about stress or problems can feel very supportive but can also lead to an excessive focus on the problem, which leads to negative feelings (Rose & Rudolph, 2006).

There are some aspects of intimacy for which research has not found gender differences. Boys and girls report nearly equivalent knowledge about their best friends (McNelles & Connolly, 1999). Perhaps boys learn about their close friends during activities, whereas girls may do so in conversations. There also seem to be certain topics for which boys and girls self-disclose similar amounts of information to their friends. For example, boys and girls are equally likely to share information about romantic relationships with friends (Azmitia, Kamprath, & Linnet, 1998). Another study found that boys and girls are equally likely to share what kind of mood they are in when they see their friends (McNelles & Connolly, 1999). Thus, although boys' friendships do seem more oriented toward shared activities than intimacy, there may be subtle processes and certain topics for which this is not the case. It has also been suggested that the development of intimacy in boys may be more delayed than in girls, and gender differences in friendships are less extreme in later adolescence and adulthood (Way & Greene, 2006). Further, most research on gender differences in intimacy has been done with European American samples. Gender differences may be less prevalent in the friendships of adolescents from other ethnic groups. One study of African American, Latino, and Asian American adolescents found no gender differences in support from friends for African American and Latinos. For Asian American adolescents, boys reported greater social support from friends as compared with girls (Way & Chen, 2000).

undermine the formation of mature intimate relationships; the insecurity left over from pre- or early adolescence will interfere with adolescents' progression into further intimate relationships. Sullivan thought it could have a long-term impact into later adolescence or adulthood. Research has validated Sullivan's ideas that insecurities in earlier life present challenges later in life, but has also shown that people are capable of learning to be intimate and experience closeness with others at any point in adulthood (Aron & Aron, 1986).

Mutual Responsiveness. **Mutual responsiveness** refers to the extent to which friends share resources and help one another. However, mutual responsiveness goes beyond prosocial behavior, which is evident and expected in friendships of even young children. Mutual responsiveness refers to simultaneously considering both one's own needs and those of a friend and acting in a way that maximizes both parties' happiness. During adolescence, individuals are more cognizant and attentive to their friends' needs (Berndt, 1982). Mutual responsiveness is grounded in the ability to engage in mutual perspective taking and is related to intimacy. However, it goes beyond self-disclosure and knowledge of friends and refers to thinking and acting in a way that ensures both friends are satisfied. It encompasses the features of equality, reciprocity, and fairness, and contributes to the development of trust and loyalty. As a teacher, you are likely to notice these issues in students' conflicts as they learn to figure out how to balance their needs with others and, at times, test the limits of their friendships.

The work of James Youniss (1980) has provided insights into how mutual responsiveness changes during adolescence. Youniss drew on Piaget's theory of the development of reciprocity in children. Young children view reciprocity as an exchange of actions or goods between two people or "tit for tat." Early adolescents view reciprocity as treating others as you want them to treat you. Youniss (1980) found that children of all ages comment that friends share with each other, but comments about sharing when one friend was worse off than the other increased from the ages of 6 through 14. He attributed this finding to the development of reciprocity—adolescents realize that both friends need to be happy, and so it is especially important to help friends when they are in need.

Friendship Provisions and Friendship Quality

As we have reviewed, the nature of friendships undergoes much change and matters for development during adolescence. Within friendships there is the potential for many benefits to adolescent development. However, friendships are complicated and dynamic relationships between two people that at times can also present challenges for adolescent development. The capacities for intimacy and mutual responsiveness are developing during adolescence but not always fully realized. Further, adolescents have to figure out with whom they want to spend their time and be intimate and responsive. As we defined at the outset of this section, a friendship is a mutual, close, and voluntary relationship. A true friendship requires two people committed to the relationship. Some friendships endure for long periods of time, whereas others dissolve as people or circumstances evolve. Whether or not friendships last and contribute in a positive way to development depends on a delicate balance of friendship provisions (benefits and costs) and the overall friendship quality (Berndt, 2004; Wentzel, Donlan & Morrison, 2012). The potential benefits and costs of friendships also play out in the classroom setting in ways that affect students' motivation, engagement, and achievement.

Benefits. The benefits or positive features of friendships include companionship, positive emotions, support, and validation. At the most basic level, friends are companions to spend time with and do things together. One of the most important aspects of friendships is simply having someone with whom to hang out with, talk, and go places. Adolescents generally want someone to eat lunch with in the cafeteria or go to school events with, such as a sports game or dance. Friendships are the source of a range of positive emotions, from feeling safe or simply comfortable to providing entertainment, humor, and fun. Friends provide different types of support ranging from information to help with a problem, guidance, or advice on practical or personal issues. When an adolescent needs a ride home, loses her wallet, has a question about homework, or has a misunderstanding with a teacher, parent, or another peer, friends cooperate or give aid to address the issue. Finally, friends provide validation for an adolescent's sense of self-worth. Friends accept

MyEdLab
Video Example 8.1

As 17-year-old Paul talks about friendship, pay attention to his description of friendships, activities with friends at his age, and how they deal with conflicts.

FIGURE 8.2
Provisions of Friendships

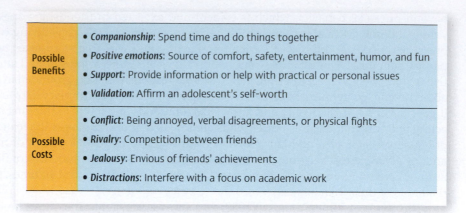

Possible Benefits	• *Companionship*: Spend time and do things together • *Positive emotions*: Source of comfort, safety, entertainment, humor, and fun • *Support*: Provide information or help with practical or personal issues • *Validation*: Affirm an adolescent's self-worth
Possible Costs	• *Conflict*: Being annoyed, verbal disagreements, or physical fights • *Rivalry*: Competition between friends • *Jealousy*: Envious of friends' achievements • *Distractions*: Interfere with a focus on academic work

you for who you are and provide assurance to adolescents that they matter and belong. Validation from friends is important to adolescents as they develop a sense of identity. Figure 8.2 summarizes these provisions of friendships.

As a teacher, it is important to appreciate the potential benefits of friendships for students' motivation, engagement, and achievement in the classroom. With companionship, positive emotions, and validation in the classroom, adolescents are more likely to feel safety, enjoyment, and a sense of belonging that sets the stage for positive engagement. Safety and belonging are basic social needs that when met can facilitate adolescents' engagement in their academic work. Adolescents' friends can make the classroom feel like a welcoming place that they enjoy spending time in. Friends can be a critical source of support in the classroom in ways that enhance their learning and achievement. Teachers are the main source of instruction and help in the classroom, but with 25 to 30 different students in the classroom, they often cannot provide the needed help to everyone. Thus, friends are an important source of help for students when they do not understand the directions or how to do their work. In middle and high school the amount of homework increases, and friends are an important source of help outside the classroom as well. Having friends that one can turn to for help increases students' efficacy that they can do their work and be successful at school.

Costs. Of course, not all friendships are characterized by such positive qualities. Some friendships offer more benefits than others. And sometimes even good friends have problems. Negative features of friendships that represent costs to well-being include conflict, rivalry, and jealousy. For some friendships, conflict can exist, including feelings of annoyance, verbal disagreements, or even physical fights with the other person. Sometimes friends develop rivalries, with one adolescent trying to do better than the other. And when one friend does better than the other, there can be jealousy. However, this is not to say that all problems in friendships represent a threat to well-being. Generally, it is only when these are regular or enduring features of a friendship that they may be unhealthy. If a friendship goes on long enough, some form of conflict is inevitable. Conflict resolution is important to sustaining the friendship over time. Handling problems and resolving conflicts are important skills that adolescents learn with their friends and with the support of teachers.

Friendships sometimes create problems in the classroom and require teachers' attention. Conflicts, rivalries, and jealousy can interfere with students' comfort and sense of belonging in the classroom. These issues can distract students from focusing on their work (and distract other students in the class as well). When these situations emerge, teachers often need to address these issues to get students back on track and focused on their work. Further, sometimes students are getting along so well that they do not do their work. Not all friends are able to balance social and academic goals in the classroom. Perhaps you remember how important it was to have friends in your classes. As a teacher, you both need to recognize the importance of peers yet balance it with the responsibility to ensure that all students are learning. For example, teachers often have to rearrange seats or provide clear consequences to keep students focused on their work (e.g., students will be split up if they do not get their work done).

Friendship Quality. Taken together, we can see that adolescent friendships can be characterized by a wide array of features with the potential to provide many benefits but also costs to adolescents' adjustment outside and inside the classroom. There is much variability in the presence and magnitude of the different features across friendships. Friendship quality refers to the overall value of a friendship and has been conceptualized as a higher ratio of positive to negative features (Berndt, 2004). As long as the benefits are more salient than the costs, the friendship may be valuable to an adolescent. However, it is hard to quantify friendship quality and why certain features may be so appealing (or tolerable) to an adolescent at any given point in time. Ultimately, friendship quality may be the overall satisfaction that an adolescent feels regarding a friendship. Friendship quality predicts adolescent well-being and adjustment at school.

Cross-Ethnic and Same-Ethnic Friendships

With the population becoming more racially and ethnically diverse, researchers have investigated the prevalence and provisions of cross-ethnic friendships. In general, students show a preference for same-ethnic friendships (Moody, 2001). This preference for same-ethnic friendships increases during adolescence, likely due to the increased importance of race and ethnicity for identity during this stage of life (Tatum, 1997). However, the diversity of the setting affects friendship choices. The more ethnically diverse the classroom and school setting are, the more likely an adolescent is to have cross-ethnic friends (Graham, Munniksma, & Juvonen, 2014).

Once formed, same-ethnic and cross-ethnic friendships have similar and different benefits. Adolescents rate their same-ethnic and cross-ethnic friendships as having similar overall friendship quality (Graham et al., 2014). Thus, in general the overall benefits and level of satisfaction with same-ethnic and cross-ethnic friends seem to be similar. However, cross-ethnic friendships do have unique benefits. Specifically, having cross-ethnic friends has been linked to having more positive intergroup attitudes and less tolerance of exclusion of others (Killen, Kelly, Richardson, Crystal, & Ruck, 2010). Further, having cross-ethnic friendships is associated with a greater sense of safety, less loneliness, and fewer experiences of peer victimization at school (Graham et al., 2014).

A unique benefit of same-ethnic friendships is that they are associated with higher levels of positive ethnic identity. Specifically, having same-ethnic friends promotes positive feelings of belonging to their ethnic groups for African American and Asian American students (Graham et al., 2014). For minority students, same-ethnic friendships likely provide a context to discuss ethnic identity and share experiences related to race. As discussed in Chapter 5, a positive ethnic identity acts as a protective factor when adolescents experience racial discrimination. Unfortunately, some minority adolescents report experiencing racial discrimination at school (as well as other settings), but if they have a positive ethnic identity they are better able to maintain high academic engagement and achievement (Chavous, Rivas-Drake, Smalls, Griffen, & Cogburn, 2008). Beverly Tatum's (1997) widely acclaimed book *"Why Are All the Black Kids Sitting Together in the Cafeteria?" and Other Conversations About Race* is a great reference for teachers wanting to understand more about identity development, discrimination, and peer relations at school.

What Educators Can Do

In this section, we reviewed the nature and development of friendship during adolescence. What we have learned about adolescent friendships has important implications for teachers:

1. *Appreciate the importance of friends for adolescents.* We discussed in this section that friendship is a key interpersonal bond. Friends matter for well-being and adjustment at school. Having friends helps adolescents feel comfortable and makes school an enjoyable place, which sets the stage for engagement and participation in school. Friendships become more intense during adolescence, and as a teacher you will witness the emotional investment that adolescents put into their friendships. Cross-ethnic and same-ethnic friendships have important benefits for students. As a teacher, it is important to keep in mind the significance of friends for your adolescent students when you try to understand their behavior and adjustment.

2. *Remember that adolescents (especially early adolescents) are learning what it means to be a good friend and get along with peers in more mature ways.* In this section, we learned about the tremendous changes in the nature of friendship during adolescence. Although adolescents are more sophisticated than children in their beliefs and behaviors regarding peers, they are still developing the skills needed for more mature relationships. At times, adolescents may need guidance in their social relations. For example, the development of mutual responsiveness takes time and support; teachers can help students gain insights by drawing attention to the needs and views of their peers in the classroom, particularly when resolving conflicts or addressing behavioral issues.

3. *Strive to facilitate friendships when needed and possible.* As a teacher, you will make decisions about where to seat students and whom to partner together for activities. These decisions can be especially important for shy or new students who might need some help in forging friendships in the classroom. Collaborating on a challenging and interesting task together is a great context for a friendship to develop. Teachers can create and manage social opportunities in subtle ways in the classroom. Teachers can also encourage participation in after-school activities such as sports, volunteering, and clubs or programs at local youth centers, where adolescents may find peers with interests similar to their own. Of course, this does not mean that teachers can ensure that all students have friends. Friendships are a voluntary relationship between students, but, at times, teachers can provide some opportunities for students to connect in the classroom or another setting that set the stage for friendships to flourish. This is important because, as we reviewed, friends provide numerous benefits that support overall well-being as well as motivation, engagement, and achievement at school.

4. *Intervene when friendships are not working well at school.* Friendships are complicated and dynamic relationships, and challenges are inevitable. At times, problems with friends can distract students from their work, and students can benefit from teacher assistance in smoothing things out. Especially in early adolescence, students can use help in seeing a friend's point of view and may need space to calm their emotions, as well as suggestions about how to reframe the issue so it does not seem so earth-shattering to them. It is helpful to remember how important friendships are to adolescents, and their seemingly overdramatic reaction to problems makes more sense when we think about the many changes they are negotiating in their peer relationships.

Peer Groups

Another important aspect of adolescents' social experience is the time they spend in peer groups (also known as cliques). A **peer group** consists of individuals who frequently interact with one another. As a teacher, you will notice groups of students who tend to hang out and talk to each other and often do activities together. Adolescents' close friends are often, but not always, in their peer groups at school. For many adolescents, their peer group consists of a broader group of individuals than their close friends. You might recall a close friend during high school from your neighborhood who wasn't part of the group of friends you most often hung around with at school. This is partly due to the fact that when students move into larger middle and high schools, their class and extracurricular schedules bring them into contact with a wide array of peers. Even close friends will have different social experiences that may result in different peer groups.

Thomas Kindermann is a scholar who has extensively studied the nature of adolescents' peer groups at school. In one study, Kindermann (2007) studied the peer groups and friends of over 360 sixth-grade students in their first year of middle school. Peer groups ranged in size from 2 to 12 members, with the typical group having 5 members. About 80% of students in the study were members of a peer group. There was only partial overlap between peer groups and close friends, as most students who did not belong to a peer group did have a reciprocated close friend at school. Conversely, most of the children without any close friends did belong to a peer group. Seven percent of sixth graders had neither a reciprocated friend nor a peer group in the fall of the school year. Across the school year, there was both stability and change in peer groups. For example:

- Most peer groups lost some and added some members across the school year.
- About 1 in 5 students had identical peer groups in the fall and spring.
- On average, most youth maintained ties with three peer group members from fall to spring.
- Half of the students with no peer group in the fall did become a member of a peer group by the spring.

Thus, although some adding and changing of members occurs across the school year, most students remain in contact with at least a few members from the fall to the spring. It takes some adolescents longer to find their peer groups than others. Similar stability and change has been documented when students transition into high school (Chan & Poulin, 2007).

Although friendship and peer groups may overlap (see Figure 8.3), they are different phenomena with their own attributes and features. One attribute that differentiates them is closeness. Friendships are close relationships and the setting where intimacy and mutual responsiveness are likely to unfold. Conversely, peer groups are based on frequent social interactions, and members may never have a close emotional bond. Indeed, adolescents who only share peer group membership, and not friendship, rate those relationships as less close than their relationships with friends (Kindermann & Skinner, 2012). It is likely that peer groups provide additional companionship and positive emotions beyond close friends, especially in larger middle and high schools where it would be unlikely for adolescents to be in the same classes all day with their close friends. However, some adolescents are satisfied with a small number of close friendships (Rubin et al., 2014).

Changes in Peer Groups in Adolescence

There are several changes in peer groups from childhood to adolescence. Some of these changes are similar to the changes we described in relation to friendship,

FIGURE 8.3

A Social Network Showing Friends and Peer Groups

Note: Lines depict reciprocated friendships, and circles depict peer groups.

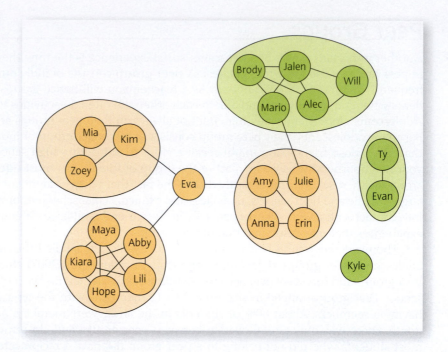

namely, the amount of time and the nature of supervision during that time. Specifically, during adolescence, youth are likely to spend more time in peer groups and this time is less likely to be supervised by an adult. Time spent with friends and peer groups is increasing during adolescence, whereas time spent with parents is decreasing (Brown, 2004). As discussed previously, puberty brings changes that draw adolescents together around topics that they would rather discuss away from adults. Increases in autonomy at this stage allow for less supervision. Further, many adolescents transition to larger middle and high school settings where they come into contact with a wider array of peers from different neighborhoods; their peer groups become less familiar to their parents, and accordingly parents have less knowledge and exert less control over time with peer groups.

Most theory and research on changes in peer groups during adolescence is based on the experiences of youth from Western countries (i.e., United States, Canada, and Europe). In a cross-cultural analysis, Schlegal and Barry (1991) noted that in other countries around the world, adolescence is also characterized by declines in time spent with family and increases in time spent with peers, and that interactions with friends and peers become more intense and complex. However, they note that, overall, adolescents in traditional cultures spend more time with family than with peers. Further, there are more stark gender differences in traditional cultures, with boys spending greater time with peers as compared with girls, who are more likely to spend time at home with their family members. Another difference is in the extent to which peer groups become mixed-sex groups during adolescence, the issue we turn to next.

One of the most notable changes to peer groups during adolescence in Western countries is that they increasingly involve cross-sex interaction (Brown, 2004). In childhood and early adolescence, peer groups are highly gender segregated. In childhood and even early adolescence, boys and girls are not interested in each other romantically. Peer groups spend time hanging out, talking, watching TV or movies, and going to the pool or other community spots with peers of the same sex. Although there is variability, common activities for boys' peer groups are playing video games or engaging in athletics or other physical pursuits. Topics for discussion or activities seen in girls' but not boys' peer groups include grooming, clothing, and fashion (Mehta & Strough, 2009). At this stage, same-gender peers play a powerful role in shaping conformity to gender-typed norms, and youth who go against the norms and hang around with members of the opposite sex may be teased or ostracized by peers (Leaper, 2015).

At some point, romantic and sexual interests bloom, and for many adolescents this involves cross-sex interactions. Initially, it may be limited and involve more of shared space and sparse and infrequent interactions. Eventually, romantic and sexual interests intensify and transform the peer group (Brown, 2004; Dunphy, 1963). In Western countries, mixed-sex peer groups are formed. Leaders in peer groups often have romantic relationships, and these serve as the catalyst for members from each individual's respective peer group to start hanging out. By middle adolescence (high school), mixed-sex peer groups are more common. In late adolescence, couples start to spend time together and break off from the peer group. Many adolescents will start to spend more time with their boyfriends or girlfriends and less time with their peer groups. Groups of couples may hang out instead of larger mixed-sex groups. Much of the research has considered this issue in the context of heterosexual adolescents, but romance and sexual interests are likely to affect lesbian, gay, bisexual, transgender, and questioning (LGBTQ) peer groups as well.

Peer Influence

Adolescent peer groups get much attention because it is thought that in this setting peer influence, or "peer pressure," is most prevalent. As a teacher at a middle or high school, you will likely observe that students who hang out together tend to be quite similar. Students who work hard in school, get good grades, and want to go to college tend to hang out with students with these same characteristics (Flashman, 2012; Ryan, 2001). Students who do not value school, frequently skip classes, and earn poor grades also tend to cluster together. Students who share similar extracurricular activities such as sports or theater also tend to hang out together (Brown & Larson, 2009). Such similarity among peer-group members is called **homophily** and extends to behavior off the school grounds as well, including smoking, drinking, drug use, dating, and sexual behavior (de la Haye, Green, Kennedy, Pollard, & Tucker, 2013; Osgood et al., 2013).

Similarity: Socialization or Selection?
Similarity among peer-group members is due to socialization and selection. **Socialization** refers to the tendency for peers to influence similar attributes in one another over time and includes modeling and social reinforcement processes. **Modeling** processes involve learning by observing peers. For example, observing a peer's effort on schoolwork or voicing of a belief about the importance of school could introduce an individual to new behaviors and viewpoints. Depending on whether the observed behavior leads to positive or negative results, observation of a model can strengthen or weaken the likelihood that the observer will engage in such behavior or adopt such beliefs in the future (Bandura, 1986). **Social reinforcement** plays a role in that beliefs and behaviors that are discouraged or received negatively by the peer group are less likely to be displayed again by an individual. Conversely, beliefs and behaviors that are encouraged or positively received by the peer group are more likely to surface again in the presence of one's peers.

TV shows and movies often depict peer influence occurring in a dramatic and direct manner (think of the bully in a teen show sneering as he says "What? You don't want to try some? Why? Are you chicken?"). However, much of peer influence is likely to occur through subtle means such as gossip, teasing, and humor. Gossiping about others, for example, is a means of clearly communicating unacceptable behavior without direct confrontation (Eder & Sanford, 1986). Thus, students share experiences and exchange information in subtle and not-so-subtle ways. Out of these interactions among peer-group members, a context emerges regarding norms and values. This peer-group context influences many beliefs and behaviors, including adolescents' motivation and engagement in school. These subtle processes, although more challenging to identify as peer influence, are important to appreciate. Indeed, past campaigns to curb alcohol and drug use ("Just say no!") were ineffectual, probably in large part because they oversimplified the dynamics that unfold within peer groups.

However, students also tend to select friends with attributes similar to their own. So when you notice that students hanging out together in the cafeteria are similar, it is not all due to peer influence. Similar interests can be the basis for shared activities together and make it easier for friends to find common ground. Adolescence, especially early adolescence, may be a time when insecurities and self-consciousness peak, and being around similar others may be reassuring. However, it is unlikely that similarity is the sole basis for adolescents' selection of friends and peer-group members. Adolescents also choose friends with complementary interests and traits, whom perhaps they admire, or friends who engage in behaviors that intrigue them but that they are not comfortable performing themselves. Adolescents themselves may not be completely aware of why they choose certain friends or peers. Further, in peer groups, a complex blend of shared and novel interests by group members may be present but hard to pinpoint. And of course peer groups are always changing, perhaps in pursuit of that delicate balance that gives each individual connection but uniqueness, predictability but stimulation.

Susceptibility to Peer Influence in Adolescence

Adolescence is characterized as the stage of life when peer influence is strongest (Brown, 2004). Few would disagree that the effect of peer influence is stronger in adolescence as compared with childhood or adulthood. Conventional wisdom and popular stereotypes depict adolescents as highly conforming to their peers in a wide range of behaviors, including the music they listen to and the clothes they wear (Steinberg & Monahan, 2007). Susceptibility to peer influence is the product of two forces: the pressure to conform and the capacity of the individual to resist peer influence. The pressure to conform is thought to increase in adolescence as peer relations become much more intense during this stage of life. The capacity of individuals to resist peer influence increases from ages 14 through 18, but not between the ages 10 to 14 or 18 to 21. Thus, early adolescence may be the peak of susceptibility to peer influence, as pressure for conformity is high but the capacity to resist peer influence does not start to increase until the age of 14. These developmental patterns are similar for boys and girls and across ethnic groups (Steinberg & Monahan, 2007).

Some of the intensity of peer relationships and increased susceptibility to peer influence seen at this stage of development may have roots in how social information is processed in the brain. Recent work on brain development has shown that adolescents' brains are not fully mature (Galvan, 2013). Experimental studies that involve brain scans find that when adolescents are with their peers, the regions in the brain associated with experiencing rewards and pleasure show much more activity than when adolescents are alone. No such differences are found in adult brains (Chein, Albert, O'Brien, Uckert, & Steinberg, 2011). Additionally, adolescents' risk-taking behavior differs depending on whether they are with their peers or alone. In the presence of peers, when scans of adolescents' brains indicate the reward circuitry is activated, they are more likely to make risky decisions. In contrast, adults' risk-taking behavior is similar whether they are alone or with peers (Chein et al., 2011). Although this work examined the implications for risky behavior, it may also mean that adolescents are more susceptible to peer influence for prosocial behavior as well.

It is important to remember that there is variability among adolescents in their susceptibility to peer influence. Although adolescence is a time of heightened peer influence, all adolescents do not conform all the time to the behaviors of their peers. Peer influence is a complex and dynamic process. Whether or not an adolescent is susceptible to peer influence in any given situation reflects both characteristics of the adolescent and the characteristics of the peer context (Allen, Chango, Szwedo, Schad, & Marston, 2012). Some adolescents are better able to maintain their personal ideals and goals for behavior when they are in a peer-group setting. Some of this may be related to personality, but as we discussed in Chapter 6, parenting style also plays a role. However, situations also vary in ways that can greatly affect adolescents' behavior with peers. It can be highly tempting to go along with the behavior of peers in certain situations, perhaps because there is a peer who is highly persuasive or because an adolescent wants to maintain existing, or develop new, bonds with the peers involved. In addition, when it is perceived that the behavior involved is widespread, or "everyone is doing it," adolescents are more likely to conform to peers. For example, in classrooms where disruptive behavior is more common, adolescents are more likely to engage in disruptive behavior. As disruptive behavior spreads in a classroom there is increased peer reinforcement for conforming to the norm and increased peer sanctions for defying the norm (Dijkstra & Gest, 2014; McFarland, 2001). This process of peer influence reinforces the importance of teachers "nipping problems in the bud" and proactively teaching and reinforcing norms, findings that have been associated with more effective classroom teaching (Brophy, 2010).

> Do you recall a time when you went along with peers even though you thought it was wrong? What factors contributed to your decision? What were your motives? What was the situation? Did peer pressure ever affect your schoolwork? What can teachers do to help adolescents make good decisions at school?

Adolescents are surrounded by peers in school and classrooms. As a teacher, you will need to decide how to best handle peer influence in your work with students. At times, you may choose to openly discuss peer influence with your students to aid them in their decision making around peers. As we noted in Chapter 3, capabilities to self-regulate behavior are improving in adolescence. Decision making about behavior around peers is an important aspect of self-regulation in the classroom and school. Drawing attention to the process, as well as your expectations for their behavior, can support students in this realm. Being consistent about your expectations is important in shaping students' behavior. However, the social dynamics among your students will also be affected by the nature of your classroom climate. As we described, susceptibility to peer influence reflects the peer context, not just individual adolescent characteristics. As a teacher, you are the leader and can exert much influence in how peer groups and peer influence operate in your classroom by the overall climate you work to create as well as specific strategies regarding peer groups. Later on in this chapter, we will discuss what constitutes a positive classroom social-emotional climate for your adolescent students. In the next section, we focus more specifically on teachers' attunement to peer groups.

Teachers' Attunement to Peer Groups

Peer-group dynamics play out in the classroom. An accurate understanding of peer groups may help teachers better manage and instruct students in their classes, as well as promote positive social relationships (Farmer, Lines, & Hamm, 2011). There is much variability in teachers' attention to, and knowledge of, students' friends and peer groups (Gest, 2006). When teachers understand the peer-group dynamics in their classrooms, it may help them to manage student behavior in the classroom. Teachers' attention to, and knowledge of, students' friends and peer groups, known as **teacher attunement to peer groups**, may be a more difficult task for middle and high school teachers because they teach a larger number of students than do elementary teachers, and because students change classes throughout the day and teachers do not get to know their students as well. With this problem in mind, a group of scholars designed a professional development program for middle school teachers that would enhance teachers' attunement to peer groups (Hamm, Farmer, Dadisman, Gravelle, & Murray, 2011). In a study to test its effectiveness, six schools were recruited; three received the program and three served as a control group. As part of the professional development program, teachers were asked to recall the different peer groups when they were in middle school. Teachers discussed the social dynamics within and between those groups and the purpose and function of those groups. Teachers also identified the peer groups of students they had the previous year and discussed the social dynamics and instructional implications of those groups (Hamm et al., 2011).

At the end of the study, teachers from schools who participated in this program differed from the teachers in the control schools in several ways (Hamm et al., 2011). First, they showed better knowledge of peer groups (measured by comparing teachers' and students' reports of peer groups in the school). Second, they were rated by observers as more responsive and attentive to the peer-group dynamics, social interactions, and infractions in their classes. Third, their students reported a more positive and supportive school social environment. Collectively, these results indicate that teacher attunement to peer groups can be enhanced and leads to better management of social dynamics in classrooms.

What Educators Can Do

As we have discussed throughout this section, peer groups and peer influence can be powerful forces during the adolescent years. As a teacher, there is much you can do to have peer influence work in a positive direction in your class. As we discussed, peer influence is a complex phenomenon that reflects the attributes of individual adolescent decisions as well as the context (your school and your classroom) within which the adolescent is situated. As a teacher, you can target both of these underlying issues by supporting individual students to make good decisions and creating a classroom environment where the norm is for peers to work together in an adaptive manner. Specific strategies include the following:

1. *When appropriate, discuss peer influence to help students better understand the nature of peer influence.* Adolescents are often not fully aware of how peers affect their behavior. You might consider discussing peer influence at the beginning of the year when you discuss rules, expectations, and norms for your classroom and school. When an issue arises, you can take the opportunity to help students reflect on their decision making among peers. This can be done individually, as a whole class, or in small groups, as appropriate for your particular situation. As a teacher, you are in a position to reinforce good decision making in your adolescent students on a regular basis.

2. *Be attuned to peer-group dynamics in your classroom.* Teacher attunement to peer-group dynamics involves monitoring peer-group dynamics in the classroom and making adjustments promptly if peer-group dynamics begin to undermine your instructional goals. One powerful tool that you can use to limit or promote contact between different students is seating assignments within your classroom. Where you seat students in the classroom also diminishes or increases their distance from you. Some students are able to stay focused on a task while seated across the room from the teacher, whereas other students benefit from your physical presence in keeping them on task. Peer-group dynamics are salient when teachers use

collaborative projects or cooperative groups with students. If you use these instructional strategies, you will need to teach students how to work productively in groups and monitor peer-group dynamics while they are working, and reteach norms as necessary. This is particularly important to do at the beginning of the school year and after students return to school after long vacations or holidays. Group assignment, rotation of group members, and assignment of roles within groups are ways that teachers can manage group dynamics.

Crowds

Another aspect of adolescents' peer experience at school concerns crowds. **Crowds** are larger, reputation-based groups of similarly stereotyped individuals who may or may not spend time together. Crowd labels that might be found at an American high school include "jocks," "brains," "loners," "druggies," "populars," and so forth. In other countries, crowd labels also emerge but can vary depending on the activities offered at the school. For example, in some European and Asian countries, sports teams are not affiliated with high schools, and thus there may not be a salient jock crowd. In contrast to the interaction-based peer groups that we discussed in the last section, crowds are larger, reputation-based groups of similarly stereotyped individuals who may or may not spend much time together (Brown, 2004). Friends and peer groups might belong to the same crowd, or they might belong to different crowds. Whereas friends and peer groups spend time together, adolescents in the same crowd do not necessarily spend time together (for example, all jocks in a high school do not hang out with each other). Some adolescents may belong to more than one crowd. One study found that about half of high school students were associated with one crowd, about one-third were associated with two crowds, and about one-sixth did not fit into any crowd (Brown, 2004).

MyEdLab
Video Example 8.2

Teens and parents often use the word clique to describe all groups of friends. In these examples, are they talking about cliques, or are they talking about crowds?

The specific labels of different crowds vary from school to school. In homogeneous high schools (regardless of race) crowds emerge along similar lines (that is, there are jocks and "populars" and nerds as well as some other groups in most schools, regardless of whether that school is predominantly Black or White or another race). In multi-ethnic schools, there is often a division along racial lines, and then within each race there are divisions into crowds. Adolescents sometimes perceive students of another race as one crowd, whereas adolescents within that race make distinctions among in-crowd membership within their group (for example, a White student perceives that there is an Asian crowd, but Asians themselves distinguish several crowds within Asians; Brown, 1990).

B. Bradford Brown is a psychologist who has done much research on crowds in adolescence. He thinks crowds are important because they represent the multiple peer cultures that exist in schools. Brown notes that, all too often, adults make sweeping generalizations that characterize teens as "irresponsible, hedonistic and recalcitrant in the face of adult expectations" (Brown, 1990, p. 172). Brown's work on crowds shows how this view is overly simplistic. There is not one monolithic adolescent peer culture, but rather multiple peer cultures that encompass and encourage a diverse range of values and behaviors (Brown, 1990). Crowds feature different clothing, language, and activity choices. Crowds have their own norms and values; they are a subcontext in schools, each of which encourages different beliefs and behaviors. Crowds represent the different peer cultures that coexist in high schools, and they are not all oppositional to the goals that educators and parents have for adolescents in those settings.

Adolescent crowds can be placed along two dimensions: (1) how involved they are in adult-controlled institutions such as school or extracurricular activities

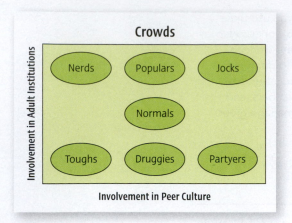

Crowds

Involvement in Adult Institutions

Nerds   Populars   Jocks

Normals

Toughs   Druggies   Partyers

Involvement in Peer Culture

FIGURE 8.4

Crowds

Source: Based on Brown, B.B., 1990.

and (2) how involved they are in peer culture. In Figure 8.4 you can see that jocks are high in involvement in adult-controlled institutions and high in involvement in peer culture, nerds are high in involvement in adult-controlled institutions and low in involvement in peer culture, and partyers are low in involvement in adult-controlled institutions and high in involvement in peer culture. This depiction highlights the complexity of peer cultures that emerge out of the goals of educators in schools in tandem with adolescents' informal peer cultures.

Crowd membership is thought to influence adolescent behavior through **social reinforcement**. Crowds have different norms and values for behaviors. When members act in ways that are valued by the crowd they are likely to get positive reinforcement from other peers in the crowd, which makes them feel good and increases that type of behavior in the future. More broadly, the positive reinforcement solidifies their group membership and identity as part of that crowd (Brechwald & Prinstein, 2011). However, views of members outside the crowd also contribute to the reputation of different crowds. Imagine a girl who dyes her hair black and shaves off the section above her left ear. She was inspired by the hairstyles of some of the older students in the "theater" crowd at her high school. At the bus stop, one of her neighborhood friends, who would be characterized as a jock, comments that she is being too dramatic. When she goes to school, students from the theater crowd (many of whom she doesn't know very well) make positive comments about her new look. She feels good about her new hairstyle and thinks it totally represents who she is. She doesn't mind the comment from her friend because she wants to be more alternative; she doesn't want a boring hairstyle like the mainstream people.

Our example highlights how adolescents can admire and act in ways to align themselves with certain crowds, and how reactions from peers outside and within the crowd contribute to a sense of group membership. This is similar to the process of social reinforcement that happens within peer groups. At the crowd level these processes can play out with peers that an adolescent does not hang around with and interact with on a regular basis. Crowd leaders may inspire behavior, and crowd members may provide reinforcement without regular interaction. In our hairstyle example, the adolescent is striving for, and pleased with, her crowd membership, but this is not always the case. Sometimes adolescents see themselves differently than their peers do, and the role of crowd membership and identity becomes more complicated. Sometimes adolescents belong to two crowds and have to navigate the tension in norms and values between two crowds.

Changes in Crowds During Adolescence

Crowds emerge in early adolescence, become most salient around ninth grade, and then diminish in importance by the end of high school (Brown, 2004). In middle school there is usually one smaller "in" group and then everyone else. In early high school, numerous crowds emerge and are salient to most adolescents in the school. Across the high school years, the structure of crowds becomes more differentiated and flexible and less hierarchical, which allows more movement for adolescents into different crowds.

The quest for identity is thought to be a catalyst for the emergence and development of crowds during adolescence. Initially, when most young adolescents are less sure about their identity, crowds help to provide a rudimentary sense of identity and an understanding of self and others. The changes in cognitive development that we discussed in Chapter 2 allow adolescents to think about themselves and their peers in more sophisticated ways are also related to the emergence of crowds.

To appreciate the concept of crowds requires thinking along multiple dimensions about a rather abstract phenomenon, something children cannot readily do. Changes in school setting also contribute to the phenomenon of crowds. Many youth move into larger middle schools and then even larger high schools during adolescence. Sorting peers into crowds may be a strategy used to make sense of a much larger social scene. Seeking out similar others with common interests may be a way to navigate a larger and more anonymous school setting.

However, ultimately crowd labels are not a satisfying way for adolescents to think about themselves and their peers. As adolescents become more secure in their sense of self and their understanding of themselves and others becomes more nuanced, they see crowds as stifling interactions and limiting identity. By the end of high school, crowds lose much of their importance to adolescents.

Popularity

Within and across peer groups and crowds, social hierarchies emerge in which some adolescents garner attention from peers and are popular, whereas others get little attention and are not popular. Popularity is a topic that attracts much attention and interest by teachers, parents, TV shows and movies, and, of course, adolescents themselves. Popular students are often well liked, attractive, athletic, and seen as "cool," and they often do well in school (Cillessen & van den Bergh, 2012). However, popularity is not always a uniformly positive force. Whereas some popular students are well liked and do well in school, other popular students are bullies who may not excel academically. Others may engage in risky behaviors that jeopardize their health and grades at school. Popular students may also influence other students who look up to them to engage in similar behaviors. Thus, popular status is multifaceted and complex, and has the potential for benefits as well as risks for adolescent development. We consider two different kinds of popularity during adolescence, peer acceptance and popular reputation, and the implications for educators.

Peer Acceptance

Peer acceptance is one form of popularity at school. Peer acceptance concerns the extent to which a student is generally liked or disliked by peers at school. Peer acceptance is distinct from friendship or peer-group membership because it is possible to have a few close friends but not be widely liked, or even noticed, by most students at school. The way researchers have measured peer acceptance is to provide adolescents with a list of the other students in the class or grade at school and have the students nominate whom they like the most and whom they like the least. By examining the frequency and type of nominations by peers, researchers have identified five categories of students that differ in their peer acceptance (see Figure 8.5).

Well-liked adolescents are widely accepted by other students at school. They are liked by many and disliked by few. Sometimes these students are referred to as popular. Well-liked adolescents tend to be cooperative, are sensitive to other students' feelings, easily join others in social activities, and often take on a leadership role (Cillessen & van den Bergh, 2012). In short, well-liked adolescents have strong social skills. Well-liked adolescents also tend to be good students (Wentzel et al., 2012). Because they are well connected with their peers and cooperative, they

FIGURE 8.5

Peer Acceptance

easily cooperate with other students on academic tasks. Social interactions tend to go well for these students. They are willing to help others, and others are willing to help them. Other students like to work with them, so small-group work tends to be positive and productive for these students. They feel comfortable in the classroom and tend not worry too much about what others think of them. For these students, coming to school is rewarding in both social and academic ways.

In contrast, **rejected** adolescents have low levels of peer acceptance by their peers. They are disliked by many and liked by few. Their lives at school are dramatically different than those of well-liked adolescents. Some rejected students often have trouble managing their emotions and tend to be aggressive. Other rejected adolescents are withdrawn and quiet around their peers. Other rejected adolescents are both aggressive and withdrawn (Brown, 2004). Basically, they are rejected because other students do not find them enjoyable to be around due to their difficulty in interacting positively with others. Rejected students are also more likely to struggle academically (Wentzel & Asher, 1995). These adolescents face numerous issues in the classroom that interfere with them doing their work. For rejected students who have issues with aggression, they may be focused on conflicts with peers rather than their schoolwork. For rejected students who are withdrawn, they may often worry about why others do not like them. Overall, students who are rejected are often isolated in the classroom. They have a harder time finding classmates to work with, and they face more difficulties in getting help with their schoolwork from their peers when needed. For all of these reasons, rejected students face a number of challenges that are not faced by students who are well accepted. Rejected students have less positive attitudes toward school, lower academic achievement, and higher absenteeism and dropout rates as compared with well-liked students (Cillessen & van den Bergh, 2012).

Many children are categorized somewhere in between these two extremes. **Average** children are average on both dimensions. They are liked by some of their classmates and may also have a few students who do not like them, but they do not stand apart from others in regard to widespread liking or disliking. **Neglected** adolescents are neither liked nor disliked by their peers. They are low in peer interaction of any kind and generally do not call attention to themselves. They are the students whom others cannot recall their names or do not recognize at all. In regard to social and academic adjustment, average and neglected children tend to not stand out in positive ways (as do the well-liked students) or negative ways (as do the rejected students). In terms of on-task behavior and following the rules, teachers view these students as similar to well-liked students (Wentzel & Asher, 1995). Neglected students are likely to be more at risk academically than average children, however, due to the fact that they have few, if any, peers reporting that they like them and thus are likely to have few friends and the support and benefits that friends provide in the classroom and at school (Wentzel & Asher, 1995).

Controversial adolescents are liked by many peers and disliked by many peers. They are often described as high impact because many students notice them but their acceptance by others is quite mixed. Similarly, their adjustment profile is mixed too. Teachers view them as less likely to follow rules and more likely to start fights than well-liked and average students, although their problems are not as extreme as those of rejected students (Wentzel & Asher, 1995). Controversial students often can interact with peers in positive ways and benefit from those relationships. However, their behavior is not as consistent or predictable as that of well-liked students. They also develop conflictual relationships or draw out antagonism from other peers at school.

Popular Reputation

Having a **popular reputation** is another form of popularity at school. Research on peer acceptance examines which students are liked (or disliked), whereas research on popular reputation examines which students are seen as popular in their class or school. Not all students with a popular reputation are widely liked. You can probably recall students from your middle or high school who would have been considered popular but you didn't particularly like. To identify adolescents with a popular reputation, researchers provide adolescents with a list of the other students in their class or grade at school and have the students nominate who is the most popular. In most classrooms and schools there is an elite group of students who are seen as popular. These students get lots of attention from other students at school. They are seen as "cool." Adolescent boys with a popular reputation are often seen as athletic, funny, and defiant. Adolescent girls with a popular reputation are often seen as attractive and sociable but also snobby and mean. Not surprisingly, unpopular children can have especially negative attitudes toward their popular peers (Closson, 2008).

Students with a popular reputation have a different profile from students who are well liked. Students who are well liked are model students who tend to do well socially and academically. In contrast, students with a popular reputation show a mixture of prosocial and aggressive or defiant behaviors (Cillessen & van den Bergh, 2012). Having a popular reputation is associated with more aggression (physical and relational) and problem behaviors (substance use and early sexual activity). The association between popular reputation and academic achievement is variable; sometimes it has been found to be negative, and other times null or positive.

Antonious Cillessen is a scholar who has conducted much research on the nature and meaning of popularity. He posits that the two types of popularity, peer acceptance and popular reputation, represent two different forms of social competence that adolescents may have at school: Peer acceptance represents the ability to be prosocial, perceive others accurately, take others' perspectives, and interpret others' emotions, all of which enable an adolescent to be empathic, supportive, and responsive to the needs of others, and ultimately be accepted and well liked. A popular reputation represents the ability to be interpersonally effective and achieve goals in social situations, either for oneself or the group. If needed, students with a popular reputation will resort to convincing argumentation, coercion, or manipulation to achieve their goals. Such adolescents are well-connected leaders who are seen as domineering, aggressive, or manipulative by some, but as assertive, socially savvy, and effective by others (Cillessen & van den Bergh, 2012).

> Do you think having a popular reputation is a form of social competence? If having a popular reputation often has drawbacks for the adolescent and others, then is it socially competent?

Power and Risks Associated with a Popular Reputation. Having a popular reputation puts an adolescent in a position of power and having influence over others. Popular peers have influence over others because of their position of high status and their social skills (Sandstrom, 2011). Due to their status as cool and admired, when popular students engage in behavior, it may spread to others who want to emulate them (McFarland, 2000). However, being in a position of high status often comes with the desire to maintain it (e.g., Eder, 1985; Merten, 1997). As a result, popular students not only influence others but are also susceptible to influence from others. To maintain their position of prominence, peers may adopt behaviors that carry high status in the peer group even if they are risky (e.g., drinking or drug use; Mayeux, Sandstrom, & Cillessen, 2008). Further, maintaining a popular reputation is hard work and may fail. That may be why stress and depression are associated with popularity (Sandstrom & Cillessen, 2010). Finally, aggression and manipulation invite retaliation from others, which places popular aggressive youth at risk for victimization (see Eder, 1985; Merten, 1997).

These processes can affect academics. If a popular student has a negative attitude toward school and engages in disruptive off-task behaviors in the classroom, other students may be motivated to emulate the student's behavior. If a popular student perceives that achievement is not cool and that disruptive behavior garners attention, then the student may adopt such behaviors to enhance his or her status. There is a dynamic and reciprocal relation between the behavior of popular students and the norms among students in a classroom or school setting. It is possible for a vicious cycle to emerge between the two if teachers do not intervene in situations involving such negative peer dynamics when necessary.

Changes in Characteristics Associated with Popularity During Adolescence

The characteristics associated with popularity change during early adolescence (Cillessen & Rose, 2005). Aggressive behavior is more likely to be associated with popularity over the course of adolescence (e.g., Cillessen & Mayeux, 2004; Rose, Swenson, & Waller, 2004). Being a high achiever is less likely to be associated with popularity during adolescence (Bukowski, Sippola, & Newcomb, 2000). Peer culture changes in adolescence to be more supportive of deviant behavior and to be less supportive of compliant and/or effortful classroom behavior. This is in line with other research finding that early adolescents are more likely than children to hide or downplay their effort toward schoolwork in front of their peers (Juvonen & Murdock, 1995). Most of the research to date has involved Western countries. One recent study found similar patterns in China for changes in the characteristics associated with popularity during adolescence, but the pattern was less pronounced and did not extend to academic achievement (French, Niu, Xu, Jun, & Ling, 2015). Popularity was positively related to academic achievement in both childhood and adolescence.

Why do these changes occur in early adolescence? Terrie Moffitt is a well-known psychologist who theorizes it is due to a "maturity gap" that characterizes early adolescence in contemporary times in Western countries (Moffitt, 1993). Moffitt postulates that adolescence is a time when youngsters use the peer system as a means of acquiring some of the features of adult status while leaving the features of childhood behind. During early adolescence, children's physical maturity due to puberty spurs an interest in adult status before our society grants expanded adult rights or responsibilities. In response to this "maturity gap," early adolescents become less attracted to characteristics that represent childhood norms and values and become more attracted to peers who embody nonnormative characteristics or features that represent increased autonomy and less childlike behaviors. Thus, aggressive peers become more attractive, and compliant classmates become less attractive (Bukowski et al., 2000; Rose et al., 2004).

Kiefer and Ryan (2011) studied students' perceptions of what characteristics were associated with popularity during early adolescence, across the transition to middle school. They included numerous characteristics to compare the relative ranking as well as changes over time. In the fall of sixth grade, students rated sincerity as the most important characteristic associated with popularity, followed by being a good student (see Figure 8.6). Being attractive and athletic were in the middle. Tough and aggressive behaviors had the lowest ratings in terms of being important to popularity. However, these perceptions changed during early adolescence. Consistent with prior research, the researchers found that students viewed sincerity and being a good student as less important to popularity over time. In contrast, students viewed tough, aggressive, as well as being attractive and athletic as more important to popularity over time.

However, early adolescents' endorsement of positive characteristics (being sincere and good student) were either higher or equal to the ratings for other characteristics (Kiefer & Ryan, 2011). Although early adolescence is a vulnerable time for changes in characteristics associated with social status, the developmental trends indicated

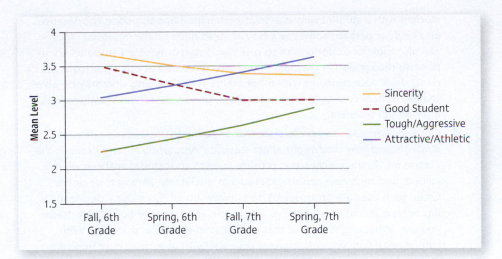

FIGURE 8.6

Student Perceptions of What Characteristics Are Associated with Popularity Changes During Early Adolescence.

Source: Kiefer and Ryan, 2011

Note: Mean level refers to student ratings about the importance of different characteristics with 1 indicating not at all important and 4 indicating very important.

that the overall picture is not wholly negative. Student endorsement of dominant and aggressive behaviors is always lowest. Prior research has shown that there is increasing support for aggressive behaviors, but it is important to note that students view other behaviors as more important, or equally important, to social success.

What Educators Can Do

In this section, we discussed the nature of popularity during adolescence. In schools and classrooms, social hierarchies emerge, with some adolescents being more popular than others. These differences in social status can play an important role in the social dynamics in schools and classrooms. We discussed several implications for educators, and specific strategies regarding popularity issues include the following:

1. *Appreciate and attend to the social dynamics concerning popularity among your adolescent students.* Who are the leaders? Who is rejected? The positions that students have in the social hierarchy at school and in your classroom matter for their social and academic adjustment and can provide you insights into their behavior. Strive to develop and use your knowledge of the social dynamics among your students to support your instruction and classroom management.

2. *Aim for a cohesive and inclusive, rather than hierarchical, classroom.* Ideally, you will develop a classroom climate in which all students belong and feel valued. As a teacher, you want all your students to be engaged and active participants in the classroom. If you have a few students who garner most of the attention in your classroom, it is not beneficial to the other students. If you have students who are rejected and not integrated into the social fabric of the classroom, they are more likely to withdraw and avoid their schoolwork. One good practice as a new teacher is to invite more experienced teachers whom you trust to observe your classroom. They may see things you do not, and together you can brainstorm how to deal with potential issues.

3. *Students who are rejected by their peers may need special attention and support from teachers.* Without any support, rejected students are unlikely to have positive interactions in your classroom. As a teacher, you can try to scaffold social opportunities that correspond to their developmental needs. For example, when assigning work partners you can try to pair a rejected

student with a student who is a good match (perhaps someone cooperative and kind, or perhaps someone who seems to have similar interests). You can also look for opportunities to give neglected or rejected students some positive recognition in the class. If you are concerned about a particular student, share your concerns with other adults in the building who may be able to help: school counselors, other teachers, principals, school social workers, after-school teachers.

4. *Contemplate your own preferences for or ability to understand different students and how they might affect students' reputation among peers in the classroom.* As the teacher, you provide cues to your students about what is valued, and such cues can shape students' social role among their peers. Often such cues are unconscious and unintentional. Consider video recording or tape recording yourself as you teach, and pay attention to the praise you use. What might it signal that you value in particular students? With careful reflection, you can improve your ability to effectively communicate your appreciation and recognition of the different positive attributes of each of your students, which will facilitate students having positive views of one another.

5. *Intervene quickly if a social dynamic emerges that is undermining your instructional goals.* As we discussed in this section, popular students garner more attention and are more likely to be emulated than other students. If a situation emerges with a popular student being disruptive in your class, intervene to change the dynamic. Examine what structures are facilitating this dynamic and make changes (for example, seating arrangements or group assignments). Talking to your students can always provide insights into what they are trying to achieve and ideas for change. Further, developing a personal relationship with students can help quell disruptive behavior. A supportive personal relationship with students generally makes them more receptive to your goals for the class and less willing to defy or alienate you.

MyEdLab **Self-Check 8.1**

MyEdLab **Self-Check 8.2**

MyEdLab
Application Exercise 8.1
Peer Influence Reflect on the ways that Tim and his peers influence one another.

Bullying, Aggression, and Victimization

The issue of bullying in schools has received much attention in recent years. High-profile shootings and suicides by adolescents over the last 15 years have garnered much media attention and galvanized public support for laws requiring that schools have policies and programs in place to prevent and punish bullying. Increasingly, school administrators and teachers are responsible for identifying and addressing bullying among students at school. In this section we define and describe bullying, the consequences for victims and bullies, how bullying behavior changes during adolescence, the conditions that affect bullying, and what schools and teachers can do to minimize the problem of bullying.

A student is bullied when he or she is exposed, repeatedly and over time, to negative actions on the part of one or more students (Juvonen & Graham, 2014). Bullying is the intention to harm another student and often involves a power imbalance that favors the bully or bullies over the victim. Victims often feel helpless to avoid being bullied. Bullying can be direct or indirect. Direct bullying is overt in nature and can involve **physical aggression** such as hitting or pushing or **verbal aggression** such as name calling or insulting someone. Indirect bullying is more subtle and involves **relational aggression**, which refers to the manipulation of someone's social status and friend-ships. Relational aggression can involve intentional exclusion by withdraw-ing attention and friendship, or it can involve efforts to damage someone's reputation by spreading rumors and gossip or making fun of someone behind his or her back. Bullying can be done in person or through digi-tal media such as text messages or social media websites, which is known as **cyberbullying**. Although the definition of bullying includes an element of rep-etition, experts implore educators not to wait around for repetition of aggres-sive acts. One traumatic incident can cause much fear and constitute abuse (Juvonen & Graham, 2014). Any act of aggression or experience of victimization should be responded to promptly by adults (American Educational Research Association, 2013).

Large-scale survey studies indicate that approximately 20 to 25% of youth at school are directly involved in bullying as perpetrators, victims, or both (Juvonen & Graham, 2014). It is estimated that about 4 to 9% of youth frequently bully, and that anywhere from 9 to 25% of school-aged children and adolescents are victims of bullying (Stassen Berger, 2007). There is some overlap among bully and victim groups over time. In one of the few studies that examined the overlap of bullying and victimization longitudinally, Scholte, Engels, Overbeek, Kemp, and Haselager (2007) found that 9% of the sample of students who had reputations as bullies in childhood developed reputations as victims by adolescence, whereas 6% of the students who had reputations as victims in childhood became bullies in adolescence.

In a recent review of the literature, Juvonen and Graham (2014) concluded that much research shows that bullying has negative consequences at school for not only the victims, but also the bullies. Victims of bullying have higher rates of anxi-ety, depression, physical health problems, and social adjustment problems. When students are bullied, they become less engaged in school and their grades and test scores decline. Being bullied in childhood and adolescence can have long-term consequences and affect adjustment in adulthood. Bullies also have adjustment problems. Not surprisingly, students who bully are more likely to also have other conduct problems at school. In addition, bullies are more likely to have physical health problems than are non-bullies. The group that is most at risk for negative outcomes consists of students who bully others and are also victims of bullying. These "bully–victim" students have higher rates of externalizing problems and psychological problems, and are reported by teachers to be the least academically engaged of all their students.

In recent years, there is much concern about cyberbullying because a picture or comment can be quickly disseminated to a large audience, causing greater humilia-tion for victims (see also Chapter 7). As technology and media devices have become more widely used by adolescents, cyberbullying has become more prevalent. Simi-lar to experiences with traditional bullying, being a victim of cyberbullying is asso-ciated with depression, declines in academic performance, and suicide ideation (Tokunaga, 2010). Tragic cases of adolescent suicide following cyberbullying appear on a far too regular basis. For example, the untimely deaths of Megan Meier (2006), Jessica Logan (2008), Hope Witsell (2009), Tyler Clemente (2010), and Amanda Todd (2012) make clear the dire consequences of harassment by peers online. In September 2013, Rebecca Sedwick jumped off a cement factory tower to her death after being bullied by other girls on sites like Ask.com, Kik, Instagram, and Voxer. The cyberbullying followed her even after she transferred schools to escape the abuse. In this case, two girls, aged 12 and 14, were arrested, perhaps a sign that the response by schools and law enforcement to cyberbullying issues is becoming more serious.

MyEdLab
Video Example 8.3

Seventh-grade teacher Chris Gammon explains that all stu-dents at his school participate in anti-cyberbullying education. What might be appropriate to include in a program for young adolescents?

Changes in Bullying During Adolescence

The nature of bullying changes during adolescence. In a recent analysis of a large, nationally representative sample, Yeager, Fong, Lee, and Espelage (2015) found that reports of being the victim of direct, observable aggression declined from about 80% of the bullying in 6th grade to about 50% in 12th grade. Reports of being the victim of indirect, less observable aggression increased from about 60% in 6th grade to about 75% in 12th grade. As youth progress through middle and high school, bullying is less likely to involve hitting and directly insulting someone and more likely to involve relational aggression, such as exclusion or spreading rumors. Notably, however, many bullying incidents still involve physical or direct verbal aggression, even at the end of high school (see Volk, Craig, Boyce, & King, 2006, for identical results in a large, nationally representative Canadian sample).

There are also changes in the relation of social skills to bullying from childhood to adolescence (Yeager et al., 2015). In childhood, bullying is more likely to be related to a deficit in social skills. In elementary school and sometimes in early middle school, bullies are less popular and have fewer social skills, such as abilities in perspective taking, problem solving, and impulse control. In adolescence, bullying is more likely to represent the presence of strong social skills that are used to manipulate others. As bullying evolves from direct forms of physical and verbal aggression to more indirect forms of relational aggression, different skills are involved. The advances in cognition during adolescence, such as increased ability for perspective taking, seem to usher in more complex and sophisticated bullying.

An interesting study by Faris and Felmlee (2011) found that much of the bullying in a high school was done by students who were moderate or above average in the number of friends they had at school. They found that very little bullying occurred at the very low and very high ends of the spectrum of number of friends. In this high school, it was not students with social skill deficits who were engaged in bullying, but rather the students who had friends and some level of popularity. Interestingly, the students with the most friends were also not engaged in bullying, perhaps because their very high social status made them feel secure and they did not have to resort to bullying.

Indeed, research indicates the motive for bullying in adolescence is often derived from a combination of insecurity about social status in tandem with the desire to achieve high status or popularity (Yeager et al., 2015). Insecurity about one's peer groups and social status often peak when students make the transition to middle and high school, times when bullying has also been found to peak (Pelligrini & Long, 2002). One study of students during their first year in middle school asked adolescents what they do when someone at school is mean or spreads a rumor about them (Shin & Ryan, 2012). Adolescents who were high in the desire for popularity were the most likely to "play it cool" around their friends and actively portray that this problem did not bother them. However, they were also the most likely to be aggressive. It seems that when their status is threatened, adolescents who desire popularity act to protect their image in their own peer group while simultaneously using aggression to deal with peers outside of the group.

Finally, bullying related to sexual relationships, sexual orientation, and gender orientation issues increases during adolescence (Pepler et al., 2006; Poteat, O'Dwyer, & Mereish, 2012). Competition over romantic partners emerges as a cause of girls' bullying in high school (Guerra, Williams, & Sadek, 2012;). LGBTQ students are more likely to be victims of bullying than are heterosexual students (D'Augelli, Pilkington, & Hershberger, 2002). Bullying of students who are gender nonconforming also increases (Meyer, 2008). During high school, boys use and are called gay epithets with increased frequency (Poteat et al., 2012). Boys who direct such epithets toward others often minimize it as harmless banter and teasing, whereas those who are targets of such epithets report finding them stigmatizing and offensive (Thurlow, 2001).

MyEdLab
Video Example 8.4

This language arts teacher approaches the topic of bullying language as part of a student assignment to read a novel addressing the topic. This sort of discussion can help to minimize bullying and victimization.

In summary, as youth progress from elementary school into middle and high school, bullying is more likely to involve indirect behaviors and be committed by socially competent students who are motivated to protect or enhance their social status. Further, as children develop into adolescents, bullying related to sexuality or gender issues increases. However, bullying among adolescents still takes many forms and involves a myriad of issues. Physical and verbal aggressions occur in middle and high school and need to be addressed by teachers. However, the task of addressing bullying becomes more challenging for teachers of adolescent students because bullying at this stage also involves more subtle, harder-to-detect behaviors by students who seem socially well adjusted at school.

Conditions That Affect Bullying

Research has identified several conditions that affect bullying. First, conditions that create a lack of empathy with the victims of bullying allow it to flourish. When witnesses to bullying chant in support of the attacker, for example, the bullying behavior is likely to persist. On the other hand, when witnesses step in to try to prevent the attack, or get into the habit of reporting bullying to adults, the culture of the school can change to one in which bullying is not tolerated. Many bullying-prevention programs focus on creating empathy for victims and empowering witnesses to report bullying.

Second, victimization and bullying tend to occur in what Astor, Meyer, and Behre (1999) referred to as "unowned places." Astor and his colleagues (1999) mapped the areas of a high school where bullying was most likely to occur and found that it was those areas that were least likely to be monitored by adults that had the most frequent incidents of bullying. They encourage teachers and other school personnel to take greater responsibility for monitoring such areas and to intervene when they witness bullying or fighting occurring.

Third, teachers' attitudes toward bullying matter (Swearer, Espelage, & Napolitano, 2009). Some teachers view bullying as normal adolescent behavior, whereas other teachers view bullying as unacceptable behavior. When teachers (or other adults) view bullying as normal adolescent behavior, they are more likely to ignore or dismiss bullying behaviors, and the prevalence of bullying is higher. When teachers view bullying as a problem that can have serious consequences for victims, they are more likely to respond quickly to bullying incidents, and the prevalence of bullying is lower.

Fourth, the lack of reporting of bullying by victims, perpetrators, and witnesses allows bullying to continue. Victims are often embarrassed about being bullied, and perpetrators have little incentive to report these incidents. According to data from the National Center for Educational Statistics (2011), only 40% of the students who reported being bullied at least once in the 2010–2011 academic year told an adult about it. If the bullying happened via the Internet, only 26% reported it to an adult. Schools and teachers need to encourage students to report bullying incidents and respond when students do come forward with such information. Further, if a teacher suspects a student is being victimized, the teacher can privately ask the student about it in an open-ended manner to provide the student a safe space for talking about the issue. Additionally, a teacher might inquire with parents about what is affecting their son or daughter's adjustment at school.

What Educators Can Do

In this section, we described the types of aggression that can constitute bullying and have negative consequences for students in school. Teachers' awareness of bullying among their students can become more challenging during adolescence, when the repertoire of bullying behaviors is more likely to include indirect forms of aggression that are harder to spot. Efforts teachers can make to minimize bullying include the following:

- View bullying as a problem that can have serious consequences for victims.
- Monitor spaces outside the classroom because this is often where bullying occurs.
- Encourage students to report bullying, and be responsive when they do.

Further, school-level policies can guide all staff at a school to respond to bullying effectively. In fact, laws in almost all states now mandate that schools and school districts have policies in place to address bullying and victimization. In a recent report published by the American Educational Research Association (2013), a panel of experts on bullying concluded that schools can make a significant difference in the rates of bullying. In schools where teachers and staff work with students to address bullying, victimization can be reduced. In the report, the experts make several recommendations for educators to consider in regard to bullying policies at their school:

1. *Involve all stakeholders in working together.* It is important to include students, parents, teachers, and administrators in creating or revising the school policy so that it reflects the commitment of the entire school community.

2. *Consider nondiscrimination and antibullying policies that specifically include gender identity or sexual orientation.* These have been found to increase the feeling of safety among LGBTQ students.

3. *Encourage school leaders to create and maintain open lines of communication for students and parents to report bullying.* Schools should respond promptly to incidents of bullying and victimization.

4. *Establish clear and developmentally appropriate consequences for individuals or peer groups that encourage or engage in bullying.* As discussed in Chapter 4, emphasizing suspensions as the key disciplinary strategy has been shown to be ineffective (American Psychological Association Zero Tolerance Task Force, 2008).

5. *Beyond the bullying policy, evaluate whether the overall mission of the school encompasses the social and emotional needs of students and whether it is evident and communicated to constituents.* Toward this end, social and emotional learning can help students become more considerate and respectful of each other (discussed in the next section).

6. *If a school or school district wants to institute an antibullying program, teachers can encourage the use of one that has been evaluated and found to be effective.* Information about such programs can be found in the National Registry of Evidence-Based Programs and Practices (http://www .nrepp.samsha.gov/), Blueprints for Healthy Youth Development (http:// www.colorado.edu/cspv/blueprints), and the Model Programs Guide (http://www.ojjdp.gov/mpg/). Such programs involve publicizing school rules that bullying behavior will not be tolerated, classroom discussions to promote a positive and respectful peer culture, and training of teachers regarding how to intervene effectively. Interventions are most successful when the majority of the teachers are invested in the program. When selecting a program, schools should choose a program that was developed and tested in schools with characteristics similar to their own school. Finally, in general, antibullying programs have been shown to be most effective in elementary and middle schools, and thus the content of a program and its applicability to older adolescent issues should be a consideration for high schools (Yeager et al., 2015).

Supporting Students' Peer Relationships at School

As we have described throughout this chapter, students' peer relationships are important to their well-being and their learning at school. There is growing recognition that schools need to meet students' social and emotional needs for students to reach their full potential (Weissberg & Cascarino, 2013). Schools are social places where educators need to address not only academic growth but also social and emotional development for effective teaching and learning. Given the great changes that unfold during adolescence, it is especially important for middle and high school teachers to support students' positive peer relationships. In this section, we discuss two approaches for how educators can support students' social development. First, we discuss programs that focus on social and emotional learning. Second, we discuss the importance of a caring and emotionally supportive classroom environment and what teachers can do to establish such a climate with their adolescent learners.

Social-Emotional Learning Programs

Social and emotional learning (SEL) refers to the process through which individuals acquire and apply the knowledge, attitudes, and skills for managing emotions, setting positive goals, feeling and showing empathy for others, forming and maintaining relationships, and making responsible decisions (Weissberg & Cascarino, 2013). Such skills are viewed as critical for youth to be good students and ultimately good citizens and workers. SEL programs offer explicit instruction regarding social and emotional competencies. SEL programs are described as a positive youth development program in that they promote positive outcomes by enhancing skills and building assets rather than reducing risk by targeting problems (Brackett & Rivers, 2014).

The Collaborative for Academic, Social and Emotional Learning (CASEL) is a nonprofit group that advocates and provides leadership for high-quality SEL programs. CASEL's website (http://www.casel.org) provides a guide for best practices to promote SEL and a review of over 220 different programs. As illustrated in Figure 8.7 CASEL identifies five core competencies associated with SEL:

- **Self-awareness:** the ability to accurately recognize one's emotions and thoughts and their influence on behavior.
- **Self-management:** the ability to regulate one's emotions, thoughts, and behaviors effectively in different situations, and to set and work toward personal and academic goals.
- **Social awareness:** the ability to take the perspective of and empathize with others from diverse backgrounds and cultures and to recognize family, school, and community resources and supports.
- **Relationship skills:** the ability to establish and maintain healthy and rewarding relationships with diverse individuals and groups through communicating clearly, listening actively, cooperating, negotiating conflict constructively, and seeking and offering help when needed.
- **Responsible decision making:** the ability to make constructive and respectful choices about personal

FIGURE 8.7

Social and Emotional Learning

Source: Used by permission from CASEL: Collaborative for Academic, Social, and Emotional Learning.

behavior and social interactions based on consideration of ethical standards, safety concerns, social norms, the realistic evaluation of the consequences that stem from actions, and the well-being of self and others.

There are currently a wide variety of SEL programs available, some more effective than others. In an analysis of the effectiveness of 213 of SEL programs used in schools, Durlak and his colleagues (Durlak, Weissberg, Dymnicki, Taylor, & Schellinger, 2011) found that when SEL programs were administered well by teachers, and had certain characteristics, students from kindergarten through high school experienced gains in achievement, developed improved social and emotional skills, and displayed less antisocial behavior than did students who did not participate in such programs. The four key components to effective SEL programs are easily remembered using the acronym SAFE, which stands for sequenced, active, focused, and explicit. Programs that do not have these characteristics, such as a one-time school assembly that simply encourages students to report bullying or to be respectful of others, are generally ineffective in teaching social and emotional skills. The SAFE components are as follows:

1. *Sequenced:* A coordinated set of activities to help students develop SEL skills is presented rather than teaching the skills in a disjointed manner.
2. *Active:* Students are engaged with active learning, including such activities as role-playing and practicing of new skills.
3. *Focused:* At least part of the program is devoted specifically to teaching students personal or social skills.
4. *Explicit:* The program targets specific SEL skill development rather than focusing on prosocial skills more generally.

Although SEL programs have much potential, their effectiveness is often limited by two factors: the difficulty for teachers to find the time to dedicate to SEL programming and the fact that SEL programs are rarely integrated into classrooms and schools in ways that are meaningful, sustained, and embedded in the daily interactions of students, teachers, and staff (Jones & Bouffard, 2012). To be developed, social and emotional skills need to be practiced in the context of ongoing relationships in real life. However, educators in today's schools are under much pressure to maximize instructional time and meet accountability requirements. With such pressures, it is hard to implement SEL programs in meaningful and sustained ways.

State-based standards, such as the Common Core, are increasingly being used to affect educational practice. Most standards concern academic content, but some states are starting to adopt SEL standards to encourage schools to promote these competencies in students. What do you think? Should states adopt SEL standards?

Jones and Bouffard (2012) advocate for a new approach: embedding SEL into teachers' daily practice with students and the overall school mission. In their view, SEL should not compete for instructional time. It should be integrated with daily practice and interactions with students. This would promote students' social and emotional growth in more sustainable, feasible, and effective ways. Such an approach would require training and support for teachers, administrators, and staff, as most training and support has tended to focus on academic content.

The Emotionally Supportive Classroom

Students spend the majority of their time each day at school within classrooms. What type of classroom context best supports students' growth and development?

Academic content and instructional issues have always received much attention, and of course are important considerations for students' learning and performance. More recently, the emotional/social dimension of classrooms is receiving attention. There is now much evidence that an emotionally supportive classroom climate promotes social adjustment as well as academic achievement (Allen et al., 2013; Brophy, 2010; Gregory, Allen, Mikami, Hafen, & Pianta, 2014; Patrick & Mantzicopoulos, 2012). In emotionally supportive classrooms, students feel safe and comfortable and are more likely to form positive peer relationships. When students feel socially connected to others they are more likely to be invested in school, to be willing to comply with the teachers' wishes, and to try to get along with other students. As a teacher, you are the leader in the classroom, and you will play an important role in creating the social climate that develops in your classroom. In this section, we consider the nature of an emotionally supportive classroom and how teachers can create such an environment with their students.

What are the essential ingredients of an emotionally supportive classroom? An emotionally supportive classroom is characterized by positive relationships, positive affect, respect, and communication. Negative affect such as conflict, sarcasm, and disrespect is rare. Teachers are sensitive to student needs and show regard for student perspectives (Pianta & Hamre, 2009). Barnes and Knowles (2014) assert that in a truly caring classroom environment, teachers genuinely know their students, communicate effectively with their students, and encourage positive relationships among students.

Let's imagine walking into an emotionally supportive classroom. What might we see? There would be an emotional connection between teachers and students seen through both students and teachers seeming to enjoy their work. The relationships among teachers and students would be characterized by warmth. Verbal and nonverbal interactions would be respectful in tone. There would be enthusiasm and possibly humor. Peers would be interacting with one another in positive ways. The teacher and students would smile often. Students would listen when their classmates spoke and respond to their ideas respectfully. The teacher would use student names, and words like *we, please,* and *thank you* would be frequent. The teacher would make encouraging and specific comments about student work, such as "Your purposeful use of color to demonstrate change really helps the results of your experiment stand out." At the beginning of a Monday class, you might see the teacher inquire about what the students did over the weekend.

Sensitivity to student needs is important to building an emotionally supportive classroom (Pianta & Hamre, 2009). In classrooms where teachers are sensitive to student needs, teachers would monitor students and respond to signs of frustration or confusion. You might see the teacher walking around the room and checking on student progress. If a teacher is lecturing, she might stop periodically and ask if everyone understands something. Or when the teacher notices that some students are still working, she waits for them to finish up before moving on. In classrooms where there is regard for student perspectives, you would see the teacher showing an interest in student opinions and soliciting student ideas. For example, you might see a comment that a student makes shape the course of a discussion or alter the direction of an activity.

Now let's imagine visiting a classroom that is not emotionally supportive. What might we see? Teachers and students might appear distant or disinterested in one another. There would be few positive comments. Enjoyment might be rarely seen. Or there might be salient negative dynamics in a classroom. For example, you might see consistent displays of irritability, annoyance, or even anger and hostility by the teacher and/or students. The teacher might attempt to control student behavior by threatening them with punishment or yelling at

MyEdLab
Video Example 8.5
Mr. Gammon describes some of the ways in which he encourages an emotionally supportive classroom.

them to change their behavior. The teacher might snap at students, use a harsh voice, or overreact to minor problems with disproportionate punishment. Bullying, teasing, exclusion, or use of discriminatory language might be seen (Pianta, Hamre, & Mintz, 2010).

When we contrast an emotionally supportive classroom environment with one that is flat in affect or has negative social-emotional dynamics, it is easy to see why an emotionally supportive context facilitates positive social and academic development.

What Educators Can Do

In this section, we discussed two approaches to supporting students' peer relationships in schools: social-emotional learning programs and emotionally supportive classroom environments. There are important implications for educators, and specific strategies include the following:

1. *Realize that school-based SEL programs have the potential to positively affect students' social and emotional skills.* The implementation of social and emotional learning programs in schools has grown greatly in recent years. It is important for teachers to be aware of the role that such programs can play in creating a positive school climate and supporting student needs within that climate. However, it is critical to appreciate that the success of such programs hinges on teachers' dedication and consistent nurturing of students' social skills on a regular basis in the classroom.

2. *Create an emotionally supportive classroom.* The following list is not exhaustive but describes some of the teacher behaviors that are thought to facilitate positive relationships, positive affect, respect, and communication in a classroom (Brown & Knowles, 2014; Charney, 2002; Patrick & Mantzicopoulos, 2012; Pianta et al., 2010):

   • **Build relationships with your students.** Show an interest in your students as people. Ask questions. Share something about your hobbies or interests outside of school. Some teachers might set aside a few minutes at the beginning or end of class as a time to make a personal connection with the class. The period when students are entering the classroom and settling down is a great time to have brief relationship-building conversations with students.

   • **Build in activities to allow students to get to know one another.** This can be especially helpful for students to feel comfortable and build relationships early in the school year.

   • **Show positive affect.** Smile. Laugh. Show enthusiasm. If you want your students to be positive, you need to be positive!

   • **Communicate in a positive manner.** Compliment students when they do well, describing what it is they did well. Show appreciation for positive behavior. Express positive expectations. Emphasize what you would like to see in your students rather than what you would not like to see.

   • **Encourage respect.** Use your students' names. Use respectful language like "please" and "thank you." Encourage students to respect one another by listening and constructively responding to their classmates' ideas.

   • **Manage negative emotions.** It is inevitable that teachers will feel stress, irritation, or even anger at times in the classroom. However, as the leader and role model of the classroom, it is important to stay calm and not respond to students when you are angry. Taking a deep breath and counting to 10 can work wonders.

- **Check in with students.** Monitor their progress as they work. Scan the room to see if students are having problems. Periodically ask students how they are doing.
- **Listen to your students.** Try to hear students' perspectives. Ask questions to elicit their thinking. Often we think we understand how others think, but after some questioning we realize we were mistaken. When possible, make adjustments, follow students' lead, or incorporate their ideas into classroom activities or products. Really listening to others is not easy to achieve and impedes many relationships, not just student–teacher relationships. Strive to be empathetic and work on truly listening to and understanding your students.
- **Respond when students need help.** Make adjustments as needed for students who struggle. Reassure students when they have difficulty and strive to assist them.

As a teacher, all of your interactions with students will convey your caring and commitment to them. Schools can be a stressful place for teachers and students. Certainly, adolescents can be unpredictable, and teachers are only human too. An emotionally supportive climate requires consistent nurturing by teachers, day in and day out. However, when an emotionally supportive classroom is achieved and maintained, it is a more pleasant and productive environment for the students and the teacher. Being proactive and working to establish positive norms and values with your students at the beginning of the year can be helpful for you and your students (see "Creating Classroom Rules and Norms" In-Depth box that follows).

In-Depth 8.2

Creating Classroom Rules and Norms

Ruth Charney is a well-known author and education consultant. She was a public school teacher in New York City for 35 years and drew on her extensive experience when writing her groundbreaking book *Teaching Children to Care* (Charney, 1993, 2002). She developed the Responsive Classroom, an approach for creating an emotionally supportive classroom environment, which is widely used around the country. Charney has written extensively about the importance of teachers co-creating rules and norms with their students in the beginning of the school year. Including students in the process of creating behavioral norms is thought to increase their investment in the classroom and create a partnership with students. The goal is to create a concise set of rules and norms to post in the classroom that can serve as a guide and be referenced often. Charney calls the process "Hopes and Dreams," and we outline it here for you. Interestingly, it was initially developed for elementary-aged children but has gained wide support from teachers of adolescent learners as well. The process is as follows:

- In the beginning of the school year the teacher invites the students to share their hopes for the school year. The teacher asks students to reflect on what kind of classroom environment would help them learn the most. What behaviors would they see in the classroom? How would students treat one another? The teacher focuses students on observable behaviors that are specific enough to guide daily action. The idea is that students can easily picture themselves enacting the norms. Note that norms are meant to be general for the whole class. A separate and parallel exercise might be to have students set their personal hopes and goals.
- The teacher begins by modeling for the students. For example, a teacher might say, "I hope you will

be interested in the work we do and do your best work each day."

■ Students brainstorm ideas. Students might reflect and write on their own to get ideas flowing before opening up discussion to the whole class.

■ The teacher encourages students to frame items positively so they can guide students in what to do rather than what to avoid.

■ The teacher helps students narrow down the list by grouping similar ideas together and having students decide which are the most important rules and norms. A short list that students can remember is better than a long list that everyone forgets. Generally, norms and rules reflect how students take care of themselves, others, and their environment.

■ The teacher encourages discussion around why students think certain norms are important. Depending on students' energy level, the process may be split over 2 days.

Of course there are variations on how to co-construct rules and norms with students. The key idea is to set a positive and productive tone for the year. Regardless of the exact procedure used to create the rules, the rules need to be used each day if they are to truly create norms in a classroom. The teacher needs to reference the rules and model appropriate behavior. Much positive reinforcement and redirecting might be necessary in the beginning of the school year or after breaks from school. Charney (1993, 2002) thinks it takes 6 weeks for routines and norms to be solidified in a classroom.

Recommendations for Educators

In this chapter, we have examined the different facets of students' peer relationships, how they change during adolescence, and the implications for students' adjustment at school. We examined what is currently known about bullying and victimization. We discussed how social-emotional learning programs and an emotionally supportive classroom environment can facilitate positive peer relationships for students at school. Next, we review the important implications that these topics have for teachers of adolescents.

Insights into the Nature and Development of Peer Relationships Can Help Teachers Manage the Social Dynamics Among Adolescents in Classrooms and at School

We discussed the nature and development of friendship, peer groups, peer influence, crowds, and popularity. As a teacher, your appreciation of the importance of adolescent peer relationships can help you support students' adjustment at school. Throughout the chapter, we described numerous ways teachers can support students' social development and manage social dynamics in their classrooms to optimize learning. In your work with adolescent learners, you can help students learn how to be a good friend and get along with peers in more mature ways. When needed and possible, you can strive to facilitate friendships for students. By being attuned to peer-group dynamics, you can manage the nature and extent of peer influence on achievement-related behaviors. You can notice the social dynamics around popularity among your students and aim for an inclusive classroom where all students belong and feel valued.

The Attitudes and Efforts of Teachers and Schools Can Reduce Bullying and Victimization

We described bullying, the consequences for victims and bullies, and how bullying behavior changes during adolescence. Teachers' awareness of bullying can become more challenging during adolescence when bullying behaviors include not only direct physical and verbal aggression but also indirect forms (relational aggression and cyberbullying) that are more subtle and harder to spot. We discussed efforts that teachers can make to minimize bullying, including viewing bullying as a problem, monitoring spaces outside the classroom where bullying often occurs, encouraging students to report bullying, and being responsive when they do. We also discussed recommendations for school-level policies that can help educators reduce bullying.

Social-Emotional Learning and Antibullying Programs Are Options for Schools to Promote Positive Social Skills and Minimize Bullying Behavior Among Students

Interventions and programs that schools can adopt to address social developmental issues have proliferated in recent years. We described these programs and provided information about where teachers can go to find more information regarding numerous popular programs and their effectiveness. It is important for teachers to appreciate that the success of such schoolwide programs hinges on the majority of teachers being invested in the program and integrating the principles into their daily practice with students.

By Creating an Emotionally Supportive Classroom Environment, Teachers Can Support Adolescents' Social and Academic Development

We described that an emotionally supportive classroom includes building positive relationships, striving for positive affect, insisting on mutual respect, and being sensitive to student needs. We discussed numerous behaviors that teachers can engage in to create such a classroom. As a teacher, co-creating rules and norms with your adolescent students at the beginning of the year can be an effective way to gain the investment of your students in their classroom environment.

MyEdLab Self-Check 8.4

MyEdLab Self-Check 8.5

MyEdLab

Application Exercise 8.2 Creating an Emotionally Supportive Classroom Consider the ways in which Mr. Wimberley leads the classroom instruction, manages classroom behavior, and works individually with two students involved in a longstanding conflict.

Conclusion

In conclusion, there are numerous direct and subtle ways that teachers provide social opportunities and convey expectations for students' social interactions with their peers at school. At times, managing students' peer relations is likely to overlap with your strategies for classroom management, instruction, and student engagement, but it is also likely to be a distinct issue to which you will need to attend. Overall, an appreciation of, and attention to, facilitating students' friendships, managing peer-group and social-status dynamics, and addressing social problems will enhance your efforts to create an emotionally supportive classroom and school environment.

oscar williams/Fotolia

9

Motivation, Classrooms, and Schools

Learning Outcomes

9.1 You will be able to explain the nature of motivation, how it affects adolescents' engagement and achievement in school, and what teachers can do to support students' motivation to learn.

9.2 You will be able to describe four important dimensions of classrooms and what teachers can do to create an effective classroom environment.

9.3 You will be able to explain how the different features of schools affect adolescents' experiences.

9.4 You will be able to describe how socioeconomic resources and student ethnicity affect adolescents' school experiences.

Introduction

Adolescents spend more time in schools than anywhere else but home. The experiences that adolescents have in schools shape their development in many ways. Students may be inspired and learn to think critically or be bored and disengaged. Students may form a meaningful bond with a teacher or another adult at school or feel unimportant and neglected by staff. Students may make cherished friends for life or feel marginalized, unsafe, and untethered to the school community in any way. Or the reality might fall somewhere in between. An important part of the adolescent experience is defined by the nature of students' time in middle and high schools. There is tremendous variability in adolescents' school experiences. Consider the following examples:

>>>

Ella leaves rehearsal exhilarated. The school performance of *Much Ado About Nothing* is 4 days away. Just a week ago she thought Shakespeare was so hard and doubted whether she would ever get her lines down. She is so proud of her progress. The director, Ms. Kilgallon, actually complimented her stage voice today! Ella can't wait to get home and practice some more. She really wants her performance to be perfect. That evening, she stays up until midnight practicing her lines. The next morning when she arrives at school, Ella and several other members of the cast gather at her locker discussing the play. As Ella parts with her friends and makes her way to first period, she thinks about how much she loves school this year.

Nathaniel looks down at the worksheet on his desk. He marks true or false next to each statement in the list. The work in this class has been pretty easy. Nathaniel doubts he has learned much of anything this year at school. Last year he took several honors classes, but this year his school stopped offering most of the honors classes. His chemistry teacher rarely has a lesson planned for his class. His AP English class is taught by a new teacher who is not certified to teach it. When his city school was taken over by the state last year, a quarter of the student body opted to transfer out of the failing school, taking valuable funds with them and depleting the school of much-needed resources. Most of Nathaniel's favorite teachers left too. As Nathaniel looks around at his classmates, many of whom have their heads down and are sleeping, he thinks about how school is a complete waste of time this year.

In these examples, we can see differences in students' motivation, engagement, and achievement at school. Classroom experiences as well as other endeavors at school, such as music, theater, clubs, or sports, can be important to adolescent development. As students move into adolescence they have many more choices at school in terms of what classes they take and what activities they pursue. The choices that adolescents make regarding academics and extracurricular activities, and the satisfaction they derive from their choices, depend, in part, on the school context in which they make such choices. As a teacher, you will play an important role in many adolescents' school experiences.

OVERVIEW OF THE CHAPTER

In this chapter we examine the ways in which schools affect adolescent development, with a focus on motivation, engagement, and achievement. First, we learn about the nature of adolescents' motivation and how it affects their engagement and achievement at school. We discuss several prominent theories to help us appreciate the multifaceted and complex nature of motivation. Throughout this section, we discuss how teachers can support and encourage students' motivation to learn.

Second, we consider the classroom environment. We discuss four important dimensions of classrooms: organization and behavior management, instruction, the motivational climate, and the social-emotional climate. We consider what teachers can do to create an effective classroom environment.

Third, we turn our attention to the larger school environment. We consider many different features of schools, such as public versus private, urban or suburban or rural, and school size. We consider different grade configurations and school transitions. We discuss how academic tracking can affect students' school experiences.

Fourth, we examine how social-economic resources and student ethnicity affect school experiences for adolescents.

Motivation

MyEdLab
Video Example 9.1

Motivation is a multifaceted topic. Note how this adolescent describes his academic motivation in many different ways.

Imagine strolling around a high school on a fall day. You walk by one classroom in which some students are working hard at their desks while a few others gaze out the window or have their heads down on their desks. A few students in the back corner are engrossed in a conversation. The bell rings and most students gather their things and leave the classroom. Two students approach the teacher to discuss the material and an assignment that is due at the end of the week. You walk by the gym, where a class is participating in physical education. The teacher has students organized into several stations where they are doing fitness tests. One group of students is intensely competing to see who can do the most push-ups. Several other students hang back and seem to be avoiding doing any of the activities. In the library, you see dozens of students working in pairs under a large banner titled "Student Express Tutoring." You walk by the office and overhear the vice principal chastising several students for skipping class. As a teacher, on any given day in school, you are likely to notice tremendous variability in students' behavior. Differences in adolescents' choices and investment in their schoolwork is of great interest to educators and parents and concerns their motivation.

Broadly, the term **motivation** refers to why people think and behave the way that they do (Wigfield et al., 2014). Motivation concerns the initiation, direction, intensity, persistence, and quality of behavior (Schunk, Meece, & Pintrich, 2014). In the classroom, motivation concerns students' choices about which tasks and activities to pursue and the level of effort they put into those tasks and activities. Motivation is distinct from ability. Two students could have equal reading and verbal ability but do quite different on a vocabulary test. Motivation captures differences in whether, why, and how much students study for a vocabulary test. In this section we provide an overview of some key ideas from various theories about student motivation.

Intrinsic Versus Extrinsic Motivation

There has been much attention to the distinction between intrinsic and extrinsic motivation. **Intrinsic motivation** refers to motivation that comes from within a person or is inherent in the task itself. Students who are intrinsically motivated work on tasks because they find them enjoyable or interesting. **Extrinsic motivation** refers to motivation that comes from factors external to the student and is unrelated to the task itself. Students who are extrinsically motivated work on tasks because they believe that it will get them something desirable, such as a reward or a good grade. Basically, when a student is extrinsically motivated, doing well on a task is a means to an end. When an individual is intrinsically motivated, doing the task is all that is desired.

There are numerous benefits associated with intrinsic motivation as compared with extrinsic motivation. Adolescents who are intrinsically motivated for a task are inclined to approach it with a more positive attitude and engage with the material for longer and in more meaningful ways, which increases their learning and creativity. In contrast, when adolescents are extrinsically motivated, they are more likely to only do what is necessary to get the outcome that they desire. Because they are focused on the outcome rather than the task itself, they are more likely to engage in a more superficial manner, which diminishes learning and creativity (Lepper & Henderlong, 2000). For example, imagine a student completing an assignment to write out definitions for important terms in a unit on the ancient city of Mesopotamia. If the assignment is approached with intrinsic motivation, a student might reflect on the meaning of the different terms and make connections among the different concepts as the student looked up and wrote down the definitions. Perhaps the student would become engaged with the text beyond the term and look at the pictures and think about what the world was like at that time. If the assignment is approached with extrinsic motivation, a student might rush to find the terms, copy down the definitions, and complete the assignment as quickly as possible.

Given the benefits of intrinsic motivation, there has been much attention to what teachers can do to promote intrinsic motivation (Brophy, 2010; Lepper & Henderlong, 2000; Schunk et al., 2014). Strategies for teachers to increase students' intrinsic motivation center around two basic ideas. First, teachers can design learning activities that foster intrinsic motivation. One way they can do this is to incorporate elements of novelty, variety, or fantasy into tasks or routines, which tend to pique students' interest or curiosity. This might include presenting students with surprising or incongruous information. Or it might mean giving students the opportunity to do something different in the classroom, such as a new type of project or activity that involves role-playing, simulation, or an educational game. Another way to do this is to adapt tasks to incorporate students' interests. For example, teachers might use examples or apply the concepts that are being learned to topics their students will find interesting. This might include current events, local issues, popular games or movies, or celebrities of interest to most teenagers.

Second, teachers can allow students choices about their work. For example, students can have some input into how class time is organized. Or the teacher can present several options and students can choose which tasks to do during class time, or the teacher can give students the same moderately challenging problem but let students decide how to approach solving the problem. Such an approach has the added benefit of teaching problem-solving strategies and critical thinking skills, core parts of the Common Core State Standards (2010) in the United States and international standards for student learning. Regarding assignments, teachers can allow students to choose from several alternatives. Or teachers might allow students to tailor a project to incorporate their own personal interests. There are two reasons giving students choice can support their autonomy. First, when students make their own choices, their decisions come from them rather than an external source, which makes them feel autonomous (doing things of one's own volition) and not controlled by external forces, which is part of intrinsic motivation. Second, when students make their own choices they are more likely to choose options that are things they like to do. When students are allowed to individualize a project it is more likely to reflect their interests.

As teachers, we must realize that our students at times will feel both intrinsically and extrinsically motivated. Consider the students represented in Table 9.1.

TABLE 9.1	Intrinsically and Extrinsically Motivated Students	
	Low Intrinsic	**High Intrinsic**
Low Extrinsic	Caleb can't stand his Spanish class. He is not interested in learning Spanish, he finds the class and the language boring, and he does not care about getting good grades in Spanish class.	Keira loves her music classes; she is in the band and the choir and she takes her school's course on music theory; however, she really doesn't focus much on her grades, and sometimes gets low grades because she is so caught up in the joy of playing music.
High Extrinsic	Jordan is focused on getting good grades in his social studies class, but he really doesn't care about the information that he is learning.	Anna strives to get good grades in her chemistry class, but she also is very interested in chemistry and really enjoys what she is learning.

As you can see, these four students have different motivational beliefs in some of their classes. Some students (e.g., Keira and Anna) are highly intrinsically motivated—they enjoy specific school subjects, and are eager to learn about those topics and to be engaged in class. Other students (e.g., Caleb and Jordan) are extrinsically motivated—they are concerned about their grades, and they strive to achieve at high levels in class. It is useful to note that these students are described in terms of both intrinsic and extrinsic motivation. Thus Anna is highly intrinsically motivated toward chemistry (she likes it and wants to learn it), but she also cares deeply about getting good grades. Caleb is the student who probably poses the most challenges for teachers, because he does not enjoy his Spanish class, and he doesn't care about his grades either.

There has been much attention to the effect that extrinsic rewards have on intrinsic motivation. Some educators and scholars have expressed concern that using extrinsic rewards will diminish students' intrinsic motivation (Lepper & Henderlong, 2000). Given the widespread use of extrinsic rewards, it is not surprising that this idea has sparked much debate. The current view is that extrinsic rewards, when used properly, often can support positive educational outcomes (American Psychological Association, Coalition for Psychology in Schools and Education, 2015). There are many skills students need to master that initially are unlikely to be intrinsically motivating, and in these instances extrinsic rewards can be helpful. The intrinsic value of an activity may not be apparent until the student has acquired some basic level of expertise, and the use of extrinsic rewards at this stage of skill development also may be beneficial. However, there are two caveats to keep in mind about extrinsic rewards (Anderman & Anderman, 2014). First, avoid offering awards for activities that students are already willing to do. If a student is engaged, then there is no need to offer rewards. This is when awards can have drawbacks, as they can shift a student from having intrinsic to extrinsic motivation. Second, when rewards are used, they should be informational and not controlling. Rewards should be contingent on specific accomplishments, and students should know why they are receiving them. When rewards are used to get students to merely complete a task or elicit behavior such as sitting quietly, they are perceived as controlling and undermine intrinsic motivation in the classroom.

Although intrinsic motivation is desirable, it may be difficult for teachers to facilitate intrinsic motivation in their students on a regular basis (Brophy, 2010; Lepper & Henderlong, 2000; Urdan & Turner, 2005). Intrinsic motivation is most likely when people freely engage in self-chosen activities. Recreational activities often provide such opportunities, but classrooms often do not. Teachers can strive to give students some opportunities to foster their intrinsic motivation, but there are constraints for what teachers can do to intrinsically motivate students in the classroom. Teachers are not running a day camp or acting as recreational workers whose goal is to provide enjoyable experiences (Brophy, 2010).

Brophy (2010) identified four reasons why it is difficult for teachers to facilitate intrinsic motivation in the classroom. First, school attendance is compulsory and the curriculum is assigned, not chosen. This is especially true with current educational policies, which emphasize that all students progress through the same core curriculum to prepare for standardized tests. Second, teachers must work with classes of 20 or more students and cannot focus on the individual needs of students. Third, classrooms are social settings and their public nature can make failure embarrassing. Fourth, student work is graded and report cards are sent home to parents. In combination, these factors focus students' attention on concerns about meeting external demands rather than intrinsic motivation. Thus, it is unlikely to be feasible for teachers to have intrinsic motivation be their primary goal on a daily basis in the classroom.

> Recall a time when you were intrinsically motivated in the classroom. What about the classroom setting or the teacher supported your intrinsic motivation? Do you agree with Brophy that it is difficult for teachers to facilitate intrinsic motivation on a regular basis in the classroom?

If intrinsic motivation is not suitable to be a key guiding principle for middle and high school teachers, then what should be? Jere Brophy, an educator and psychologist, spent his career studying motivation, with a focus on what motivational principles were most suitable for teachers to apply in the classroom. Brophy (1998; 2010) proposed that teachers should strive to facilitate the motivation to learn. At times, teachers may be able to promote intrinsic motivation and by all means should do so. But a more realistic goal in the classroom setting that can be pursued on a daily basis is focusing on students' motivation to learn.

Motivation to Learn

Motivation to learn refers to "the tendency to find learning activities meaningful and worthwhile and to try and get the intended benefits from them" (Brophy, 2010, p. 11). As described by Brophy (2010), the motivation to learn is different from both intrinsic and extrinsic motivation, although it may coexist with either of them. Learning refers to the information-processing, sense-making, comprehension, and mastery process when a student acquires new knowledge or skill. Performance refers to the demonstration of that knowledge or skill after it has been acquired. Promoting students' motivation to learn includes encouraging them to use thoughtful information-processing and skill-building strategies to advance their learning. This is different than offering students incentives for good performance.

An important difference between intrinsic motivation and the motivation to learn is the difference between affective and cognitive experiences. A defining feature of intrinsic motivation is the affective experience or the enjoyment that comes from engaging in a task or activity. In contrast, a defining feature of the motivation to learn is the cognitive experience or the process of making sense of information and mastering the skills involved in an activity. Brophy (2010) argues that students may be motivated to learn from a lesson regardless of whether or not they find it enjoyable. Although students may not find something fun or even interesting, they can become engaged, learn, and feel some satisfaction in that process.

Brophy (2010) argues that by focusing on motivation to learn, teachers hone in on what is really the most important process in the classroom. Teachers socialize students' motivation and engagement in the classroom. We all adapt our thinking and behavior in different settings. As a teacher, if your expectations, instructions, feedback, and consequences are focused on students' engagement in learning, you will promote your students' motivation to learn. There are two main strategies teachers can use to encourage students to take academic activities seriously and want to acquire knowledge and skills in the classroom. First, teachers can model the motivation to learn. When teachers routinely show students that they value learning and experience satisfaction from the process of learning, students are more likely to develop motivation to learn. In addition to positive comments about topics in class, you can share with your students your interests in learning outside of the classroom, for example, books you like to read or activities you like to engage in that help you learn more about the world and yourself as a person. Second, teachers can communicate positive expectations about students' motivation to learn. When teachers are positive and optimistic in their beliefs and expectations that students are curious, want to learn new information, and want to master new skills, students are more likely to develop the motivation to learn.

Think back to a classroom where you felt intrinsic motivation. Was it actually motivation to learn? Thinking of your future classroom, what evidence would you look for to know if the students in your classroom are intrinsically motivated or motivated to learn?

We continue to examine how teachers foster their students' motivation to learn in the next several sections of this chapter. In the following sections, we consider how an appreciation of students' expectancies and values, as well as mindsets, can support their motivation to learn.

Expectancy-Value Framework and the Motivation to Learn

A widely used framework to understand motivation is the Expectancy-Value framework (Wigfield et al., 2014). This framework asserts that motivation is the result of both the degree to which students expect to be able to complete an activity successfully if they try and the degree to which they value the activity. Before engaging in a task or activity, students ask themselves, "Can I do this task?" (expectancy) and "Do I want to do this task?" (value). Both expectancies for success and value are necessary preconditions for the motivation to learn.

Expectancies for Success.

A student's response to "Can I do this task?" concerns the student's expectancies for success at a task or activity. Students' expectancies for success are a combination of their perceptions of their own competence in combination with their estimation of the difficulty of the task and fairness of the evaluation (Schunk et al., 2014). Generally, when students think they will be successful, they are more likely to engage and persist in a task or activity as compared with when they do not think they will be successful. However, if a task is perceived to be so easy that it provides no challenge at all, an individual is unlikely to desire to engage in it. Finally, students' perceptions of the fairness of evaluation can play an important role. For example, if students do not believe that a teacher systematically and carefully reviews students' work, this could diminish their expectancies for success despite the fact that they believe they can do a good job on the assignment. Perhaps you can recall a time when you got a lower grade than expected with little rationale or evidence that the teacher read your work carefully, or you were told that your work did not meet the criteria, but those criteria were not made clear in the description of the assignment or in the feedback on your first draft. What were your expectancies for success on the next assignment in that class?

As a teacher, you will need to make sure students can be successful if they put in reasonable effort on the learning activities you assign. Instruction needs to take into account students' existing knowledge and skills and move at an appropriate pace for most students. Tasks and activities need to be at an appropriate level of challenge and difficulty. If instruction is too slow, or tasks are too easy, then students will be bored. If instruction moves too fast, students will get lost. If tasks are too difficult, students will be frustrated. Of course, when teaching 20 or 30 students, it is not always possible to match instruction and activities to each learner's needs. However, as you design instruction to scaffold students to develop essential skills necessary to meet learning goals, their needs will become more similar over time. Nevertheless, as a teacher, you will need to offer opportunities for struggling students to get extra help or do makeup work. Finally, you need to be clear about the criteria for evaluation in advance, systematically evaluate student work in light of those criteria, and provide specific feedback when student work falls short of the mark.

A critical component of expectancies for success is appropriate goal setting. Goals that are proximal (what is to be done immediately) rather than ultimate (the final product), specific (clearly stated actions) rather than global (broad objectives), and appropriately challenging rather than too easy or too hard support expectancies for success. As a teacher, you can help students develop and pursue proximal, specific, and achievable goals. When you have students who are not trying because they do not believe they can do something, it is often helpful to assist them in breaking down the task or assignment into smaller steps and specify the initial step they need to take. Sometimes a task or assignment can seem overwhelming when viewed in its entirety, but it can seem more manageable when broken down into a series of small and specific steps.

Mindsets and Expectancies for Success

Learning is hard work. At times students will start a class or task expecting to succeed but then encounter difficulty or struggle in their learning. Responding adaptively to challenge is crucial to sustaining the motivation to learn, and in the long term, to success in school. Much research has found that a key factor that determines how a student responds to challenge is the student's mindset, also known as the student's implicit theory of intelligence (Yeager & Dweck, 2012). With a **fixed mindset**, students view intelligence as fixed and unchanging. With a **growth mindset**, students view intelligence as malleable and something that can change and develop over time with effort.

As described by Yeager and Dweck (2012), these two different mindsets create two different psychological worlds. The interpretation of adversity leads to quite different reactions, with different implications for their expectancies for success. With a fixed mindset, the world is about measuring your ability. Effort, mistakes, and challenge all indicate something about natural ability and are potentially threatening. With a growth mindset, the world is about learning and growth. Effort, mistakes, and challenge are all helpful to learning and development. When students with a fixed mindset experience difficulty, they are more likely to think it signals that they lack ability. This threat undermines their expectancies for success and leads them to give up, consider cheating, or become defensive. Both high and low achievers are vulnerable to the negative processes that result from a fixed mindset. When students with a growth mindset experience difficulty, they are more likely to think they need to work harder or try different strategies. Setbacks and challenges do not undermine their expectancies for success, and they are more likely to respond with increased effort and new approaches.

As a teacher, you can support students' expectancies for success and response to challenge by encouraging a growth mindset and providing students with success experiences on appropriately difficult tasks. Key to a growth mindset is for students to see the link between their effort and performance. The goal-setting strategies we discussed in the previous section can help students see this link because they make progress on the task as they tackle proximal and specific goals. When students see that effort leads to progress, they are more likely to have a positive view of effort and a growth mindset. As a teacher, you can draw attention to how the amount and quality of effort that students put into a task affects their learning and performance.

MyEdLab
Video Example 9.2

In this video, Professor Carol Dweck of Stanford University explains the differences between a growth and a fixed mindset.

You can portray learning and skill development as incremental and something that unfolds in small steps. As teachers, we need to be aware that we have our own mindset beliefs about our students' abilities (e.g., Gutshall, 2014). Some teachers may believe that student ability is malleable, whereas others may believe that it is fixed. As a teacher, you need to reflect on and foster your own growth mindset about students' abilities to effectively encourage students to have one.

As a teacher, your use of praise also has important implications for students' mindsets and how they respond to adversity. Carol Dweck is a psychologist who has done extensive research on mindsets and praise. Her work has shown that praising ability (for example, a comment such as "Excellent! You are so smart!") gives a short burst of pride followed by all the vulnerabilities of a fixed mindset. In contrast, praising effort encourages a growth mindset and supports students' confidence. Praising effort, perseverance, strategies, and improvement indicates to students what they did to be successful and what they need to do to be successful again in the future. Dweck (2007) provides the following examples of effort-based praise:

"You really studied for your English test, and your improvement shows it. You read the material over several times, outlined it, and tested yourself on it. That really worked!" (37)

"I like the way you tried all kinds of strategies on that math problem until you finally got it. That's great!" (37)

"I like that you took on that challenging project for your science class. It will take a lot of work—doing the research, designing the machine, buying the parts, and building it. You're going to learn a lot of great things." (37)

When students get an A without trying, Dweck suggests a comment such as "All right, that was too easy for you. Let's do something more challenging that you can learn from," which does not offer admiration for something done quickly. When a student works hard and does not do well, Dweck suggests a comment such as "I liked the effort you put in. Let's work together some more and figure out what you don't understand," to keep the student focused on effort.

Value. Students' responses to "Do I want to do this task?" concern their beliefs about the value of the task, which is another important part of their motivation. Even if students think they can be successful at something, if they do not value it then they are unlikely to put much effort into it. There are many are different reasons that a student might have high value for a task or activity. The Expectancy-Value framework outlines three types of reasons: intrinsic, importance, and utility (Eccles, 2005). **Intrinsic value** refers to enjoyment or liking activities in a certain domain. **Importance value** refers to reverence for success in a given domain. **Utility value** refers to perceptions that skills in a certain domain would be useful to other future endeavors. For example, if a student likes doing math problems and finds it enjoyable, that would be intrinsic value. If a student viewed doing well in math as a worthy and meaningful endeavor, one that all students should take seriously, that would be importance value. If a student thought learning math would come in handy in the future, perhaps in a future science class or in functioning as an adult in life (e.g., paying bills and balancing a checkbook), that would be utility value. In addition to these three positive types of value, perceptions of cost can detract from the value a student has for a task or activity. **Cost** refers to the negatives associated with task involvement. For example, a student might view taking an honors class as important, useful, and even interesting, but thinks it requires a great deal of time to do well. Given other classes and activities, that student may decide not take the honors class.

As a teacher, you will need to help your students see the value in your subject matter in general and in the specific learning activities you assign. You likely noticed

In-Depth 9.1

Providing Effective Feedback

Alison Koenka
The Ohio State University

Feedback is one of the most pervasive and powerful mechanisms for altering student learning (Hattie & Timperley, 2007). However, its power is a double-edged sword; depending upon how it is delivered, feedback can be as harmful as it can be helpful. As a teacher, you will have countless opportunities to provide feedback to adolescents and will quickly learn that there are many decisions involved in how to most effectively do so. For example:

- In an English class, students submit a critique of William Shakespeare's *Hamlet*. Will you provide your students with written feedback? If so, what components of the students' performance will you focus on? How and when will you assign grades?

- In a math class, you are teaching a lesson on geometry and ask for a student volunteer to write the solution on the board. The student's solution is perfect. How will you respond?

As these examples illustrate, opportunities to deliver student feedback occur frequently in both structured and unstructured contexts. These interactions can have profound effects on adolescents' motivation and learning. Research points to the following recommendations to consider when delivering feedback:

- **Assigning Grades.** Grading academic activities can undermine adolescents' performance and desire to learn for learning's sake (Pulfrey, Darnon, & Butera, 2013).
  - *Recommendations:* Assigning grades often cannot be avoided. However, students will benefit from: (a) nongraded assignments and activities to complement graded ones and (b) an opportunity to review written feedback and/or revise work based on suggestions before a grade is assigned.
- **Written Comments.** When appropriately crafted, written comments on tests and assignments foster adolescent motivation and learning as compared

with when students solely receive grades without any written feedback (Butler, 1987).
  - *Recommendation:* Accompany grades with specific written feedback on tests and assignments. Even a single sentence can heighten motivation and learning.
- **Normative Versus Individual-Oriented Feedback.** *Normative feedback* is feedback that compares individual performance to the group. For instance, teachers may note that one student's work was the best in the class. Alternatively, they may deliver feedback that is oriented toward the individual student. It may be *task focused* (e.g., "You have demonstrated a solid understanding in applying the correct formula to calculate the volume of a cone and cylinder") or *self-referenced* (e.g., "You have demonstrated significant improvement in applying the correct formula from the previous geometry assignment"). Research consistently indicates that feedback that is oriented toward the individual students fosters adaptive motivation outcomes (e.g., enhanced mastery goals and intrinsic motivation), whereas normative feedback produces suboptimal ones (e.g., performance-avoidance goals; Butler, 1987; Pekrun, Cusak, Murayama, Elliot, & Thomas, 2014).
  - *Recommendation:* Avoid providing percentiles, class average scores, comments emphasizing a student's standing relative to others, or other forms of normative feedback. Instead, opt for feedback that focuses on the individual student's performance.
- **Changeable Versus Unchangeable Characteristics.** The reasons a teacher cites for a student's success or failure when delivering feedback are important to consider. For example, whether adolescents are praised for ability or hard work can influence reactions to subsequent failure experiences: Those praised for hard work are more persistent, report higher levels of enjoyment, and perform better (Mueller & Dweck, 1998). However, there can also be drawbacks to effort praise, particularly when a student's hard work is unsuccessful. Adolescents

may interpret feedback in this context to signal low ability, leading to frustration and a decline in feelings of efficacy (Henderlong & Lepper, 2002).

- *Recommendations:* Regardless of whether the student has succeeded or fell short of expectations, deliver feedback with a focus on changeable behaviors rather than unchangeable ones,

such as ability. Especially in circumstances under which a student continues to experience failure, avoid providing solely effort-focused feedback and instead offer other process-oriented information, such as feedback on the strategies the student is adopting (Henderlong & Lepper, 2002).

that the multifaceted aspects of value as outlined in the Expectancy-Value framework give you additional options beyond intrinsic motivation. According to this framework, intrinsic value is just one type of reason students will want to do a task or activity. There are scholars who argue that intrinsic motivation is the ideal type of motivation and carries the most benefits in terms of affect, quality of engagement, learning, and creativity (Ryan & Deci, 2000). But not all scholars or educators share this viewpoint, and there is much evidence that importance and utility value also contribute to students' commitment to do their work in many circumstances (Hulleman, Godes, Hendricks, & Harackiewicz, 2010). Further, it is possible for students to have multiple reasons for doing their work or for one type of value to lead to another. For example, utility value might be the reason why students decide to take Latin. They believe that Latin will help them better understand the origins of many words, enhance their vocabulary, and help them do well on the verbal portion of the SAT. However, once they are taking the course, they come to truly enjoy it and develop intrinsic value for Latin.

There are two main points for educators to bear in mind in regard to helping students see the value in the work in your course. First, your instruction and learning activities need to be meaningful. If students are not learning anything new, or most of their time is spent on rote memorization or boring worksheets, then obviously they are not going to find much value in the coursework. It is often appropriate for students to memorize or practice skills, but, at times, try to allow students to work on and complete larger projects that integrate or apply what they are learning. Students will find greater value and satisfaction in the context of a project such as a report that includes cover art, a table of contents, multiple chapters, and supporting figures than isolated worksheets or quizzes (Brophy, 2010). Moreover, in the context of projects that require a baseline of knowledge or certain skills to complete successfully, students may begin to see the utility value in memorizing needed information and practicing isolated skills.

Second, you can help students see the value in topics or learning activities. You can do this in a general way by pointing out why what they are learning is interesting, important, or useful. Students are not experts and can benefit from your explanations of how the knowledge and skills in your course relate to various types of work or are foundational to future academic success. You can also do this in a more individualized way by encouraging students to find their own personal value in topics or learning activities. In one classroom-based experimental study, researchers had half of the students select a course topic and write a one- to two-page essay to a significant person in their lives describing the relevance of their topic to their lives. The other half of the students selected a course topic and wrote a one- to two-page summary of the topic. Students who wrote relevance essays increased in their perceptions of both utility and intrinsic value and performed better by the end of the course as compared with students who wrote summaries (Hulleman et al., 2010). Students may not often stop and reflect on the value of their work, but teachers can encourage them to do so.

MyEdLab
Application Exercise 9.1 Motivation and STEM Consider how teachers can incorporate the four components of achievement values into lessons in order to enhance students' motivation in STEM.

Changes in Motivation During Adolescence

Many aspects of students' motivation tend to decline during adolescence (Wigfield et al., 2014). Several large-scale longitudinal studies have examined changes in students' perceptions of competence and values during adolescence (Wigfield et al., 2014). More so than at younger ages, adolescents doubt their abilities to do their schoolwork and question the value of their schoolwork. In regard to perceptions of competence, the decline starts around the ages of 7 or 8. This decline likely reflects increasing realism that comes with cognitive maturity and experience in the world. Children are overly optimistic about their abilities, but as they age they have more opportunities to get evaluative feedback as well as compare themselves with peers. During adolescence, such social comparisons start to affect students' estimation of their own capabilities. Another period of decline is often seen in early adolescence, when youth make the transition to middle school. School environments in the United States (as well as Europe and Asia) tend to change in ways that make evaluation more salient. The context of middle (and high school) is more competitive in nature and generally has a larger pool of peers with whom students can compare themselves to. Thus, changes in experience, cognitive maturity, and school context all contribute to declining perceptions of competence in adolescence.

Studies in the United States, Europe, and Australia also show that perceptions of value for schoolwork decline during adolescence (Wigfield et al., 2014). Adolescents have lower levels of intrinsic, importance, and utility value than younger children for all school subjects. Declines in value have been found in math, language arts, and sports (Jacobs, Lanza, Osgood, Eccles, & Wigfield, 2002). The declines in value during adolescence may be due to the declines in perceptions of competence. That is, over time, adolescents will attach value to the things they believe they do well. In contrast, they will start to devalue activities and subjects in which they have difficulty in order to maintain their self-esteem. For example, imagine a student named Daniel who gets to high school and tries out for soccer, basketball, and baseball but gets cut from all three teams. His perceptions of his athletic competence are likely to decline. Daniel might start to think to himself that sports are not that important. He is glad he is so good at math because that is actually important. This line of thinking serves to protect Daniel's self-esteem.

What Educators Can Do

As we have discussed throughout this section, students' motivation is a critical component of their engagement and achievement at school. Motivation tends to decline during adolescence. However, as a teacher, there is much you can do to foster students' motivation and promote their engagement in your class. There are several implications for educators, and strategies include the following:

1. *Encourage intrinsic motivation when possible.* There are numerous benefits to intrinsic motivation, and when possible teachers should strive to promote intrinsic motivation. Teachers can design learning activities to foster intrinsic motivation (for example, incorporate elements of novelty, variety, or fantasy into tasks, or use examples that your students are likely to find interesting). Teachers can also look for opportunities to allow students some choice in their work, which promotes intrinsic motivation.

2. *Promote students' motivation to learn on a daily basis.* Although intrinsic motivation is desirable, it is not always feasible or the priority in classrooms. However, as a teacher, you can promote students' motivation to learn on a regular basis by modeling your value, enthusiasm, and satisfaction in the process of learning. You can also consistently communicate positive expectations about students' motivation to learn.

3. *Support students' expectancies for success.* As a teacher, there is much you can do to foster student beliefs that they can be successful in your classroom. Have your instruction and learning activities be at an appropriate level of challenge. Offer additional opportunities for instruction and practice for struggling students. Be clear and systematic in regard to evaluation. Help students set proximal, specific, and challenging, yet achievable, goals. Make criteria for success on assignments clear, continually assess how students are progressing toward those goals, and provide constructive feedback before assignments are turned in.

4. *Encourage students to have a growth mindset.* Help students see the link between effort and performance. Encourage students to view mistakes as opportunities for learning. Portray learning and skill development as incremental. Praise effort, perseverance, and improvement and avoid praising ability.

5. *Help your students see the value in learning activities and subject matter.* Strive for meaningful instruction, tasks, and assignments. Point out why information is interesting, important, or useful, or ask them to reflect on what value they see in the topic. Encourage students to make their own connections and find personal value in the topics in your course.

MyEdLab **Self-Check 9.1**

MyEdLab
Application Exercise 9.2
Goal Setting In this exercise, we'll practice setting appropriate goals to help adolescents learn various topics.

Classrooms

At the heart of students' school experience is their time in classrooms. In several large-scale studies of student achievement, classrooms have been found to be the most important source of variation in explaining differences in what students learn (Pianta & Hamre, 2009). What type of classroom best supports adolescent development? This question has been the focus of much research. In this section, we examine the core dimensions of effective classrooms. Overall, your goal as a teacher is to establish a community in your classroom with norms and practices that encourage students to come to class each day ready and willing to learn in collaboration with you and their peers (Brophy, 2010; Patrick et al., 2012). We focus on four dimensions of classrooms that extensive theory and research have shown to be important to creating an effective classroom for adolescent development: organization and behavior management, instruction, the motivational climate, and the social-emotional climate.

What was one of your favorite classes when you were in high school? Did you learn a lot? Did you value the material? Why? What did the teacher do? What was one of your least favorite classes? Why? What did the teacher do?

Organization and Behavior Management

A classroom needs to be well organized and managed for students to be motivated and engaged in learning. In a well-organized classroom, students know what is expected of them and they know how to meet these expectations. When behavior is managed effectively, students feel secure because the procedures and routines are predictable and the teacher is dependable. We start with this dimension of the classroom because it is a necessary precondition for the other dimensions of an effective classroom. A well-organized and well-managed classroom environment sets the stage for instruction, positive relationships, and students' motivation to learn. In this section, we consider the nature of a well-organized classroom and how teachers can create such an environment.

In a recent report put out by the American Psychological Association's Coalition for Psychology in Schools and Education (2015), a panel of experts described several key principles that are important for creating an organized and well-managed classroom. First, expectations for classroom conduct and social interactions are taught and retaught throughout the year. The first 2 weeks are thought to be a crucial time for teachers to communicate expectations and establish rules and norms. However, behavior is continuously shaped and responsive to the classroom environment and teacher guidance. To effectively teach (and reteach) expectations, there needs to be clear communication of goals, opportunities for practice, timely and specific feedback, reinforcement of positive behavior, and correction of undesired behavior. Additionally, it is better to use proactive strategies to avoid problems than reactive strategies to address problems. For example, if you find you are reacting to a lot of disruptive behavior in the classroom, this is a signal that you may need to reteach and practice certain norms or procedures. Even the most experienced teachers need to do this periodically.

Second, as we discussed earlier in the chapter, high expectations are very important; however, high expectations should be coupled with high support in the context of nurturing, positive relationships. High expectations alone, especially if overly punitive, will not result in a positive classroom community. Part of a structured environment is a safe and well-arranged physical classroom environment and a predictable schedule. Overall, there should be more positive reinforcement than punishment, and teachers should resist overreacting to relatively minor student infractions.

Let's imagine walking into a well-organized and well-managed classroom. What might we see? The teacher would give clear directions at the beginning of the class. Overall, students would exhibit on-task behavior and would be interacting with one another in a respectful way. It would be an environment conducive to working, with few disruptions from students. If students displayed inappropriate behavior, the teacher would notice quickly and redirect the behavior in an efficient manner so that little time was lost from the lesson. The teacher might call the students' attention to an expectation that was communicated earlier in the year. If two students started to giggle and joke, the teacher might move closer to them to provide a subtle cue for them to return their focus on the lesson. The teacher would notice and comment on instances of positive behavior. When the class transitioned from one activity to another, there would be little time lost and students would seem familiar with the rules and expectations.

Now let's imagine walking into a classroom that is not very well organized and managed. What might we see? The teacher does not start the lesson on time. The teacher is inefficient in her use of time. She spends more than 10 minutes collecting homework and talking to several students about missing assignments instead of teaching the group. At the beginning of an activity, the teacher tells students that they will need to raise their hands if they want to make a contribution, but then as the activity unfolds the teacher allows some students to call out their answers. The teacher does not seem prepared for the lesson and stops several times to check her planner. Two students are having a personal conversation in the corner of the room, but the teacher fails to notice. The teacher asks a student to stop reading a book several times; he ignores her without consequence. There is a lengthy disruption that detracts from the lesson. While the teacher talks to the disruptive student, some students put their heads down on their desks, others talk, and one student wanders out of the room. Near the end of the class, students are working individually on a worksheet. Some students finish and then have nothing to do.

When we contrast an organized and well-managed classroom with one that is not, it is easy to see why behavior management is a critical part of an effective classroom. However, it is not sufficient to create an effective learning environment. Organization, structure, predictability, and efficiency lay the foundation for instruction, the issue we turn to next.

Instruction

The quality of instruction matters for student motivation, engagement, and learning in the classroom. There has been much attention devoted to what constitutes effective instruction (e.g., Bransford, Brown, & Cocking, 1999; Brophy, 1998; Gage, 1978; Pressley et al., 2003). Pianta & Hamre (2009) examined the literature on what effective teaching should look like and offered an overarching framework that synthesized prior work. They focused on general dimensions that were relevant across different subject areas. They identified four key dimensions regarding different ways that teachers provide instructional supports to their adolescent learners: (a) the explanation of content, (b) the encouragement of higher-order thinking skills, (c) the nature of dialogue that is prompted in the classroom, and (d) the quality of feedback.

Adolescents learn best when teachers have high expectations and provide the necessary instructional supports to meet those standards. In terms of explanations of content, effective teachers activate prior knowledge when they introduce new material. New material is presented in small steps and teachers give different examples, model, and provide opportunities for guided practice, group work, independent practice, and guided inquiry, as appropriate. Effective teachers organize instruction around "big ideas" and help students see the connections between topics they are learning. Teachers facilitate students' higher-order thinking skills, such as analysis, application to new problems, and synthesis of information. Effective teachers are purposeful in their dialogue with students; they use questioning to encourage students to think more deeply about their ideas and prompt reflection on what students have learned (Pianta, Hamre, & Mintz, 2010).

High-quality feedback is also essential to student learning and is most effective when it is clear, explanatory, and timely. A comment like "good job" is vague and does not facilitate student motivation or learning. More specific comments, such as "You made three excellent points. If you could provide some examples that would be even more convincing," are more direct and push the student to develop his or her work further. Feedback is best when it is in relation to learning goals that were made clear at the beginning of an activity because then students can gain insight into the level of their current performance and what else is needed to attain their goal. Finally, students are most receptive to feedback that recognizes their prior effort and is encouraging in tone.

Let's imagine walking into a history classroom where the teacher provides high levels of instructional support. What might we see? The teacher starts the class with questions about what students recall about World War I before starting the unit on World War II. "What were the triggers and causes?" "Who was the conflict between?" "What was the outcome?" "What was the reaction of different countries to the Treaty of Versailles?" Several times the teacher asks a student to explain further or asks the class if someone else can build on a comment. The teacher uses the review to diagnose students' initial understanding and identify any misconceptions, and then introduces some of the issues that led to World War II. At one point, a student seems confused and the teacher stops and asks if he has a question. In response to his question, she checks if other students are confused, and then explains communism to the whole class in a different way. About halfway through the class period, the teacher has the students work in groups to develop a concept map that outlines the main issues that led to World War II. The teacher walks around the room making comments on the groups' concept maps and assessing patterns in student thinking to see if she needs to adjust the next stage of instruction. For each group she notes something the group is doing well and points out something the group could improve. To one group she says, "I like how you grouped some of the similar issues together. Check the directions. I think you are missing one category."

MyEdLab
Video Example 9.3

This teacher provides timely and specific feedback to a student while he is working on an assignment in class.

Let's imagine walking into another history classroom where the teacher provides low levels of instructional support. What might we see? The teacher starts a lesson on World War II with no connections to any prior units. When a student asks a question about what fascism is, the teacher repeats the same information given previously. At one point, a student offers an opinion on the fairness of the Treaty of Versailles that followed World War I. The teacher says that is an interesting point and moves on without further comment or questioning. The teacher has students work individually and look up information about the different nations involved in the war, such as the geography, economy, and political leaders of each country. The teacher walks around the room. To one student she says, "Nice work," and to another she says, "You have a lot of work to do." Near the end of class, the teacher calls the class together for a whole-class discussion. She asks them about their opinions regarding the most important issue that led to World War II. When no student responds, the teacher spends the remaining class time telling them her opinion.

Motivational Climate

Much research has shown that when teachers create a **mastery goal structure** in their classrooms, it facilitates students' motivation to learn (Ames, 1992; Anderman & Wolters, 2006). With a mastery goal structure, teachers communicate to students that the main purpose for doing schoolwork is to develop their competence. Real learning and understanding are what are most valued. Intrapersonal and absolute standards are used to judge success. With intrapersonal standards, students are encouraged to focus on their own personal progress and improvement. With absolute standards, the focus is on task mastery. With such standards all students can be successful in the classroom. A mastery goal structure can be contrasted with a **performance goal structure**, in which teachers communicate to students that the main purpose for doing schoolwork is to demonstrate their competence, especially relative to other students. Interpersonal standards are used to judge success. With interpersonal standards, students strive to outperform others. Doing well in school is a means to achieving recognition and validating one's sense of self-worth. In such a classroom environment, only the top-performing students are considered successful.

In classrooms where the teacher emphasizes a mastery goal structure, students are more likely to be motivated to learn as well as to have a range of adaptive beliefs, behaviors, and feelings about their schoolwork (Wigfield et al., 2014). These include perceptions of competence, effort, the use of effective learning strategies, help-seeking skills, positive school-related affect, satisfaction with learning, and achievement. In contrast, in classrooms where the teacher emphasizes a performance goal structure, students are less likely to be motivated to learn and more likely to have maladaptive beliefs, behaviors, and feelings about their schoolwork. These include procrastination, avoiding asking for help when it is needed, cheating, and negative affect toward school.

There has been much attention devoted to understanding how teachers can create a mastery goal structure in the classroom (Ames, 1992; Brophy, 2010). The key issue is to emphasize individual progress and task mastery and minimize social comparison among students in the classroom. The nature of tasks, basis for recognition, and types of evaluation practices are especially relevant. First, when tasks and assignments are introduced, teachers can help students see them as opportunities for learning. The strategies we talked about for teachers fostering students' motivation to learn would foster a mastery goal structure in the classroom. Further, when there is some variety in the nature of the tasks (or the order in which students work on them), it can minimize social comparison between students. Some flexibility on the time limits students have for tasks can also help students focus on their own learning and not worry about finishing before or after other students.

Second, when teachers recognize students' effort, progress, and mastery of skills and concepts, it reinforces that effort, improvement, and mastery are valued. Recognition should be for improved or good performance, not performance relative to others. In this way, all students have the chance to earn positive recognition or rewards. Further, making salient the skills and knowledge learned, not the reward, encourages a focus on mastery.

Third, the nature and standards for evaluation and assessment of student learning and performance can communicate different goals to students. When evaluation is conducted privately, it conveys to students that they should only be concerned with their own progress. When evaluation practices are public, they encourage social comparison. Practices such as posting all student grades on a bulletin board make social comparisons salient to students. In addition, there are two types of assessments that differ in the standards by which achievement is marked: criterion referenced and norm referenced. When teachers use criterion-referenced assessments, they grade students based on predetermined standards or criteria. Norm-referenced assessments indicate how students do relative to their peers. Criterion-referenced standards orient students to focus on their own task mastery in comparison with norm-referenced standards, which encourage students to focus on how they compare to others. Finally, when there are opportunities for students to revise their work, or re-take exams, it encourages them to put forth more effort to learn material and master skills. However, teachers also want students to learn to put forth their best effort the first time and not take advantage of opportunities to redo work. Accordingly, teachers can give only partial credit on revisions and re-takes. This can minimize the workload for teachers but still provide incentives for students who do not do well.

Social-Emotional Climate

The social-emotional dimension of the classroom is important to students' social and academic adjustment (see Chapter 8). Research shows that the social-emotional climate of classrooms is intimately related to the motivational climate. When students perceive their teacher as caring about them as individuals, they are much more likely to think that the teacher really wants them to learn and improve academically (Patrick, Kaplan, & Ryan, 2011; Patrick & Ryan, 2008; Wentzel, 1997). A close teacher–student relationship seems a critical building block for the motivation to learn.

Further, the social-emotional climate with peers is also related to the motivational climate. Working with peers can be enjoyable and support the motivation to learn (see Chapter 8). This is especially true in adolescence, when peer relationships take on special significance. Further, working with others can support expectancies for success. When students perceive that they are part of a group or community working together toward learning, peers become an important resource for help and support. Thus, it is recommended that teachers provide students opportunities to interact with their peers around learning tasks. There are many possibilities (pairs, small groups, discussions), but it is most important that the tasks promote collaboration and involve worthwhile learning objectives.

In-Depth 9.2

TARGET

The TARGET acronym is helpful for teachers to think about the modifiable dimensions of classrooms that affect student motivation (Ames, 1992; Epstein, 1983; Kaplan & Maehr, 2007; Schunk et al., 2014). It refers to task design, distribution of authority, recognition of students, grouping arrangements, evaluation practices, and how time is allocated across academic tasks. Although we discuss each individually here, in classrooms they are likely to overlap. TARGET can be used by teachers when they create their lesson plans. Here we summarize the key recommendations for educators in relation to TARGET in regard to intrinsic motivation, motivation to learn, expectancies, value, growth mindset, and a mastery goal structure.

- *Tasks* are meaningful, challenging, and interesting, with a range of options available so that ability differences are not accentuated. Introduction of tasks emphasizes the opportunities they offer for students to develop their competence and helps students appreciate their value. Goal setting is encouraged so that students can approach and self-regulate their progress toward task completion.
- *Authority* and responsibility for rules, decisions, and tasks are shared between the students and teacher. Students' interests and questions about the content and tasks are solicited and addressed. Students are given some choices and control over activities in the classroom.
- *Recognition* is available to all students who put forth effort and make progress, not just the high achievers. There are few opportunities for social comparison among students.
- *Grouping* is flexible and heterogeneous, and students are not grouped by ability. Students have opportunities to work with other students. Group composition varies and does not highlight ability differences between students.

- *Evaluation* is criterion-referenced to help students recognize and appreciate their progress and task mastery. There are opportunities for revision or makeup work to improve upon initially poor performance. Evaluation is private rather than public.
- *Time* use is flexible, with opportunities for students to pace themselves. Students have some opportunity to manage their own time in accordance with their learning. Students who need it are given extra time.

As a teacher, you might use the TARGET acronym as a daily or weekly checklist. You can customize the checklist depending on which aspects of your practices you want to improve. The following are possible questions that you might ask yourself as you plan lessons:

- *Tasks:* Are the tasks that I am assigning interesting? Are they relevant? Can the students relate these tasks to the larger unit that I am teaching?
- *Authority:* Do students have the opportunity to make some meaningful choices?
- *Recognition:* How do I recognize students? Does everyone get recognized, or do only a few students get recognized? Do students get recognized for effort and improvement, or just for reaching a certain standard of performance?
- *Grouping:* How are students grouped for instruction? Is grouping flexible? Do the groups that students work in send particular messages to students about their ability or potential?
- *Evaluation:* How are students evaluated? Is the same form of evaluation used all the time for all students?
- *Time:* How is time used? Do I follow the same schedule every day, or do I sometimes arrange the schedule differently in order to stimulate motivation and engagement?

What Educators Can Do

The nature of the classroom context matters for adolescents' adjustment at school. As a teacher, it will be important for you to create a classroom that is organized and well managed, with high-quality instruction. You will want to develop a mastery goal structure in your classroom to motivate your students to learn. You will want a supportive social-emotional climate in which students perceive that you and their peers care about and support them personally and in their learning. Together these features should work together to create a community in your classroom in which students come to class each day ready and willing to learn with you and in collaboration with their peers. Throughout this section we discussed practices and strategies teachers can use to achieve such a classroom. However, effective teaching is incredibly hard work. Achieving such ideals will never be easy, and each new group of students will present new challenges. And, of course, curriculum and standards are always evolving, and teachers need to adapt their teaching practice over time. Part of what makes teaching an exciting profession is that it is so dynamic and complex. As a teacher, you will always be striving to improve and gain insights into effective practice. Here are a few suggestions for what educators can do in their pursuit of honing their practice and creating a classroom context that best supports their adolescent learners:

1. *Reflect on your teaching practice often.* Analyzing your practice will give you insights for improvement. However, be selective and work on only a few goals at a time. Apply the effective goal-setting techniques we discussed to your goals for your teaching. Set proximal, specific, and appropriately challenging goals for your practice.

2. *Critically evaluate the organizational structure of your classroom.* Recall the two classrooms that we described at the beginning of this section. Your students will learn more (and behave better) in a classroom that is well-managed and well-organized. Try to be consistent in how you implement your policies and procedures.

3. *Have a growth mindset about your teaching practice.* Earlier in this chapter we talked about the importance of a growth mindset for students. It is also important for teachers to have a growth mindset about teaching. Teaching is hard work and requires great effort. Challenges and setbacks are inevitable. Focus on growth and improvement.

4. *Establish supportive professional relationships.* Strive to find a colleague or colleagues with whom you can discuss your teaching practice. As a new teacher, seek out mentorship. Whom do you admire in your school or perhaps in other schools? How might you learn from that colleague? Which of your fellow teachers are invested in their practice? Find ways that you might support one another in improving your practice. Professional support comes in all shapes and sizes. It might be informal and happen during a discussion over lunch. Or you might try to organize something more formal, such as a meeting to discuss a certain issue. You might be lucky and enter a school where support is abundant or there are structures in place that facilitate communication among teachers. Or you may have to take an active role in developing such relationships, perhaps through seeking out online professional learning communities.

MyEdLab **Self-Check 9.2**

Schools

Classrooms are not islands. Classrooms are situated in schools, and the characteristics of the school also influence adolescent development. Schools vary tremendously within the United States. Consider the following examples:

- Dominic is a 12th grader. He attends a suburban public high school, with a traditional grade configuration (grades 9–12).
- Lucia is a 7th grader. She attends a private K–12 school that charges very high tuition.
- Jacob is an 8th grader. He attends a private Catholic school with grades 6–12.
- Jillian is a 10th grader. She does not attend a traditional school; she is home-schooled by her parents.
- Arvena is an 11th grader. She also is home-schooled, but her family is connected to an online learning environment.

What do you imagine is a typical day for each of these students? How might some of their experiences be similar? How will their experiences differ? How might what they learn by the end of 12th grade be different? How might their experiences affect their beliefs about their abilities and prospects for the future? How might their experiences affect their preferences for different subject areas? How might their experiences affect their future goals and career aspirations? We pose these questions to you to encourage you to think about how different features of schools and school experiences might affect development during adolescence.

In some cases, parents have choices about which types of school their sons and daughters can attend; however, often such choice is not available. The availability of choice is often related to family income. Families with high incomes often have the option of sending their children to private or parochial schools that charge tuition, instead of the local public school; families with lower incomes may not be able to send their children to private schools, unless they qualify for competitive scholarships. In addition, home-schooling is often not an option for families in which both parents hold full-time jobs. There are different types of schools available for adolescents, but students and parents don't always have autonomy in making these decisions.

The distribution of students across schools in the United States is summarized in Table 9.2. It is interesting to compare the numbers in the table to similar data reported just for early adolescents from about 20 years ago (Mac Iver & Epstein, 1991), which indicated that the majority of schools serving early adolescents were of the K–8 configuration, followed closely by traditional middle schools (mostly grades 6–8).

Does School Type Matter?

An obvious question for parents, students, and teachers is whether or not attending one type of school is beneficial over others. The answer is complex, because it depends on individual students' characteristics, preferences, and resources. There is some evidence that attending a private over a public school does not afford as many benefits as is often assumed. For example, results of one study suggest that high school students who graduate from private schools have higher SAT scores than do their peers who attend public schools; however, after 1 year of college, grade point averages are higher for the students who attended the public schools

TABLE 9.2	Distribution of U.S. Students Across Schools, 2010–2011		
		n	%
Total Schools Reporting		97,767	
Total Elementary grade 6 or below through no higher than 8		67,086	68.62%
Middle school grade 4, 5, or 6 through 6, 7, and 8		13,045	13.34%
One-teacher schools		224	0.23%
Other elementary schools		53,817	55.05%
Total Secondary no grade lower than 7		24,544	25.10%
Junior high grades 7–8 or 7–9		2855	2.92%
3- to 4-year high school		16,321	16.69%
5- to 6-year high school		4047	4.14%
Other high school		1321	1.35%
Combined Elementary and Secondary		6137	6.28%
Other schools		1050	1.07%

Source: Adapted from National Center for Educational Statistics, 2011.

(Monto & Dahmen, 2009). Data from the National Center for Education Statistics suggest that achievement differences are small when comparing public and private schools (Braun, Jenkins, & Grigg, 2006), but others who have examined the same data and computed alternative statistical models report that there is an advantage to attending private schools (Peterson & Llaudet, 2007).

The complexity of the decision regarding the type of school to attend is further complicated for adolescents, because the many changes and transitions described in this book are occurring simultaneously. Given all of the changes that are occurring in all aspects of adolescents' lives, clearly the decision about the type of school to attend during the adolescent years is extremely important.

School Types

Schools can be described along many dimensions. One of the most common distinctions is related to whether or not schools are public (i.e., funded by tax dollars) or private (i.e., funded by tuition payments, endowments, or scholarships). In recent years, several additional options have become available, including charter schools and various home-schooling options. In the next sections, we consider the characteristics of these various types of schools.

Public Schools. Most adolescents in the United States attend public schools. The National Center for Education Statistics (NCES) collects and reports data on school enrollments. Data from 2007–2008 indicate that of all of the U.S. schools serving children and adolescents, 73% are public (NCES, 2012b). Projections suggest that enrollments in schools serving students in kindergarten through the eighth grade (K–8) will increase more than will enrollments in schools serving adolescents over the next several years (e.g., grades 9–12 schools), although there will be some variation across states; for example, increases in high school enrollments are projected to be unusually large in the state of Texas (NCES, 2012a).

Enrollments in public schools are extremely diverse. Students of varying ethnic groups, religions, and income brackets all attend these schools. Some public schools are internally quite homogeneous, whereas others are more diverse. Public schools are located across urban, suburban, and rural regions.

Private and Religious Schools. Private schools generally charge tuition and various other fees for students to attend. In 2007–2008, 23.6% of the schools serving students in the United States were private (NCES, 2012b). Private schools include both religious schools that charge tuition and other nondenominational schools that also charge tuition.

Many parents choose to send adolescents to private schools because they feel that their sons and daughters will receive a better education in these settings. Nevertheless, research suggests that, overall, there are few social and psychological benefits to attending a private school. For example, results of a longitudinal study of adolescents using the National Longitudinal Study of Adolescent Health indicate that attending a private school does not afford any benefits in terms of emotional adjustment (Watt, 2003). A similar study examining middle school students in Chicago indicated that achievement differences were small when comparing students who attended either Catholic schools or public schools (Hallinan & Kubitschek, 2012). Other research also indicates few achievement differences for students attending private schools (Lubienski & Lubienski, 2006).

There also is some evidence that there are important achievement-related differences in students attending Catholic schools versus other types of private schools. In a large-scale national study, Lee and her colleagues found that although students who attend private schools take more advanced math courses than do students who attend public schools, the distribution of students of varying ability levels across advanced math courses is greater in Catholic schools than in other types of private schools or public schools (Lee, Chow-Hoy, Burkam, Geverdt, & Smerdon, 1998). Thus, although adolescents who come from lower-socioeconomic-status households are less likely to enroll in advanced mathematics courses in public schools, those students are more likely to enroll in advanced classes when they attend Catholic schools.

Nevertheless, some research does indicate that the climates in private and religious schools may be more positive than they are in public schools. For example, Fan, Williams, and Corkin (2011) found that students who attended Catholic or private schools reported a more positive school climate than did students who attended public schools. Other research suggests that minority students in particular who attend Catholic schools are more likely to report that they believe that teachers care for them (Bempechat, Boulay, Piergross, & Wenk, 2008).

Charter Schools. Charter schools are public schools, but they have their own governing boards and do not have to adhere to many of the bureaucratic rules that most other public schools do (Allen, 2013). Therefore, teachers in charter schools often have the opportunity to try out innovative instructional techniques. In 2007–2008, approximately 3% of schools in the United States were charter schools (NCES, 2012b). Enrollments in charter schools have grown quite dramatically over the past decade. The graph presented in Figure 9.1 demonstrates this growth; in the United States, there were about 1.1 million students enrolled in charter schools during the 2005–2006 academic year; this grew to almost 2.3 million by 2012–2013.

There has not been much research comparing the performance of students in charter schools and regular public schools. The research that exists so far does not indicate that there are many notable advantages to attending charter schools (Zimmer & Buddin, 2006). For example, Berends, Goldring, Stein, and Cravens (2010)

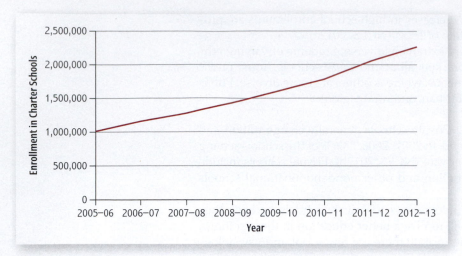

FIGURE 9.1

Growth in Enrollments in Charter Schools in the United States, 2005–2013

Source: Prepared using data from U.S. Department of Education, NCES, Common Core of Data, 2015.

found that math achievement gains did not differ when comparing students who attended charter schools with those attending more traditional schools.

Indeed, research indicates that in charter schools, as in other public schools, socioeconomic status (SES) is still related strongly to student achievement (Bancroft, 2009). Because students from lower-SES households are more likely to attend charter schools than are their more affluent peers (Ni, 2010), the negative relations between SES and achievement are still present in many charter schools. Lower-SES adolescents are more likely to attend charter schools than higher-SES students because charter schools are still public schools that are open to anyone; however, families often may choose charter schools as an alternative to regularly assigned public schools because lower-SES families are more likely to live in neighborhoods that contain low-performing schools. Thus the academic benefits to adolescents of attending charter schools are not evident, at least at this time.

Home-Schooling. The number of students who are home-schooled is increasing in the United States. Whereas in 1999 there were approximately 850,000 students being home-schooled, in 2007, there were about 1.5 million (representing approximately 2.9% of the school-aged population), and in 2012 there were over 1.7 million (NCES, 2012c, 2013).

The experience of being home-schooled varies across students. Whereas some students spend all of their time being educated in their homes, some students spend at least some portion of each week in a more traditional school setting. White students have a higher rate of being home-schooled (3.9%) than do Black students (0.8%) and Hispanic students (1.5%). The rate for other ethnicities is similar to that of White students (3.4%; NCES, 2012c).

Parents report varying reasons for preferring home-schooling to other types of education. These are summarized in Table 9.3. Clearly, the most common reasons are religious and moral in nature. Many parents feel that their religious beliefs should be incorporated into their children's education; because public schools do not offer courses on specific religions or espouse the practice of any single type of

TABLE 9.3 Reasons Why Parents Home-School Their Children

Rank	Reason	Percentage of Students
1	Provide religious or moral instruction	36%
2	Concerns about school environments (e.g., drugs, safety, peer pressure, etc.)	21%
3	Dissatisfaction with academic instruction at schools	17%
4	Other reasons (e.g., family time, finances, travel, distance, etc.)	14%
5	Desire to provide a nontraditional approach to education	7%
6	Health problems	6%

Source: National Center for Education Statistics, 2012c.

religious belief in school, many parents see home-schooling as the most economical and viable means of providing religion-infused education to adolescents.

A small portion of parents choose home-schooling because of the medical or psychological conditions of their children or teens. Although not much research has been conducted on the efficacy of home-schooling, there is some evidence that early adolescents with attention-deficit hyperactivity disorder (ADHD) may fare better on some educational outcomes when home-schooled (Duvall, Delquadri, & Ward, 2004). Parents of some exceptional students (e.g., students with autism spectrum disorders) sometimes report that they choose home-schooling because they believe that the public schools are either unwilling or unable to provide appropriate and effective services (Hurlbutt, 2011).

Urbanicity

In the United States, distinctions often are made based on the proximity of schools to urban centers. Schools that are located within urban centers are referred to as urban schools, those that are located in suburbs of urban centers are referred to as suburban schools, and those that are located at longer distances from urban centers are referred to as rural schools.

Some research indicates that there are differences in the experiences and outcomes for students who attend schools in these varied settings. For example, adolescents who attend rural schools are less likely to enroll in or graduate from college than are urban and suburban students, primarily due to their lower average SES (Byun, Meece, & Irvin, 2012). Nevertheless, the availability of community resources for rural students is related to ultimately attaining a college degree. This is important, because other research indicates that rural adolescents do not have access to

In-Depth 9.3

Dropping Out of School

Students' school experiences have the potential to play a profound role in their educational trajectory. Of major concern is students who drop out of school. Dropping out of school is related to a lower overall quality of life for many individuals, as many future job opportunities are severely limited when students drop out of school. Dropping out can occur at any time; indeed, many adolescents drop out during middle school, and never even make it to high school (Rumberger, 1995).

Although dropout rates have declined in recent years, they remain unacceptably high, particularly for Hispanic students (NCES, 2012a). For example, in 2010, the national dropout rate was 7.4% overall, but 15.1% for Hispanic adolescents in the United States. Risk factors for dropping out include grade retention (being "held back"; Rumberger, 1995), experiencing excessive academic problems upon the transition into high school (Pharris-Ciurej, Hirschman, & Willhoft,

2012), and having switched schools (Gasper, DeLuca, & Estacion, 2012).

As a prospective educator, knowing the warning signs for students at risk for dropping out of school is important. Based on the research on this topic, the American Psychological Association (APA, 2012) identified characteristics of students at risk for dropping out:

- Not having mastered reading by the third grade
- Displaying poor academic performance, disengagement, and absenteeism during grades 6 through 8
- Having poor beliefs about one's competence
- Displaying little effort
- Associating with peers who do not value school
- Experiencing a difficult transition into high school
- Being held back in the ninth grade
- Displaying poor grades, absenteeism, and disengagement during high school

as many school and family resources that are related to academic success as compared with students from nonrural regions (Roscigno & Crowley, 2001).

Interestingly, there is little variation in psychological outcomes for adolescents across these settings. Using a nationally representative sample, Anderman (2002) found few differences among rural, urban, and suburban adolescents in terms of depression, optimism, social rejection, school problems (i.e., trouble getting homework finished, getting along with teachers, etc.), and grade point average. In fact, the only difference that emerged was that urban students reported feeling less optimistic overall than did suburban students (Anderman, 2002).

There also has been some research examining differences in dropout rates across urban regions. Research comparing dropout rates of rural and urban high school students indicates that although dropout rates have increased by about 3 percentage points since the 1980s, after family characteristics are considered, differences in dropout rates between rural and urban schools are quite small (Jordan, Kostandini, & Mykerezi, 2012).

It is important to note that there is much heterogeneity within rural, urban, and suburban settings. Indeed, being an adolescent in inner-city Chicago is not an identical experience to growing up in inner-city San Francisco or Dallas. Similarly, there is much variation even across different rural settings (Jordan et al., 2012) and suburban settings.

School Size

The size of the schools that adolescents attend is an important consideration. There are clearly both advantages and disadvantages to attending either small or large schools. Advantages of attending large schools may include the availability of more courses for students to take, numerous after-school extracurricular activities, and a broader and larger group of peers. In contrast, advantages of small schools may include more personal attention from teachers, greater cohesion among peers, and a greater likelihood of developing a sense of place or belonging in the school.

Research on the relations between school size and achievement outcomes for adolescents is mixed. Some research indicates that optimal learning for adolescents is achieved in schools with medium-sized student populations (e.g., between 600 and 900 students; Lee & Smith, 1996; Weiss, Carolan, & Baker-Smith, 2010). However, other data suggest that achievement is greater in small and very large schools than in schools with medium-sized enrollments (Werblow & Duesbery, 2009). Some data suggest that students learn less in smaller schools, and that attending very large schools (i.e., those with over 2100 students) is related to the poorest achievement. However, more recent data suggest that school size is only minimally if at all related to student achievement, once SES is controlled for (Lindahl & Cain, 2012). There is some research suggesting that the larger size of middle schools (as compared with elementary schools) may be related to the poorer engagement often seen in early adolescents who attend middle-grades schools (Holas & Huston, 2012). Thus the transition from the smaller, more intimate elementary school into the larger, less personal middle school may be problematic; however, as we review later in the chapter, the negative effects of this transition for adolescents are not only related to the move from a smaller to a larger school (i.e., there are other important variables also at play).

The size of a school can be related to more than just academic achievement. For example, it is plausible that students who attend larger schools may experience greater levels of victimization than do students who attend smaller schools. Research suggests that the teacher-to-student ratio is more strongly related to victimization than is actual school size. In general, when students attend schools in which the ratio of teachers to students is high (i.e., there are a lot of teachers working with fewer students), victimization is more likely to occur (Gottfredson &

DiPietro, 2011). Other research indicates that students who attend smaller-sized high schools are less likely to drop out than are students who attend larger schools (Werblow & Duesbery, 2009).

In summary, the size of the school that an adolescent attends often is related to educational outcomes. However, as you have seen from our discussion, the relation between school size and these outcomes is complex. Overall, in looking at the entire body of research on school size, researchers generally argue that smaller schools facilitate learning better than do larger schools, particularly for students from lower-SES backgrounds. In addition, the optimal size for schools serving diverse or disadvantaged adolescents should be less than 600, whereas the recommended size for schools serving socioeconomically mixed or advantaged students should be less than 1000 (Leithwood & Jantzi, 2009).

Grade Configurations and School Transitions

There are many different grade configurations in schools that serve adolescents. School districts need to decide how to group students together, and different configurations have emerged, often due to building constraints, population surges, and crowding. In rural settings, a school might contain students from kindergarten through 12th grade. Other configurations include kindergarten through 8th followed by 9th through 12th, or kindergarten through 5th grade followed by a middle school containing grades 6 through 8 and then a high school containing grades 9 through 12. However, some school districts house kindergarten through 6th grade, then 7th- through 9th-grade students, and then high school for 10th- through 12th-grade students. Consider the following examples:

>>> ────────────

Tasha just completed the sixth grade. For seventh grade, she will be enrolling in her local middle school; that school serves students in grades 7 through 9. After the ninth grade, she will transition into a high school that serves students in grades 10 through 12.

Jerry is in the sixth grade. For seventh grade, he will remain in the same school, because he is enrolled in a school that serves students in grades kindergarten through grade 8. After the 8th grade, he will transition into a high school that serves students in grades 9 through 12.

Jann is in the fifth grade. He will transition into a middle school that serves students in grades 6 through 8 next year. After the 8th grade, he will transition into a high school that serves students in grades 9 through 12.

The experiences of Tasha, Jerry, and Jann during adolescence are quite different. If one looks just at the eighth-grade year, Tasha will be enrolled in a school with students who are both 1 year older and 1 year younger than her; Jerry will be enrolled in a school that serves students who are all younger than him; and Jann will be enrolled in a school that serves younger students, but only students who are within 2 years of Jann's age. Thus the contexts of and experiences within these schools for these early adolescents will be quite different.

During adolescence, students often make several transitions between schools. Typically, students move from smaller schools to larger and more diverse schools. These transitions at times can be stressful for students because they require students to adapt to a new environment. We will examine two common transitions: the transition to middle school and the transition to high school.

MyEdLab
Video Example 9.4

Student motivation changes as they move from early childhood and then middle childhood into adolescence. Note how the students in this video talk about motivation differently depending on their age and their levels of cognitive and social development.

MyEdLab
Video Example 9.5

Educators can plan for school transitions with students and their parents to make the transition a positive and successful experience for students who may need extra resources to support their learning.

The Transition from Elementary School into Middle School.

Many students experience their first major school transition when they graduate from elementary school and move into a middle-grades school. Most students make this transition after either the fifth or sixth grades; they typically move into schools that serve other early adolescents (e.g., schools with configurations of grades 6 through 8 or grades 7 through 9). The transition into middle school can be a stressful time for early adolescents (Goldstein, Boxer, & Rudolph, 2015).

There has been much research on the transition from elementary school into middle school (Anderman & Mueller, 2010). Much of this research yields several consistent findings:

- Achievement often decreases across the transition.
- Motivation often changes across the transition (students often become more focused on grades and test scores [extrinsic motivation], and less focused on learning for the sake of learning [intrinsic motivation].
- Middle school teachers feel less efficacious (i.e., confident in their abilities to positively affect student learning) than do elementary school teachers.
- Students often report having poorer interpersonal relationships with their teachers after the transition.

However, another important finding is that the transition does not necessarily lead to negative shifts in achievement and motivation for all students (Anderman, Maehr, & Midgley, 1999). Indeed, some middle schools provide outstanding environments for early adolescents; when students attend such schools, negative effects are less common.

Eccles, Midgley, and their colleagues characterize the problems associated with the middle school transition as being a problem of stage–environment fit (Eccles, Lord, & Buchanan, 1996; Eccles, Lord, & Roeser, 1996; Eccles & Midgley, 1989; Eccles et al., 1993; Feldlaufer, , Midgley, , & Eccles, 1988; Midgley, Middleton, Gheen, & Kumar, 2002). They specifically argue, and have demonstrated, that many middle-grades schools do not provide for the developmental needs of early adolescents. This is exemplified by the trends described in Table 9.4.

Specifically, early adolescents have very particular needs. As we discuss elsewhere in this book, early adolescents desire autonomy and opportunities to

TABLE 9.4 **The Mismatch Between Adolescents' Needs and Typical Middle Schools**

Domain	What Adolescents Need	What Schools Often Provide
Relationships with adults	Strong, supportive, caring relationships	Relationships that are focused on behavior management
Cognition	Opportunities to engage in abstract thinking and more complex problem solving	Fill-in-the-blank worksheets
Peers	Opportunities to constructively engage with peers	Control of behavior; students often asked to stay in their seats and work alone on tasks and assignments
Autonomy	Opportunities to make choices	Fewer opportunities to make choices than in elementary school
Academic tasks	Opportunities to engage in meaningful tasks where creativity and risk taking are encouraged	An increased focus on testing and assessment

Sources: Anderman & Midgley, 1997; Anderman & Mueller, 2010; Eccles & Midgley, 1989; Eccles et al., 1993; Eccles et al., 1996; Midgley et al., 1995; Midgley, Eccles, & Feldlaufer, 1991; Midgley & Feldlaufer, 1987; Midgley, Feldlaufer, & Eccles, 1988; Wigfield & Eccles, 1994; Wigfield, Eccles, MacIver, Reuman, & Midgley, 1991.

engage in meaningful work; however, many middle schools actually afford early adolescents fewer opportunities for autonomy and engagement with meaningful educational tasks. In addition, from a Piagetian perspective, early adolescents are entering into the period of formal operations, when they are able to think about complex, abstract issues (Piaget, 2008); nevertheless, in many middle schools, students actually receive assignments that do not require much higher-order thinking. This may be because of the increased concerns that many middle-grades teachers have about behavior management—many teachers may be providing a lot of "busywork" to keep students on task and to keep them from engaging in potentially disruptive behaviors (Anderman & Mueller, 2010; Eccles & Midgley, 1989).

Nevertheless, the transition from elementary to middle school does not have to be a negative experience for early adolescents. Indeed, research indicates that when the middle school context supports their developmental needs, students do not suffer negative consequences from such transitions (Anderman et al., 1999). Moreover, some researchers are now conceptualizing difficult middle school transitions as interruptions in students' achievement trajectories, rather than as markers of permanent decline (e.g., Akos, Rose, & Orthner, 2015). Two recommended practices for middle schools are teaming and advisory periods. **Teaming** refers to the practice in which students within grades in a middle school are broken down into smaller units called teams. Students on the same team have the same set of teachers. So, for example, the 250 sixth graders in a given middle school would be divided into two teams of 125 each, and each team would have a math, language arts, social studies, and science teacher. Teaming creates a smaller peer group that students have to interact with in school each day and makes it easier for students to make friends in their classes. Further, teachers on the same team have the same set of students, which can facilitate communication among teachers about students.

Advisory periods are an opportunity for groups of students to meet with a teacher or a school counselor during the school day. There are a variety of models that can be used to organize group advisory periods. For example, in some schools, all students have a block of time daily (e.g., one half-hour) when the same group of students meets with one teacher. The time can be used as a traditional study hall, but the advantage of organizing this into a consistent group of students with a constant teacher is that the teacher can meet daily with smaller groups of students to discuss various issues. In addition, the teacher can devote some sessions to talking with the entire group about issues that do not fit into traditional subject matter. Often, advisory periods are when special programs, such as social-emotional learning programs, take place.

Although group advisory periods can be very beneficial for adolescents in many ways, it is important for school administrators to provide appropriate support and training for teachers. Many teachers understand the value of providing advisory support for adolescents but also report that they do not feel adequately prepared to do so (Rothi, Leavey, & Best, 2008). Therefore, it is important for teachers to receive and to request this important support. Teachers need in particular to know their limits, and to know when they should seek support and consult with others.

The Transition into High School.

There has been less research on the transition into high school than on the transition into middle school. Nevertheless, this transition is particularly important. When students decide to drop out of school, it often occurs during the high school years (Benner, 2011). In addition, research indicates that students' academic performance during the ninth grade (which is often the first year of high school) is predictive of dropping out of school, after controlling for numerous other variables (Neild, Stoner-Eby, & Furstenberg, 2008).

Thus, students' experiences at the high school transition are critical determinants of subsequent academic success.

Although results of some studies indicate that high school students like school less, feel more depressed, have lower self-esteem, and receive less support from teachers and administrators (Barber & Olsen, 2004), other studies suggest that students do not have much difficulty making this transition (Akos & Galassi, 2004). In addition, other studies report mixed results. For example, Benner and Graham (2009) found that high school students reported liking school more than when they were in middle school; however, those same students reported feeling more anxious and lonelier than before (Benner & Graham, 2009).

Academic Tracking

Tracking refers to the practice of assigning students to different classes on the basis of ability (Oakes, 2000). Prior to the 20th century, high schools in the United States were elite, focused on a classic liberal arts education and preparation for college. In the 1920s, enrollment in secondary education increased, and high schools expanded their role to prepare students for careers. At this time, students were assigned to college preparation, general education, or vocational education tracks, which would dictate all of their classes at high school. Over time, these broad tracks were replaced and subject-specific courses were designated as advanced or honors, regular, basic, and remedial. Tracking is most prevalent in math and language arts but many schools track in science and social studies courses as well. There is much variation in how tracking is done at different schools. Some schools are inclusive and allow much student choice, whereas other schools are more restrictive and students must qualify. Qualifications would include prior grades, test scores, and teacher and counselor recommendations.

Tracking has been the source of much debate in the United States. The rationale for tracking is to permit teachers to tailor instruction to the ability levels of their students. When instruction is too advanced, students struggle because they lack the requisite skills. When instruction is too easy, students are bored and do not learn. Tracking allows for a better fit between students' abilities and instructional level. Thus, the advantage of tracking and why it is often promoted is that it has the potential to be more efficient and effective in promoting the cognitive growth of students.

However, critics have identified several problems that can arise with tracking. The quantity and quality of instruction have been found to be different across tracks (Carbonero, 2005; Lucas & Berends, 2002; Montt, 2011). The curriculum and instruction are often better in the higher tracks. The amount of time spent on teaching as opposed to administrative and disciplinary tasks is greater in classes in higher tracks. Instructional methods have also been found to vary, with more student-centered and active approaches in higher-level courses. Differences in teacher quality can explain some of these effects, as less experienced teachers are often assigned to lower-level courses.

Tracking affects friendship patterns between students because it limits contact between adolescents with different levels of achievement and engagement (Crosnoe, Riegle-Crumb, Field, Frank & Muller, 2008). For low-achieving students, tracking promotes friendships with other low-achieving students who are more likely to be engaged in delinquent behavior. As we learned in Chapter 8, adolescents are highly susceptible to peer influence (Ryan, 2001). Grouping low achievers together also contributes to differences in instruction between tracks. When numerous students with low achievement and conduct problems are placed together in classes, it creates a more challenging classroom environment for teachers.

These differences contribute to the findings that tracking does not equally benefit all students. Students in high-ability classes learn more than students in low-ability classes (Carbonero, 2005). These differential patterns contribute to the continued controversy around tracking. Advocates for high-achieving students want them in environments where they will excel and reach their full potential. Advocates for students from disadvantaged backgrounds (who are more likely to be low-achieving students) point out that tracking contributes to a widening gap between high- and low-achieving students in high schools. Low-achieving students get an inferior education, which dampens their opportunities and exacerbates the achievement gap. Further, the longer a student is in a lower track, the harder it can be to move up to a higher track.

Another concern with tracking is that a greater proportion of minority and low-income students end up in lower tracks. Some of this is due to differences in prior achievement, but even when prior achievement is taken into account there are still differences in student track enrollment by race and income (Carbonero, 2005). These patterns may be partially explained by differences in the extent to which parents get involved in the process either through lobbying on behalf of their students or by counseling their children to choose more advanced classes. Further, students themselves may opt out of the choice to take coursework at an advanced level (Hallinan & Kubitschek, 2011). One way to address the inequity that often results from having tracked coursework involves eliminating students' options to choose different levels of classes, especially for gateway classes early in high school. For example, the federal Gear Up program aimed to improve academic preparedness for low-income students by having all 9th grade students entering high school automatically take biology with no option for a less rigorous course (U. S. Department of Education, 2012). Evaluations of such programs have found positive effects on student achievement. It seems that when students are forced to take more challenging coursework they show great achievement gains. Thus, such policies have the potential to reduce the inequities in achievement gaps by race and socioeconomic background. However, an important caveat is that such benefits have not been found in the most advanced courses (e.g., calculus; Crosnoe & Benner, 2015). Policies to reduce tracking and increase educational opportunities might be most appropriate early in high school.

What Educators Can Do

In summary, schools have many different characteristics. The size, location, funding structures, and grade configurations of schools all can have varying effects on adolescents. We discuss two implications and related suggestions for teachers:

1. *Know the context of your school and local community.* As an educator of adolescents, it is essential to understand the nature of the community in which you are teaching. In order to provide schooling that will lead to optimal engagement of adolescents, educators need to understand their students' lives. For example, if you are teaching in a region that has experienced a great deal of unemployment, it is important to be aware of this. Indeed, some students may be experiencing economic hardships that can have an impact on their performance at school (McLoyd et al., 2009). An awareness of the contexts in which adolescents are living can enhance your ability as a teacher to positively engage and influence your students.

2. *Support students during transitions.* Transitions can be stressful times for students. Knowing about some of the research on grade configurations and school transitions will help you to meet the developmental needs of your students. Be aware of some of the problems that arise for some adolescents as they transition into middle and high school, and support students at these junctures.

MyEdLab **Self-Check 9.3**

Socioeconomic Status, Ethnicity, and Schooling

Adolescents come to schools from vastly differing backgrounds. These background characteristics represent important parts of students' identities, and are related in important ways to how students learn, to the valuing of education, and to important educational decisions that both students and parents make. Two of the most important variables that need to be considered are (a) students' socioeconomic status and (b) students' ethnic backgrounds. Much can and has been written about the importance of these topics; in this chapter, we briefly review some of the most important considerations for teachers of adolescents.

Socioeconomic Status

Socioeconomic status (SES) refers to the resources of students' home environments. Definitions of SES vary (Murdock, 2000), but generally include aspects of parental education, occupation, and income. There is much debate among researchers about how to define SES, and whether or not income is a reliable indicator of SES. Nevertheless, in general, researchers agree that higher levels of SES are related to access to resources (i.e., high-SES families are more likely to have more disposable income and live in safer neighborhoods than are lower-SES families). A large body of research indicates that SES is related positively and quite strongly to students' academic achievement (Entwisle, Alexander, & Olson, 2010; Hattie, 2009; Perry & McConney, 2010; Ransdell, 2012; Sirin, 2005; Tomul & Savasci, 2012; van Ewijk & Sleegers, 2010). It is important to note that both the SES of students' families and the aggregated SES of schools is related positively to student achievement (Entwisle et al., 2010; Rumberger & Palardy, 2005). Thus, in addition to personal family income, attending a school that primarily serves students from high-SES backgrounds is related to individual students' achievement.

One of the important questions that educators and policymakers wrestle with concerns the mechanisms by which higher SES is related to enhanced academic achievement for students. Research generally suggests that students who reside in higher-SES homes are exposed to a more heterogenous quality of resources than are students who reside in lower-SES homes. For example, these students are more likely to have higher-quality childcare, to have parents in the home for extended periods of time (i.e., paying attention to the students and monitoring their homework and behavior), and to attend schools where high achievement is the norm among peers (Dupere, Leventhal, Crosnoe, & Dion, 2010). Some research indicates that the relation between having emotional and/or behavioral difficulties and academic achievement is stronger for low-income than for higher-income students (Ansary, McMahon, & Luthar, 2012). Moreover, emerging evidence suggests that growing up in poverty may adversely affect brain development, which consequently may adversely affect academic achievement (e.g., Hair, Hanson, Wolfe, & Pollak, 2015).

Some research also indicates that students from lower-SES backgrounds experience a poorer quality of education overall. For example, there is some evidence that lower-SES students are tracked into ability groups more often, and receive lower-quality educational experiences, than do students from higher-SES backgrounds (Entwisle et al., 2010). In addition, for adolescents, research indicates that the relation between SES and achievement is stronger for students who attend schools that use a great deal of tracking of students by ability level (i.e., separating students by class based on their ability levels; Marks, Cresswell, & Ainley, 2006). Nevertheless, research also indicates that lower-SES adolescents may experience achievement gains when they are able to attend high-achieving schools (Wong et al., 2014).

Ethnicity

Although ethnicity is often discussed as it relates to a variety of aspects of schooling and education, there has not been a *comprehensive* meta-analysis examining the relations between ethnicity and academic achievement (Hattie, 2009). Nevertheless, student ethnicity does play an extremely important role in adolescents' school experiences. Indeed, ethnic segregation still occurs in the United States, and is particularly evident for Latino and Black students. As a classroom teacher, the amount of ethnic variation that you encounter among your students will vary depending on the school in which you teach; thus it is extremely important to be aware of student ethnicity, whether you have only one or many students of diverse backgrounds in your classes.

Consider a classroom that consists of primarily White students, where there is only one ethnic-minority student; what would the experience be like for this student? Now consider a classroom that is highly diverse (i.e., there are students representing multiple ethnicities)—what would the experience be like for the students? Clearly these experiences will vary considerably, and may have powerful effects on the motivation, achievement, and attitudes of both the minority and majority students in the classes (Adams, 2012). These experiences also may vary according to other factors. For example, the number of students in the class is an important consideration in discussions of ethnicity and schooling. In general, research indicates that minority students achieve at higher levels when class sizes are smaller (Nye, Hedges, & Konstantopoulos, 2004). The ethnicity of the teacher also is important; in some cases, minority students may feel more comfortable when the teacher is of the same ethnic heritage as the student.

For ethnic-minority adolescents, being the only person (or one of only a few people) representing one's ethnicity can be a difficult experience. For example, stereotypes about Asian students being good at mathematics can have deleterious psychological consequences for Asian students in predominantly White classrooms (Au & Chang, 2012). In a now classic article, Holloway (1988) compared beliefs about ability and effort in Japan and the United States. She found that in Japan, effort is viewed as an extremely important predictor of academic achievement, whereas in the United States, ability is emphasized. In addition, the families of Japanese students emphasize cooperation over competition (Holloway, 1988). These patterns that were noted for Japanese students may at least partially explain why students of Asian descent often outperform their peers in the United States.

For Latino students, segregation has been particularly evident in the western United States. Most Latino students attend schools where the majority of students also are Latino, and where many are quite poor. California, New York, and Texas are particularly segregated for Latino students (Orfield, Kuscera, & Siegel-Hawley, 2012). The patterns are quite similar for Black students. The typical Black student in the United States attends schools in which about two-thirds of the students in the school are poor. New York, Illinois, and Michigan contain the most highly segregated schools for Black students. In addition, in the southern regions of the United States, segregation is now on the rise for Black students (Orfield et al., 2012). The quality of the buildings, materials, and resources in schools serving Black adolescents often is inferior to that in schools serving primarily majority students (Orfield & Lee, 2006).

Minority students also are more likely to be severely reprimanded for bad behavior than are other students. African American students are more likely to report feeling discriminated against than are students of other ethnicities (Rosenbloom & Way, 2004; Rowley, Kurtz-Costes, & Cooper, 2010). A study conducted at UCLA found that during the 2009–2010 school year, 17% of Black students across the United States were suspended from school, compared with 7% of Latino students and 5% of White students (Losen & Gillespie, 2012).

What Educators Can Do

As a teacher, you will inevitably wrestle with questions about paying "too much" or "too little" attention to ethnicity and SES. Whereas on one level it is important to be aware of these distinctions, at another level, teachers may become criticized for being classist or racist if they pay too much attention to such differences. Our view is that it is important for educators to be aware of research examining how SES and ethnicity are related to achievement. Students may not come to schools having had equal opportunities or resources in the past, but as a teacher, you can work diligently to provide equitable access to those opportunities in the future. Teachers make critical decisions about how to best educate their students on a daily basis, and being well equipped with knowledge about the research base on SES and ethnicity is the best tool that teachers can have so that they can make informed and thoughtful decisions.

MyEdLab **Self-Check 9.4**

Recommendations for Educators

In this chapter, we have examined the nature of students' motivation, classrooms, and schools. We first considered the multifaceted nature of motivation and the important role it plays in students' engagement and learning at school. We examined four important dimensions of effective classrooms: organization and behavior management, instruction, motivational climate and the socioemotional climate. We then discussed contextual differences across schools and the implications for adolescent development. Throughout, we considered the implications for educators. Next, we review some of the implications that these topics have for middle and high school teachers.

Foster Students' Motivation

Students are always motivated to do something. You want to motivate your students to learn and engage in school. An appreciation of the multifaceted nature of motivation will help you do so. Whenever possible, encourage students' intrinsic motivation. On a daily basis, promote students' motivation to learn, which means helping them find learning activities meaningful and worthwhile and try to get the intended benefits from them. Students will only be motivated to learn when they believe they can be successful and when they see the value in doing so. Toward that end, support students' expectancies for success, encourage a growth mindset, and help them see the value in schoolwork.

Create an Effective Classroom Context Characterized by Organization, High-Quality Instruction, and a Motivationally and Socially-Emotionally Supportive Climate

Teaching is a profession that will always require reflection and adjustment. Each year will bring new and different dynamics with students. Some years there will be new curriculum and standards. And there are endless possibilities when it comes to discovering new ways to motivate, instruct, and connect with your students. We suggested that a growth mindset and working to establish supportive professional relationships will serve you well to meet your goals in the exciting profession of teaching.

Know the Context of Your School and Local Community to Better Meet the Needs of Your Students

Schools and communities vary tremendously. Meeting the needs of your students can only be accomplished when your practice is tailored to the needs of your constituents. This includes supporting students at critical junctures such as transitions to middle and high school. Be aware of the role of socioeconomic status and ethnicity in students' experiences at school and work to provide equitable access to opportunities for all students in your classes and school.

Conclusion

The experiences that adolescents have in classrooms and schools can have long-lasting effects on social and academic outcomes, and ultimately on future career choices. Every day teachers make important decisions about their practice in their classrooms and contribute in important ways to the school setting. Teachers can and do make a difference in students' lives daily. Whether it is a brief conversation with a student or advocating for a change in school policy, every action that we take as teachers can greatly benefit adolescents in both the short and the long term.

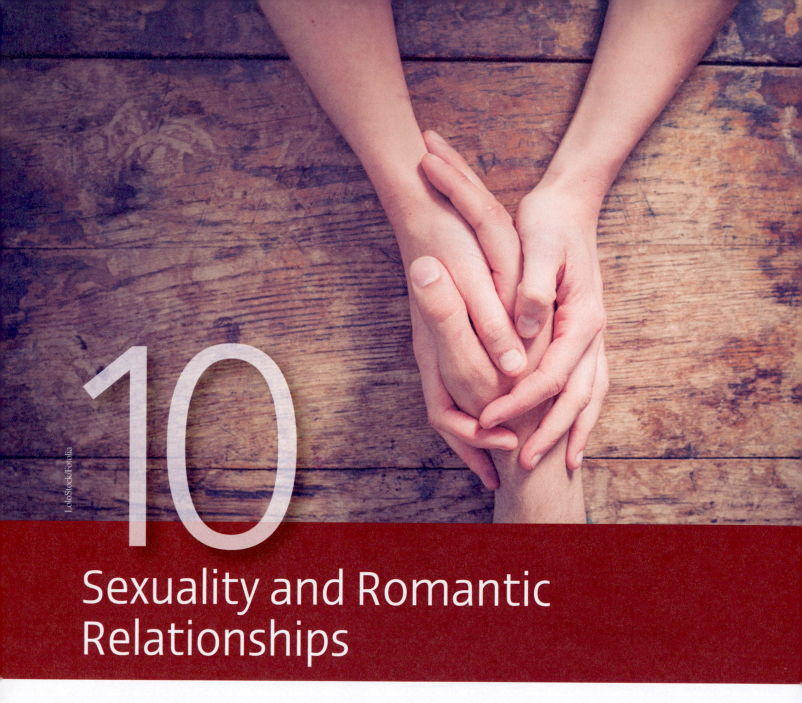

LoloStock/Fotolia

10

Sexuality and Romantic Relationships

Learning Outcomes

10.1 You will be able to describe the percentages of adolescents who engage in various sexual activities by age, ethnicity, and gender.

10.2 You will be able to describe the nature of adolescents' romantic relationships, their attitudes about them, and different kinds of sexuality.

10.3 You will be able to identify the various sources that adolescents rely upon for information about sex and romantic relationships and describe the strengths and shortcomings of each source.

10.4 You will be able to identify the various physical and emotional consequences of engaging in sexual behavior and romantic relationships.

10.5 You will be able to describe what educators can do to foster healthy sexual development among their adolescent students.

Introduction

One of the consequences of the biological changes that usher in the adolescent period of development is that teenagers become sexually mature, at least physically. The same hormonal processes that produce the development of primary and secondary sex characteristics also produce urges for sexual activity. These urges are both exciting and confusing for teenagers, as their physical development is accompanied by societal messages about the appropriateness of sexual behavior, information (and misinformation) from peers and adults about how they should feel and act on their sexual desires, and their own developing beliefs about what sex and romantic relationships mean to them.

Teachers who work with adolescent students often witness the emerging romantic and sexual relationships of their students, and sometimes these relationships and their effects encroach on classroom life. Consider these two examples:

>>>

> Mr. Jones has decided to organize his 11th-grade students into teams of four to work on their science projects. He wanted to make the team projects enjoyable to students, so he decided to try to group friends with one another as much as he could. He knew that Jason and Erica were friends, so he put them on the same team. What Mr. Jones did not know was that Jason and Erica had been a romantic couple until last weekend, when they had an ugly argument and decided to break up. After class, Erica approached Mr. Jones and asked to be moved to a different team so she wouldn't have to work with Jason.

> Ms. Kincaid teaches eighth-grade social studies, and her class has arrived at the point in the year where they are beginning the unit on sexuality. This unit often involves several awkward moments as her students snicker, make jokes, and reveal very personal information about themselves and one another. This year, as Ms. Kincaid begins the discussion about developing bodies and emerging sexuality, one of the students blurts out that one of the girls in the class is rumored to be pregnant. The class gasps and turns to look at the girl who has been named, and she bursts into tears.

Because sexuality and romantic relationships are new urges and experiences for adolescent students, it is common for them to respond to these developments in a variety of ways, ranging from embarrassment to immaturity to confusion, and to recklessness. It can also be very confusing for teachers because sex and romance are topics that are usually private. In addition, these are topics that are fraught with potential dangers whenever children and adults interact, as teachers and adolescent students do. As students seek advice and guidance from their peers, most of whom have their own misconceptions about sex, they may put themselves at risk for anything from hurt feelings to serious disease. Teachers and schools are in a position to help adolescents navigate these confusing developmental waters, but how can teachers walk the tightrope of providing valuable information without appearing to advocate sexual activity or meddling in teenagers' private lives?

OVERVIEW OF THE CHAPTER

Sexual behavior is a very complex phenomenon that has implications for physical and psychological well-being. In many countries, including the United States, sex is linked with moral and religious beliefs, and it is also an important part of the social culture of adolescents. In this chapter, we consider sexual behavior among adolescents as well as their attitudes and knowledge about sexual behavior and romantic relationships. We begin with a definition of healthy sexual development, then move on to an examination of the occurrence rates of sexual activity among U.S. adolescent. Next, we consider how adolescents think about and understand sexual behavior, their attitudes about romantic relationships, and varieties of sexual orientations. Finally, we explore where adolescents get their information about sex and sexuality, some of the problems associated with sexual activity, and the role that teachers and schools can play in helping adolescents develop healthy attitudes and behaviors about sex and romantic relationships.

What Is Healthy Sexual Development?

In a country as diverse as the United States, there will never be universal agreement regarding what constitutes appropriate sexual beliefs or behaviors. Whereas some believe that the only acceptable sexual behavior is between married heterosexual adults, others disagree with this view. With this diversity of perspectives in mind, Brooks-Gunn and Paikoff (1993) offered a model of **healthy sexual development** in adolescence (summarized in Table 10.1). The first piece of the model calls for an acceptance of the physical changes associated with puberty, such as changes in body shape and weight gain. Adolescents, particularly girls, often develop feelings of dissatisfaction with their bodies when these changes occur, leading to feelings of unattractiveness. So coming to terms with one's new body shape and proportions is an important first step in developing sexual well-being.

How does this model of healthy sexual development fit with your own beliefs and attitudes about teenage sexual behavior and with those of the community in which you live?

The second step in the model involves developing comfort and acceptance with new sexual desires. Many adolescents feel confused and ashamed by these desires, so it is important to learn that these feelings are a normal part of development rather than unhealthy or immoral.

The third step in the model is about being comfortable in choosing to engage in, or not engage in, sexual activity. Brooks-Gunn and Paikoff (1993) emphasize the importance

TABLE 10.1	Summary of Brooks-Gunn and Paikoff's Model of Healthy Sexual Development	
Components	**Explanation**
Positive feelings about one's body	Puberty brings a tremendous amount of change to the body, and it is important for adolescents to develop healthy and positive perceptions of their bodies.
Feelings of sexual arousal and desire	Puberty also brings increases in sexual desires. Despite ubiquitous messages about sexuality in popular culture, many adolescents do not feel safe to discuss their new desires with others. This inhibits gaining important information and promotes feelings of shame. Adolescents need to understand that these feelings and desires are a normal part of development.
Sexual behavior	Most adolescents engage in some sort of sexual behavior (e.g., masturbation, kissing, petting) in the years before engaging in intercourse. Adolescents should understand that these behaviors are a normal part of development. They should also be aware that sexual behavior is often associated with emotional connections to partners.
Safe sex	For those adolescents who are engaging in sexual intercourse, it is important that they know about methods of safer sex to avoid disease and unwanted pregnancy.

Source: Based on Brooks-Gunn and Paikoff, 1993.

of feeling that sexual behaviors are engaged in by choice rather than coercion if healthy sexual development is to occur.

Finally, for adolescents who do choose to engage in sexual activity, healthy sexual activity involves making smart choices about safe sex practices. Given the fact that most adolescents do choose to engage in sexual activity, it is important that they understand the risks involved and the precautions they can take to minimize these risks.

Rates of Sexual Activity

It is important to note at the outset of this section that researchers must rely on the reports of adolescents themselves to determine how frequently they engage in various sexual activities. This may not always produce reliable data, as adolescents are not always anxious to tell some researcher how many times in the last month they made out with their boyfriends or girlfriends. Most researchers assume that the actual rates of sexual behavior are probably a bit higher than adolescents report, although it is always possible that some adolescents (i.e., boys) may be prone to overreporting their sexual activities. With that caveat in mind, here are the numbers.

Intercourse

According to data collected by the Centers for Disease Control and Prevention (CDC, 2013), 47% of all adolescents in high school in the United States have had sexual intercourse. This rate increases to 64% by the time they are in 12th grade. (By the early-adult age of 23, about 90% of the U.S. population has engaged in sexual intercourse.) The percentage of sexually active adolescents varies quite dramatically depending on the adolescents' gender, ethnicity, and region of the country. For example, in Alabama 50% of high school students reported having had intercourse, compared to 39% of the high school students in Alaska. Across all of the United States, African American youth were more likely to have had intercourse by 12th grade (77%) than were adolescents of other ethnic groups. Asian Americans were the least likely to have had intercourse (33%). Although African American and Hispanic males were more likely to report having had intercourse by 12th grade than were African American and Hispanic females, the percentage of White adolescent males and females who reported having had sexual intercourse by 12th grade was equal (61%). Tables 10.2 and 10.3 summarize the data on adolescents who have had sexual intercourse, and Figure 10.1 shows trends over time.

TABLE 10.2 **Percentage of High School Students Who Have Had Sexual Intercourse by Gender and Grade Level, 2013 Data**

	9th Grade	10th Grade	11th Grade	12th Grade	Total
Male	32	41	54	65	48
Female	28	42	54	63	46
Total	30	41	54	64	47

Source: Data from Centers for Disease Control and Prevention, 2013b.

TABLE 10.3 **Percentage of High School Students Who Have Had Sexual Intercourse by Race and Gender, All Grade Levels, 2013 Data**

	Asian	Black	Hispanic	White	Multiple Race
Male	24	68	52	42	48
Female	22	53	47	45	49
Total	23	61	49	44	49

Source: Data from Centers for Disease Control and Prevention, 2013b.

FIGURE 10.1

Percentage of High School Students Who Have Had Sexual Intercourse, 1991–2013

Source: Data from Centers for Disease Control and Prevention, 2013b.

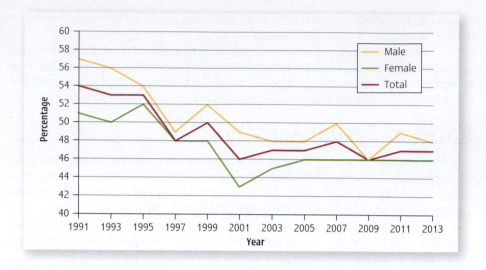

Among those teenagers who have had intercourse, the median age of first intercourse is 16.9 years for boys and 17.4 for girls (Kaiser Family Foundation, 2013). About 6% of all high school students report losing their virginity before the age of 13, ranging from a low of about 3% percent for Asian and White adolescents to a high of 14% for African American adolescents. Fifteen percent of American high school students (13% for females, 17% for males) report having had sex with four or more partners in their lifetimes (not at once), again with wide variation between the racial, age, and gender groups. For example, 49% of Black male high school seniors reported having had at least four sexual partners, compared with 30% of Hispanic males and 20% of White males. Predictably, the percentage of adolescents who have had multiple sexual partners increases as students move from 9th through 12th grade.

It is interesting to note that the percentage of adolescent females (ages 15 to 19) who reported *never* having had vaginal intercourse increased from 1995 to 2010 (Figure 10.2). Across all ethnic groups, there was a decrease of 16% over this time period. In 1995, 48.9% of girls and women between the ages of 15 and 19 reported that they had never had sexual intercourse. During the 2006–2010 time period, this percentage increased to 56.7% (CDC, 2012). This increase in the percentage of adolescent females who report never having had intercourse

FIGURE 10.2

Changes in Percentages of Self-Reported Virginity of Female Adolescents Ages 15–19, by Race, 1995–2010

Source: Data from Centers for Disease Control and Prevention, 2012.

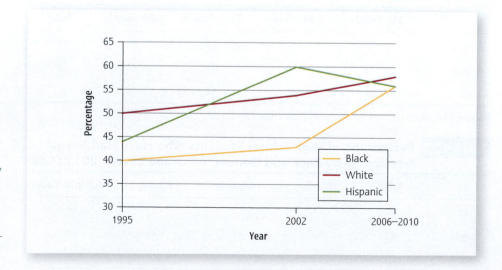

was significant across all ethnic groups, but was steepest for African American girls and women (a 34% drop) and Hispanics (a 29% decline). For males between the ages of 15 and 19, the increase in the percentage who had *never* had vaginal intercourse was even more dramatic. In 1995, 44.8% of this population reported that they had never had intercourse. By the 2006–2010 period, 58.2% of U.S. males between the ages of 15 and 19 said they had never had vaginal intercourse (Martinez & Abma, 2015).

Other Types of Sexual Activity

Of course, sexual intercourse is not the only, or usually the first, form of sexual behavior in which adolescents engage. Masturbation, kissing, **petting**, and **oral sex** are all frequent sexual behaviors for teenagers and early adolescents. Most U.S. boys begin masturbating by the time they are 13, and the practice is practically universal among U.S. boys by the time they reach 19 years of age (Robbins et al., 2011). And boys practice the activity often—five times per week, on average. Girls are less likely than boys to report that they masturbate, both in early adolescence and into early adulthood. Whereas 62% of boys in the 13 to 14 age range reported having masturbated, only 40% of girls in this age range said they had masturbated (Figure 10.3). By the early-adult period of 20 to 24 years old, these percentages were 83% for men and 64% for women. Those girls and young women who do report masturbating tend to engage in the practice less often than boys (Masters, Johnson, & Kolodny, 1994).

There are interesting ethnic differences in the progression of sexual behaviors from masturbation to intercourse. Whereas White adolescents tend to follow a pattern from masturbating to kissing to petting above the waist to then petting below the waist and then sexual intercourse and oral sex, African American teenagers often report moving through these stages more quickly, or skipping stages entirely. For many African American adolescents, their first sexual experience with a partner includes intercourse (Smith & Udry, 1985).

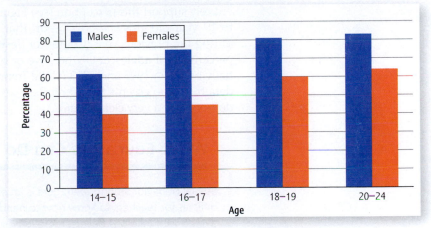

FIGURE 10.3

Percentage of Males and Females Who Report Having Masturbated, by Age Group

Source: Data from Center for Sexual Health Promotion, 2010.

Oral sex among adolescents is a topic that has received a considerable amount of attention in the media because of alleged changes in attitudes about its meaning. Specifically, there is a perception that adolescents have developed a much more cavalier attitude about oral sex, viewing it as a less serious form of sexual behavior than their parents did. Some media reports have suggested that adolescents no longer view oral sex as sex, perceiving it as more akin to kissing or petting (Stepp, 1999). Indeed, some research indicates that adolescents tend to view oral sex as less risky, both physically and emotionally; less likely to violate their own values; and more acceptable for people in their age group than is vaginal sex (Halpern-Felsher & Kropp, 2005). But research indicates that adolescent girls still regard oral sex as a serious form of sexual activity, with 50% viewing it as less serious than vaginal intercourse but 41% viewing it as just as intimate as vaginal intercourse, and 9% saying it is even more intimate (Malacad & Hess, 2010). Some have argued that the increasing emphasis on abstinence in sexual education courses has led to more teenagers having oral sex so that they can engage in sexual behavior while technically remaining a virgin. Research

FIGURE 10.4

Percentage of Adolescents and Early Adults Who Have Given or Received Oral Sex, by Gender And Age Group

Source: Data from Center for Sexual Health Promotion, 2010.

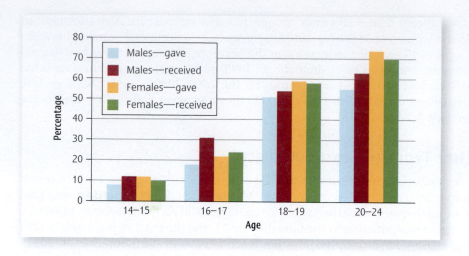

indicates that 14% adolescent girls and 15% of adolescent boys who have never had vaginal intercourse have engaged in oral sex with an opposite-sex partner (Child Trends, 2015). Most adolescents who have engaged in oral sex have also had vaginal intercourse.

Although the perception is that oral sex has become much more common among adolescents, especially girls performing **fellatio** on boys, the data do not entirely support this perception (see Figure 10.4). First, between 55 and 64% of 18- to 19-year-old girls *and* boys report that they have given and/or received oral sex during the previous year (Center for Sexual Health Promotion, 2010). Second, the percentage of adolescents who gave or received oral sex did not change substantially between 1995 and 2013 (Child Trends, 2015). As with much of the self-report data from adolescents regarding their sexual activity, these data regarding oral sex do not paint a very clear picture.

What Educators Can Do

Sexual behavior among teenagers is an extremely controversial topic, making it difficult for teachers to know how to handle the issue. Because sexuality is intertwined with religious beliefs, morality, issues of privacy, and health (both physical and emotional), many states and school districts have placed restrictions on the kinds of information that teachers and other school personnel can provide to students. Therefore, it is important for you to make yourself aware of the policies in your state and school regarding what you can and cannot say to students regarding sex. It is also important to realize that most adolescents become engaged in some sort of sexual activity, and this activity can be confusing, exhilarating, and risky for teens. By making yourself aware of the prevalence, effects, and risks of adolescent sexual activity, you can be better prepared to recognize the effects of this activity and provide appropriate counsel (or referral) if that is allowable where you work.

MyEdLab **Self-Check 10.1**

Romantic Relationships in Adolescence

Until the 1990s, adolescent romantic relationships generally revolved around the concept of dating. A couple would go on a first date, and if that went well they would go on more dates until they were either going steady or no longer dating.

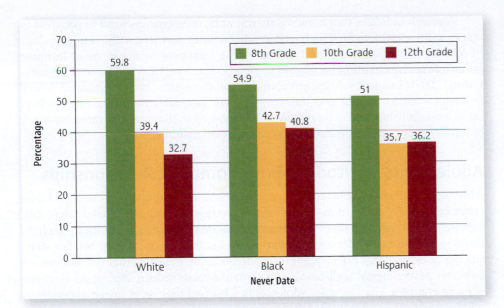

FIGURE 10.5

Percentage of 8th-, 10th-, and 12th-Grade Students Who Never Date, by Grade and Race/Hispanic Origin, 2012

Source: Child Trends' (2014) original analysis of the Monitoring the Future Survey, 1976 to 2013.

This clear beginning and ending of the relationship made it relatively easy to determine the duration of a romantic relationship for a particular adolescent. But in the last generation or so, one-on-one dating has become less prevalent among teenagers. From 1991 to 2012, the percentage of teenagers in grades 8, 10, and 12 who reported never having dated increased, and the percentage of adolescents who reported dating more than once per week decreased (Child Trends, 2014). As you would expect, the percentage of adolescents who have never dated declines as they get older, and the steepest decline is among White adolescents (from 60% in 8th grade to 33% in 12th grade; see Figure 10.5). Instead of one-on-one dating, a more informal form of romantic relationship has taken its place. Teenagers are more likely to talk about hanging out or **hooking up** with a romantic partner, and the relationship often begins as a friendship formed within a group of adolescents that later evolves into a romantic relationship. All of this has made it more difficult for researchers to determine the length of romantic relationships during adolescence (Furman & Hand, 2006; Sax, 2005).

Most teenagers report that they have been in a romantic relationship in the previous 18 months (Carver, Joyner, & Udry, 2003). Generally speaking, younger adolescents often have relatively short romantic relationships, lasting a few weeks or months for 15-year-olds. As adolescents get older, however, romantic relationships tend to last longer, with girls reporting a median length of 16 months, and boys reporting 12 months (Karney, Becket, Collins, & Shaw, 2007). In addition to having longer relationships as they get older, adolescents and young adults also report different values in their relationships. Whereas younger adolescents tend to focus more on physical attractiveness of their "crushes," older adolescents and young adults focus more on issues of intimacy, companionship, support, and shared goals as important qualities of romantic partners (Connolly & Goldberg, 1999; Connolly & Johnson, 1996). In addition, younger adolescents viewed dating behavior as a vehicle for gaining social status with peers, whereas young adults generally did not (Montgomery, 2005). Whatever the perceived purpose of dating, adolescent romantic relationships are often quite intimate, and high school students report spending more time interacting with their romantic partners than they do with parents or with friends (Laursen & Jensen-Campbell, 1999).

Research indicates that adolescents' romantic relationships tend to progress in stages, with social activities such as hanging out with partners within larger groups of friends, then spending time together alone, then proceeding to more intimate behaviors such as holding hands and kissing (O'Sullivan, Cheng, Harris, & Brooks-Gunn, 2007). In most adolescent romantic relationships, more advanced sexual behavior such as petting and intercourse occur last, after declaring one's self to be in a relationship, and is less likely to be engaged in than are the more innocent behaviors that represent earlier stages of the relationship.

Adolescents' Attitudes About Romantic Relationships

Although relatively brief by adult standards, romantic relationships during adolescence can involve quite intense emotions. Some research suggests that adolescents, especially girls, who become involved in romantic relationships are more likely to develop symptoms of depression than adolescents who are not in relationships (Joyner & Udry, 2000). Subsequent research, however, indicates that the association between psychological well-being and romantic relationships during adolescence is more complex. For example, adolescents who had their first sexual experiences within the context of a romantic relationship did not develop more depressive symptoms, but those who engaged in casual sex did (Grello, Welsh, Harper, & Dickson, 2003). In addition, researchers have found that certain qualities of romantic relationships (e.g., a lack of closeness or other problems) were associated with negative mood and depression, but simply being in a romantic relationship without these negative features was not (La Greca & Harrison, 2005; Williams, Connolly, & Segal, 2001). Experiencing a breakup is associated with depressive symptoms (Monroe, Rohde, Seeley, & Lewinsohn, 1999), but being in a steady relationship is actually associated with higher levels of self-esteem (Samet & Kelly, 1987). It appears that being in a romantic relationship exposes adolescents to both risk for negative mood (when there are problems or a breakup in the relationship) but also to opportunities for feelings of intimacy, closeness, and esteem.

The way that adolescents think about their sexual experiences and romantic relationships depends to a large extent on their gender and their age. Regarding their first experience with sexual intercourse, adolescent boys tend to view the experience more favorably than girls. Boys tend to view the experience as physically enjoyable (Ott, Ghani, McKenzie, Rosenberger, & Bell, 2012) and often report feelings of increased intimacy and closeness with their partners. Girls, in contrast, report a more mixed reaction to their first experience with sexual intercourse. Although many teenage girls say that the experience was physically pleasurable and led to increased feelings of closeness with their partners, they also are quite likely to report that they experienced physical pain and feelings of guilt, shame, and fear (Thompson, 1990; Zimmer-Gembeck & Helfand, 2008). Fears about pregnancy and contracting a sexually transmitted disease are higher among girls than boys. In addition, girls are acutely aware of the societal double standard regarding the sexuality of girls as compared with boys. Whereas boys are generally not viewed negatively for engaging in premarital sex, and are even encouraged to engage in such behaviors, girls are often viewed as morally flawed if they have premarital sex or multiple sexual partners (Crawford & Popp, 2003). This undoubtedly contributes to girls' more ambivalent views of their early sexual experience (Carpenter, 2002).

The "Hook-Up Culture"

A number of popular books and social commentators have noted that adolescents and early adults are increasingly moving away from committed relationships in favor of casual, noncommitted "hook-ups." Hooking up has no clear definition and can range from kissing to sexual intercourse. Whatever the specific sexual

MyEdLab
Video Example 10.1

Listen to these college students as they discuss their feelings about the "hook-up culture." Think about how it fits with the research about how sexual practices and attitudes have changed or stayed the same over the last few decades. Then, in the last part of the video, listen to the woman's advice about the importance of finding a husband at college and think about whether you agree or disagree with her opinion.

acts involved in a particular hook-up, most agree that hooking up involves casual sexual encounters with little commitment. Although casual sexual activity without long-term commitment has long horrified adults, it is difficult to argue that casual sexual encounters are new to the current generation of adolescents. Going back at least to the 1960s, and likely well before that, adolescents have engaged in sexual activity outside of committed romantic relationships. What has changed in recent years, according to some, is the prevalence of hooking up and the potential damage the "hook-up culture" is doing to the sexual attitudes of adolescents and early adults. In her popular book *Unhooked*, Laura Sessions Stepp (2007) argues that dating has been replaced by hooking up, and this change has hurt women the most because it has changed their ability to develop enduring and committed romantic relationships. In essence, she and others (e.g., Freitas, 2013) argue that this shift to the hook-up culture has changed the sex and dating scripts. Whereas men used to actively pursue women and women were the gatekeepers (i.e., the ones who said "no" when sexual progress was moving too fast), now women are expected to behave as men always have—sexually aggressive with few limits.

Does the claim that dating and courting have been replaced by casual "hook-ups" fit with your experience and observations of adolescents? If it is true, what are some of the implications of this change for adolescents' attitudes about sex and dating?

Does the research evidence support the perception that the hook-up culture has become pervasive in high schools and colleges? To date, most of the evidence on this topic is anecdotal and not longitudinal. In other words, most of the research has relied on the self-reports of small, unrepresentative samples and has not clearly defined the terms. For example, Paul and his colleagues (Paul & Hayes, 2002; Paul, McManus, & Hayes, 2000) studied the self-reported sexual behavior of students at a single college campus and found that roughly 4 in 5 men and women had hooked up at least once. In this study, about half of the men and one-third of the women said that they had engaged in sexual intercourse during a hook-up. In other words, they had had a **one-night stand**.

So has hooking up replaced dating? And are these casual sexual encounters any more common than they used to be? Or have we just given a new name to an old practice (i.e., the "one-night stand") and decided it was a harmful epidemic that is ruining adolescents' and young adults' abilities to form meaningful romantic relationships? Research using large, representative samples and examining trends across several years suggests that there have not been major changes in the sexual behaviors of college students in recent years (Monto & Carey, 2014). For example, college students who were studied between 2004 to 2012 did not report having sex more often, or having more sexual partners, than did college students studied from 1988 to 1996. Slightly more students from the 1988–1996 group (55%) reported having sex at least once a week and having more than one partner since turning 18 years old (67%) than did students in the 2004 to 2012 group (51% and 63% for these two questions, respectively). In addition, students in both eras—about 80% of them—agreed that sex outside of wedlock is acceptable. Although more recent college students were more likely to report that they have had sex with a friend (71% in the 2004–2012 group, 56% in the 1988–1996 group), the idea that the current hook-up culture has produced a group of college students who have sex more often and with more partners than their peers of yesteryear does not appear to be true.

Homosexuality

On June 26, 2015, the Supreme Court of the United States decided that state prohibitions on gay marriage were unconstitutional, making gay marriage legal throughout the country. Before this historic decision, several states had already legalized gay marriage, and there were other victories in the fight for equal rights for homosexuals,

In-Depth 10.1

It Gets Better

On September 19, 2010, Tyler Clementi was an 18-year-old freshman at Rutgers University. As many college students do, Tyler went to his dorm room that day to enjoy what he thought would be a private sexual encounter with a friend. What Tyler did not know was that his roommate and his roommate's friend had secretly set up a camera and were live-streaming Tyler's encounter via the Internet. In addition, Tyler's sexual encounter was with another man. Tyler was gay and had not "come out" yet, choosing to keep his sexual orientation hidden. Shortly after Tyler discovered that his encounter had been made public, along with his sexual orientation, Tyler posted a brief suicide note on his Facebook page and then jumped off a bridge to his death (Friedman, 2010).

Three weeks before Tyler Clementi's suicide, Dan Savage founded the It Gets Better Project. As a gay man and author of the syndicated column "Savage Love," an advice column about sex and sexuality, Dan Savage understood the difficulties that many gay, lesbian, transgender, and bisexual youth experience. Gender-minority adolescents and young adults are more likely to be bullied, harassed, and assaulted than are straight adolescents. As the It Gets Better Project (2015) website states, many LGBT youth cannot imagine themselves as adults who are openly gay. They fear for their safety; fear being rejected by family, friends, and society; and often struggle with feelings of shame about their sexuality. The purpose of the It Gets Better Project is to support LGBT youth, partly by posting videos of openly gay adults who can speak from experience about some of the difficulties they faced as adolescents, and how they have found love, acceptance, and happiness as adults. To date, thousands of the website's users have uploaded videos, including many celebrities. To learn more about the project and view some of the videos, you can visit the website at http://www.itgetsbetter.org/.

such as the elimination of the **"Don't Ask, Don't Tell"** policy in the military. Despite these recent advances for gay rights, gay, lesbian, bisexual, and transgender youth and adults still face a tremendous amount of **homophobia**, social stigma and discrimination, both in the United States and in other countries. (See In-Depth 10.1 on the It Gets Better Project.) According to Rich Savin-Williams (2010), a leading researcher of adolescent sexuality and sexual preference, the percentage of adolescents who are gay is almost impossible to determine because of the differences that researchers, and adolescents themselves, have in their definitions of gay. If a teenager has one same-sex experience, is he gay? If an adolescent tends to engage in sexual activities with boys but prefers girls, is she homosexual or heterosexual? As a result, estimates of the percentage of adolescents who are gay range from 1% to 25%. Ultimately, Savin-Williams questions whether it even matters what the actual number is. Given the experiences of gay, lesbian, and bisexual youth, even if the percentage of adolescents who are gay is small, the consequences are large and should be addressed. It is also important to note that not all adolescents fit nicely into the two categories of gay and straight. In recent years, there has been increasing recognition that some adolescents are **bisexual**, **transsexual**, **pansexual**, **transgender**, **queer**, or in the processes of trying to figure out what their **sexual orientation** is (i.e., **questioning**). The familiar **LGBT** acronym has expanded to the more inclusive LGBTQ or **LGBTQI** (lesbian, gay, bisexual, and trans; *trans* refers to transgender, transsexual, and transvestite) acronyms. Some celebrities, most notably Caitlyn Jenner and Laverne Cox from the television show *Orange Is the New Black*, have raised public awareness of the transgender and transsexual communities.

Gay, lesbian, bisexual, and trans youths in the United States experience a number of difficult situations that can make adolescence, already an awkward and difficult period of development for many, even more difficult. For example, one of the most difficult decisions for gay, bisexual, and trans adolescents (and adults) is whether to "come out" (i.e., declare their sexual orientation) to others, including family and friends. This decision is a dilemma because there are dangers and difficulties associated with either decision. Those who choose to keep their sexual orientation secret often feel that they are living dishonestly, hiding an important aspect of their identity from loved ones. In addition, they often must take extreme measures to maintain the secret, such as meeting boyfriends or girlfriends in secret and lying about their whereabouts and behaviors. On the other hand, adolescents who choose to reveal their sexual orientation to others run the risk of alienating family and friends who may disapprove of, or having difficulty relating to, homosexuality and homosexuals. Therefore, this decision is a major stressor for many gay, lesbian, bisexual, and trans adolescents.

It appears that LGBT youth have reason to fear revealing their sexual orientation. This population is more likely than straight adolescents to be bullied and harassed at school (Nationwide Children's Hospital, 2010). In addition, gay, lesbian, and bisexual adolescents are 40% more likely than heterosexual youths to be punished, both in school and in the court system (Himmelstein & Brückner, 2010). They are more likely to be expelled from school, stopped by police, arrested, and convicted. Although gay, lesbian, and bisexual youths are actually less likely to engage in violent behavior, they are more likely to be punished for it.

Given the difficulties many LGBT youths face, it is perhaps not surprising that they experience psychological and behavioral troubles more often than heterosexual youth. LGBT adolescents are more prone to depression and are more likely to think about, attempt, and commit suicide (Cochran, 2001; Savin-Williams, 1994, 2009). Interestingly, it does not appear that homosexual behavior is the key risk factor for psychological distress. Rather, it is self-identification as homosexual that is associated with depression and suicide attempts. Some research has revealed that gay and lesbian adolescent youth are more prone to delinquency and drug abuse than are heterosexual youth (Lanza, Cooper, & Bray, 2014). Although this evidence suggests that the stressors associated with being a homosexual teenager in the United States lead many to engage in delinquent or self-destructive behavior, other research indicates that the majority of this behavior is committed by a relatively small subgroup of gay and lesbian adolescents and that most LGBT youth are psychologically healthy and not especially prone to engaging in delinquent behavior (Savin-Williams, 2010).

> Think about how you might react to a student who "came out" to you and asked for your advice about whether he or she should be open about his or her sexual orientation with parents and peers. How would you advise this student? Similarly, what would you do if a student in your class used a homophobic slur during a class discussion?

MyEdLab
Video Example 10.2

This is one of over 50,000 user-created videos from the It Gets Better Project. In this video, two gay men talk openly about the difficulty they had coming out and being open about their sexuality and provide words of encouragement to others who are struggling with the challenges of being LGBT.

What Educators Can Do

Romantic relationships become a central concern for many adolescents, and the consequences of these relationships—physical, social, and emotional—are often brought to the attention of teachers. There is some evidence that teenagers who begin dating and having sex at an early age, especially girls, have lower levels of academic achievement than those who delay dating and sexual activity (Pawlby, Mills, & Quinton, 1997). (It is important to remember that correlations between two variables such as early dating and lower achievement do not necessarily mean that dating causes lower achievement.) There are also many indicators of adolescent sexuality and romantic relationships—from flirting to distress over a breakup to sexual harassment—that you, as a teacher, are likely to witness. So what can, and should, you do about any of this?

As mentioned, your ability to discuss issues of sexuality and romantic relationships with your students will depend on the policies of the schools and states in which you work. Similarly, there may be policies and laws that require you to report evidence of sexual harassment or dating violence that you witness. Therefore, it is important to make yourself aware of the policies and laws in your state and school regarding these issues. It is also important for you to be aware of the importance of dating and romantic relationships in the lives of adolescent students, and how these may affect their mood, behavior, and achievement in your classroom. Learn about the resources available in your school and community to help students handle the emotional and physical challenges and risks associated with sexual behavior and romantic relationships so that you can, if allowed by law and school policy, steer students toward these resources.

LGBTQ adolescents are more likely to be bullied and sexually harassed, more likely to attempt suicide, and more likely to be depressed than their straight peers. Entry into the world of sex and dating is confusing for just about every adolescent. For LGBTQ youth who must also confront peers, family, and a society that may disapprove of their sexuality, the general angst of adolescent sexuality is compounded. To help LGBTQ adolescents survive this tumultuous period, educators can follow these strategies:

- Create a safe space for adolescents of all sexual orientations, especially LGBTQ youths, in the school and classroom. This can be done by letting students know that you are open to talking with them and by discouraging sexual harassment and bullying in the classroom and school.

- Encourage LGBTQ youths to take a longer-term view of their lives and to realize that the difficulties of adolescence often subside as they enter the more mature world of adulthood (see the In-Depth 10.1 discussion of the It Gets Better Project).

- Steer LGBTQ youths toward resources such as the Trevor Project (http://www.thetrevorproject.org/) and the It Gets Better Project (http://www.itgetsbetter.org/) that offer support to LGBTQ adolescents as they struggle through issues related to their sexual orientation.

- Educate yourself about the issues that LGBTQ adolescents face, and how you, as an educator, can help your students understand and navigate the challenges that LGBTQ students face. One resource for information and ideas is the Gay, Lesbian, and Straight Education Network (GLSEN; https://www.glsen.org/).

MyEdLab **Self-Check 10.2**

Where Adolescents Get Their Information About Sex

Imagine the following class discussion during a 10th-grade biology lesson:

During a lesson on genetics and inheritable disease in Mr. Wilson's class, some students spontaneously begin discussing sexually transmitted diseases.

"I heard that you can only get AIDS if you're a gay man," Lisa says. "I'm neither so I don't need to worry about that."

"That's not true," counters William. "Anybody can get AIDS, but only if they have anal sex. So just avoid that and you'll be all right."

"You're both wrong," Elaine says. "You can get AIDS from any kind of sex, so you should always use a condom. Except if it's your first time having sex—then you're safe. You can't catch anything, or even get pregnant, the first time. That's what my older sister told me, and she should know."

Because most adolescents engage in sexual activity by the time they finish high school, it is important to understand where they get their information about sex and to ensure that the information they receive is accurate. For decades, research has consistently revealed that there are four primary sources that teenagers use to gain information about sex: parents, friends, school, and the media (e.g., movies, television, Internet). Although the primary source of information shifts among these four groups periodically (Brown, 2008), these have remained the top-four sources of information since at least 1974. In one study, 42% of youth said they received information about sex from their doctors, a percentage that is below those for the four major sources, which tend to be in the 55% to 75% range. Adolescents also report receiving information about sex from their grandparents and churches, but these percentages were substantially lower (in the 12 to 14% range).

Adolescents have reported that their preferred sources for information about sex are parents, then peers and school sources (Somers & Surmann, 2004). In addition, adolescents reported having clearer personal values about sex when they received information from parents rather than from peers or the media (Somers & Surmann, 2005). But adolescents often turn to their peers for advice and information about sex because there is less risk of shame and punishment than there might be when discussing sex with parents. Many parents disapprove of any sexual behavior that their teenage children may want to engage in, so their advice is often to abstain from sex. Although this may be sound advice, it is clear that most adolescents do not follow it all the way through high school, so teenagers are often in need of practical information about pregnancy, sexually transmitted diseases, and safer-sex practices. Unfortunately, teenagers are often woefully uninformed or misinformed about these issues, leading them to give bad information and advice to their friends. Adolescents often tell each other that they cannot get pregnant the first time they have sex, that sexually transmitted diseases (STDs) cannot be transmitted via oral sex, and that taking a bath or shower immediately after intercourse prevents pregnancy.

Peers are not the only unreliable sources of information about sex. Parents are also frequently misinformed about issues, such as the efficacy of various forms of contraception, and 2 out of every 3 male teens and 80% of female teens in the United States talk with their parents about at least some aspect of sexual behavior (e.g., birth control methods, how to use a condom, how to say no to sex, etc.; Martinez, Abma & Casey, 2010). Although it is encouraging news that most adolescents talk with their parents about sex, unfortunately parents often do not have all of their facts straight. In one study, fewer than half of the parents believed that frequent use of condoms effectively guarded against STDs or pregnancy (Eisenberg, Bearinger, Sieving, Swain, & Resnick, 2004). Similarly, many parents do not realize how effective oral contraceptives are at preventing pregnancy. The Internet, another frequent source of information about sex for teens, is also somewhat unreliable. In a study of 177 health-related websites examined by Buhi et al., 46% that focused on **contraception** included false information. In addition, more than one-third of the sites with information about abortion included misinformation (Buhi et al., 2010).

Because American adolescents often are sexually active, and because teenagers often receive misinformation about sex from their friends or fail to discuss sex with a knowledgeable adult, rates of teenage pregnancy and STDs in the United States are among the highest in the industrialized world (Darroch, Frost, Singh, & the Study Team, 2001; McKay & Barrett, 2010,). Some have also argued that adolescents in the United States are more likely than youth in other countries to have unprotected sex because of the mixed messages that U.S. teenagers receive

MyEdLab
Video Example 10.3
Josh says there's no peer pressure to have a girlfriend, but he also says that some classmates brag or lie about having a sexual relationship. Think about how this kind of bragging can affect what adolescents think is normal sexual behavior.

Suppose that one of your students told you that her friend had given her some information about sex that was clearly false (e.g., "Girls cannot become pregnant the first time they have sex," or "Oral sex is safe because saliva kills all STDs"). The student asks you whether this information is correct. How would you handle this situation?

about sex. On the one hand, popular media is saturated with images and depictions of sex and sexuality. On the other hand, the United States is a highly religious country (compared to most Western European countries, for example), and there are moral taboos against premarital or recreational sex. Therefore, many U.S. teens develop **ambivalent attitudes** about sex, and often engage in sex without much planning (Crockett, Raffaelli, & Moilanen, 2002).

To combat the scourge of unplanned teenage pregnancies and the spread of STDs such as HIV/AIDS, many schools have adopted sex education programs. Of course, the content of these programs varies dramatically, with some focusing exclusively on the virtues of sexual abstinence (abstinence-only programs) and others taking a more comprehensive approach (comprehensive sex education). These more comprehensive programs include information about sexual development, contraception, teenage pregnancy, and abstinence. Both programs have generated an enormous amount of controversy. Critics of comprehensive sex education argue that teaching adolescents about contraception, and even making it easily available to them, encourages teens to engage in sexual activity. On the other hand, critics of abstinence-only education note that teenagers already engage in sexual activity, so it is important to provide them with accurate information they can use to protect themselves from unwanted pregnancies and STDs.

During the presidential administration of George W. Bush (2000–2008), the federal government provided money to support abstinence-only education programs in schools, but not comprehensive sex education programs. This led to an increase in the number of schools offering abstinence-only education programs that prohibit any discussion of contraception, except for failure rates for condoms. In a nationwide study of school superintendents, 35% reported having abstinence-only education programs in place, compared with 14% who reported utilizing truly comprehensive sex education (Collins, Alagiri, Summers, & Morin, 2002). These percentages seem to be at odds with what most Americans want. A poll on the beliefs of Americans regarding what topics should be discussed in sex education courses in schools found that only 15% of Americans favored teaching abstinence only; indeed, the majority of Americans believe schools should teach adolescents a wide variety of topics about sex, ranging from the value of abstinence to how to obtain and use contraception (National Public Radio/Kaiser Family Foundation/ Kennedy School of Government, 2004; see Table 10.4).

MyEdLab

Video Example 10.4

As this science teacher introduces a demonstration on how the HIV virus is transmitted, notice how he describes the benefits of abstinence and think about how this is related to research on effective sex education programs.

TABLE 10.4   **Percentage of Americans Who Endorse Coverage of Various Topics in School-Based Sex Education and When They Should be Covered**

Topic	Middle School	High School	Both	Total
STDs	9	15	75	99
How babies are made	14	13	69	97
Birth control	8	29	57	94
Abstinence until marriage	8	13	72	93
How to obtain and use contraception	5	37	44	86
Abortion	5	30	50	85
Homosexuality and sexual orientation	5	24	44	73
How to put on a condom	5	38	40	83

Source: Data from National Public Radio/Kaiser Family Foundation/Kennedy School of Government, 2013.

Recent research suggests that this may have been unwise policy, as students in abstinence-only programs were no more likely to delay initiation of sexual activity, to abstain from sex altogether, or to have fewer sexual partners than were other students. In contrast, students in comprehensive sexual education programs were likely to alter their sexual behavior as a result of these programs. For example, 40% of students in these programs delayed sexual initiation, had fewer sexual partners, and were more likely to use condoms and other contraception when engaging in sex. In addition, 30% of students in comprehensive sexual education programs reduced the frequency of their sexual activity, and 60% reduced their rates of engaging in unprotected sex (Boonstra, 2010). In contrast, there is little evidence that adolescents in abstinence-only education programs delay sexual activity. There is, however, evidence that participation in abstinence-only education programs is associated with a lower rate of contraception use when adolescents do engage in sexual activity.

MyEdLab **Self-Check 10.3**

Problems Associated with Adolescent Sexual Behavior

Although sexual activity is a source of physical pleasure and social bonding for many adolescents, there are also a number of problems associated with sex. These problems range from teenage pregnancy and the spread of STDs to unwanted sexual behavior, such as sexual harassment and assault. In this section we consider some of these problems.

Pregnancy

As mentioned earlier, the United States has one of the highest rates of teenage pregnancy in the industrialized world. As of 2010, about 6% of all female teenagers in the United States between the ages of 15 and 19 get pregnant at some point. That is a rate of about 57.4 out of every 1000 U.S. women in this age group. The pregnancy rate was about three times higher for girls in the 18 to 19 age group compared to girls in the 15 to 17 age group. Among African American and Latina girls and women, the rate is roughly 126.5 women per 1000; for White girls and women in this age group, the rate is 44 per 1000, or 4.4%. Teenage pregnancy rates also differ by region of the country, with adolescents in the South and Southwest much more likely to become pregnant than are girls in the Northeast portion of the United States (Kost & Henshaw, 2014).

The pregnancy rates for adolescent girls and early adults (ages 20 to 24) in the United States increased steadily from the early 1970s to the early 1990s, rising 21% among teenage girls and 17% among early adults (Kost & Henshaw, 2014). This increase in pregnancy rates was most likely due to a combination of more liberal attitudes about sexual behavior (i.e., the so-called sexual revolution of the late 1960s and early 1970s) and the legalization of abortion in 1973. Evidence of the link between abortion and pregnancy rates is readily available, as abortion rates increased during the 1970s and 1980s, right alongside pregnancy rates, but live birth rates remained stable from the 1970s through the 1980s (see Figure 10.6).

Between 1990 and 2010, the rates of both pregnancy and abortion for adolescents and early adults declined substantially, reaching 30-year lows in 2010. In 2006, adolescents between the ages of 15 and 19 accounted for 16.5% of all abortions performed in the United States (Pazol et al., 2009). Interestingly, the rates of live births for these age groups also declined during this period, indicating that the decline in abortions was probably not due to a greater number of adolescents and young adults deciding to avoid abortion by keeping their babies or giving them up for adoption (Martin, Hamilton, & Ventura, 2013; see Figure 10.7). Instead, it

FIGURE 10.6

Adolescent Pregnancy Rate, Birth Rate, and Abortion Rate, 1970–2010

Source: Guttmacher Institute, 2014.

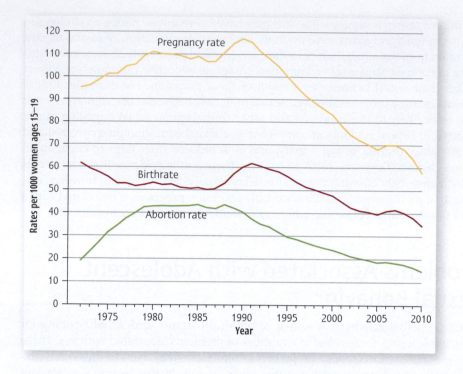

appears that teenagers and young adults were simply becoming pregnant less often between 1990 and 2010 than they did between the mid-1970s and 1990. There are only two known ways of reducing pregnancy: reduced rates of sexual activity and increased rates of contraception use. It appears that virtually all of the decrease in pregnancy among young women aged 18 to 19 was due to increased contraception use. For teenage girls between the ages of 15 and 17, about 25% of the decrease in pregnancy rates was caused by lower rates of sexual activity (i.e., abstinence), and 75% was attributable to greater use of contraception (Kost & Henshaw, 2014).

For the first time in about 15 years, 2006 brought an overall increase in the rates of pregnancy, live births, and abortion for adolescent girls in the United States. Definitive explanations for this increase are difficult to come by, but the changing demographics

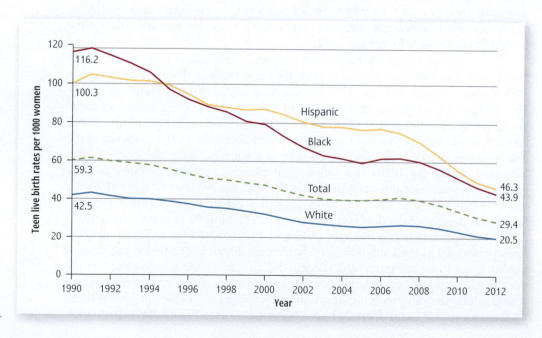

FIGURE 10.7

Trends in Live Birth Rates to Teens of Different Ethnicities, 1990–2012

Source: Martin et al., 2013.

of the adolescent population (i.e., more Latinos who, as a group, have higher teenage pregnancy rates than Whites) and changes in the sexual education programs to which adolescents are exposed (i.e., more abstinence-only education) have been mentioned as contributing factors (Kost & Henshaw, 2014). Whatever the cause, the trend seems to have reversed again in recent years. The most recent data, from 2012, indicate that the birth rate for 15- to 19-year-old females in the United States reached its lowest level on record, at 29.4 live births per 1000 females in this age group. The decline in the birth rate was true for all age groups, including young teens, older teens, and young adults, and cut across all ethnic groups as well (Martin et al., 2013).

Sexually Transmitted Diseases

Another unwelcome side effect of sexual activity is **sexually transmitted diseases (STDs)**. Approximately 4 million adolescents contract an STD each year, and 1 in 4 sexually active adolescents females have at least one STD (CDC, 2015a). According to a 2014 survey conducted by the CDC, the infection rates for **chlamydia**, **gonorrhea**, **syphilis**, and **HIV/AIDS** vary considerably depending on the age and gender of the person. Among 15- to 19-year-olds, for example, approximately 718 of every 100,000 males has chlamydia, compared with 2,941 of every 100,000 females. Whereas syphilis is almost nonexistent among the adolescent and early-adult populations in the United States, and the rate of gonorrhea infections has declined to its lowest level since the CDC began tracking the disease in 1941 (except for a slight increase in recent years for men aged 20 to 24), the rate of AIDS diagnoses has increased for both adolescents (ages 15 to 19) and early adults (ages 20 to 24) (CDC, 2015b). Table 10.5 presents information about the various types of STDs, their effects, and their frequency of occurrence in adolescent and early-adult populations.

TABLE 10.5 **Sexually Transmitted Diseases, Their Effects, and Their Rates of Incidence Among Adolescents and Early Adults**

Disease	Effects of the Disease	Incidence Rates
Chlamydia	If untreated by antibiotics, can cause damage to the urethra in males, infertility in females.	In 2014, 718 males and 2,941 females per 100,000 between the ages of 15 and 19 were reported.[a]
Gonorrhea	If untreated by antibiotics, can cause pelvic inflammatory disease and infertility in females, painful discharge in males.	In 2014, 221 males and 431 females per 100,000 between the ages of 15 and 19 were reported.[a]
Syphilis	If untreated by antibiotics, can cause death.	In 2014, 7 males and 2.5 females per 100,000 between the ages of 15 and19 were reported.[a]
Human papillomavirus (HPV)	In men, genital warts can develop on the penis and develop into penile cancer. In women, genital warts can develop into cervical cancer.	There are dozens of varieties of HPV, so estimates of prevalence are difficult to find. Estimate of 26.8% infection rate among women aged 14–59, with highest rates in the 20–24 age group.[b]
HIV/AIDS	Causes deficiency of the immune system, creating susceptibility to many illnesses and death.	Estimated 9,961 new cases of diagnosed HIV/AIDS diagnoses for 13- to 24-year-olds in the United States in 2013. Infection rate is much higher than diagnosis rate.[c]
Genital herpes	Causes periodic outbreaks of painful blisters on or around the genitals. Linked to meningitis.	Estimate of 640,000 new infections each year among 15- to 24-year-olds in United States. Estimate of 11% of this age group infected with genital herpes.[d]

[a]Centers for Disease Control and Prevention, 2014.
[b]Dunne et al., 2007.
[c]Centers for Disease Control and Prevention, 2015.
[d]Weinstock, Berman, and Cates, 2004.

In an effort to reduce the spread of HIV/AIDS, the American Psychological Association (APA) adopted a resolution in 2005 urging the Congress of the United States to provide funding for effective, comprehensive sex education programs. The resolution cited evidence that more than half of all HIV infections occur during adolescence and early adulthood (Rosenberg, Biggar, & Goedert, 1994), and that HIV infections during adolescence occur disproportionately among females and adolescents of color (National Center for Health Statistics, 2001). Because research has documented that adolescents who participate in **abstinence-only sex education** programs or take "**virginity pledges**" (i.e., vow to remain virgins until marriage) are not less likely to engage in sexual activity but are less likely to use condoms when they do have sex (Bearman & Bruckner, 2001, 2004; Kirby, Korpi, Barth, & Cagampang, 1997), the APA resolution recommends that schools and communities use **comprehensive sex education** programs that have been proven effective at informing adolescents about safer-sex practices and increasing condom use among sexually active teens (Kirby, 2001; O'Donnell et al., 2002). Comprehensive sex education programs discuss the benefits of abstinence and of delaying the onset of sexual activity while also providing information about contraception, STDs, and safer-sex practices.

Failure to Use Contraception

Given the shortcomings in adolescents' abilities to think through the future consequences and ramifications of their actions (see Chapters 2 and 3), it is probably not surprising that many teenagers fail to use contraception during sexual activity. The sense of invincibility that accompanies the **personal fable** that adolescents develop often causes teenagers to engage in a number of risky behaviors, and unprotected sex is one such behavior.

Almost all (98%) sexually active adolescents between the ages of 15 and 19 report having used some form of contraception at least once. Condoms (92%) and "**the pill**" (68%) are the two most commonly used forms of birth control. But when asked about what form of contraception they used the last time they engaged in sexual intercourse, 17.9% of females between the ages of 15 and 19 reported using no birth control (CDC, 2012). Given the pressure adolescents are under to be responsible, it is quite likely that adolescents are overreporting their actual use of contraceptives, so the percentage of adolescents who did not use any form of birth control the last time they had sex is probably quite a bit higher than reported. Even with the social desirability of responses indicating contraceptive use, only 25% of adolescents reported using a condom the last time they engaged in sexual intercourse.

There are several possible explanations regarding why adolescents fail to use contraception, especially condoms, more consistently. First, as already mentioned, adolescents are often not as planful as adults. Purchasing condoms and having them on hand when the moment arrives requires thinking ahead, both in terms of anticipating sexual activity will happen and thinking about the longer-term consequences of sexual activity. But the anticipation of sexual activity has at least two complications for adolescents. One, teenagers tend to have sex irregularly. They may have sex with a partner once or twice and then go several months, or years, without having sex again. Almost two-thirds of the adolescents in the CDC (2012) survey said they had not had any sexual intercourse during the 3 months prior to the survey. Sexual activity during adolescence is often not planned. Romantic relationships are often short lived, and sexual intercourse may not occur until soon before the relationship ends. It is difficult to plan for sexual activity if you have little idea when you will again engage in sexual activity. Two, as mentioned earlier, adolescents' ambivalent attitudes about sex, due in part to mixed messages from society about the appropriateness of sexual activity, may also contribute to the lack of preparation many adolescents have for engaging in sex.

A second reason that many sexually active adolescents do not use condoms, the most effective method (besides abstinence) for curbing the transmission of STDs, is that they reduce pleasure. In a study of sexually active teens at high risk for pregnancy and the transmission of STDs, Brown and his colleagues (2008) found that nearly two-thirds of the 1410 adolescents in their sample did not use a condom during their last sexual encounter. In addition, this sample reported an average of 15.5 unprotected sexual encounters during the last 90 days. The adolescents in the study said that reduction of sexual pleasure, the insistence of partners, and the lack of discussion about condoms with partners were the three main reasons that they did not use condoms. These results suggest the importance of helping adolescents learn how to have discussions with their sexual partners about the importance of using condoms.

Another reason that some adolescents do not use contraception is that they have more fears and misgivings about the contraception itself than they do about the consequences of not using contraceptives (i.e., creating a baby). For example, in one study of African American and Latino youth, Aarons and Jenkins (2002) found that adolescents were often afraid of the side effects of hormonal contraceptives such as the pill, and therefore avoided using them. Moreover, only about half of the participants in this study viewed teenage pregnancy as having undesirable consequences. For some adolescents, it appears that ambivalent attitudes about pregnancy and fears about the health effects of some contraceptives contribute to their lack of use.

Sexual Harassment

Sexual harassment is defined as unwelcome sexual advances, requests for sexual favors, and other verbal or physical contact of a sexual nature. Such harassment is often severe enough, or persistent enough, to interfere with a student's right to receive an equal educational opportunity that is afforded by law. It is a serious problem and one that is remarkably widespread. It often begins quite early, with 38% of girls reporting that they were first sexually harassed in the sixth grade (American Association of University Women [AAUW], 1993). More recent studies by the AAUW report that 83% of girls and 78% of boys in grades 8 through 11 report having been sexually harassed. Most sexual harassment occurs between students (i.e., with a student perpetrator and a student victim), but 38% of the students who reported being harassed said that they had been victimized by teachers or other school staff.

Sexual harassment can range from unwanted verbal or nonverbal taunts or gestures (e.g., whistles, lewd gestures) to physical violence such as groping or forced sexual contact. Perhaps the most prevalent form of sexual harassment among middle schoolers is targeting one's sexual orientation or behaviors. For example, in middle school adolescents often use homophobic slurs or spread rumors that someone is gay or lesbian (Espelage & Stein, 2007). Spreading rumors about one's sexual orientation or using homophobic slurs is not limited to middle school students, however (e.g., Chiodo, Woolfe, Crooks, Hughes, & Jaffe, 2009). This kind of harassment has become much easier, and potentially more damaging, with the growth of the Internet and social media (see In-Depth 10.2).

Research suggests that boys are more likely than girls to be the perpetrators of sexual harassment. African American girls are more likely to be harassed by their peers than are Latina or White girls. For boys, the perpetration rates were similar for African American and White boys, but lower for Latino boys (AAUW, 1993). The contextual factors that predict sexual harassment and violence are not well

MyEdLab
Video Example 10.5

In this brief video, students discuss the difficulties they've experienced from sexual harassment and information is provided about what constitutes sexual harassment, why it often goes unreported, and why perpetrators engage in sexual harassment.

In-Depth 10.2

Sex and Dating in the Internet Age

Digital technologies such as the Internet and camera-equipped cell phones have added a new and complicating wrinkle to the world of adolescent dating and sexual behavior. Before the 1990s, it took a bit more effort to smear a person's reputation with accusations of various sexual exploits. Today, any teenager with a cell phone can publish pictures and videos of their ex-boyfriends or ex-girlfriends on the Internet for all to see. Similarly, adolescents' exposure to pornography used to be restricted to stealing whatever old issues of *Playboy* their fathers left lying around. Today, a kid with an iPhone or other Internet-enabled phone can instantly access hard-core pornography for free. It is a different world.

One technology-enabled behavior that has received a lot of media attention is the practice of "sexting." This involves sending pictures of one's own sexual body parts (e.g., breasts, genitalia) to a love interest. There is no consensus about the definition of sexting, but it can include sending picture texts via cell phone, posting pictures to online social media sites such as Facebook or Instagram, and sending pictures via e-mail. Students have been suspended from school for sexting, and a number of laws have been proposed to curb the practice. Indeed, when sexting involves sending or receiving nude or seminude photographs of minors (i.e., anyone under 18 years old), the activity may constitute distribution of child pornography and be considered illegal. This may even apply to teenagers who send naked pictures of themselves to boyfriends and girlfriends. Although reports of the prevalence of sexting have been as high as 50% of sexually active teens, these reports often use flawed methodologies, such as including adults in the sample or not clearly defining what was meant by sexting (Lounsbury, Mitchel, & Finkelhor, 2011). If adolescents were asked specifically about sending nude or semi-nude pictures of *themselves* to others, the actual percentage of teenagers who engaged in sexting would probably be much lower. For example, in a study of teenagers between the ages of 12 and 17, the Pew Internet and American Life Project found that only 4% of teens sent sexually revealing pictures of themselves and only 15% received such pictures,

often forwarded from friends who were the original targeted recipients of the "sext" (Lenhart, Ling, Campbell, & Purcell, 2010).

The Internet has also opened the door for more dangerous sexuality-related activities. Because social networking sites allow strangers to interact in an anonymous forum, sexual predators have a new way of gaining access to adolescents. These predators often search the Internet for adolescents who have posted information about themselves online. A predator then initiates contact with the adolescent, often posing as someone with good intentions and as someone who is closer to the adolescent's age. The Internet allows a 50-year-old pedophile to present himself as a friendly 17-year-old, complete with fake pictures of himself. The adolescent is often fooled and, after getting to know each other through an exchange of e-mails or instant chat messages, agrees to meet the predator. In addition, research suggests that many adults soliciting sex from adolescents online do not try to hide their age or intentions, and a fair number of adolescents agree to meet them anyway. Reliable statistics about the prevalence of the online sexual solicitation of adolescents are difficult to come by. A study by Wolak, Finkelhor, and Mitchell (2005) put the number at 17%, but in a subsequent article the authors noted that the 1-in-7 statistic did not apply only to overt sexual solicitations from sexual predators. The statistic referred to any unwanted sexual contact online, including the occasional rude comment (e.g., "What is your bra size?"; Wolak, Finkelhor, Mitchell, & Ybarra, 2008). In addition, they found that about 4% of the participants in their study received aggressive sexual solicitations online, and 4% were upset by an online sexual solicitation. Only two of the participants were actually sexually victimized by someone they had met online.

Although the prevalence of dangerous or illegal sexual activity using digital media, such as aggressive online sexual solicitations or underage sexting, may be less common than is portrayed by the media, it is certainly a relatively new development with potentially deleterious consequences for those who engage in it. As adolescents' access to graphic sexual images increases, one has to wonder how this will affect their attitudes about themselves and others as sexual beings. Will teenage boys, the overwhelming consumers of online pornography, increasingly come to view women as sexual objects? Will adolescent girls feel pressure to become ever-more sexualized as society becomes desensitized to graphic sexual images available on the Internet? These questions deserve attention, from both the research and educational communities, in the years to come.

understood, but some evidence suggests that adolescents who have witnessed violence, particularly of a sexual nature, at home are more likely to perpetrate sexual violence at school (Espelage & Holt, 2012). Factors at school also appear to affect the rates of sexual harassment. The AAUW study conducted in 1993 found that sexual harassment at school often occurs in public places, with many witnesses. Victims of sexual harassment reported that they wanted to talk to someone about their experiences but had difficulty obtaining help from school staff. Moreover, more than one-third of participants in the AAUW study said that sexual harassment was just an accepted and normal part of school.

Whatever the causes of sexual harassment may be, the consequences can be quite severe. In a study comparing the rates and consequences of bullying and sexual harassment, Gruber and Fineran (2008) found that although bullying was more common among middle and high school students, sexual harassment had more negative effects on health. Gays, lesbians, and bisexuals were subjected to more bullying and sexual harassment than were other students. Although both bullying and sexual harassment had negative effects on health, sexual harassment was more strongly associated with lowered self-esteem, poorer physical and mental health, and more symptoms of trauma. These effects were especially prevalent for girls and for gay and lesbian adolescents.

What Educators Can Do

The research on sexual harassment in schools has clear implications for teachers and school administrators. First and foremost, educators need to be vigilant about witnessing sexual harassment, especially as it is perpetrated on girls and sexual minorities. Second, when they witness it, teachers and school staff need to intervene. Although hearing adolescents hurl homophobic slurs at one another or catcalls at girls may seem like normal teen behavior, teachers and administrators need to make it clear to students that sexual harassment is not acceptable, even when it is of a verbal nature. Third, teachers and school staff need to solicit from students stories of their experience of sexual harassment at school. Research shows that harassment is common but that adolescents do not feel like their complaints are taken seriously, so they often do not report it. Attempts to make the reporting of sexual harassment as simple as possible should be adopted in schools. Just as schools have taken bullying more seriously in recent years, so too must they crack down on sexual harassment.

Dating Aggression

Romantic relationships in adolescence and emerging adulthood may not share the same levels of commitment and dependence as adult relationships, but they do share many other characteristics. Just as adult relationships sometimes involve physical and emotional abuse, so do the relationships of teenagers and early adults. The numbers of adolescents and emerging adults who report being the victims of **dating aggression** are alarmingly high. For example, as many as 15% of adolescent girls and 1 in 4 emerging adults between the ages of 18 and 24 report having been sexually assaulted while on a date (i.e., date raped; Rickert & Wiemann, 1998; Vezina & Hebert, 2007; Vicary, Klingaman, & Harkness, 1995). Precise numbers regarding the prevalence of dating aggression are difficult to come by, as adolescents often fail to report such aggression (CDC, 2014). Therefore, estimates of the percentages of adolescents who experience physical aggression within a dating relationship range from 9 to 46% (Espelage & Holt, 2012; Gray & Foshee, 1997; Katz, Kuffel, & Coblentz, 2002; Roscoe & Callahan, 1985). Rates for nonphysical violence are alarming as well, with one estimate of 1 in 5 adolescents reporting **emotional aggression** (Halpern et al., 2001). Another study with a sample of high school students found that 37% experienced physical dating violence and 62% were victimized by emotional abuse in dating relationships (Holt & Espelage, 2007). Of course, many adolescents who are the victims of physical violence in a dating relationship also experience emotional abuse.

Whatever the exact numbers, the consequences of dating aggression are often quite serious. Victims of dating aggression report being saddened, confused, and angered by the experience (Carlson, 1987; CDC, 2014). One study found that being the victim of dating aggression was associated with higher levels of anxiety and depression (Holt & Espelage, 2007). Adolescent victims of dating violence are more likely than nonvictims to be engaged in risky behaviors such as substance abuse and risky sexual activity and are more likely to experience academic difficulties. Perhaps most disturbingly, being involved in an emotionally or physically abusive dating relationship during adolescence predicts being involved in violent adult relationships (Magdol et al., 1998; Smith, White, & Holland, 2003), indicating a strong need for early intervention to promote healthy relationships.

Efforts to reduce dating violence among adolescents have often focused on targeting the risk factors that are associated with the problem. For example, because substance abuse and risky sexual behavior are predictors of dating violence victimization and perpetration, programs designed to reduce risky sexual behavior and illicit substance use and abuse can also reduce dating violence. Another precursor to dating violence is the belief that violence toward romantic partners is acceptable. To combat such beliefs, some school-based programs focus on teaching adolescents (and educators) about the various forms dating aggression can take, and why all forms are damaging and unacceptable (e.g., Wolfe et al., 2009). By understanding some of the precursors of dating aggression, educators can take steps to counter these antecedents and reduce dating aggression and violence.

Recommendations for Educators

The world of adolescent romance, dating, and sexuality is an awkward place where adults fear to tread. It is one of the most private and personal aspects of adolescent development, yet it is also a very confusing issue and an aspect of life that is filled with many potential dangers, both physical and psychological. Teenagers are often misinformed or underinformed about how common sexual activity is among their peers, ways to protect themselves against unwanted pregnancy or STDs, and the long-term consequences of **sexting** nude photographs of themselves to boyfriends and girlfriends. And despite stereotypes of adolescents closing themselves off to adult influence and relying solely on their peers for information, most adolescents say that they

MyEdLab **Self-Check 10.4**

MyEdLab
Application Exercise 10.1
Teenage Pregnancy Stephanie is a teenager pregnant with her first child. Watch as she and her mother describe their feelings about the pregnancy. Think about how this is related to teen pregnancy rates, adolescents' attitudes about sex, and where adolescents get their information about sex.

rely on the adults in their lives, from parents to teachers to clergy, for important information about sex and dating. With this last point in mind, we offer some suggestions for what educators can do to help adolescents navigate this strange new world.

Inform Yourselves

Because adolescents depend heavily on the adults in their lives to provide information about sex and dating, it is important that these adults have their facts straight. Research suggests that teachers and parents often exaggerate the risks of sex, overestimating the failure rates of condoms and the likelihood of contracting an STD. Although these scare tactics are understandable, they can reduce the credibility of the adult messenger and drive adolescents to seek advice from less reliable sources, such as peers and the Internet. Therefore, educators and parents need to learn about adolescent sexuality and make themselves available to adolescents as providers of accurate information about a variety of topics related to sexuality, including the following:

- The sexual behavior of adolescents, including the percentages of adolescents of different ages who engage in various sexual activities
- The efficacy, availability, and correct usage of various forms of contraception
- The most effective methods for communicating relevant and appropriate information to teens

Create Space for Safe and Open Communication

Too many adolescents report that they feel like they must confront some of the most confusing and difficult sexual situations without the guidance of an adult. Whether it is a gay 16-year-old boy who is being bullied by his peers or a 15-year-old girl who is receiving aggressive and unwanted sexual advances from a fellow student, adolescents often do not feel like there is a sympathetic adult at school in whom they can confide. Some schools have adopted "Safe Space" programs with stickers to indicate that teachers are ready and willing to listen to youth who want to discuss issues of sexual orientation. Teachers can also create space for communication by openly confronting acts of sexual harassment and bullying as they arise in the classroom, the hallway, or other public spaces at school. When adolescents see educators who are unafraid to discuss issues of sexuality and confront instances of sexual injustice, they are more willing to discuss their own sexual concerns with them.

Address the Difficult Subjects

Discussions of sexuality and dating in school have long been a controversial issue. A large segment of the U.S. population believes that educators should limit their treatment of the issue to telling adolescents that premarital sex is immoral and dangerous and that abstinence is the only acceptable sexual behavior. In addition, there are many who believe that homosexuality should be treated as though it were a curable disease or an unfortunate life choice. One state has even gone so far as to introduce legislation that would ban teachers from using the word *gay* in class before the ninth grade (Fallon, 2013).

Unfortunately, discouraging the open discussion of sexual topics in school does not change the fact that many adolescents engage in premarital sex; do not use condoms or other forms of contraception as often as they should; are gay, lesbian, transgender, or transsexual; and are engaged in dating relationships that involve emotional or physical abuse. By ignoring these issues, educators miss an opportunity to teach adolescents about appropriate and safe behavior. Researchers agree that romantic relationships during adolescence often provide the framework for adult marital relationships (Collins & Sroufe, 1999; Furman & Shaffer, 2003). When these relationships in adolescence involve abuse, infidelity, or risky sexual behavior, the likelihood of entering into relationships with similar qualities as adults increases. Perhaps just as importantly, when teachers and schools fail to acknowledge and address these issues directly, students do not feel that they can turn to teachers or other school personnel for advice when they need it.

Rather than ignoring the difficult issues involved in adolescent sexuality and dating, numerous school districts have adopted curricula that address them directly. Comprehensive sexual education programs discuss the benefits of abstinence but also teach adolescents about contraception, STDs and their consequences, and the physical and emotional risks of engaging in sexual activity. Similarly, there are a variety of curricular programs available that teach adolescents about what constitutes a healthy romantic relationship, including the absence of verbal and physical abuse. Research tells us that children and adolescents begin thinking about romantic relationships from a young age and often experiment with sexual activity such as kissing before they even reach their teens. Unfortunately, we also know that some of the more negative behaviors, such as bullying and sexual harassment, also begin very early and may even be modeled at home. It is important, therefore, that as children and adolescents begin to form their own sexual identities they are provided with information and modeling that will keep them safe and help them develop a pattern of beliefs and behaviors that is respectful and healthy. To facilitate this, educators can do the following:

- Demonstrate to students that they are willing to discuss issues of sexuality and romantic relationships with students.
- Model appropriate behavior, such as avoiding the use of derogatory language about sexual orientation, women, or sexual behavior (e.g., "slut") and immediately addressing such language when it is used by students.
- Create an environment where students feel safe to discuss issues of sexuality without fear of ridicule.

Sex and dating will always be controversial topics, especially when adolescents are involved. Although there is a real need for adolescents to be able to talk about these topics with adults whom they trust, navigating this issue can be a dangerous minefield for teachers. Offering advice to a teenager, even innocuous-seeming advice, such as "If you are going to have sex, be safe," can get a teacher in trouble with parents, school administrators, or both. Before counseling an adolescent or engaging the class in discussion about sexuality issues, it is a good idea for teachers to talk with administrators at the school to get guidelines about appropriate topics and methods for discussing these issues with students. Fortunately, several good models of comprehensive sex education currently exist (e.g., the Safer Choices program, Reducing the Risk), and these include recommendations for how to discuss issues of sexuality and romantic relationships with students.

MyEdLab **Self-Check 10.5**

Conclusion

Many teachers feel unprepared to deal with the awkward and personal issues of adolescent sexuality, dating, and romantic relationships. But the reality of working with adolescents, especially high school students, is that these issues will arise. By the time they graduate from high school, most adolescents will have become sexually active, and many will have become romantically involved with a boyfriend or girlfriend. These relationships are deeply important to students and can influence all aspects of their physical, social, and emotional lives, including their engagement and performance in school. In addition, adolescents often need guidance from trusted adults in their lives to help them cope with the confusion and social pressures involved in sexual behavior and dating relationships. To help adolescents make smart and safe choices and decisions, teachers should equip themselves with the requisite knowledge and communication skills.

11

Mental Health, Coping Strategies, and Problems

Learning Outcomes

11.1 You will be able to identify various types of internalizing mental disorders, their symptoms, and the frequency with which they occur among adolescents.

11.2 You will be able to identify various types of externalizing disorders, their symptoms, and the frequency with which they occur among adolescents.

11.3 You will be able to describe adolescent substance use and abuse in terms of the types of substances used, rates of use, and problems associated with their abuse.

11.4 You will be able to describe what educators can do to identify mental and behavioral problems among their adolescent students and help their students cope with or get help for these problems.

Introduction

Teachers of adolescent students often are faced with a common dilemma: They must decide whether their students' behavior is "normal" or indicative of a serious problem. Compare these two examples:

>>>

In Ms. Jordan's 10th-grade geometry class, Andre is a student who might best be described as mercurial. One minute he is happy, playful, animated, and friendly. The next minute he can seem angry, surly, and distant. Andre has never threatened or harmed anyone, but his mood swings are disconcerting.

Another student in Ms. Jordan's class is Angela. She rarely smiles and tends to sit quietly at her desk. She almost never participates in class, seems lethargic for weeks at a time, and has often failed to show up for class at all.

Although the behaviors of both students in these examples would be considered odd by adult standards, teachers might need to consider whether one of these students, both of them, or neither of them should potentially be referred for mental health services. How do we know whether an adolescent's behavior falls within the range of normal or is indicative of a serious problem that needs help? Are the frequent changes in mood displayed by Andre simply normal adolescent behavior, or a sign of a serious problem? Is Angela simply tired in the morning, as many adolescents are, or is she depressed? What kinds of problematic behaviors and disorders are most common during adolescence? What are the symptoms of these disorders, and what should educators do if they observe these symptoms in their students? These are some of the topics that we discuss in this chapter.

OVERVIEW OF THE CHAPTER

In this chapter we focus on the kinds of disorders and problematic behaviors that are most common among adolescents, particularly those in the U.S. The chapter is divided into four broad sections. First, we discuss **internalizing disorders**. These are problems associated with internal or self-directed thoughts, moods, and behaviors and include depression, stress, anxiety, and eating disorders. Next, we describe **externalizing disorders** that are most common during adolescence, including conduct disorder, aggression, and oppositional-defiant disorder. The third section of this chapter presents information about substance use and **substance abuse** among adolescents, including the use of alcohol, tobacco, and illicit drugs. The chapter ends with a section that summarizes what schools and educators can do to identify these disorders and problems and, where appropriate, try to help.

Each of the first three sections of the chapter includes information about the prevalence of the behavior or disorder among U.S. adolescents, a description of the symptoms and behaviors associated with each problem, a consideration of the cause or causes of the disorder or problematic behavior, and information about what educators and schools can do to recognize the problems and offer help, when appropriate, to students who are afflicted with the disorder or engaged in problematic behavior.

As you read this chapter, it is important to remember that adolescence is a unique period of life, with unique challenges. As we have discussed in other chapters of this book, adolescence is a period that is marked by numerous changes occurring both within the individual (e.g., changes in the body, cognitive developments) and in the contexts (peers, school, family, society) in which adolescents live. These changes and transitions are stressful, can create conflict in social relationships with friends and family, and can be confusing to adolescents as they try to make sense of who they are and how they fit into their various social roles. As a result, adolescents may often seem moody, engage in risky behaviors, express anger, and seem distant from parents and teachers. Much of this behavior is considered normal, and most adolescents emerge from adolescence with their physical and mental health intact. But some adolescents experience emotional distress or engage in behavior that is beyond the range of normal, and is genuinely unhealthy. It is these problems that are the focus of this chapter.

Internalizing Disorders Common Among Adolescents

Internalizing disorders take many forms. Because they stem from thoughts and feelings that are internal to the individual, it is not always easy to recognize or understand the symptoms. For example, one common symptom of depression is lethargy and a lack of enthusiasm or energy for normal behaviors. As most teachers of adolescents can attest, these are common characteristics of nondepressed teenagers as well. In this section of the chapter we discuss some of the more common internalizing disorders, including their symptoms, consequences, and prevalence among adolescents. We also discuss what teachers and schools can do to recognize and try to address these disorders, focusing specifically on some of the effective programs already in place in some schools.

Anxiety and Stress

Adolescence is a life stage that includes many stressful events, from social interactions with peers to increased discord with parents to pressure to succeed academically. **Stress** is very common among adolescents, with roughly half reporting feeling stressed in any given week (de Anda et al., 2000). Some research also indicates that **anxiety** and **depression** among adolescents have become more common over the last 30 years (Collishaw, Maughan, Goodman, & Pickles, 2004; Hagell, 2012). In fact, recent research by the American Psychological Association (APA, 2014) indicates that adolescents in the United States are even more stressed out than adults. Unfortunately, teens are less likely than adults to understand the negative consequences that stress has on their physical and mental health.

White adolescents report the highest levels of stress, followed by Latino/a and then African American adolescents. Some research indicates that adolescents in the United States currently exhibit more symptoms of anxiety as compared with adolescents 20 years ago (Twenge, 2000). It appears that, in general, adolescents feel more stress about schools, grades, and future plans than they do about their relationships with peers, although the specific causes of stress will vary dramatically across individuals and even over time within individuals (de Anda et al., 2000). For example, a 15-year-old girl may be particularly anxious about a big test in biology one week, and then stressed about not being invited to a party the next week. In addition, adolescents' experiences of stress will depend quite strongly on the stressors in their environment (e.g., violent crime rates in their neighborhoods, family discord at home) as well as their own physiological reactions to stress.

Although stress and anxiety are normal parts of adolescent life, for some adolescents stress and anxiety can interfere with healthy functioning. High levels of stress and fear can lead some adolescents to experience **panic attacks**. These are debilitating episodes of fear that can cause individuals to feel disoriented and experience nausea, loss of breath, and trembling. These symptoms tend to be short in duration (about 10 minutes on average). In addition, some adolescents develop

generalized anxiety disorders. These are longer-lasting (at least 6 months) periods of fear and anxiety. Although it is very common for adolescents to experience mild and brief episodes of anxiety, the incidence of more serious, longer-lasting anxiety disorders is about 2% for boys and 3% for girls (Costello, Mustillo, Erkanli, Keeler, & Angold, 2003). Unfortunately, frequent experiences of stress and anxiety are one cause of depression among adolescents, a topic we turn to next.

Depression and Mood Disorders

Everybody experiences periods of sadness, low energy, and hopelessness from time to time. Getting a bad grade in a class, breaking up with a boyfriend or girlfriend, and not being selected for a team are just a few of the common experiences of adolescents that can trigger negative affect. Although it is common for people to say they are depressed (e.g., "My favorite show on TV was canceled—I'm so depressed!"), brief periods of negative affect are very common and are considered normal. To rise to the level of a disorder, the symptoms of depression must be persistent, lasting for several weeks or more. The disorder of depression has a few different names—**major depressive disorder (MDD)**, clinical depression, major depression—but they all refer to the same set of symptoms. These include feelings of hopelessness and despair, lack of interest in many or most activities, sadness, and sometimes lethargy and lack of appetite. To be categorized as having MDD, a person must show at least five of the common symptoms of depression nearly every day for at least 2 weeks (American Psychiatric Association, 2013). These symptoms include:

- Depressed mood or irritability most of the day
- Decreased interest or pleasure in most activities most of the day
- Significant weight change (5% or more), or change in appetite
- Changes in sleep patterns (insomnia or hypersomnia)
- Change in activity
- Fatigue or loss of energy
- Feelings of worthlessness or guilt
- Diminished ability to think or concentrate
- Thoughts of death or suicide (**suicidal ideation**)

Many people experience periods of depression without being clinically depressed. Some experience so-called "minor depression," which is defined as having at least two (but fewer than five) of the symptoms of depression present for at least 2 weeks. There are also those who have mild, moderate, or severe depressive episodes. These are experiences of depression that can be quite intense, but that do not last as long as minor or major depression.

Prevalence of MDD in Adolescence. It is difficult to know exactly what percentage of adolescents in the United States experience MDD because most adolescents with the disorder never seek professional treatment for it (Sen, 2004). This is particularly true for boys. In the United States, the common stereotype of adolescents as moody and lethargic may cause the adults in their lives, such as teachers and parents, to overlook symptoms of depression, writing them off as normal adolescent behavior. As a result, the estimates of the percentage of adolescents who have MDD are most likely *under*estimates. In addition, there is evidence that the rates of depression are not equal across all cultural and gender groups. Keep this in mind as you consider the prevalence rates presented here.

The National Survey on Drug Use and Health (Substance Abuse and Mental Health Services Administration, 2015) revealed that about 11% of adolescents in the United States reported having at least one major depressive episode in the previous 12-month period, and the American Academy of Child and Adolescent

TABLE 11.1	Percentage of Adolescents Aged 12 to 17 with a Major Depressive Episode (MDE) in the Last Year, by Gender and Ethnic Group			
	White	**Black**	**Asian**	**Hispanic/Latino/a**
Males	5.6	3.0	6.5	5.7
Females	16.3	14.4	13.9	17.4

Source: Data from Substance Abuse and Mental Health Services Administration, 2015.

Psychiatry (2013) reported that about 5% of U.S. adolescents are believed to have MDD at any given time. Although there are no differences between boys and girls in their rates of depression before the age of 12, during the adolescent years, girls are more likely than boys to be diagnosed with MDD, both in the United States (Nolen-Hoeksema & Girgus, 1994) and in Europe (Wichstrom, 1999). The gender difference is quite large, with adolescent girls being diagnosed with clinical depression about twice as often as adolescent boys, and these differences appear across ethnic groups (Ge, Lorenz, Conger, & Elder, 1994).

In addition to the large gender differences in the rates of depression, there may also be ethnic differences (see Table 11.1), although the evidence for these differences is not entirely clear. When controlling for socioeconomic status (SES), Mexican American adolescents reported higher levels of depression than did youth from other ethnic groups. Cummings and Druss (2011) found that among 12- to 17-year-olds who experienced MDD, non-Hispanic White students were more likely than Black, Hispanic, or Asian adolescents to receive treatment for their depression, with Asian students being the least likely to receive treatment. Less than half of all adolescents with MDD received any form of treatment for their disorder (Cummings & Druss, 2011).

In addition to ethnic differences in the prevalence of depression among adolescents, there may be differences between adolescents from different social classes. Because poverty exposes adolescents to serious stressors (e.g., insecurities about having basic needs met, more frequent moves from one home to another, more exposure to crime and violence), and because stress is one cause of depression, it makes sense that adolescents from less affluent families might experience higher rates of depression (Lorant et al., 2003; Melchoir et al., 2013). It is also true, however, that adolescents from lower-SES families are less likely to receive treatment for their depression, so the rates of depression among lower-income adolescents are most likely higher than what is reported. Roberts, Roberts, and Chen (1997) found evidence that among middle school students, those who *believed* they were from a lower-SES background than their peers, whether they actually were or not, were more likely to suffer from depression.

Suicide. Depression can lead to a reduction in effective functioning and quality of life, and some adolescents who are depressed consider or ultimately attempt suicide. Suicide ideation can be anything from fleeting thoughts about committing suicide to more persistent, detailed thoughts about when and how one might commit suicide. Although suicidal ideation often accompanies depression, one does not need to be depressed to contemplate suicide, and most adolescents who do consider suicide never actually attempt to kill themselves. Suicide is the third leading cause of death among high school students, accounting for 15% of all deaths in this population (Centers for Disease Control and Prevention, 2014). Suicide rates are more common in older than younger students—fewer than 1 in 100,000 early adolescents (10 to 14 years of age) commits suicide, whereas the rate increases to 9 suicides per 100,000 for adolescents between the ages of 15 and 19, and to 12.7 per 100,000 for early adults between 20 and 24 years old (CDC, 2014).

More concern can be raised when looking at the numbers of adolescents who report having attempted suicide. In their study of adolescents, Jiang, Perry, and Hesser (2010) found that about 8% of boys and 10% of girls reported having attempted suicide at least once. Data from the Centers for Disease Control indicates that 10.6% of high school females and 5.4% of high school boys reported a suicide attempt that resulted in care from a medical professional within the 12-month period preceding the survey (Kann et al., 2014). The wide disparity between the reported rates of attempted suicide (nearly 10% of all high school students in the United States in the Jiang et al. study) and the actual suicide rate (less than 1/100th of a percent of high-school-aged U.S. adolescents) indicates that many adolescents who report having attempted suicide do not actually commit suicide. Because of this disparity between reports of attempted suicides and the number of actual suicides among adolescents, researchers and psychiatric health professionals distinguish between **suicidal gestures** and **suicidal acts**. The former are intentional, self-injurious behaviors that are not lethal, sometimes made as a way to garner attention or sympathy. The latter are behaviors that individuals with suicidal ideation do to injure themselves, even if the injuries do not actually result in the person's death.

There are gender and ethnic-group differences in the rates of suicide attempts and actual suicides (see Figure 11.1). White male adolescents in the United States have a higher suicide rate than do African American adolescents or White female adolescents. Although White males are more likely to *commit* suicide, White female adolescents are more likely to *attempt* suicide (Maltsberger, 1988). Overall, the suicide rate for males between 10 and 24 years of age is 11.9 per 100,000 for males and 3.2 per 100,000 for females (Sullivan et al., 2015). This disparity is most likely the result of the methods of suicide used most frequently by each gender, with males using more lethal methods (e.g., guns) and females using slower, less lethal methods (e.g., pills).

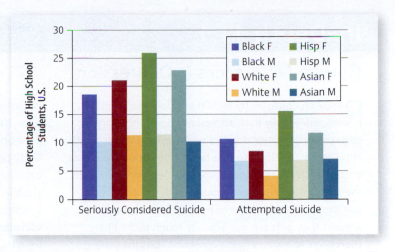

FIGURE 11.1

Suicide Rates (Considered and Attempted), by Ethnicity and Gender, High School Students, Grades 9–12

Source: Data from Centers for Disease Control and Prevention, 2013.

Note: Attempted suicide at least once in the last 12 months.

Causes of Depression. Most researchers agree that depression and other internalizing disorders are caused by the combination of a genetic predisposition and environmental stressors. This model of causation that involves the combination of biological and environmental factors is known as the **diathesis-stress model** (see Figure 11.2), and has been employed to understand a variety of physical and psychological maladies, including schizophrenia and obesity. According to the diathesis-stress model, adolescents who develop depression and other internalizing disorders most likely have a **genetic predisposition** for the disorder that they inherited from one or both parents. But simply possessing the genotype is not enough to produce a depressive disorder. In addition to the genetic predisposition (the "diathesis" part of the diathesis-stress model), the individual must also experience acute (e.g., the death of a loved one) or chronic (e.g., bullying, continual academic failure, ongoing dissatisfaction with one's appearance, loneliness) stressors. The diathesis-stress model explains why

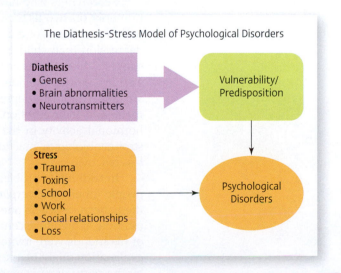

FIGURE 11.2

Diathesis-Stress Model

In-Depth 11.1

Gender Differences in Depression

Research consistently finds that adolescent girls are more likely than adolescent boys and women to experience major depressive disorder (Nolen-Hoeksema, 2001) despite a lack of gender differences in depressive symptoms before adolescence. To date, there is little consensus about why this might be, but there is no shortage of hypotheses. Some have argued that girls are not actually much more likely than boys to experience depression, but they are more likely to seek help for it, and are therefore more likely to be diagnosed. Others have argued that girls are genuinely more likely than boys to experience depression and that this difference stems from the different social roles assigned to boys and girls in society. Whereas boys are socialized to express their negative emotions outwardly, sometimes physically, girls are encouraged to be quiet and well behaved. This socialization process causes girls to turn their negative emotions inward, increasing their levels of depression. In addition, girls may feel more pressure than boys to be popular and to achieve an ideal body type, and these kinds of anxiety-producing expectations can increase depressed mood. Girls are also socialized to be particularly sensitive to, and invested in, interpersonal relationships. All of these socialization processes are potential sources of stress for girls, and stress is strongly associated with depression. A third explanation for this gender difference is biological. Even when girls and boys have the same genetic predisposition toward depression, as inherited from their parents, this predisposition is more likely to be expressed as depression among girls than among boys. The reason for this is not clear, but it may be that the genetic predisposition is triggered into manifested depression by the kinds of stressors that girls experience as a result of gender socialization processes.

some adolescents who experience a lot of stress in their lives, such as living in poverty and enduring repeated exposure to violence, do not develop depression: They lack the genetic predisposition. Similarly, many adolescents who inherit the genetic predisposition for depression never develop symptoms because they are able to avoid the **environmental stressors** that turn the predisposition into the disorder.

Researchers who have examined the diathesis part of the model have focused primarily on two factors. First, there is evidence that depression runs in families, with the children of a depressed parent being three times more likely to develop depression than children of nondepressed parents (Graber & Sontag, 2009). This suggests that there is a strong genetic component to depression; in fact, researchers have produced evidence that genes that are associated with reactions to stress are associated with depression. Specifically, some adolescents have more difficulty regulating their emotions in response to stressful events because of problematic hormonal activity in the brain and nervous system. Individuals who experience stronger biological reactions to stress are more prone to depression than those with less reactivity.

In addition to problems with hormonal regulation, there is some evidence that people inherit their *explanatory style* from their parents. An **explanatory style** is the pattern of beliefs one has for explaining the events that occur in one's life. For example, if an adolescent learns that he has not been invited to a party that many of his friends were invited to, he will attempt to explain this event. An optimistic explanation might blame the party slight on a fixable problem, such as an oversight by the party organizers or the lack of opportunity to befriend the person who is throwing the party. This type of explanation involves no self-blame and offers an opportunity to easily fix the problem. In contrast, a pessimistic explanatory style may lead the individual to explain his lack of an invitation as being the result of some persistent personal shortcoming—a disagreeable personality or physical unattractiveness, for example. Individuals with more pessimistic explanatory styles often develop helpless and hopeless feelings because they tend to explain events, particularly negative events, with stable and internal causes. For example, suppose that two students in the same high school math class both receive disappointing grades on an exam. One may explain this outcome in a manner that provides some hope for future success (e.g., "I was really busy this week and didn't have time to study. I'm sure I'll be more prepared for the next test."). The other student may attribute his poor performance to factors that are internal and not likely to change (e.g., "I'm not surprised that I failed. I am just really stupid at math."). Not surprisingly, the explanatory style of the second student in this example is more associated with depression and other internalizing disorders than is an optimistic explanatory style (Seligman, 2011).

One reason that rates of depression tend to increase in adolescence is that the "stress" side of the diathesis-stress model increases in severity and frequency during adolescence. Biological changes associated with puberty, changing social roles, increased pressure to perform academically, social pressures to be popular, and initial forays into romantic relationships all occur during adolescence, and all can be sources of stress. Research indicates that adolescents who experience a breakup with a boyfriend or girlfriend, live in families that have a lot of conflict and are not close, are unpopular with their peers, or are not performing up to expectations academically are more likely to be depressed than are adolescents who do not

> One of the primary causes of stress for adolescents is the demands of schoolwork. Teachers want to be sensitive to student stress, but they also want to challenge their students and prepare them for college. What can you do, as a teacher, to find the right balance?

In-Depth 11.2

Stress and the Race to Nowhere

In recent years there has been increasing attention given to the overscheduled, super-busy, overachieving culture of adolescents in the United States. As articulated in the documentary film called *Race to Nowhere* (Ables & Congdon, 2011), several commentators have noted that the relative freedom of youth has been replaced by a series of scheduled practices, rehearsals, school, tutors, test preparation, jobs, and community service activities. High school students are faced with ever-increasing pressure to get perfect grades, take leadership roles in community service projects, excel athletically, and be popular with their peers. The by-product of this pressure to excel in all areas of life is stress. Tragically, some students who find it difficult to cope with stress turn to self-harming behaviors, such as cutting or, in extreme cases, suicide. But even less dramatic responses to stress can be detrimental to motivation, achievement, and mental health. A theory of motivation known

as *self-determination theory* (SDT) has spawned scores of studies that have documented the negative consequences of feeling pressured and coerced into behavior (Deci & Ryan, 2000). Based on the idea that human beings have a need to feel autonomous, SDT researchers have produced evidence that when autonomy is thwarted, such as when adolescents feel pressured into performing at high levels in many areas of life with little downtime, stress increases and emotional well-being suffers. This has negative consequences for health as well as for motivation and achievement. Allowing adolescents the time they need to explore interests and socialize with friends can reduce anxiety and increase well-being. We should also note that some research evidence suggests that most adolescents are not overly busy and that participation in extracurricular activities has more positive than negative effects for youth (Mahoney, Harris, & Eccles, 2008).

MyEdLab
Video Example 11.1

In this TedXYouth talk, Megan Shinnick discusses her own experience with depression and talks about adolescent anxiety and depression and what schools can do to combat it.

have these stressors (Ge et al., 1994; Williamson, Birmaher, Anderson, al-Shabbout, & Ryan, 1995). Of course, an adolescent's subjective experience of stress is going to depend, in part, on how he or she perceives and copes with these stressors. As previously discussed, some adolescents are more likely, because of hormonal causes or a negative explanatory style, to have an extreme negative reaction to these stressors, whereas others are more likely to take these difficulties in stride. There is evidence that the hormones associated with reactivity to stress also increase during adolescence, thereby further explaining the increased levels of depression during this period of development.

Risk and Resilience

Some adolescents who seem to have a lot of challenges that may cause them to become anxious and depressed do not exhibit these reactions, whereas others do. What explains this difference between teens in their response to stressful situations? Researchers have focused on the combination of **risk** and **resilience** factors in adolescents' lives as a method for understanding these differences. Risk factors include biological factors (e.g., impulsiveness, hormonal changes, genetic inheritance), personality traits (e.g., aggressiveness, detachment, perfectionist tendencies, poor social skills leading to feelings of isolation), difficulties within the family (e.g., divorce, conflict, loss of income or chronic poverty, alcoholism, abuse), challenges with peers or school (e.g., conflict with teachers, being bullied by peers, a breakup with a romantic partner, low achievement, being retained a grade, pressure to achieve), and larger societal pressures (e.g., pressure to conform, pressure to have a certain body type, concerns about the environment or social justice; Dabkowska & Dabkowska-Mika, 2015; Merikangas & Pine, 2002). Although any of these stressors, by themselves, can increase the risk for developing anxiety and depression, risk-and-resiliency models generally posit that the more of these risks an adolescent experiences, the greater the likelihood of developing anxiety.

Just as there are multiple stressors that place adolescents at risk for becoming anxious and depressed, there are also a number of factors, both within the individual and in the environment, that can buffer adolescents from these risks, making them resilient. For example, having parents who set limits and hold high expectations for their children, yet are warm toward and supportive of their children (known as an **authoritative parenting style**) is one protective factor that can help adolescents be resilient to the harmful effects of various risks (Steinberg, Mounts, Lamborn, & Dornbusch, 1999). In general, having relationships with caring and supportive adults is an important protective factor for adolescents exposed to stressors and at risk for developing anxiety. In addition, research has consistently found that high cognitive functioning (i.e., intelligence) is another protective factor (Masten & Coatsworth, 1998). One possible explanation for the association between intelligence and resilience is that high levels of intelligence may allow adolescents to think of solutions to some of the challenging problems that they face.

There are many other factors that can contribute to resilience in the face of difficulties. Belonging to a tight-knit family that is free from high levels of discord and disruption (e.g., divorce, serious illness) is generally a protective factor against anxiety and depression (Duncan, Duncan, & Strycker, 2000). Similarly, explanatory style (i.e., **attributions**; Weiner, 1985) can serve as a protective factor. Just as believing that negative events in one's life are due to stable and uncontrollable causes can cause feelings of helplessness and depression, when adolescents believe that they have the power to change or to avoid negative situations or to create positive outcomes, they can have a sense of hope and optimism that guards against anxiety and depression (Seligman, 2011; Seligman et al., 1984). Positive feelings about school, such as a strong feeling of **belonging** and the belief that one is a valued member of the school community, can also protect adolescents against feelings of detachment and anxiety (Goodenow, 1993). These are a few of the many protective factors that can help adolescents, even those who face tremendous difficulties in their lives, avoid feelings of anxiety and depression. Just as risk factors are believed to be additive (i.e., the more risk factors one faces, the more likely one is to develop a disorder), so too are protective factors. The more protective factors adolescents have, the greater their level of resilience to the stressors in their lives. Of course, it does not work this way for all adolescents, but as a general model of risk and resilience, it is sound.

Eating Disorders

As we discussed in Chapter 2, it is very common for adolescents in the United States, both male and female, to be concerned about their body shape and to be unsatisfied with their bodies. These concerns lead many adolescents to engage in unhealthy behaviors, such as frequent dieting and taking laxatives to manage their weight. For a smaller percentage of adolescents, the desire to obtain their ideal body shape and size leads to the development of an eating disorder and may be accompanied by risky behaviors, such as excessive exercise paired with limited caloric intake, binging and purging of food, and frequent use of diet pills and laxatives. The most common eating disorders are *anorexia nervosa*, *binge eating*, and *bulimia nervosa*.

Anorexia nervosa is a disorder that causes people to obsess about their weight, their body shape, and what they eat. It is usually accompanied by a focus on becoming thin and perceptions of a healthy body shape that are out of sync with reality. People suffering from anorexia nervosa often perceive themselves to be quite fat, even when they are very thin (Stice & Shaw, 2002). This disconnect between perception and reality often leads those with anorexia to starve themselves, sometimes to death. **Bulimia nervosa** is a mental disorder in which people eat large amounts of food (known as **binge eating**) and then engage in unhealthy practices to eliminate the food from their bodies, such as self-induced vomiting or abuse of laxatives.

Prevalence. For many years, eating disorders and unhealthy eating habits were thought to be a problem primarily constrained to middle- and upper-middle class White girls (Yuan, 2010). But the evidence suggests that disordered eating may affect girls across ethnic groups. In a study comparing different ethnic groups, Shaw, Ramirez, Trost, Randall, and Stice (2004) found that there were no differences across ethnic groups in their reported eating disorder symptoms or the relationship between various risk factors and the development of eating disorders; in their words, "[E]thnic minority groups have reached parity with Whites in this domain" (p. 12). Similarly, Story and colleagues, using a large sample of Minnesota high school students, found that Hispanic adolescent girls were more likely than White girls to use diuretics to control their weight, and that African American girls were more likely than White girls to use vomiting as a weight-control technique (Story, French, Resnick, & Blum, 1995). Research has found, however, that White adolescent girls are more likely than African American, Hispanic, or Native American adolescent girls to seek treatment for their disordered eating. This may be one reason that the prevalence of eating disorders among minority adolescents has been underestimated for so long (National Eating Disorders Association, n.d.).

In addition to the common perception that eating disorders are primarily limited to White adolescents, there has also been a belief that males rarely suffer from eating disorders. Although the evidence suggests that disordered eating is more common among females, there is increasing evidence that many male adolescents also suffer from eating disorders. Some research suggests that one reason eating disorders among male adolescents have been overlooked is that males with eating disorders present them differently than do females (Campbell & Peebles, 2014). For example, adolescent males with eating disorders are less likely than adolescent females to engage in **purging** behavior. In addition, male adolescents are more likely than female adolescents to couch their eating behavior as a desire to be "fit and healthy" rather than a desire to be thin (Campbell & Peebles, 2014). These factors have made it more difficult to diagnose disordered eating among adolescent boys, thereby leading to underestimations of the prevalence in this population.

Causes. Disordered eating appears to be the result of a combination of factors. There is little doubt that the high value in many societies, including the United States, on being thin contributes to adolescents' dissatisfaction with their own bodies. Body dissatisfaction, even more than body shape as measured by the **body-mass index (BMI)**, is the strongest predictor of disordered eating among adolescents. The fact that adolescent girls are more likely than adolescent boys to suffer from body dissatisfaction and from eating disorders, coupled with the frequent images of thin women as representatives of the beauty ideal on television, in movies, and in advertising, suggests that disordered eating is caused, at least in part, by societal factors. Indeed, adolescent girls who frequently read fashion magazines with many images of thin women are more likely to report dissatisfaction with their own bodies and to have disordered eating habits (Botta, 2003).

There is interesting evidence that the causes of anorexia and bulimia may be somewhat different. For example, anorexia is much more likely to be inherited (i.e., run in the family) than is bulimia, suggesting there may be a stronger genetic component to anorexia. Similarly, whereas anorexia is found throughout the world, bulimia tends to be limited to Western cultures, such as the United States and Western Europe (Keel & Klump, 2003), where the thin-body ideal is more prevalent. There is also evidence that eating disorders, particularly anorexia nervosa, are more common among adolescents who experience other symptoms of psychological distress, such as depression, anxiety, and **obsessive-compulsive disorder** (Jacobi, Hayward, de Zwaan, Kraemer, & Agras, 2004; Stice, Presnell, & Bearman, 2001). All of this suggests that the roots of bulimia may be more culturally based and socialized, whereas the etiology of anorexia may be more hereditary and based in the brain.

What are some of the possible social factors that influence body dissatisfaction among adolescents, and what are some ways to help adolescents feel more satisfied with their body shape and size?

What Educators Can Do

Because internalizing disorders such as depression and anxiety can be difficult to identify and even more difficult to treat, teachers often feel that there is little they can do to help their students who suffer from depression. In one sense, they are correct about this. Teachers should not attempt to treat students' depression. But if they observe students displaying some of the symptoms of depression, they can consult local mental health professionals. Many schools employ counselors and other mental health professionals. Teachers who suspect that they have one or more students who are struggling with depression or anxiety can discuss the situation with a mental health professional such as the school psychologist and, if appropriate, discuss ways for encouraging the students to seek treatment for this depression or anxiety.

In recent years, various school-based programs designed to address mental health problems have been developed and tested, both in the United States and abroad. The focus of several of these programs is to openly discuss life issues that create stress for adolescents and, in some cases, develop strategies for coping with them. For example, Srikala and Kumar (2010) described a program in India in which teachers are trained, and provided with a curriculum and activities, to teach their adolescent students life skills. Students who participated in the life-skills training program had higher levels of self-esteem, better adjustment with teachers and school, and higher levels of prosocial behavior than did students who did not participate in the program, but there were no differences between the two groups in overall levels of psychopathology. Similarly, a program in New Zealand and Australia called the Gatehouse Project focuses on creating a whole-school approach to promoting well-being in an effort to prevent depression among students (Patton et al., 2000). This program includes the development of mental health teams within schools and the use of intervention strategies to prevent depression. It includes a strong emphasis on integrating health-related materials into the normal curriculum of classroom teachers, making the material relevant to the lives of adolescents, and training teachers in ways of developing and implementing health-promoting curricula and pedagogy in their classrooms.

The Gatehouse Project is an example of a whole-school and whole-classroom approach to addressing mental health issues in school. In contrast, there are also modular programs. These programs are generally focused more on treatment rather than prevention, and are characterized by relatively short interventions delivered through school-based health centers. For example, Lyon, Charlesworth-Attie, Vander Stoep, and McCauley (2011) described a program in which seven therapists from school-based mental health centers (SBHCs) participated. These therapists were trained in the use of mental health modules. Through this program, the therapists were able to identify students suffering from depression and/or anxiety and to provide treatment using one or more of the treatment modules. Because this study was focused on therapists' participation and understanding of the module approach to treatment (which did increase during the study), information about the benefits for students was not reported.

There have also been a number of programs designed specifically to address stress and anxiety among adolescents. Most of these programs have adopted principles from **cognitive-behavioral therapy** to help adolescents reframe their thoughts about stressful events, and to develop **coping strategies**. For example, Hampel, Meier, and Kummel (2008) described an anti-stress training program in which teachers were trained to help students develop coping strategies, such as relaxation techniques and seeking social support. The results of their study indicate that teachers and adolescents, particularly early adolescents, found the training useful, and adolescents who participated in the program reported lower-levels of stress. de Anda (1998) described a 10-week program designed to teach adolescents how to use coping self-talk (e.g., problem-solving techniques) and positive coping behaviors (e.g., relaxation, exercise, distracting activities) to reduce anxiety and stress. The results of this study revealed that adolescents who learned these techniques were more likely to engage in positive coping behaviors and felt less stressed than their peers who did not participate in the program. Similar programs have been used, with success, to address adolescents struggling with social anxiety (Miller et al., 2011).

It is worth noting that school-based stress-reduction programs are needed, in part, because of the stress that school-related activities introduce into adolescents' lives. Middle and high schools often place a constant emphasis on the importance of getting good grades, gaining college admission, and performing well on standardized achievement tests. Because career planning and the pressure to succeed academically are two of the primary sources of stress for adolescents, it is ironic that schools are trying to help students cope with the school-induced stress that adolescents experience. But it appears that cognitive-behavioral approaches to stress reduction are effective, so teachers and schools should learn and use these techniques with their adolescent students. Given the source of the stress, one might argue that it is the least schools could do.

School-based efforts to reduce the symptoms of disordered eating have focused primarily on encouraging adolescents, particularly girls, to change their perceptions of the ideal body type and their own body dissatisfaction (Stice, Rohde, Gau, & Shaw, 2009). For example, one study attempted to alter high school girls' perceptions of the thin-body ideal by having them develop oral and written arguments against it. For example, they were asked to write about the costs associated with trying to attain the ideal, thin body type. Taking a stance against one's beliefs is known as **dissonance training**. All of the girls in the study had expressed dissatisfaction with their bodies. The program did produce some reduction in the thin-body ideal, but these effects disappeared after 3 years. There was also a slight reduction in disordered eating symptoms among participants in the dissonance group.

In another study conducted with early-adolescent girls in Germany, Wick and her colleagues (2011) employed a similar dissonance-training program. After 9 weeks of dissonance-training exercises, they found that study participants had an increase in body self-esteem and in their awareness of health and body issues, but no decrease in symptoms of disordered eating. Taken together, these intervention studies suggest that engaging adolescents in activities designed to help them think differently about the thin-body ideal can help them develop a greater awareness of healthy body types. But this research also suggests that disordered eating symptoms can be very resistant to change (Stice et al., 2009; Wick et al., 2011).

This review of several school-based programs designed to reduce the prevalence and hardships associated with internalizing disorders can be summarized with a set of recommendations for educators:

1. *Become aware of the symptoms of different internalizing disorders.* Because these disorders are, by definition, internal to the individuals that are suffering from them, the visible signs of distress can be easy to miss. In addition, several symptoms of depression, anxiety, and eating disorders are quite similar to what one would expect to observe in a healthy adolescent, including some moodiness, anxiety about academic and social problems, and a desire for control. With training, however, teachers can learn to recognize the signs of internalizing disorders and better distinguish between normal adolescent behaviors and the symptoms of more serious problems.

2. *Do not try to treat the disorder yourself.* Mental disorders are very complex phenomena that are generally not subject to quick and easy fixes. If you suspect that one of your students is suffering from an internalizing disorder, your best option is to seek the advice of your building administrator and a mental health professional at your school.

3. *If appropriate, provide opportunities for students to discuss the stressors in their lives.* Stress and anxiety can become debilitating, and lead to depression, when adolescents feel they must cope with their problems on their own. When given the opportunity to discuss their anxieties, they often discover that many of their peers share their fears and concerns. In addition, these discussions can lead to sharing of strategies for coping with these tensions. There are several programs and materials available to help teachers structure these kinds of discussions. Before inviting students to discuss these issues, however, teachers should be aware that adolescents may raise issues that are difficult for teachers or other students to handle. Therefore, it

is important to seek assistance and training in how to lead open discussions about stress and anxiety, and to prepare for any uncomfortable revelations that may emerge from such discussions.

4. *If appropriate, teach students stress-reduction and other coping strategies.* The normal stresses of daily life can become overwhelming for adolescents who lack the perspective and skills needed to cope with them. Teaching students relaxation techniques and coping strategies (e.g., to break a large, overwhelming school assignment into smaller, more manageable parts; time management skills) can reduce anxiety, stress, and incidents of depression.

5. *Integrate mental health policies and care into the school.* Several school-based programs that address the internalizing problems discussed in this chapter are clearly beyond the efforts and control of individual teachers. To really confront these problems, some schools have developed integrated services that include a variety of support services. These can range from resources to help teachers recognize the symptoms of internalizing disorders all the way to on-staff mental health professionals to help diagnose and treat adolescents who suffer from these problems.

MyEdLab **Self-Check 11.1**

MyEdLab
Application Exercise 11.1 Eating Disorders In these two videos, two young adult women discuss their struggles with eating disorders and describe how their thought processes, events in their lives, and personality traits contributed to their disordered thoughts and behaviors.

Externalizing Disorders Most Common During Adolescence

>>>

Jason is a 15-year-old boy in his first year of high school. He is generally a good kid, but he has been disciplined by school personal twice during his freshman year. He was caught writing graffiti on the bathroom wall once and served a detention. He was also involved in a fight with another student and was suspended from school for a day.

Gregory is another student at the school that Jason attends. Like Jason, Gregory has also gotten in trouble in school. Unlike Jason, Gregory has a pattern of misbehavior that includes fights with other students and repeatedly vandalizing property on school grounds and around his neighborhood.

Many adolescents engage in antisocial or aggressive behaviors from time to time. From the occasional fight on the playground to petty thievery or vandalism, adolescent misdeeds are both common and annoying. But these occasional behaviors, such as those of Jason in the previous example, do not rise to the level of a disorder. For a much smaller percentage of adolescents, those who repeatedly vandalize property or behave aggressively toward others, such as Gregory in the previous example, there is a class of externalizing disorders that describe those adolescents and their behaviors. These disorders include *conduct disorder, oppositional-defiant disorder,* and *aggression.* All of these disorders, as well as other externalizing behaviors that are not psychological disorders but are problematic, all fall under the umbrella of **antisocial behavior.**

Conduct Disorder and Oppositional-Defiant Disorder

Conduct disorder is a clinically diagnosable pattern of behaviors that is marked by repetitive and persistent antisocial behavior. These behaviors often (but not always) involve aggression toward other people or animals and cause problems in the perpetrator's social relationships or functioning in school or work. The *Diagnostic and*

TABLE 11.2	Symptoms of Conduct Disorder	
Category	**Behavior**
Aggression to people or animals	• Often bullies or intimidates others • Often initiates fights • Use of a weapon • Cruelty to people or animals • Stealing while confronting victim (e.g., mugging) • Sexual assault
Destruction of property	• Deliberately setting fires with intent to cause damage • Intentionally destroying property
Deceitfulness or theft	• Breaking into someone's house or car • Often lies to others to gain something; "cons" • Shoplifting (without forcible entry), forgery
Serious violations of rules	• Often violates guardian-set curfew, beginning before age 13 • Running away from home multiple times or once for a lengthy period • Truancy from school, beginning before age 13

Source: Based on American Psychiatric Association, 2013.

Statistical Manual of Mental Disorders, fifth edition (American Psychiatric Association, 2013), referred to as the **DSM-V**, lists a number of symptoms of conduct disorder, and to be diagnosed with the ailment a person must display at least three of these behaviors over the last 12 months, and at least one in the last 6 months. Examples of these behaviors include bullying or intimidating others, initiating physical fights, being physically cruel to people or animals, mugging or robbing people, destroying other people's property intentionally, and engaging in age-inappropriate behavior such as running away from home, staying out late, or being truant from school, all before the age of 13 (see Table 11.2). **Oppositional-defiant disorder** is a somewhat milder form of conduct disorder that is marked by angry and spiteful interactions with others but often lacks the aggressive, violent aspect found among those with conduct disorder. Estimates of the prevalence of conduct disorder vary from sample to sample, but most research suggests that it is more common among boys (about 12%) than girls (about 7%) in the United States (Nock, Kazdin, Hiripi, & Kessler, 2006). Research suggests that the average age of onset for conduct disorder is about 12 years of age, but some children are diagnosed with the disorder before the age of 10.

Most adolescents who have conduct disorder do not grow into violent or antisocial adults, but some do. Individuals with conduct disorder who persist in their antisocial behaviors into adulthood can be diagnosed with a different disorder: **antisocial personality disorder**. This disorder is marked by an almost total disregard for societal rules or moral standards and a clear inability to get along with others. A subclass of those with antisocial disorder includes individuals known as **sociopaths** or **psychopaths**. A sociopath (or psychopath) is a person who has no moral compass and, as a result, often engages in extremely cruel and violent behavior. Sometimes sociopaths appear outwardly charming or affable, and they use this guise as a means of ingratiating themselves to others for the purposes of subsequent manipulation and violence. Some high-profile criminals, such as Ted Bundy and Jeffrey Dahmer, were considered psychopaths. Both were serial killers who used the outward appearance of geniality to lure their victims. Because many juveniles who engage in antisocial behavior do not continue such behavior into adulthood, terms such as *antisocial personality*, *psychopath*, and *sociopath* are not applied to minors.

Aggression

Aggression is a common form of problematic externalizing behavior that is marked by intentional hurting of others. Many adolescents with conduct disorder engage in aggressive behavior, but one can be aggressive without having conduct disorder. Aggression can be physical or relational, such as purposefully smearing another's reputation by posting hurtful gossip about him or her on social media, or shunning others for the sake of hurting their feelings. Adolescent boys are more likely than adolescent girls to engage in physically aggressive behavior. The reasons for this most likely include a combination of physical and social causes, such as more testosterone among adolescent males and lower societal acceptance of physically aggressive behavior among girls. Some have argued that societal prohibitions against girls' use of physical violence has caused them to resort to **relational aggression**. A book called *Queen Bees and Wannabes* (Wiseman, 2002) and a movie based on the book called *Mean Girls* (Michaels & Waters, 2004) argued that relational aggression was epidemic among adolescent girls. Although it is not possible to calculate the percentage of adolescents who engage in physical or relational aggression, it is clear that these forms of externalizing behaviors are serious problems, especially for the victims of such aggression.

Causes of Antisocial Behavior

There is evidence that serious physical aggression declines with age. Crime statistics reveal that violent criminal activity increases throughout the adolescent years, peaks around the age of 18, and then declines steadily throughout adulthood, with the decline becoming quite steep after age 24 (Federal Bureau of Investigation, 2014; see Figure 11.3). This trend has remained consistent over the last several decades, even as violent crime rates rose through the 1980s and have declined since the mid-1990s. During periods of relatively high or relatively low crime, late-adolescent males have always been the most likely to commit violent crimes. Indeed, this trend of increasing likelihood to commit violent crime throughout adolescence followed by a long and steady decline in adulthood led Moffitt (2006) to distinguish between *adolescence-limited offenders* and *life-course-persistent offenders*. **Adolescence-limited offenders** are those who generally do not begin their antisocial behavior until adolescence and only engage in such behavior during adolescence. This group is in quite stark contrast to **life-course-persistent offenders**, who often begin engaging in antisocial behavior before adolescence and continue to engage in antisocial and criminal behavior well into adulthood.

The implications of this difference between adolescence-limited and life-course-persistent offenders are profound. The punishment of a 16-year-old boy who assaults another person should perhaps differ if the assailant has little history of violent or antisocial behavior than if the assailant has a pattern of violent and antisocial behavior dating back to his childhood. The 16-year-old with no history of violence is not likely to continue his violent behavior into adulthood, whereas the 16-year-old with a pattern of antisocial behavior is likely to persist in that behavior as an adult (Moffitt, 2003).

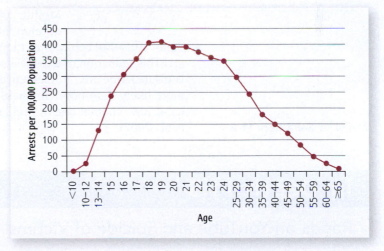

FIGURE 11.3

Arrest Rates for Violent Crime (Murder, Rape, Robbery, Aggravated Assault), by Age, United States, 2011

Source: Data from Federal Bureau of Investigation, 2014.

MyEdLab
Video Example 11.2

As Tim talks about his antisocial behavior and his mother describes her actions to curb it, think about the different kinds of adolescent delinquents and the social influences on antisocial behavior.

Given that adolescents engage in delinquent and antisocial behavior for different reasons and different lengths of time, should these factors be taken into account when they are punished for these behaviors? Or should all adolescents receive the same punishment for the same kinds of misbehavior?

MyEdLab Self-Check 11.2

There is also considerable evidence that the underlying causes of the antisocial or violent behavior differ quite dramatically for these two different types of offenders. Life-course-persistent offenders are likely to suffer from a combination of biological, cognitive, and environmental problems that all contribute to the behavior. For example, these adolescents are often raised in highly stressful environments that include chaotic homes and harsh parents, a relatively high amount of criminal activity in their neighborhoods, and high poverty (Susman, 2006). In addition to a possible genetic predisposition to engage in violent and antisocial behavior (chronic delinquent behavior tends to run in families), these chronic sources of stress can trigger stress hormones that are associated with more violent behavior and lower levels of impulse control. This inability to regulate one's emotions and behavior can lead some adolescents to respond to certain situations violently, whereas others who are better able to regulate their emotions and suppress their impulses will handle their anger in less aggressive ways. In addition to hormonal and genetic contributions to aggressive behavior, there is also evidence that adolescents who tend to respond to situations in an aggressive manner may have a **hostile attribution bias**. This refers to the tendency among some adolescents to interpret ambiguous acts (e.g., a look or a comment from another person) as being hostile, thereby triggering an aggressive response (Helfritz-Sinville & Stanford, 2014). This inability to regulate oneself may contribute to poor relations with peers, a common trait among chronically delinquent and aggressive adolescents (Raine et al., 2005).

In contrast, adolescence-limited delinquents do not appear to suffer from the cognitive and neurological problems seen among many life-course-persistent offenders. For those who begin their antisocial behavior during the adolescent years and tend to end it there as well, low parental supervision combined with associating with peers who tend to engage in antisocial behaviors appear to contribute to the problem behavior (McCabe, Hough, Wood, & Yeh, 2001; Moffitt, 2006). Most adolescence-limited delinquents do not develop into serious criminals. Indeed, they tend to mature out of antisocial behavior as they enter adulthood.

This reduction in antisocial behavior, however, does not mean that this group is trouble-free after adolescence. As adults, adolescence-limited delinquents are more likely than nondelinquent adolescents to develop drug and alcohol problems, have mental health problems, and experience financial difficulties (Moffitt et al., 2002).

In-Depth 11.3

Rapes on YouTube and Suicide of Victims

One of the disturbing new trends in social media use by teens is the sharing of photos and videos that provide evidence of drunken, semi-conscious adolescent girls being sexually assaulted. In a series of highly publicized cases, one adolescent girl after another experienced not only the pain of the assault, but the humiliation and harassment of their peers once the pictures and videos of the assaults were

posted online for all to see. Some of these crimes resulted in the victims taking their own lives. Audrie Pott, a 15-year-old, committed suicide a week after the three high school boys who allegedly raped her posted pictures of their crime online. Rehtaeh Parsons, a 17-year-old Canadian girl, also committed suicide after images of her rape were posted online. And in a particularly high-profile case, a 16-year-old girl in Ohio was raped by two teenage football players on the celebrated high school team.

Rape is certainly not a recent invention, and there is no evidence that the frequency of rapes has increased since the creation of the Internet. What is new is the ability of the perpetrators to subject their victims to increased shame and bullying by posting evidence of the crimes online and allowing everybody to see the victim being assaulted. In each of the cases just described, the *victims* of the assaults were bullied online by their peers and by strangers who had not participated in the crimes. As

Ron Astor and his colleagues have noted, bullying and violence tend to occur more often in the "unclaimed" spaces of schools and society (Astor, Meyer, & Behre, 1999). Perpetrators are emboldened when no adult is present to monitor their behavior. In many ways, the Internet represents the ultimate unclaimed space, where people can harass and humiliate others, often anonymously. It may not be surprising that social media and the Internet have ushered in new opportunities for adolescents to bully and humiliate each other, but it certainly is revolting.

Substance Use and Abuse Among Adolescents

As mentioned in Chapter 2, adolescence tends to be the healthiest time of life for most people, and the majority of adolescents are strong and healthy. Indeed, the most common ailments affecting adolescent health are self-inflicted: engaging in risky behavior and abusing substances. Although most adolescents and early adults experiment with one or more types of drugs or alcohol, such as drinking a beer or smoking a cigarette, it is the *abuse* of these substances that often begins in adolescence and causes damage to physical health, mental health, and daily functioning.

Alcohol

The national Youth Risk Behavior Survey (YRBS; CDC, 2013) collects data about the substance use of high school students. It is conducted every 2 years and provides a representative picture of substance use among students in grades 9 through 12 in the United States since 1991. In 2013 (the last year for which data are reported), the following statistics about high school students' use of alcohol were gathered in the YRBS (CDC, 2013):

- 66% have tried at least one alcoholic drink in their lives;
- 35% had at least one alcoholic drink within the 30 days prior to completing the survey;
- 21% had consumed at least five alcoholic drinks within a short period of time (i.e., a few hours) during the 30 days prior to completing the survey (this is the definition of **binge drinking**); and
- 6% had consumed at least 10 drinks within a short period of time (i.e., a few hours) during the 30 days prior to completing the survey.

Over the last 20 years, would you guess that the prevalence of drinking among high school students has increased, decreased, or stayed the same? According to the statistics from the YRBS (CDC, 2013), the numbers *decreased* from 1991 to 2013 in all four categories of drinking rated by the survey. For example, in 1991 82% of high school students reported having had at least one drink in their lives, and 51% had consumed at least one drink within the month before taking the survey. In addition, almost a third of all high school students (31.3%) in 1991 reported engaging in binge drinking at least once within the 30 days prior to completing the survey, compared with less than a quarter of students who reported binge drinking in the 2013 survey. The good news is that alcohol consumption and abuse among

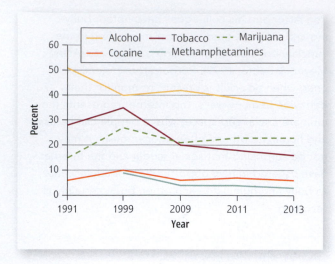

FIGURE 11.4

Drug and Alcohol Use by Adolescents, 1991–2013

Source: Data from Centers for Disease Control and Prevention, 2013.

MyEdLab

Video Example 11.3

Several teens discuss why they use drugs and how they got deeper into drug use and abuse.

adolescents appears to be on the decline. The bad news is that roughly three-quarters of high school students have at least tried alcohol (almost all illegally), and almost one-quarter have engaged in binge drinking. How do the trends in alcohol use among adolescents compare to the trends for the use of other drugs?

Illicit Drugs

According to data collected by the YRBS (CDC, 2013), the use of **illicit drugs** such as marijuana, cocaine, and methamphetamines has followed an interesting pattern over the last 20 years or so. After a period of steady increase from 1991 to 2001, there was a slow decline in the use of these drugs by adolescents from 1999 to 2013 (see Figure 11.4). The use of some of these drugs (e.g., alcohol, tobacco) continued to decline between 2009 and 2013. In contrast, after a decade of decline, adolescents' use of marijuana increased between 2009 and 2013. A similar but smaller increase was reported for the use of cocaine. Even among newer drugs such as Ecstasy, there has been a decline in use among high school students. In 2001, 11% of high school students said they had used Ecstasy at least once. By 2007, this percentage had declined to 5.8%. Although there was a slight uptick to 6.6% in 2013, the percentage of high school students who report having tried Ecstasy is still down substantially from where it was in 2001.

Besides alcohol, the drug most commonly used by U.S. high school students is tobacco. Almost half (41%) of all high school students reported having smoked at least one cigarette in their lives, and the percentage was roughly equal for boys and girls (CDC, 2013). This number is down substantially from the 1990s, when the percentage of high schoolers who had tried a cigarette hovered around 70%. Thankfully, the percentage has dropped about 4% every 2 years since 2001. There has been a similar decline among frequent smokers. After reaching a peak in 1999 of 17% of high school students who said they smoked cigarettes on at least 20 of the previous 30 days, by 2013 only 5.6% reported smoking that often. Of course, the frequency of use is quite a bit higher among 12th graders than it is among 9th graders, but the pattern of change, and in particular of decline over the last decade, is similar for all age groups.

Differences by Ethnicity and Gender in the Use of Drugs and Alcohol

Adolescents' use of drugs and alcohol differs by gender and race as well as by age, with older adolescents being more likely to use drugs and alcohol than are younger adolescents. In the 2013 YRBS survey (CDC, 2013), girls (67.9%) were significantly more likely than boys (64.4%) to report having tried alcohol, but the difference was slight. There were no gender differences in the percentages of adolescents who engaged in binge drinking or were current users of alcohol, but boys were more likely to have had a drink by the age of 13 (21% compared with 17% for girls). Similarly, there were no differences in boys' and girls' current smoking behaviors, but boys were more likely than girls to begin smoking before the age of 13. For illicit drug use, high school boys were significantly more likely than high school girls to have ever tried Ecstasy, cocaine, and marijuana, and were also significantly more likely to be current users of cocaine or marijuana. Keep in mind that in 2013, whereas nearly three-quarters of high school students had tried alcohol and a little less than half had tried cigarettes and/or marijuana, less than 15% had tried cocaine, methamphetamines, or Ecstasy.

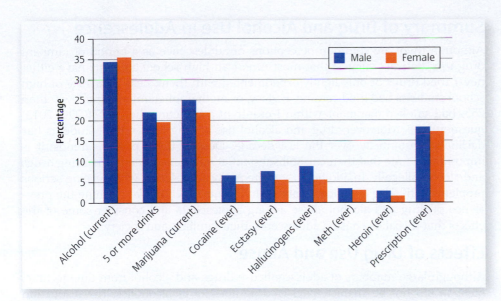

FIGURE 11.5

Gender Differences in Drug and Alcohol Use, Grades 9–12, 2013

Source: Data from Centers for Disease Control and Prevention, 2013.

Note: Prescription drug use was without a doctor's prescription.

In addition to the minor differences between boys and girls (see Figure 11.5), the YRBS (CDC, 2013) reported several differences among ethnic groups in their use of drugs and alcohol. Table 11.3 presents the percentages of high school students in five different ethnic groups who used various types of drugs and alcohol. Some notable differences among the ethnic groups are apparent. Asian students tend to use drugs and alcohol significantly less than all of the other ethnic groups across all of the drugs and alcohol examined, except for methamphetamine use (which was low). On the more worrisome side, the American Indian/Alaskan Native group tends to have a higher percentage of adolescents who use drugs and tobacco than do the other ethnic groups. Whereas Hispanic adolescents as a group were relatively high in their use of all of the drug and alcohol categories in Table 11.3, African American high school students were relatively high in some categories (e.g., marijuana use) and relatively low in others (e.g., binge drinking, current smoking).

TABLE 11.3 Drug and Alcohol Use (Percentages), by Ethnicity

	Black	White	Hispanic	Asian	American Indian/ Alaskan Native
Ever used alcohol	63.4	65.9	72.4	51.3	70
Current alcohol use	29.6	36.3	37.5	21.7	33.4
Binge drink	12.4	23.2	22.6	10.2	18.3
Ever smoked tobacco	34.0	42.9	43.2	24.7	62.3
Current tobacco smoking	8.3	18.6	14.0	10.3	24.6
Ever used marijuana	46.8	36.7	48.8	24.4	46.2
Current marijuana use	28.9	20.4	27.6	16.4	35.3
Ever used cocaine	2.1	4.8	9.5	5.3	13.3
Ever used Ecstasy	4.4	5.8	9.4	7.9	9.7
Ever used methamphetamines	1.3	3.0	4.5	3.8	10.6

Source: Data from Centers for Disease Control and Prevention, 2013.

Summary of Drug and Alcohol Use in Adolescence

Although there are common perceptions of adolescence as a period of rampant drug use, statistics suggest that most American high school students have either never tried drugs or only lightly experimented with them. Less than 15% of high school students had tried cocaine, Ecstasy, or methamphetamines, and fewer than 25% had smoked marijuana within 1 month of completing the YRBS (CDC, 2013) questionnaire. Moreover, drug and alcohol use among high school students has declined substantially over the last decade. Despite these positive trends, it is important to note that there are still substantial numbers of teenagers using drugs and alcohol illegally. In addition, there are many adolescents who develop serious problems with drug and alcohol abuse. In the next section, we examine the prevalence of drug and alcohol abuse among adolescents and consider some of the effects that this abuse has on adolescents, their families, and society.

Effects of Drug Use and Abuse

Although large numbers of adolescents use drugs and alcohol from time to time, most would not be characterized as drug abusers or alcoholics. The distinction between an occasional user and an abuser is an important one. To rise to the level of abuse, the use of drugs or alcohol must cause some problems for the user, such as missing work or deterioration of relationships or negative feelings about the self. The use of drugs is considered an **addiction** when the user feels a loss of control over his or her ability to cease using the substance. In essence, the drug use becomes a compulsion rather than merely a willful act.

Data collected on large samples of 8th, 10th, and 12th graders in the United States from 2011 to 2014 in the Monitoring the Future Study (University of Michigan, 2014) reveal the wide disparity between the occasional versus frequent users of drugs during adolescence (see Table 11.4). For example, whereas

TABLE 11.4	Trends in Adolescent Drug Use, by Grade Level and Frequency						
Drug	**Time Period**	**8th Grade**		**10th Grade**		**12th Grade**	
		2011	**2014**	**2011**	**2014**	**2011**	**2014**
Alcohol	Lifetime	33.1	26.8	56.0	49.3	70.0	66.0
	Past Month	12.7	9.0	27.2	23.5	40.0	37.4
	Daily	.40	.30	.80	.80	2.10	1.90
Cigarettes (any use)	Lifetime	18.4	13.5	30.4	22.6	40.0	34.4
	Past Month	6.1	4.0	11.8	7.2	18.7	13.6
	Daily	2.4	1.4	5.5	3.2	10.3	6.7
E-cigarettes	Past Month		6.7		16.2		17.1
Marijuana/hashish	Lifetime	16.4	15.6	34.5	33.7	45.5	44.4
	Past Month	7.2	6.5	17.6	16.6	22.6	21.2
	Daily	1.3	1.0	3.6	3.4	6.6	5.8
Prescription drugs	Lifetime					21.7	19.9
	Past Month					7.2	6.4
Cocaine (any kind)	Lifetime	3.7	3.0	4.9	3.6	7.1	6.4
	Past Month	1.3	0.8	1.1	0.9	1.6	1.7

Source: Johnston et al, 2012.

66% of 12th graders in 2014 reported that they had tried alcohol at least once in their lives, and 60.2% said they had consumed alcohol at least once in the last year, only 1.9% indicated that they drank alcohol daily. These disparities between occasional use and frequent use were present for just about all drugs.

The data from the Monitoring the Future Study (University of Michigan, 2014) presented in Table 11.4 also reveal that, for most drugs (i.e., alcohol, cigarettes, marijuana, cocaine), and at each of the three grade levels included in the study, drug use decreased from 2011 to 2014. The one exception to this trend is the use of electronic cigarettes, which are new and continue to gain popularity with adolescents.

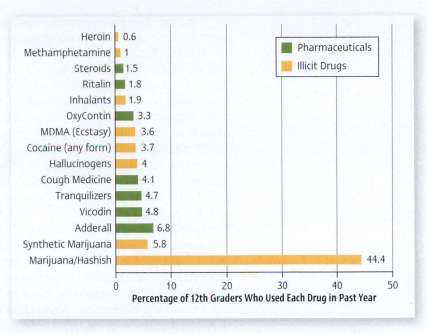

FIGURE 11.6

Use of Illicit and Prescription Drugs by 12th Graders in Past Year

Source: Data from University of Michigan, 2014.

Two additional features of adolescent drug use are worth noting. First, the use of most drugs (besides alcohol, tobacco, and marijuana) among adolescents is quite low. By 12th grade, 6.4% of adolescents had tried cocaine and 1.7% had used it in the past month. Similarly, 6.3% had tried some sort of hallucinogen (e.g., LSD; MDMA, a.k.a. "Ecstasy") at least once in their lives, and 1.5% in the previous month. Second, the most commonly used drugs among 12th graders in the United States, after marijuana, are prescription drugs that are not being used for prescribed purposes. In other words, these are prescription drugs that adolescents take from their parents, receive from their friends, or buy off the street for the purposes of getting high. More than 1 in 5 12th graders had taken some sort of prescription drug for nonmedical reasons at least once, and 6.4% had taken them within the last 30 days (amphetamines and tranquilizers were the two most common types of prescription drugs taken). As presented in Figure 11.6, after marijuana, the four most commonly used drugs among 12th graders were prescription drugs used for nonmedical reasons.

Reasons for Drug Use

Adolescents receive a lot of mixed messages about drugs and alcohol. On the one hand, they receive frequent warnings from teachers, public service announcements, and parents not to use them. On the other hand, adolescents are bombarded with images of people around their age using and enjoying alcohol, cigarettes, and, sometimes, illegal drugs (e.g., in movies). It can be difficult to heed the warnings when the competing messages about the fun these vices provide are so attractive. For example, many of the advertisements for alcohol and cigarettes, although supposedly not targeted at adolescents, show relatively young people, usually attractive, engaged in the types of activities that adolescents enjoy, such as playing on the beach or socializing with friends at a party.

When considering the reasons that adolescents might use drugs and alcohol, it is important to remain mindful of the distinction between an infrequent user and an abuser. For example, a high school student may use a stimulant such as Ritalin every once in a while when he has several exams to study for. Another student, in contrast, may use a stimulant such as methamphetamine daily because he has become addicted to it. Both are using stimulants, but they are using them for different reasons and with different frequency.

Perhaps the most common reasons that adolescents begin using drugs and alcohol are curiosity and peer pressure. With increasing cognitive sophistication (as discussed in Chapter 3) comes a desire to discover for themselves how drugs and alcohol make them feel. Because most drugs produce some sort of pleasurable effect, adolescents (like adults) often continue to use drugs and alcohol because they enjoy the effects. Many adolescents are encouraged by their peers to try a drink or a drug, and the pressure can be difficult to resist when the benefits of joining include social bonding and a sense that one is being cool.

In addition to these fairly innocent reasons for trying drugs and alcohol, there are several other factors that may be influencing adolescents' decisions. One is that adolescents often have a false sense of **invincibility**. They feel strong and healthy, and the problems of old age, such as cancer and sclerosis of the liver, seem remote and far away. This explains why many adolescents who know that smoking and drinking are unhealthy choose to engage in these behaviors anyway. Another reason is that many adolescents quickly discover that some drugs, most notably marijuana and alcohol, can relieve stress, at least temporarily. As we discussed earlier in this chapter, stress and anxiety are common problems among adolescents, so they often welcome the relief provided by drugs and alcohol.

One of the interesting reasons that adolescents use drugs and alcohol is that they often perceive there to be little risk involved in the use of these substances. For example, data from the Monitoring the Future Study (University of Michigan, 2014) indicate that 12th graders' use of marijuana has increased as their perceptions about the risks of marijuana use have declined (see Figure 11.7). Similarly, electronic cigarettes are now more commonly used by teens in the United States than regular tobacco cigarettes, partly because only 14.2% of 12th graders believe that e-cigarette use (i.e., **vaping**) is harmful (University of Michigan, 2014). These perceptions reflect the changing views of American society at large regarding marijuana use and may be influenced further by the increasing liberalization of marijuana laws. Similarly, adolescents tend to view alcohol use, even binge drinking, as relatively safe. According to a 2013 study, only 39% of adolescents believed that having five or more drinks at one sitting once or twice per week was highly risky. Similarly, about a quarter of adolescents believed that smoking pot

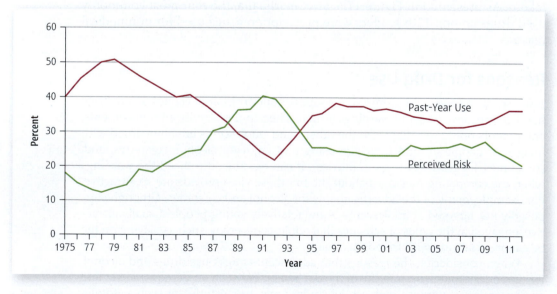

FIGURE 11.7

Trends in Marijuana Use and Perceived Risk of Marijuana Use Among 12th Graders

Source: Data from University of Michigan, 2014.

once per month was risky behavior (Substance Abuse and Mental Health Services Administration, 2014).

It is also important to note that certain personality traits are associated with engaging in risky behaviors during adolescence, including taking drugs. **Impulsivity** and high **sensation seeking** are two personality traits associated with such risky behaviors (Andrucci, Archer, Pancoast, & Gordon, 1989; Donohew et al., 1999). Some research suggests that high sensation seekers are drawn toward deviant peers who talk favorably about drug use, which increases the likelihood of these sensation-seeking adolescents to engage in drug use (Yanovitsky, 2005). As discussed in the section of Chapter 2 on brain development, adolescents often experience an increase in sensation seeking, pleasure seeking, and the desire for intense experiences, and drugs often provide these effects. Helping adolescents find other, safer methods of satisfying these needs for pleasure and thrills, such as sports or performing arts, may reduce their likelihood of taking drugs.

Comorbidity of Internalizing Disorders, Externalizing Disorders, and Substance Abuse

Although we have presented information about internalizing disorders, externalizing disorders, and substance abuse separately, it is important to note that there is a fair amount of **comorbidity** among these kinds of problems during adolescence. For example, research with adolescents who have sought treatment for substance abuse has found that slightly more than 40% of adolescents seeking treatment for a substance use problem also had symptoms of both internalizing *and* externalizing disorders (Chan, Dennis, & Funk, 2008). In addition, research has found that roughly 70% of adolescents seeking treatment for substance use also had some sort of mental disorder. Internalizing disorders in this population of substance users increased with age, from roughly 50% for adolescents between the ages of 12 and 17 to over 60% for adolescents and young adults between 18 and 25 years old (Chan et al., 2008). The comorbidity rates for substance problems and externalizing disorders decreased with age, from about 65% among adolescents younger than 18 to about 50% among young adults aged 18 to 25. Some of the disorders that co-occur most frequently among adolescents with substance use problems are conduct disorder, **attention deficit hyperactivity disorder (ADHD)**, major depressive disorder, and **posttraumatic stress disorder (PTSD)** (Clark et al., 1997). Research also indicates that the comorbidity of mental health problems with substance use problems increases substantially when substance use becomes an addiction. For example, whereas over 70% of adolescents and young adults who were dependent on drugs or alcohol also had some form of internalizing disorder, that percentage dropped to about 33% among adolescents who used, but were not addicted to, these substances (Chan et al., 2008).

What Educators Can Do

Because the use of drugs and alcohol during adolescence is unhealthy, can lead to engaging in unsafe behaviors such as driving while intoxicated or engaging in unprotected sex, and can lead some adolescents to develop drug dependency and abuse, educators have long been concerned with developing strategies for preventing adolescents from using drugs or alcohol. What can teachers and schools do to prevent or reduce drug use and abuse among adolescents?

One approach that shows some promise is a **life-skills training** program (Griffin, Botvin, Nichols, & Doyle, 2003). This program is based upon the belief that adolescents sometimes turn to drugs because they have difficulty coping with the stresses in their lives and lack the self-confidence and social skills to resist pressure from peers and the larger culture to engage in behavior such as drinking or drug use. Adolescents who are exposed to a lot of stressors in their lives—for example, low income, living in urban areas with high crime rates, experiencing trauma—may be particularly at risk for taking drugs and drinking. The life-skills training program teaches adolescents how to develop social and coping skills, with the goal of helping students develop the internal resources to allow them to resist the pressure to engage in drug use. Results of this study indicated that at-risk adolescents who participated in the program were less likely to use a variety of drugs (e.g., tobacco, alcohol, inhalants) than were a similar group of adolescents who did not participate in the program.

Another approach, called Climate Schools, provides students with online and in-class information and activities to show adolescents some of the risks of alcohol and marijuana use. This approach is based on the principles of **modeling** and **observational learning** developed by Bandura (1986). In a series of sessions, students follow a cartoon storyline depicting adolescents having difficulties with alcohol or marijuana use. The students then complete activities and lessons related to the storyline in their classrooms, delivered by teachers. Results of a study examining the effectiveness of the Climate Schools program found that adolescents who participated in the program were more knowledgeable of the problems associated with alcohol and marijuana use and were less likely to drink alcohol than were their peers who did not participate in the program (Newton, Teesson, Vogl, & Andrews, 2010). These results suggest that there are benefits to observing models, even fictional models, engaged in real-life activities associated with drug and alcohol use.

As we have discussed in previous chapters (i.e., in the discussions of physical development in Chapter 2, cognitive development in Chapter 3, and sexuality in Chapter 10), adolescents are prone to certain cognitive errors that increase their willingness to engage in risky behaviors and reduce their willingness to be convinced not to. For example, adolescents often have feelings of invincibility that lead them to disregard the potential dangers of certain activities. There are very few teenagers who do not know that smoking is bad for one's health. Yet every day thousands of adolescents start smoking, led in part by the false belief that the health risks do not apply to them. Similarly, adolescents are vulnerable to the belief that "everyone is doing it." In other words, they often overestimate the number or percentage of their peers who engage in a behavior, whether that behavior is cheating in school, having sex, or smoking pot. Some long-established and well-funded drug-prevention programs, most notably the Drug Abuse Resistance Education (D.A.R.E.) program, have been found to be ineffective in reducing or preventing adolescent drug use (Lilienfeld, 2007; Singh et al., 2011). It appears that simply telling adolescents that they should not do drugs, and even asking them to sign a contract saying they will not take drugs, does not reduce the likelihood that they will actually take drugs. Just as with sex education, drug-prevention programs that are based on fear and scaring adolescents straight are generally ineffective. Why? Because adolescents do not believe the dangers apply to them, and because they believe lots of their peers are engaged in the behavior without negative consequences.

Given these characteristics of adolescent thinking, the most effective approaches to reducing and preventing teen drug use and abuse are those that provide adolescents with accurate information and with alternative strategies besides saying "yes" when drugs are offered. For example, telling adolescents that most kids their age did not smoke, drink, or take any drugs in the last 30 days may help teens realize that drinking and taking drugs is *not* the norm for their age group. This information, coupled with some skills training, can provide adolescents with the confidence they need to resist pressure to take drugs. Rumors and popular media can make drug use seem to be the norm among teenagers, when in fact it is not.

It also appears that the ability to talk openly with trusted adults about drug and alcohol use may reduce adolescents' likelihood of using and abusing drugs

(Mayo Clinic, 2013). When adults try to scare teenagers away from behaviors such as sex and drug use, young people can feel uneasy discussing their own interest in and questions about these activities. On the other hand, presenting teens with accurate information about drugs, including why people take them and how many adolescents do not use drugs, can build trust between adolescents and adults, such as their teachers. It can also open the door for teachers to help their adolescent students develop alternative social and coping skills to deal with their stress, anxiety, or boredom, thereby reducing their desire to turn to drugs to alleviate these problems.

Because there is an association between impulsivity, sensation seeking, and engaging in risky behavior such as drug use during adolescence, some researchers have suggested that efforts to reduce these behaviors need to target adolescents with these personality traits specifically. For example, antidrug messages presented in the media, such as public service announcement commercials on television, appear to be more effective if they are designed to appeal to adolescents who are high in sensation seeking (Donohew, Palmgreen & Lorch, 1994; Palmgreen, Donohew, Lorch, Hoyle, & Stephenson, 2001).

Considering the various reasons that adolescents use alcohol and drugs, evaluate the substance-use-prevention programs that you are aware of. How effective do you think commercials, warning labels, programs like D.A.R.E., and other efforts that you are familiar with are in keeping adolescents off of drugs and alcohol? Why do you think so?

MyEdLab **Self-Check 11.3**

Trauma

There are many reasons why different kinds of disorders may co-occur within certain groups of adolescents. For example, a genetic predisposition to abuse drugs and alcohol may contribute to anxiety and antisocial behavior. Similarly, chronic stress caused by persistent poverty can contribute to the development of several disorders, causing comorbidity among them. Traumatic experiences in childhood and adolescence can also lead to the development of both internalizing and externalizing disorders, as well as the use and abuse of substances to cope with the trauma and after-effects.

A remarkably high number of adolescents are exposed to **traumatic life events**, which are defined as events that threaten "physical injury, death, or the physical integrity of self or others and also causes horror, terror, or helplessness at the time it occurs" (APA Zero Tolerance Task Force, 2008, p. 2). These traumatic events can either be experienced personally or be witnessed as they happen to others. Examples of such events include being the victim of, or witness to, natural disasters; automobile accidents; sexual abuse; physical abuse; acts of violence in the home, school, or community; terrorism; and war. Although estimates of the percentage of adolescents who experience or witness traumatic life events vary widely, the numbers are alarming. For example, between 39% and 85% of adolescents have witnessed violence in their communities, and up to 65% have been victims of such violence (APA Zero Tolerance Task Force, 2008). In addition, millions of adolescents have been victims or witnesses of sexual abuse, domestic violence, and unintentional injury. And millions more experience or witness earthquakes, floods, tornadoes, wars, and other natural and human-made disasters.

Many children and adolescents develop short-term anxieties as a result of their exposure to such traumatic events. This can result in behaviors, beliefs, and emotions that are symptomatic of some of the disorders discussed earlier in this chapter, such as sadness, irritability, anxiety, and anger. These symptoms tend to decline as the reaction to the traumatic event fades. But for some adolescents, particularly those who repeatedly experience traumatic events, the trauma creates longer-lasting effects that can lead to posttraumatic stress disorder (PTSD).

The best estimate is that roughly 5% of U.S. adolescents have experienced PTSD, with higher rates for girls than for boys (Kessler, 2013). Adolescents with PTSD, or those who have simply experienced a traumatic event but not developed PTSD, often experience other mental health problems as well. For example, it is quite common for adolescents with PTSD to also suffer from anxiety and depression. Similarly, experiencing trauma can lead to externalizing disorders such as conduct disorder and aggressive behavior. Substance use and abuse are more common among adolescents who have experienced trauma than those who have not, as is suicide ideation, academic difficulties, and problems with interpersonal relationships (Giaconia et al., 1995). Although it is clear that exposure to trauma can impair the healthy functioning of adolescents, there is evidence that most adolescents who suffer the negative effects of trauma exposure do not receive any treatment from health care professionals to cope with these problems (APA Zero Tolerance Task Force, 2008). This is particularly true for minority and immigrant adolescents, who tend to live in lower-income households with less access to mental health services.

Because large numbers of adolescents have experienced and witnessed traumatic events but have never received psychological services to help them cope with these events, and because exposure to trauma can interfere with healthy functioning and academic performance, some schools have decided to address the issues themselves. In Massachusetts, for example, the Department of Elementary and Secondary Education is providing grants to schools that want to develop programs for helping students who have been exposed to trauma. Projects such as the Trauma and Learning Policy Initiative (TLPI; see http://traumasensitiveschools.org/) are providing information and resources to educators to help them learn about the effects of trauma on learning and develop strategies for helping traumatized students. Because some traumatized students engage in problematic behavior in school, they are often punished for their behavior rather than treated for their trauma. This led to a class-action lawsuit in Compton, California, aimed at getting trauma recognized as a disability that deserves treatment rather than as a behavior that warrants punishment and expulsion (National Public Radio, 2015). (For more information on this lawsuit and the effects of trauma on adolescent learning, read or listen to the story at http://www.npr.org/sections/ed/2015/08/20/432885473/are-traumatized-students-disabled-a-debate-straight-outta-compton). As schools become more aware of the symptoms and consequences of trauma on their students' learning and behavior, they will develop better, more sensitive strategies for working with traumatized students.

Recommendations for Educators

MyEdLab
Video Example 11.4

In this video a middle school teacher and her students discuss bullying, aggression, and what students, teachers, and schools can do to reduce it.

It would be easy for teachers and schools to view the problems described in this chapter, whether internalizing or externalizing, as beyond their jurisdiction. After all, teachers are not trained to treat depression, anxiety, conduct disorders, or drug addiction. In addition, many of these problems have their roots in causes that are beyond the school's control, such as biological predispositions or stresses in the adolescents' homes and neighborhoods. But all of these problems can have serious consequences for student motivation, achievement, and behavior in school, and there are practices and programs that teachers and schools can employ to help students cope with anxiety, resist the urge to take drugs, and choose not to engage in antisocial behavior. And because these problems are often comorbid (i.e., occur together and influence one another), even treating just one type of problem can reap numerous benefits. For example, anxiety, aggressive behavior, and drug use can all be reduced by helping adolescents develop effective strategies for coping with stressful situations.

The approach that teachers and schools take to addressing the kinds of problems discussed in this chapter can take many forms, and will vary depending on the nature of the specific problem. Several specific treatment programs have already been discussed. Here is a more general list of steps that teachers and schools can take to help adolescents cope with their challenges:

- Learn the signs of different types of problems, from depression to PTSD, so that you can increase your awareness of and ability to recognize problems.
- Teachers can and should take some ownership of the problem (e.g., monitoring public spaces, talking about stressors and problems openly) rather than thinking of these problems as beyond their control or responsibility. This does not mean that teachers should diagnose and treat every problem they witness among their students. But if you suspect that an adolescent is engaged in risky behavior or suffering from a mental or behavioral disorder, do not look the other way. Seek assistance from an administrator, a school psychologist/counselor, and a health professional if possible.
- Teachers can make themselves credible to students by being honest and by listening openly. When teachers and other adults are perceived as credible, students are more likely to talk with them about their problems and to listen to their advice.
- Teachers and schools should look for and implement good, evidence-based programs to help with problems.
  - Beware of "hyped" programs with little evidence of efficacy (e.g., some drug-prevention programs, self-esteem-boosting programs).
- Teachers and administrators should beware of biases and prejudices that influence their beliefs about, and treatment of, student problems. For example, believing that all adolescents are naturally moody can cause some teachers to overlook more serious problems, such as depression. Similarly, stereotypes about African American students can lead school personnel to administer harsher penalties for their misconduct.

MyEdLab **Self-Check 11.4**

Conclusion

Although most adolescents navigate their way through adolescence without becoming addicted to drugs or engaging in problematic antisocial behavior, some adolescents are confronted with serious psychological problems that impair their functioning in and out of school. Anxiety, depression, aggression, and substance abuse are just some of the problems that teachers of adolescents witness or hear about frequently. By observing these problems, discussing them openly and honestly with students, and employing sound, evidence-based programs for addressing these problems, teachers and schools can do much to help their adolescent students cope with and overcome these difficulties. It is important to remember, however, that some of the problems adolescents face, especially psychological disorders and addictions, cannot be adequately treated by teachers. These problems need to be addressed by professional therapists and counselors who have been trained to deal with these issues. Teachers can recognize the signs of problems and refer students and their families for counseling, but they should not try to treat students' psychological problems themselves.

12

Moving Into Adulthood

Learning Outcomes

12.1 You will be able to describe the phenomenon of emerging adulthood, and explain how teachers can facilitate the transition into emerging adulthood for high school students.

12.2 You will be able to describe issues related to the transition to college, and how teachers can help adolescents to make informed decisions about their postsecondary educational options.

12.3 You will be able to describe the transition into the workforce or the military, and how teachers can support students who make these choices.

Introduction

Adolescence does not end when students leave school. Whereas there used to be clear societal delineations or boundaries between adolescence and adulthood, those have become blurred in recent years, particularly in the United States (Gilmore, 2002; Hendry & Kloep, 2012). There are some 20-year-old young adults who engage in what society would deem as highly adult-like activities (e.g., working full-time, raising children, caring for aging parents, etc.), and there are simultaneously other 20-year-old adults who engage in what many would deem as "finding themselves" (e.g., constantly switching jobs, trying out many different majors in college, backpacking across the United States or Europe, etc.). Thus some young adults are truly living the lives of adults, whereas others are living what would seem to many to be a continuation of their adolescence. In general, many aspects of adolescents' lives change as they move into adulthood. These changes include changes in living arrangements, changes in relationships with other family members, and numerous other transitions (Scabini, Marta, & Lanz, 2006).

The fact that the boundaries between adolescence and adulthood are less clear than ever has implications for teachers; those implications are particularly relevant for high school teachers who are working with students who are about to transition out of school and into new realms of life. These issues also are important for middle school teachers, because even early adolescents often consider what they will do after they complete high school. As educators, we need to be aware of these forthcoming transitions, and to help our students to make wise choices and to be prepared for the next stages of their lives.

Middle school and high school teachers can play meaningful roles in the preparation of their students for life after high school. As educators, we need to be particularly cognizant of our own values and beliefs. Although licensed teachers almost always have college degrees, some of our students may not value higher education, even though they may have achieved highly during high school. As educators, we need to be particularly sensitive to the values of our students, their families, and their communities, and our own beliefs and values, so that we can best help our students in making wise choices regarding their postsecondary plans.

OVERVIEW OF THE CHAPTER

In this chapter, we explore these transitions. In particular, we examine some of the more common transitions that adolescents make after high school, and we also discuss how we as teachers can help students to navigate those transitions successfully. In addition, we examine these transitions within the larger context of how young adulthood is viewed by educators, researchers, and policymakers in contemporary society; specifically, we examine the period of life roughly between the ages of 18 through 29, which in recent years has been referred to as the period of emerging adulthood.

Although adolescents can pursue many different types of life choices after high school, there are several that are particularly common. These include transitions into the working world, transitions into college, and transitions into the military. In this chapter, we examine these three transitions carefully. We consider the characteristics of students who choose these varied life trajectories (including current demographic trends), and we also discuss ways in which teachers can help students to think about and plan for their futures while still in high school. We also discuss the outcomes of these transitions—although most adolescents experience positive transitions, some experience unpleasant transitions, and we examine some of the reasons in this chapter.

Emerging Adulthood

Consider the following descriptions of young adults:

>>>

Jonah is 19 years old. He graduated from high school last year, and he probably could have gone to college if he had wanted to, but he just isn't sure what he wants to do with his life. His grandmother left him several thousand dollars when she died, and he has decided to backpack through Europe for as long as he can (until his money runs out). He'll figure out what to do with the rest of his life after he is finished with his journey through Europe.

Keisha is 21 years old. She is in college, and has switched majors several times. Although she should be graduating at the end of this academic year, she has not earned enough credit hours yet to complete a major. She has been taking many different courses, in many different subject areas, before she commits to a major.

Ray is 23 years old. He has a steady job, and he has been in several different types of relationships during the past few years. For one year, he had a steady girlfriend; for another year, he and a different girlfriend moved in and lived together; for several other years, Ray was single but dated many different women.

Mandy enlisted in the army right after high school. She comes from a military family, and she has always envisioned a career in the military as a possibility for herself. She has thought about going to college, but she decided to try the military first. Many of her friends don't understand why she has made this choice, but Mandy is determined to try the military, at least until she is ready to start a family; after that, she might move on to other career.

What do Ray, Keisha, Mandy, and Jonah have in common? In some respects, they have very little in common—Jonah is backpacking through Europe, Keisha is a college student, Ray is successfully employed, and Mandy is going to try life in the military. However, on another level, they do have something in common—each, in her or his own way, is experimenting with different options and opportunities; none of the four has firmly committed to a particular permanent lifestyle. Jonah doesn't know what he wants to do with himself, so he spends time gallivanting around Europe; Keisha does not know what she wants to do for her career, so she dabbles in many majors while in college; Ray does not know what kind of relationships he wants, so he tries out many different kinds of relationships (single life, steady girlfriend, living together); Mandy isn't sure about college or her long-term goals, so she decides to try being in the military for a while.

These four individuals are representative of the period of development that is referred to as **emerging adulthood.** Emerging adulthood is the period between the ages of 18 through 29; this period is distinct from both adolescence and early adulthood, and represents a time during which individuals explore various life options, without necessarily committing to any of those possibilities (Arnett, 2000). Emerging adults explore many different facets of life, and generally are free of most forms of parental authority, but also do not have many of the responsibilities of adults (Arnett, 2004). They may try out different career options; they may move from one area of study to another; they may try out different religious or political viewpoints; they may entertain a number of different kinds of relationships; they may try out different types of hobbies; they may move from one city to another; and they may interact with a variety of peer groups. Jonah, Keisha, Ray, and Mandy all have made different life choices, but all four of them are emerging adults.

Jeffrey Arnett and some of his colleagues have identified several demographic trends that support the emergence of this phenomenon in the United States. Specifically, these demographic data indicate that the life choices that young adults between the ages of 18 through 29 make have changed in recent decades. Numerous aspects of young adults' lives are different in the 21st century than they were in the past. For example, Arnett and his colleagues note that most men and women got married in their early 20s in 1960, whereas by 1997 the median ages for marriage were 25 for women and 27 for males (Arnett, 2000; Arnett, Ramos, & Jensen, 2001). They also noted that the median ages for the birth of one's first child have risen, as has the number of students pursuing a higher education (Arnett, 2000; Arnett et al., 2001). Indeed, a recent article in the *New York Times* described this time of life as follows:

MyEdLab
Video Example 12.1
Jeffrey Arnett describes emerging adulthood.

> The 20s are a black box, and there is a lot of churning in there. One-third of people in their 20s move to a new residence every year. Forty percent move back home with their parents at least once. They go through an average of seven jobs in their 20s, more job changes than in any other stretch. Two-thirds spend at least some time living with a romantic partner without being married. And marriage occurs later than ever. (Marantz-Henig, 2010, p. MM28)

Characteristics of Emerging Adults

How can we describe the typical "emerging adult"? Actually, there is much variation among young people in this age group. Nevertheless, most emerging adults do have a few characteristics in common. First, in general, most emerging adults are deeply engaged in **identity** exploration (recall Chapter 5), and generally are content with their lives (Arnett, 2004). Thus, although emerging adults often explore many different opportunities, overall they are generally content with this period of life. Think about your own "emerging adulthood" (you may be in it right now)—overall, do you recall being content with this time in your life? Most people do!

Second, although many emerging adults are moving away from their parents' homes and trying out new living arrangements (e.g., living with roommates, residing in college residence halls, etc.), *their relationships with parents actually improve when they leave home* (Arnett, 2015). In Chapter 6 we discussed family relationships during adolescence. Although many adolescents do generally experience positive relationships with their parents, there is always some turmoil that occurs, particularly during the middle school and high school years. Nevertheless, during emerging adulthood, those relationships in general tend to improve.

Third, emerging adults tend to be politically disengaged (Snell, 2010). This may be surprising to hear—often we think of young adults in their early 20s as finally being able to vote, and as becoming politically active. Although this is certainly true for many emerging adults (particularly those on college campuses), there are many who are quite uninvolved in politics. Consider the visits that presidential candidates always make to college campuses during campaigns; those visits occur both because college students represent a large group of the voting population and also because many college students are politically neutral and may not have strong allegiance to a particular candidate or political party. Thus those visits to campus are designed because politicians know that emerging adults often have not fully committed to highly specific political beliefs.

Fourth, for most emerging adults, involvement with **behavioral aspects of religion** (e.g., going to church services) generally declines (Stoppa & Lefkowitz, 2010). Whereas adolescents may have regularly attended church or synagogue with their parents, attendance may sharply decline during emerging adulthood.

For many adolescents, religious affiliations may be important sources of social networks, and thus many adolescents spend much time involved in religious activities; however, after high school, adolescents' social networks expand, and they do not need all of the social resources that they did during high school. Thus, attendance at religious services often declines during this period.

Finally, sexual activity increases during emerging adulthood. Although many adolescents become sexually active prior to graduation from high school (see Chapter 10), those who did not become sexually active during adolescence generally do become sexually active during emerging adulthood (Lefkowitz & Gillen, 2006). The fact that many emerging adults reside outside of their parents' homes facilitates sexual activity for many emerging adults.

Emerging Adults in the 21st Century

As we work with our students, we need to consider what it means to be an emerging adult in the 21st century. Young adults are living today in a very unique time in history. The world is changing dramatically, and the experiences of emerging adults are not the same today as they were even 10 years ago.

In particular, globalization has occurred as a result of the rapid advent of technology, and this globalization has altered the pathways into emerging adulthood (e.g., Jensen & Arnett, 2012). For example, whereas emerging adults often lived in cultural isolation prior to the emergence of the Internet, today's emerging adults have access to a plethora of social relationships and novel possibilities to consider via communications through **social media** (Natriello, 2016). Indeed, much of the communication among emerging adults, particularly related to social relationships and dating, involves the use of technology (e.g., Facebook; Fox & Warber, 2013; Natriello, 2016; Nitzburg & Farber, 2013; Taylor, Rappleyea, Fang, & Cannon, 2013). Thus, today's emerging adult is living in a world in which information is readily and immediately available, and communication throughout the world can occur instantaneously. Consider your experiences during emerging adulthood, and what your parents experienced—the differences in those experiences may be quite surprising!

Does Everyone Experience Emerging Adulthood?

Do all young adults experience emerging adulthood? Or is this period of life a luxury for privileged young adults? It has been argued that emerging adulthood is not a universal experience; rather, it is a unique period of life that is particularly associated with Western, wealthy societies. Arnett (2000, 2010) notes that emerging adulthood generally occurs in industrialized nations, particularly those in which adolescents can delay taking on adult responsibilities (e.g., marriage and parenthood). Thus for those adolescents who need to begin taking on adult roles and responsibilities early (e.g., those who need to begin working at a young age in agriculturally focused societies), emerging adulthood is less likely to be universally experienced.

Cross-cultural research indicates that although emerging adulthood is not universal, it nevertheless is a developmental possibility for young adults when the contexts are supportive. In one recent study, Manago (2012) studied Mayan university students in Mexico. Individuals living in Mayan communities for many years adhered to traditional values and responsibilities. However, changes in the economy have forced many young Mayans from the Chiapas region of Mexico to move from rural to more urban areas. The participants in this study all moved from rural regions of Mexico into the city to attend the university. Data from this study indicated that these students perceived the development of a sense of emerging adulthood as they moved into this new urban and collegiate context. For example, some of the participants noted that they had more independence than did their parents; one participant stated

MyEdLab
Video Example 12.2

This young man, who is now 30 years old, reflects back on his emerging adult years, and his struggles figure out what he wanted to do with his life.

that "nobody is obligated to do something that they don't want to do, before yes, they were like enslaved to a thing and now no" (Manago, 2012, p. 678). Participants in the study also noted that with their moves to the city, they acquired more freedom to engage in different types of activities, and to pursue alternatives that traditional Mayans living in rural areas would not normally consider. Thus these students, by moving to the city and attending the university, were able to delay the onset of adult responsibilities, and to subsequently explore a variety of possibilities. Whereas emerging adulthood would not have been a part of these individuals' lives if they had stayed in their rural villages, the move to the city and the university setting allowed these individuals to experience emerging adulthood.

The Varied Experiences of Emerging Adults

We noted earlier that there are some commonalities among emerging adults. However, it is also important to recall that emerging adulthood is *not* experienced in the same ways by all individuals. For example, although emerging adulthood represents a time of great exploration, and although many emerging adults report being happy during this time of life, there is no guarantee that all emerging adults will be content. In fact, although emerging adults *overall* are quite content with their lives, some recent research indicates that contentedness varies daily; for example, some research indicates that emerging adults' satisfaction with their lives is higher on days in which emerging adults are more physically active (Maher et al., 2013). This is an important distinction—although generally the period of emerging adulthood is a pleasant time for most individuals, there is much variation from day to day.

Whereas emerging adulthood represents a time of overall contentment for many, there are of course individuals who do not experience overall positive emotional well-being; indeed, some emerging adults experience substantial sadness. Although there is some evidence that overall mean levels of depression decrease during emerging adulthood (compared with adolescence; e.g., Galambos & Krahn, 2008), there also is much individual variation in depression, and some emerging adults do experience substantial depression.

In addition, family stressors still exist, and can impact the lives of emerging adults (Valdez, Chavez, & Woulfe, 2013). An emerging adult who is away from home and in college may still have to deal with family issues, such as parents who are going through a bitter divorce, siblings who are experiencing problems with school, or financial crises. Finally, it is important to note that for ethnic-minority emerging adults, racial identity issues and family obligations may induce stress that is not experienced by majority peers (Hood, Brevard, Nguyen, & Belgrave, 2013; Sanchez, Esparza, Colon, & Davis, 2010). Thus, emerging adults who are members of ethnic-minority groups often may not be able to experience as much freedom to explore various life options as do nonminority emerging adults, and may experience greater stress (Hood et al., 2013).

It also is important to consider emerging adulthood for vulnerable populations, such as youth who lived in foster care during adolescence. A large-scale longitudinal study conducted by researchers at the University of Chicago was designed to examine the experiences of these individuals during emerging adulthood. Unfortunately, the data indicated that, in general, emerging adults who come from the foster care system do not fare well. For example, only 11% of females and 5% of males had earned an associate's degree by the age of 26; less than half of the former foster-care children were employed at the age of 26, and many of those who were employed were not earning sufficient money on which to live; and many of these individuals had been incarcerated (Courtney et al., 2011).

Finally, we need to consider the fact that there is much diversity in the living arrangements of emerging adults (Hendry & Kloep, 2012). In recent years, a growing

MyEdLab
Application Exercise 12.1
Emerging Adulthood Let's consider some of the experiences that are characteristic of emerging adulthood.

MyEdLab
Video Example 12.3
Teachers of high school seniors can help them to achieve their long-term goals. In this video, this teacher helps a student develop a portfolio that he can use for review by the College Board.

What was your senior year like? Do you think that you were beginning to enter into "emerging adulthood"?

MyEdLab Self-Check 12.1

MyEdLab
Application Exercise 12.2
Teaching Seniors What is it like to teach high school seniors? What are some issues that teachers of seniors might encounter?

trend has been for emerging adults (as well as some older young adults) to live with their parents (Arnett, 2004). This trend has emerged for several reasons. One of the most prominent reasons is because of the high costs of living on one's own. In the United States, the proportion of young adults living with their parents increased between the year 2000 through 2012; the rise was greater for emerging adults (ages 18 through 24) than for older emerging adults and young adults (ages 25 through 34), although both groups displayed increases (Vespa, Lewis, & Kreider, 2013). Recent estimates are that 36% of young adults between the ages of 18 through 31 in the United States live with their parents (Fry, 2013). This trend is not unique to the United States. For example, the trend has been growing in Great Britain as well. In Canada, recent data indicated that 42.3% of the 4,318,400 young adults between the ages of 20 and 29 lived with their parents (Statistics Canada, 2011).

Senior Year: The Beginning of Emerging Adulthood

Issues of emerging adulthood are relevant to you as a teacher because you can do much to help students to prepare for the entry into emerging adulthood. In particular, you may start to see evidence of movement into this new developmental phase as students move into the final years of high school.

The phrase "senior year" probably brings up many stereotypes (some positive and some negative). Some high school seniors may see their senior year as a potential vacation, whereas others may see it as a year that should be devoted to hard work. Many students need to acquire important skills during their final year of high school that will be needed either in college or in the workforce (Roderick, Coca, Moeller, & Kelley-Kemple, 2013). However, for many high school seniors, social events become particularly important; students realize that this is the last year that they will be able to socialize with some of their closest friends. In addition, many students have drivers' licenses, and therefore have the ability to travel to a wide range of social events. Seniors often also may be absent from school more often than younger students, because of visits to colleges or interviews for jobs. As teachers, we need to be aware of seniors' academic demands, social priorities, and family situations. Although as teachers we often need to be strict and consistent with our rules and assignments and due dates, we also need to remember that seniors are at a significant transition point, and may have many responsibilities and goals to balance as they enter into emerging adulthood.

In-Depth 12.1

Do Emerging Adults Get Enough Sleep?

As we have discussed, emerging adulthood is a period of development in which individuals get to try out many different identities and lifestyles. But all of these opportunities to engage in all of these different activities may affect time for rest. Sleep is essential for our cognitive abilities (Alhola & Polo-Kantola, 2007). When we don't get enough sleep, we can suffer severe consequences.

Although our bodies are generally quite strong and healthy between the ages of 18 and 25, sleep does matter. Results of a recent study conducted on emerging adults in Israel suggests that when emerging adults get sufficient amounts of sleep, they engage in more activities during the day and consequently are better able to cope with stressors and experience less negative affect (Lev Ari & Schulman, 2013). According to the Mayo Clinic (2014), adults need at least 7 to 8 hours of sleep per night to maintain their health. Thus, although emerging adults have many opportunities, they still need to get their sleep!

What Educators Can Do

As a teacher, you might be wondering what you can do to assist your current students with a period of life that has not yet begun for most of them. Because emerging adulthood generally begins at about the age of 18, most of your students will have graduated from high school at the inception of emerging adulthood. Nevertheless, as we have discussed, emerging adulthood is a time of great exploration for many individuals. Thus, you can engage your students in many discussions and activities during high school that will help to prepare them for this new period.

For your college-bound students, you can help to prepare them for the future by exposing them to information about the various academic choices that they will be able to make in college. As we will review later in this chapter, college students make choices about their majors, their electives, their living situations, their activities, their peer groups, and many other facets of their lives. High school teachers can help to prepare them by giving them information while still in high school that will help them to make educated choices once they start their higher education.

For example, many high school students do not really understand all of the options for what they can potentially study in college. Some students might not know what "sociology" is or what "philosophy" is; others might not know the difference between chemical engineering, electrical engineering, and civil engineering; and others might not really understand what one studies when majoring in English. These students, once in college, may spend much time taking different courses and experimenting with various areas of study. This is an important part of the college experience. However, college students might have an easier time making these choices if they are exposed to some of this information while they are still in high school. Indeed, a high school that provides students with preparatory information about the college experience might make part of emergent adulthood easier to traverse. Similar information can be provided for students who are planning to join the workforce or the military. Exposing students to practical information about potential future careers and life options may make their subsequent transitions and choices easier for them.

Transitions into College

After high school, many adolescents choose to pursue **higher education.** This is an important transition, as the college experience is usually extremely instrumental in helping young adults determine their future careers. The transition occurs for most individuals during the period of emerging adulthood, and consequently affords individuals opportunities to take a variety of courses, live in an assortment of settings, and interact with different peer groups and social networks.

Rates of Postsecondary Education Attendance

The percentage of students deciding to attend college immediately after graduating from high school has increased in recent decades. Specifically, this percentage increased from 51% in 1975 to 68% by 2011 (National Center for Education Statistics [NCES], 2014). Rates have increased both for females and males, although increases have been greater overall for females. Over the past three decades, although the overall percentage of youth who chose to attend college increased, the increase has been larger for 2-year colleges as compared with 4-year colleges. Thus, many students are initially choosing to attend **community colleges.** Interestingly,

MyEdLab
Video Example 12.4
Barack Obama proposed free community college for anyone in the United States. In this video, he describes why he thinks this is an important initiative to consider.

the rates of graduation from 4-year colleges for students who first started in community colleges (and later transferred into 4-year colleges) as compared with students who started in 4-year colleges are equal (Attewell & Monaghan, 2014). Rates of college attendance within 2 years of graduating from high school have increased in recent decades for African Americans, Hispanics, and Whites, but have remained stable for Asian Americans (NCES, 2012).

Changes in Emerging Adults' Lives During the College Years

Many contemporary college students simultaneously work, at least part-time, while attending college. Indeed, given the high costs of tuition, this is not surprising. Similar to the patterns with higher education enrollment figures, the number of students who simultaneously work also has changed in recent decades; specifically, the percentage of college students who worked while attending college was 63% in 1974, and increased to 78% by 2006 (NCES, 2012).

Many aspects of emerging adults' lives change substantially during the college years. If you were to speak to a graduating high school senior and then speak to the same person again 4 years later, you probably would note that several changes have occurred in the person's attitudes and behaviors. Let's look at the example of a student named Mary. Table 12.1 presents some questions and Mary's possible answers right after high school graduation, and again right after college graduation.

Although Mary's responses are not going to be the same as other emerging adults' responses, there are some clear patterns evident that are somewhat typical. When you look at the two columns in Table 12.1, you will probably notice that overall Mary becomes more open to newer and broader ideas after her 4 years in college. Prior to college, she is considering at least three different career paths; however, after graduation, she knows that she wants to go into marketing, and she has a plan for how to achieve this goal. Whereas ultimately Mary may veer from this plan and end up in an entirely different career, she clearly has explored her options during her time in college, and has a clearer sense of what she wants to do in the long term.

> Think about your own experiences. If you are within the age range of the typical emerging adult, do you think that the description of this developmental phase applies to you? If you are older than that age range, do you think that it did apply to you?

TABLE 12.1 **Mary: Before and After College**

Question	12th-Grade Response	Response After College Graduation
What career do you see yourself in?	"I don't really know. I am seriously thinking about becoming a nurse, but I also like math, so might be an accountant. I also might go into business."	"I am going to work in marketing. I plan to get a job for 2 years to learn the trade, and then I hope to get my MBA."
Where do you want to live in the future?	"I love the beach, so I will definitely move to Florida or to California; whatever I do in the future, it has to be near a beach."	"I am going to live wherever I get the best job opportunity. I would prefer to be in a big city, but in the end, I'll go wherever I have to go."
Describe your relationship with your parents.	"It's pretty good. We don't see eye to eye on everything, but we don't fight too much. They don't treat me like I'm an adult sometimes, and I am 18, so I am an adult!"	"It's good. I really understand them better now; my relationship with my dad in particular has gotten much better. I understand his politics, and although I don't always agree with him, I understand why he believes what he believes, and I respect all that he has done."
With whom do you tend to socialize?	"My best friend is the person I spend the most time with; I also have a great group of friends who are on the debate team with me."	"I spend time with my boyfriend and we spend a lot of time with his friends, but I also spend a lot of time with my friends who are in the marching band with me, and I still see a few of my old high school friends whenever possible."

In addition, prior to college, Mary has a small circle of friends, but after college, she has a more diverse group in her social network.

The changes that Mary experienced are borne out in research on college student development. One area that develops in particular during this period of life is the emerging adult's identity (recall our discussion of identity from Chapter 5). When adolescents go to college, they have the opportunity to meet and interact with a diverse group of peers; they become exposed to varied ways of thinking about political and social issues; and they can study a variety of topics, and thus entertain diverse career possibilities. They also, often for the first time, are separated from their parents. All of these new experiences contribute to identity formation. After college, many (but certainly not all!) emerging adults have a better sense of "who they are" and "who they want to be."

During college, obvious changes occur in the domain of learning. College often is quite rigorous for students, and they clearly learn new information and skills during this time. In terms of academics, college students generally advance in their verbal skills, their quantitative skills, their knowledge in their major areas of study, their oral and written communication skills, their reasoning skills, their appreciation of the arts, and their abilities to deal with conceptually complex issues (Pascarella, Bohr, Nora, & Terenzini, 1995). Advances in these and other domains contribute to how college students develop a sense of identity and also to how they form long-term life goals. Although high school achievement is an important predictor of college achievement, research also indicates that academic achievement during the first few semesters after the transition into college is perhaps even more strongly related to subsequent college achievement (Martin, Wilson, Liem, & Ginns, 2013).

After the transition to college, adolescents and emerging adults also may engage in risky behaviors. As these young adults meet new peers and move into apartments, residence halls, and other living situations (e.g., fraternities and sororities), many will face temptations to engage in a variety of risky behaviors. Research indicates that adolescents who engaged in **risky behaviors** during high school (e.g., drinking, using illicit drugs, having unsafe sexual relationships) are likely to continue to engage in those behaviors in college. However, across the transition from high school to college, alcohol use, marijuana use, and numbers of sexual partners all increase. Alcohol abuse is a particular risk factor after the college transition for adolescents who came from rural high schools, and for those who reside in dormitories. Interestingly, in general, drunk driving, aggression, and property crimes tend to decrease after transitioning into college (e.g., Fromme, Corbin, & Kruse, 2008).

Having a Positive College Experience

Some students succeed in college and have a wonderful experience, whereas others do not. Research conducted in recent years has identified some of the variables that are associated with having a successful college experience. We discuss some of these in this section.

College Student Belonging. The academic learning that occurs during college may be more effective in certain types of postsecondary settings; specifically, when students feel secure and comfortable in their college environments, they accrue greater benefits (Strayhorn, 2012). More specifically, recent research indicates that when college students perceive a sense of **belonging,** academic learning during college may be enhanced. A sense of belonging at the college level involves feeling connected with, committed to, and supported by the college or university community. Research indicates that when feelings of belonging increase during the first year of college and beyond, students are more likely to report academic efficacy, feelings of social acceptance, and lower levels of **internalizing behaviors** (i.e., feeling depressed, anxious, withdrawn, etc.), and are less likely to experience serious mental health issues than are students who do not experience increases in feelings of belonging (Pittman & Richmond, 2008). In addition, when college students experience positive transitions and consequently develop healthy identities with which they are satisfied and content, and experience emotional support from their friends and their family members, they are less likely to experience poor mental health during college (Azmitia, Syed, & Radmacher, 2013).

In college, students can experience a sense of belonging within a number of contexts. At the college or university level, students may feel that they "belong" within a specific university. Thus one student who chooses to attend a large state university may feel extremely comfortable in such a setting, whereas another student may not experience a sense of belonging in the same large institution; that student might experience greater feelings of belonging in a smaller, more intimate school. In addition, students also experience a sense of belonging within individual classes. We can all think of classes in which we have felt either more or less comfortable. Research indicates that when students experience a sense of belonging within specific college courses, those students are more likely to feel efficacious about learning in the course, and also to be more intrinsically motivated in the course; in addition, when students experience feelings of belonging within a particular course, they also are more likely to perceive that the instructor creates a positive climate for learning (i.e., being open, warm, encouraging participation, etc.; Freeman, Anderman, & Jensen, 2007).

There are a number of ways that new college students can develop a sense of belonging. One particularly important part of this equation is the relationships between students and faculty. University faculty sometimes work diligently to develop positive relationships with their students; however, particularly in large research universities, faculty may focus on developing relationships with their graduate students, and thus undergraduates may not receive as much attention. Nevertheless, research indicates that when first-year college students try to build relationships with faculty, those students are more likely to earn higher grade point averages and to engage in student activities (Wang, Cullen, Yao, & Li, 2013).

In-Depth 12.2

STEP

An example of a program that has been developed to facilitate belonging among college students is STEP, offered at The Ohio State University. STEP, an acronym for Second-Year Transformational Experience Program, represents a large-scale attempt at creating a positive university experience and a sense of belonging for college sophomores. The university found that the strongest predictors of student success during the sophomore year were:

- Participating in campus events
- Living on campus
- Interacting with peers
- Interacting with faculty
- A commitment to the institution

In STEP, students must live on campus during their sophomore year. They are arranged into STEP groups of about 20 students and one faculty member. The student groups meet with the faculty member weekly in both formal and informal contexts. During the academic year, students and the faculty member attend at least three co-curricular activities related to a variety of areas (e.g., global citizenship, career exploration, etc.). Participants also complete a financial literacy program. The students, in collaboration with the faculty member, plan a project that the students complete during the summer after STEP participation or during the following year. Students receive $2000 toward funding their project upon completion of the program. Projects can involve community outreach, service learning, travel abroad, or a variety of other possibilities. By participating in the program throughout an entire year, students develop a strong commitment to and sense of belonging at the university (Ohio State University, 2015).

Transitioning from a 2- to a 4-Year College. An area that is seldom considered but is quite important is the transition from attendance at a community college to a 4-year college or university. Many students attend community colleges, either before transitioning into a 4-year college or for a terminal degree. The numbers of individuals who choose to enroll in community colleges is staggering; for example, in California, community colleges enroll more than 2 million students per year (Boroch & Hope, 2009). The American Association of Community Colleges (2014) estimates that almost 7 million students are enrolled annually in community colleges in the United States, with 59% attending part-time and 41% attending full-time.

The transition from a 2-year to a 4-year college can be facilitated when students are introduced to the larger university into which they plan to transfer prior to the transition. An interesting example occurred between Compton Community College (CCC) and California State University at Northridge (CSUN). In this case, mentors from CSUN worked with students from CCC in a garden once per week. The CSUN students came to the CCC campus to work on the garden, and then CCC students also went to the CSUN campus for campus tours and informational sessions. The community college students also were introduced to CSUN faculty during these visits. Compared with students in a comparison condition, the CCC students who went through this mentoring program displayed increases in grade point average, academic confidence, self-esteem, and locus of control (Hoffman & Wallach, 2005).

Special Considerations for Low-Income Students. High school students who live in low-income households or who come from families with lower socioeconomic status (SES) may in particular benefit from rigorous high school programs that provide the skills and backgrounds that will be needed to succeed in college (Rosenbaum & Becker, 2011). Students who come from lower-SES backgrounds often have to contend with issues that other college students may not ever need to consider. In particular, they are likely to experience financial strains that other students may not encounter (recall our discussion of SES and achievement from Chapter 9). They may have to negotiate loans, financial aid, and not knowing if their tuition will be paid from semester to semester; these scenarios can cause much stress for college students. As educators, we can help our students by providing them with information about sources of financial assistance for college. Some examples are presented in Table 12.2.

It is particularly important to remember that low-income and ethnic-minority students in particular may experience new forms of **discrimination** once they move into college. Whereas peers in high school may have been from similar backgrounds, in college there will be a larger mix of peers, and some of those peers may discriminate in either subtle or not-so-subtle ways. In addition, even if students do not experience discrimination at college, they still must live in a larger world in which discrimination still occurs. Results of a recent study of college freshmen found that although ethnic-minority students' perceptions of discrimination declined during the first 2 years of college, perceptions of society at large devaluing and not respecting their ethnic group increased over the same time period (Huynh & Fuligni, 2012).

Using Social Media to Facilitate the Transition. Social media can also help students to successfully transition into college. Whereas 20 years ago the use of computers for facilitating social connections might have been perceived as detrimental to academic success, there is some indication that the use of social media may actually benefit students in several ways. For example, Gray, Vitak, Easton, and Ellison (2013) found that for first-year college students, the number of Facebook friends that a student has is related positively to social adjustment at college; social adjustment in

TABLE 12.2 Funding a College Education

Funding Source	Description
Scholarships	Funds available to directly pay tuition, room, or board; some are based on merit (i.e., achievement during high school), some are based on achievements in athletics or artistic endeavors (e.g., music), and some are designated for specific types of students (e.g., first-generation students; students from a particular county or city).
Fellowships	Same as scholarships, but more typical for graduate students
Student loans	Loans available at lower interest rates for students
Scholarships to encourage employment in some fields	Some organizations and professions provide scholarships to encourage students to major in content areas that will increase number of qualified job applicants in fields with shortages.
Work study	Federal program allowing students to work on campus for pay; these funds are subsidized by the government.
Part-time jobs	Many students find employment on and off-campus during college. Jobs must be balanced with studies, but can help greatly in financing one's education.
Part-time attendance	Some students choose to attend college on a part-time basis; this lowers tuition costs, and also allows students to have more time to work and earn money.
Grants	Funds provided by colleges, universities, and other organizations to pay some or all of a student's tuition or fees
Community college	Community colleges generally cost less than do 4-year colleges. Many students choose to attend a community college and graduate with an associate's degree, or to spend a year or two at a community college, and then transfer into a 4-year institution.
Dual enrollment	Programs that allow students to take college-level courses while still in high school; these courses may cost little or nothing, and students often can receive both high school and college credit for such coursework.

turn is related to re-enrolling in college the following year. Interestingly, adolescents' overall number of Facebook friends did not predict social adjustment—it is only the number of friends who are simultaneously enrolled in the same college. Thus the social connections that students make and reinforce via Facebook and other social media websites may contribute to successful transitions into college.

Social media also can be used so that students can obtain support from others. Through the use of social media, students can stay connected to their families and their friends from home. Many college students who initially are lonely or not adjusting well to their new surroundings probably find solace in being able to instantaneously reconnect with these social networks. In addition, social media sites allow college students to stay in close contact with their high school friends; thus students who are experiencing homesickness or loneliness may find comfort in the ability to communicate with old friends instantaneously via computers, smart-phones, tablets, and other communication devices.

Dual Enrollment. There also are strategies that can be implemented while adolescents are still in high school that may help them to adjust to their future lives in college. Dual-enrollment programs during the senior year in high school can facilitate the transition. Although these programs vary in design, **dual-enrollment programs** usually allow for students to enroll in college or university courses, and to receive both high school and college credit for the coursework (with the college tuition usually paid for by local school systems or the state). For example, a high school student could enroll in a college calculus course offered by a neighboring university, and the student could receive both mathematics credit that can be applied to high school graduation *and* math credit that could later be used toward a college degree. Although these courses traditionally have been aimed at advanced or honors students, dual-enrollment opportunities are growing in popularity, and are becoming available to a wider array of students. Participation in these programs may facilitate the transition into college because experience with college-level curricula, college syllabi, and college faculty prior to enrollment in college may better prepare some students for the increased workloads and rigor associated with many college courses. In addition, by completing some credit hours prior to the entry into college, students may be able to take fewer courses during their first year of college, thus alleviating some of the stress that heavy course loads may induce.

An example of a large-scale dual-enrollment program can be found in Miami, Florida. Students enrolled in the Miami Dade County public schools (one of the largest school systems in the United States) can participate in this program. In order to participate, students must have at least a 3.0 grade point average, must have passed certain basic skills assessments, must have parental and school permission, must have met with a dual-enrollment coordinator, and must understand that the college courses will probably require more effort than most high school courses. Courses are available across a large array of subject domains, including mathematics, journalism, music, philosophy, the sciences (e.g., physics, oceanography, chemistry), psychology, foreign languages, English, history, and numerous other areas. In this program, students are not charged tuition for participation—even textbooks are provided at no cost (Miami Dade Community College, 2014).

College Now is one of the most extensive dual-enrollment programs. This is a partnership between the New York City Department of Education and the City University of New York (CUNY). The goals of College Now are to improve high school graduation rates, to improve the preparation of students for college, and to ensure the success of high school graduates in college. Participants take a sequence of structured courses that are designed to fill foundational requirements. These courses also help high school students to develop the academic skills that will help them to be successful after the transition into college. Results of a recent study indicate that participants in College Now who later enrolled in CUNY schools had higher grade point averages than did nonparticipants (on average, .71 point higher), and also on average earned 1.6 more credits in college during their first two semesters of study (Allen & Dadgar, 2012).

High school students also can take many college courses for free via the Internet. For example, there are many courses now available at no cost through iTunes university. Courses sponsored by hundreds of universities are now readily available online. Thus high school students who want to get a head start on college studies and to better prepare for the academic rigor of college can take or audit courses on a wide range of topics, offered by many colleges and universities.

Health and Well-Being. Emotional and psychological health also are important factors to consider in the college transition. If students are not physically and psychologically well, their experience and potential success will be hurt. The transition into college in particular can be highly stressful for some students; thus students who have better coping skills may fare better across the transition. Research indicates that students who have self-compassion (i.e., they treat themselves kindly) experience lower levels of homesickness and depression in college and greater satisfaction with their college experience than do students who do not experience self-compassion (Terry, Leary, & Mehta, 2013).

Colleges and universities often provide many services and programs to ensure the health and well-being of their students. College students in particular are taught and reminded about the availability of various resources and support services. In addition, students can still rely on their families to support their physical and mental health. In fact, research indicates that adolescents who retain close emotional bonds with their parents but who also report that they feel independent in terms of decision making experience greater psychological well-being during their freshman year than do students who do not feel close to their parents and do not feel able to make independent decisions (Kenyon & Koerner, 2009).

Later Transitions into College. What about adolescents who choose to pursue other life goals, and then later decide to attend college (e.g., after spending several years in another occupation or in the military)? For these individuals, it may be particularly difficult to navigate their way through college admissions and subsequent enrollment. These students may be within the stage of "emerging adulthood" (or older), but may not be able to rely on their parents for advice or for financial support.

Luckily, there are some model programs that exist to help these students. One program is the Maine College Transitions program (Maine Adult Education, 2014). This program, which began in 2006, is a state-funded initiative that was designed to assist nontraditional students (i.e., those who are not right out of high school) with the transition to college. The program is run through local adult education programs throughout the state. Participants vary in age, but results of a recent study indicated that 9% of the participants were between the ages of 16 and 18, 31% were between the ages of 19 and 24, and 60% were over the age of 25 (Levinson, 2009).

Participants explore various career options through job shadowing, obtain individual counseling, and are taught how to conduct online job searches. Students are taught about college admissions processes, and learn how to successfully complete applications and how to navigate the financial aspects of admission. For those who need to improve their academic skills, coursework is available. Students are able to learn many of the skills that are necessary to be successful in college; these include how to use various forms of technology (e.g., spreadsheets and word-processing programs), time-management skills, and study strategies (Ruff, 2011).

What Educators Can Do

Educators at both the high school and college level can use a variety of strategies to ensure the success of college students. When educators work with and support adolescents in high school and after the transition into college, students are more likely to experience success and ultimately to graduate from college. So what can we do?

First, high school teachers and guidance counselors can carefully and strategically advise adolescents prior to college admissions or enrollment. Indeed, educators need to be aware of the factors that are most strongly related to college student success. Some predictors of academic success during the first year of college, as determined by American College Testing (ACT), are listed in Table 12.3.

TABLE 12.3 Predictors of Successful Performance in First-Year College Courses

Academic preparation during high school
Students who take a core curriculum in high school are more successful in first-year college courses.
Taking additional social studies in high school is related to a small advantage in first-year social science courses.
Taking high-level math during high school is related to increased success in first-year college math courses.
Taking high-level science during high school is related to success in first-year science courses.

Source: ACT, 2008.

The data in particular reinforce the fact that when students take high-level courses in a particular subject domain (e.g., mathematics), they are more likely to succeed academically in that area in college (ACT, 2008). Although this may seem quite obvious to many, it is important to recall that high-school-aged adolescents are still developing cognitively (see Chapter 3), and may not always be able to make goal-oriented decisions. Consequently, as teachers, we need to encourage adolescents to consider what they might study in college, and to advise them, when possible, to consider enrolling in higher-level (e.g., Advanced Placement) courses in those areas. Clearly, advanced coursework will not be an option or viable choice for all high school students, but when a student is considering taking an "easier" high school course in order to have fun during senior year, as educators we can advise them to consider taking the more challenging course, and remind them of the potential longer-term benefits.

In addition, as educators we can continue to work on building our students' **self-regulatory skills**. As we discussed in Chapter 3, **self-regulated learners** are able to monitor their progress on academic tasks and to carefully and appropriately apply various learning strategies (Boekaerts, Pintrich, & Zeidner, 2000; Zimmerman & Moylan, 2009). College students who effectively engage in self-regulatory strategies are more successful in their academic pursuits during college (Kitsantas, Winsler, & Huie, 2008). Thus, high school teachers can have a tremendously positive influence on their students' later success by consistently reinforcing the appropriate use of various effective academic strategies (e.g., note-taking tips, study skills, how to avoid procrastination, etc.).

MyEdLab **Self-Check 12.2**

Transitions into the Workforce

Not all adolescents decide to go to college directly after high school. For a variety of reasons, some prefer to pursue work opportunities. For some adolescents, this is for financial reasons—college may not be affordable. For others, it is simply a life choice—some adolescents, who may not have been highly engaged in academics or who do not see a purpose to obtaining a higher education—may choose to pursue work instead. In addition, some adolescents choose to pursue work opportunities because it is a cultural expectation in their communities. For example, in some parts of Appalachia, working in coal mines is a traditional career for males, and because a college education is not a prerequisite for entry into that profession, students may not see any purpose in attending college. In addition, some students who do not complete high school are thrust into the workforce at younger ages than are students who graduate from high school.

Did you have a job during high school? Did you ever consider staying in your job after graduation, and pursuing a career related to that job? Why might some students make this choice?

Data from the National Center for Education Statistics (NCES) indicate that 2 years after high school graduation, approximately 79% of high school graduates had enrolled in college, 20% worked and had never enrolled in college, and 1% neither worked nor enrolled in college. Nevertheless, it is important to remember that of the 79% who had enrolled in college, many of those young adults also were employed at least some of the time (NCES, 2006). As we discussed earlier in this chapter, many emerging adults need to work in order to pay for their tuition and living expenses. Data suggest that of the adolescents who chose not to enroll in postsecondary education and instead decided to enter the workforce, most work about 36 hours per week (compared with 39 hours per week in 1974; NCES, 2012). More of these individuals worked in clerical jobs in the 1970s than since the turn of the century, and more worked as skilled operatives in the 1970s as compared with the present; however, the percentage of those working in service or sales industries has risen over the past three decades (NCES, 2012). Of those emerging adults who are working, disruption in work experiences during emerging adulthood (e.g., being fired from a job) may be related to depressed moods, excessive drinking, and declines in self-reports of the quality of one's life (Aseltine & Gore, 2005).

It is particularly important to consider job options for students who do not complete high school. Such individuals, who often were disengaged in high school, are less competitive for many jobs (Lippman, Atienza, Rivers, & Keith, 2008), for several reasons. First, they have not earned a high school diploma, which is a requirement for many jobs. Second, due to dropping out, they often do not acquire the skills that are needed to be successful in many 21st-century jobs. Technological skills (e.g., the ability to use a computer) are now necessary in many professions that did not require such skills in the past. Third, there is often a stigma attached to being a "dropout," and that label may cause some potential employers to be reluctant to offer jobs to students who did not complete high school. Although some dropouts do eventually transition into successful careers, the majority of students who drop out of high school appear to remain in low-status jobs (National Education Association, 2006).

We discussed academic motivation and achievement in Chapter 9 and provided a variety of strategies that educators can use to try to reach potential dropouts and engage them in academic work. Nevertheless, some adolescents will be determined to leave school. In the next section, we discuss vocational education, which is often a viable option for students who are determined to drop out of school; if such students are directed toward these programs, they may learn valuable skills that will help them to succeed and to obtain good jobs.

The Benefits of Vocational Education

For adolescents who are not considering college, or who are uncertain about whether or not they want to attend college, one viable option is **vocational education.** Vocational education programs generally consist of a planned set of courses and experiences that are designed to prepare individuals for future employment in a variety of trades and professions. Vocational education, as well as other forms of career and technical education, involves much experiential learning (Clark, Threeton, & Ewing, 2010). Specifically, participants in vocational education programs spend time both in classrooms and also in learning their actual future jobs by engaging with other professionals in internships and apprenticeships. Vocational education has existed for many years, and its importance was reaffirmed when the Carl D. Perkins Vocational and Technical Education Act, which was originally authorized in 1984, was reauthorized in 2006 (U.S. Department of Education, 2006). In some other countries, participation in vocational education after mandatory schooling is quite popular. For example, in Switzerland, about two-thirds of adolescents continue their education with some form of vocational training (Bachmann, 2012). In fact, in Switzerland, vocational training is available for 230 different professions (Swiss Education, 2013).

There are potential benefits to enrolling in vocational education programs while still in high school (Brown, 2003; Wonacott, 2000). Students who do not enjoy or value traditional subject areas (e.g., English, math, foreign language, science), and who often do not experience success in those subject domains, may experience success and feel better about school if they simultaneously can enroll in a vocational education program that is preparing them for specific types of jobs. In addition, students who under other circumstances might drop out of school may be more likely to stay in school if they can enroll in vocational education programs. Indeed, those students may see true utility value in vocational training, because it often will lead to gainful employment. Interestingly, there also is an additional beneficial side effect of participation in vocational training programs. Specifically, research indicates that high school students who enroll in vocational education programs actually also increase the number of academic courses that they take, as well as their achievement in those courses (U.S. Department of Education, 2004).

Vocational education courses can be offered on-site (i.e., within schools). However, they also can be offered at worksites, so that students can receive on-the-job training. Although online courses and instructional methods are less often used in vocational education as compared with more traditional academic areas, growth in online learning in vocational education is occurring (Metz, 2010). In addition, vocational education also can be offered by community colleges (Shulock & Offenstein, 2012).

In-Depth 12.3

Transitions for Disabled Adolescents

As teachers, we will have students in our classes who are exceptional in a number of ways. Some of our students may have physical disabilities (e.g., they may be unable to walk without assistance), others may have specific learning disabilities (e.g., in the area of reading), others may have more general cognitive impairments, and others may have various social or emotional concerns.

Many of these students will qualify for special educations services; as part of those services, they will be able to receive special considerations and assistance in planning their transitions from high school into other situations. The Individuals with Disabilities Act (IDEA) requires the provision of such transition services for these students (U.S. Department of Education, 2007).

There are several important predictors of postsecondary success for students with disabilities. First, students who have been taught how to make decisions, set goals, and solve problems are likely to be successful once they leave high school. Second, students who have taken a well-developed, appropriate program of study that is related to their postsecondary plans also are likely to be successful (Morningstar & Maz-

zotti, 2014). Although all students with disabilities are eligible for postsecondary transition planning, students with intellectual disabilities often are less likely to have clear postsecondary educational or employment goals (Grigal, Hart, & Migliore, 2011) and less likely to take on leadership roles in the planning process (Shogren & Plotner, 2012); thus, those students in particular may need support in the planning process.

Here are some things that you can do to assist students in making these transitions:

- Advocate for programs that provide instruction in self-regulatory skills such as goal setting and effective problem solving.
- Encourage school counselors to work with special educators, teachers, and parents to plan appropriate coursework for students with disabilities. This should include appropriate training in independent living skills, as well as vocational training for specific jobs.
- Talk to school administrators (e.g., the principal) about the importance of providing support and resources for planning these transitions (Levinson & Palmer, 2005).

Transitions into the Military

In the United States, many adolescents choose to enter the military after graduation. Data from 2011 indicate that 43.3% of members of the U.S. military are ages 25 and younger; this trend has remained consistent for the past two decades, and this percentage is fairly consistent across all branches of the military, although, interestingly, 68.5% of those enlisted in the U.S. Marine Corps. are aged 25 and younger (U.S. Department of Defense, 2012). Nevertheless, the percentage of young adults/late adolescents who serve in the military overall has decreased in recent decades; whereas 7% of young adults served in 1974 and 6% in 1982, only 3% were enlisted in 2006 (NCES, 2012). Overall, the percentage of young adults who had served in the military was smaller in 2006 than in 1974 and 1982—3% for young adults in 2006, but 7% for young adults in 1974, and 6% for young adults in 1982. In 2011, about 14.5% of active-duty military forces consisted of females (CNN, 2013).

The proportions of military personnel who are members of minority and low-income groups is high. Members of ethnic-minority groups made up 20% of the total population of U.S. veterans in 2011, with the majority of veterans being African American (11%) and Hispanic (6%; U.S. Department of Veterans Affairs, 2013). In addition, data indicate that the relation between time served in the military and increased future income in the civilian sector is higher for African American and Hispanic veterans than for others (Ryan, Meredith, & David, 2010). Projections from the U.S. Department of Veterans Affairs (2013) indicate that the greatest expected increases in minority participation in the military through 2040 are for African Americans and Hispanics.

It is important to acknowledge that participation in the military differs across cultures and countries, both in terms of rates of participation and reasons for enlisting. Those differences can have long-term effects. For example, data indicate that in Israel, where military service is mandatory after high school (Nurmi, Poole, & Seginer, 1995), students acknowledge that their hopes and their fears about educational goals will be actualized later in life as compared with adolescents in other countries who do not encounter mandatory military service. Interestingly, research on women transitioning into the military during late adolescence in Israel suggests that those who have troubled relationships with their parents have a particularly difficult time adjusting to life in the military (Scharf, Mayseless, & Kivenson-Baron, 2011).

Despite stereotypes that often are perpetrated by the media, there are no definitive personality types that are associated with joining the military, although there are some personality correlates related to highly specialized military positions. However, the one element that unites all members of the military is perhaps an attraction to the military culture (i.e., the "military way of life"), which is quite different from the ways that most civilians live on a daily basis (DeVries & Wijnans, 2013; Ryan et al., 2010). It is important for adolescents who are considering joining the military to understand what life in the military will be like.

Research on those enlisted in the military indicates that finding meaning in one's life while enlisted in the military is related to being well adjusted and experiencing success across many parts of one's life (e.g., work, family, social relationships, etc.)—not just one's work (Bryan et al., 2013). Thus educators can be helpful to adolescents who are considering careers in the military by helping them to find resources that will allow them to fully explore what military life will be like, and to carefully consider if they will be able to thrive in the military environment.

Educators also must recognize that some adolescents will choose to enter the military after high school, and then, after several years of service, will transition back into either the workforce or into college. In particular, colleges and universities need to consider devoting resources toward easing the transition from military life into college life for young veterans; these services are especially important for individuals who experience injuries and subsequently suffer from disabilities after military service (Burnett & Segoria, 2009).

Finally, the phenomenon of emerging adulthood also may influence adolescents transitioning into the military (Settersten & Ray, 2010). As adolescents take more time to explore their options and to come to terms with what they want to do with their lives, some adolescents who have chosen to enter the military may have second thoughts and doubt their decisions. Indeed, as some young members of the military return home for visits and see that some of their friends are engaged in other endeavors (e.g., attending college, working in a profession), they may develop doubts about their decisions. It is important for families of adolescents who have transitioned into the military to support their decisions, to empathize with their feelings, and to understand that they may experience multiple stressors.

Think about what it might be like to transition into the military immediately after high school. You may, in fact, have done this yourself, or you may have peers who have made this choice. What are some of the challenges that these individuals might face, particularly during high school, when they are thinking about the military as an option?

What Educators Can Do

As teachers, we need to be aware of the diversity within our students. Whereas some students may want to attend college, we should not assume that attending college will be a goal for all of our students. Moreover, being aware of the forthcoming period of emerging adulthood, when our students are likely to consider a variety of options for their lives and their careers, it is important for us to support our students in their choices.

In many high schools, college admissions staff visit the schools to meet with students interested in gaining admission. However, since some of our students will be considering other options, something very helpful that we can do is to work with school counselors to ensure that visits also are made by representatives from the military and from various occupations. Even if prospective employers are not interested in coming to the high school to recruit or interview students for specific jobs, we can invite representatives in to discuss the skills that students should acquire if they want to become employed in a particular field after graduation.

Finally, we need to make sure that our students are aware of options such as vocational education. Students who might otherwise drop out of school might choose to remain in school and to graduate if they can enroll in vocational education programs that can help them to feel successful and to be prepared for employment upon graduation.

MyEdLab **Self-Check 12.3**

Recommendations for Educators

There are many actions that educators can take and strategies that educators can use to help to prepare their current adolescent students for the transition into adult roles and responsibilities.

1. *Provide opportunities for students to explore career possibilities.* As noted in Chapter 5, adolescents often consider many possibilities for their futures while they are negotiating identity development. If adolescents are exposed early to multiple career options, they may be more likely to consider a variety of trajectories. For example, an adolescent might not know what an entomologist is (someone who studies insects). In fact, many adolescents probably could not even imagine such a career; nevertheless, a guest lecture by an entomologist from the local university could spark an interest in an unknowing adolescent and change his or her life.

2. One way to assist adolescents with transitions into new roles is through *discussion groups* (Goodnough & Ripley, 1997). Separate groups can be formed for students transitioning into 4-year colleges, community colleges, the military, or the workforce. Such groups generally are run by school counselors, although with appropriate training, other school personnel may be able to organize such groups as well.

3. *Remind students that the ways in which they manage their time are important.* As an educator, you can help your students understand that what they do during their school time and their nonschool time has important implications for their futures. During adolescence, students spend much of their time engaged in activities that both they and their parents may perceive as being unproductive. For example, adolescents spend much time watching television and engaging with others through social media. It is particularly important for adolescents to develop strong time-management skills and to feel that they are spending their time in meaningful ways (Csiksezentmihalyi & Schneider, 2000).

4. *Incorporate into high school curricula skills that adolescents will need in college and in the workforce.* Given the importance of 21st-century skills in education and work settings (see Chapter 3), it is essential for educators to nurture the development of these skills in adolescents and emerging adults. Whether our students are planning to go to college, enter the military, or join the workforce, we need to provide them with academic experiences that focus on creativity, flexibility, and working with others (Csiksezentmihalyi & Schneider, 2000).

Conclusion

In this chapter we have discussed the period of development referred to as emerging adulthood. This represents a time during which older adolescents and young adults explore various life options. This is general a happy, positive time for most individuals, although there is much variation as life circumstances change.

As educators, we can help high school students be prepared for this stage of life by providing them with support and with helpful information while they are still in high school. Educators can help their current students learn about various post-secondary options. Whereas some of our students will want to go to college, others may be interested in different options, including joining the workforce or enlisting in the military. We need to do all that we can to prepare them so that they can successfully achieve their post-secondary goals.

Glossary

abstinence-only sex education An educational program that provides students with information about the importance and health benefits (physical and emotional) of remaining a virgin until marriage and does not include other information about contraception.

academic cheating Engaging in dishonest or unethical behavior in academic work.

academic self-concept Perceptions of the self as a student (e.g., "I am a good student"; "I do well in math").

accommodation The cognitive process wherein individuals change their current ways of thinking as a result of acquiring new information.

acculturation The process of learning about, and adopting, the beliefs, behaviors, and customs of the host or dominant culture in a society.

acting White The idea that performing well academically or using certain mannerisms of speaking, dressing, or behaving is acting as though one were White. It is a term most often applied to African American students.

actual self or real self How one perceives himself or herself to be at the present time.

adaptive thinking Using background/prior knowledge to alter one's thinking in order to effectively solve problems.

addiction A need, either physical or psychological, for a habit-forming substance.

adolescence-limited offenders Individuals who engage in antisocial and/or delinquent behavior during adolescence but end such behaviors after the adolescent period.

adolescent growth spurt A period of very rapid growth in height that occurs during adolescence.

advisory periods An opportunity for groups of students to meet with a teacher or a school counselor during the school day.

aggression Hostile and/or violent behaviors directed toward the self, others, or objects, often unprovoked.

ambivalent attitudes Having both positive and negative attitudes toward sexual activity simultaneously.

androgen A type of hormone that includes testosterone and androsterone and is responsible for producing some of the characteristic traits of males. Androgen levels increase dramatically in boys during adolescence.

androgynous When one has a set of beliefs, behaviors, and appearance characteristics that are a roughly equal combination of stereotypically male and stereotypically female traits or do not conform to either male or female stereotypes.

anorexia nervosa An eating disorder marked by an obsessive concern with body weight and shape, a refusal to eat, and distorted perceptions of body weight and shape.

antisocial behavior Disruptive acts that are either overtly or covertly hostile and aggressive toward others.

antisocial personality disorder A personality disorder that is marked by a lack of empathy or conscience, cruelty, deceit, and manipulation. Aggressive or violent behavior is also a common characteristic.

anxiety Fear or worry. To rise to the level of an anxiety disorder, the psychological discomfort produced by the fear or worry is persistent rather than short term and may get worse over time.

anxious-avoidant An attachment between parent and child characterized by a lack of an emotional bond with a caregiver and is the results of a caregiver who is neglectful even when a child is distressed.

anxious-resistant An attachment between parent and child characterized by anxiety by the child and is due to an inconsistent pattern of appropriate and neglectful caregiving behavior.

assimilation The cognitive process wherein individuals acquire new information, and subsequently fit that new information in with their current thinking.

attention deficit hyperactivity disorder (ADHD) A chronic condition marked by an inability to pay attention for extended periods of time, high levels of activity, an inability to control one's behavior, and impulsivity at times.

attributions Explanations that people develop to understand events that occur.

authoritarian parents Parents who are high in demandingness and low in responsiveness.

authoritative parenting style A style of parenting that is marked by a combination of warmth and responsiveness with high expectations and accountability. Authoritative parents listen to their children and solicit their perspective but also set limits and reasonable boundaries.

authoritative parents Parents who are high in both demandingness and responsiveness.

automaticity The ability to engage in highly familiar tasks without exerting much mental effort.

average Adolescents who do not stand apart from other students in terms of widespread liking or disliking by their peers at school.

axons The long part of nerve cells that transmit the nerve impulse from the body of the nerve to the synapse or to another nerve.

background knowledge Prior information that has previously been learned, and that is necessary for learning and understanding more complex information.

barometric self-esteem Fluctuations in self-esteem that occur over time and across situations and contexts.

baseline self-esteem The general sense of global self-esteem that is mostly stable and consistent over time and across situations and contexts.

behavioral aspects of religion Actions and activities associated with religious participation, such as attending religious services or meetings of religious organizations.

behavioral autonomy Characterized by more mature decision-making and taking responsibility for one's own behavior.

belonging Feeling respected and valued in a context (e.g., school, family).

bicultural identity For students who simultaneously operate in two or more cultural or ethnic groups, this refers to adopting the beliefs, values, and behaviors of both the dominant cultural or ethnic group and the minority or non-dominant cultural or ethnic group. It may involve switching between the two.

binge drinking Having at least four (for women) or five (for men) alcoholic drinks in one sitting and within a 2-hour period.

binge eating or binging Frequently consuming large amounts of food with a feeling that one cannot stop oneself.

bio-psycho-social model Model of development that acknowledges that development is influenced by biological, psychological, and social factors, and that these factors all interact with each other.

bioecological model Model of development focusing on how individuals develop within a multilayered social and environmental system.

biracial Belonging to, or identifying with, two racial or ethnic groups.

bisexual Engaging in both heterosexual and homosexual activities.

blended family A family in which both parents bring children from previous marriages.

body dissatisfaction Unhappiness with one's weight or body shape, which is common among adolescent girls in the United States.

body-mass index (BMI) A measure of the ratio of weight to height that is used to determine whether individuals are overweight or underweight.

bulimia nervosa An eating disorder marked by binge eating followed by purging through vomiting, laxatives, extreme exercising, or a combination of these behaviors. It involves a preoccupation with weight and body shape.

care A moral focus on the importance of relationships between individuals.

central executive The part of working-memory that oversees all of the processes involved in working memory.

centrality An aspect of ethnic identity that refers to how important one's ethnic identity is to his or her overall sense of self.

centration The phenomenon in which young children focus on one specific aspect of an object.

chlamydia A sexually transmitted disease that can be transmitted through oral, anal, or vaginal sex. It can cause serious problems with a woman's reproductive system, making it difficult to become pregnant or carry a pregnancy to term. It is a bacterial infection that is treatable with antibiotics.

chum A special friendship children form during the preadolescent/ early adolescent stage that Harry Stack Sullivan thought played a pivotal role in the development of intimacy by providing the foundation for future intimacy in sexual relationships.

chunking A strategy that can be used to enhance working memory, in which information that needs to be memorized is consolidated into fewer, easier to remember groups.

circadian rhythm Our internal pattern, or rhythm, that controls when we feel tired and sleepy and when we feel more awake.

civic engagement Participation in socially-oriented activities focused on the well-being of others, often within one's community.

co-rumination Extensive discussion of problems between friends.

cognitive dissonance When learners encounter new information that counters what is already known, they experience discomfort, which motivates them to resolve the feelings of discomfort.

cognitive or value autonomy Characterized by the development of one's own opinions guided by a personal set of principles and values

cognitive-behavioral therapy A therapeutic approach that focuses on challenging and changing negative or damaging thoughts with the hope that changing these thoughts will produce a change in maladaptive behavior as well.

collectivism A cultural definition of the self that emphasizes one's membership in a particular cultural or familial group and the importance of that group's cohesiveness and well-being. The individual's role within the group is emphasized.

commitment An aspect of ethnic identity that refers to how important one's ethnicity is to one's self. It comes after the exploration stage.

community colleges Usually these are two-year post-secondary institutions that offer an Associate's degree; students can transfer into four-year colleges after attending a community college.

comorbidity The co-occurrence of two or more disorders or psychological problems.

complex carbohydrates Food or tissue compounds that are comprised of three or more sugars and therefore take longer to break down and have more fiber than simple carbohydrates. Complex carbohydrates have health benefits for digestion and longer-term energy.

comprehensive sex education A model of education about sex that includes information about the benefits of abstinence along with information about contraception, sexually transmitted diseases, pregnancy prevention, and various sexual behaviors.

concrete operations Piagetian stage of cognitive development that occurs between the ages of 7–11, wherein students become able to engage in complex cognitive operations (e.g., conservation of mass), but are still unable to engage in complex, hypothetical reasoning.

conditional knowledge Knowledge of when and how to use procedural and declarative knowledge.

conduct disorder A psychological disorder that encompasses many different kinds of behavior, such as bullying, initiating fights with others, being cruel to people or animals, running away from home, and destroying other people's property, all before the age of 13. To be diagnosed with conduct disorder one must display at least three of these behaviors within a 12-month period.

conservation The ability to understand that the amount of an entity stays the same, even if the configuration or shape of the entity is changed, as long as no additional amount of the entity is added.

contraception A general term that refers to any method of preventing pregnancy during or after sexual intercourse.

controversial Adolescents who are liked by many and disliked by many of their peers at school.

Conventional Stage Middle-levels of Kohlberg's stages of moral development; focus is on engaging in appropriate behaviors in order to receive approval from others or out of respect for authority.

coordinated school health plan A plan, developed by the Centers for Disease Control and Prevention, that promotes the development of integrated health services for students, their families, and their teachers.

coping strategies Behaviors or thoughts that adolescents use to manage difficult situations and circumstances in their lives.

cost The negatives associated with task involvement.

crowd Larger, reputation-based groups of similarly stereotyped individuals who may or may not spend much time together (e.g., jocks, brains, druggies).

crystallized The type of intelligence resulting from what has been learned through interactions with others and with the environment.

cultural identity The same as ethnic identity, but about one's cultural group (e.g., Italian culture, the culture of one's age group or regional group, etc.).

cyberbullying Bullying done through digital media such as text messages or social media websites.

dating aggression Physical or emotional aggression or violence that occurs within a dating or romantic relationship. This often refers to sexual aggression, such as coercion and date rape.

de-idealization of parents Adolescents' realizing that their parents are not perfect and, like other adults, they have their unique strengths and challenges.

decision making Choosing from among several alternatives.

declarative knowledge The knowledge of facts.

delayed phase preference The shift during adolescence toward preferring to stay up later at night and to sleep later in the morning.

depression Persistent feelings of sadness, hopelessness, lethargy, and loss of interest in common, once-enjoyable activities.

diathesis-stress model A model of mental disorder that postulates a combination of genetic or biological predisposition and environmental stressors as the cause of the disorder.

digital citizenship The norms of appropriate and responsible technology use and the information and skills that one needs to be active, informed, and responsible in the digital world.

digital divide The gap between groups of people who have access to and knowledge of technology and the Internet and those who do not.

digital footprint The traces one leaves in the electronic environment.

digital natives Adolescents and young adults in contemporary times who were born and grew up immersed in digital technology and therefore have high levels of familiarity with computers and the Internet.

discrimination Treatment of an individual by standards different than those used for others; often is based on group membership (e.g., gender, ethnicity, religion, etc.).

disequilibrium State that occurs when new information is encountered that conflicts with current understanding.

disordered eating Problematic eating habits that might include not eating enough, binging and purging, and using laxatives to avoid weight gain.

displacement effect The time that youth spend with technology and media is time away from family and friends and time spent outdoors.

dissonance training A method of countering, and trying to change, irrational fears or beliefs that involves asking adolescents to take a stance that is contrary to those beliefs.

"don't ask, don't tell" A policy in the U.S. military, instituted under President Bill Clinton in 1994, to neither ask whether members are homosexual or bisexual nor for homosexual or bisexual members of the military tell others that they are homosexual or bisexual. The policy was designed to protect gay, lesbian, and bisexual members of the military from discrimination as long as they were not open about their sexual orientation. The policy was repealed in 2011 as restrictions on openly homosexual and bisexual members of the military were relaxed.

downward assimilation The idea that some cultural or ethnic groups, particularly those that experience the most discrimination and oppression, will eschew working hard in school or adopting the cultural values of the majority and instead adopt the beliefs, values, and behaviors of the lower-income and disenfranchised members of society.

DSM-V   Acronym for the *Diagnostic and Statistical Manual of Mental Disorders*, Fifth Edition. This is the widely used publication that defines and categorizes most known psychological and psychiatric disorders. Produced by the American Psychiatric Association.

dual-enrollment programs   Programs in which high school students can simultaneously enroll in college or university courses, and simultaneously receive both high school and college credit.

dual-systems model   A model, developed by Robert Steinberg, demonstrating that adolescents' ability to control their impulses is tied to growth in the prefrontal cortex, but reward seeking is tied more to increases in certain hormones.

dynamic systems theory   Developmental theory emphasizing the ever-changing nature of the systems within which adolescents operate, and the adjustments that adolescents must make to adapt to these changes.

dystopian perspective   The view that changes in technology and media are troubling and cause for concern.

ecological systems theory   Bronfenbrenner's model of development, in which the individual is nested within the microsystem, mesosystem, exosystem, and macrosystem.

edible schoolyard   A program that originated in Berkeley, California, that emphasizes educating students about nutrition, growing food in gardens on school property, and learning how to cook healthy food.

efficacy beliefs   Beliefs in one's abilities to accomplish specific tasks.

elaboration   Relating newly learned information to knowledge already stored in long-term memory.

emerging adulthood   Period between the ages of 18 through 29, during which individuals explore different facets of life before taking on major responsibilities of adulthood.

emotional aggression   Hostility expressed toward another person without involving physical contact. It is meant to threaten or to cause emotional harm and discomfort to others.

emotional autonomy   Characterized by self-sufficiency and feeling comfortable and confident when making decisions without excessive guidance from parents.

empty-nest syndrome   The idea that parents, especially mothers, are distressed when children grow up and leave home.

endocrine system   The system of glands that produces hormones involved in the onset and development of puberty.

environmental stressors   Factors in the individual's context that can contribute to the development or expression of a psychological disorder. These can include anything from poverty to trauma to a breakup of a romantic relationship to environmental toxins.

equilibrium   State that occurs when new information as been accommodated.

estrogens   A set of hormones responsible for the development of several female traits that increases dramatically in girls during adolescence.

ethnic identity   How one thinks about one's self in terms of one's ethnicity. This includes the importance of ethnicity to one's overall sense of self, positive and negative feelings about one's ethnic group, and beliefs about how members of one's ethnic group should think and behave.

exosystem   Social system that includes extended family, the neighborhood, and community organizations.

experience sampling method (ESM)   A method of collecting data that involves remotely notifying research participants, several times a day, that it is time for them to answer questions about what they are doing and how they are feeling at the moment.

explanatory style   The attributions one makes to understand the events that occur in one's life. Whereas some people are prone to making hopeful or positive attributions (a positive or hopeful explanatory style), others are prone to generating more negative or hopeless explanations for these life events (a negative or hopeless explanatory style).

exploration   An aspect of ethnic identity that refers to the process of seeking out information about the beliefs, behaviors, values, and mannerisms of one's ethnic group.

externalizing disorder   A category of mental disorders that is characterized by thoughts, feelings, and behaviors that are outwardly expressed and directed toward others.

extrinsic motivation   Motivation that comes from factors external to the student and is unrelated to the task itself.

false self   The feeling that one is a phony or a fake because one thinks and behaves differently in different situations and contexts.

family process model   A model that conceptualizes a family's economic circumstances affect child and adolescent well-being by influencing interpersonal dynamics within the family.

feared selves   Future or possible selves that are perceived as undesirable by the individual; what one is afraid of becoming.

fellatio   Oral sex involving mouth-to-penis stimulation.

feminine traits   A set of behaviors, mannerisms, and appearance characteristics that are commonly associated with being female.

fixed mindset   Students view intelligence as fixed and unchanging.

fluid intelligence   Cognitive processes that are directly related to the physiological functions of the brain.

follicle-stimulating hormone (FSH)   A hormone released by the pituitary gland at the beginning of puberty that causes the ovaries in girls to produce hormones, primarily estrogens, that are associated with the development of female traits.

formal operations   Ability to think logically and reason about abstract, hypothetical, and theoretical concepts.

friendship   A mutual, close, and voluntary relationship.

full assimilation   For adolescents who simultaneously operate in two or more cultural or ethnic groups, this refers to fully adopting the beliefs, values, and behaviors of the majority or dominant cultural or ethnic group.

full separation For adolescents who simultaneously operate in two or more cultural or ethnic groups, this refers to fully adopting the beliefs, values, and behaviors of the minority or nondominant cultural or ethnic group.

g A general measure of overall intelligence.

gender identity How one thinks about one's self in terms of gender and what it means to be a person of that gender.

gender roles Information in the society and culture about appropriate beliefs, behaviors, and mannerisms for each gender.

gender-intensification hypothesis The idea that during adolescence there is increasing pressure from various socializing agents (e.g., parents, teachers, peers, media) to appear and behave in ways that are appropriate to one's gender.

gender-stereotypical Behaviors or mannerisms that are consistent with stereotypes about a particular gender.

generalized anxiety disorder Persistent fear and worry that is not attached to a specific issue. It is marked by excessive worry about several aspects of life (e.g., career, relationships, natural disasters, etc.) that is chronic.

genetic predisposition Inheriting genes that make one prone to developing a disorder or trait.

gonorrhea A sexually transmitted disease that that can be transmitted through oral, anal, or vaginal sex. It often causes a painful, burning sensation when urinating, discharge from the penis or vagina, and swelling. It is a bacterial infection that is treatable with antibiotics.

good-boy/nice-girl orientation Stage of Kohlberg's theory focused on behaving appropriately in order to receive the approval of others.

gray matter The part of the brain that contains nerve cells, axons, dendrites, and neurotransmitters, in which the processing of information and responses to the information occur in the brain.

growth mindset Students view intelligence as malleable and something that can change and develop over time.

healthy sexual development A model that focuses on beliefs, attitudes, and behaviors associated with safe and healthy sexual development.

heinz dilemma Scenario developed by Kohlberg, used to examine levels of moral development.

high-sensation-seekers Individuals who like exciting, stimulating activities.

high-stakes exams Tests in which results often have important consequences, and often are reported to the public in aggregated format.

higher education Formal education that occurs after graduation from high school.

HIV/AIDS HIV is an acronym that stands for human immunodeficiency virus. This is the virus that causes AIDS. AIDS is an acronym that stands for acquired immune deficiency syndrome.

homophily Similarity among peer group members.

homophobia A fear of, dislike of, or discrimination toward homosexuals.

hooking up Sexual encounters, ranging from kissing to sexual intercourse, with little or no ongoing commitment to or relationship with the hook-up partner.

hoped-for selves Future or possible selves that are perceived as desirable by the individual; what one hopes to become.

horizontal decalage Occurs when an aspect of cognitive development emerges in some domains prior to others.

hormones Chemicals developed in various glands in the body that influence physical development, mood, and behavior during adolescence.

hostile attribution bias The tendency to interpret neutral cues, such as facial expressions or behaviors of others, as having hostile intent.

hypothalamus A portion of the brain that produces many hormones. At the beginning of adolescence, it produces a hormone that disinhibits the pituitary gland, allowing it to begin releasing hormones associated with the beginning of the puberty process.

ideal self How one wishes he or she were, in the present or the future.

identity The understanding and appreciation of both how individuals perceive themselves and how they believe they are perceived by others.

identity achievement In Marcia's theory, identity achievement is the most advanced status of identity development in which one has committed to a path after exploring and considering various other pathways.

identity diffusion In Marcia's theory, identity diffusion is the identity status in which one is neither exploring various pathways or identities nor has committed to an identity. It is the least mature identity status.

identity foreclosure In Marcia's theory, identity foreclosure is the status in which one has decided on a path (e.g., career, life partner) without exploring other options or pathways.

identity interview An interview protocol and procedure developed by James Marcia to determine one's status of identity development and commitment.

identity moratorium In Marcia's theory, identity moratorium is the identity status in which one is exploring several different potential paths but has not yet committed to any.

ideology An aspect of ethnic identity that refers to how one thinks that members of one's ethnic group should think and behave.

illicit drugs Substances that are either illegal or legal but used for purposes other than their prescribed use (e.g., using prescription drugs without a prescription).

immigrant paradox The tendency for immigrants to have more positive achievement and wellness profiles (e.g., mental health, academic achievement, lack of delinquent behavior) than native-born peers.

importance value Perceptions that skills in a certain domain are important and success in that domain is revered or admired

impulsivity Personality trait wherein individuals make decisions quickly and without considering consequences.

independent self or individualism A cultural definition of the self that emphasizes independent accomplishment, goals, and uniqueness. The individual's personal goals and self-sufficiency are emphasized.

indifferent parents Parents who are low in both demandingness and responsiveness.

individuation The process of gradually achieving a sense of self separate from parents.

information processing The system of processes that help us to remember information.

intellectual risk taking Feeling comfortable in providing creative responses to questions and taking novel approaches to solving problems.

interdependent self A cultural definition of the self that emphasizes one's membership in a particular cultural or familial group and the importance of that group's cohesiveness and well-being. The individual's role within the group is emphasized.

internal working model A mental representation for understanding the self with others.

internalizing behaviors Negative feelings that are directed inward, including depression, anxiety, and feeling withdrawn.

internalizing disorder A category of mental disorders that is characterized by thoughts, feelings, and behaviors that are kept inside or directed toward the self.

intimacy The closeness of a relationship.

intrinsic motivation Motivation that comes from within a person or is inherent in the task itself.

intrinsic value Enjoyment or liking activities.

invincibility A feeling that one cannot be hurt, injured, or killed. Adolescents often feel a sense of invincibility, making them more prone to engage in risky behavior.

justice A moral focus on fairness and equity.

knowledge-acquisition components How individuals learn to solve problems and acquire information.

Knowledge Is Power Program (KIPP) A network of charter schools that emphasizes academic rigor and a "no-excuses" approach to helping low-income students achieve well.

law-and-order orientation Stage of Kohlberg's theory focused on behaving appropriately because of respect for authorities, rules, and the social order.

Let's Move A program initiated by Michelle Obama to increase health and reduce obesity among children and teens. The program focuses on exercise and nutrition.

LGBT Acronym that stands for lesbian, gay, bisexual, trans (i.e., transsexual, transgender, transvestite).

LGBTQI Acronym that stands for lesbian, gay, bisexual, trans, queer, and intersex (i.e., someone whose sex characteristics are not exclusively male or female).

life-course-persistent offenders Individuals who engage in antisocial and/or delinquent behavior during adolescence as well as at other periods of development, including childhood and/or adulthood.

life-skills training Programs designed to teach adolescents various social, problem-solving, and self-regulatory skills as a method of improving their ability to cope with challenging situations and circumstances.

long-term memory The virtually unlimited capacity to store information.

luteinizing hormone (LH) One of the hormones produced by the pituitary gland during adolescence. It stimulates the testes to begin producing androgens, such as testosterone in boys.

macrosystem The larger society and culture in which one lives.

major depressive disorder (MDD) Exhibiting at least five symptoms of depression every day for at least 2 weeks.

marginalized For students who simultaneously operate in two or more cultural or ethnic groups, this refers to feeling that one is not really accepted by, or a full member of, either the majority/dominant or the minority/nondominant ethnic group.

masculine traits A set of behaviors, mannerisms, and appearance characteristics that are commonly associated with being male.

mastery goal structure When teachers communicate to students that the main purpose for doing schoolwork is to develop their competence. Real learning and understanding are what are most valued.

mean world syndrome The phenomenon where media exposure cultivates the belief that the world is a more violent and mean place than it is in reality.

media literacy The ability to access, analyze, evaluate, create, and participate in the images, words, and sounds that make up our contemporary mass-media culture.

melatonin A hormone that helps humans determine the time of day and, therefore, when the body should sleep.

memory Storage of information that has been learned.

menarche The beginning of the first ovulation process for adolescent girls, resulting in their first menstrual period.

mesosystem Linkages and processes that take place between two or more microsystems.

meta-analysis A method of research in which the results from several studies on a single issue are combined to find the average effects across studies.

metacognition   The ability to think about one's own thinking.

metacomponents   Ability to recognize problems, select appropriate strategies to solve problems, and to evaluate responses to problems.

metamemory   The ability to think about one's memory.

microsystem   Close social systems within which the individual operates, such as family, school, and close friends.

mixed race   Belonging to, or identifying with, more than one racial or ethnic group.

mnemonic devices   Strategies that can be used to summarize information (e.g., use of acronyms), so that the information can be more easily remembered.

modeling   Learning by observing others.

moral   Beliefs and behaviors related to what is considered to be either right or wrong.

moral development   Changes in individuals' beliefs and behaviors related to issues of fairness and right versus wrong.

motivation   Why people think and behave the way that they do; motivation concerns the initiation, direction, intensity, persistence, and quality of behavior.

motivation to learn   The tendency to find learning activities meaningful and worthwhile and to try and get the intended benefits from them.

multidimensional self   The idea that individuals possess different self-perceptions in different domains (e.g., physical, academic, social) and that one's identity is comprised of these self-perceptions from many domains.

multiple intelligences   Theory of intelligence suggesting that humans have distinct intelligences across a range of domains.

multiracial   Belonging to, or identifying with, more than one racial or ethnic group.

mutual responsiveness   The extent to which friends share resources and help one another.

myelin and myelination   Myelin is a fatty sheath of insulation that is comprised of proteins and phospholipids. It forms around some axons and helps to speed up the transfer of impulses from the nerve cell down the axon.

neglected   Adolescents who are neither liked nor disliked by their peers at school.

neurons   Cells in the nervous system; nerve cells.

neurotransmitters   Chemicals in the brain that facilitate the communication between neurons.

novelty seeking   The tendency among adolescents to search for, and engage in, new experiences.

obese/obesity   Having a body-mass index in the 95th percentile or above as compared with adolescents of the same age and sex.

observational learning   Learning what to do or how to behave by watching others and noticing how they are reinforced or punished for their behavior.

obsessive-compulsive disorder (OCD)   A psychological disorder marked by unreasonable thoughts and fears that are difficult to put out of one's mind (obsession) and repetitive behaviors (compulsion). One can have OCD with only obsessive thoughts or compulsive behaviors, as well as having both.

one-night stand   Euphemism for a brief sexual encounter.

oppositional-defiant disorder   A milder form of conduct disorder that is characterized by angry, spiteful, and disrespectful interactions with others, but without the violence or level of aggression present in those with conduct disorder.

oral sex   Stimulation of another's sexual organs (e.g., penis, vagina) with the mouth.

organization   Systematically arranging information so that it can more easily be learned.

overweight   Having a body-mass index between the 85th and 95th percentile as compared with adolescents of the same age and sex.

panic attacks   Acute, brief episodes of fear and worry that can cause nausea, shortness of breath, disorientation, and trembling.

pansexual   Being attracted to and/or being able to fall in love with members of any gender.

parental demandingness   The extent to which parents create clear expectations and rules, expect mature and responsible behavior, and require children and adolescents to comply, with a willingness to confront disobedience.

parental responsiveness   The extent to which parents recognize their adolescent as an individual and attune to their needs in an accepting, supportive manner.

parietal lobe   Region of the brain that controls visual-spatial acuity and subsequent motor responses.

peer acceptance   One form of popularity among peers at school which refers to the extent to which a student is generally liked or disliked by peers at school.

peer group   Groups of students who tend to hang out and talk to each other and often do activities together.

performance components   The ways individuals carry out metacomponents.

performance goal structure   When teachers communicate to students that the main purpose for doing schoolwork is to demonstrate their competence, especially relative to other students.

permissive parents   Parents who are low in demandingness but high in responsiveness.

personal fable   The tendency of adolescents to make up stories about themselves of which they are the protagonist and, as such, they are special, unique, and immune from the problems and hazards that confront more normal individuals. It can provide a dangerous sense of invincibility, making adolescents more prone to engage in risky behavior.

perspective taking   The ability to consider issues and situations from others' points of view.

petting   Sexual activity that involves touching of parts of the body (e.g., breasts, buttocks, penis, vagina) with the hands, either over or under clothing.

phonological loop   Component of working memory that allows for the temporary storage of small bits of information.

physical aggression   Aggressive behavior that is physical like hitting or pushing.

pituitary gland   One of the glands in the endocrine system. At the beginning stages of puberty, the pituitary gland stimulates release of luteinizing hormone and follicle-stimulating hormone.

popular reputation   One form of popularity among peers which refers to which students are seen as popular at their school.

possible selves (or future selves)   Perceptions about how or what one might become in the future.

postconventional stage   Highest levels of moral development in Kohlberg's theory; focus is on societal needs and the ethical treatment of all people.

posttraumatic stress disorder (PTSD)   A persistent condition of heightened stress and fear that occurs after experiencing or witnessing a traumatic event. Symptoms can include lack of sleep, frequent flashbacks to the event, an inability to stop thinking about the event, and withdrawal from people.

preconventional stage   Lowest levels of moral development in Kohlberg's theory; focus is on obedience and rules.

prefrontal cortex   Region of the brain associated with planning, impulse control, abstract reasoning, and self-regulation.

preoperational stage   Piagetian stage in which children obtain the ability to use symbols and language.

primary sex characteristics   Physical characteristics that are directly involved in sexual reproduction. These include parts of the anatomy such as the penis, vagina, testes, and ovaries.

procedural knowledge   The knowledge of how to do things.

pruning   The process whereby neural connections and pathways fade away as they are no longer used.

punishment/obedience orientation   Stage of Kohlberg's theory in which decisions are made based on obedience to authority and avoidance of punishment.

purging   Expulsion of food and drink, most often by vomiting, as a method of weight control. It is commonly associated with the eating disorder bulimia.

queer   An umbrella term that some people use to refer to the LGBT community. It is not a reference to a particular sexual orientation. Rather, it refers to an entire set of beliefs, practices, orientations, and personal expression. The word has a long history as a pejorative term used against homosexuals and is still considered offensive by many, but is an accepted term without the negative connotation among many in the LGBT community.

questioning   A term for sexual orientation that refers to someone who has not decided on a sexual orientation label and is exploring different sexual orientations.

regard   An aspect of ethnic identity that refers to how one feels, positively and/or negatively, about one's ethnic group and one's membership in it.

rehearsal   Continuous repetition of information, in order to keep the information active in working memory.

rejected   Adolescents who are disliked by many and liked by few of their peers at school.

rejection sensitivity   A heightened sensitivity and fear of rejection in adolescence which may be due to lack of a secure attachment in early childhood.

relational aggression   Aggressive behavior that aims to manipulate someone's social status or friendships such as exclusion, spreading rumors or gossip.

resilience   The ability to avoid developing a psychological disorder or problematic behavior even when one encounters one or more stressors that might put the individual at risk for developing a disorder or problematic behavior.

risk   Factors that increase the adolescent's likelihood of developing psychological and behavioral problems or disorders.

risky behaviors   Behaviors that potentially are physically or psychologically dangerous (e.g., using drugs, abuse of alcohol, unprotected sex, drunk driving).

role confusion   The negative outcome in Erikson's fifth stage of psychosocial development. Role confusion involves an unclear sense of what one values and of the path one wants to commit to in terms of career, relationships, or other important areas of life.

salience   An aspect of ethnic identity that refers to how conscious one is of his or her ethnicity in a given situation.

sandwich generation   When parents are caught in the middle of responsibilities for both older (i.e., aging parents) and younger generation (i.e., children).

scaffolding   Providing supports to learners to help them to develop particular skills or abilities.

schema   The ways that individuals represent concepts in their memories.

school Health Centers   Offices, either mobile or within a school or community building, that provide health-care services and information to students.

secondary sex characteristics   Physical characteristics that are associated with sexual maturity, such as breasts in females and facial hair in males. These characteristics develop during puberty.

secular trend   The tendency for children to begin adolescence and the development of secondary sex characteristics at younger ages than they did in previous generations.

secure   An attachment between parent and child characterized by trust and built from a caregiver who responds consistently and appropriately to a child's needs.

segmented assimilation theory   The theory that immigrant families living in low-income neighborhoods with few available role models of academic success adopt the values, beliefs, and behaviors of the underclass of society, which are often in opposition to those of the dominant or majority cultural or ethnic group in society.

selective perception Adolescents see and interpret media messages in different ways depending on their personal characteristics.

self-concept Perceptions of the self.

self-disclosure The sharing of personal or private thoughts and feelings with friends.

self-efficacy Judgments about one's own ability to perform a specific task (e.g., "I am confident that I will get an A on my history exam this afternoon.")

self-esteem (or global self-esteem) Overall perceptions of one's value or worth.

self-regulated learners Learners who can monitor their progress on academic tasks and apply appropriate learning strategies.

self-regulatory skills Ability to monitor one's progress on tasks and to apply appropriate learning strategies

self-worth (or global self-worth) Overall judgments about one's own value and worth.

semenarche The beginning of the production of semen during puberty.

sensation seeking A desire for, and seeking out of, experiences that are novel, intense, thrilling, and rewarding.

sensorimotor stage First Piagetian stage, featuring the most simplistic forms of thought.

sensory register Instantaneous retention of information perceived by one's senses.

service learning An educational experience in which students participate actively in activities that both meet community needs and are integrated into academic curricula.

sexting Sending texts via phone of a sexual nature, including sexually explicit photographs or videos.

sexual behavior Behavior that involves any aspect of sexuality, from flirting to sexual intercourse.

sexual harassment Unwanted sexual advances, requests for sexual favors, or other remarks or behaviors of a sexual nature that cause the target of such remarks and behaviors discomfort, fear, or offense.

sexual orientation The inclination to be physically and/or romantically attracted to a particular gender: one's own (homosexual), not one's own (heterosexual), or both (bisexual). There are other sexual orientations besides these three. For example, some people identify as asexual (not being physically attracted to members of either gender), pansexual (attracted to members of any gender), and skoliosexual (attracted to those who do not identify as exclusively male or female), among others.

sexually transmitted diseases (STDs) Diseases that are spread through sexual contact. This is a generic term that refers to any such disease.

sexy world syndrome The phenomenon where media exposure cultivates the belief that people have more sex and sex-related issues than is typical in real life.

short-term memory Temporary storage of information while paying attention to that information.

sleep debt Accumulating lack of sleep as the adolescent regularly sleeps fewer hours than he or she needs to feel fully rested.

social comparison The action of comparing one's self to others.

social contract/legalistic orientation Stage of Kohlberg's theory in which moral reasoning is based on laws, one's own values and beliefs, and the needs of society.

social media Communication via technology in which individuals can readily share information and communicate.

social reinforcement The process whereby beliefs/behaviors that are discouraged by peers are less likely to be displayed again by an individual and beliefs/behaviors encouraged by peers are more likely to be displayed again by an individual.

socialization The tendency for peers to influence similar attributes in one another over time.

socioeconomic status (SES) A family's economic or social position, including aspects of parental education, occupation, and income.

sociopaths or psychopaths Individuals with a personality disorder marked by a lack of conscience and a high level of antisocial attitudes and behavior.

stereotype threat When a member of a group about which there is a negative stereotype is in a situation where the possibility of fulfilling the negative stereotype is present.

storm-and-stress view A view of the adolescent period as one that is marked by high levels of emotionality and stress, caused primarily by changes in hormone levels.

storm-and-stress view Perspective that adolescence is a biologically based period of heightened stress and emotionality.

stress Mental or emotional strain caused by difficult circumstances or experiences.

substance abuse Continued overuse of substances (e.g., drugs, alcohol), even if the abuse causes problems in one's life (e.g., legal problems, relationship problems, an inability to work effectively).

successful intelligence Conception of intelligence focusing on the skills that individuals need.

suicidal acts Intentional, self-injurious behaviors, committed by those with suicidal ideation, that may or may not result in death.

suicidal gestures Intentionally hurting or injuring oneself by not lethally.

suicidal ideation   Thoughts about committing suicide, ranging from passing thoughts to detailed planning.

syphilis   A sexually transmitted disease that can be transmitted through oral, anal, or vaginal sex. It causes sores on the mouth, anus, vagina, or penis. If untreated, it can develop into a rash and cause symptoms such as headache, fever, body aches, and weight loss. If left untreated for more than a year, serious consequences can develop, including blindness, problems with the nervous system, mental disorders, and death. It is a bacterial infection that is treatable with antibiotics.

systems theories   Theories that acknowledge that development and behavior are influenced by multiple factors simultaneously, and that individuals are nested within complex systems that mutually influence each other.

tanner scale   A system developed by Dr. James Tanner that documents the development of secondary sex characteristics in males and females at different stages of adolescence.

teacher attunement to peer groups   Teachers' attention to, and knowledge of, students friends and peer groups.

teaming   The practice in which students within grades in a middle school are broken down into smaller units called teams.

temporal lobe   A region of the brain that is located behind the ears and is associated with memory, emotion, hearing and vision, and the understanding of speech.

testosterone   An androgen that is produced in greater amounts in boys during adolescence and is responsible for the development of several male traits.

the pill   A form of oral contraceptive.

thin-body ideal   The idea, promoted in popular media, that the ideal body shape for women is thin and tall.

title IX   A federal law, passed in 1972, prohibiting discrimination in participation or funding for boys' and girls' athletic programs in public schools.

transgender   When one's gender identity and gender expression are different from one's assigned sex as determined by his or her anatomy.

transsexual   When one strongly desires to adopt the physical features of the opposite gender and may take steps to fulfilling that desire through hormone treatments and/or surgery.

traumatic life events, trauma   Events, either personally experienced or witnessed, that cause intense psychological or physical harm to the person who experienced or witnessed them.

triggers   Events and experiences that can cause one to become aware of his or her culture or ethnicity.

true self   The idea that one should have a single, true self that is the same across situations and contexts.

21st-century skills   The skills that are necessary in order to be able to be cognitively prepared to be competitive in the workforce in the 21st century.

universal/ethical principle orientation   Stage of Kohlberg's theory in which moral reasoning is based on individual beliefs, with a focus on justice, human rights, and the ethical treatment of others.

utility value   Perceptions that skills in a certain domain would be useful to other future endeavors

utopian perspective   The view that changes in technology and media represent new opportunities and are a force for positive changes in the world.

values affirmation   A method of reducing the negative effects of stereotype threat by reminding oneself of something, or things, that one finds important.

vaping   Inhaling and exhaling the vapor produced by e-cigarettes.

verbal aggression   Aggressive behavior that is verbal such as name calling or teasing someone.

vicarious learning   Learning that takes place through observation rather than first-hand experience.

virginity pledge   A promise to remain a virgin until marriage. Some adolescents take this pledge as a sign of their commitment to virginity until marriage.

visuospatial sketchpad   Component of working memory that allows us to temporarily hold and manipulate images.

vocational education   Planned sets of courses and experiences designed to prepare individuals for future employment in a variety of trades and professions.

volunteering   Participating in activities that meet the needs of individuals or organizations in the community, without receiving any form of remuneration.

well-liked   Adolescents who are liked by many and disliked by few of their peers at school.

working memory   Temporary storage of information while paying attention to that information.

zero tolerance   Behavioral policies in which punishments are consistently applied when certain behavioral infractions occur, regardless of circumstances.

zone of proximal development (ZPD)   The difference between an individual's ability to solve problems independently versus when working in collaboration with more experienced peers or adults.

References

Aarons, S. J., & Jenkins, R. R. (2002). Sex, pregnancy, and contraception-related motivators and barriers among Latino and African-American youth in Washington, DC. *Sex Education, 2,* 5–30.

Ables, V. (Producer & Director), & Congdon, J. (Director). (2011). *Race to nowhere* [Motion picture]. United States: Reel Link Films.

Abrams, K. K., Allen, L. R., & Gray, J. J. (1993). Disordered eating attitudes and behaviors, psychological adjustment, and ethnic identity: A comparison of Black and White female college students. *International Journal of Eating Disorders, 14,* 49–57.

Abrams, L. S., & Stormer, C. C. (2002). Sociocultural variations in the body image perceptions of urban adolescent females. *Journal of Youth and Adolescence, 31,* 443–450.

Adams, D. M. (2012). Racism, trauma, and being the other in the classroom. In H. Curtis-Boles, D. M. Adams, & V. Jenkins-Monroe (Eds.), *Making our voices heard: Women of color in academia* (pp. 35–46). Hauppauge, NY: Nova Science Publishers.

Agliata, D., & Tantleff-Dunn, S. (2004). The impact of media exposure on males' body image. *Journal of Social and Clinical Psychology, 23,* 7–22.

Ainsworth-Darnell, J. W., & Downey, D. B. (1998). Assessing the oppositional culture explanation for racial/ethnic differences in school performance. *American Sociological Review, 63,* 536–553.

Ainsworth, M., Blehar, W., Waters, E., & Wall, S. (1978). *Patterns of attachment.* Hillsdale, NJ: Erlbaum.

Akos, P., & Galassi, J. P. (2004). Gender and race as variables in psychosocial adjustment to middle and high school. *Journal of Educational Research, 98*(2), 102–108.

Akos, P., Rose, R. A., & Orthner, D. (2015). Sociodemographic moderators of middle school transition effects on academic achievement. *Journal of Early Adolescence, 35*(2), 170–198.

Albrecht, A. K., Galambos, N. L., & Jansson, S. L. (2007). Adolescents internalizing and aggressive behaviors and perceptions of parents' psychological control: A panel study examining the direction of effects. *Journal of Youth and Adolescence, 36,* 673–684.

Alfieri, T., Ruble, D. N., Higgins, E. T. (1996). Gender stereotypes during adolescence: Developmental changes and the transition to junior high school. *Developmental Psychology, 32,* 1129–1130.

Alhola, P., & Polo-Kantola, P. (2007). Sleep deprivation: Impact on cognitive performance. *Neuropsychiatric Disease and Treatment, 3*(5), 553–567.

Allen, A. (2013). Charter schools and academic achievement. In J. Hattie & E. M. Anderman (Eds.), *International guide to student achievement* (pp. 113–115). New York, NY: Routledge.

Allen, D., & Dadgar, M. (2012). Does dual enrollment increase students' success in college? Evidence from a quasi-experimental analysis of dual enrollment in New York City. *New Directions for Higher Education, 158,* 11–19.

Allen, J. P., Chango, J., Szwedo, D., Schad, M., & Marston, E. (2012). Predictors of susceptibility to peer influence regarding substance use in adolescence. *Child Development, 83*(1), 337–350.

Altschul, I., Oyserman, D., & Bybee, D. (2008). Racial-ethnic self-schemas and segmented assimilation: Identity and the academic achievement of Hispanic youth. *Social Psychology Quarterly, 71,* 302–320.

Amato, P. R. (2010). Research on divorce: Continuing trends and new developments, *Journal of Marriage and Family, 72,* 650–666.

Amato, P. R., & Cheadle, J. E. (2008). Parental divorce, marital conflict and children's behavior problems: A comparison of adopted and biological children. *Social Forces, 86,* 1139–1161.

American Academy of Child and Adolescent Psychiatry (2013). *The depressed child.* https://www.aacap.org/AACAP/Families_and_Youth/Facts_for_Families/FFF-Guide/The-Depressed-Child-004.aspx. Retreived on January 8, 2016.

American Academy of Pediatrics. (2000). *Joint statement on the impact of entertainment violence on children.* Retrieved from http://www.aap.org/advocacy/releases/jstmtevc.htm

American Association of Community Colleges. (2014). *Community college enrollment.* Retrieved from http://www.aacc.nche.edu/ABOUTCC/TRENDS/Pages/enrollment.aspx

American Association of University Women. (1993). *Hostile hallways: The AAUW survey on sexual harassment in America's schools.* Washington, DC: Author.

American College Testing. (2008). *What we know about college success: Using ACT data to inform educational issues.* Retrieved from https://www.act.org/research/policymakers/pdf/what_we_know.pdf

American Educational Research Association. (2013). *Prevention of bullying in schools, colleges, and universities: Research report and recommendations.* Washington, DC: Author.

American Psychiatric Association. (2013). *Diagnostic and statistical manual of mental disorders* (5th ed.). Arlington, VA: American Psychiatric Association Press.

American Psychological Association. (2005). *Resolution in favor of empirically supported sex education and HIV prevention programs for adolescents.* Washington, DC: Author.

American Psychological Association. (2012). *Facing the school dropout dilemma.* Washington, DC: Author. Retrieved from http://www.apa.org/pi/families/resources/school-dropout-prevention.aspx

American Psychological Association. (2014). *Stressed in America: Are teens adopting adults' stress habits?* Washington, DC: Author.

American Psychological Association, Coalition for Psychology in Schools and Education. (2015). *Top 20 principles from psychology for preK–12 teaching and learning.* Retrieved from http://www.apa.org/ed/schools/cpse/top-twenty-principles.pdf

American Psychological Association (APA) Zero Tolerance Task Force (2008). Are zero tolerance policies effective in the schools?: An evidentiary review and recommendations. *American Psychologist, 63*(9), 852–862.

Ames, C. (1992). Classrooms: Goals, structures, and student motivation. *Journal of Educational Psychology, 84,* 261–271.

Amey, C. H., Albrecht, S. L., & Miller, M. K. (1996). Racial differences in adolescent drug use: The impact of religion. *Substance Use and Misuse, 31*(10), 1311–1332.

Anderman, E. M. (1995). Achievement goals and the transition to middle grades school. *Dissertation Abstracts International Section A: Humanities and Social Sciences, 55*(8–A), 2320.

Anderman, E. M. (2002). School effects on psychological outcomes during adolescence. *Journal of Educational Psychology, 94,* 795–809.

Anderman, E. M. (2007). The effects of personal, classroom, and school goal structures on academic cheating. In E. M. Anderman & T. B. Murdock (Eds.), *Psychology of academic cheating* (pp. 87–106). San Diego, CA: Elsevier.

Anderman, E. M., & Danner, F. (2008). Achievement goals and academic cheating. *International Review of Social Psychology, 21,* 155–180.

Anderman, E. M., & Midgley, C. (1997). Changes in achievement goal orientations, perceived academic competence, and grades across the transition to middle-level schools. *Contemporary Educational Psychology, 22*(3), 269–298.

Anderman, E. M., & Midgley, C. (2004). Changes in self-reported academic cheating across the transition from middle school to high school. *Contemporary Educational Psychology, 29,* 499–517.

Anderman, E. M., & Mueller, C. (2010). Middle school transitions and adolescent development. In J. Meece & J. S. Eccles (Eds.), *Handbook of research on schools, schooling, and human development* (pp. 198–215). New York, NY: Routledge.

Anderman, E. M., & Turner, J. C. (2004). *Changes in academic cheating across the transition to middle school.* Paper presented at the American Educational Research Association, San Diego, CA.

Anderman, E. M., & Wolters, C. A. (2006). Goals, values, and affect: Influences on student motivation. In P. Alexander & P. Winne (Eds.), *Handbook of educational psychology* (2nd ed., pp. 369–389). Mahwah, NJ: Erlbaum.

Anderman, E. M., Cupp, P. K., & Lane, D. R. (2010). Impulsivity and academic cheating. *Journal of Experimental Education, 78,* 135–150.

Anderman, E. M., Griessinger, T., & Westerfield, G. (1998). Motivation and cheating during early adolescence. *Journal of Educational Psychology, 90,* 84–93.

Anderman, E. M., Maehr, M. L., & Midgley, C. (1999). Declining motivation after the transition to middle school: Schools can make a difference. *Journal of Research and Development in Education, 32,* 131–147.

Anderman, E. M., Sinatra, G. M., & Gray, D. L. (2012). The challenges of teaching and learning about science in the twenty-first century: Exploring the abilities and constraints of adolescent learners. *Studies in Science Education, 48*(1), 89–117.

Anderman, E., & Maehr, M. L. (1994). Motivation and schooling in the middle grades. *Review of Educational Research, 64,* 287–309.

Anderman, E.M. (2015). *Students cheat for good grades. Why not make the classroom about learning and not testing?* Retrieved from https://theconversation.com/students-cheat-for-good-grades-why-not-make-the-classroom-about-learning-and-not-testing-39556

Anderman, E.M., & Anderman, L.H. (2014). *Classroom motivation,* 2nd ed. Boston: Pearson.

Anderson, C. A., & Bushman, B. J. (2001). Effects of violent video games on aggressive behavior, aggressive cognition, aggressive affect, physiological arousal, and pro- social behavior: A meta-analytic review of the scientific literature. *Psychological Science, 12,* 353–359.

Anderson, J., & Applebome, P. (2011). Exam cheating on Long Island hardly a secret. *New York Times.* Retrieved from: http://www.nytimes.com/2011/12/02/education/on-long-island-sat-cheating-was-hardly-a-secret.html?_r=0

Anderson, S. E., & Must, A. (2005). Interpreting the continued decline in the average age at menarche: Results from two nationally representative surveys of U.S. girls studied 10 years apart. *Journal of Pediatrics, 147,* 753–760.

Andrucci, G. L., Archer, R. P., Pancoast, D. L., & Gordon, R. A. (1989). The relationship of MMPI and sensation seeking scales to adolescent drug use. *Journal of Personality Assessment, 53,* 253–266.

Angier, N. (2013, November 25). The changing American family. *New York Times.* Retrieved from http://www.nytimes.com/2013/11/26/health/families.html?pagewanted=all&_r=0

Ansary, N. S., McMahon, T. J., & Luthar, S. S. (2012). Socioeconomic context and emotional-behavioral achievement links: Concurrent and prospective associations among low- and high-income youth. *Journal of Research on Adolescence, 22*(1), 14–30.

Archibald, A. B., Graber, J. A., & Brooks-Gunn, J. (2003). Pubertal processes and physiological growth in adolescence. In G. R. Adams, M. D. Berzonsky, & M. A. Malden (Eds.), *Blackwell handbook of adolescence* (pp. 24–47). Malden, MA: Blackwell.

Arcia, E., Reyes-Blanes, M. E., & Vazquez-Montilla, E. (2000). Constructions and reconstructions: Latino parents' values for children. *Journal of Child and Family Studies, 9,* 333–350.

Armbruster, B. B., Echols, C. H., & Brown, A. L. (1982). The role of metacognition in reading to learn: A developmental perspective. *The Volta Review, 84*(5), 45–56.

Armenta, B. E. (2010). Stereotype boost and stereotype threat effects: The moderating role of ethnic identification. *Cultural Diversity and Ethnic Minority Psychology, 16,* 94–98.

Arnett, J. J. (1995). Broad and narrow socialization: The family in the context of a cultural theory. *Journal of Marriage and Family, 57,* 617–628.

Arnett, J. J. (1999). Adolescent storm and stress, reconsidered. *American Psychologist, 54,* 317–326.

Arnett, J. J. (2000). Emerging adulthood: A theory of development from the late teens through the twenties. *American Psychologist, 55*(5), 469–480.

Arnett, J. J. (2004). *Emerging adulthood: The winding road from the late teens through the twenties.* New York: Oxford University Press.

Arnett, J. J. (2006). G. Stanley Hall's *Adolescence:* Brilliance and nonsense. *History of Psychology, 9,* 186–197.

Arnett, J. J. (2010). *Adolescence and emerging adulthood* (4th ed.). Boston, MA: Prentice Hall.

Arnett, J. J. (2012). *Adolescence and emerging adulthood: A cultural approach* (5th ed.). Boston, MA: Pearson.

Arnett, J. J. (2015). *Emerging adulthood: The winding road from the late teens through the twenties* (2nd ed.). New York: Oxford University Press.

Arnett, J. J., Ramos, K. D., & Jensen, L. A. (2001). Ideological views in emerging adulthood: Balancing autonomy and community. *Journal of Adult Development, 8*(2), 69–79.

Aron, A., & Aron, E. (1986). *Love and the expansion of self: Understanding attraction and satisfaction.* New York, NY: Hemisphere.

Aronson, J., Fried, C. B., & Good, C. (2002). Reducing the effects of stereotype threat on African American college students by shaping theories of intelligence. *Journal of Experimental Social Psychology, 38,* 113–125.

Arunkumar, R., & Midgley, C. (April 1999). Listening to students' voices: Reasons for experiencing cultural dissonance between home and school. Biennial meeting of the Society for Research on Child Development, Albuquerque, NM.

Aseltine, R. R., & Gore, S. (2005). Work, postsecondary education, and psychosocial functioning following the transition from high school. *Journal of Adolescent Research, 20*(6), 615–639.

Astor, R. A., Meyer, H. A., & Behre, W. J. (1999). Unowned places and times: Maps and interviews about violence in high schools. *American Educational Research Journal, 36,* 3–42

Atkins, R., Hart, D., & Donnelly, T. M. (2005). The association of childhood personality type with volunteering during adolescence. *Merrill-Palmer Quarterly, 51*(2), 145–162.

Atkinson, R. C., & Shiffrin, R. M. (1968). Human memory: A proposed system and its control processes. In K. W. Spence & J. T. Spence (Eds.), *The psychology of learning and motivation: Advances in theory and research* (pp. 89–195). New York, NY: Academic Press.

Attewell, P., & Monaghan, D. (2014). The community college route to the bachelor's degree. *Educational Evaluation and Policy Analysis,* 1–22.

Au, W., & Chang, B. (2012). You're Asian, how could you fail math? Unmasking the myth of the model minority. In E. K. Shrake & E. Chen (Eds.), *Asian Pacific American experiences: Past, present, and future* (pp. 161–166). Dubuque, IA: Kendall Hunt.

Azmitia, M., Kamprath, N., and Linnet, J. Intimacy and conflict: On the dynamics of boys' and girls' friendships during middle childhood and adolescence. In L. Meyer, M. Grenot-Scheyer, B. Harry., H. Park, & I. Schwartz (Eds.), *Understanding the social lives of children and youth.* Baltimore, MD: P.H. Brookes Publishing Co., 1998.

Azmitia, M., Syed, M., & Radmacher, K. (2013). Finding your niche: Identity and emotional support in emerging adults' adjustment to the transition to college. *Journal of Research on Adolescence, 23*(4), 744–761.

Bachmann, H. (2012). Who needs college? The Swiss opt for vocational school. *Time World.* Retrieved from http://world.time.com/2012/10/04/who-needs-college-the-swiss-opt-for-vocational-school/

Baddeley, A. D. (2001). Is working memory still working? *American Psychologist, 56,* 851–864.

Bagwell, C. L., Newcomb, A. F., & Bukowski, W. M. (1998). Preadolescent friendship and peer rejection as predictors of adult adjustment. *Child Development, 69,* 140–153. doi:10.2307/1132076

Bailey, K., West, R., & Anderson, C. A. (2010). A negative association between video game experience and proactive cognitive control. *Psychophysiology, 47,* 34–42.

Baker, C. N. (2005). Images of women's sexuality in advertisements: A content analysis of Black- and White-oriented women's and men's magazines. *Sex Roles, 52,* 13–27.

Bancroft, K. (2009). To have and to have not: The socioeconomics of charter schools. *Education and Urban Society, 41*(2), 248–279.

Bandura, A. (1986). *Social foundations of thought and action: A social cognitive theory.* New York: Prentice Hall.

Bandura, A. (1986). *Social foundations of thought and action: A social cognitive theory*. Englewood Cliffs, NJ: Prentice-Hall.

Bandura, A. (1986). *Social foundations of thought and action*. Upper Saddle River, NJ: Pearson.

Bandura, A. (2002). Social cognitive theory of mass communication. In J. Bryant & D. Zillman (Eds.), *Media effects: Advances in theory and research* (2nd ed., pp. 121–153). Mahwah, NJ: Lawrence Erlbaum.

Bandura, A., & Walters, R. H. (1963). *Social learning and personality development*. New York, NY: Holt, Rinehart & Winston.

Bangert-Drowns, R. L., Hurley, M. M., & Wilkinson, B. (2004). The effects of school-based writing-to-learn interventions on academic achievement: A meta-analysis. *Review of Educational Research, 74,* 29–58.

Barber, B. K., & Olsen, J. A. (2004). Assessing the transitions to middle and high school. *Journal of Adolescent Research, 19*(1), 3–30.

Barry, D. T., & Grilo, C. M. (2002). Eating and body image disturbances in adolescent psychiatric inpatients: Gender and ethnicity patterns. *International Journal of Eating Disorders, 32,* 335–343.

Bartholow, B. D., Bushman, B. J., & Sestir, M. A. (2006). Chronic violent video game exposure and desensitization to violence: Behavioral and event-related brain potential data. *Journal of Experimental Social Psychology, 42,* 532–539.

Bartsch, K. (1993). Adolescents' theoretical thinking. In R. M. Lerner (Ed.), *Early adolescence: Perspectives on research, policy, and intervention* (pp. 143–157). Hillsdale, NJ: Lawrence Erlbaum Associates.

Basow, S. (2004). The hidden curriculum: Gender in the classroom. In M. A. Paludi (Ed.), *Praeger guide to the psychology of gender* (pp. 117–131). Westport, CT: Praeger/Greenwood Publishing Group.

Basow, S. A., & Rubin, L. R. (1999). Gender influences on adolescent development. In N. G. Johnson, M. C. Roberts, & J. Worell (Eds.), *Beyond appearance: A new look at adolescent girls* (pp. 25–52). Washington, DC: APA Books.

Batanova, M. D., & Loukas, A. (2012). What are the unique and interacting contributions of school and family factors to early adolescents' empathic concern and perspective taking? *Journal of Youth and Adolescence, 41,* 1382–1391.

Baumeister, R. F., Campbell, J. D., Krueger, J. I., & Vohs, K. D. (2003). Does high self-esteem cause better performance, interpersonal success, happiness, or healthier lifestyles? *Psychological Science in the Public Interest,* 1–44.

Baumgartner, S. E., Weeda, W. D., van der Heijden, L. L., & Huizinga, M. (2014). The relationship between media multitasking and executive function in early adolescents. *Journal of Early Adolescence.* doi:0272431614523133

Baumrind, D. (1991). Parenting styles and adolescent development. In J. Brooks-Gunn, R. Lerner, & A. C. Peterson (Eds.), *The encyclopedia of adolescence* (pp. 746–758). New York, NY: Garland.

Bearman, P., & Bruckner, H. (2001). Promising the future: Virginity pledges and first intercourse. *American Journal of Sociology, 106,* 859–912.

Bearman, P., & Bruckner, H. (2004, March). *The relationship between virginity pledges in adolescence and STD acquisition in young adulthood: After the promise: The long-term consequences of adolescent virginity pledges.* Paper presented at the National STD Conference, Philadelphia, PA.

Beausang, C. C., & Razor, A. (2000). Young Western women's experiences of menarche and menstruation. *Health Care for Women International, 21,* 517–528.

Beaver, K. M., & Wright, J. P. (2007). A child effects explanation for the association between family risk and involvement in an antisocial lifestyle. *Journal of Adolescent Research, 22,* 640–664.

Becker, M. W., Alzhabi, B. S., & Hopwood, C. J. (2013). Media multi-tasking is associated with symptoms of depression and social anxiety. *Cyberpsychology, Behavior, and Social Networking, 16*(2), 132–135.

Beede, D., Julian, T., Langdon, D., McKittrick, G., Khan, B., & Doms, M. (2011). Women in STEM: A gender gap to innovation. *Economics and Statistics Administration Brief No. 4-11.* Retrieved from http://www.esa.doc.gov/sites/default/files/reports/documents/womeninstemagaptoinnovation8311.pdf

Bem, S. L. The measurement of psychological androgyny. *Journal of Consulting and Clinical Psychology, 1974, 42,* 155–162.

Bempechat, J., Boulay, B. A., Piergross, S. C., & Wenk, K. A. (2008). Beyond the rhetoric: Understanding achievement and motivation in Catholic school. *Education and Urban Society, 40*(2), 167–178.

Benner, A. D. (2011). The transition to high school: Current knowledge, future directions, *Educational Psychology Review, 23*(3), 299–328.

Benner, A. D., & Graham, S. (2009). The transition to high school as a developmental process among multiethnic urban youth. *Child Development, 80*(2), 356–376.

Benner, A. D., Graham, S., & Mistry, R. S. (2008). Discerning direct and mediated effects of ecological structures and processes on adolescents' educational outcomes. *Developmental Psychology, 44,* 840–854.

Berends, M., Goldring, E., Stein, M., & Cravens, X. (2010). Instructional conditions in charter schools and students' mathematics achievement gains. *American Journal of Education, 116*(3), 303–335.

Berndt, T. J. (1982). The features and effects of friendship in early adolescence. *Child Development, 53,* 147–1460.

Berndt, T. J. (2004). Children's friendships: Shifts over a half century in perspectives on their development and their effects. *Merrill Palmer Quarterly, 50,* 206–223.

Berry, J. (1990). Psychology of acculturation. In J. Berman (Ed.), *Cross-cultural perspectives: Nebraska symposium on motivation* (pp. 201–234). Lincoln, NE: University of Nebraska Press.

Berry, J. W. (2006). Contexts of acculturation. In D. L. Sam & J. W. Berry (Eds.), *The Cambridge handbook of acculturation psychology* (pp. 27–42). Cambridge, England: Cambridge University Press.

Berry, J. W., Phinney, J. S., Sam, D. L., & Vedder, P. (2006). Immigrant youth: Acculturation, identity, and adaptation. *Applied Psychology: An International Review, 55,* 303–332.

Bessant, J. (2008). Hard wired for risk: Neurological science, "the adolescent brain," and developmental theory. *Journal of Youth Studies, 11,* 347–360.

Biener L., & Siegel, M. (2000). Tobacco marketing and adolescent smoking: More support for a causal inference. *Journal of Public Health, 90,* 407–411.

Biener, L., Ji, M., Gilpin, E. A., & Albers, A. B. (2004). The impact of emotional, tone, message, and broadcast parameters in youth anti-smoking advertisements. *Journal of Health Communication, 9,* 259–274.

Billingsley, K. L. (2010). Retrospective: A state of esteem? Retrieved from CalWatchdog website: http://calwatchdog.com/2010/07/29/retrospective-a-state-of-esteem/

Bleakely, A., Vaala, S., Jordan, A. B., & Romer, D. (2014). The Annenburg media environment survey: Media access and use in U.S. homes with children and adolescents. In A. B. Jordan & D. Romer (Eds.), *Media and the well-being of children and adolescents* (pp. 1–19). New York, NY: Oxford University Press.

Bodenhausen, G., Schwartz, N., Bless, H., & Wanke, M. Effects of atypical exemplars on racial beliefs: Enlightened racism or generalized appraisals? *Journal of Experimental Social Psychology, 31,* 48–63.

Bodrova, E., Leong, D. J., & Akhutina, T. V. (2011). When everything new is well-forgotten old: Vygotsky/Luria insights in the development of executive functions. *New Directions for Child and Adolescent Development, 133,* 11–28.

Boekaerts, M., Pintrich, P. R., & Zeidner, M. (2000). *Handbook of self-regulation.* San Diego, CA: Academic Press.

Bogin, B. (2015). *Adolescent growth spurt.* Retrieved from CARTA: Center for Academic Research and Training in Anthropogeny website: http://carta.anthropogeny.org/moca/topics/adolescent-growth-spurt

Boonstra, H. (2010). Sex education: Another big step forward—and a step back. *Guttmacher Policy Review, 13,* 27–28.

Boroch, D., Hope, L., & Academic Senate for California Community. (2009). *Effective practices for promoting the transition of high school students to college: A review of literature with implications for California Community College practitioners.* Retrieved from http://www.cccbsi.org/Websites/basicskills/Images/High-School-Transition.pdf

Borzekowski, D. L. G. (2014). Examining media's impact of children's weight: Amount, content and context. In A. B. Jordan & D. Romer (Eds.), Media and the well-being of children and adolescents (pp. 44–51). New York, NY: Oxford University Press.

Botta, R. A. (1999). Television images and adolescent girls' body image disturbance. *Journal of Communication, 49,* 22-41.

Botta, R. A. (2000). The mirror of television: A comparison of Black and White adolescents' body image. *Journal of Communication,* 144–159.

Botta, R. A. (2003). For your health? The relationship between magazine reading and adolescents' body image and eating disturbances. *Sex Roles, 48,* 389–399.

Bowlby, J. (1969). *Attachment and loss. Vol. 1: Attachment.* New York, NY: Basic Books.

Boyd, D. (2014). It's complicated: The social lives of networked teens. New Haven, CT: Yale University Press.

Brackett, M. A., & Rivers, S. E. (2014). Transforming students' lives with social and emotional learning. In R. Pekrun & L. Linnenbrink-Garcia (Eds.), *International handbook of emotions in education* (pp. 368–388). New York, NY: Taylor & Francis.

Bransford, J. D., Brown, A. L., & Cocking, R. R. (Eds.). (1999). *How people learn: Brain, mind, experience, and school.* Washington, DC: National Academy Press.

Braun, H., Jenkins, F., & Grigg, W. (2006). *Comparing private schools and public schools using hierarchical linear modeling.* Washington DC: U.S. Department of Education, Institute of Education Sciences, National Center for Education Statistics.

Brechwald, W., & Prinstein, M. (2011). Beyond homophily: A decade of advances in understanding peer influence processes. *Journal of Research on Adolescence, 21,* 166–179.

Broadbent, D. E. (1958). *Perception and communication.* New York, NY: Pergamon Press.

Broadbent, D. E. (1963). Flow of information within the organism. *Journal of Verbal Learning and Verbal Behavior, 4,* 34–39.

Broh, B. A. (2002). Linking extracurricular programming to academic achievement: Who benefits and why? *Sociology of Education, 75,* 69–96.

Bronfenbrenner, U. (1989). Ecological systems theory. In R. Vasta (Ed.), *Annals of child development* (Vol. 6, pp. 187–249). Greenwich, CT: JAI Press.

Bronfenbrenner, U., & Morris, P. A. (2006). The bioecological model of human development. In R. M. Lerner (Ed.), *Handbook of child psychology. Vol. 1: Theoretical models of human development* (6th ed., pp. 793–828). Hoboken, NJ: Wiley.

Brooks-Gunn, J., & Paikoff, R. L. (1993). Sex is a gamble, kissing is a game: Adolescent sexuality and health promotion. In S. G. Millstein, A. C. Petersen, & E. O. Nightingale (Eds.), *Promoting the health of adolescents: New directions for the twenty-first century* (pp. 180–208). New York, NY: Oxford University Press.

Brophy, J. (1981). Teacher praise: A functional analysis. *Review of Educational Research, 51,* 5–32.

Brophy, J. (1998). *Motivating students to learn* (1st ed.). Boston, MA: McGraw Hill.

Brophy, J. (2010). *Motivating students to learn* (3rd ed.). New York, NY: Routledge.

Brown J. (Ed.). (2008). *Managing the media monster: The influence of media (from television to text messages) on teen sexual behavior and attitudes.* Washington, DC: National Campaign to Prevent Teen and Unplanned Pregnancy.

Brown, A. L. (1987). Metacognition, executive control, self-regulation, and other more mysterious mechanisms. In F. Weinert & R. Kluwe (Eds.), *Metacognition, motivation, and understanding* (pp. 65–116). Mahwah, NJ: Lawrence Erlbaum.

Brown, B. (2003). *The benefits of career and technical education.* Washington, DC: ERIC Clearinghouse on Adult Education. (ERIC Document Reproduction Service No. ED 481326)

Brown, B. B. (1990). Peer groups and peer culture. In S. S. Feldman & G. R. Elliott (Eds.), *At the threshold: The developing adolescent* (pp. 171–196). Cambridge, MA: Harvard University Press.

Brown, B. B. (2004). Adolescents' relationships with peers. In R. Lerner & L. Steinberg (Eds.), *Handbook of adolescent psychology* (2nd ed., pp. 363–394). New York, NY: Wiley.

Brown, B. B., & Dietz, E. L. (2009). Informal peer groups in middle childhood and adolescence. In K. H. Rubin, W. M. Bukowski, & B. Laursen (Eds.), *Handbook of peer interactions, relationships, and groups* (pp. 361–375). New York, NY: Guilford Press.

Brown, B. B., & Larson, J. (2009). Peer relationships in adolescence. In R. M. Lerner & L. Steinberg (Eds.), *Handbook of adolescent psychology* (3rd ed., pp. 74–103). Hoboken, NJ: Wiley.

Brown, D. F. and Knowles, T. (2014). *What every middle school teacher should know.* College of Education Faculty Books.

Brown, J. D. (2000). Adolescents' sexual media diets. *Journal of Adolescent Health, 27,* 35–40.

Brown, J. D., & Bobkowski, P. (2011). Older and newer media: Patterns of use and effects on adolescents' health and well-being. *Journal of Research on Adolescence, 21,* 95–113.

Brown, J. D., & L'Engle, K. L. (2009). X-rated: Sexual attitudes and behaviors associated with U.S. early adolescents' exposure to sexually explicit media. *Communication Research, 36,* 129–151.

Brown, J. D., & Pardun, C. J. (2004). Little in common: Racial and gender differences in adolescents' television diets. *Journal of Broadcasting and Electronic Media, 48,* 266–278.

Brown, J. D., El-Toukhy, S., & Ortiz, R. (2014). Growing up sexually in a digital world: The risks and benefits of youths' sexual media use. In A. B. Jordan & D. Romer (Eds.), *Media and the well-being of children and adolescents* (pp. 90–108). New York, NY: Oxford University Press.

Brown, J. D., L'Engle, K. L., Pardun, C. J., Guo, G., Kenneavy, K., & Jackson, C. (2006). Sexy media matter: Exposure to sexual content in music, movies, television, and magazines predicts Black and While adolescents' sexual behavior. *Pediatrics, 117,* 1018–1027.

Brown, K. L., DiClemente, R., Crosby, R., Fernandez, M. I., Pugatch, D., Cohn, S., et al. (2008). Condom use among high-risk adolescents: Anticipation of partner disapproval and less pleasure associated with not using condoms. *Public Health Reports, 123,* 601–607.

Bryan, C. J., Elder, W. B., McNaughton-Cassill, M., Osman, A., Hernandez, A., & Allison, S. (2013). Meaning in life, emotional distress, suicidal ideation, and life functioning in an active duty military sample. *Journal of Positive Psychology, 8*(5), 444–452. doi:10.1080/17439760.2013.823557

Buchanan, C. M., Eccles, J. S., & Becker, J. B. (1992). Are adolescents the victims of raging hormones: Evidence of activational effects of hormones on moods and behavior at adolescence. *Psychological Bulletin, 111,* 62–107.

Buchanan, C. M., Maccoby, E. E., & Dornbusch, S. M. (1996). *Adolescents after divorce.* Cambridge, MA: Harvard University Press.

Buhi, E. R., Daley, E. M., Oberne, A., Smith, S. A., Schneider, T., & Fuhrmann, H. J. (2010). Quality and accuracy of sexual health information websites visited by young people. *Journal of Adolescent Health, 47*(2), 206–208.

Bukowski, W. M., Sippola, L., & Newcomb, A. (2000). Variations in patterns of attraction to same- and other-sex peers during early adolescence. *Developmental Psychology, 36,* 147–154. doi:10.1037/0012-1649.36.2.147

Burbules, N. (2010). *Ubiquitous learning and the future of teaching.* Paper presented at the Boyd Bode Memorial Lecture in Philosophy of Education, Columbus, OH.

Burnett, S. E., & Segoria, J. (2009). Collaboration for military transition students from combat to college: It takes a community. *Journal of Postsecondary Education and Disability, 22*(1), 53–58.

Burt Solorzano, C. M., & McCartney, C. R. (2010). Obesity and the pubertal transition in girls and boys. *Reproduction, 140,* 339–410.

Bushman, B. J., & Anderson, C. A. (2001). Media violence and the American public: Scientific facts versus media misinformation. *American Psychologist, 56,* 477–489.

Butler, J. C., Doherty, M. S., & Potter, R. M. (2007). Social antecedents and consequences of interpersonal rejection sensitivity. *Personality and Individual Differences, 43,* 1376–1385.

Butler, R. (1987). Task-involving and ego-involving properties of evaluation: Effects of different feedback conditions on motivational perceptions, interest, and performance. *Journal of Educational Psychology, 79*(4), 474–482.

Byun, S.-Y., Meece, J. L., & Irvin, M. J. (2012). Rural-nonrural disparities in postsecondary educational attainment revisited. *American Educational Research Journal, 49,* 412–437.

Calabrese, R. L., & Cochran, J. T. (1990). The relationship of alienation to cheating among a sample of American adolescents. *Journal of Research and Development in Education, 23,* 65–72.

California State Department of Education. (1986). *Toward a state of self-esteem*. Report of the California Task Force to Promote Self Esteem and Personal and Social Responsibility. Sacramento, CA: Author.

Calvert, S.L. (1999). *Children's Journey through the Information Age*. Boston, MA: McGraw Hill.

Campbell, K. & Peebles, R. (2014). Eating disorders in children and adolescents: State of the art review. *Pediatrics, 134,* 582–592.

Campione, J. C., Brown, A. L., & Connell, M. L. (1988). Metacognition: On the importance of understanding what you are doing. In R. I. Charles & E. A. Silver (Eds.), *The teaching and assessing of mathematical problem solving* (Vol. 3, pp. 93–114). Hillsdale, NJ: Lawrence Erlbaum Associates.

Carbonaro, W. (2005). Tracking, students' effort, and academic achievement. *Sociology of Education, 78,* 27–49.

Carnagey, N. L., Anderson, C. A., & Bartholow, B. D. (2008). Media violence and social neuroscience: New questions and new opportunities. *Current Directions in Psychological Science, 16,* 178–182.

Carnagey, N. L., Anderson, C. A., & Bushman, B. J. (2007). The effect of video game violence on physiological de-sensitization to real-life violence. *Journal of Experimental Social Psychology, 43,* 489–496.

Carpenter, L. M. (2002). Gender and the meaning and experience of virginity loss in the contemporary United States. *Gender and Society, 16,* 345–365.

Carskadon, M., & Acebo, C. (2002). Regulation of sleepiness in adolescence: Update, insights, and speculation. *Sleep, 25,* 606–616.

Carver, K., Joyner, K., & Udry, R. J. (2003). National estimates of adolescent romantic relationships. In P. Florsheim (Ed.), *Adolescent romantic relationships and sexual behavior: Theory, research, and practical implications* (pp. 23–56). Mahwah, NJ: LEA.

Caskadon, M., Vieira, C., & Acebo, C. (1993). Association between puberty and delayed phase preference. *Sleep, 16,* 258–262.

Caspi, A., Lynam, D., Moffitt, T., & Silva, P. (1993). Unraveling girls' delinquency: Biological, dispositional, and contextual contributions to adolescent misbehavior. *Developmental Psychology, 29,* 19–30.

Cattell, R. B., & Horn, J. L. (1978). A check on the theory of fluid and crystallized intelligence with description of new subtest designs. *Journal of Educational Measurement, 15*(3), 139–164.

Caulfield, P. (2011). Seven Long Island teens busted for SAT cheating scam; college whiz charged cash, took test for others. *New York Daily News*. Retrieved from: http://www.nydailynews.com/new-york/7-long-island-teens-busted-sat-cheating-scam-college-whiz-charged-cash-test-article-1.958528

Cavanagh, S. E., & Huston, A. C. (2008). The timing of family instability and children's social adjustment. *Journal of Marriage and Family, 70,* 1258–1270.

Cavanagh, S. E., Crissey, S. R., & Raley, R. K. (2008). Family structure history and adolescent romance. *Journal of Marriage and Family, 70,* 698–714.

CBS News. (2014). *Severe childhood obesity on the rise in U.S., study shows*. Retrieved from http://www.cbsnews.com/news/in-the-us-childhood-obesity-is-a-heavy-burden/

Cemalcilar, Z. (2009). Understanding individual characteristics of adolescents who volunteer. *Personality and Individual Differences, 46,* 432–436.

Center for Sexual Health and Promotion. (2010). *National Survey of Sexual Health and Behavior (SSHB)*. Retrieved from http://www.nationalsexstudy.indiana.edu/

Centers for Disease Control and Prevention. (2012, May 4). Sexual experience and contraceptive use among female teens—United States, 1995, 2002, and 2006–2010. *Morbidity and Mortality Weekly Report, 61*(17).

Centers for Disease Control and Prevention (CDC). (2013a). *Youth Risk and Behavior Surveillance—United States, 2013*. Retrieved from http://www.cdc.gov/mmwr/pdf/ss/ss6304.pdf

Centers for Disease Control and Prevention. (2013b). *Youth Risk Behavior Survey (YRBS)*. Retrieved from http://www.cdc.gov/healthyyouth/data/yrbs/index.htm

Centers for Disease Control and Prevention (2014). *Understanding teen dating violence*. http://www.cdc.gov/violenceprevention/pdf/teen-dating-violence-factsheet-a.pdf. Retrieved January 6, 2016.

Centers for Disease Control and Prevention. (2014). Youth risk behavior surveillance—United States, 2013. *Surveillance Summaries, 63*(4), 1–168.

Centers for Disease Control. (2015). *Adolescent health*. Retrieved from http://www.cdc.gov/nchs/fastats/adolescent-health.htm

Centers for Disease Control and Prevention (2015a). STD's in adolescents and young adults. *2014 Sexually Transmitted Diseases Surveillance*. http://www.cdc.gov/std/stats14/adol.htm#foot1. Retreived January 10, 2016.

Centers for Disease Control and Prevention. (2015b). *HIV among youth*. Retrieved from http://www.cdc.gov/hiv/pdf/risk_youth_fact_sheet_final.pdf

Cesar, M. (1998). *Social interactions and mathematics learning*. Paper presented at the Annual Meeting of International Mathematics Education and Society Conference.

Chagnon, J. H., & Simon, W. (1987). The sexual scripting of oral genital contact. *Archives of Sexual Behavior, 16,* 1–25.

Chakroff, J. L., & Nathanson, A. I. (2009). Parent and school interventions: Mediation and media literacy. In S. L. Calvert & B. J. Wilson (Eds.), The handbook of children, media and development (pp. 552–576). Singapore: Blackwell.

Chan, A., & Poulin, F. (2007). Monthly changes in the composition of friendship networks in early adolescence. *Merrill-Palmer Quarterly, 53,* 578–602. http://dx.doi.org/10.1353/mpq.2008.0000

Chan, P. A., & Rabinowitz, T. (2006). A cross-sectional analysis of video games and attention deficit hyperactivity disorder symptoms in adolescents. *Annals of General Psychiatry, 5*, 1–10.

Chan, Y. F., Dennis, M. L., & Funk, R. R. (2008). Prevalence and comorbidity of major internalizing and externalizing problems among adolescents and adults presenting to substance abuse treatment. *Journal of Substance Abuse and Treatment, 34*, 14–24.

Chandra, A., Martino, S., Collins, R., Elliott, M., Berry, S., Kanouse, D., et al. (2008). Does watching sex on television predict teen pregnancy? Findings from a national longitudinal survey of youth. *Pediatrics, 122*, 1047–1054.

Chao, R. K., & Otsuki-Clutter, M. (2011). Racial and ethnic differences: Sociocultural and contextual explanations. *Journal of Research on Adolescence, 21*, 47–60.

Charney, R. S. (1993). *Teaching Children to Care: Management in the Responsive Classroom.* Pittsfield, MA: Northeast Foundation for Children.

Charney, R. S. (2002). *Teaching Children to Care: Classroom Management for Academic and Ethical Growth, K–8.* Pittsfield, MA: Northeast Foundation for Children.

Chase-Lansdale, P. L., Moffitt, R. A., Lohman, B. J., Cherlin, A. J., Coley, R. L., Pittman, L. D., Votruba Drzal, E. (2003). Mothers' transitions from welfare to work and the well-being of preschoolers and adolescents. *Science, 299*(5612), 1548–1552.

Chavous, T. M., Rivas-Drake, D., Smalls, C., Griffen, T., & Cogburn, C. (2008). Gender matters too: The influence of school racial discrimination and racial identity on academic engagement outcomes among African American adolescents. *Developmental Psychology, 44*(3), 637–654.

Chavous, T., Bernat, D., Schmeelk-Cone, K., Caldwell, C., Kohn-Wood, L., & Zimmerman, M. (2003). Racial identity and academic attainment among African American adolescents. *Child Development, 74*, 1076–1090.

Chein, J., Albert, D., O'Brien, L., Uckert, K., & Steinberg, L. (2011). Peers increase adolescent risk taking by enhancing activity in the brain's reward circuitry. *Developmental Science, 14*, F1–F10.

Cheung, C., & Lee, T. (2010). Contributions of moral education lectures and moral discussion in Hong Kong secondary schools. *Social Psychology of Education, 13*(4), 575–591. doi:10.1007/s11218-010-9127-x

Cheung, C., & Pomerantz, E. M. (2012). Why does parents' involvement in children's learning enhance children's achievement? The role of parent-oriented motivation. *Journal of Educational Psychology, 104*, 820–832.

Child Trends. (2013). *Watching television.* Retrieved from http://www.childtrends.org/?indicators=watching-television

Child Trends. (2013a). Religiosity among youth. Retrieved from: http://www.childtrends.org/wp-content/uploads/2012/05/35_Religiosity.pdf

Child Trends. (2013b). Attendance at religious services. Retrieved from: http://www.childtrends.org/?indicators=religious-service-attendance

Child Trends. (2014). *Children in poverty.* Bethesda, MD: Author.

Child Trends. (2015). Volunteering. Retrieved from: http://www.childtrends.org/wp-content/uploads/2012/11/20_Volunteering.pdf

Child Trends Data Bank. (2014, December). *Dating: Indicators on children and youth.* http://www.childtrends.org/wp-content/uploads/2012/05/73_Dating.pdf. Retrieved January 6, 2016.

Child Trends Databank. (2015). Oral sex behaviors among teens. Available at: http://www.childtrends.org/?indicators=oral-sex-behaviors-among-teens. Retrieved January 6, 2016.

Chiodo, A. J., Hernández-Murillo, R., & Owyang, M. T. (2010). Nonlinear Effects of School Quality on House Prices. *Review (00149187), 92*(3), 185–204.

Chiodo, D., Wolfe, D. A., Crooks, C. V., Hughes, R., & Jaffe, P. (2009). The impact of sexual harassment victimization by peers on subsequent adolescent victimization and adjustment: A longitudinal study. *Journal of Adolescent Health, 45*, 246–252.

Chrisler, J. C., & Zittel, C. B. (1998). Menarche stories: Reminiscences of college students from Lithuania, Malaysia, Sudan and the United States. *Health Care for Women International, 19*, 303–312.

Christenson, P. G., Henriksen, L., & Roberts, D. F. (2000). *Substance use in popular prime-time television.* Washington, DC: Office of National Drug Control Policy.

Chua, A. (2011) *Battle hymn of the tiger mother.* London, England: Penguin Books.

Cillessen, A. H. N., & Mayeux, L. (2004). From censure to reinforcement: Developmental changes in the association between aggression and social status. *Child Development, 75*, 147–163. doi:10.1111/j.1467-8624.2004.00660.x

Cillessen, A. H. N., & Rose, A. J. (2005). Understanding popularity in the peer system. *Current Directions in Psychological Science, 14*, 102–105.

Cillessen, A. H. N., & van den Berg, Y. H. M. (2012). Popularity and school adjustment. In A. M. Ryan & G. W. Ladd (Eds.), *Peer relationships and adjustment at school* (pp. 135–164). Charlotte, NC: Information Age Press.

Cizek, G.J. (2001). *An overview of issues concerning cheating on large scale tests.* Proceedings from the National Association of Test Directors 2001 Symposia (pp. 1–30). Retrieved from: http://national-associationoftestdirectors.org/wp-content/uploads/2012/12/natd2001.pdf

Clark D. B., Pollock N., Bukstein O., Mezzich A., Bromberger J. T., & Donovan J. E. (1997). Gender and comorbid psychopathology in adolescents with alcohol dependence. *Journal of the American Academy of Child and Adolescent Psychiatry, 36*, 1195–1203.

Clark, R. W., Threeton, M. D., & Ewing, J. C. (2010). The potential of experiential learning models and practices in career and technical education. *Journal of Career and Technical Education, 25*(2), 46–62.

Clavel-Chapelon, F. (2002). The E3N-EPIC group: Evolution of the age at menarche and at onset of regular cycling in a large cohort of French women. *Human Reproduction, 17,* 228–232.

Clavel-Chapelon, F., et al. (1997). E3N: A French cohort study on cancer risk factors. *European Journal of Cancer Prevention, 6,* 473–478.

Closson, L. M. (2008). Status and gender differences in early adolescents' descriptions of popularity. *Social Development, 18*(2), 412–426. doi:10.1111/j.1467-9507.2008.00459

CNN. (2013, January 24). By the numbers: Women in the U.S. military. CNN.com. Retrieved from http://www.cnn.com/2013/01/24/us/military-women-glance/

Cochran, S. D. (2001). Emerging issues in research on lesbians' and gay men's mental health: Does sexual orientation really matter? *American Psychologist, 56*(11), 929–947.

Coles, R. L. (2016). *Race and Family: A Structural Approach,* 2nd Edition. Lanham, MD: Rowman & Littlefield Publishing Group.

Coll, C. G., Flannery, P., Yang, H., Suarez-Aviles, G., Batchelor, A., & Marks, A. (2009, March). *The immigrant paradox: A review of the literature.* Paper presented at the Is Becoming American a Developmental Risk: Children and Adolescents from Immigrant Families conference, Brown University, Providence, RI.

Collaborative for Academic, Social, and Emotional Learning (CASEL). (2015). Social and Emotional Learning Core Competencies. Retrieved from http://www.casel.org/social-and-emotional-learning/core-competencies/.

Collier, A. (2013, June 5). Though reports about bullying are increasing, the behavior itself is not. *Christian Science Monitor.* Retrieved from http://www.csmonitor.com/The-Culture/Family/Modern-Parenthood/2013/0605/Though-reports-about-bullying-are-increasing-the-behavior-itself-is-not

Collins, C. C., Alagiri, P., Summers, T., & Morin, S. F. (2002). *Abstinence only vs. comprehensive sex education: What are the arguments? What is the evidence?* San Francisco, CA: AIDS Research Institute, University of California.

Collins, W. A. & Sroufe, L. A. (1999). Capacity for intimate relationships: A developmental construction. In W. Furman, B. B. Brown, & C. Feiring, (Eds.) (1999), *The development of romantic relationships in adolescence* (pp. 125–147). New York: Cambridge University Press.

Collins, W. A., & Steinberg, L. (2006). Adolescent development in interpersonal context. In W. Damon & N. Eisenberg (Eds.), *Handbook of child psychology: Socio-emotional processes* (pp. 1003–1067). New York, NY: Wiley.

Collishaw, S., Maughan, B., Goodman, R., & Pickles, A. (2004). Time trends in adolescent mental health. *Journal of Child Psychology and Psychiatry, 45,* 1350–1362.

Coltrane, S., & Messineo, M. (2000). The perception of subtle prejudice: Race and gender imagery in 1990's television advertising. *Sex Roles, 42,* 363–369.

Commission on National and Community Service (1993). *What you can do for your country.* Washington, DC: Government Printing Office.

Common Core State Standards. (2010). National Governers Association Center for Best Practices. Washington, DC: Council of Chief State School Officers.

Common Sense Media. (2012). *Social media, social life, how teens view their social lives.* Retrieved from https://www.commonsensemedia.org/research/social-media-social-life-how-teens-view-their-digital-lives

Common Sense Media. (2014a). *Advertising to children and teens: Current practices.* Retrieved from https://www.commonsensemedia.org/research/advertising-to-children-and-teens-current-practices

Common Sense Media. (2014b). *Children, teens, and reading.* San Francisco, CA: Author.

Conger, R. D., Wallace, L. E., Sun, Y., Simons, R. L., McLoyd, V. C., & Brody, G. H. (2002). Economic pressure in African American families: A replication and extension of the family stress model. *Developmental Psychology, 38,* 179–193.

Conger, R.D., Conger, K.J., & Martin, M.J. (2010). Socioeconomic status, family processes and individual development. *Journal of Marriage and the Family, 72*(3), 685–704.

Connolly, J. A., & Goldberg, A. (1999). Romantic relationships in adolescence: The role of friends and peers in their emergence and development. In W. Furman, B. B. Brown, & C. Feiring (Eds.), *The development of romantic relationships in adolescence* (pp. 266–290). New York, NY: Cambridge University Press.

Connolly, J. A., & Johnson, A. (1996). Adolescents' romantic relationships and the structure and quality of their close interpersonal ties. *Personal Relationships, 2,* 185–195.

Cook, P. J. and Ludwig, J. (1997), Weighing the "burden of 'acting white'": Are there race differences in attitudes toward education?. *Journal of Policy Analysis and Management, 16,* 256–278.

Costello, E. J., Mustillo, S., Erkanli, A., Keeler, G., & Angold, A. (2003). Prevalence and development of psychiatric disorders in childhood and adolescence. *Archives of General Psychiatry, 60,* 837–844.

Costenbader, V., & Markson, S. (1998). School suspension: A study with secondary school students. *Journal of School Psychology, 36,* 59–82.

Côté, J. E., & Schwartz, S. J. (2002). Comparing psychological and sociological approaches to identity: Identity status, identity capital, and the individualization process. *Journal of Adolescence, 25,* 571–586.

Courtney, M., Dworksy, A., Brown, A., Cary, C., Love, K., & Vorhies, V. (2011). *Midwest evaluation of the adult functioning of former foster youth: Outcomes at age 26.* Chicago, IL: Chapin Hall, University of Chicago.

Covington, M. (1992). *Making the grade: A self-worth perspective on motivation and school reform.* Cambridge, England: Cambridge University Press.

Cowan, N., & Alloway, T. (2009). Development of working memory in childhood. In M. L. Courage & N. Cowan (Eds.), *The development of memory in infancy and childhood* (2nd ed., pp. 303–342). New York, NY: Psychology Press.

Cowan, N., AuBuchon, A. M., Gilchrist, A. L., Ricker, T. J., & Saults, J. S. (2011). Age differences in visual working memory capacity: Not based on encoding limitations. *Developmental Science, 14,* 1066–1074.

Crain, R. M. (1996). The influence of age, race, and gender on child and adolescent self-concept. In B. A. Bracken (Ed.), *Handbook of self-concept: Developmental, social, and clinical considerations* (pp. 395-420). New York: Wiley.

Crandall, C. (1988). Social contagion of binge eating. *Journal of Personality and Social Psychology, 55,* 588–598.

Crawford, M., & Popp, D. (2003). Sexual double standards: A review and methodological critique of two decades of research. *Journal of Sex Research, 40,* 13–26.

Crepinsek, M. K. Gordon, A. R., McKinney, P. M., Condon, E. M., & Wilson, A. (2009). Meals offered and served in U.S. public schools: Do they meet nutrient standards? *Journal of the American Dietary Association, 109*(Suppl. 2), S31–S43.

Crocetti, E., Jahromi, P., & Meeus, W. (2012). Identity and civic engagement in adolescence. *Journal of Adolescence, 35,* 521–532.

Crockett, L. J., Rafaelli, M., & Moilanen, K. L. (2003). Adolescent sexuality: Behavior and meaning. In G. Adams & M. Borzonsky (Eds.), *Blackwell handbook of adolescence* (pp. 371–392). Malden, MA: Blackwell.

Crone, E. A., Bullens, L., van der Plas, E. A. A., Kijkuit, E. J., & Zelazo, P. D. (2008). Developmental changes and individual differences in risk and perspective taking in adolescence. *Development and Psychopathology, 20*(4), 1213–1229.

Crosnoe, R. & Benner, A. (2015). Children at School. In M. Bornstein & T. Leventhal (Eds.), *Handbook of Child Psychology and Developmental Science, Vol. 4: Ecological Settings and Processes* (pp. 268–304). New York: Wiley.

Crosnoe, R., & Cavanagh, S. E. (2010). Families with children and adolescents: A review, critique and research agenda. *Journal of Marriage and Family, 72,* 594–611.

Crosnoe, R., & Lopez-Turley. R. (2011). The K-12 educational outcomes of immigrant youth. *Future of Children, 21,* 129–152.

Crosnoe, R., Riegle-Crumb, C., Field, S., Frank, K., & Muller, C. (2008). Peer group contexts of girls' and boys' academic experiences. *Child Development, 79,* 139–155.

Cross, W. E., Jr. (1971). The Negro-to-Black conversion experience. *Black World, 20*(9), 13–27.

Cross, W. E., Jr. (1995). The psychology of nigrescence: Revising the Cross model. In J. G. Ponterotto, J. M. Casas, L. A. Suzuki, & C. M. Alexander (Eds.), *Handbook of multicultural counseling* (pp. 93–122). Thousand Oaks, CA: Sage.

Cross, W. E., Jr., & Vandiver, B. J. (2001). Nigrescence theory and measurement: Introducing the Cross Racial Identity Scale (CRIS). In J. G. Ponterotto, J. M. Casas, L. A. Suzuki, & C. M. Alexander (Eds.), *Handbook of multicultural counseling* (2nd ed., pp. 371–393). Thousand Oaks, CA: Sage.

Csiksezentmihalyi, M., & Schneider, B. (2000). *Becoming adult: How teenagers prepare for the world of work.* New York, NY: Basic Books.

Csikszentmihalyi, M., & Larson, R. (1984). *Being adolescent.* New York, NY: Basic Books.

Cummings, J. R., & Druss, B. G. (2011). Racial/ethnic differences in mental health service use among adolescents with major depression. *Journal of the American Academy of Child and Adolescent Psychiatry, 50,* 160–170.

Cusumano, D. L. & Thompson, J. K. (1997). Body image and body shape ideals in magazines: Exposure, awareness, and internalization. *Sex Roles, 37,* 701–721.

D'Augelli, A. R., Pilkington, N. W., & Hershberger, S. L. (2002). Incidence and mental health impact of sexual orientation victimization of lesbian, gay, and bisexual youths in high school. *School Psychology Quarterly, 17,* 148–167. doi:10.1521/scpq.17.2.148.20854

Dabkowska, M., & Dabkowska-Mika, A. (2015). Risk factors of anxiety disorders in children. In F. Durbano (Ed.), *A fresh look at anxiety disorders.* InTech Open Access. Retrieved from http://www.intechopen.com/books/a-fresh-look-at-anxiety-disorders. doi:10.5772/59525

Dahl, R. E. (2004). Adolescent brain development: A period of vulnerabilities and opportunities, keynote address. *Annals of the New York Academy of Sciences, 1021,* 1–22.

Danaher, K., & Crandall, C. S. (2008). Stereotype threat in applied settings re-examined. *Journal of Applied Social Psychology, 38,* 1639–1655.

Darling, N., & L. Steinberg (1993). Parenting style as context: An integrative model. *Psychological Bulletin 113,* 487–496.

Darmon, N., & Drewnowski, A. (2008). Does social class predict diet quality? *American Journal of Clinical Nutrition, 87,* 1107–1117.

Darroch, J. E., Frost, J., Singh, S., & the Study Team. (2001). Teenage sexual and reproductive behavior in developed countries: Can more progress be made? (Occasional Report No. 3). New York, NY: The Alan Guttmacher Institute.

Davila, A., & Mora, M. T. (2007). *Fact sheet: An assessment of civic engagement and educational attainment.* Retrieved from Center for Information and Research on Civic Learning and Engagement (CIRCLE) website: http://www.civicyouth.org/PopUps/FactSheets/FS_Mora.Davila.pdf

Davis, J. A. (2011). *A generation of attitude trends among U.S. householders as measured in the NORC General Social Survey, 1972–2010.* Chicago, IL: National Opinion Research Center.

Davis, S. F., Grover, C. A., Becker, A. H., & McGregor, L. N. (1992). Academic dishonesty: Prevalence, determinants, techniques, and punishments. *Teaching of Psychology, 19,* 16–20.

de Anda, D. (1998). The evaluation of a stress management program for middle school adolescents. *Child & Adolescent Social Work Journal, 15,* 73–85.

de Anda, D., Baroni, S., Boskin, L., Buchwald, L., Morgan, J., Ow, J., . . . Weiss, R. (2000). Stress, stressors, and coping among high school students. *Children and Youth Services Review, 22,* 441–463.

de la Haye, K., Green, H. D., Kennedy, D., Pollard, M., & Tucker, J. (2013). Selection and influence mechanisms associated with marijuana initiation and use in adolescent friendship networks. *Journal of Research on Adolescence, 23,* 474–486.

Deci, E. L., & Ryan, R. M. (2000). The "what" and "why" of goal pursuits: Human needs and the self-determination of behavior. *Psychological Inquiry, 11,* 227–268.

Delaney, W., & Lee, C. (1995). Self-esteem and sex roles among male and female high school students: Their relationship to physical activity. *Australian Psychologist, 30,* 84–87.

Delpit, L. (2012). *"Multiplication is for White people." Raising expectations for other people's children.* New York: New York Press.

Demerath, E. W., Towne, B., Chumlea, W. C., Sun, S. S., Czerwinski, S. A., Remsberg, K. E., & Siervogel, R. M. (2004). Recent decline in age at menarche: The Fels longitudinal study. *American Journal of Human Biology, 16,* 453–457.

Denton, M. L., Pearce, L. D., & Smith, C. (2008). *Religion and spirituality on the path through adolescence.* Chapel Hill, NC: Carolina Population Center.

DeRose, L. M., & Brooks-Gunn, J. (2006). Transition into adolescence: The role of pubertal processes. In L. Balter & C. S. Tamis-LaMonda (Eds.), *Child psychology: A handbook of contemporary issues* (2nd ed., pp. 385–414). New York, NY: Psychology Press.

DeVries, M. R., & Wijnans, E. K. (2013). Personality and military service. In B. A. Moore & J. E. Barnett (Eds.), *Military psychologists' desk reference* (pp. 26–30). New York, NY: Oxford University Press.

Dewald, J. F., Meijer, A. M., Oort, F. J., Kerkhof, G. A., & Bögels, S. M. (2010). The influence of sleep quality, sleep duration and sleepiness on school performance in children and adolescents: A meta-analytic review. *Sleep Medicine Reviews, 14,* 179–189.

Diekelmann, S., & Born, J. (2010). The memory function of sleep. *Nature Reviews Neuroscience, 11,* 114–126.

Dijkstra, J., & Gest, S. D (2014). Peer norm salience for academic achievement, prosocial behavior, and bullying: Implications for adolescent school experiences. *Journal of Early Adolescence. 20,* 942–958.

Dockett, S., & Perry, B. (1996). Young children's construction of knowledge. *Australian Journal of Early Childhood, 21*(4), 6–11.

Donohew, L., Palmgreen, P., & Lorch, E. P. (1994). Attention, sensation seeking, and health communication campaigns. *American Behavioral Scientist, 38,* 310–332.

Donohew, L., Zimmerman, R., Cupp, P., Novak, S., Colon, S., & Abell, R. (2000). Sensation seeking, impulsive decision-making, and risky sex: Implications for risk-taking and design of interventions. *Personality and Individual Differences, 28*(6), 1079–1091.

Donohue, R. L., Hoyle, R. H., Clayton, R. R., Skinner, W. F., Colon, S. E., & Rice, R. E. (1999). Sensation seeking and drug use by adolescents and their friends: Models for marijuana and alcohol. *Journal of Studies on Alcohol, 60*(5), 622–631.

Dorner, L. M., Orellana, M. F., & Jiménez, R. (2008). "It's one of those things that you do to help the family": Language brokering and the development of immigrant adolescents. *Journal of Adolescent Research, 23,* 515–543.

Douvan, E., & Adelson, J. (1966). *The adolescent experience.* New York, NY: John Wiley & Sons.

Downs, A. C., & Harrison, S. K. (1985). Embarrassing age spots or just plain ugly?: Physical attractiveness as an instrument of stereotyping on American television commercials. *Sex Roles, 13,* 9–19.

Doyne, S. (2013). Considering the varying viewpoints on a pregnancy prevention campaign. *The Learning Network, The New York Times.* Retrieved from: http://learning.blogs.nytimes.com/2013/08/30/reader-idea-considering-the-varying-viewpoints-on-a-pregnancy-prevention-campaign/

Duncan, S. C., Duncan, T. E., & Strycker, L. A. (2000). Risk and protective factors influencing adolescent problem behavior: A multivariate latent growth curve analysis. *Annals of Behavioral Medicine, 22,* 103–109.

Dunifon, R., Kalil, A., & Bajracharya, A. (2005). Maternal working conditions and child well-being in welfare-leaving families. *Developmental Psychology, 41,* 851–951.

Dunne, E. F., Unger, E. R., Sternberg, M., McQuillan, G., Swan, D. C., Patel, S. S., & Markowitz, L. E. (2007). Prevalence of HPV infection among females in the United States. *Journal of the American Medical Association, 297*(8), 813–819.

Dunphy, D. (1963). The social structure of urban adolescent peer groups. *Sociometry, 26,* 230–246.

Dupere, V., Leventhal, T., Crosnoe, R., & Dion, E. (2010). Understanding the positive role of neighborhood socioeconomic advantage in achievement: The contribution of the home, child care, and school environments. *Developmental Psychology, 46*(5), 1227–1244.

Duran, E., Yaussy, D., & Yaussy, L. (2011). Race to the Future: Integrating 21st Century Skills into Science Instruction. *Science Activities, 48*(3), 98–106.

Durham, M. G. (1998). Gender socialization in girls' teen magazines. *Youth and Society, 29,* 369–389.

Durlak, J. A., Weissberg, R. P., Dymnicki, A. B., Taylor, R. D., & Schellinger, K. B. (2011). The impact of enhancing students' social and emotional learning: A meta-analysis of school-based universal interventions. *Child Development, 82*(1), 405–432.

Durm, M. W., & Pitts, S. (1993). Heinz dilemma? Let the subject choose! *Psychological Reports, 73,* 1399–1402.

Duvall, S. F., Delquadri, J. C., & Ward, D. L. (2004). A preliminary investigation of the effectiveness of homeschool instructional environments for students with attention-deficit/hyperactivity disorder, *School Psychology Review, 33*(1), 140–158.

Dweck, C.S. (2007). The perils and promises of praise. *Educational Leadership, 65,* 34–39.

Dworkin, J., & Larson, R. (2001). Age trends in conflict in mother-headed single parent families across adolescence. *Journal of Adolescence, 24,* 529–534.

Eccles, J. S. (1987). Gender roles and women's achievement-related decisions. *Psychology of Women Quarterly, 11,* 135–172.

Eccles, J. S. (2005). Subjective task value and the Eccles et al. model of achievement-related choices. In A. Elliot & C. Dweck (Eds.), *Handbook of competence and motivation* (pp. 105–121). New York, NY: Guilford Press.

Eccles, J. S. (2007). Where are all the women? Gender differences in participation in physical science and engineering. In S. J. Ceci & W. M. Williams (Eds.), *Why aren't more women in science? Top researchers debate the evidence* (pp. 199–210). Washington, DC: American Psychological Association.

Eccles, J. S., & Midgley, C. (1989). Stage-environment fit: Developmentally appropriate classrooms for young adolescents. In C. Ames & R. Ames (Eds.), *Research on motivation in education. Vol. 3: Goals and cognitions* (pp. 13–44). New York, NY: Academic Press.

Eccles, J. S., & Midgley, C. (1989). Stage-environment fit: Developmentally appropriate classrooms for young adolescents. In C. Ames & R. Ames (Eds.), *Research on motivation in education: Goals and cognitions* (Vol. 3, pp. 139–186). New York, NY: Academic

Eccles, J. S., & Midgley, C. (1989). Stage/environment fit: Developmentally appropriate classroom for early adolescents. In R. Ames & C. Ames (Eds.), *Research on motivation in education* (Vol. 3, pp. 139–181). San Diego, CA: Academic Press.

Eccles, J. S., Lord, S. E., & Roeser, R. W. (1996). Round holes, square pegs, rocky roads, and sore feet: The impact of stage-environment fit on young adolescents' experiences in schools and families. In D. Cicchetti & S. L. Toth (Eds.), *Adolescence: Opportunities and challenges. Rochester symposium on developmental psychopathology, Vol. 7* (pp. 47–92). Rochester, NY: University of Rochester Press.

Eccles, J. S., Lord, S., & Buchanan, C. M. (1996). School transitions in early adolescence: What are we doing to our young people? In J. A. Graber (Ed.), *Transitions through adolescence: Interpersonal domains and context* (pp. 251–284). Hillsdale, NJ: Lawrence Erlbaum Associates.

Eccles, J. S., Midgley, C., Wigfield, A., Miller-Buchanan, C. M., Reuman, D., Flanagan, C., et al. (1993). Development during adolescence: The impact of stage-environment fit on young adolescents' experiences in schools and in families. *American Psychologist, 48*(2), 90–101.

Eder, D. (1985). The cycle of popularity: Interpersonal relations among female adolescents. *Sociology of Education, 58,* 154–165.

Eder, D. (1995). *School talk: Gender and adolescent culture.* New Brunswick, NJ: Rutgers University Press.

Eder, D., & Sanford, S. (1986). The development and maintenance of interactional norms among early adolescents. In P. Adler & P. Adler (Eds.), *Sociological studies of child development* (Vol. 1, pp. 283–300). Greenwich, CT: JAI Press.

Educational Testing Service. (1999). *Cheating is a personal foul.* Retrieved from: http://www.glass-castle.com/clients/www-nocheating-org/adcouncil/research/cheatingfactsheet.html

Egan, S., & Perry, D. (2001). Gender identity: A multidimensional analysis with implications for psychosocial adjustment. *Developmental Psychology, 37,* 451–463.

Eisenberg, M. E., Bearinger, L. H., Sieving, R. E., Swain, C., & Resnick, M. D. (2004). Parents' beliefs about condoms and oral contraceptives: Are they medically accurate? *Perspectives on Sexual & Reproductive Health, 36*(2), 50–57.

Ellis, B. J. (2004). Timing of pubertal maturation in girls: An integrated life history approach. *Psychological Bulletin, 30,* 920–958.

Engel, G. L. (1977). The need for a new medical model: A challenge for biomedicine. *Science, 196,* 129–136.

Entwisle, D. R., Alexander, K. L., & Olson, L. S. (2010). Socioeconomic status: Its broad sweep and long reach in education. In J. L. Meece & J. S. Eccles (Eds.), *Handbook of research on schools, schooling, and human development* (pp. 237–255). New York, NY: Routledge.

Epstein, J. L. (1995). Family/school/community partnerships: Caring for the children we share. *Phi Delta Kappa, 76,* 701–712.

Erikson, E. H. (1963). *Childhood and society.* New York, NY: Norton.

Erikson, E. H. (1968). *Identity: Youth and crisis.* New York, NY: Norton.

Erikson, E. H. (1980). *Identity and the life cycle.* New York, NY: Norton.

Ernst, M., & Spear, L. (2008). Reward systems. In M. de Haan & M. Gunnar (Eds.), *Handbook of developmental neuroscience* (pp. 324–341). New York, NY: Guilford Press.

Erol, R.Y., & Orth, U. (2011). Self-esteem development from age 14 to 30 years: a longitudinal study. *Journal of Personality and Social Psychology, 101*, 607–619.

Espelage, D. L., & Holt, M. K. (2012). Understanding & preventing bullying, Sexual harassment & dating violence in school. In K. Harris, S. Graham, & T. Urdan (Eds.), *APA educational psychology handbook*. Washington, DC: American Psychological Association.

Espelage, D.L., & Stein, N. (2007). *Middle school bullying & sexual violence: Measurement issues and methodological issues*. American Psychological Association: Washington, DC.

Fallon, K. (2013). "Don't say gay" is back: 5 things to know about the Tennessee bill. *The Daily Beast, January 31, 2013*. Retrieved on January 6, 2016.

Faltis, C. (1990). Spanish for native speakers: Freirian and Vygotskian perspectives. *Foreign Language Annals, 23*(2), 117–126.

Fan, W., Williams, C. M., & Corkin, D. M. (2011). A multilevel analysis of student perceptions of school climate: The effect of social and academic risk factors. *Psychology in the Schools, 48*(6), 632–647.

Faris, R., & Felmlee, D. (2011). Status struggles: Network centrality and gender segregation in same- and cross-gender aggression. *American Sociological Review, 76*, 48–73. Retrieved from http://dx.doi.org/10.1177/0003122410396196

Farmer, T. W., Lines, M. M., & Hamm, J.V. (2011). Revealing the invisible hand: The role of teachers in children's peer experiences. *Journal of Applied Developmental Psychology, 32*(5), 247–256.

Federal Bureau of Investigation. (2014). *Uniform crime statistics*. Retrieved from http://www.fbi.gov

Federal Interagency Forum on Child and Family Statistics. *America's Children: Key National Indicators of Well-Being, 2015*. Washington, DC: U.S. Government Printing Office.

Feinstein, B. A., Herschenberg, R., Bhatia, V., Latack, J. A., Meuwly, N., & Davila, J. (2013). Negative social comparison on Facebook and depressive symptoms: Rumination as a mechanism. *Psychology of Popular Media Culture, 2*, 161–170.

Feldlaufer, H., Midgley, C., & Eccles, J. S. (1988). Student, teacher, and observer perceptions of the classroom environment before and after the transition to junior high school. *Journal of Early Adolescence, 8*(2), 133–156.

Feng, J., Spence, I., & Pratt, J. (2007). Playing an action video game reduces gender differences in spatial cognition. *Psychological Science, 18*, 850–855.

Ferguson, C. J., Garza, A., Jerabeck, J., Ramos, R., & Galindo, M. (2013). Not worth the fuss after all? Cross-sectional and prospective data on violent video game influences on aggression, visuospatial cognition and mathematics ability in a sample of youth. *Journal of Youth and Adolescence, 42*(1), 109–122.

Festinger, L. (1962). *A theory of cognitive dissonance*. Stanford, CT: Stanford University Press.

Field, A. E., Cheung, A. M., Wolf, D. B., Herzog, S. L., & Colditz, G. A. (1999). Exposure to the mass media and weight concerns among girls. *Pediatrics, 103*(3), doi: 10.1542/peds.103.3.e36.

Fields, S. A., Sabet, M. M., & Reynolds, B. B. (2013). Dimensions of impulsive behavior in obese, overweight, and healthy-weight adolescents. *Appetite, 70*, 60–66. doi:10.1016/j.appet.2013.06.089

Finkelhor, D., Mitchell, K. J., & Wolak, J. (2000). *Online victimization: A report on the nation's youth*. Alexandria, VA: National Center for Missing & Exploited Children.

Fisch, S., Truglio, R., & Cole, C. (1999). The impact of *Sesame Street* on preschool children: A review and synthesis of 30 years of research. *Media Psychology, 1*, 165–190.

Fischer, K. W., & Bidell, T. R. (2006). Dynamic development of action and thought. In R. M. Lerner (Ed.), *Handbook of child psychology. Vol. 1: Theoretical models of human development* (6th ed., pp. 313–399). Hoboken, NJ: Wiley.

Fisher, D. A., Hill, D. L., Grube, J. W., & Gruber, E. L. (2007). Gay, lesbian, and bisexual content on television: A quantitative analysis across two seasons. *Journal of Homosexuality, 52*, 167–188.

Fiske, S. T., & Taylor, S. E. (1991). *Social cognition* (2nd ed.). New York, NY: McGraw-Hill.

Flashman, J. (2012). Academic achievement and its impact on friend dynamics, *Sociology of Education, 85*(1), 61–80.

Flavell, J. H. (1979). Metacognition and cognitive monitoring: A new area of cognitive–developmental inquiry. *American Psychologist, 34*(10), 906–911.

Flavell, J. H. (1985). *Cognitive development* (2nd ed.). Englewood Cliffs, NJ: Prentice Hall.

Flegal, K. M., & Troiano, R. P. (2000). Changes in the distribution of body mass index of adults and children in the U.S. population. *International Journal of Obesity Related Metabolism Disorders, 24*, 807–818.

Fletcher, J., & Kumar, S. (2014). Religion and risky health behaviors among U.S. adolescents and adults. *Journal of Economic Behavior & Organization, 104*, 123–140. doi:10.1016/j.jebo.2014.03.018

Flint, J. (2012). Teens are watching more TV, not less, report says. *Los Angeles Times*. Retrieved from http://articles.latimes.com/2012/mar/09/business/la-fi-ct-teen-tv-study-20120309

Flum, H., & Kaplan, A. (2006). Exploratory orientation as an educational goal. *Educational Psychologist, 41*, 99–110.

Flum, H. & Kaplan, A. (2012). Identity formation in educational settings: A contextualized view of theory and research in practice. *Contemporary Educational Psychology, 37*, 240–245.

Foehr, U. G. (2006). Media multitasking among youth: Prevalence, predictors and pairings. Menlo Park, CA: The Henry J Kaiser Family Foundation.

Fogel, A., & Garvey, A. (2007). Alive communication. *Infant Behavior and Development, 30*, 251–257.

Fomby, P., & Cherlin, A. J. (2007). Family instability and child well-being. *American Sociological Review, 72*, 181–204.

Food Research and Action Center. (2010). *National School Lunch Program*. Retrieved from http://frac.org/federal-foodnutrition-programs/school-breakfast-and-lunch/national-school-lunch-program/

Fordham, S., & Ogbu, J. (1986). Black students' school success: Coping with the "burden of 'acting White.'" *Urban Review, 18*, 176–206.

Fox, E., & Riconscente, M. (2008). Metacognition and self-regulation in James, Piaget, and Vygotsky. *Educational Psychology Review, 20*, 373–389.

Fox, J., & Warber, K. M. (2013). Romantic relationship development in the age of Facebook: An exploratory study of emerging adults' perceptions, motives, and behaviors. *Cyberpsychology, Behavior, and Social Networking, 16*(1), 3–7. doi:10.1089/cyber.2012.0288

Franklyn-Stokes, A., & Newstead, S. E. (1995). Undergraduate cheating: Who does what and why? *Studies in Higher Education, 20*, 159–172.

Fredricks, J. A., & Eccles, J. S. (2002). Children's competence and value beliefs from childhood through adolescence: Growth trajectories in two male-sex-typed domains. *Developmental Psychology, 38*(4), 519–533.

Freeman, T. M., Anderman, L. H., & Jensen, J. M. (2007). Sense of belonging in college freshmen at the classroom and campus levels. *Journal of Experimental Education, 75*(3), 203–220.

Freitas, D. (2013). *The end of sex: How hookup culture is leaving a generation unhappy, sexually unfulfilled, and confused about intimacy*. New York, NY: Basic Books.

French, D. C., Niu, L., Xu, S., Jun, S., Ling, L. (2015). *Popularity and social preference in Chinese adolescents: Associations with social and behavioral adjustment*. Paper presented at the Society for Research in Adolescence bi-annual meeting, Philadelphia, PA.

Freud, A. (1958). Adolescence. *Psychoanalytic Study of the Child, 13*, 255–278.

Friedman, E. (2010). Victim of secret dorm sex tape posts Facebook goodbye, jumps to his death. *ABC News*. Retrieved from http://abcnews.go.com/US/victim-secret-dorm-sex-tape-commits-suicide/story?id=11758716

Frome, P., & Eccles, J. (1996, March). *Gender role identity and self-esteem*. Paper presented at the meetings of the Society for Research on Child Development, Boston, MA.

Fromme, K., Corbin, W. R., & Kruse, M. I. (2008). Behavioral risks during the transition from high school to college. *Developmental Psychology, 44*(5), 1497–1504.

Frontline. (2002). *Inside the adolescent brain* <Documentary>. Retrieved from Public Broadcasting Service website: http://www.pbs.org/wgbh/pages/frontline/shows/teenbrain/

Fry, R. (2013). *A rising share of young adults live in their parents' home*. Washington, DC: Pew Research Center. Retrieved from http://www.pewsocialtrends.org/2013/08/01/a-rising-share-of-young-adults-live-in-their-parents-home/

Fuligni, A. J. (1997). The academic achievement of adolescents from immigrant families: The roles of family background, attitudes, and behavior. *Child Development, 68*, 261–273.

Fuligni, A. J., & Tseng, V. (1999). Family obligation and the academic motivation of adolescents from immigrant and American-born families. In T. Urdan (Ed.), *Advances in Motivation and Achievement* (Vol. 11, pp. 159–183). Stamford, CT: JAI Press.

Fuligni, A., Witkow, M., & Garcia, C. (2005). Ethnic identity and the academic adjustment of adolescents from Mexican, Chinese, and European backgrounds. *Developmental Psychology, 41*, 799–811.

Furman, W., & Hand, L. S. (2006). The slippery nature of romantic relationships: Issues in definition and differentiation. In A. C. Crouter & A. Booth (Eds.), *Romance and sex in adolescence and emerging adulthood: Risks and opportunities* (pp. 171–178). Mahwah, NJ: Lawrence Erlbaum Associates.

Furman, W., & Shaffer, L. (2003). The role of romantic relationships in adolescent development. In P. Florsheim (Ed.), *Adolescent romantic relations and sexual behavior: Theory, research, and practical implications* (pp. 3–22). Mahwah, NJ: Lawrence Erlbaum Associates.

Furnham, A., & Calnan, A. (1998). Eating disturbance, self-esteem, reasons for exercising, and body weight dissatisfaction in adolescent males. *European Eating Disorders Review, 6*, 58–72.

Gage, N. L. (1978). *The scientific basis of the art of teaching*. New York NY: Teachers College Press.

Galambos, N. L., & Krahn, H. J. (2008). Depression and anger trajectories during the transition to adulthood. *Journal of Marriage and Family, 70*, 15–27.

Galambos, N. L., Berenbaum, S. A., & McHale, S. M. (2009). Gender development in adolescents. In R. M. Lerner & L. Steinberg (Eds.), *Handbook of adolescent psychology. Vol. 1. Individual bases of adolescent development* (3rd ed., pp. 305–337). Hoboken, NJ: Wiley.

Galvan, A. (2013). The teenage brain: Sensitivity to rewards. *Current Directions in Psychological Science, 22*, 88–93.

Gantz, W., Schwartz, N., Angelini, J., & Rideout, V. (2007). *Food for thought: Television food advertising to children in the United States*. Menlo Park, CA: The Henry J. Kaiser Family Foundation.

Garbarino, J. (1999). *Lost boys: Why our sons turn violent and how we can save them*. New York, NY: Simon & Schuster.

Gardner, H. (1993). *Multiple intelligences: The theory in practice*. New York, NY: Basic Books.

Gardner, H. (1999). *Intelligence reframed: Multiple intelligences for the 21st century*. New York, NY: Basic Books.

Gardner, H. (2006). *Multiple intelligences: New horizons in theory and practice*. New York, NY: Basic Books.

Garrod, A., Beal, C., & Shin, P. (1990). The development of moral orientation in elementary school children. *Sex Roles, 22*, 13–27.

Gasper, J., DeLuca, S., & Estacion, A. (2012). Switching schools: Revisiting the relationship between school mobility and high school dropout, *American Educational Research Journal, 50*(6), 1188–1218.

Gates, G. (2013). Family formation and raising children among same-sex couples, *National Council of Family Relations*, issue FF51. Retrieved from Williams Institute website: http://williamsinstitute. law.ucla.edu/wp-content/uploads/Gates-Badgett-NCFR-LGBT-Families-December-2011.pdf

Gates, G. (2015). Marriage and Family: LGBT Individuals and Same-sex couples. *Future of Children, 25*(2), 67–87.

Gathercole, S. E., Pickering, S. J., Ambridge, B., & Wearing, H. (2004). The structure of working memory from 4 to 15 years of age. *Developmental Psychology, 40*, 177–190.

Gauvain, M. (2009). Vygotsky's theory. In E. M. Anderman & L. H. Anderman (Eds.), *Psychology of classroom learning* (Vol. 1, pp. 200–204). Detroit, MI: Gale Cengage Learning.

Gavassi, S. M. (2011). *Families with adolescents: Bridging the gaps between theory, research, and practice*, New York: Springer.

Gay, G. (2010). *Culturally responsive teaching: Theory, research, and practice, 2nd Edition (In J. Banks, Series Ed. Multicultural Education Series)*. New York: Teachers' College Press.

Ge, X., & Natsuaki, M. N. (2009). In search of explanations for early pubertal timing effects on developmental psychopathology. *Current Directions in Psychological Science, 18*, 327–331.

Ge, X., Conger, R. A., & Elder, G. H. Jr. (2001). The relation between puberty and psychological distress in adolescent boys. *Journal of Research on Adolescence, 11*, 49–70.

Ge, X., Lorenz, F., Conger, R., & Elder, G. H. (l994) Trajectories of stressful life events and depressive symptoms during adolescence. *Developmental Psychology, 30*, 467–83.

Gebbia, M. I., Maculaitis, M. C., & Camenzuli, C. A. (2012). The relationship between volunteer experience quality & adolescent bullying. *North American Journal of Psychology, 14*(3), 455–470.

Gelman, R. (2000). Domain specificity and variability in cognitive development. *Child Development, 71*(4), 854–856.

General Records of the United States Government. (1916). *An act to prevent interstate commerce in the products of child labor, and for other purposes, September 1, 1916; Enrolled Acts and Resolutions of Congress, 1789-; General Records of the United States Government; Record Group 11; National Archives*. Retrieved from http://www.ourdocuments.gov/doc.php?flash=true&doc=59

Genereux, R. L., & McCleod, B. A. (1995). Circumstances surrounding cheating: A questionnaire study of college students. *Research in Higher Education, 36*, 687–704.

Gennetian, L. A., Duncan, G., Knox, V., Vargas, W., Clark-Kauffman, E., & London, A. S. (2004). How welfare policies affect adolescents' school outcomes: A synthesis of evidence from experimental studies. *Journal of Research on Adolescence, 14*, 399–423.

Gentile, B., et al., (2009). Gender differences in domain-specific self-esteem: A meta-analysis. *Review of General Psychology, 13*, 34–45.

Gentile, D. A., Lynch, P. J., Linder, J. R., & Walsh, D. A. (2004). The effects of violent video game habits on adolescent hostility, aggressive behaviors, and school performance. *Journal of Adolescence, 27*, 5–22.

Gerbner, G., Gross, L., Morgan, M., Signorelli, A., & Shanahan, J. (2002). Growing up with television: Cultivation processes. In J. Bryant & D. Zillman (Eds.), *Media effects: Advances in theory and research* (2nd ed., pp. 43–67). Mahwah, NJ: Lawrence Erlbaum.

Gest, S. D. (2006). Teacher Reports of Children's Friendships and Social Groups: Agreement with Peer Reports and Implications for Studying Peer Similarity. *Social Development, 15*, 248–259.

Ghanem, M., Gamaluddin, H., Mansour, M., Samiee', A., Shaker, N., & El Rafei, H. (2013). Role of impulsivity and other personality dimensions in attempted suicide with self-poisoning among children and adolescents. *Archives of Suicide Research, 17*(3), 262–274. doi:10.1080/13811118.2013.805645

Giaconia, R. M., Reinherz, H. Z., Silverman, A. B., Bilge, P., Frost, A. K., & Cohen, E. (1995). Traumas and post-traumatic stress disorder in a community population of older adolescents. *Journal of the American Academy of Child and Adolescent Psychiatry, 34*, 1369–1380.

Giannotti, F., Cortesi, F., Sebastiani, T., & Ottaviano, S. (2002). Circadian preference, sleep and daytime behaviour in adolescence. *Journal of Sleep Research, 11*, 191–199.

Gibson, M. A. (1988). *Accommodation without assimilation: Sikh immigrants in an American high school*. Ithaca, NY: Cornell University Press.

Giedd, J., et al. (1999). Brain development during childhood and adolescence: A longitudinal MRI study. *Nature Neuroscience, 2*, 861–863.

Gil-Rivas, V., Greenberger, E., Chen, C. S., & Lopez-Lena, M. M. Y. (2003). Understanding depressed mood in the context of a family-oriented culture. *Adolescence, 149*, 93–109.

Gilligan, C. (1982). *In a different voice: Psychological theory and women's development*. Cambridge, MA: Harvard University Press.

Gilligan, C., & Attanucci, J. (1994). Two moral orientations: Gender differences and similarities. In B. Puka (Ed.), *Caring voices and women's moral frames: Gilligan's view* (pp. 123–137). New York, NY: Garland Publishing.

Gilmore, D. (2002). Requirements for manhood in an East African culture. In J. J. Arnett (Ed.), *Readings on adolescence and emerging adulthood* (pp. 95–100). Upper Saddle River, NJ: Prentice Hall.

Gitlin, A., Buendia, E., Crosland, K., & Doumbia, F. (2003). The production of margin and center: Welcoming-unwelcoming of immigrant students. *American Educational Research Journal, 40,* 91–122.

Glascock, J. (2001). Gender roles on prime-time network television: Demographics and behaviors. *Journal of Broadcasting and Electronic Media, 45,* 656–669.

Gluckman, P. D., & Hanson, M. A. (2006). Evolution, development, and timing of puberty. *Trends in Endocrinology and Metabolism, 17,* 7–12.

Goldstein, S. E., Boxer, P., & Rudolph, E. (2015). Middle school transition stress: Links with academic performance, motivation, and school experiences. *Contemporary School Psychology, 19*(1), 21–29.

Goleman, D. (1995). *Emotional intelligence: Why it can matter more than IQ.* New York, NY: Bantam.

Gonzales, N. A., Fabrett, F., C., & Knight, G. P. (2009). Acculturation, enculturation, and the psychosocial adaptation of Latino youth. In F. A. Villarruel et al. (Eds.), *Handbook of U.S. Latino psychology* (pp. 115–134). Los Angeles, CA: Sage.

Goodenow, C. (1993). The psychological sense of school membership among adolescents: Scale development and educational correlates. *Psychology in the Schools, 30,* 79–90.

Goodnough, G. E., & Ripley, V. (1997). Structured groups for high school seniors making the transition to college and to military service. *The School Counselor, 43,* 230–234.

Gopnik, A. (2012). Scientific thinking in young children: Theoretical advances, empirical research, and policy implications. *Science, 337*(6102), 1623–1627.

Gottfredson, D. C., & DiPietro, S. M. (2011). School size, social capital, and student victimization. *Sociology of Education, 84*(1), 69–89.

Gottfried, A. E., Marconlides, G. A., Gottfried, A. W., & Oliver, P. H. (2009). A latent curve model of parental motivational practices and developmental decline in math and science academic intrinsic motivation. *Journal of Educational Psychology, 101,* 729–739.

Graber, J. A., & Sontag, L. M. (2009). Internalizing problems during adolescence. In R. M. Lerner & L. R. Steinberg (Eds.), *Handbook of adolescent psychology* (3rd ed., pp. 642–682). New York, NY: Wiley & Sons.

Graber, J., Seeley, J., Brooks-Gunn, J., & Lewinsohn, P. (2004). Is pubertal timing associated with psychopathology in young adulthood? *Journal of the American Academy of Child and Adolescent Psychiatry, 43,* 718–726.

Gracia, E., Fuentes, M. C., Garcia, F., & Lila, M. (2012). Perceived neighborhood violence, parenting styles, and developmental outcomes among Spanish adolescents. *Journal of Community Psychology, 40*(8), 1004–1021.

Graham, S. (2006). Writing. In P. A. Alexander & P. H. Winne (Eds.), *Handbook of educational psychology* (2nd ed., pp. 457–478). Mahwah, NJ: Lawrence Erlbaum Associates.

Graham, S., Munniksma, A., & Juvonen, J. (2014). Psychosocial benefits of cross-ethnic friendships in middle school. *Child Development, 85,* 469–483.

Gray, H. M. & Foshee, V. (1997). Adolescent dating violence: Differences between one-sided and mutually violent profiles. *Journal of Interpersonal Violence, 12,* 126–141.

Gray, P., & Feldman, J. (2004). Playing in the zone of proximal development: Qualities of self-directed age mixing between adolescents and young children at a democratic school. *American Journal of Education, 110*(2), 108.

Gray, R., Vitak, J., Easton, E. W., & Ellison, N. B. (2013). Examining social adjustment to college in the age of social media: Factors influencing successful transitions and persistence. *Computers & Education, 67,* 193–207. doi:10.1016/j.compedu.2013.02.021

Gredler, M. E. (2009). Hiding in plain sight: The stages of mastery/self-regulation in Vygotsky's cultural-historical theory. *Educational Psychologist, 44*(1), 1–19.

Greenberg, B. S., & Mastro, D. E. (2008). Children, race, ethnicity and the media. In S. L. Calvert & B. J. Wilson (Eds.), *The handbook of children, media and development* (pp. 74–97). Singapore: Blackwell.

Greenleaf, C., Boyer, E. M., & Petrie, T. A. (2009). High school sport participation and subsequent psychological well-being and physical activity: The mediating influences of body image, physical competence, and instrumentality. *Sex Roles, 61,* 714–726.

Greenspan, L., & Deardorff, J. (2014). *The new puberty: How to navigate early development in today's girls.* New York, NY: Rodale.

Gregory, A., Allen, J. P., Mikami, A., Hafen, C. A., & Pianta, R. (2014). Effects of a professional development program on behavioral engagement of students in middle and high school. *Psychology in the Schools, 51*(2), 143–163.

Greitemeyer, T. (2009). Effects of songs with prosocial lyrics on prosocial thoughts, affect and behavior. *Journal of Experimental Social Psychology, 45,* 186–190.

Grello, C. M., Welsh, D. P., Harper, M. S., & Dickson, J. W. (2003). Dating and sexual relationship trajectories and adolescent functioning. *Adolescent and Family Health, 3,* 103–112.

Griffin, K. W., Botvin, G. J., Nichols, T. R., & Doyle, M. M. (2003). Effectiveness of a universal drug abuse prevention approach for youth at high risk for substance use initiation. *Preventive Medicine, 36* (1), 1–7.

Grigal, M., Hart, D., & Migliore, A. (2011). Comparing the transition planning, postsecondary education, and employment outcomes of students with intellectual and other disabilities. *Career Development for Exceptional Individuals, 34*(1), 4–17.

Grolnick, W. S., Benjet, C., Kurowski, C. O., & Apostoleris, N. H. (1997). Predictors of parent involvement in children's schooling. *Journal of Educational Psychology, 89,* 538–548.

Grolnick, W. S., Raftery-Helmer, J. N., Marbell, K., Flamm, E., Cardemil, E. V., & Sanchez, M. (2014). Parental provision of structure: Implementation, correlates and outcomes in three domains. *Merrill-Palmer Quarterly, 60,* 354–385.

Grotevant, H. D., Thorbecke, W., & Meyer, M. L. (1982). An extension of Marcia's identity status interview into the interpersonal domain. *Journal of Youth and Adolescence, 11,* 33–47.

Gruber J. E., & Fineran, S. (2008). Comparing the impact of bullying and sexual harassment victimization on the mental and physical health of adolescents. *Sex Roles, 59,* 1–13. doi:10.1007/s11199-008-9431-5

Gruber, J., & Zinman, J. (2001). Youth smoking in the United States. In J. Gruber (Ed.), *Risky behavior among youths: An economic analysis* (pp. 69–120). Chicago, IL: University of Chicago Press.

Guerra, N. G., Williams, K. R., & Sadek, S. (2011). Understanding bullying and victimization during childhood and adolescence: A mixed methods study. *Child Development, 82,* 295–310. Retrieved from http://dx.doi.org/10.1111/j.1467-8624.2010.01556.x

Gunter, W. D., & Daly, K. (2012). Causal or spurious: Using propensity score matching to detangle the relationship between violent video games and violent behavior. *Computers in Human Behavior, 28*(4), 1348–1355.

Gutshall, C. A. (2014). Pre-service teachers' mindset beliefs about student ability. *Electronic Journal of Research in Educational Psychology, 12*(3), 785–802.

Guttmacher Institute. (2012). *Facts on American teens' information sources of information about sex.* Retrieved from http://www.guttmacher.org/pubs/FB-Teen-Sex-Ed.html

Guttman, L. M., & Eccles, J. S. (2007). Stage-environment fit during adolescence: Trajectories of family relations and adolescent outcomes. *Developmental Psychology, 43,* 522–537.

Guyll, M., Madon, S., Prieto, L., & Scherr, K. C. (2010). The potential roles of self-fulfilling prophecies, stigma consciousness, and stereotype threat in linking Latino/a ethnicity and educational outcomes. *Journal of Social Issues, 66,* 113–130.

Hagell, A. (2012). *Changing adolescents: Social trends and mental health.* Bristol, England: Policy Press.

Hagenauer, M. H., Perryman, J. I., Lee, T. M., & Carskadon, M. A. (2009). Adolescent changes in the homeostatic and circadian regulation of sleep. *Developmental Neuroscience, 31,* 276–284.

Hair, N. L., Hanson, J. L., Wolfe, B. L., & Pollak, S. D. (2015). Association of Child Poverty, Brain Development, and Academic Achievement. *JAMA Pediatrics, 169*(9), 822-829. doi:10.1001/jamapediatrics.2015.1475

Hall, G. S. (1904). *Adolescence: Its psychology and its relations to physiology, anthropology, sociology, sex, crime, religion, and education* (Vols. I & II). New York, NY: D. Appleton & Co.

Hall, R. E. (2009). Cool pose, Black manhood, and juvenile delinquency. *Journal of Human Behavior in the Social Environment, 19,* 531–539.

Hallinan, M., & Kubitschek, W. N. (2012). A comparison of academic achievement and adherence to the common school ideal in public and Catholic schools. *Sociology of Education, 85*(1), 1–22.

Halpern-Felsher, B. L., & Kropp, R. Y. (2005). Oral versus vaginal sex among adolescents: Perceptions, attitudes, and behavior. *Pediatrics, 115,* 845–851.

Halpern, C. T., Oslak, S. G., Young, M. L., Martin, S. L., & Kupper, L. L. (2001). Partner violence among adolescents in opposite-sex romantic relationships: Findings from the National Longitudinal Study of Adolescent Health. *American Journal of Public Health, 91,* 1679–1685.

Hamilton, R. (1989). The effects of learner-generated elaborations on concept learning from prose. *Journal of Experimental Education, 57*(3), 205–217.

Hamilton, S. F., & Fenzel, L. M. (1988). The impact of volunteer experience on adolescent social development: Evidence of program effects. *Journal of Adolescent Research, 3*(1), 65–80.

Hamm, J. V., Farmer, T. W., Dadisman, K., Gravelle, M., & Murray, A. (2011). Teachers' attunement to students' peer group affiliations as a source of the improved social context following the middle school transition in rural schools. *Journal of Applied Developmental Psychology, 32,* 267–277.

Hampel, P., Meier, M., & Kummel, U. (2008). School-based stress management training for adolescents: Longitudinal results from an experimental study. *Journal of Youth and Adolescence, 37,* 1009–1024.

Harrison, K., & Cantor, J. (1997). The relationship between media consumption and eating disorders. *Journal of Communication, 47,* 40–67.

Harter, S. (1990). Adolescent self and identity development. In S. S. Feldman & G. R. Elliot (Eds.), *At the threshold: The developing adolescent* (pp. 352–387). Cambridge, MA: Harvard University Press.

Harter, S. (1999). *The construction of the self: A developmental perspective.* New York: Guilford Press.

Harter, S. (2006). The development of self-representations in childhood and adolescence. In W. Damon & R. Lerner (Eds.), *Handbook of child psychology* (6th ed.). New York: Wiley.

Harter, S., & Monsour, A. (1992). Developmental analysis of conflict caused by opposing attributes in the adolescent self-portrait. *Developmental Psychology, 28,* 251–260.

Harter, S., & Whitesell, N. R. (2003). Beyond the debate: Why some adolescents report stable self-worth over time and situation, whereas others report changes in self-worth. *Journal of Personality, 71,* 1027–1058.

Harter, S., Bresnick, S., Bouchey, H. A., & Whitesell, N. R. (1997). The development of multiple role-related selves during adolescence. *Development and Psychopathology, 9,* 835–853.

Harter, S., Waters, P. L., Whitesell, N. R., & Kastelic, D. (1998). Level of voice among female and male high school students: Relational context, support, and gender orientation. *Developmental Psychology, 34*, 892–901.

Hattie, J. (2009). *Visible learning*. New York, NY: Routledge.

Hattie, J., & Timperley, H. (2007). The power of feedback. *Review of Educational Research, 77*, 81–112. doi: 10.3012/003465430298487

Hausenblas, H. A., & Down, D. S. (2001). Comparison of body image between athletes and non-athletes: A meta-analytic review. *Journal of Applied Sport Psychology, 13*, 328–339.

Helfritz-Sinville, L. E., & Stanford, M. S. (2014). Hostile attribution bias in impulsive and premeditated aggression. *Personality and Individual Differences, 56*, 45–50.

Helms, J., & Cook, D. (1999). *Using race and culture in counseling and psycho-therapy: Theory and process*. Needham Heights, MA: Allyn & Bacon.

Helms, S. W., Gallagher, M., Calhoun, C. D., Choukas-Bradley, S., Dawson, G. C., & Prinstein, M. J. (2015). Intrinsic religiosity buffers the longitudinal effects of peer victimization on adolescent depressive symptoms. *Journal of Clinical Child and Adolescent Psychology, 44*(3), 471–479. doi:10.1080/15374416.2013.865195

Helms, S.E. (2013). Involuntary volunteering: The impact of mandated service in public schools. *Economics of Education Review, 36*, 295–310.

Henderlong, J., & Lepper, M. R. (2002). The effects of praise on children's intrinsic motivation: A review and synthesis. *Psychological Bulletin, 128*, 774–795. doi:10.1037//0033-2909.128.5.774

Hendry, L. B., & Kloep, M. (2012). *Adolescence and adulthood: Transitions and transformations*. New York, NY: Palgrave Macmillan.

Henry, S. (2010, September 23). Berkeley's new school food study: A victory for Alice Waters. *The Atlantic*. Retrieved from http://www.theatlantic.com/health/archive/2010/09/berkeleys-new-school-food-study-a-victory-for-alice-waters/63465/

Herman-Giddens, M. E., et al. (2012). Secondary sexual characteristics in boys: Data from the Pediatric Research in Office Settings network. *Pediatrics, 130*, 1058–1068.

Herman-Giddens, M. E., Slora, E. J., Wasserman, R. C., Bourony, C. J., Bhapkar, M. V., Koch, G. G., & Hasemeier, C. M. (1997). Secondary sexual characteristics and menses in young girls seen in office practice: A study from the Pediatric Research in Office Settings network. *Pediatrics, 99*, 505–512.

Herrett-Skjellum, J., & Allen, M. (1996). Television programming and sex stereotyping and sex stereotyping: A meta-analysis. In B. R. Burleson (Ed.), *Communication yearbook* (Vol. 19, pp. 157–185). Thousand Oaks, CA: Sage.

Herting, M. M., & Nagel, B. J. (2012). Aerobic fitness relates to learning on a virtual Morris water task and hippocampal volume in adolescents. *Behavioral Brain Research, 233*, 5127–5525.

Herting, M. M., & Nagel, B. J. (2013). Differences in brain activity during a verbal associative memory encoding task in high- and low-fit adolescents. *Journal of Cognitive Neuroscience, 25*, 595–612.

Hetherington, E. M. (Ed.). (1999). *Coping with divorce, single parenting, and remarriage: A risk and resiliency perspective*. Mahwah, NJ: Lawrence Erlbaum.

Hetherington, E. M., & Stanley-Hagan, M. (2000). Diversity among stepfamilies. In D. H. Demo & K. R. Allen (Eds.), *Handbook of family diversity* (pp. 172–196). New York, NY: Oxford University Press.

Hetherington, E. M., & Stanley-Hagan, M. (2002). Parenting in divorced and remarried families. In M. H. Bornstein (Ed.), *Handbook of parenting. Vol. 3: Being and becoming a parent* (2nd ed., pp. 287–315). Mahwah, NJ: Erlbaum.

Hill, J. P., & Lynch, M. E. (1983). The intensification of gender-related role expectations during early adolescence. In J. Brooks-Gunn & A. Petersen (Eds.), *Girls at puberty: Biological and psychosocial perspectives* (pp. 201–228). New York: Plenum.

Hill, N. E., & Tyson, D. F. (2009). Parental involvement in middle school: A meta-analytic assessment of the strategies that promote achievement. *Developmental Psychology, 45*, 740–763.

Hill, N. E., Bush, K. R., & Roosa, M. W. (2003). Parenting and family socialization strategies and children's mental health: Low-income Mexican American and Euro-American mothers and children. *Child Development, 74*, 189–204.

Himmelstein, K. E. W., & Brückner, H. (2011). Criminal-justice and school sanctions against nonheterosexual youth: A national longitudinal study. *Pediatrics, 127*, 48–57.

Hoffman, A. J., & Wallach, J. (2005). Effects of mentoring on community college students in transition to university. *Community College Enterprise, 11*(1), 67–78.

Holas, I., & Huston, A. C. (2012). Are middle schools harmful? The role of transition timing, classroom quality and school characteristics. *Journal of Youth and Adolescence, 41*(3), 333–345.

Holloway, S. D. (1988). Concepts of ability and effort in Japan and the United States. *Review of Educational Research, 58*(3), 327–345.

Holt, M. K., & Espelage, D. L. (2007). Perceived social support among bullies, victims, and bully-victims. *Journal of Youth and Adolescence, 36*, 984–994.

Holz, J., Piosczyk, H., Landmann, N., Feige, B., Spiegelhalder, K., Riemann, D., et al. (2012). The timing of learning before night-time sleep differentially affects declarative and procedural long-term memory consolidation in adolescents. *PLoS ONE, 7*.

Hood, K., Brevard, J., Nguyen, A., & Belgrave, F. (2013). Stress among African American emerging adults: The role of family and cultural factors. *Journal of Child and Family Studies, 22*(1), 76–84. doi:10.1007/s10826-012-9639-4

Hooks, B. (1981). *Yearning: Race, gender and culture politics*. London, England: Turnaround.

Hoover-Dempsey, K. V., Bassler, O. C., & Brassie, J. S. (1992). Explorations in parent-school relations. *Journal of Education Research, 85*, 287–294.

Horn, J. L., & Cattell, R. B. (1966). Refinement and test of the theory of fluid and crystallized general intelligences. *Journal of Educational Psychology, 57*(5), 253–270.

Horn, J. L., & Cattell, R. B. (1967). Age differences in fluid and crystallized intelligence. *Acta Psychologica, 26*(2), 107–129.

Horzog, D. B., Dorer, D. J., Keel, P. K., Selwyn, S. E. Ekeblad, E. R., Flores, A. T., … Keller, M. B. (1999). Recovery and relapse in anorexia and bulimia nervosa: A 7.5-year follow-up study. *Journal of American Academy of Child Adolescent Psychiatry, 38*, 829–837.

Howard Gardner's multiple intelligences theory. (2013). Retrieved from Public Broadcasting Service website: http://www.pbs.org/wnet/gperf/education/ed_mi_overview.html

Huang, B., Biro, F. M., & Dorn, L. D. (2009). Determination of relative timing of pubertal maturation through ordinal logistic modeling: Evaluation of growth and timing parameters. *Journal of Adolescent Health, 45*, 483–488.

Huang, C. (2013). Gender differences in academic self-efficacy: a meta-analysis. *European Journal of Psychology of Education, 28*, 1–35.

Hudak, M. A., & Anderson, D. E. (1990). Formal operations and learning style predict success in statistics and computer science courses. *Teaching of Psychology, 17*(4), 231–234. doi:10.1207/s15328023top1704_4

Hudley & Irving, (2012). Ethnic and racial identity in childhood and adolescence. In K. Harris, S. Graham, and T. Urdan (Eds.) *APA Educational Psychology Handbook, Vol. 2*. Washington, DC: American Psychological Association.

Huesmann, L. R. (1986). Psychological processes promoting the relation between exposure to media violence and aggressive behavior by the viewer. *Journal of Social Issues, 42*, 125–139.

Hulleman, C. S., & Harackiewicz, J. M. (2009). Promoting interest and performance in high school science classes. *Science, 326*, 1410–1412.

Hulleman, C. S., Godes, O., Hendricks, B., & Harackiewicz, J. M. (2010). Enhancing interest and performance with a utility value intervention. *Journal of Educational Psychology, 102*(4), 880–895.

Hupkens, C. L. H., Knibbe, R. A., & Drop, M. J. (2000). Social class differences in food consumption: The explanatory value of permissiveness and health and cost considerations. *European Journal of Public Health, 10*, 108–113.

Hurlbutt, K. S. (2011). Experiences of parents who homeschool their children with autism spectrum disorders. *Focus on Autism and Other Developmental Disabilities, 26*, 239–249.

Hust, S. J., & Brown, J. D. (2008). Gender, media use and effects. In S. L. Calvert & B. J. Wilson (Eds.), *The handbook of children, media and development* (pp. 98–120). Singapore: Blackwell.

Huynh, V. W., & Fuligni, A. J. (2012). Perceived ethnic stigma across the transition to college. *Journal of Youth and Adolescence, 41*(7), 817–830.

Inhelder, B., & Piaget, J. (1977). The growth of logical thinking from childhood to adolescence (A. Parson & S. Milgram, Trans.). In H. E. Gruber & J. J. Voneche (Eds.), *The essential Piaget* (pp. 405–444). New York, NY: Basic Books.

Inman, D. D., van Bakergem, K. M., LaRosa, A. C., & Garr, D. R. (2011). Evidencebased health promotion programs for schools and communities. *American journal of preventive medicine, 40*(2), 207–219.

INSERM. (2007). *Collective reports*. Growth and puberty secular trends, environmental and genetic factors. Retrieved from National Center for Biotechnology Information website: http://www.ncbi.nlm.nih.gov/books/NBK10786/

It Gets Better Project. (2015). Retrieved from http://www.itgetsbetter.org/

Jackson, L. (2008). Adolescents and the Internet. In P. Jamieson & D. Romer (Eds.), *The changing portrayal of adolescents in the media since 1950* (pp. 377–411). New York, NY: Oxford University Press.

Jacobi, C., Hayward, C., de Zwaan, M., Kraemer, H. C., & Agras, W. S. (2004). Coming to terms with risk factors for eating disorders: Application of risk terminology and suggestions for a general taxonomy. *Psychological Bulletin, 130*, 19–65.

Jacobs, J. E., Lanza, S., Osgood, D. W., Eccles, J. S., & Wigfield, A. (2002). Changes in children's self-competence and values: Gender and domain differences across grades one through twelve. *Child Development, 73*, 509–527.

Jacobsen, K., & Rowe, D. (1999). Genetic and environmental influences on relationships between family connectedness, school connectedness, and adolescent depressed mood. *Developmental Psychology, 35*, 926–939.

Jaffee, S., & Hyde, J. S. (2000). Gender differences in moral orientation: A meta-analysis. *Psychological Bulletin, 126*(5), 703–726.

James, C., Davis, K., Flores, A., Francis, J. M., Pettingill, L., Rundle, M., & Gardner, H. (2009). Young people, ethics and the new digital media: A synthesis from the Good Play Project. Cambridge, MA: MIT Press. Retrieved from https://mitpress.mit.edu/sites/default/files/titles/free_download/9780262513630_Young_People_Ethics_and_New_Digital_Media.pdf

Jennsen, B., Klein, J., Salazar, M., Daluga, R., & DiClemente, R. (2009). Exposure to tobacco on the Internet: Content analysis of adolescents' Internet use. *Pediatrics, 124,* e180–e184.

Jensen, L. A., Arnett, J. J., Feldman, S. S., & Cauffman, E. (2002). It's wrong, but everybody does it: Academic dishonesty among high school and college students. *Contemporary Educational Psychology, 27,* 209–228.

Jensen, L., & Arnett, J. (2012). Going global: New pathways for adolescents and emerging adults in a changing world. *Journal of Social Issues, 68*(3), 473–492. doi:10.1111/j.1540-4560.2012.01759.x

Jeynes, W. (1999). Effects of remarriage following divorce on the academic achievement of children. *Journal of Youth and Adolescence, 28,* 385–393.

Jeynes, W. (2007). The relationship between parental involvement and urban secondary school student academic achievement: A meta-analysis. *Urban Education, 42,* 82–110.

Jiang, Y., Ekono, M., & Skinner, C. (2015). *Basic Facts about Low-Income Children: Children 12 through 17 Years, 2013.* New York: National Center for Children in Poverty, Mailman School of Public Health, Columbia University.

Jiang, Y., Perry, D. K., & Hesser, J. E. (2010). Suicide patterns and associations with predictors among Rhode Island public high school students: a latent class analysis. *American Journal of Public Health, 100,* 1701–1707.

Johns, M., Schmader, T., & Martens, A. (2005). Knowing is half the battle: Teaching stereotype threat as a means of improving women's math performance. *Psychological Science, 16,* 175–179.

Jones, D. C., Vigfusdottir, T. H., & Lee, Y. (2004). Body image and the appearance culture among adolescent girls and boys: An examination of friend conversations, peer criticism, appearance magazines, and the internalization of appearance ideals. *Journal of Adolescent Research, 19,* 323–339.

Jones, S. M., & Bouffard, S. M. (2012). Social and emotional learning in schools: From programs to strategies. *Social Policy Report, 26*(4), 3–22.

Jordan-Irvine, J. (2008). I dared to proclaim: The influence of African American women teachers. In F. Pajares and T. Urdan (Eds.) *The ones we remember: Scholars reflect on teachers who made a difference* (pp. 95–102). Charlotte, NC: Information Age Publishing.

Jordan, J. L., Kostandini, G., & Mykerezi, E. (2012). Rural and urban high school dropout rates: Are they different? *Journal of Research in Rural Education, 27,* 1–21.

Joyner, K. & Udry, J. R. (2000). You don't bring me anything but down: Adolescent romance and depression. *Journal of Health and Social Behavior, 41,* 369–391.

Jutte, D. P., Burgos, A., Mendoza, F., Ford, C. B., & Huffman, L. C. (2003). Use of the pediatric symptom checklist in a low-income, Mexican-American population. *Archives of Pediatric and Adolescent Medicine, 157,* 1169–1176.

Juvonen, J., & Graham, S. (2014). Bullying in schools: The power of bullies and the plight of victims. *Annual Review of Psychology, 65,* 159–183.

Juvonen, J., & Murdock, T. B. (1995). Grade-level differences in the social value of effort: Implications for self-presentation tactics of early adolescents. *Child Development, 66,* 1694–1705.

Juvonen, J., Wang, Y., & Espinoza, G. (2011). Bullying experiences and compromised academic performance across middle school grades. *Journal of Early Adolescence, 31,* 152–173.

Kaiser Family Foundation. (2013). *U.S. teen sexual activity.* Retrieved from http://kff.org/womens-health-policy/fact-sheet/sexual-health-of-adolescents-and-young-adults-in-the-united-states/

Kandel, W. A. (2011). *The U.S. Foreign-born population: Trends and selected characteristics* (Congressional Research Service Report for Congress). Washington, DC: Congressional Research Service.

Kann, L. et al. (2014). Youth risk behavior surveillance—United States, 2013. *Morbidity and Mortality Weekly Report, 63 (SS04).* 1–168. Centers for Disease Control and Prevention. http://www.cdc.gov/mmwr/preview/mmwrhtml/ss6304a1.htm

Kanner, A. D., Coyne, J. C., Schaefer, C., & Lazarus, R. S. (1981). Comparisons of two modes of stress measurement: Daily hassles and uplifts versus major life events. *Journal of Behavioral Medicine, 4,* 1–39.

Kaplan, A., & Maehr, M. L. (2007). The contribution and prospects of goal orientation theory. *Educational Psychology Review, 19,* 141–184.

Kaplan, A., Sinai, M., & Flum, H. (2014). Design-based interventions for promoting students' identity exploration within the school curriculum. In S. Karabenick & T. C. Urdan (Eds.), *Advances in motivation and achievement* (Vol. 18). Bingley, England: Emerald.

Karney, B. R., Becket, M. K., Collins, R. L., & Shaw, R. (2007). *Adolescent romantic relationships as precursors of healthy adult marriages: A review of theory, research, and programs.* Santa Monica, CA: RAND.

Katz, J., Kuffel, S., & Coblentz, A. (2002). Are there gender differences in sustaining dating violence?: An examination of frequency, severity, and relationship satisfaction. *Journal of Family Violence, 17,* 247– 271.

Keel, P. K., & Klump, K. L. (2003). Are eating disorders culture-bound syndromes? Implications for conceptualizing their etiology. *Psychological Bulletin, 129,* 747–796.

Kelley, R. M., Young, M., Denny, G., & Lewis, C. (2005). Liars, cheaters, and thieves: correlates of undesirable character behaviors in adolescents. *American Journal of Health Education, 36*(4), 194–201.

Kelly, A., Wall, M., Eisenberg, M., Story, M., & Neumark-Sztainer, D. (2005). Adolescent girls with high body satisfaction: Who are they and what can they teach us? *Journal of Adolescent Health, 37,* 391–396.

Kennedy, S., & Bumpass, L. (2008). Cohabitation and children's living arrangements: New estimates from the United States. *Demographic Research, 19*, 1663–1692.

Kenniston, A. H., & Flavell, J. H. (1979). A developmental study of intelligent retrieval. *Child Development, 50*, 1144–1152.

Kenyon, D. B., & Koerner, S.S. (2009). College student psychological well-being during the transition to college: Examining individuation from parents. *College Student Journal, 43*, 1145–1160.

Kessler, R. C. (2013). *National Comorbidity Survey: Adolescent Supplement (NCS-A), 2001–2004* (ICPSR28581–v5). Ann Arbor, MI: Inter-university Consortium for Political and Social Research. doi:10.3886/ICPSR28581.v5

Kiefer, S. M., & Ryan, A. M. (2011). What characteristics are associated with social success?: Changes in students' perceptions of social success during early adolescence. *Applied Developmental Psychology, 32*, 218–226.

Killen, M., Kelly, M., Richardson, C., Crystal, D., & Ruck, M. (2010). European American children's and adolescents' evaluations of interracial exclusion. *Group Processes & Intergroup Relations, 13*, 283–300.

Kindermann, T. (2007). Effects of naturally existing peer groups on changes in academic engagement in a cohort of sixth graders. *Child Development, 78*, 1186–1203.

Kindermann, T., & Skinner, E. (2012). Will the real peer group please stand up?: In A. M. Ryan & G. W. Ladd (Eds.), *Peer relationships and adjustment at school* (pp. 51–78). Charlotte, NC: Information Age Press.

King, P. E., & Roeser, R. W. (2009). Religion and spirituality in adolescent development. In R. M. Lerner, L. Steinberg, R. M. Lerner, & L. Steinberg (Eds.), *Handbook of adolescent psychology, Vol 1: Individual bases of adolescent development* (3rd ed.) (pp. 435–478). Hoboken, NJ: John Wiley & Sons Inc.

King, P. E., Ramos, J. S., & Clardy, C. E. (2013). Searching for the sacred: Religion, spirituality, and adolescent development. In K. I. Pargament, J. J. Exline, J. W. Jones, K. I. Pargament, J. J. Exline, & J. W. Jones (Eds.), *APA handbook of psychology, religion, and spirituality (Vol. 1): Context, theory, and research* (pp. 513–528). Washington, DC: American Psychological Association.

Kirby, D. (2001). *Emerging answers: research findings on programs to reduce teen pregnancy*. Washington, DC: The National Campaign to Prevent Teen Pregnancy.

Kirby, D., Korpi, M., Barth, R. P., & Cagampang, H. H. (1997). The impact of the postponing sexual involvement curriculum among youths in California. *Family Planning Perspectives, 29*, 100–108.

Kisker, E., & Brown, R. (1996). Do school-based health centers improve adolescents' access to health care, health status, and risk-taking behavior? *Journal of Adolescent Health, 18*, 335–343.

Kitsantas, A., Winsler, A., & Huie, F. (2008). Self-regulation and ability predictors of academic success during college: A predictive validity study. *Journal of Advanced Academics, 20*(1), 42–68.

Klass, P. (2013, February 11). How advertising targets our children [blog]. *New York Times*. Retrieved from http://well.blogs.nytimes.com/2013/02/11/how-advertising-targets-our-children/

Kling, K. C., Hyde, J. S., Showers, C. J., & Buswell, B. N. (1999). Gender differences in self-esteem: A meta-analysis. *Psychological Bulletin, 125*, 470–500.

Kobasigawa, A. (1974). Utilization of retrieval cues by children in recall. *Child Development, 45*, 127–134.

Kohlberg, L. (1975). The cognitive-developmental approach to moral education. *Phi Delta Kappan, 56*, 670–677.

Kost, K., & Henshaw, S. (2014). *U.S. teenage pregnancies, births, and abortions, 2010: National and state trends by age, race, and ethnicity*. New York, NY: Guttmacher Institute.

Kraft, R. J. (1996). Service learning: An introduction to its theory, practice, and effects. *Education and Urban Society, 28*(2), 131–159.

Kramer, L. (2010). The essential ingredients of successful sibling relationships: An emerging framework for advancing theory and practice. *Child Development Perspectives, 4*, 80–86.

Kulik, L. (2008). Responses to volunteering among adolescent volunteers in Israel: The contribution of personal and contextual variables. *Megamot, 45*(3), 576–605.

Kunkel, D., Eyal, K., Donnerstein, E., Farrar, K. M., Biely, E., & Rideout, V. J. (2007). Sexual socialization messages on entertainment television: Comparing content trends 1997–2002. *Media Psychology, 9*, 595–622.

Kunsch, C., Jitendra, A., & Sood, S. (2007). The effects of peer-mediated instruction in mathematics for students with learning problems: A research synthesis. *Learning Disabilities Research & Practice, 22*, 1–12.

Kuzmak, S. D., & Gelman, R. (1986). Young children's understanding of random phenomena. *Child Development, 57*(3), 559–566.

La Greca, A. M., & Harrison, H. M. (2005). Adolescent peer relations, friendships, and romantic relationships: Do they predict social anxiety and depression? *Journal of Clinical Child and Adolescent Psychology, 34*, 49–61.

Lachman, M. E. (2004). Development in midlife. *American Review of Psychology, 55*, 305–331.

LaFromboise, T., Coleman, H., & Gerton, J. (1993). Psychological impact on biculturalism: Evidence and theory. *Psychological Bulletin, 114*, 395–412.

Lakin, R. & Mahoney, A. (2006). Empowering youth to change their world: Identifying key components of a community service program to promote positive development. *Journal of Social Psychology, 44*, 513–531.

Lansford, J., Criss, M., Laird, R., Shaw, D., Pettit, G., Bates, J., & Dodge, K. (2011). Reciprocal relations between parents' physical discipline and children's externalizing behavior during middle childhood and adolescence. *Development and Psychopathology, 23*, 225–238.

Lanza, S. T., Cooper, B. R., & Bray, B. C. (2014). Population heterogeneity in the salience of multiple risk factors for adolescent delinquency. *Journal of Adolescent Health, 54*, 319–325.

Lareau, A. (1987). Social class differences in family-school relationships: The importance of cultural capitol. *Sociology of Education, 60*, 73–85.

Larson, R. (1983). Adolescents' daily experience with family and friends: Contrasting opportunity systems. *Journal of Marriage and the Family, 11*, 739–750.

Larson, R. W., & Armstrong, J. (2014). Adolescents' development of new skills for prospective cognition: Learning to anticipate, plan, and think strategically. *Journal of Cognitive Education and Psychology, 13*(2), 232–244.

Larson, R. W., Wilson, S., & Rickman, A. (2009). Globalization, societal chance, and adolescence across the world. In R. Lerner & L. Steinberg (Eds.), *Handbook of adolescent psychology*. Hoboken, NJ: John Wiley & Sons.

Larson, R., & Lampman-Petraitis, C. (1989). Daily emotional states as reported by children and adolescents. *Child Development, 60*, 1250–1260.

Larson, R., & Richards, M. H. (1994). Family emotions: Do young adolescents and their parents experience the same states? *Journal of Research on Adolescence, 4*(4), 567–583.

Larson, R., Richards, M., Moneta, G., Holmbeck, G., & Duckett, E. (1996). Changes in adolescents' daily interactions with their families from the age of 10 to 18: Disengagement and transformation. *Developmental Psychology, 32*, 744–754.

Lau, A. S., McCabe, K. M., Yeh, M., Garland, A. F., Wood, P. A., & Hough, R. L. (2005). The acculturation gap–distress hypothesis among high-risk Mexican American families. *Journal of Family Psychology, 19*, 367–375.

Laursen, B., & Collins, W. A. (2009). Parent-child relationships during adolescence. R. In M. Lerner & L. Steinberg (Eds.), *Handbook of adolescent psychology* (3rd ed., pp. 3–42). Hoboken, NJ: Wiley.

Laursen, B., & Jensen-Campbell, L. A. (1999). The nature and functions of social exchange in adolescent romantic relationships. In W. Furman, B. B. Brown, & C. Feiring (Eds.), *The development of romantic relationships in adolescence* (pp. 50–74). Cambridge, England: Cambridge University Press.

Lauzen, M. M., & Dozier, D.M. (2004). Evening the score in prime time: The relationship between behind-the-scenes women and on-screen portrayals in the 2002–2003 season. *Journal of Broadcasting and Electronic Media, 48*, 484–500.

Law, B. M. F., & Shek, D. T. L. (2009). Family influence on volunteering intention and behavior among Chinese adolescents in Hong Kong. *Adolescence, 44*, 665–683.

Leany, B. D. (2013). Brain development and health implications in adolescents. In W. T. O'Donohue, L. Benuto, & L. W. Tollie (Eds.), *Handbook of adolescent health psychology* (pp. 235–244). Springer Science + Business Media: New York.

Leaper, C. (2015). Gender and social-cognitive development. In R. M. Lerner, L. S. Liben, & U. Mueller (Eds.), *Handbook of child psychology and developmental science* (7th ed., Vol. 2, pp. 806–853). Hoboken, NJ: John Wiley & Sons, Inc.

Lee, J. S., & Bowen, N. K. (2006). Parent involvement, cultural capital, and the achievement gap among elementary school children. *American Educational Research Journal, 43*(2), 193–218.

Lee, V. E., & Smith, J. B. (1996). *High school size: which works best, and for whom? Draft.* Paper presented at the meeting of the American Educational Research Association, New York, NY. Retrieved from http://proxy.lib.ohio-state.edu/login?url=http://search.ebscohost.com/login.aspx?direct=true&db=eric&AN=ED396888&site=ehost-live

Lee, V. E., Chow-Hoy, T. K., Burkam, D. T., Geverdt, D., & Smerdon, B. A. (1998). Sector differences in high school course taking: A private school or Catholic school effect? *Sociology of Education, 71*(4), 314–335.

Lefkowitz, E. S., & Gillen, M. N. (2006). "Sex is just a normal part of life": Sexuality in emerging adulthood. In J. J. Arnett & J. L. Tanner (Eds.), *Emerging adults in America* (pp. 235–255). Washington, DC: American Psychological Association.

Leithwood, K., & Jantzi, D. (2009). A review of empirical evidence about school size effects: A policy perspective. *Review of Educational Research, 79*(1), 464–490.

Lenhart, A. (2012). *Teens, smartphones and texting*. Retrieved from Pew Research Center website: http://www.pewInternet.org/2012/03/19/teens-smartphones-texting/

Lenhart, A. (2015). *Teens, social media and technology overview*. Retrieved from Pew Research Center website: http://www.pewinternet.org/files/2015/04/PI_TeensandTech_Update2015_0409151.pdf

Lenhart, A., Kahne, J., Middaugh, E., Macgill, A., Evans, C., & Vitak, J. (2008). *Teens, video games and civics*. Retrieved from Pew Research Center website: http://www.pewInternet.org/2008/09/16/teens-video-games-and-civics/

Lenhart, A., Ling, R., Campbell, S., & Purcell, K. (2010). *Teens and mobile phones: Text messaging explodes as teens embrace it as the centerpiece of their communication strategies with friends*. Pew Research Center. Retrieved from http://pewinternet.org/Reports/2010/Teens-and-Mobile-Phones.aspx.

Lepper, M., & Henderlong, J. (2000). Turning "play" into "work" and "work" into "play": 25 years of research on intrinsic versus extrinsic motivation. In C. Sansone & J. Harackiewicz (Eds.), *Intrinsic and extrinsic motivation: The search for optimal motivation and performance* (pp. 257–307). San Diego, CA: Academic Press.

Lev Ari, L., & Shulman, S. (2013). Sleep, daily activities, and their association with mood states among emerging adults. *Biological Rhythm Research, 44*(3), 353–367. doi:10.1080/09291016.2012.692251

Levine, M. P., & Harrison, K. (2009). Effects of media on eating disorders and body image. In J. Bryant & M. B. Oliver (Eds.), *Media effects: Advances in theory and research* (3rd ed., pp. 490–516). New York, NY: Routledge.

Levinson, E. M., & Palmer, E. J. (2005, April). Preparing students with disabilities for school-to-work transition and postschool life. *Principal Leadership*, 11–15.

Levinson, L. (2009). *Evaluation summary: Main College Transitions Program, fiscal year 2008*. Retrieved from Maine Adult Education website: http://mct.maineadulted.org/news/article/2009/01/25/mct_evaluation_report_available

Levitt, M., Guacci-Franci, N., & Levitt, J. (1993). Convoys of social support in childhood and adolescence: Structure and function. *Developmental Psychology, 29*, 811–818.

Lilienfeld, S. O. (2007). Psychological treatments that cause harm. *Perspectives on Psychological Science, 2*, 53–70.

Lin, C. C. H., Hsiao, C. K., & Chen, W. J. (1999). Development of sustained attention assessed using the Continuous Performance Test among children 6–15 years of age. *Journal of Abnormal Child Psychology, 27*(5), 403–412.

Lindahl, R. A., & Cain, P. M., Sr. (2012). A study of school size among Alabama's public high schools. *International Journal of Education Policy and Leadership, 7*(1), 1–27.

Linver, M., Brooks-Gunn, J., & Kohen, D. E. (2002). Family processes as pathways from income to young children's development. *Developmental Psychology, 38*, 719–734.

Lippman, L., Atienza, A., Rivers, A., & Keith, J. (2008). *A developmental perspective on college and workplace readiness*. Bethesda: Child Trends.

Livingstone, S. (2014). Risk and harm on the Internet. In A. B. Jordan & D. Romer (Eds.), *Media and the well-being of children and adolescents* (pp.129–146). New York, NY: Oxford University Press.

Livson, N., & Peskin, H. (1980). Perspectives on adolescence from longitudinal research. In J. Adelson (Ed.), *Handbook of adolescent psychology* (pp. 47–98). New York, NY: Wiley.

López-Pérez, B., Gummerum, M., Keller, M., Filippova, E., & Gordillo, M. V. (2015). Sociomoral reasoning in children and adolescents from two collectivistic cultures. *European Journal of Developmental Psychology, 12*(2), 204–219.

Lorant, V., Deliege, D., Eaton, W., Robert, A., Philippot, P., & Ansseau, M. (2003). Socioeconomic inequalities in depression: A meta-analysis. *American Journal of Epidemiology, 157*(2), 98–112.

Losen, D. J., & Gillespie, J. (2012). *Opportunities suspended: The disparate impact of disciplinary exclusion from school*. Los Angeles, CA: UCLA, The Civil Rights Project.

Lounsbury, Mitchel, & Finkelhor, (2011). Prevalence and characteristics of youth sexting: A national study. *Pediatrics, 129*, 13–20.

Lubienski, S. T., & Lubienski, C. (2006). School sector and academic achievement: A multilevel analysis of NAEP mathematical data. *American Educational Research Journal, 43*(4), 651–698.

Lucas, S. R., & Berends, M. (2002). Sociodemographic diversity, correlated achievement, and de facto tracking. *Sociology of Education, 75*, 328–348.

Luu, T. M., Ment, L., Allan, W., Schneider, K., & Vohr, B. R. (2011). Executive and memory function in adolescents born very preterm. *Pediatrics, 127*, e639–e646.

Lyon, A., Charlesworth-Attie, S., Vander Stoep, A., & McCauley, E. (2011). Modular psychotherapy for youth with internalizing problems: Implementation with therapists in school-based health centers. *School Psychology Review, 40*, 569–581.

Mac Iver, D. J., & Epstein, J. L. (1991). Responsive practices in the middle grades: Teacher teams, advisory groups, remedial instruction, and school transition programs. *American Journal of Education, 99*(4), 587–622.

Maccoby, E. E. (2002). Gender and group process: A developmental perspective. *Current Directions in Psychological Science, 11*, 54–57.

MacLeod, J. (2009). *Ain't no makin' it: Aspirations and attainments in a low-income neighborhood*, 3rd ed. Boulder, CO: Westview Press.

Madden, M. (2013). *Teens haven't abandoned Facebook yet*. Retrieved from Pew Research Center website: http://www.pewInternet.org/2013/08/15/teens-havent-abandoned-facebook-yet/

Madden, M., Lenhart, A., Duggan, M. Cortesi, S., & Gasser, U. (2013). *Teens and technology*. Retrieved from Pew Research Center website: http://www.pewInternet.org/2013/03/13/teens-and-technology-2013/

Magdol, L., Moffitt, T. E., Caspi, A., & Silva, P. A. (1998). Developmental antecedents of partner abuse: a prospective-longitudinal study. *Journal of Abnormal Psychology, 107*, 375–389.

Magnusson, D., Stattin, H., & Allen, V. (1986). Differential maturation among girls and its relation to social adjustment in a longitudinal perspective. In P. Baltes, D. Featherman, & R. Lerner (Eds.), *Life span development and behavior* (Vol. 7, pp. 135–172). Hillsdale, NJ: Erlbaum.

Maher, J. P., Doerksen, S. E., Elavsky, S., Hyde, A. L., Pincus, A. L., Ram, N., & Conroy, D. E. (2013). A daily analysis of physical activity and satisfaction with life in emerging adults. *Health Psychology, 32*(6), 647–656. doi:10.1037/a0030129

Mahoney, J. S., Harris, A. L., & Eccles, J. S. (2008). Organized activity participation, positive youth development, and the over-scheduling hypothesis. *Social Policy Report, 20,* 1–30.

Maine Adult Education. (2014). *Maine College Transitions.* Retrieved from http://mct.maineadulted.org/

Malacad, B. L., & Hess, G. C. (2010). Oral sex: Behaviours and feelings of Canadian young women and implications for sex education. *European Journal of Contraception and Reproductive Health Care, 15,* 177–185.

Maltsberger, J. T. (1988). Suicide danger: Clinical estimation and decision. *Suicide and Life-Threatening Behavior, 18,* 47–54.

Manago, A. M. (2012). The new emerging adult in Chiapas, Mexico: Perceptions of traditional values and value change among first-generation Maya university students. *Journal of Adolescent Research, 27*(6), 663–713.

Marantz-Henig, R. (2010, August 18). What is it about 20-somethings? *New York Times Magazine.* Retrieved from http://www.nytimes.com/2010/08/22/magazine/22Adulthood-t.html?pagewanted=all&_r=0

Marcia, J. (1980). Identity in adolescence. In J. Adelson (Ed.), *Handbook of adolescent psychology* (pp. 159–187). New York: Wiley.

Marcia, J. E. (1966). Development and validation of ego-identity status. *Journal of Personality and Social Psychology, 3,* 551–558.

Marcia, J. E. (1993). The status of the statuses. In J. E. Marcia, A. S. Waterman, D. Matteson, S. Archer, & J. Orlofsky (Eds.), *Ego identity* (pp. 22–41). New York, NY: Springer-Verlag.

Marin, L. M., & Halpern, D. F. (2011). Pedagogy for developing critical thinking in adolescents: Explicit instruction produces greatest gains. *Thinking Skills and Creativity, 6*(1), 1–13. doi:10.1016/j.tsc.2010.08.002

Marks, G., Cresswell, J., & Ainley, J. (2006). Explaining socioeconomic inequalities in student achievement: The role of home and school factors. *Educational Research and Evaluation, 12*(2), 105–128.

Markstrom-Adams, C. (1989). Androgyny and its relation to adolescent psychological well-being: A review of the literature. *Sex Roles, 21,* 469–473.

Markus, H., & Nurius, P. (1986). Possible selves. *American Psychologist, 41,* 954–969.

Marsh, H. W., & Yeung, A. S. (1998). Longitudinal structural equation models of academic self-concept and achievement: Gender differences in the development of math and English constructs. *American Education Research Journal, 35,* 705–738.

Marsh, H. W., Byrne, B. M., & Shavelson, R. J. (1988). A multi-faceted academic self-concept: Its hierarchical structure and its relation to academic achievement. *Journal of Educational Psychology, 80,* 366–380.

Martens, A., Johns, M., Greenberg, J., & Schimel, J. (2006). Combating stereotype threat: The effect of self-affirmation on women's intellectual performance. *Journal of Experimental Social Psychology, 42,* 236–243.

Martin, A. J., Wilson, R., Liem, G. D., & Ginns, P. (2013). Academic momentum at university/college: Exploring the roles of prior learning, life experience, and ongoing performance in academic achievement across time. *Journal of Higher Education, 84*(5), 640–674.

Martin, J.A., Hamilton, B.E., & Ventura, S. J. (2013). *Births: Final data for 2012.* Hyattsville, MD: National Center for Health Statistics.

Martin, M., Bascoe, S., & Davies, P. (2011). Family relationships. In B. Brown & M. Prinstein (Eds.), *Encyclopedia of adolescence* (Vol. 2, pp. 84 – 94). New York, NY: Academic Press.

Martinez, G. M. & Abma, J. C. (2015). Sexual activity, contraceptive use, and childbearing of teenagers aged 15–19 in the United States. *NCHS Data Brief, 209.* Centers for Disease Control and Prevention. Retrieved from http://www.cdc.gov/nchs/data/databriefs/db209.htm

Martinez, G., Abma, J., & Casey C. (2010). *Educating teenagers about sex in the United States* (NCHS Data Brief No. 44). Hyattsville, MD: National Center for Health Statistics.

Marx, D. M., & Roman, J. S. (2002). Female role models: Protecting women's math test performance. *Personality and Social Psychology Bulletin, 28,* 1183–1193.

Masten, A. S., & Coatsworth, J. D. (1998). The development of competence in favorable and unfavorable environments. *American Psychologist, 53,* 205–220.

Masters, W. H., Johnson, V. E., & Kolodny, R. C. (1994). *Heterosexuality.* New York, NY: Harper-Collins.

Mastro, D. (2003). A social identity approach to understanding the impact of television messages. *Communication Monographs, 70,* 98–113.

Mastro, D. & Kopacz, M. (2006). Media representations of race, prototypicality and policy reasoning: An application of self-categorization theory. *Journal of Broadcasting and Electronic Media, 50,* 305–322.

Mastro, D., & Stern, S. (2003). Representation of race in television commercials: A content analysis of prime time advertising. *Journal of Broadcasting and Electronic Media, 47,* 638–647.

Mathews, J. (2009). *Work hard. Be nice.: How two inspired teachers created the most promising schools in America.* Chapel Hill, NC: Algonquin.

Matusov, E., & Hayes, R. (2000). Sociocultural critique of Piaget and Vygotsky. *New Ideas in Psychology, 18*(2–3), 215–239.

Mayer, R. E. (2012). Information processing. In C. B. McCormick, G. M. Sinatra, & J. Sweller (Eds.), *APA educational psychology handbooks* (Vol. 1, pp. 85–99). Washington, DC: American Psychological Association.

Mayeux, L., Sandstrom, M. J., & Cillessen, A. H. N. (2008). Is being popular a risky proposition? *Journal of Research on Adolescence, 18*, 49–74.

Mayo Clinic. (2013). *Teen drug abuse.* Retrieved from http://www.mayoclinic.com/health/teen-drug-abuse/My01099

Mayo Clinic. (2014). *How many hours of sleep are enough for good health?* Retrieved from http://www.mayoclinic.org/healthy-living/adult-health/expert-answers/how-many-hours-of-sleep-are-enough/faq-20057898

McCabe, K. M., Hough, R., Wood, P. A., & Yeh, M. (2001). Childhood and adolescent onset conduct disorder: A test of the developmental taxonomy. *Journal of Abnormal Child Psychology, 29*, 305–316.

McCaslin, M. & Good, T. L. (1992). The misalliance of management and instructional goals in current school reform. *Educational Researcher, 21*, 4–17.

McCaslin, M., & Murdock, T. B. (1991). The emergent interaction of home and school in the development of students' adaptive learning. In M. Maehr & P. Pintrich (Eds.), *Advances in motivation and achievement* (Vol. 7, pp. 213–259). Greenwich, CT: JAI Press.

McElhaney, K. B., Allen, J., Stephenson, C., & Hare, A. (2009). Attachment and autonomy during adolescence. In R. M. Lerner & L. Steinberg (Eds.), *Handbook of adolescent psychology* (3rd ed., pp. 358–403). Hoboken, NJ: Wiley.

McFarland, D. A. (2001). Student resistance: How the formal and informal organization of classrooms facilitate everyday forms of student defiance. *American Journal of Sociology, 107*, 612–678.

McGinley, M., Lipperman-Kreda, S., Byrnes, H. F., & Carlo, G. (2010). Parental, social and dispositional pathways to Israeli adolescents' volunteering. *Journal of Applied Developmental Psychology, 31*(5), 386–394.

McIntryre R. B., Paulson, R. M., & Lord, C. G. (2003). Alleviating women's mathematics stereotype threat through salience of group achievements. *Journal of Experimental Social Psychology, 39*, 83–90.

McKay, A., & Barrett, M (2010). Trends in teen pregnancy rates from 1996–2006: A comparison of Canada, Sweden, USA and England/Wales. *Canadian Journal of Human Sexuality, 19*(1–2), 43–52.

McLoyd, V. C., Kaplan, R., Purtell, K. M., Bagley, E., Hardaway, C. R., & Smalls, C. (2009). Poverty and socioeconomic disadvantage in adolescence. In R. M. Lerner & L. Steinberg (Eds.), *Handbook of adolescent psychology, Vol 2: Contextual influences on adolescent development* (3rd ed., pp. 444–491). Hoboken, NJ: John Wiley & Sons.

McNelles, L., & Connolly, J. (1999). Intimacy between adolescent friends: Age and gender differences in intimate affect and intimate behaviors. *Journal of Research on Adolescence, 9*, 143–159.

Meezan, W. (2005). Gay marriage, same-sex parenting, and America's children. *The Future of Children, 15*(2), 97–115.

Mehta, C. & Strough, J. (2009). Sex segregation in friendship and normative contexts across the life span. *Developmental Review, 29*, 201-201-220.

Melchoir, M., Chastang, J.-F., Head, J., Goldberg, M., Zins, M., Nabi, H., & Younes, N. (2013). Socioeconomic position predicts long-term depression trajectory: a 13–year follow-up of the GAZEL cohort study. *Molecular Psychiatry, 18*, 112–121.

Mendle, J., & Ferrero, J. (2012). Detrimental psychological outcomes associated with pubertal timing in adolescent boys. *Developmental Review, 32*, 49–66.

Mendle, J., Turkheimer, E., & Emery, R. E. (2007). Detrimental psychological outcomes associated with early pubertal timing in adolescent girls. *Developmental Review, 27*, 151–171.

Mensah, F. K., Bayer, J. K., Wake, M., Carlin, J. B., Allen, N. B., & Patton, G. C. (2013). Early puberty and childhood social and behavioral adjustment. *Journal of Adolescent Health, 53*, 118–124.

Merikangas, K. R. & Pine, D. (2002). Genetic and other vulnerability factors for anxiety and other disorders. In K. L. Davis, D. Charney, J. T. Coyle, & C. Nemeroff (Eds.), *Neuropsychopharmacology: The fifth generation of progress* (pp. 867–882). Brentwood, TN: American College of Neuropsychopharmacology.

Merten, D. E. (1997). The meaning of meanness: Popularity, competition, and conflict among junior high school girls. *Sociology of Education, 70*, 175–191.

Metz, K. (2010). Benefits of online courses in career and technical education. *Techniques: Connecting Education and Careers, 85*(6), 20–23.

Metzger, A., & Ferris, K. (2013). Adolescents' domain-specific judgments about different forms of civic involvement: Variations by age and gender. *Journal of Adolescence, 36*, 529–538.

Meyer, E. J. (2008). Gendered harassment in secondary schools: Understanding teachers' (non)interventions. *Gender and Education, 20*(6), 555–572.

Miami Dade Community College. (2014). *High school opportunities.* Retrieved from https://www.mdc.edu/asa/dual_enrollment.asp

Michaels, L. (Producer), & Waters, M. (Director). (2004). *Mean girls* [Motion picture]. United States: Paramount Pictures.

Midgley, C., & Edelin, K.C. (1998). Middle school reform and early adolescent well-being: The good news and the bad. *Educational Psychologist, 33*(4), 195–206.

Midgley, C., & Feldlaufer, H. (1987). Students' and teachers' decision-making fit before and after the transition to junior high school. *Journal of Early Adolescence, 7*(2), 225–241.

Midgley, C., Anderman, E. M., & Hicks, L. H. (1995). Differences between elementary and middle school teachers and students: A goal theory approach. *Journal of Early Adolescence, 15*(1), 90–113.

Midgley, C., Eccles, J. S., & Feldlaufer, H. (1991). Classroom environment and the transition to junior high school. In B. J. Fraser & H. J. Walberg (Eds.), *Educational environments: Evaluation, antecedents and consequences* (pp. 113–139). Elmsford, NY: Pergamon Press, Inc.

Midgley, C., Feldlaufer, H., & Eccles, J. S. (1988). The transition to junior high school: Beliefs of pre- and posttransition teachers. *Journal of Youth and Adolescence, 17*(6), 543–562.

Midgley, C., Middleton, M. J., Gheen, M. H., & Kumar, R. (2002). Stage-environment fit revisited: A goal theory approach to examining school transitions. In C. Midgley (Ed.), *Goals, goal structures, and patterns of adaptive learning* (pp. 109–142). Mahwah, NJ: Lawrence Erlbaum Associates.

Mikolajczyk, R. T., Iannotti, R. J., Farhat, T., & Thomas, V. (2012). Ethnic differences in perceptions of body satisfaction and body appearance among U.S. schoolchildren: a cross-sectional study. *BioMed Central Public Health, 12,* 425.

Milbrath, C., Ohlson, B., & Eyre, S. L. (2009). Analyzing cultural models in adolescents accounts of sexual relationships. *Journal of Research on Adolescence, 19,* 313–351.

Miller, A., Murdock, T., Anderman, E. M., & Poindexter, A. L. (2007). Who are all these cheaters? Characteristics of academically dishonest students. In E. M. Anderman & T. B. Murdock (Eds.), *Psychological perspectives on academic cheating* (pp. 9–32). San Diego, CA: Elsevier.

Miller, L. D., Gold, S., Laye-Gindhu, A., Martinez, Y. J., Yu, C. M., & Waechtler, V. (2011). Transporting a school-based intervention for social anxiety in Canadian adolescents. *Canadian Journal of Behavioural Science/Revue Canadienne Des Sciences Du Comportement, 43,* 287–296.

Millman, R. P., Working Group on Sleepiness in Adolescents/Young Adults, & AAP Committee on Adolescence. (2005). Excessive sleepiness in adolescents and young adults: Causes, consequences, and treatment strategies. *Pediatrics, 115,* 1774–1786.

MIT(n.d.). *Young Adult Development Project.* Retrieved from http://hrweb.mit.edu/worklife/youngadult/brain.html

Miyake, A., Kost-Smith, L. E., Finkelstein, N. D., Pollock, S. J., Cohen, G. L., & Ito, T. A. (2010). Reducing the gender achievement gap in college science: A classroom study of values affirmation. *Science, 330,* 1234–1237.

Moffitt, T. E. (1993). Adolescence-limited and life-course-persistent antisocial behavior: A developmental taxonomy. *Psychological Review, 100,* 674–701.

Moffitt, T. E. (2003). Life-course-persistent and adolescence-limited antisocial behavior: A 10–year research review and a research agenda. In B. B. Lahey, T. E. Moffitt, & A. Caspi (Eds.), *Causes of conduct disorder and juvenile delinquency* (pp. 49–75). New York, NY: Guilford.

Moffitt, T. E. (2006). Life-course persistent versus adolescence-limited antisocial behavior: Research review. In D. Cicchetti & D. J. Cohen (Eds.), *Developmental psychopathology, Vol. 3: Risk, disorder, and adaptation* (pp. 49–74). New York, NY: Wiley

Molloy, L., Gest, S., & Ruilson, K. (2011). Peer influences on academic motivation: Exploring multiple methods of assessing youth's most "influential" peer relationships. *Journal of Early Adolescence, 31*(1), 13–40.

Molock, S. D., & Barksdale, C. L. (2013). Relationship between religiosity and conduct problems among African American and Caucasian adolescents. *Journal of Child and Family Studies, 22,* 4–14.

Monahan, R. (2013). What happens when kids don't have Internet at home? *The Atlantic.* Retrieved from http://www.theatlantic.com/education/archive/2014/12/what-happens-when-kids-dont-have-internet-at-home/383680/

Monroe, S. M., Rohde, P., Seeley, J. R., & Lewinsohn, P. M. (1999). Life events and depression in adolescence: Relationship loss as a prospective risk factor for first onset of major depressive disorder. *Journal of Abnormal Psychology, 108,* 606–614.

Montgomery, K. C., Grier, S. A., Chester, J., & Dorfman, L. (2013). The digital food marketing landscape: Challenges for researchers. In J. D. Williams, et al. (Eds.), Advances in communication research to reduce childhood obesity (pp. 221–242). New York, NY: Springer.

Montgomery, M. J. (2005). Psychosocial intimacy and identity: From early adolescence to emerging adulthood. *Journal of Adolescent Research, 20,* 346–374.

Monto, M. A., & Carey, A. G. (2014). A new standard of sexual behavior? Are claims associated with the "hook up" culture supported by general social survey data? *Journal of Sex Research, 51,* 605–615.

Monto, M. A., & Dahmen, J. (2009). College success among students graduating from public and private high schools. *Journal of School Choice, 3*(3), 307–312.

Montt, G. (2011). Cross-national differences in educational achievement inequality. *Sociology of Education, 84,* 49–68.

Moody, J. (2001). Race, school integration, and friendship segregation in America. *American Journal of Sociology, 107,* 679–716. doi:10.1086/338954

Moore, K. E. S., & Rideout, V. (2007). The online marketing of food to children: Is it just fun and games? *Journal of Public Policy and Marketing, 26*(2), 202–220.

Moran, S., Kornhaber, M., & Gardner, H. (2006). Orchestrating multiple intelligences. *Educational Leadership, 64*(1), 22–27.

Moreno, R., Ozogul, G., & Reisslein, M. (2011). Teaching with concrete and abstract visual representations. *Journal of Educational Psychology, 103*(1), 32–47.

Morningstar, M. E., & Mazzotti, V. L. (2014). *Teacher preparation to deliver evidence-based transition planning and services to youth with disabilities* (Document No. IC-1). Retrieved from University of

Florida, Collaboration for Effective Educator Development, Accountability, and Reform Center website: http://ceedar.education.ufl.edu/tools/innovation-configuarations/

Mueller, C. M., & Dweck, C. S. (1998). Praise for intelligence can undermine children's motivation and performance. *Journal of Personality and Social Psychology, 75*(1), 33–52.

Murdock, T. B. (2000). Incorporating economic context into educational psychology: Methodological and conceptual challenges. *Educational Psychologist, 35*(2), 113–124.

Murdock, T. B., & Anderman, E. M. (2006). Motivational perspectives on student cheating: Toward an integrated model of academic dishonesty. *Educational Psychologist, 41*(3), 129–145.

Murphy, J. M., & Gilligan, C. (1994). Moral development in late adolescence and adulthood: A critique and reconstruction of Kohlberg's theory. In B. Puka (Ed.), *The great justice debate: Kohlberg criticism* (pp. 75–102). New York, NY: Garland Publishing.

Mwamwenda, T. S. (1993). Formal operations and academic achievement. *Journal of Psychology: Interdisciplinary and Applied, 127*(1), 99–103. doi:10.1080/00223980.1993.9915547

National Association of Anorexia Nervosa and Associated Disorders (2015). *Eating disorder statistics.* http://www.anad.org/get-information/about-eating-disorders/eating-disorders-statistics/. Retreived December 23, 2015.

National Cancer Institute. (2008). *The role of the media in promoting and educing tobacco use, smoking and tobacco control.* Retrieved from http://cancercontrol.cancer.gov/tcrb/monographs/19/m19_complete.pdf.

National Center for Education Statistics. (2006). *Career/technical education statistics.* Retrieved from https://nces.ed.gov/surveys/ctes/tables/h101.asp

National Center for Educational Statistics (2011). The condition of education, 2011. Washington.

National Center for Educational Statistics. (2011). *Digest of education statistics tables and figures.* Retrieved from http://nces.ed.gov/programs/digest/d12/tables/dt12_098.asp

National Center for Educational Statistics. (2012a). *Fast facts: Dropout rates.* Retrieved from http://nces.ed.gov/fastfacts/display.asp?id=16

National Center for Educational Statistics. (2012b). *The condition of education.* Washington, DC: National Center for Education Statistics/Institute of Education Sciences.

National Center for Educational Statistics. (2012c). *Fast facts: Public and private school comparison.* Retrieved from http://nces.ed.gov/fastfacts/display.asp?id=55

National Center for Educational Statistics. (2013). *Digest of education statistics.* Retrieved from https://nces.ed.gov/programs/digest/d13/tables/dt13_206.10.asp?current=yes

National Center for Education Statistics. (2012). *Trends among young adults over three decades, 1974–2006.* Washington, DC: Institute of Education Sciences.

National Center for Education Statistics. (2014). *Fast facts: Immediate transition to college.* Retrieved from https://nces.ed.gov/fastfacts/display.asp?id=51

National Center for Educational Statistics. (2013). The Nation's Report Card: Trends in Academic Progress 2012 (NCES 3013-456). National Center for Education Statistics, Institute of Education Sciences, U.S. Department of Education, Washington, DC. Retrieved from http://nces.ed.gov/nationssreportcard/

National Center for Health Statistics. (2001). *National vital statistics report.* Hyattsville, MD: Author.

National Eating Disorders Association. (n.d.). *Eating disorders affect us all.* Retrieved from http://www.nationaleatingdisorders.org/eating-disorders-affect-us-all

National Education Association. (2006). Research talking points on dropout statistics. Retrieved from http://www.nea.org/home/13579.htm

National Federation of State High School Associations. (2014). 2013–2014 High School Athletics Participation Survey. Retrieved from http://www.nfhs.org/ParticipationStatics/PDF/2013-14_Participation_Survey_PDF.pdf

National Heart, Lung, and Blood Institute, Growth and Health Study Research Group. (1992). Obesity and cardiovascular disease risk factors in Black and White girls: The NHLBI Growth and Health Study. *American Journal of Public Health, 82,* 1613–1620.

National Institutes of Health. (2015). *Death among children and adolescents.* Retrieved from http://www.nlm.nih.gov/medlineplus/ency/article/001915.htm.

National Opinion Research Center. (2011). *General Social Survey, 2011.* Chicago, IL: Author.

National Public Radio. (2012, July 12). How stereotypes can drive women to quit science. *All Things Considered.* Retrieved from http://www.npr.org/2012/07/12/156664337/stereotype-threat-why-women-quit-science-jobs

National Public Radio. (2013). *Are traumatized students disabled? A debate straight outta Compton.* Retrieved from http://www.npr.org/sections/ed/2015/08/20/432885473/are-traumatized-students-disabled-a-debate-straight-outta-compton

National Public Radio/Kaiser Family Foundation/Kennedy School of Government. (2013). *Sex education in America.* Retrieved from http://kff.org/hivaids/poll-finding/sex-education-in-america/

Nationwide Children's Hospital. (2010, February 1). Sexual minority youth bullied more than heterosexual youth. Retrieved from Science Daily website: http://www.sciencedaily.com/releases/2010/01/100127182503.htm

Natriello, G. (2016). Networked learning. In L. Corno & E. M. Anderman (Eds.), *Handbook of Educational Psychology,* 3rd ed. (pp. 337–348). New York: Routledge.

Neild, R. C., Stoner-Eby, S., & Furstenberg, F. (2008). Connecting entrance and departure: The transition to ninth grade and high school dropout. *Education and Urban Society, 40*(5), 543–569.

Nesi, J., & Prinstein, M. J. (2015). Using social media for social comparison and feedback-seeking: Gender and popularity moderate associations with depressive symptoms. *Journal of Abnormal Child Psychology, 43*(8), 1427–1438.

Newton, N. C., Teesson, M., Vogl, L. E., & Andrews, G. (2010). Internet-based prevention for alcohol and cannabis use: final results of the Climate Schools course. *Addiction, 105*(4), 749–759. doi:10.1111/j.1360–0443.2009.02853

Neymotin, F., & Downing-Matibag, T. M. (2013). Religiosity and adolescents' involvement with both drugs and sex. *Journal of Religion and Health, 52,* 550–569.

Ni, Y. (2010). The sorting effect of charter schools on student composition in traditional public schools. *Educational Policy, 26,* 215–242.

Niederdeppe, J., Davis, K. C., Farrelly, M. C., & Yaresevich, J. (2007). Stylistic features, need for sensation, and confirmed recall of national smoking prevention advertisements. *Journal of Communication, 57,* 272–292.

Nitzburg, G. C., & Farber, B. A. (2013). Putting up emotional (Facebook) walls? Attachment status and emerging adults' experiences of social networking sites. *Journal of Clinical Psychology, 69*(11), 1183–1190. doi:10.1002/jclp.22045

Nock, M. K., Kazdin, A. E., Hiripi, E., & Kessler, R. C. (2006). Prevalence, subtypes, and correlates of DSM-IV conduct disorder in the National Comorbidity Survey replication. *Psychological Medicine, 36,* 699–710.

Nolen-Hoeksema, S. (2001). Gender differences in depression. *Current Directions in Psychological Science,* 173–176.

Nolen-Hoeksema, S., & Girgus, J. S. (1994). The emergence of gender differences in depression during adolescence. *Psychological Bulletin, 115,* 424–443.

Noller, P. (2005). Sibling relationships in adolescence: Learning and growing together. *Personal Relationships, 12,* 1–22.

Norman, D. A. (1969). *Memory and attention.* New York, NY: John Wiley & Sons.

Nurmi, J., Poole, M. E., & Seginer, R. (1995). Tracks and transitions: A comparison of adolescent future-oriented goals, explorations, and commitments in Australia, Israel, and Finland. *International Journal of Psychology, 30*(3), 355–375.

Nye, B., Hedges, L. V., & Konstantopoulos, S. (2004). Do minorities experience larger lasting benefits from small classes? *Journal of Educational Research, 98*(2), 94–100.

O'Donnell, L., Stueve, A., O'Donnell, C., Duran, R., San Doval, A., Wilson, R., … Pleck, J. H. (2002). Long-term reductions in sexual initiation and sexual activity among urban middle schoolers in the Reach for Health service learning program. *Journal of Adolescent Health. 31,* 93–100.

O'Sullivan, L. F., Cheng, M. M., Harris, K. M., & Brooks-Gunn, J. (2007). I wanna hold your hand: The Progression of Social, Romantic and Sexual Events in Adolescent Relationships. *Perspectives of Sexual and Reproductive Health, 39,* 100–107.

Oakes, J. (2000). Grouping and tracking. In A. E. Kazdin, A. E. Kazdin (Eds.), *Encyclopedia of psychology, Vol. 4* (pp. 16–20). Washington, DC; New York, NY: American Psychological Association. doi:10.1037/10519-009

Office for National Statistics. (2012). *Young adults living with parents in the UK, 2011.* Retrieved from http://www.ons.gov.uk/ons/dcp171776_266357.pdf

Ogbu, J. U. (1992). Understanding cultural diversity and learning. *Educational Researcher, 21,* 5–14.

Ogden, C. L., Carroll, M. D., Kit, B. K., & Flegal, K. M. (2014). Prevalence of childhood and adult obesity in the United States, 2011-2012. *Journal of the American Medical Association, 311,* 806–814.

Ogden, C., Carroll, M., & Flegal, K. (2008). High body mass index for age among U.S. children and adolescents, 2003–2006. *Journal of the American Medical Association, 299,* 2401–2405.

Ohio State University. (2015). STEP. Retrieved from http://step.osu.edu

Ophir, E., Nass, C., & Wagner, W. D. (2009). Cognitive control in media multi-taskers. *Proceedings of the National Academy of the Sciences, 106,* 15583–15587.

Orfield, G., & Lee, C. (2006). *Racial transformation and the changing nature of segregation.* Cambridge, MA: Harvard University.

Orfield, G., Kuscera, J., & Siegel-Hawley, G. (2012). *E pluribus… separation: Deepening double segregation for more students.* Los Angeles, CA: UCLA, The Civil Rights Project.

Orr, E., & Ben-Eliahu, E. (1993). Gender differences in idiosyncratic sex-typed self- images and self-esteem. *Sex Roles, 29,* 271–296.

Orwin, R., Cadell, D., Chu, A., Kalton, G., Maklan, D., Morin, C., et al. (2004). Evaluation of the National Youth Anti-Drug Media Campaign: 2004 report of findings. Rockville, MD: Westat.

Osgood, D. W., Ragan, D. T., Wallace, L., Gest, S. D., Feinberg, M. E., & Moody, J. (2013). Peer and the emergence of alcohol use: Influence and selection processes in adolescent friendship networks, *Journal of Research on Adolescence, 23*(30), 500–512.

Ott, M. A., Ghani, N., McKenzie, F., Rosenberger, J. G., & Bell, D. L. (2012). Adolescent boys' first experiences of sex. *Culture, Health, and Sexuality: An International Journal for Research, Intervention, and Care, 14,* 781–793.

Oyserman, D. (2014). Identity-based motivation: Core processes and intervention examples. In S. Karabenick & T. C. Urdan (Eds.), *Advances in motivation and achievement* (Vol. 18). Bingley, England: Emerald.

Oyserman, D., Bybee, D., & Terry, K. (2006). Possible selves and academic outcomes: How and when possible selves impel action. *Journal of Personality and Social Psychology, 91*, 188–204.

Oyserman, D., Terry, K., & Bybee, D. (2002). A possible selves intervention to enhance school involvement. *Journal of Adolescence, 25*, 313–326.

Ozer, E. J. (2005). The impact of violence on urban adolescents: Longitudinal effects of perceived school connection and family support. *Journal of Adolescent Research, 20*, 167–192.

Padilla, A. M. (2006). Bicultural social development. *Hispanic Journal of Behavioral Sciences, 28*, 467–497.

Paik, H., & Comstock, G. (1994). The effects of television violence on anti-social behavior: A meta-analysis. *Communication Research, 21*, 516–546.

Pajares, F. (1997). Current directions in self-efficacy research. In P. R. Pintrich & M. L. Maehr (Eds.), *Advances in motivation and achievement* (Vol. 10, pp. 1–49). Greenwich, CT: JAI Press.

Pajares, F. (2005). Gender differences in mathematics self-efficacy beliefs. In A. M. Gallagher & J. C. Kaufman (Eds.), *Gender differences in mathematics: An integrative psychological approach* (pp. 294–315). New York: Cambridge University Press.

Pajares, F., & Valiante, G. (1999). Grade level and gender differences in the writing self-beliefs of middle school students. *Contemporary Educational Psychology, 24*, 390-405.

Palincsar, A. S., & Brown, A. L. (1984). Reciprocal teaching of comprehension-fostering and comprehension-monitoring activities. *Cognition and Instruction, 1*(2), 117–175.

Palincsar, A. S., & Brown, A. L. (1989). Instruction for self-regulated reading. In L. B. Resnick & L. E. Klopfer (Eds.), *Toward the thinking curriculum: Current cognitive research* (pp. 19–39). Alexandria, VA: ASCD.

Palmgreen, P., Donohew, L., Lorch, E. P., Hoyle, R. H., & Stephenson, M. T. (2001). Television campaigns and adolescent marijuana use: Tests of sensation seeking targeting. *American Journal of Public Health, 91*, 292–296.

Paris, S. G., & Flukes, J. (2005). Assessing children's metacognition about strategic reading. In S. E. Israel, C. C. Block, K. L. Bauserman, & K. Kinnucan-Welsch (Eds.), *Metacognition in literacy learning: Theory, assessment, instruction, and professional development* (pp. 121–139). Mahwah, NJ: Lawrence Erlbaum Associates.

Paris, S. G., Lipson, M.Y., & Wixson, K. K. (1983). Becoming a strategic reader. *Contemporary Educational Psychology, 8*(3), 293–316.

Parker, S., Nichter, M., Nichter, M., Vuckovic, N., Sims, C., & Ritenbaugh, C. (1995). Body image and weight concerns among African American and White adolescent females: Differences that make a difference. *Human Organization, 54*, 103–114.

Pascarella, E., Bohr, L., Nora, A., & Terenzini, P. (1995). Cognitive effects of 2-year and 4-year colleges: New evidence. *Educational Evaluation and Policy Analysis, 17*(1), 83–96.

Patrick, H., & Ryan, A., M. (2008). What do students think about when evaluating their classroom's mastery goal structure? An examination of young adolescents' explanations. *Journal of Experimental Education, 77*, 99–123.

Patrick, H., Kaplan, A., & Ryan, A.M. (2011). Positive classroom motivational environments: Convergence between mastery goal structure and the classroom social climate. *Journal of Educational Psychology, 103*, 367–382.

Patrick, H., Mantzicopoulos, P., & Sears, D. (2012). Effective classrooms. In K. R. Harris, S. Graham, & T. Urdan (Eds.), *APA educational psychology handbook. Volume 2: Individual differences and cultural and contextual factors* (pp. 443–469). Washington, DC: American Psychological Association.

Patrick, H., Mantzicopoulos, P., & Sears, D. (2012). Effective classrooms. In K. Harris, S. Graham, & T. Urdan (Eds.), *Educational psychology handbook, Vol. 2* (pp. 443–469). Washington DC: American Psychological Association Publications.

Patton, G. C., Glover, S., Bond, L. L., Butler, H., Godfrey, C., Pietro, G., & Bowes, G. (2000). The Gatehouse Project: A systematic approach to mental health promotion in secondary schools. *Australian & New Zealand Journal of Psychiatry, 34*(4), 586–593.

Paul, E. L., & Hayes, A. (2002). The casualties of "casual" sex: A qualitative exploration of the phenomenology of college students' hookups. *Journal of Social and Personal Relationships, 19*, 639–661.

Paul, E. L., McManus, B., & Hayes, A. (2000). "Hook-ups": Characteristics and correlates of college students' spontaneous and anonymous sexual experiences. *Journal of Sex Research, 37*, 76–88.

Pawlby, S. J., Mills, A., & Quinton, D. (1997). Vulnerable adolescent girls: Opposite-sex relationships. *Journal of Child Psychology and Psychiatry, 38*, 909–920.

Pazol, K., Gamble, S. B., Parker, W.Y., Cook, D. A., Zane, S. B., & Hamdan, S. (2009). *Abortion surveillance, United States—2006.* Retrieved from CDC website: http://www.cdc.gov/mmwr/preview/mmwrhtml/ss5808a1.htm?s_cid=ss5808a1_e

Pechmann, C., Zhao, G., Goldberg, M. E., & Reibling, E. T. (2003). What to convey in antismoking advertisements for adolescents: The use of protection motivation theory to identify effective message themes. *Journal of Marketing, 67*, 1–18.

Peebles, R., Wilson, J. L., Borzekowski, D. L. G., Hardy, K. K., Lock, J. D., Mann, J. R., & Lift, I. L. (2012). Disordered eating in a digital age: Eating behaviors, health, and quality of life in users of websites with pro-eating disorder content. *Journal of Medical Internet Research, 14*(5), e148.

Pekrun, R., Cusak, A., Murayama, K., Elliot, A., & Thomas, K. (2014). The power of anticipated feedback: Effects on students' achievement goals and achievement emotions. *Learning and Instruction, 29,* 115–124. doi:10.1016/jlearninstruc.2013.09.002

Pellegrini, A. D., & Long, J. D. (2002). A longitudinal study of bullying, dominance, and victimization during the transition from primary school through secondary school. *British Journal of Developmental Psychology, 20,* 259–280.

Pepler, D. J., Craig, W. M., Connolly, J. A., Yuile, A., McMaster, L., & Jiang, D. (2006). A developmental perspective on bullying. *Aggressive Behavior, 32,* 376–384.

Perry, L. B., & McConney, A. (2010). Does the SES of the school matter? An examination of socioeconomic status and student achievement using PISA 2003. *Teachers College Record, 112*(4), 1137–1162.

Peskin, H. (1973). Influence of the developmental schedule of puberty on learning and ego functioning. *Journal of Youth and Adolescence, 2,* 273–290.

Peterson, P. E., & Llaudet, E. (2007). The NCES private-public school study: Findings are other than they seem. *Education Next, 7*(1), 75–79.

Pew Charitable Trusts. (2010). Collateral costs: Incarceration's effect on economic mobility. Washington, DC: Author.

Pew Hispanic Center. (2009). *Between two worlds: How young Latinos come of age in America.* Washington, DC: Author.

Pew Internet Research Center. (2013). *How teachers are using technology at home and in their classrooms.* Retrieved from: http://www.pewinternet.org/2013/02/28/how-teachers-are-using-technology-at-home-and-in-their-classrooms/

Pew Research Center. (2010). *Religion among the millennials.* Retrieved from http://www.pewforum.org/2010/02/17/religion-among-the-millennials/

Pew Research Center. (2015). Raising Kids and Running a Household: How Working Parents Share the Load.

Pharris-Ciurej, N., Hirschman, C., & Willhoft, J. (2012). The 9th grade shock and the high school dropout crisis. *Social Science Research, 41,* 709–730.

Phelan, P., Davidson, A. L., & Cao, H. T. (1991). Students' multiple worlds: Negotiating the boundaries of family, peer, and school cultures. *Anthropology and Education Quarterly, 22,* 224–250.

Phelan, P., Yu, H. C., & Davidson, A. L. (1994). Navigating the psychosocial pressures of adolescence: The voices and experiences of high school youth. *American Educational Research Journal, 31,* 415–447.

Phillips, J. L., Shiffrin, R. M., & Atkinson, R. C. (1967) Effects of list length on short-term memory. *Journal of Verbal Learning & Verbal Behavior, 6*(3), 303–311.

Phinney, J. (1990). Ethnic identity in adolescents and adults: A review of research. *Psychological Bulletin, 108,* 499–514.

Phinney, J. S. (1989). Stages of ethnic identity development in minority group adolescents. *Journal of Early Adolescence, 9,* 34–49.

Phinney, J. S. (1992). The Multigroup Ethnic Identity Measure: A new scale for use with diverse groups. *Journal of Adolescent Research, 7*(2), 156–176.

Phinney, J. S. (1996). When we talk about American ethnic groups, what do we mean? *American Psychologist, 51,* 918–927.

Phinney, J. S. (2003). Ethnic identity and acculturation. In K. M. Chun, P. B. Organista, & G. Marín (Eds.), *Acculturation: Advances in theory, measurement, and applied research* (pp. 63–82). Washington, DC: American Psychological Association.

Phinney, J. S. & Devich-Navarro, B. (1997). Variations in bicultural identification among African American and Mexican American adolescents. *Journal of Research on Adolescence, 7,* 3–32.

Phinney, V. G., Jensen, L. C., Olsen, J. A., & Cundick, B. (1990). The relationship between early development and psychosexual behaviors in adolescent females. *Adolescence, 25,* 321–332.

Piaget, J. (1929). *The child's conception of the world.* London, England: Routledge & Kegan Paul.

Piaget, J. (1952). *The origin of intelligence in children.* New York, NY: International Universities Press.

Piaget, J. (1954). *The construction of reality in the child.* New York, NY: Basic Books.

Piaget, J. (1972). Intellectual evolution from adolescence to adulthood. *Human Development, 15,* 1–12.

Piaget, J. (2008). Intellectual evolution from adolescence to adulthood. *Human Development, 51*(1), 40–47.

Piaget, J. & Inhelder, B. (1969). *The psychology of the child* (H. Weaver translation). New York: Basic Books. (Originally published in 1966).

Piaget, J., & Inhelder, B. (1973). *Memory and intelligence.* London, England: Routledge & Kegan Paul.

Pianta, R. C., & Hamre, B. K. (2009). Conceptualization, measurement, and improvement of classroom processes: Standardized observation can leverage capacity. *Educational Researcher, 38*(2), 109–119.

Pianta, R. C., Hamre, B. K., & Mintz, S. (2010). Classroom Assessment Scoring System (CLASS) Manual: Upper Elementary. University of Virginia, Charlottesville, VA.

Pintrich, P. R., & Schunk, D. H. (2002). *Motivation in education: Theory, research, and applications.*

Pittman, L. D., & Richmond, A. (2008). University belonging, friendship quality, and psychological adjustment during the transition to college. *Journal of Experimental Education, 76*(4), 343–361.

Pollack, E. (2013, October 3). Why are there still so few women in science? *New York Times.* Retrieved from http://www.nytimes.com/2013/10/06/magazine/why-are-there-still-so-few-women-in-science.html?_r=0

Pomerantz, E. M., & Kim, E. M., & Cheung, C. S. (2011). Parents' involvement in children's learning. In K. Harris, S. Graham, & T. Urdan (Eds.), *Educational psychology handbook* (pp. 417–440). Washington DC: American Psychological Association Publications.

Pomerantz, E. M., & Wang, Q. (2009). The role of parental control in children's development in Western and East Asian countries. *Current Directions in Psychological Science, 18,* 285–289.

Pomerantz, E. M., Moorman, E. A., & Litwack, S. D. (2007). The how, whom, and why of parents' involvement in children's academic lives: More is not always better. *Review of Educational Research, 77*(3), 373–410.

Pomerantz, E. M., Ng, F. F., & Wang, Q. (2006). Mothers' mastery-oriented involvement in children's homework: Implications for the well-being of children with negative perceptions of competence. *Journal of Educational Psychology, 98,* 99–111.

Pomerantz, E. M., Ng, F. F., Cheung, C. S., & Qu, Y. (2014). Raising happy children who succeed in school: Lessons from China and the United States. *Child Development Perspectives, 2,* 71–76.

Portes, A., & Fernandez-Kelly, P. (2008). No margin for error: Educational and occupational achievement among disadvantaged children of immigrants. *Annals of the American Academy of Political and Social Science, 620,* 12–36.

Portes, A., & Rumbaut, R. G. (1996). *Immigrant America: A portrait.* Berkeley, CA: University of California Press.

Portes, A., & Rumbaut, R. G. (2001). *Legacies: The story of the immigrant second generation.* New York, NY: Russell Sage Foundation.

Portes, A., & Schauffler, R. (1996). Language and the Second generation: Bilingualism yesterday and today. In A. Portes (Ed.), *The new second generation* (pp. 8–29). New York, NY: Russell Sage Foundation.

Portes, A., & Zhou, M. (1993). The new second generation: Segmented assimilation and its variants. *Annals of the American Academy of Political and Social Sciences, 530,* 74–96.

Poteat, V. P., & Rivers, I. (2010). The use of homophobic language across bullying roles during adolescence. *Journal of Applied Developmental Psychology, 31*(2), 166–172.

Poteat, V. P., O'Dwyer, L. M., & Mereish, E. H. (2012). Changes in how students use and are called homophobic epithets over time: Patterns predicted by gender, bullying and victimization status. *Journal of Educational Psychology, 104,* 393–406.

Potkin, K. T., & Bunney, W. E., Jr. (2012). Sleep improves memory: The effect of sleep on long term memory in early adolescence. *PLoS ONE, 7.*

Potter, D. (2010). Psychosocial well-being and the relationship between divorce and children's academic achievement. *Journal of Marriage and Family, 72,* 933–946.

Pressley, M., & McCormick, C. B. (1995). *Cognition, teaching, and assessment.* New York, NY: Harper Collins College.

Pressley, M., Roehrig, A. D., Raphael, L. M., Dolezal, S. E., Bohn, C., Mohan, L., et al. (2003). Teaching processes in elementary and secondary education. In W. M. Reynolds & G. E. Miller (Eds.), *Handbook of psychology, Volume 7: Educational psychology* (pp. 153– 175). New York, NY: John Wiley.

Prot, S., Anderson, C. A., Gentile, D. A., Brown S. L., & Swing, E. L. (2014). The positive and negative effects of video game play. In A. B. Jordan & D. Romer (Eds.), *Media and the well-being of children and adolescents* (pp. 109–128). New York, NY: Oxford University Press.

Pulfrey, C., Darnon, C., & Butera, F. (2013). Autonomy and task performance: Explaining the impact of grades on intrinsic motivation. *Journal of Educational Psychology, 105,* 39–57. doi:10.1037/a0029376

Purcell, K., Rainie, L., Heaps, A., Buchanan, J., Friedrich, L., Jacklin, A., … Zickhur, K. (2012). *How teens do research in the digital world.* Retrieved from Pew Research Center website: http://www.pewInternet .org/2012/11/01/how-teens-do-research-in-the-digital-world/

Qin, D. B. (2006). "Our child doesn't talk to us anymore": Alienation in immigrant Chinese families. *Anthropology and Education Quarterly, 37,* 162–179.

Quintana, S. M. (1998). Development of children's understanding of ethnicity and race. *Applied and Preventive Psychology: Current Scientific Perspectives, 7,* 27–45.

Raine, A., Moffitt, T. E., Caspi, A., Loeber, R., Stouthamer-Loeber, M., & Lynam, D. (2005). Neurocognitive impairments in boys on the life-course persistent antisocial path. *Journal of Abnormal Psychology, 114,* 38–49.

Ramdass, D., & Zimmerman, B. J. (2011a). Developing self-regulation skills: The important role of homework. *Journal of Advanced Academics, 22,* 194–218.

Ramdass, D., & Zimmerman, B. J. (2011b). The effects of modeling and social feedback on middle school students' math performance and accuracy judgments. *International Journal of Educational and Psychological Assessment, 7,* 4–23.

Ramos, E., Frontera, W. R., Llopart, A., & Feliciano, D. (1998). Muscle strength and hormonal levels in adolescence: Gender related differences. *International Journal of Sports Medicine, 19,* 526–531.

Randler, C. (2008). Morningness-eveningness and satisfaction with life. *Social Indicators Research, 86,* 297–302.

Ransdell, S. (2012). There's still no free lunch: Poverty as a composite of SES predicts school-level reading comprehension. *American Behavioral Scientist, 56,* 908–925.

Raver, C. C., Gershoff, E. T., & Aber, J. L. (2007). Testing equivalence of mediating models of income, parenting, and school readiness for White, Black, and Hispanic children in a national sample. *Child Development, 78*(1), 96–115.

Regan, P. C., Durvasula, R., Howell, L., Ureno, O., & Rea, M. (2004). Gender, ethnicity, and the developmental timing of first sexual and romantic experiences. *Social Behavior & Personality, 32*, 667–676.

Reichert, T., & Carpenter, C. (2004). An update on sex in magazine advertising: 1983–2003. *Journalism and Mass Communication Quarterly, 81*, 823–837.

Ribble, M. (2009). *Raising a digital child*. Washington, DC: International Society for Technology in Education.

Ribble, M. (2011). *Digital citizenship in the schools* (2nd ed.). Washington, DC: International Society for Technology in Education.

Richards, M., & Larson, R. (1993). Pubertal development and the daily subjective states of young adolescents. *Journal of Research on Adolescence, 3*, 145–169.

Rickert, V. I., & Wiemann, C. M. (1998). Date rape among adolescents and young adults. *Journal of Pediatric and Adolescent Gynecology, 11*, 167–175.

Rideout, V. J., Foehr, U. G., & Roberts, D. F. (2005). *Generation M²: Media in the lives of 8- to 18-year-olds*. Menlo Park, CA: Kaiser Family Foundation.

Rideout, V. J., Foehr, U. G., and Roberts, D. F. (2010). *Generation M²: Media in the lives of 8- to 18-year-olds*. Retrieved from Kaiser Family Foundation website: http://kff.org/other/poll-finding/report-generation-m2-media-in-the-lives/

Rivas-Drake, D., Hughes, D., & Way, N. (2008). A closer look at peer discrimination ethnic identity, and psychological well-being among urban Chinese American sixth graders." *Journal of Youth and Adolescence, 37*(1), 12–21.

Robbins, C. L., Schick, V., Reece, M., Herbenick, D., Sanders, S. A., Dodge, B., & Fortenberry, J. D. (2011). Prevalence, frequency, and associations of masturbation with partnered sexual behaviors among U.S. adolescents. *Archives of Pediatrics and Adolescent Medicine, 12*, 1087–1093.

Roberts, D. F., Henriksen, L., & Foehr, U. G. (2009). Adolescence, adolescents and the media. In R. M. Lerner & L. Steinberg (Eds.), *Handbook of adolescent psychology* (3rd ed.). Hoboken, NJ: John Wiley & Sons.

Roberts, R. E., Roberts, C. R. & Chen, Y. R. (1997). Ethnocultural differences in prevalence of adolescent depression. *American Journal of Community Psychology, 25*, 95–110.

Robins, R. W., & Trzesniewski, K. H. (2005). Self-esteem development across the lifespan. *Current Directions in Psychological Science, 14*, 158–162.

Rockquemore, K. A., & Brunsma, D. L. (2002). *Beyond Black: Biracial identity in America*. Thousand Oaks, CA: Sage.

Roderick, M., Coca, V., Moeller, E., Kelley-Kemple, T., & Consortium on Chicago Schools. (2013). *From high school to the future: The challenge of senior year in Chicago Public Schools* (Research report, Consortium on Chicago School Research). Retrieved from https://consortium.uchicago.edu/publications/high-school-future-challenge-senior-year-chicago-public-schools

Rodota, J. (2014). California's Self-Esteem Commission was no joke. Retrieved from http://www.zocolopublicsquare.org/2014/05/30/californias-self-esteem-commission-was-not-a-joke/chronicles/who-we-were/

Rogoff, B. (1990). *Apprenticeship in thinking: Cognitive development in social context*. New York, NY: Oxford University Press.

Rohrer, D., & Taylor, K. (2006). The effects of overlearning and distributed practise on the retention of mathematics knowledge. *Applied Cognitive Psychology, 20*, 1209–1224.

Rohrer, D., Taylor, K., Pashler, H., Wixted, J. T., & Cepeda, N. J. (2005). The effect of overlearning on long-term retention. *Applied Cognitive Psychology, 19*, 361–374.

Roisman, G. I., & Fraley, R. C. (2012). The legacy of early interpersonal experience. In J. B. Benson (Ed.), *Advances in child development and behavior* (Vol. 42, pp. 79–112). Burlington, MA: Academic Press.

Roisman, G.I., & Groh, A.M. (2011). Attachment theory and research in developmental psychology: An overview and appreciative critique. In M.K. Underwood & L.H. Rosen (Eds.), *Social development: Relationships in infancy, childhood, and adolescence.* (pp. 101–126). New York: Guilford.

Root, M. (1998). Experiences and processes affecting racial identity development: Preliminary results from the Biracial Sibling Project. *Cultural Diversity and Mental Health, 4*, 237–247.

Roscigno, V. J., & Crowley, M. L. (2001). Rurality, institutional disadvantage, and achievement/attainment. *Rural Sociology, 66*, 268–292.

Rose, A. J., & Rudolph, K. D. (2006). A review of sex differences in peer relationship processes: Potential trade-offs for the emotional and behavioral development of girls and boys. *Psychological Bulletin, 132*, 98–131.

Rose, A. J., & Swenson, L. P. (2009). Do perceived popular adolescents who regress against others experience emotional adjustment problems themselves? *Developmental Psychology, 45*, 868–872.

Rose, A. J., Swenson, L. P., & Waller, E. M. (2004). Overt and relational aggression and perceived popularity: Developmental differences in concurrent and prospective relations. *Developmental Psychology, 40, 378–387.*

Rose, C. A., Forber-Pratt, A. J., Espelage, D. L., & Aragon, S. R. (2013). The influence of psychosocial factors on bullying involvement of students with disabilities. *Theory into Practice, 52*(4), 272–279.

Rose, C. A., Monda-Amaya, L. E., & Espelage, D. L. (2011). Bullying perpetration and victimization in special education: A review of the literature. *Remedial and Special Education, 32*, 114–130.

Rosenbaum, J. E., & Becker, K. (2011). The early college challenge: Navigating disadvantaged students' transition to college. *American Educator, 35*(3), 14–20.

Rosenberg, M. (1986). Self-concept from middle childhood through adolescence. In J. Suls & A. G. Greenwald (Eds.), *Psychological perspectives on the self* (Vol. 3, pp. 107–135). Hillsdale, NJ: Erlbaum.

Rosenberg, M. (1989). *Society and the adolescent self-image* (Rev. ed.). Middletown, CT: Wesleyan University Press.

Rosenberg, M., Schooler, C., Schoenbach, C., & Rosenberg, F. (1995). Global self-esteem and specific self-esteem: Different concepts, different outcomes. *American Sociological Review, 60*, 141–156.

Rosenberg, P. S., Biggar, R. J., & Goedert, J. J. (1994). Declining age at HIV infection in the United States. *New England Journal of Medicine, 330*, 789–790.

Rosenbloom, S. R., & Way, N. (2004). Experiences of discrimination among African American, Asian American, and Latino adolescents in an urban high school. *Youth and Society, 35*, 420–541.

Rosenfeld, M. J. (2010). Nontraditional families and childhood progress through school. *Demography, 47*(3), 755–775.

Rosenshine, B., & Meister, C. (1994). Reciprocal teaching: A review of the research. *Review of Educational Research, 64*(4), 479–530.

Rosenthal, S., Feiring, C., & Lewis, M. (1998). Political volunteering from late adolescence to young adulthood: Patterns and predictors. *Journal of Social Issues, 54*(3), 477–493.

Rostosky, S. S., Danner, F., & Riggle, E. D. B. (2008). Religiosity and alcohol use in sexual minority and heterosexual youth and young adults. *Journal of Youth and Adolescence, 37*, 552–563.

Rothi, D. M., Leavey, G., & Best, R. (2008). On the front-line: Teachers as active observers of pupils' mental health. *Teaching and Teacher Education: An International Journal of Research and Studies, 24*(5), 1217–1231.

Rowley, S. J., Kurtz-Costes, B., & Cooper, S. M. (2010). The schooling of African American children. In J. L. Meece & J. S. Eccles (Eds.), *Handbook of research on schools, schooling, and human development* (pp. 275–292). New York, NY: Routledge.

Rubin, K. H., Bukowski, W. M., & Bowker, J. C. (2014). Children in peer groups. *Handbook of Child Psychology, 41*, 138–149.

Ruble, D. N., Martin, C. L., & Berenbaum, S. (2006). Gender development. In W. Damon & R. M. Lerner (Series Eds.) & N. Eisenberg (Volume Ed.), *Handbook of child psychology, Vol. 3: Social, emotional, and personality development* (pp. 858–932). New York, NY: Wiley.

Ruble, D., & Brooks-Gunn, J. (1982). The experience of menarche. *Child Development, 53*, 1557–1566.

Rudd Center for Food Policy & Obesity. (2012). *Trends in television food advertising to young people: 2011 update. Rudd report*. Retrieved from http://www.yaleruddcenter.org/briefs.aspx

Ruff, L. A. (2011). Successful transitions to higher education: A look at Maine's college transitions initiative. *Adult Basic Education and Literacy Journal, 5*(3), 182–185.

Rumbaut, R. (1997) *Passages to adulthood: The Adaptation of children of immigrants in Southern California.* Report to the Russell Sage Foundation.

Rumberger, R. W. (1995). Dropping out of middle school: A multilevel analysis of students and schools. *American Educational Research Journal, 32*(3), 583–625.

Rumberger, R. W., & Palardy, G. J. (2005). Does segregation still matter? The impact of student composition on academic achievement in high school. *Teachers College Record, 107*, 199–2045.

Ryan, A. M. (2001). The peer group as a context for the development of young adolescent motivation and achievement. *Child Development, 72*, 1135–1150.

Ryan, A. M., Kuusinen, C., & Bedoya-Skoog, A. (2015). Managing peer relations: A dimension of teacher self-efficacy that varies between elementary and middle school teachers and is associated with observed classroom quality. *Contemporary Educational Psychology, 41*, 147–156. doi:10.1016/j.cedpsych.2015.01.002

Ryan, A. M. (2001). The peer group as a context for the development of young adolescents' motivation and achievement. *Child Development, 72*, 1135–1150.

Ryan, K., Meredith, K., & David, R. S. (2010). The military and the transition to adulthood. *The Future of Children, 20*(1), 181–207.

Ryan, R. M., & Deci, E. L. (2000). Self-determination theory and the facilitation of intrinsic motivation, social development and well-being. *American Psychologist, 55*, 68–78.

Samet, N. R., & Kelly, E. W. (1987). The relationship of steady dating to self-esteem and sex role identity among adolescents. *Adolescence, 22*, 231–245.

Sana, F., Weston, T., & Cepeda, N. J. (2013). Laptop multitasking hinders classroom learning for both users and nearby peers. *Computers & Education, 62*, 24–31.

Sanchez, B., Esparza, P., Colon, Y., & Davis, K. E. (2010). Tryin' to make it during the transition from high school: The role of family obligation attitudes and economic context for Latino-emerging adults. *Journal of Adolescent Research, 25*(6), 858–884.

Sandstrom, M. J. (2011). The power of popularity: Influence processes in childhood and adolescence. In A. H. N. Cillessen, D. Schwartz, & L. Mayeaux (Eds.), *Popularity in the Peer System* (pp. 219–244). New York: NY: Guilford Press.

Sandstrom, M. J., & Cillessen, A. H. N. (2010). Life after high school: Adjustment of popular teens in emerging adulthood. *Merrill-Palmer Quarterly, 56*, 474–499.

Saraceni, R., & Russell-Mayhew, S. (2007). Cultural expectations of thinness in women: A partial replication and update of magazine content. *Eating and Weight Disorders, 12*, e68–e74.

Saulney, S. (2011, March 24). Census data presents rise in multiracial population of youths. *New York Times*. Retrieved from http://www.nytimes.com/2011/03/25/us/25race.html?_r=1

Savin-Williams, R. C. (1994). Verbal and physical abuse as stressors in the lives of lesbian, gay male, and bisexual youths: Associations with school problems, running away, substance abuse, prostitution, and suicide. *Journal of Consulting and Clinical Psychology, 62*, 261–269.

Savin-Williams, R. C. (2009). *The new gay teenager.* Cambridge, MA: Harvard University Press.

Savin-Williams, R. C. (2010, November 11). The gay kids are all right. *Good Men Project Magazine*. Retrieved from http://goodmenproject.com/2010/11/11/the-gay-kids-are-all-right/

Savin-Williams, R. C., Cohen, K. M., Joyner, K., & Rieger, G. (2010). Depressive symptoms among same-sex oriented young men: Importance of reference group. *Archives of Sexual Behavior, 39*, 1213–1215.

Sax, L. (2005). *Why gender matters:* New York, NY: Random House.

Scabini, E., Marta, E., & Lanz, M. (2006). *The transition to adulthood and family relations: An intergenerational perspective.* New York, NY: Psychology Press.

Scharf, M., Mayseless, O., & Kivenson-Baron, I. (2011). Leaving the parental nest: Adjustment problems, attachment representations, and social support during the transition from high school to military service. *Journal of Clinical Child and Adolescent Psychology, 40*(3), 411–423.

Scharrer, E. (2004). Virtual violence: Gender and aggression in video game advertisements. *Mass Communication and Society, 7*, 393–412.

Scharrer, E., & Leone, R. (2008). First-person shooters and the third-person effect. *Human Communication Research, 34*, 210–233.

Schlegal, A., & Barry, H. (1991). *Adolescence: An anthropological inquiry.* New York, NY: Free Press.

Schlegal, A., & Hewlett, B. L. (2011). Contributions of anthropology to the study of adolescence. *Journal of Research on Adolescence, 21*, 281–289.

Schleicher, A. (2006). Where immigrant students succeed: A comparative review of performance and engagement in PISA 2003. *Intercultural Education, 17*, 507–516.

Schmidt, J. A., Shumow, L., & Kackar, H. (2007). Adolescents' participation in service activities and its impact on academic, behavioral, and civic outcomes. *Journal of Youth and Adolescence, 36*(2), 127–140.

Schneider, W. (2010). Metacognition and memory development in childhood and adolescence. In H. S. Waters & W. Schneider (Eds.), *Metacognition, strategy use, and instruction* (pp. 54–81). New York, NY: Guilford Press.

Scholastic. (2013). *Kids and family reading report, 4th edition.* Retrieved from: http://mediaroom.scholastic.com/kfrr.

Scholnick, E. K., Nelson, K., Gelman, S. A., & Miller, P. H. (1999). *Conceptual development: Piaget's legacy.* Mahwah, NJ: Lawrence Erlbaum Associates.

Scholte, R. H. J., Engels, R., Overbeek, G., Kemp, R., & Haselager, G. (2007). Stability in bullying and victimization and its association with social adjustment in childhood and adolescence. *Journal of Abnormal Child Psychology, 35*, 217–228.

Schoppe-Sullivan, S. J., Schermerhorn, A. C., & Cummings, M. E. (2007). Marital conflict and children's adjustment: Evaluation of the parenting process model. *Journal of Marriage and Family, 69*, 1118–1134.

Schraw, G. (2006). Knowledge, structures and processes. In P. A. Alexander & P. H. Winne (Eds.), *Handbook of educational psychology* (2nd ed., pp. 245–263). Mahwah, NJ: Lawrence Erlbaum Associates.

Schunk, D. H., & Swartz, C. W. (1993). Goals and progress feedback: Effects on self-efficacy and writing achievement. *Contemporary Educational Psychology, 18*, 337–354.

Schunk, D. H., Meece, J. L. & Pintrich, P. R. (2014). *Motivation in education: Theory, research, and applications* (4th ed.). Englewood Cliffs, NJ: Merrill Prentice-Hall.

Schwartz, K. (2008). Adolescent brain development: An oxymoron no longer. *Journal of Youth Ministry, 6*, 85–93.

Schweber, N., Barker, K., & Grant, J. (2014, October 19). Football players in Sayreville, N.J. recall hazing. *New York Times*. Retrieved from http://www.nytimes.com/2014/10/20/nyregion/in-new-jersey-young-players-recall-hazing.html?_r=0

Scruggs, T. E., Mastropieri, M. A., Berkeley, S. L., & Marshak, L. (2010). Mnemonic strategies: Evidence-based practice and practice-based evidence. *Intervention in School and Clinic, 46*(2), 79–86.

Seligman, M. E. P., Peterson, C., Kaslow, N. J., Tanenbaum, R. L., Alloy, L. B., & Abramson, L. Y. (1984). Attributional style and depressive symptoms among children. *Journal of Abnormal Psychology, 93*, 235–238.

Seligman, M. P. (2011). *Learned optimism: How to change your mind and your life.* New York, NY: Vintage.

Sellers, R. M., Smith, M. A., Shelton, J. N., Rowley, S. J., & Chavous, T M. (1998). Multidimensional model of racial identity: A reconceptualization of African American racial identity. *Personality and Social Psychology Review, 2*, 18–36.

Selman, R. (1976). Social-cognitive understanding. In T. Lickona (Ed.), *Moral development and behavior* (pp. 219–316). New York, NY: Holt, Rinehart, & Winston.

Selman, R. (1980). *The growth of interpersonal understanding: Development and clinical analyses.* New York, NY: Academic Press.

Selman, R. (1981). The child as a friendship philosopher. In S. R. Asher & J. M. Gottman (Eds.), *The development of children's friendships* (pp. 242–272). Cambridge, England: Cambridge University Press.

Selman, R., & Byrne, D. (1974). A structural developmental analysis of levels of role-taking in middle childhood. *Child Development, 45,* 803–806.

Sen, B. (2004). Adolescent propensity for depressed mood and seeking help for it: Race and gender differences. *Journal of Mental Health Policy and Economics, 7,* 133–145.

Settersten, R. A., & Ray, B. (2010). What's going on with young people today? The long and twisting path to adulthood. *Future of Children, 20*(1), 19–41.

Shafer, A. S., Bobkowski, P. S., & Brown, J. D. (2013). Sexual media practice: How adolescents select, interact with and are affected by sexual media. In K. E. Dill (Ed.), *Oxford handbook of media psychology* (pp. 223–251). New York, NY: Oxford University Press.

Shaffer, D. R., & Wittes, E. (2006). Women's precollege sports participation, enjoyment of sports, and self-esteem. *Sex Roles, 55,* 225–232.

Shah, N. (June 3, 2013). Students experiencing less bullying, fear from school, new data show [Blog post]. *Education Week.* Retrieved from http://blogs.edweek.org/edweek/rulesforengagement/2013/06/students_experience_less_bullying_fear_at_school_new_data_show.html

Shapiro, J. R., & Williams, A. M. (2011). The role of stereotype threats in undermining girls' and women's performance and interest in STEM fields. *Sex Roles, 66*(3–4), 175–183.

Shapka, J. D. & Keating, D. P. (2005). Structure and Change in Self-Concept During Adolescence. *Canadian Journal of Behavioural Science/Revue canadienne des sciences du comportement, 37,* 83–96.

Shaw, H., Ramirez, L., Trost, A., Randall, P., & Stice, E. (2004). Body image and eating disturbances across ethnic groups: More similarities than differences. *Psychology of Addictive Behaviors, 18,* 12–18.

Shaw, M. E. (1998). Adolescent breakfast skipping: An Australian study. *Adolescence, 33*(132), 851–861.

Sheard, J., Markham, S., & Dick, M. (2003). Investigating differences in cheating behaviours of IT undergraduate and graduate students: The maturity and motivation factors. *Higher Education Research and Development, 22,* 91–108.

Sheldon S. B. (2002). Parents' social networks and beliefs as predictors of parental involvement. *Elementary School Journal, 102,* 301–316.

Shiffrin, R. M., & Atkinson, R. C. (1969). Storage and retrieval processes in long-term memory. *Psychological Review, 76*(2), 179–193.

Shih, M., Bonam, C., Sanchez, D., & Peck, C. (2007). The social construction of race: Biracial identity and vulnerability to stereotypes. *Cultural Diversity and Ethnic Minority Psychology, 13,* 125–133.

Shin, H., & Ryan, A. M. (2012). How do young adolescents cope with social problems?: An examination of social goals, coping with friends and social adjustment. *Journal of Early Adolescence, 32*(6), 851–875.

Shogren, K. A., & Plotner, A. J. (2012). Transition planning for students with intellectual disability, autism, or other disabilities: Data from the National Longitudinal Transition Study-2. *Intellectual and Developmental Disabilities, 50*(1), 16–30.

Shrum, L. J. (2002). Media consumption and perceptions of social reality: Effects and underlying processes. In J. Bryant & D. Zillman (Eds.), *Media effects: Advances in theory and research* (2nd ed., pp. 69–95). Mahwah, NJ: Lawrence Erlbaum.

Shulock, N., Offenstein, J., & California State University, S. (2012). *Career opportunities: Career technical education and the college completion agenda. Part I: Structure and funding of career technical education in the California community colleges.* Sacramento, CA: Institute for Higher Education Leadership & Policy. (ERIC Document Reproduction Service No. ED415392)

Signorelli, N. (1997). *Reflections of girls in the media: A content analysis.* Menlo Park: CA: Kaiser Family Foundation.

Signorielli, M. & Lears, N. (1991). Children, television, and conceptions about chores: Attitudes and behaviors. *Sex Roles* (304), 157–170.

Signorielli, N. (2003). Prime-time violence 1993–2001: Has the picture really changed? *Journal of Broadcasting and Electronic Media, 47,* 36–57.

Signorielli, N., & Kahlenberg, N. (2001). Television's world of work in the nineties. *Journal of Broadcasting and Electronic Media, 45,* 4–22.

Silverberg Koerner, S., Kenyon, D. B., & Rankin, L. A. (2006). Growing up faster? Post-divorce catalysts in the mother-adolescent relationship. *Journal of Divorce and Remarriage, 45,* 25–41.

Sinai, M., Kaplan, A., and Flum, H. (2012). Promoting identity exploration within the school curriculum: A design-based study in a junior high literature lesson in Israel. *Contemporary Educational Psychology, 37,* 171–236.

Singh, R. D., Jimerson, S. R., Renshaw, T., Saeki, E., Hart, S. R., Earhart, J., & Stewart, K. (2011). A summary and synthesis of contemporary empirical evidence regarding the effects of the Drug Abuse Resistance Education Program (D.A.R.E.). *Contemporary School Psychology, 15,* 93–102.

Sirin, S. R. (2005). Socioeconomic status and academic achievement: A meta-analytic review of research. *Review of Educational Research, 75*(3), 417–453.

Skiba, R., & Sprague, J. (2008). Safety without suspensions. *Educational Leadership, 66*(1), 38–43.

Skiba, R., Reynolds, C. R., Graham, S., Sheras, P., Conoley, J. C., & Garcia-Vasquez, E. (2008). *Are zero tolerance policies effective in the schools? An evidentiary review and recommendations.* Washington, DC: American Psychological Association.

Skinner, E., Johnson, S., & Snyder, T. (2005). Six dimensions of parenting: A motivational model. *Parenting: Science and Practice, 5,* 175–235.

Smetana, J. G. (2011). *Adolescents, families, and social development: How adolescents construct their worlds.* West Sussex, England: Wiley-Blackwell.

Smetana, L., Daddis, C., & Chuang, S. (2003). "Clean your room!" *Journal of Adolescent Research, 18,* 631–650.

Smith-Davis, J. (2004). The World of immigrant students. *Principal Leadership, 4*(7), 44–49.

Smith, E. A., & Udry, J. R. (1985). Coital and non-coital sexual behaviors of White and Black adolescents. *American Journal of Public Health, 75,* 1200–1203.

Smith, L. (1987). A constructivist interpretation of formal operations. *Human Development, 30*(6), 341–354.

Smith, P. H., White, J. W., & Holland, L. J. (2003). A longitudinal perspective on dating violence among adolescent and collegeage women. *American Journal of Public Health, 93,* 1104–1109.

Sneed, J. R., Schwartz, S. J., & Cross, Jr., W. E. (2006). A multicultural critique of identity status theory and research: A call for integration. *Identity: An International Journal of Theory and Research, 6,* 61–84.

Snell, P. (2010). Emerging adult civic and political disengagement: A longitudinal analysis of lack of involvement with politics. *Journal of Adolescent Research, 25*(2), 258–287.

Snyder, L. B., & Hamilton, M. A. (2002). A meta-analysis of U.S. health campaign effects on behavior: Emphasize enforcement, exposure and new information, and beware the secular trend. In R. C. Hornik (Ed.), *Public Health Communication: Evidence for Behavior Change* (pp. 357–384). Mahwah, NJ: Lawrence Erlbaum.

Somers, C. L., & Surmann, A. T. (2004). Adolescents' preferences for source of sex education. *Child Study Journal, 34,* 47–59.

Somers, C. L., & Surmann, A. T. (2005). Sources and timing of sex education: Relations with American adolescent sexual attitudes and behavior. *Educational Review, 57,* 37–54.

Sommers, C. H. (2000, May). The war against boys. *The Atlantic,* 59–74.

Spano, S. (2003). Adolescent brain. *Youth Studies of Australia, 22,* 36–38.

Sparks, S.D. (2013). Community service requirements seen to reduce volunteering. *Education Week,* August 21, 2013. Retrieved from: http://www.edweek.org/ew/articles/2013/08/21/01volunteer_ep.h33.html

Spearman, C. (1904). "General intelligence" objectively determined and measured. *American Journal of Psychology, 15*(2), 201–293.

Spearman, C. (1927). *The abilities of man.* London, England: Macmillan.

Spencer, M. B., Dupree, D., Swanson, D. P., & Cunningham, M. (1998). The influence of physical maturation on African American adolescents' learning behaviors. *Journal of Comparative Family Studies, 29,* 189–200.

Spotts, E. L., Neiderhiser, J. M., Hetherington, E., & Reiss, D. (2001). The relation between observational measures of social problems solving and familial antisocial behavior: Genetic and environmental influences. *Journal of Research on Adolescence, 11*(4), 351–374.

Steinberg, L. (2001). We know some things: Parent-adolescent relationships in retrospect and prospect. *Journal of Research on Adolescence, 11*(1), 1–19.

Srikala, B., & Kumar, K. (2010). Empowering adolescents with life skills education in schools—school mental health program: Does it work? *Indian Journal of Psychiatry, 52,* 344–349.

Stassen Berger, K. (2007). Update on bullying at school: science forgotten? *Developmental Review, 27,* 90–126.

Statistics Canada. (2011). *Living arrangements of young adults aged 20–29.* Retrieved from https://www12.statcan.gc.ca/census-recensement/2011/as-sa/98-312-x/98-312-x2011003_3-eng.cfm

Steele, C. M. (1997). A threat in the air: How stereotypes shape intellectual identity and performance. *American Psychologist, 52*(6), 613–629.

Steele, C. M., & Aronson, J. (1995). Stereotype threat and the intellectual test performance of African-Americans. *Journal of Personality and Social Psychology, 69,* 797–811.

Steele, J. R., & Ambady, N. (2006). "Math is hard!" The effect of gender priming on women's attitudes. *Journal of Experimental Social Psychology, 42,* 428–436.

Stein, J. H., & Reiser, L. W. (1994). A study of White, middle-class adolescent boys' responses to "semenarche" (the first ejaculation). *Journal of Youth and Adolescence, 23,* 373–384.

Steinberg, L. (1988). Reciprocal relation between parent-child distance and pubertal maturation. *Developmental Psychology, 24,* 122–128.

Steinberg, L. (2010). A dual-systems model of adolescent risk-taking. *Developmental Psychobiology, 52,* 216–224.

Steinberg, L. (2014). *Age of Opportunity: Lessons from the New Science of Adolescence.* New York: Houghton Mifflin.

Steinberg, L. & Monahan, K. (2007). Age difference in resistance to peer influence. *Development Psychology, 43,* 1531–1543. doi:10.1037/0012-1649.43.6.1531

Steinberg, L., & Monahan, K. (2007). Age differences in resistance to peer influence. *Developmental Psychology, 43,* 1531–1543.

Steinberg, L., Mounts, N. S., Lamborn, S. D., & Dornbusch, S. M. (1999). Authoritative parenting and adolescent adjustment across varied ecological niches. In R. M. Lerner & D. R. Castellino (Eds.), *Adolescents and their families: Structure, function, and parent-youth relationships* (p. 129–146). New York, NY: Garland Publishing, Inc.

Stemler, S. E., Grigorenko, E. L., Jarvin, L., & Sternberg, R. J. (2006). Using the theory of successful intelligence as a basis for augmenting AP exams in psychology and statistics. *Contemporary Educational Psychology, 31,* 344–376.

Stepp, L. S. (1999, July 8). Unsettling new fad alarms parents: Middle school oral sex. *Washington Post.* Retrieved from http://www.washingtonpost.com/wp-srv/style/features/students070899.htm

Stepp, L. S. (2007). *Unhooked: How young women pursue sex, delay love, and lose at both.* Riverhead Books: New York.

Stern, S. R. (2005). Messages from teens on the big screen: Smoking, drinking, and drug use in teen-centered films. *Journal of Health Communication, 10,* 331–346.

Sternberg, R. J. (2003). A broad view of intelligence: The theory of successful intelligence. *Consulting Psychology Journal: Practice and Research, 55*(3), 139–154.

Sternberg, R. J. (2009). The theory of successful intelligence. In J. C. Kaufman & E. L. Grigorenko (Eds.), *The essential Sternberg: Essays on intelligence, psychology, and education* (pp. 71–100). New York, NY: Springer Publishing Co.

Sternberg, R. J. (2011). The theory of successful intelligence. In R. J. Sternberg and S. B. Kaufman (Eds.), *The Cambridge handbook of intelligence* (pp. 504–527). New York, NY: Cambridge University Press.

Sternberg, R. J. (2013). Classical theories of intelligence and their contemporary counterparts. In W. M. Reynolds & G. E. Miller (Eds.), *Handbook of psychology* (2nd ed., Vol. 7, pp. 23–44). Hoboken, NJ: Wiley.

Sternberg, R. J., & Grigorenko, E. L. (2000). *Teaching for successful intelligence.* Arlington Heights, IL: Skylight Professional Development.

Stevenson, B. (2007). *Title IX and the evolution of high school sports,* CESifo working paper, No. 2159.

Stevenson, H. C. (2004). Boys in men's clothing: Racial socialization and neighborhood safety as buffers to hypervulnerability in African American adolescent males. In N. Way & JY. Chu (Eds.) *Adolescent boys: Exploring diverse cultures of boyhood* (pp. 59–77). New York, NY: Simon & Schuster.

Stice, E., & Shaw, H. E. (2002). Role of body image dissatisfaction in the onset and maintenance of eating pathology: a synthesis of research findings. *Journal of Psychosomatic Research 53,* 985–993.

Stice, E., Presnell, K., & Bearman, S. K. (2001). Relation of early menarche to depression, eating disorders, substance abuse, and comorbid psychopathology among adolescent girls. *Developmental Psychology, 37,* 608–619.

Stice, E., Rohde, P., Gau, J., & Shaw, H. (2009). An effectiveness trial of a dissonance-based eating disorder prevention program for high-risk adolescent girls. *Journal of Consulting and Clinical Psychology, 77,* 825–834.

Stoppa, T. M., & Lefkowitz, E. S. (2010). Longitudinal changes in religiosity among emerging adult college students. *Journal of Research on Adolescence, 20*(1), 23–38.

Story, M., French, S. A., Resnick, M. D., & Blum, R. W. (1995). Ethnic/racial and socioeconomic differences in dieting behaviors and body image perceptions in adolescents. *International Journal of Eating Disorders, 18,* 173–179.

Strasburger, V. (2010). Children, adolescents, substance use and the media. *Pediatrics, 126,* 791–799.

Strasburger, V. C. (2014). Wasssup? Adolescents, drugs, and the media. In A. B. Jordan & D. Romer (Eds.), *Media and the well-being of children and adolescents* (pp. 70–89). New York, NY: Oxford University Press.

Strasburger, V. C., Wilson, B. J., & Jordan, A. B. (2009). *Children, adolescents and the media.* Thousand Oaks, CA: Sage.

Strasburger, V., Jordan, A., & Donnerstein, E. (2010). Health effects of media on children and adolescents. *Pediatrics, 123,* 756–767.

Strauss, S., & Kroy, M. (1977). The child as logician or methodologist? A critique of formal operations. *Human Development, 20*(2), 102–117.

Strauss, V. (2013). How hard is teaching? *The Washington Post,* December 27, 2013. Downloaded from https://www.washingtonpost.com/news/answer-sheet/wp/2013/12/27/how-hard-is-teaching/

Strayhorn, T. L. (2012). *College students' sense of belonging: A key to educational success for all students.* New York, NY: Routledge.

Strom, S. (2014, May 5). Coca-Cola to remove an ingredient questioned by consumers. *New York Times.* Retrieved from http://www.nytimes.com/2014/05/06/business/coca-cola-to-remove-an-ingredient-questioned-by-consumers.html

Suarez-Orozco, C., & Suarez-Orozco, M. M. (1995). *Transformations: Immigration, family life, and achievement motivation among Latino adolescents.* Stanford, CA: Stanford University Press.

Substance Abuse and Mental Health Services Administration (2014). *Results from the 2013 National Survey on Drug Use and Health: Summary of National Findings, NSDUH Series H-48, HHS Publication No. (SMA) 14-4863.* Rockville, MD: Substance Abuse and Mental Health Services Administration.

Substance Abuse and Mental Health Services Administration (2015). *Behavioral Health Barometer: United States, 2014. HHS Publication No. SMA–15–4895.* Rockville, MD: Substance Abuse and Mental Health Services Administration.

Suh, J., & Seshaiyer, P. (2013). Mathematical Practices That Promote 21st Century Skills. *Mathematics Teaching in The Middle School, 19*(3), 132–137.

Sullivan, E. M., Annest, J. L., Simon, T. R., Luo, F., & Dahlberg, L. L. (2015). Suicide trends among persons aged 10–24 years—United States, 1994–2012. *Morbidity and Mortality Weekly Report, 64(08),* 201–205. Centers for Disease Control and Prevention. http://www.cdc.gov/mmwr/preview/mmwrhtml/mm6408a1.htm

Sullivan, H. S. (1953). *The interpersonal theory of psychiatry.* New York, NY: Norton.

Sullivan, P. (1995). Mortality in anorexia nervosa. *American Journal of Psychiatry, 152,* 1073–1074.

Susman, E. J. (2006). Psychobiology of persistent antisocial behavior: Stress, early vulnerabilities, and the attenuation hypothesis. *Neuroscience Behavior Review, 30,* 376–389.

Susman, E. J., & Dorn, L. D. (2009). Puberty: Its role in development. In R. M. Lerner & L. Steinberg (Eds.), *Handbook of adolescent psychology* (pp. 116–151). New York, NY: John Wiley & Sons.

Swanson, H. L., & Packiam-Alloway, T. (2012). Working memory, learning, and academic achievement. In C. B. McCormick, G. M. Sinatra, & S. Sweller (Eds.), *APA educational psychology handbook. Vol. 1: Theories, constructs, and critical Issues* (pp. 327–366). Washington, DC: American Psychological Association.

Swearer, S. M., Espelage, D. L., & Napolitano, S. A. (2009). *Bullying prevention and intervention: Realistic strategies for schools.* New York, NY: Guilford Press.

Swiss Education. (2013). *Vocational education and training.* Retrieved from https://swisseducation.educa.ch/en/vocational-education-and-training-0

Taliaferro, C. (2009). Using picture books to expand adolescents' imaginings of themselves and others. *English Journal, 99*(2), 30–36.

Tasker, F. (2005). Lesbian mothers, gay fathers, and their children: A review. *Developmental Behavioral Pediatrics, 26*(3), 224–240.

Tatum, B. D. (1997). *"Why are all the Black kids sitting together in the cafeteria?" and other conversations about race.* New York, NY: Basic Books.

Taylor, A. C., Rappleyea, D. L., Fang, X., & Cannon, D. (2013). Emerging adults' perceptions of acceptable behaviors prior to forming a committed, dating relationship. *Journal of Adult Development, 20*(4), 173–184. doi:10.1007/s10804-013-9169-3

Teachmann, J. (1997). Gender of siblings, cognitive achievement, and academic performance: Familial and nonfamilial influences on children. *Journal of Marriage and the Family, 59,* 363–374.

Terry, M. L., Leary, M. R., & Mehta, S. (2013). Self-compassion as a buffer against homesickness, depression, and dissatisfaction in the transition to college. *Self and Identity, 12*(3), 278–290. doi:10.1080/15298868.2012.667913

Thompson, M., & Kindlon, D. (2009). *Raising Cain: Protecting the emotional life of boys.* New York, NY: Random House.

Thompson, S. (1990). Putting a big thing into a little hole: Teenage girls' accounts of sexual initiation. *Journal of Sex Research, 27,* 341–361.

Thomsen, S. R., McCoy, J. K., Gustafson, R., & Williams, H. M. (2002). Motivations for reading beauty and fashion magazines and anorexic risk in college-age women. *Media Psychology, 4,* 113–135.

Thorman, E., & Jolis, T. (2005). Literacy for the 21st century: An overview and orientation guide to media literacy education. Retrieved from Center for Media Literacy website: http://www.medialit.org/cml-medialit-kit

Thornburg, H. D., Adey, K. L., & Finnis, E. (1986). A comparison of gifted and nongifted early adolescents' movement toward abstract thinking. *The Journal of Early Adolescence, 6*(3), 231–245. doi:10.1177/0272431686063003

Thurlow, C. (2001). Naming the "outsider within": Homophobic pejoratives and the verbal abuse of lesbian, gay and bisexual high-school pupils. *Journal of Adolescence, 24,* 25–38. doi:10.1006/jado.2000.0371

Tickle, J. J., Beach M. L., & Dalton, M. A. (2009). Tobacco, alcohol and other risk behavior in film: How well do MPAA ratings distinguish content? *Journal of Health Communication, 14,* 756–767.

Tokunaga, R. S. (2010). Following you home from school: A critical review and synthesis of research on cyberbullying victimization. *Computers in Human Behavior, 26,* 277–287.

Tomul, E., & Savasci, H. S. (2012). Socioeconomic determinants of academic achievement. *Educational Assessment, Evaluation and Accountability, 24*(3), 175–187.

Travis, R., & Bowman, S. W. (2012). Ethnic identity, self-esteem and variability in perceptions of rap music's empowering and risky influences. *Journal of Youth Studies, 15*(4), 455–478.

Triandis, H. C. (1989). The self and social behavior in differing social contexts. *Psychological Review, 96,* 506–520.

Triandis, H. C. (1995). *Individualism and collectivism. New directions in social psychology.* Boulder, CO: Westview Press.

Troutman, K. P., & Dufur, M. J. (2007). From high school jocks to college grads: Assessing the long-term effects of high school sport participation on females' educational attainment. *Youth & Society, 38,* 443–462.

Tuckman, B. W. (2003). The effect of learning and motivation strategies training on college students' achievement. *Journal of College Student Development, 44*(3), 430–437.

Turiel, E. (1989). Domain-specific social judgments and domain ambiguities. *Merrill-Palmer Quarterly, 35*(1), 89–114.

Turiel, E. (2008). The development of children's orientations toward moral, social, and personal orders: More than a sequence in development. *Human Development, 51*(1), 21–39. doi:10.1159/000113154

Twenge, J. M. (2000). The age of anxiety? The birth cohort change in anxiety and neuroticism, 1952–1993. *Journal of Personality and Social Psychology, 79,* 1007–1021.

Tyack, D. (1990). *Learning together: A history of coeducation in American schools.* New Haven, CN: Yale University Press.

Tynes, B. M. (2007). Internet safety gone wild?: Sacrificing the educational and psychosocial benefits of online social environments. *Journal of Adolescent Research, 22,* 575–584.

U.S. Census Bureau. (2015). *Current population survey, annual social and economic supplements.* Retrieved from http://www.childstats.gov/americaschildren/surveys2.asp#cps

U.S. Census. (2012). Retrieved from http://www.census.gov/newsroom/releases.

U.S. Department of Commerce, Economics and Statistics Administration. (2011). *Women in STEM: A gender gap to innovation.* ESA Issue Brief No. 4/11. Washington, DC: Author.

U.S. Department of Defense. (2012). *2011 Demographic profile of the military. community.* Washington, DC: Author.

U.S. Department of Education, NCES, Common Core of Data. (2015). *Public elementary/secondary school universe survey, 1990–91 through 2012–13.* Retrieved from https://nces.ed.gov/programs/digest/d14/tables/dt14_216.20.asp

U.S. Department of Education. (2004). *National assessment of vocational education: Final report to Congress, executive summary.* Washington, DC: US Department of Education. Retrieved from http://eric.ed.gov/?id=ED483151

U.S. Department of Education. (2006). Carl D. Perkins Career and Technical Education Act of 2006. Retrieved from http://www2.ed.gov/policy/sectech/leg/perkins/index.html?exp=7

U.S. Department of Education. (2007). *IDEA regulations: Secondary transition.* Washington, DC: U.S. Department of Education, Office of Special Education Programs.

U.S. Department of Education. (2012). Gaining early awareness and readiness for undergraduate programs (GEAR UP). Retrieved from http://www2.ed.gov/programs/gearup/index/html

U.S. Department of Health and Human Services. (2009). *APSE research brief: Youth from low-income families.* Retrieved from http://aspe.hhs.gov/hsp/09/vulnerableyouth/3/index.pdf

U.S. Department of Health and Human Services. (2015). *Substance abuse.* Retrieved from http://www.hhs.gov/ash/oah/adolescent-health-topics/substance-abuse/home.html

U.S. Department of Labor. (2014). *Women in the workforce in 2010.* Retrieved from http://www.dol.gov/wb/factsheets/Qf-laborforce-10.htm

U.S. Department of Veterans Affairs. (2013). *Minority veterans: 2011.* Washington, DC: Author.

United States Department of Transportation (2013). Traffic safety facts, 2011 data: Young drivers. Retrieved from http://www-nrd.nhtsa.dot.gov/Pubs/811744.pdf

University of Chicago. (2013). *Premature thelarche and adrenarche.* Retrieved from https://pedclerk.bsd.uchicago.edu/page/premature-thelarche-and-adrenarche

University of Iowa Labor Center and Center for Human Rights. (2015). *Child Labor Public Education Project.* Retrieved from https://www.continuetolearn.uiowa.edu/laborctr/child_labor/

University of Michigan. (2014). *Monitoring the Future Survey.* Ann Arbor, MI: Author

Urdan, T., & Garvey, D. (2004). The education of immigrant and native-born students: Local and national perspectives. In T. Urdan & F. Pajares (Eds.), *Educating adolescents: Challenges and strategies* (pp. 149–178). Greenwich, CT: Information Age Publishing.

Urdan, T., & Morris, S. (2010, June). *Cultural identity and academic motivation among Hispanic adolescent students.* Poster presented at the meetings of the American Psychological Association, Division 45, Ann Arbor, MI.

Urdan, T., & Turner, J. C. (2005). Competence motivation in the classroom. In A. Elliot & C. Dweck (Eds.), *Handbook of competence and motivation* (pp. 297–315). New York, NY: Guilford Press.

Uskal, A. K. (2004). Culture and menstruation experiences. *Social Science and Medicine, 59,* 667–679.

Valadez, J. R. (2008). Shaping the educational decisions of Mexican immigrant high school students. *American Educational Research Journal, 45,* 834–860.

Valdez, C. R., Chavez, T., & Woulfe, J. (2013). Emerging adults' lived experience of formative family stress: The family's lasting influence. *Qualitative Health Research, 23*(8), 1089–1102. doi: 10.1177/1049732313494271

Valenzuela, S., Park, N., & Kee, K. F. (2009). Is there social capital in a social network site?: Facebook use and college students' life satisfaction, trust and participation. Journal of *Computer Mediated Communication, 14*(4), 875–901.

Van der Veer, R. (1994). The concept of development and the development of concepts. education and development in Vygotsky's thinking. *European Journal of Psychology of Education, 9*(4), 293–300.

Van der Veer, R., & van Ijzendoorn, M. H. (1999). Vygotsky's theory of the higher psychological processes: Some criticisms. In P. Lloyd & C. Fernyhough (Eds.), *Lev Vygotsky: Critical assessments: Vygotsky's theory* (Vol. I, pp. 381–391). Florence, KY: Taylor & Frances/Routledge.

van Ewijk, R., & Sleegers, P. (2010). The effect of peer socioeconomic status on student achievement: A meta-analysis. *Educational Research Review, 5*(2), 134–150.

Vandewater, E. A., & Cummings, H. (2008). Media use and childhood obesity. In S. L. Calvert & B. J. Wilson (Eds.), *The handbook of children, media, and development* (pp. 355–380). Malden, MA: Blackwell.

Verma, S., & Larson, R. (1999). Are adolescents more emotional? A study of the daily emotions of middle class Indian adolescents. *Psychology and Developing Societies, 11,* 179–194.

Vespa, J., Lewis, J. M., & Kreider, R. M. (2013). America's families and living arrangements: 2012 (Current Population Reports, P20-570). Washington, DC: U.S. Census Bureau.

Vezina, J. & Hebert, M. (2007). Risk factors for victimization in romantic relationships of young women: A review of empirical studies and implications for prevention. *Trauma, Violence, and Abuse, 8*, 33–66.

Vicary, J. R., Klingaman, L. R., & Harkness, W. L. (1995). Risk factors associated with date rape and sexual assault of adolescent girls. *Journal of Adolescence, 18*, 289–306.

Virginia Department of Education. (2010). Tips and Strategies for Increasing Parent and Family Involvement in Virginia Schools.

Vogel, H., & Perry, J. (2009). Are drastic swings in CRCT scores valid? *Atlanta Journal Constitution.* Retrieved from: http://www.ajc.com/news/news/local/are-drastic-swings-in-crct-scores-valid/nQYQm/

Volk, A., Craig, W., Boyce, W., & King, M. (2006). Adolescent risk correlates of bullying and different types of victimization. *International Journal of Adolescent Medicine and Health, 18*, 575–586. doi:10.1515/IJAMH.2006.18.4.575

Voyer, D., & Voyer, S. D. (2014). Gender differences in scholastic achievement: A meta-analysis. *Psychological Bulletin, 140*, 1174–1204.

Vygotsky, L. S. (1978). *Mind in society: The development of higher psychological processes* (M. Cole, V. John-Steiner, S. Scribner, & E. Souberman, Trans.). Cambridge, MA: Harvard University Press.

Wahlstrom, K. (2002). Changing times: Findings from the first longitudinal study of later high school start times. *National Association of Secondary School Principals Bulletin, 86*(633), 3–21.

Waldinger, R., & Feliciano, C. (2004). Will the new second generation experience "downward assimilation"? Segmented assimilation re-assessed. *Ethnic and Racial Studies, 27*, 376–402.

Walker, L. J. (1984). Sex Differences in the Development of Moral Reasoning: A Critical Review. *Child Development, 55*(3), 677–691.

Walker, V. S. (2008). In search of Miss Steepleton. In F. Pajares and T. Urdan (Eds.) *The ones we remember: Scholars reflect on teachers who made a difference* (pp. 53–62). Charlotte, NC: Information Age Publishing.

Wallace, J. J., Forman, T. A., & Caldwell, C. H. (2003). Religion and U.S. Secondary School Students: Current Patterns, Recent Trends, and Sociodemographic Correlates. *Youth & Society, 35*(1), 98–125.

Walton, G. M., & Spencer, S. J. (2009). Latent ability: Grades and test scores systematically underestimate the intellectual ability of negatively stereotyped students. *Psychological Science, 20*, 1132–1139.

Wang, W., Parker, K., & Taylor, T. (2014). *Breadwinner moms.* Washington, DC: Pew Research Center. Retrieved from http://www.pewsocialtrends.org/2013/05/29/breadwinner-moms/

Wang, Y., & Lobstein, T. (2006). Worldwide trends in childhood overweight and obesity. *International Journal of Pediatric Obesity, 1*, 11–25.

Wang, Y., Cullen, K. L., Yao, X., & Li, Y. (2013). Personality, freshmen proactive social behavior, and college transition: Predictors beyond academic strategies. *Learning and Individual Differences, 23*, 205–212.

Ward, J. V. (1996). Raising resisters: The role of truth telling in the psychological development of African American girls. In B. J. Leadbeater & N. Way (Eds.), *Urban girls: Resisting stereotypes, creating identities* (pp. 85–99). New York, NY: New York University Press.

Ward, L. M. (2003). Understanding the role of the entertainment media in the sexual socialization of American youth: A review of the empirical research. *Developmental Review, 23*, 347–388.

Ward, L. M. (2005). Talking about sex: Common themes about sexuality in the prime-time television programs children and adolescents view most. *Journal of Youth and Adolescence, 24*, 595–615.

Ward, L. M., & Friedman, K. (2006). Using TV as a guide: Associations between television viewing and adolescents' sexual attitudes and behavior. *Journal of Research on Adolescence, 16*, 133–156.

Ward, L. M., Hansborough, E., & Walker, E. (2005). Contributions of music video exposure to black adolescents' gender and sexual schemas. *Journal of Adolescent Research, 20*(2), 143–166.

Wartella, E., Rideout, V., Lauricella, A. R., & Connell, S. L. (2013). *Parenting in the age of digital technology: A national survey.* Evanston, IL: Northwestern University.

Waterhouse, L. (2006). Multiple intelligences, the Mozart effect, and emotional intelligence: A critical review. *Educational Psychologist, 41*, 207–225.

Watt, T. T. (2003). Are small schools and private schools better for adolescents' emotional adjustment? *Sociology of Education, 4*, 344–367.

Way, N., & Chen, L. (2000). Close and general friendships among African American, Latino and Asian American adolescents from low-income families. *Journal of Adolescent Research, 15*, 274–301.

Way, N., & Greene, M. L. (2006). Trajectories of perceived friendship quality during adolescence: The patterns and contextual predictors. *Journal of Research on Adolescence, 16*, 293–320.

Weil, L. G., Fleming, S. M., Dumontheil, I., Kilford, E. J., Weil, R. S., Rees, G., et al. (2013). The development of metacognitive ability in adolescence. *Consciousness and Cognition: An International Journal, 22*, 264–271.

Weiner, B. (1985). An attributional theory of achievement motivation and emotion. *Psychological Review, 92*, 548–573.

Weiner, B. (1985). An attributional theory of achievement motivation and emotion. *Psychological Review, 92*, 548–573.

Weinstock, H., Berman, S., & Cates, W. Jr. (2004). Sexually transmitted diseases among American youth: Incidence and prevalence estimates, 2000. *Perspectives on Sexual and Reproductive Health, 36*(1), 6–10.

Weiss, C. C., Carolan, B. V., & Baker-Smith, E. C. (2010). Big school, small school: (Re)testing assumptions about high school size, school engagement and mathematics achievement. *Journal of Youth and Adolescence, 39*(2), 163–176.

Weissberg, R. P. & Cascarino, J (2013). Academic learning + social-emotional learning = national priority. *Phi Delta Kappan, 95*(2): 8–13.

Weissbourd, R. (2012). Promoting moral development in schools. *Harvard Education Letter, 28*(1). Retrieved from http://hepg.org/hel-home/issues/28_1/helarticle/promoting-moral-development-in-schools_522

Weisz, J. R., McCarty, C. A., & Valeri, S. M. (2006). Effects of psychotherapy for depression in children and adolescents: A meta-analysis. *Psychological Bulletin, 132*, 132–149.

Wentzel, K. R. (1997). Student motivation in middle school: The role of perceived pedagogical caring. *Journal of Educational Psychology, 89*, 411–419.

Wentzel, K. R. (2002). Are effective teachers like good parents? Teaching styles and student adjustment in early adolescence. *Child Development, 73*, 287–301.

Wentzel, K. R., & Asher, S. R. (1995). Academic lives of neglected, rejected, popular, and controversial children. *Child Development, 66*, 754–763.

Wentzel, K. R., Donlan, A & Morrison, D. (2012). Peer relationships and social motivational processes. In A. M. Ryan & G. W. Ladd (Eds.), *Peer relationships and adjustment at school* (pp. 79–105). Charlotte, NC: Information Age Press.

Werblow, J., & Duesbery, L. (2009). The impact of high school size on math achievement and dropout rate. *High School Journal, 92*(3), 14–23.

Wichstrom, L. (1999). The emergence of gender difference in depressed mood during adolescence: The role of intensified gender socialization. *Developmental Psychology, 35*, 232–245.

Wick, K., Brix, C., Bormann, B., Sowa, M., Strauss, B., & Berger, U. (2011). Real world effectiveness of a German school-based intervention of anorexia nervosa in preadolescent girls. *Preventative Medicine, 52*, 152–158.

Wigfield, A., & Eccles, J. S. (1994). Children's competence beliefs, achievement values, and general self-esteem: Change across elementary and middle school. *Journal of Early Adolescence, 14*(2), 107–138.

Wigfield, A., Byrnes, J. P., & Eccles, J. S. (2006). Development during early and middle adolescence. In P. Alexander & P. Winne (Eds.), *Handbook of educational psychology* (2nd ed., pp. 87–113). Mahwah, NJ: Lawrence Erlbaum Associates.

Wigfield, A., Eccles, J. S., Fredricks, J. A., Simpkins, S., Roeser, R. W., & Schiefele, U. (2014). Development in achievement motivation and engagement. In R. Lerner (Series Ed.) & M. Lamb & C. Garcia-Coll (Vol. Eds.), *Handbook of child psychology, Vol. 3* (7th ed., pp. 657–701). Hoboken, NJ: Wiley.

Wigfield, A., Eccles, J. S., Mac Iver, D., Reuman, D. A., & Midgley, C. (1991). Transitions during early adolescence: Changes in children's domain-specific self-perceptions and general self-esteem across the transition to junior high school. *Developmental Psychology, 27*(4), 552–565.

Wilkins, J. A., Boland, F. J., & Albinson, J. (1991). A comparison of male and female university athletes and non-athletes on eating disorder indices. *Journal of Sport Behavior, 14*, 129–143.

Williams, K. R., & Guerra, N. G. (2007). Prevalence and predictors of Internet bullying. *Journal of Adolescent Health, 41*, S14–S21.

Williams, S., Connolly, J., & Segal, Z. V. (2001). Intimacy in relationships and cognitive vulnerability to depression in adolescent girls. *Cognitive Therapy and Research, 25*, 477–496.

Williamson, D. E., Birmaher, B., Anderson, B. P., al-Shabbout, M., & Ryan, N. D. (1995). Stressful life events in depressed adolescents: The role of depressive events during the depressive episode. *Journal of the American Academy of Child & Adolescent Psychiatry, 34*, 591–598.

Willingham, D. T. (2008–2009). What will improve a student's memory? *American Educator*, 17–25.

Willingham, D. T. (2010). *Why don't students like school?* San Francisco, CA: Jossey-Bass.

Wilson, A. E., Allen, J. W., Strahan, E. J., & Ethier, N. (2008). Getting involved: Testing the effectiveness of a volunteering intervention on young adolescents' future intentions. *Journal of Community & Applied Social Psychology, 18*, 630–637.

Wiseman, C. V., Gray, J. J., Mosimann, J. E., & Ahrens, A. H. (1992). Cultural expectations of thinness in women: An update. *International Journal of Eating Disorders, 11*, 85–89.

Wiseman, R. (2002). *Queen bees and wannabes: Helping your daughter survive cliques, gossip, boyfriends, and the new realities of girl world.* New York, NY: Three Rivers Press.

Witte, S. (2007). "That's online writing, not boring school writing": Writing with blogs and the Talkback Project. *Journal of Adolescent & Adult Literacy, 51*(2), 92–96.

Wojciki, J. M., & Heyman, M. B. (2006). Healthier choices and increased participation in a middle school lunch program: Effects of nutrition policy changes in San Francisco. *American Journal of Public Health, 96*, 1542–1547.

Wolak, J., Finkelhor, D., & Mitchell, K. J. (2005a). Child pornography possessors arrested in Internet-related crimes: Findings from the National Juvenile Online Victimization Study (NCMEC 06–05–023). Alexandria, VA: National Center for Missing & Exploited Children.

Wolak, J., Finkelhor, D., Mitchell, K. J., & Ybarra, M. L. (2008). Online "predators" and their victims: Myths, realities, and implications for prevention and treatment. *American Psychologist, 63*, 111–128.

Wolak, J., Finkelhor, D., & Mitchell, K. J. (2007). Does online harassment constitute bullying? An exploration of online harassment by known peers and online-only contacts. *Journal of Adolescent Health, 41*, S51–S58.

Wolf, A. (2002). *"Get out of my life, but first could you drive me and Cheryl to the mall?": A parent's guide to the new teenager.* New York, NY: Farrar, Straus and Giroux.

Wolfe, D. A., Crooks, C., Jaffe, P., Chiodo, D., Hughes, R., Ellis, W., … Donner, A. (2009). A school based program to prevent adolescent violence: A cluster randomized trial. *Archives of Pediatric and Adolescent Medicine, 163*, 692–699.

Wolters, C. A., & Rosenthal, H. (2000). The relations between students' motivational beliefs and their use of motivational regulation strategies. *International Journal of Education Research, 33*, 801–820.

Wonacott, M. E. (2000). *Benefits of vocational education. Myths and realities, no. 8.* Washington, DC: ERIC Clearinghouse on Adult, Career, and Vocational Education.

Wong, M. D., Coller, K. M., Dudovitz, R. N., Kennedy, D. P., Buddin, R., Shapiro, M. F., & … Chung, P. J. (2014). Successful schools and risky behaviors among low-income adolescents. *Pediatrics, 134*(2), e389–e396. doi:10.1542/peds.2013-3573

Wood, B., Rea, M. S., Plitnick, B., & Figueiro, M. G. (2013). Light level and duration of exposure determine the impact of self-luminous tablets on melatonin suppression. *Applied Ergonomics, 44*, 237–240.

Woolfolk Hoy, A., Davis, H., & Pape, S. J. (2006). Teacher knowledge and beliefs. In P. A. Alexander & P. H. Winne (Eds.), *Handbook of educational psychology* (2nd ed., pp. 715–737). Mahwah, NJ: Lawrence Erlbaum Associates.

Wright, P. (2011). Mass media effects on youth sexuality: Assessing the claim for causality. In C. T. Salmon (Ed.), *Communication yearbook* (pp. 343–386). New York, NY: Routledge Press.

Yanovitsky, I. (2005). Sensation seeking and adolescent drug use: The mediating role of association deviant peers and pro-drug discussions. *Health Communication, 17*, 67–89.

Ybarra, M. L., Espelage, D. L., & Mitchell, K. J. (2007). The co-occurrence of Internet harassment and unwanted sexual solicitation victimization and perpetration: Associations with psychosocial indicators. *Journal of Adolescent Health, 41*, S31–S41.

Yeager, D. S., & Dweck, C. S. (2012). Mindsets that promote resilience: When students believe that personal characteristics can be developed. *Educational Psychologist, 47*(4), 302–314.

Yeager, D. S., Fong, C. J., Lee, H. Y., Espelage, D. (2015). Declines is efficacy of anti-bullying programs among older adolescents: Theoretical considerations and a three-level meta-analysis. *Applied Developmental Psychology, 37*, 36–61.

Youniss, J. (1980). *Parents and peers in social development: A Sullivan-Piaget perspective.* Chicago, IL: University of Chicago Press.

Yuan, A. S. V. (2010). Body perceptions, weight control behavior, and changes in adolescents' psychological well-being over time: A longitudinal examination of gender. *Journal of Youth and Adolescence, 39*, 927–939.

Yuan, A. S. V. (2010). Body perceptions, weight control behavior, and changes in adolescents' psychological well-being over time: A longitudinal examination of gender. *Journal of Youth and Adolescence, 39*, 927–939.

Zhang, X., Anderson, R. C., Dong, T., Nguyen-Jahiel, K., Li, Y., Lin, T., & Miller, B. (2013). Children's moral reasoning: Influence of culture and collaborative discussion. *Journal of Cognition and Culture, 13*(5), 503–522.

Zickuhr, K. (2013). *In a digital age, parents value printed books for their kids.* Retrieved from Pew Research Center website: http://www.pewresearch.org/fact-tank/2013/05/28/in-a-digital-age-parents-value-printed-books-for-their-kids/

Zimmer-Gembeck, M. J., & Helfand, M. (2008). Ten years of longitudinal research on U.S. adolescent sexual behavior: Developmental correlates of sexual intercourse, and the importance of age, gender and ethnic background. *Developmental Review, 28*, 153–224.

Zimmer-Gembeck, M. J., Ducat, W. H., & Collins, W. A. (2011). Autonomy, development of. In B. B. Brown & M. Prinstein (Eds.), *Encyclopedia of adolescence* (Vol. 1, pp. 66–76). Oxford, England: Elsevier.

Zimmer, R., & Buddin, R. (2006). Charter school performance in two large urban districts. *Journal of Urban Economics, 60*, 307–326.

Zimmerman, B. J. (1990). Self-regulated academic learning and achievement: The emergence of a social cognitive perspective. *Educational Psychology Review, 2*, 173–201.

Zimmerman, B. J. (2002). Becoming a self-regulated learner: An overview. *Theory into Practice, 41*, 64–70.

Zimmerman, B. J., & Moylan, A. R. (2009). Self-regulation: Where metacognition and motivation intersect. In D. J. Hacker, J. Dunlosky, & A. C. Graesser (Eds.), *Handbook of metacognition in education* (pp. 299–315). New York, NY: Routledge.

Zong, J. & Batalova, J. (2015). Frequently Requested Statistics on Immigrants and Immigration in the United States. Migration Policy Institute. Retrieved from: http://www.migrationpolicy.org/article/frequently-requested-statistics-immigrants-and-immigration-united-states#Current and Historical

Zuckerman, D. M., Colby, A., Ware, N. C., & Lazerson, J. S. (1986). The prevalence of bulimia among college students. *American Journal of Public Health, 76*, 1135–1137.

Name Index

Subject Index

including equations, graphs, and scientific notation, may be created for both print or testing online.

TestGen is available exclusively from Pearson Education publishers. You install TestGen on your personal computer (Windows or Macintosh) and create your own tests for classroom testing and for other specialized delivery options, such as over a local area network or on the web. A test bank, which is also called a Test Item File (TIF), typically contains a large set of test items, organized by chapter and ready for your use in creating a test, based on the associated textbook material. The tests can be downloaded in the following formats:

TestGen Testbank file–MAC
TestGen Testbank file–PC
Angel TestGen Conversion
Test Bank for Blackboard Learning System
Desire to Learn TestGen Conversion
Moodle TestGen Conversion
Sakai TestGen Conversion
Test Bank for Blackboard CE/Vista